D0205009

THE PICKERING MASTERS

The Collected Letters of Rosina Bulwer Lytton

Drawing of Rosina Bulwer Lytton (1852) by A. E. Chalon, engraved by J. Jewell Penstone.

THE COLLECTED LETTERS OF
ROSINA BULWER LYTTON

Volume 2

Edited by
Marie Mulvey-Roberts
with the assistance of
Steve Carpenter

LONDON
PICKERING & CHATTO
2008

Published by Pickering & Chatto (Publishers) Limited
21 Bloomsbury Way, London WC1A 2TH

2252 Ridge Road, Brookfield, Vermont 05036-9704, USA

www.pickeringchatto.com

BRITISH LIBRARY CATALOGUING IN PUBLICATION DATA

Lytton, Rosina Bulwer Lytton, Baroness, 1802–1882
The collected letters of Rosina Bulwer Lytton. – (The Pickering masters)
1. Lytton, Rosina Bulwer Lytton, Baroness, 1802–1882 – Correspondence 2.
Novelists, English – 19th century – Correspondence 3. Women novelists, English – 19th century – Correspondence
I. Title II. Mulvey-Roberts, Marie III. Carpenter, Steve
   823.8

ISBN-13: 9781851968039

This publication is printed on acid-free paper that conforms to the American
National Standard for the Permanence of Paper for Printed Library Materials.

Typeset by Pickering & Chatto (Publishers) Limited
Printed in the United Kingdom at the University Press, Cambridge

CONTENTS

7 1853–4   Llangollen   1
8 1855–7   Taunton   167

CHAPTER 7 (1853–4) LLANGOLLEN

... you will think there is no end to my scribbledom ...

RBL to Rebecca Ryves 17 December 1855.

To Rebecca Ryves

Wednesday January 5th 1853

I have only a quarter of a minute Dearest Rebecca to thank you and Mr T Lloyd for the Bride cake which arrived quite safely to day – c'est a dire[1] at 10 o'clock this morning – it being a June day the sun, burning and the Primroses blooming (in profusion). I walked down to Lady Hothams with her piece she was out taking her constitutional walk. James greatly wanted me to go in and stay till she returned as he said she would be angry if he let me go – but as I hate infesting a House, I would not. – And now my dear Rebecca you will wish me, and my troublesome Commissions Au Diable[2] and no wonder – but only fancy Byrne sending me down here with but One!! Flanel Dressing gown and saying you would bring the other! – now if you have that other would you kindly make a parcel of it, or put it in a little Box – or Hamper and send it me down by rail – it need not be carriage paid but must be Booked in a few days I will enclose you a Draft for my £97 on the 10th out of which Mr Hodgson has to recieve £50 for Mr Wheeler – and out of the rest you can pay for the screen, and the Strasbourg Bacon and with the remaining £43 or 44 I have about £90! to pay which you will own would puzzle an Irish – or even a Jewish! Chancellor of the Exchequer![3] – We are all hoping to see you here very soon so we hope your Brothers wont disappoint us – With kind regards to them, and best love to yourself – Believe me in Electric Telegraph Haste – and unnumbered visits looming in Kemp Town Ever Affectly yours and mine ownest of Tibs R Bulwer Lytton.

HALS
1. That is to say (French).
2. To the devil (French).

3.   Benjamin Disraeli, who was Chancellor of the Exchequer in 1852 (and later in 1858–9
     and 1866) had been brought up as a Jew but later converted to Christianity.

To Rebecca Ryves

Sunday 4 o'clock January 9th 1853

Dearest Rebecca Here is a Postscription to my long letter, and an other tire-some Commission! but would you when you get my Parish allowance,[1] kindly call at Pagetts,[2] and tell him that I cannot settle my Bill till April but that "Mrs Hardinge Tyler"[3] a Lady who tasted his sherry at my House wishes a Dozen of the <u>same</u> at £2"8"0 a dozen sent down to her immediately it must not be <u>too</u> high colored, yet not what is called <u>pale</u> sherry but the same I had last – for this Dozen <u>pay</u> and get the receipt let him direct it to Mrs Hardinge Tyler – 23 Montpelier Crescent Brighton and be sure it is <u>Booked</u>, and <u>carriage</u> <u>paid</u>.- It seems the Chevaliers[4] scarlettina[5] was all a conbotherification of <u>Gorges</u>[6] the poor man only had sciatica! – with shoals of kisses to mine dearest of Tibs, Ever your affect R Bulwer Lytton

---

HALS
1.   A reference to payments by Edward Bulwer Lytton (EBL), which Rosina Bulwer Lytton
     (RBL) considers too meagre.
2.   Wine merchant.
3.   RBL's friend, who lives in Brighton. See RBL, 12 December 1852.
4.   Chevalier de Birard is described by RBL in a letter to A. E. Chalon, 24 March 1855, as
     an impoverished 'little wizen old Frenchman' and Lady Hotham's 'toady and hanger-on'.
     See *Unpublished Letters of Lady Bulwer Lytton to A. E. Chalon*, ed. S. M. Ellis (London:
     Eveleigh Nash, 1914), p. 175.
5.   Scarlet fever (Italian).
6.   RBL's nickname for George Beauclerk. See RBL, 26 October 1835. In RBL's novel *Very*
     Successful!, she caricatures him as Mr Gorge Beaucherche.

To Rebecca Ryves

23 Montpelier Crescent [Brighton]
January 11th 1853

My dearest Rebecca I have only three quarters of a minute to thank you for your very kind letter, and all the trouble you are kind enough to take about my both-ersome commissions, between Mrs Lloyd and me, St Paul[1] with the care of all the Churches! must have had a sinecure, compared to you with the care of all the Blenheims, and Bonnets! there is another Subscription Ball on Friday, and I shall be too happy to see mine dearest of Tibs, again, – with ten thousand thanks to you for all the care you have taken of him, but will he follow Massy? and will Massy take de <u>biggest</u> of care of him, and bring him to me safe, and sound? – if he does <u>not</u>! woe betide him! taking his life would do nothing! but I'll do worse, – spoil his coat! wisp his cravat!! and tumble his hair!!! as I have all my life set more value on a Dog – than a Puppy! Me hopes him (Tib) will have de bootsest of clean coats for Travelling. Pray give your brother William, my best thanks for his kindness in going to Herries'[2] for me, – I shall not fail to give Mrs Wheeler the very <u>acceptable</u> bunch of <u>Sweet William</u> you have arranged for her, which she may spell over like an Oriental Love letter! – and thereupon consider him as one of the wise men of the East – Alas! my dear Rebecca I have no chance of getting any thing – from Mr Wheeler for my Wooverman[3]– as I think it would be indelicate even to mention to <u>him</u> that I had such a thing – for fear that he should think that I wanted him to buy it after all he has already done for me; – Mr Moores silence is Passing strange! with a big <u>P</u>! – and quite unaccountable! By all means pay Scarnell[4] when the Parish pays me – I am very glad you are going to a "Flare Up" at Mrs Culpeppers; who does that bouncing Miss White marry? it ought to be a Mr Cherry – and then she would be Cherry bounce![5] I get on very well without Byrne, as Eliza[6] is very attentive, does hair beautifully! and improves greatly upon acquaintance, nothing can be kinder than dear Mrs Tyler, and her sister Mrs Barclay[7] is equally so – she yesterday to my great annoyance, gave me a beautiful white Pishmina which is a Cashmere shawl without a border, – I really feel like a Thief in taking it. Emily who with her mother[8] desires her best love to you, is like the Priests maid always <u>going</u> – to write to you, so I suppose she will do so at last! – If Miss Hobhouse is the Belle of London Blanche Vincent (from being <u>the</u> prettiest child) is certainly the ugliest girl in London, not to say Europe; – is Mrs Herbert Lady Vincents[9] mother still alive? and still with her. The Sectarian Fever rages at Brighton and the Guelphs and Gibbelines[10] were nothing to the High and Low churchites, but where we go, must be the slow church, for I never heard such a prosey man in my life. I am still ill, and always in pain; no wonder for my hopeless affairs and terrible position prays upon me night, and day, I see nothing for it but like Mr Wyndham Flitter (in the Pottleton Legacy)[11] to go – to Cremorne and lick all my creditors by stepping into a Balloon, and soaring majestically above and – what is far more "germain to the matter" <u>beyond</u> all the Bailiffs! Tell mine Tibbist dat last night my feelings were much harrowed by hearing a German song, the chorus of which was Tib! Tib! Tab! Tab! – It seems that the poor Chevaliers <u>improvisée</u> scarlittina,[12] was only one of <u>Gorges</u> clever <u>dodges</u>; – for he wrote to the Chevalier "My dear Chevalier if you wrote to dear Lady Hotham pray <u>for Heaven sake</u>! be sure to fumigate your letter well or you might expose her to danger" – which charming <u>Bighllitto</u>[13] was of course duly forwarded to her – your last letter was overweight – and though well worth Two pence as you know, it is not always that I have <u>so</u>

large! a sum at my command. Addio[14] God Bless you, and again thanking you a thousand times for all the trouble you so kindly take about my tiresome commissions – believe me with kind regards to your brothers, and kisses to him Tibbest Ever your affect Post Haste Rosina Bulwer Lytton.

HALS
1.   St Paul the Apostle (AD 10–67) was a leader of the early Christian Church.
2.   Herries Bank, St James Street, London.
3.   A painting by a member of the Wouverman family. See RBL, 23 December 1852.
4.   Dressmaker.
5.   A drink made out of mashed cherries, sugar and whisky.
6.   Eliza is Mrs Hardinge Tyler's lady's maid. See below, n. 7.
7.   Sister to Mrs Hardinge Tyler of Montpelier Crescent, Brighton.
8.   Emily Tyler, probably Mrs Hardinge Tyler's daughter.
9.   See RBL, 14 December 1847.
10. Two warring factions fighting for control of Italy since the Middle Ages, who clashed with the Papacy and the Holy Roman Empire.
11. A character in Albert Smith's *The Pottleton Legacy: A Story of Town and Country Life*. See RBL, 24 December 1852.
12. Extemporaneous (French) scarlet fever [*scarlettina*] (Italian).
13. Card [*biglietto*] (Italian).
14. Goodbye [*adiós*] (Spanish).

To Rebecca Ryves

Brighton
Wednesday January 12th 1853

My dearest Rebecca Here is another Telegraphic Despatch! full of commissions!!! Which are dat him poorest of Tibs may not be sent off on hims Travels without hims drinking Bowl and the little basket it stands in hims Collar, chain &&& Me's got hims Whistle. I wish it was your brother Willy that was coming – as I know he would be kind to him, and smuggle him into the carriage with himself (as I used to do my poor angel Taff who was three times his size) as I dread the idea of him going in that horrid Dog Box which is a sort of Black Hole at Calcutta,[1] and I fear hims poor innocent ears – of which him has by no means too much already may be bitten off by some quarrelsome canibus.[2] – Would you also kindly go to Brownes and get me all the Frilled Pillow cases (only the frilled) that came from the wash – so that there may be no undoing of boxes – as they wisely sent me off with only one!! they will not make a very large parcel if Massy would have the kindness to bring them. It is a relief to find Jonas[3] is at length in print though not his Di—a! at least I saw in my Paper an Extract from Ainsworth Magazine headed "Jovial Jonas and his four Wives"[4] not that I think our Jonas is likely ever de faire le Diable à quatre![5] I hope there was no delay in my Parish allowance as neither of the Wines have yet come but it is only 2 o'clock yet, so they may arrive this Evening. In awful haste with kisses to Tib and best love from all here to you. Believe me Ever My Dearest Rebecca your affect Rosina Bulwer Lytton

---

HALS

1. This was a small dungeon of around 7 m by 5 m where British prisoners of war were held allegedly by the Nawab of Bengal after the capture of Fort William in the Indian city of Calcutta on 20 June 1756. According to survivor John Zephaniah Holwell in his *A Genuine Narrative of the Deplorable Deaths of the English Gentlemen and others who were suffocated in the Black Hole* (1758), 146 were imprisoned out of whom 123 died. His figures have been questioned by recent historians.
2. With dogs (Latin).
3. The name Jonas, an amalgamation of the biblical Judas and Jonah, both associated with bad luck, is RBL's nickname for George Jones, RA (1786–1869) of 8 Park Square, London, a painter, Keeper of the Royal Academy and editor of the *Saturday Review*. He was an acquaintance of the Ryves family and friend of Mrs Hardinge Tyler. See RBL, 3 June 1853.
4. *Ainsworth Magazine* was run by William Harrison Ainsworth from 1842 to 1854. There is no such heading in the magazine for 1853. There is a lavish review of EBL's *My Novel*, *Ainsworth's Magazine*, 23 (1853), pp. 314-15, which concludes '...it is also... a work of high art, and it is calculated not only to add to the already brilliant reputation of its author, but to live as long as the language in which it is written'. This may have been written by George Jones, whose nick-name was Jonas and whose role as the Keeper of the Royal Academy qualified him to comment on 'high art'.
5. Kick up a shindy (French).

To Rebecca Ryves

Brighton
Thursday night January 14th 1853

Many thanks My dearest Rebecca for the Claret, which arrived safely last night, and for your kind letter recieved at 2 to day – I was very sorry to hear that you got wet in going for the wine, it was not so pressing as all that – the bottle we opened to day was very fair, without however being as super human! as that first green sealed sample bottle we got in July. Mrs Tyler is very anxious you, and your Brothers should come to a party she gives next Tuesday week, and is so sorry she has not anything like a bed she could offer you, but if you can come; and I dont see why you cannot; I will with pleasure pay for your bed, and Breakfast at an Hotel for a few days – let us have an answer by return of post – which we all sincerely hope may be yes – as we shall be much disappointed if you are not at this "flare up" as well as your brothers. I am en disappointedest at not seeing mine poorest of Tibbums on Friday – but it will be all the better if you can come down for a few days and bring him. I dined at the Wheelers yesterday – a very pleasant party, nothing can be more <u>affect</u> than they <u>both</u> are, he said laughing that he always tells Mrs Wheeler, that he is sure he and I <u>must</u> be cousins;- I assured him that at all events I would not <u>cozen</u> him, he really is a dear good man. I feel so wretchedly ill and have done so all day, that I will now say good night and finish my scribblery tomorrow.

Friday Mng. – I had almost hoped to have heard from you this morning; – but nothing has come but another dun! from Mme de Blarer, so I have written her a poser, which pray have the goodness to give her. Thank your Brother very much for going for my Parish allowance, to add to my comfort, I must <u>now</u> throw away more money to get another pair of stays made by Mme de Blarers. Being so <u>short</u> waisted and tight in the chest that it has made a great wound in my side. – Having told "The Reved Mr Smith" that you remained in Town for your cousins Wedding he desires his love to you and says he hopes you will "soon do likewise as she may find it an agreeable change besides maid, wife and Widow looks more imposing on an Epitath – than maid alone!" this is something like the lovely Topham[1] writing – to congratulate the girl on her marriage by telling her, he felicitated her on having taken the first step towards Widowhood! I <u>cannot</u> account for Mr Moores dead silence unless he is dead. I have not a pen that will write so must with many kisses to mine Tibbest, and loves to you from all here, say addio[2] – it is now only 10 o'clock – so I may hear from you again at 2 if so; I will acknowledge the letter as I am in great want of the pence the sherry not yet come Ever your affect & obliged Rosina Bulwer Lytton.

HALS
1. This may be a reference to a letter written by the deceased playwright, journalist and correspondent, Edward Topham (1751–1820).
2. Goodbye [*adios*] (Spanish).

To Rebecca Ryves

Sunday January 16th 1853

My dearest Rebecca I have only a quarter of a minute after Church, and before our 2 o'clock Dinner to thank you for your kind letter of yesterday – and acknowledge the reciept of the £23 – and the sherry which arrived safely yesterday Evening. I hope your Wedding went off well yesterday? – I am so ill, and bothered out of my life with bills, that I cant pay – and see no chance of doing so – for the hope about that picture seems to fail me like every other! – I have got Lady Hotham to ask the Wheelers to her House, and she very kindly called on them to please me. Mrs W: seems <u>Extasicé</u>[1] at this. – I will write again tomorrow

– with Kennels of kisses to mine <u>Tibbest</u> Believe me in Electric fluid Haste Ever Affectly yours R Bulwer Lytton

HALS
1. To be in ecstasy (French).

To Rebecca Ryves

Brighton
Tuesday January 18th 1853

Many thanks my dearest Rebecca for your kind letter and account of the Wedding – I hope you got my hurried scrawl yesterday acknowledging the money order and the arrival of the sherry with many thanks you have nothing to thank me for my dear, as Mrs Tylers party is now just off or rather it is not going to take place at all – for she is frightened about Alice,[1] whose nose certainly gets worse, and she is going up to Town with her next week, to leave her at Dr Lawries.[2] – It is very odd you not hearing from Mr Hodgson either perhaps he has also gone on a trip to the stys with Mr Moore at last! We have had two fine days here yesterday, and to day but I have got a fresh cold, from taking a long drive with Lady Hotham yesterday – though it was in the close carriage she said "<u>Grace</u>!(?) Lady Webster"[3] was complaining she had not seen me – I said if she wanted me she might find me out, as I certainly should not trouble myself to go to her. Every day I feel more desponding – miserable and out of my Element & all this presses upon me the more, that I try to keep my low spirits to myself

I must end this dull scrawl as I have a set of Petticoats to finish for Alice, as her mother is in a hurry to get her things ready to go to town. Mine poorest of Tibs! Kiss him poor innocent nutmegs for me, and tell him dat Every day me feels more and more starved for my dog. – Lady Hotham has a great Party next week I begged so hard that she has let me off the Dinner – which is a reprieve, but I have to go in the Evening which I dont dislike as her rooms are charming and I feel in a congenial atmosphere in them, and with the people one meets at her House. Addio[4] – All the good people here unite in best love to you

> In great Haste
> Ever your affect
> and Obliged
> Rosina Bulwer Lytton

HUNT
1. Mrs Hardinge Tyler's daughter.
2. A London-based physician. See RBL to Rebecca Ryves, first letter, 26 January 1853.
3. A friend of Lady Hotham.
4. Goodbye [*adios*] (Spanish).

To Rebecca Ryves

Brighton
Wednesday January 19th 1853

My dearest Rebecca I have one of my excruciating rheumatic headaches so terribly bad to day that I am scarcely able to thank you (which I do very much) for all the trouble you have so kindly taken about all my bothering Commissions – and for the Post office order for £1"2"6"!! which makes just £3'2'6 to last me till April! Out of which £2-2- are to be paid for stays! – a nice proposal and one that is daily shattering my brain for it <u>is</u> too much to bear up against without one ray of hope from any quarter – however Gods will be done and may he grant me strength to endure it. – I yesterday got the incloseds Billet <u>doux</u>[1] from Elton[2] the Dyer in Sloane St.[3] would you some day kindly go – and tell him that I shall be returning to Town – in April and it will not be convenient to me to settle his account before – I twice sent Gates about it to tell him he had charged me for a set of chair covers that I had never had cleaned but she said she could not find him at home <u>all</u> he has done for me since I paid his bill Xmas twelvemonth was cleaning (and very badly they were done) 9 strips of White Merinos – for curtain draperies – and dying 7 strips of thin green silk black – so that I dont know how his bill can amount to £2"14'8! though I recollect there was a Baby's white satin quilted quilt cleaned – about 2 yards square – with my servants bills I have nothing to do – neither had I any servant of the name of Mrs Rogers – I dare say it is that impudent Brown. The blinking woman you saw at Mrs Culpeppers – <u>is</u> the wife of the nimble-fingered Fitzgerald – she always did wink in that way even at her Husbands goings on – till he went off and left her there. We all hope that we shall see you at Brighton one of these days – though at present there seems to be little hope of it. Thousand of kisses to mine poorest of Tibs Me has made up all de respectable Pup Dogs in de Town dat him may have a large circle of acquaintance when him comes – all unite with me in affect love to you Ever my dearest Rebecca Affectly yours Rosina Bulwer Lytton.

HALS
1.   Love letter (French).
2.   Mr Elton is also a furniture cleaner.
3.   A London street forming a boundary between the exclusive districts of Knightsbridge, Belgravia and Chelsea.

To Rebecca Ryves

Brighton
Friday January 21ˢᵗ 1853

My dearest Rebecca Always bothering you about something! but here is a Dun
from collier the Silversmith Sloane St, touching that Bracelet of Miss Hodgsons[1]
would you kindly when it is <u>fine</u> & your cough is <u>better</u> call, and tell him that I
am very sorry but that I have been disappointed in money I was to have recieved,
and I cannot therefore possibly settle his bill before the middle of April. – I gave
your kind message to Mrs Tyler, about your brothers meeting her at the station,
and she desired me to tell you with her best love how much obliged to you she
was, but that she would not trouble them, as a man will be there to meet her. Did
you see the touch of Massy! in this Weeks "Punch" – "Irritated swell – dressing
– to little maid who has answered the bell "Ring"! yes to be sure; how the deuce
do you think I am to do my back hair with only one candle?" <u>Mise</u> <u>en</u> <u>scéne</u>,[2]
the room strewed with repudiated cravats, and rejected boots – Irritated swell,
with a large Battledore[3] looking brush in each hand. – I do hope to hear to day
that your cough is better. I am still suffering dreadfully from rheumatism, but far
more from <u>exhaustion</u> of the <u>chest</u>; for all these never ending money worries are
killing me; I only wish they would do it a little faster Addio[4] – God Bless you My
dearest Rebecca and with a thousand kisses to mine poorest of Tibs – Believe me
Ever your obliged & affect Rosina Bulwer Lytton.

HALS
1. A relative of RBL's lawyer, Mr Hodgson.
2. Setting the scene (French).
3. 'An instrument like a small racket used in playing with a shuttlecock' (*OED*).
4. Goodbye [*adios*] (Spanish).

To Rebecca Ryves

Brighton
Sunday January 23ʳᵈ 1853

I did not thank you My dearest Rebecca yesterday for you last kind letter, because
you would not have got mine before Monday. I am grieved to hear that your
cough, and cold still continue, pray take care of them, and above all do not go
out to do commissions for me, because though I am constantly boring you with
them, I do not mean you should go out rain, hale, or snow. – My "Gout" still
continues very painful, and I wish (to continue Lord Limericks[1] charming Phraseology) that I could find a "<u>Prostitute</u>"! (vulgo substitute) for it. By not writing
to you yesterday I am enabled to send you a letter from good Mrs Hodgson,[2]

in which honorable mention is made of my "amiable young friend Miss Ryves" – and also of de <u>booty</u> and <u>doodness</u> of Mr Tib, whom me is starving to see. I do wish Mrs Tyler would bring him back with her. I don't like to ask her to do so, but you might; she goes up next Thursday after Lady Hothams party, will you therefore have the goodness to get my frilled pillow cases from Brownes (only those that have come from the wash) that she may bring them back with her; and also beg of Browne to get that picture of my poor Fairy – <u>cleaned</u> <u>immediately</u>; that is, to get all that nasty lumpy linseed oil off of it, he said he could get it beautifully done; let him <u>lose no time</u> about it, Mrs Tyler is always at me to sell it; this is a sore trial to me, but I suppose in my most wretched, and hopeless position, I should have no right to retain my skin, if I could get money for it; but whatever you do; dont tell <u>Browne</u> I am going to sell it or he might get frightened about his bill. I should think if he set about it <u>immediately</u>, it would not take more than a day or two to clean – and then Mrs Tyler might bring it back with her; – but as she will only stay a couple of days in London, he had better <u>begin</u> it on Tuesday; – if you wrote to him, he would come to you, without your going out. I must also bore you with another commission; which is to take a Bracelet of mine to Killicks,[3] to be repaired which Mrs Tyler will bring you. – I have written to him all the directions with the bracelet (which I want back <u>as soon as possible</u>) so you will only have the trouble of leaving it, or sending it to him. I do indeed most sincerely wish my dear Rebecca that one, or both of your brothers would marry a rich Heiress – that you might have a comfortable Home; – I have always felt for those without one, and now of course a fellow feeling makes me sympathize doubly with them. À propos[4] of Marriage what think you of Louis Napoleons marriage with the Spanish Countess?[5] he has always tried to get all the <u>Spanish</u> he could; – and small blame to him! We think Sir Liar is at his dirty work again as two days ago – a woman called here, wanted to know if I was here? then to see my maid? and then to know <u>how long I had taken the lodgings for</u>? that is how long I was going to remain here, I only wish I could catch any of his emissaries – and the brute should have a surgeons bill to pay for their broken bones. – Tell mine Tibbest dat de most <u>heartrendingest</u> of <u>tings</u> happened to me yesterday, as we drove up to a door, an Innocent Blenheim Dog started back and looked up into my face with just such a pair of big moons of eyes as dose of b[l]ack Eyed Tibbiana. Have you ever been able to see the poor cat? It would gratify my <u>Felines</u> to hear some tidings of him. – Forgive this stupid scrawl but I am ill in body, and mind, but with the united love of all here Ever My dearest Rebecca your obliged and affect Rosina Bulwer Lytton

HALS
1.   William Henry Tennison Pery, second Earl of Limerick (1812–66).
2.   The wife of Mr Hodgson, RBL's lawyer.
3.   A London jeweller.

4. In connection with (French).
5. Charles Louis Napoleon Bonaparte (1808–73), shortly after becoming Emperor Napoleon III (see RBL, 28 May 1853), set out to make a dynastic marriage in order to secure a legitimate heir, but the royal families of Europe were unwilling to marry into the parvenu Bonaparte family. After being rejected by Princess Caroline Stephanie of Sweden and Queen Victoria's German niece, Princess Adelaide von Hohenlohe-Langenburg, Napoleon decided to marry for love and chose the beautiful Spanish Countess of Teba, Eugenie-Marie of Montijo of Guzman, in 1853.

To Rebecca Ryves

Brighton
Tuesday January 25th 1853

I really wish My dearest Rebecca that you would take care of your cold and not go out doing commissions for me while it lasts, – for even Browne and poor Fairys picture (which is the only pressing one) you could write and tell him to come to you. I got your letter too late yesterday – to write and tell you this your account of the Australian Shares[1] (which I had heard of in several instances before) makes one writhe in spirit about ones empty coffers at ones ill luck and the sustained and savage onslaught of Fortune against me; and yet and yet [*sic*] there is no use in "kicking against the pricks"[2] – Thank you for your Hospitality to poor Mr Hodgson, for hospitality is among the rarest virtues in this vulgar and detestable country. I will send you by Mrs Tyler – three Madeira Cakes – the only thing Eatable that Brighton is famed for, or rather the only Eatable things here, yes I suppose for my sins I shall have to go to Mrs Wheelers Ball on the 8th – but balls delighteth me not, nor dinners either, though we have an other at Lady Boyntons[3] on the 3rd of February – she was at Bath when I was there and remembers me though to my shame be it said, I had quite forgotten her. – Lady Hothams flare up is tonight I wish you were to be there, or that there was any chance of your coming to Brighton which I begin to despair of I am sure you would be much happier here; for your brothers always going about and amusing themselves – while you remain at home – en rôle de[4] patient Grizzle[5] must be dull work for you. – We went last night with Lady Hothams tickets to a concert at the Pavilion[6] (all Teapots and taste!???) Those Destius – on the saxe Horn[7] were really wonderful, and worth going any distance to hear but such a set of people! I never saw – I have not got the effluvia of them off my nerves yet – I have just got a long letter from little de Birard which I must answer to good Mrs Hodgson I will write in a day or two – and as between letters – visits partys – and mending my clothes all of which havings to do! I detest – I really don't know which way to turn – I must say good bye, and God Bless you and with a sack full of kisses to my poor innocent Tib whom me does long to see Believe me Ever My dearest Rebecca your obliged & affect Rosina Bulwer Lytton

I hope your brother William means to go to Mrs Wheelers ball? or what will be the use of her having it?

HALS
1. In 1851, gold was discovered in New South Wales, which led to a gold rush and investment opportunities. See RBL, 2 February 1853.
2. Acts 26:14.
3. This may be Harriet Lightfoot (d. 1889) who in 1843 became the second wife of Sir Henry Boynton, tenth Baronet (1811–69).
4. In the role of (French).
5. *Patient Grissel* is a play, dating from 1599. Grizzel is an anglicization of Griselda, a figure from folklore, who appears in the last story of Boccaccio's *Decameron*, composed 1348–53. Griselda is also the model for Chaucer's 'The Clerk's Wife' in *The Canterbury Tales* (1400).
6. George IV transformed the neo-classical building called the Marine, originally a farmhouse, into the Royal Pavilion at Brighton. John Nash created the Indian-style exterior and Chinese interior between 1815 and 1822, collaborating with the firm Crace. EBL hired John Crace to work on the interior design of Knebworth, when he inherited the house after his mother's death in 1843. In 1851, a year after Brighton's municipal authority bought the Pavilion from Queen Victoria, the rate-paying public were admitted free on two days a month.
7. Developed during the mid to late 1830s, the saxhorn family was patented in Paris in 1845 by Adolphe Sax.

To Rebecca Ryves

Brighton
Wednesday January 26th 1853

I was much shocked, & grieved My dearest Rebecca on My return home last night from Lady Hothams, to find your letter telling me of poor Massys terrible accident, the great thing is to get the hemorrhage stopped as soon as possible and then to keep him as quiet as possible – I fear dancing is a dangerous exertion for him, I believe Iceland Moss in milk is a good thing for him to take, but of course the Dr who attends him, knows better than I can what is good for him, I am very sorry their pleasure should have ended in so sudden, and so sad a way – but alas! in this world sorrow is the shadow of everything & of pleasure perhaps the darkest of all. I will let you know before closing this letter, the hour Mrs Tyler can see you at Dr Lawries on Friday – but perhaps I shall have to wait more than half the day before I can find out; she goes on Thursday (tomorrow) but talks, of only remaining <u>one</u> day – and of your having the trouble of sending for the cakes and my Bracelet – which with the letter to Killick to be left with it is all ready packed. Many thanks for going to Brownes – he had better have the picture put in hand as it will take so long to do; – and send it down to me by rail There was a regular crush, at Lady Hothams last night, and so many hideous specimens of humanity (or rather inhumanity!) I have rarely seen brought into one focus; pre eminent among the Griffens[1] were Lady Henley![2] (Sir Robert Peels[3] sister, and the image of her sister the late Mrs George Dawson,[4] always considered the ugliest woman in London) next came Lady Chantry!! ye gods! goblins! And little fishes! what a monument for an artist! to leave after him – and last though by no means least among the horrors was that detestable Miss King[5] (Lord Lovelaces's[6] sister) She looked all bugles and <u>bugs</u>! for on that mangey looking crop of hers – she had a sort of dangling Fillet of what looked like scalped bugs of brown Lady bird shaped shiney beads. "Perfections self" that vulgar ugly Mrs Kemp has considerably cooled in her ardour to me since I left Lady Hothams. That brute Gorge was there, looking more disgusting than ever and actually presumed for the first time in his life to shake hands with me! – and I being taken off my guard like a fool put out my hand. I wore the black Moire[7] antique dress – dear Mrs Tyler so kindly gave me, which Madame Veergime Dornay[8] has made very nicely – Mrs Tyler and Mrs Barclay were splendidly dressed and looked charmingly I was perfectly stunned with compliments about Molière[9] which seems so strange to <u>me</u> at this time of day! – there was a ball at the Hanbury Tracy's[10] which drew off a great many people from Lady Hothams – to Mrs Wheelers despair; Colonel Lawrenson among the rest, and we went to a stupid Conversazzione[11] at the Pavilion, where I was blinded by the gas – and have an awful headache this morning – with a pendant aching heart, for every day my most miserable position stares me more gauntly in the face. – Mrs Tyler and all of them are <u>so</u> grieved to hear of poor Massy's accident, and hope as I do that he will be <u>very careful</u>. She will be very glad to see you on Friday morning at Dr Lauries 6 Boyne Terrace Notting Hill[12] between 11 – & 12 – or sooner she says if you could manage it. Try what you can do about getting her to bring me back mine poorest of Tibs – and the <u>one</u> frilled pillow case – is my box at Ramsays done? God Bless you My dearest Rebecca with our united love to yourself kind regards to your brothers best wishes for Massy – and sacks full of kisses to Mine Tibest believe me in Great haste Ever your obliged and affect Rosina Bulwer Lytton

HALS
1. A griffin is a legendary creature with the body of a lion and the head and wings of an eagle.
2. Harriet Eleonora Peel (*c.* 1803–69) was one of Sir Robert Peel's three sisters. In 1824, she married Robert Eden, who later became second Lord Henley of Chardstock, a Master in Chancery.

3.   Sir Robert Peel, second Baronet (1788–1850), was Prime Minister from 1834–5 and 1841–6.
4.   Mary Peel (d. 1848) was one of Sir Robert Peel's eight siblings. In 1816, she married the Right Hon. George Dawson, of Castle Dawson, County Derry, Ireland.
5.   Hon. Hester King (1806–48) was the sister of Lovelace. See below, n. 6.
6.   William King, first Earl of Lovelace (1805–93), married Lord Byron's half-sister, Ada Augusta Byron, in 1835.
7.   'A type of fabric (originally mohair, now usually silk) that has been subjected to heat and pressure rollers after weaving to give it a rippled appearance' (*OED*).
8.   A French dressmaker.
9.   RBL's novel *The School for Husbands: or, Molière's Life and Times* (1852).
10. Thomas Charles Hanbury-Tracy (1801–63) and his brother Henry (1802–89) were the sons of Charles Hanbury-Tracy, first Lord Sudley of Toddington (1778–1858).
11. Conversation (Italian).
12. A fashionable suburb since the 1840s, lying west of London.

To Rebecca Ryves

Brighton
Wednesday 26th January 1853 5 P.M

My dearest Rebecca although I wrote to you this morning – I now scribble you these few lines, having just returned from a drive with Lady Hotham who begged me to tell you how grieved she was to hear of Massys accident, and hopes (as we all do) that he will take every care, and not exert himself in any way. Mrs Wheeler also came posting down here at 12 o'clock with a note she had had from your brother Willy thinking I had not heard – the bad news she also was very sorry for it, but no doubt consoled herself by rejoicing that it had not happened to her correspondent. Pray pity me! Lady Hotham has <u>forced</u> me to dine with her tomorrow, because she wont be alone with <u>Gorge</u>! and yet at her age one might think <u>he might leave her alone</u>! – Unlike poor Byron I have (alas!) no "literary lady" or "smug coterie" but nevertheless must attend to the "daily Tea is ready"[1] – so God Bless you and with kind regards to your Brothers and best wishes for Massy Believe me ever your obliged & affect Rosina Bulwer Lytton.

50 sacks of kisses to mine Tibbest

HALS
1.   'I leave them to their daily "tea is ready," / Smug coterie, and literary lady', Byron, *Beppo: A Venetian Story*, ll. 607–8. See RBL, 13 March 1825.

To Rebecca Ryves

Brighton
Thursday Mng January 27th 1853

We were all rejoiced my dearest Rebecca to hear by your letter recieved late last night that poor Massy was better; but it seems to me that he should not have come down to dinner as his own room would have been the best place for him as keeping in the <u>same</u> Atmosphere as much as possible after such an accident as his is a great desideratum; – however if he does not go out till Mrs Kitchener! sends her Brougham, for him!! (if she does it as kindly as she did it for me when she volunteered it) he is not likely to catch fresh cold. – were any one else going to town I would make him a large Pitcher of Barley water, but poor Mrs Tyler is so bothered with her children that she dont like to be bothered with any other persons <u>bothers</u> and he could have drunk it out of the Glass Jug! Mrs K so generously gave me I am very glad all the others – are so kind and attentive to him, and have no doubt with <u>great care</u> he will soon get over it but he must not do imprudent things, of even going from one room to another

A bit of the Madeira cakes I send you will do him no harm, but he should chiefly live on a milk diet Iceland moss – boiled in milk Blancmange – arrowroot made with milk &&&. –

I send you to amuse you a characteristic Whirlwind I had from Lady Hotham about her party the first thing yesterday morning. I do wish Mrs Tyler would bring me back my poor Tib; but if she wont; perhaps your Brother Willy would kindly do so – when he comes down to Mrs Wheelers Ball for <u>of course</u> – he wont have the barbarity not to come! – Will you when you leave it kindly hurry Killick about my Bracelet.

Pity! and pray for me as in a few hours I shall be opposite that disgusting animalcula[1] <u>Gorge</u>,[2] whom I think grows more disgusting every day. The Chevalier writes word that Lady Hothams garden is still submerged. –

Good bye – God Bless you and with kind regards to your Brothers – best wishes for Massy and sacks full of kisses to mine poorest of Tibs whom me was dreaming of dis morning – Believe me Ever my dearest Rebecca your obliged and affect

Rosina Bulwer Lytton

HUNT
1. 'A microscopic or minute organism, such as an amoeba or paramecium, usually considered to be an animal' (*OED*).
2. RBL's nickname for George Beauclerk. See RBL, 26 October 1835.

To Mr Leyton

23 Montpellier Crescent Brighton
January 27th 1853

Sir In reply to your note of the 25th Instant, I beg to state that "Chevely"[1] was written in two months, and four days – from the time of its commencement, which may perhaps account for, without however atoning for its innumerable defects; Works of fiction ought I think to be written Post; but decidedly [ill] …

… my turn to [worry?] … also a question? an answer to which will much oblige me; – namely, by what means you became aware of my being at Brighton; – and [ill] …

years, been subjected to a system of the most despicable <u>Espionnage</u>! I have become very tenacious on this point. I Have the Honor to be Sir your obedient servant

Rosina Bulwer Lytton.

HALS
1.   *Cheveley; or The Man of Honour* was RBL's first novel, published in 1839. It is a fictionalized account of her unhappy marriage and an attack on EBL.

To Rebecca Ryves

Brighton
Friday January 28th 1853

I was much grieved my dearest Rebecca to hear by your letter recieved late last night, (though dated Wednesday night!) that poor Massy had, had a return of the blood,[1] however slight, he really should keep in <u>one</u> atmosphere and not go up, and down stairs, and so you will find the Dr will tell him. I am very sorry I had nothing better to send you than those Madeira Cakes – so called as there is no Madeira in them! I am very glad you are so soon to see your pretty little friend Miss Lloyd,[2] for I know that will be a real pleasure to you. I cannot concieve why her mother should send her to an English school where it appears to me that girls learn nothing but the most profound ignorance and vulgarity such as "I was <u>very pleased</u>"! and "I <u>expect</u>! I have" for "I <u>suspect</u> or Imagine I have" – ride – for drive, and all sorts of abominations which it is really quite disgusting to hear. – I am writing this at a hard gallop as it wants five minutes to two when we dine – I was so ill all night, and this morning, that I could not hold a pen till this minute made ill I suppose by <u>Gorges</u> disgusting flattery and <u>patronising</u>!! attention as he has now taken to toady me! – but my real illness is in the mind – for my bodily health is better. But though I do try – and pray to submit myself to

Gods will; yet every hour I feel my homeless and destitute position more keenly – from its being so utterly helpless – in short I feel as if I was dying of a sort of atrophy of the heart, but enough of me you asked me in a former letter What Charles Matthews[3] had done? why dared to complain that the Treasury of the Lyceum[4] had lost £25, 000 from the Members of the Press being on the Free list, consequently the said Press Gang, are up in arms against him. Tell dear Mrs Tyler – with my love that all here are well – and hope she and Alice got comfortably to Town? That Plated Sugar Basin you have is for her. – Good Bye God Bless you My dearest Rebecca and with kindest regards to your Brothers best wishes for poor Massy – and mountains of kisses to mine Tibbest Believe Me Ever your obliged and affect Rosina Bulwer Lytton.

HALS
1. The early stages of tuberculosis.
2. Kate Lloyd.
3. An actor who performed at the Lyceum. See below, n. 4.
4. The Lyceum Theatre in the Haymarket, London.

To Rebecca Ryves

Sunday Morning January 30th 1853

My dearest Rebecca I seize one moment before Church (for after I shall have no time, on account of the Dinner) to tell you how glad I am to hear that Massy is going on so well but I hope he will take every care of himself and not do imprudent things. Here is another bothering Commission but would you kindly some day go to Eltons[1] with the inclosed bill and shew him that he was paid for the chintz chair covers last Xmas, twelve month for as you know these were my Buff French chintz that I had in Hans Place for my Green Ones at Thurloe Cottage being all new I have had none cleaned since and certainly will not pay this 14"3 over again; – I have another horrible large dinner at Mrs Mostyns[2] on the 2nd but she is so kind to me I could not get off of it as she made a point of my coming. I like her and she has a most Charming House – wonderfully large – and a part of it quite Pompean[3] I had a long letter from the poor French women yesterday – whom I am happy to say have arrived at Marseilles[4] at last by selling everything they possessed in the world poor Creatures! their letter is overflowing with gratitude to Mrs Tyler and all of us and they are going to send us some preserved Fruits which I shall Beg of them not to do poor things – and they beg Mille Choses[5] to Mademoiselle Reeves as they will call you – the Charmant Garçon[6] the Husband – wanted his wife says to write to me a few lines expressing his gratitude – but the poor goose of a man finding that I write French like Mme de Sévigné[7] (poor Mme de Sévigné!) is afraid to venture least I should find him and his style "par trop mediocre"![8] Mine poorest of Tibs! so me is to be starved still longer for him, – I do hope nothing will prevent your brother William from coming down to Mrs Wheelers Ball and bringing him – as there will be no puppy there that me sall like half so well. I dont think Colonel Lawrenson – or any one has superceded your brother William in Mrs W's good graces, but still a Colonel, is a Colonel (more especially of Lancers) and mustachios![9] are mustachios! "for a that – and a that"! Good Bye God Bless you my dearest Rebecca with kindest regards to your brothers – best wishes for Massy – and sandwiches of sighs and kisses to Him Tibbest Believe Me Ever your grateful and affect Rosina Bulwer Lytton.

HALS
1. Tradesman.
2. Cecilia Thrale Mostyn (1777–1857). See RBL, 0D099RR21.
3. Inspired by the ruins of Pompeii, a style made fashionable by EBL's novel *The Last Days of Pompeii*, published over twenty years earlier.
4. City in south-east France.
5. A thousand times (French).
6. Charming fellow (French).
7. Marie de Rabutin-Chantal, Marquise de Sévigné (1626–96), was a French aristocrat, remembered for her letter-writing, particularly her correspondence with her daughter, Madame de Grignan, which continued for nearly thirty years.
8. Excessively mediocre (French).
9. A mustachio is 'a moustache ... which is large and luxuriant' (*OED*).

To Rebecca Ryves

Brighton
Tuesday Mng February 1ˢᵗ 1853

I am much grieved my dear Rebecca by your Bulletin this morning of poor Massy I do hope that he <u>will</u> follow Dr Williams's[1] advice, and take every care of himself, for the <u>least</u> <u>imprudence</u> is dangerous after such an attack – I am glad Mrs Kitchener is kind to you, I suppose it is my idiosyncracy to be be [*sic*] like a human spider, and extract poison from all things, and foremost, the hollow, and intense Humbug of most people. I am so sorry you should have had the trouble of going to Browns for nothing – this is more of the abominable disorder that nearly drove me mad at Thurloe Cottage for I saw the Pillowcase counted with my own eyes for the wash – and suppose they took it out after I am sorry you did not remember to give Mrs Tyler the Plated Sugar Basin as it will be an additional trouble to your Brother William to bring – Mrs Tyler returned yesterday – I was very glad to hear you were looking so well. – I did not write to you yesterday because <u>Monday</u> is worse than a Despatch day at the Foreign Office to me having to mend my things to send to the wash – I am too old to do without a maid, having had one all my life – however I suppose what is to be must be – and mine is a sort of daily and hourly martyrdom at every pore. – My "Gout" is better but then my dear Rebecca my <u>chest</u> complaint, is quite enough without any thing else as <u>that</u> creates and comprises every misery of body and mind Mine poorest of Tibs! me dreamt of him last night and dat him had become de thinnest of Dogs – which I suppose means dat him is de fattest – me sall be <u>so</u> glad to see him and am only sorry me cannot divide him so as to leave you half of him, as I am sure you must miss him when he comes back to hims poor mud. – Pray try and send Mrs Tyler a Valentine as if from Jonas[2] – they have some elegant 2"dy concerns with Phials and Pill boxes that would do I drove out with Lady Hotham yesterday – poor woman she is making herself perfectly miserable at having that incurable complaint old age! – and yet I think she is younger for her age, than any woman I ever saw. – Good Bye God Bless you, I have not a scrap of news, perhaps after Mrs Mostyns dinner, tomorrow, and Lady Boyntons on Thursday, I may all here unite with me in best love to you, kindest regards to your Brothers, & Best wishes for poor Massy. Ever your obliged and affect Rosina Bulwer Lytton.

HALS
1. Hugh Massy Ryves's physician.
2. RBL's nickname for George Jones. See RBL, 12 January 1853.

To Rebecca Ryves

Brighton
Wednesday February 2d 1853

I am rather uneasy My dearest Rebecca at not hearing from you this morning about Massy – but hope I shall have a good account of him by the 7 O'clock Post and that it is only your attendance upon him, and not any fresh bad symptom that prevented your writing yesterday. Would you when you, go out kindly call at <u>Goslings</u> the Ironmongers in Knightsbridge who has threatened to call for "his little account" as he is coming to Brighton this week! now will you tell him that I sent for his bill four times before I left Town and could not get it; and now I cannot possibly pay him before the middle of April though his "little account", is but £1"4"9 – yet considering I have but 16s to keep the D—l[1] out of my Pocket till then I cannot possibly stretch these 16 into £1"4" I wish I could! Perhaps your brother William when he comes to Mrs Wheelers Ball will kindly bring my 4 plain pillow cases that Brown has out; with him? Now I think my dear Rebecca you will own that this <u>is</u> a piece of <u>my luck</u>!! you must know that a long time ago – when dear Mrs Tyler was staying with me, she very kindly gave that Mr Swaly you have heard her speak of £50 to speculate with for me, which I was to repay her when the Harvest was gathered in – well the said Mr Swaly was entreated by a stock broker, to clench some of those very Australian 15 shares[2] that you mention having brought £300! each but in the true apathetic English style he <u>put off</u> doing so till the next day when they were all gone! now fancy my having got £20, 000!!! with this £50 it would have been the making of us all, – but no, it seems to be Gods Will, that I should be scourged with poverty to the last – and verily there is no scourge like it! – for its cat o'nine tails[3] is lashed with a rope of each individual torture that human life is heir to. – I do hope that the 2 o'clock Post will bring us good accounts of poor Massy, and I also hope that you take care of your own cough and dont get wet feet, or take care to change your shoes if you do. With our united loves to yourself kindest regards to your Brothers and best wishes for Massy – with sacks full of kisses to mine doodest of tibs – whom me hopes to see <u>vezy</u> great big soon now Believe me in Electric Telegraph haste Ever your obliged and affect Rosina Bulwer Lytton.

HALS
1. Devil.
2. See RBL, 25 January 1853.
3. Traditionally, consisting of nine thongs, this whipping device was used to inflict punishment in the Royal Navy.

To Rebecca Ryves

Brighton
Friday February 4th 1853

It was a great relief to me my dearest Rebecca to get your letter this morning – as I was very uneasy yesterday at not having heard from you for two days – fearing poor Massy might be worse; but I am now rejoiced to find he is so much better; and hope he will take proper care of himself – and do nothing imprudent. I am very sorry you could not go to the Culpeppers to hear Barker as I am sure you would have enjoyed it; pray tell your brother William with my kind regards I hope he <u>will</u> come for Mrs Wheelers Ball for <u>my sake</u>! if not for hers; as there will be no one there I shall like half so well, <u>there</u>! don't you think I am coming out strong in the <u>British</u> <u>female line</u>?! but as it is my <u>debut</u> I hope it may be successful. Lady Abinger[1] told me of the awful fog – you had in London on Tuesday and I hoped you and my doodest of Tibbianas were not caught in it; <u>Tib</u> is invited to the ball on the 8th so him must come; as hims boo sash is all ready. I hope Killick will let me have my bracelet by then; did he say he would do it soon? if you go out will you hurry him? Mrs Mostyns Party was delightful – and all the <u>crême</u> <u>de la crême</u>[2] none of the Brunswick Square, and Brunswick Terrace[3] set, Harrison Ainsworth[4] being the only such there there were 24 to Dinner, dinner first rate, and well appointed, a servant behind every chair. You would laugh to see how I have become the fashion again everyone <u>so</u> civil! and asking to be introduced to me, one good thing is I have fretted myself thinner, and so look ten years younger than I did in Town. That horrid Miss King– is an <u>Ugly</u>! likeness of Charles Kean,[5] and looks like his 'husk' she is too ridiculous – in that black velvet regulation jacket with swallow tails that she always wears, something like Jenny Linds[6] in the Fiçha – and so disgusting in her habits that it was offensive to be in the room with her; – after she (Miss Edwards)[7] left that place she had a bad brain fever – since then I have lost sight of her – she used always to be sending me Game and things (which I fear she bought poor thing) to shew her gratitude for the little kindness I had, had it in my power to shew her. The Myddleton Biddulphs[8] have returned for a fortnight on account of his having to exercise the Denbighshire Yeomanry[9] – she drove over to see me yesterday – and here is a pretty story she told me of Lord Rendelsham[10]– (Lord John Russells[11] step son) it appears that he had a <u>liaison</u> with one of those infamous women of whom English men and their Morality! are so fond; – in order to break this thing off my little Lord Nomuscle, and his other relatives – persuaded him a few months ago to victimize some poor girl and marry her, – and she is now within two months of her confinement, well, her <u>amiable</u> husband took himself off – a short time ago, with his former mistress, leaving a short note, on his wifes dressing table saying – that as he had never cared for her; – he had returned to the only woman he did care for, but that he wished her well, and hoped she would get safely over her confinement"! Now Sir Liar Coward – Blackguard Bulwer Lytton would have done all this, and ten <u>times worse</u> (as he did) but <u>he</u> never would have committed himself by Owning it; on the contrary he would have perjured himself fifty Hells deep in denying it; and have <u>cleverly</u> contrived through the medium of his infamous Press Gang, to have shifted all the Odium of his own villainy – on his victim! but then to besure – happily for the world he stands out paramount and <u>Unique</u> in the Annals of Villainy – and –

"Will leave a <u>Blackguards</u> name to other times.

Linked with <u>no</u> virtue, and ten thousand crimes"![12]

As <u>you</u> are not Massy – you will forgive this slight variation from "The Corsair". Too bad of Skeet, never to send poor Mrs Hodgson a copy of my Book; till I <u>again</u> wrote to bully him at the beginning of the week. – Such a Magnificent! bouquet of Blush roses just come from dear old Dr Price which look quite ridiculous this winter weather. God Bless you my Dearest Rebecca – and with De dogs love Believe Me Ever Your Grateful & Affect Rosina Bulwer Lytton.

HALS
1. Born in Dublin in the same year as RBL, Sarah Smith (*c.* 1802–78) married Robert Campbell Scarlett, the second Baron of Abinger.
2. Literally: 'cream of the cream' (French), the elite.

3. Areas of fashionable high society in Brighton.
4. William Harrison Ainsworth (1805–82) was a writer, particularly renowned for his historical romances.
5. Charles John Kean, the actor. See RBL, 17 September 1839.
6. Johanna Maria Lind (1820–87) was a Swedish-born opera singer, known as Jenny Lind and the 'Swedish nightingale'.
7. Possibly a relative of the Rector Revd Edwards and his wife.
8. Colonel Robert Myddleton Biddulp (1805–72) and his wife, Fanny, were the owners of Chirk Castle in Chirk, Denbighshire, north Wales. They befriended RBL, who stayed with them, sleeping in a state bed that had been occupied by Charles I.
9. A voluntary regiment of Welsh yeomen.
10. This would appear to be Thomas Lister, third Baron Ribblesdale (1828–76), an officer in the Royal Horse Guards who was the son of Thomas Lister, second Baron Ribblesdale (1790–1832) and Adelaide Lister (b. before 1811–38).
11. Adelaide Lister (see above, n. 10) remarried, becoming the first wife of Lord John Russell (1792–1878), the leader of the Whig campaign in the House of Commons for parliamentary reform. He served as Prime Minister in 1846–52 and 1865–6.
12. 'He left a Corsair's name to other times / Linked with one virtue, and a thousand crimes', Byron, *The Corsair* (1863–4), Canto 3.

To Rebecca Ryves

Monday Night February 7th 1853

Many thanks My dearest Rebecca for your kind letter which arrived by the 2 o'clock Post to day – but Monday (an interesting fact of which I have before informed you) being my patching day, I had to take in three dresses which are now a world too wide for me, – all attempts at writing to you – before this moment were impossible as I was ill in bed all yesterday. We are much rejoiced, at hearing of Massy's convalescence and hope he will do nothing to throw himself back. Great rejoicing there will be no doubt at <u>no 12</u> tomorrow night at your brother Williams advent and I also shall be most happy to see him in a quiet way – for I have a notion I shall not be well enough to go to the ball so will stay and be tucked up with mine poorest of Tibs whom me fears will have quite forgotten hims poor old mud; thank you a thousand times for having taken such good care, of him, thank you also for going to Goslings – there will be no use in his coming here as I <u>cannot</u> pay it; were you also good enough to shew Elton; that he had been paid for the chair covers? only fancy my surprise! after dinner to day about 3o'clock at having a visit from Mr Hodgson! he said that he had come down for a clients funeral (not mine unfortunately) and would not go back without calling he also gave me the pleasant intelligence that that wretch Allen is beginning his bother again about his fraudulent demand– and that <u>Brown</u> had said to Mr Hodgson I'd have to pay it! indeed? – Mr Brown may consider himself very lucky that I pay <u>his</u> exorbitant bills, without murmuring – but <u>he</u>

need not interfere to help on that fellow Allens infamous cheating which no earthly power will induce me to yield to – so as I have before told him 20 times over let him go to law, as fast as he likes, and I think it is a pity he should have wasted so much time in doing so – and all this worry, I owe to that little shuffling sneaking contemptible brute Jones– Sir Harry Darrels death[1] did not make any sensation here – I believe if all the world but one – were to die now a days it would not make any impression upon the one left. I <u>knew</u> a more original woman than Sir Harry Darrels love for my friend went into <u>Weeds</u> for the loss of her Lover! Making the <u>Husband</u>!! buy them!! – I am so ill and tired it being now past 12 – that I must say good night, and God Bless you and with kindest regards to your Brothers Believe me Ever my dearest Rebecca your obliged and affect Rosina Bulwer Lytton

HALS
1.   Sir Harry Francis Colville Darrell (1814–53).

To Rebecca Ryves

Brighton
Wednesday Night going to Bed February 9th 1853

Tired to death with the Ball last night this is the first moment I have had for the last four and twenty hours – My dearest Rebecca to announce hims safe arrival of poor Master Tib, and thank you (which I do very sincerely) for the good care, you have taken of his Darlingship him moaned after you yesterday Evening but this morning after a little reproachful look or two, which said as plainly as Dogs Eyes could speak "Why did you leave me?" him nestled up under my chin – kissed me, & knew that I was hims mud. Will you again thank your brother for his great kindness in taking the trouble of bringing him; I have not <u>forgotten</u> that I owe him for his journey but <u>alas</u>! I must owe it him till April, for my dear Rebecca after paying my last washing – bill my funds are reduced to 5"6d! which is all I shall have till April! these incessant, and degrading pecuniary worries are gnawing away my very existence and are I should think a good foretaste of "the worm that never dies"[1] – Thanks much and many also for the pillow cases, & Poor Tibs – Household gods – to wit bowl and basket. My bracelet also arrived from Killicks yesterday morning. The ball I believe was ...

Will you send Mrs Tylers sugar bason by the next opportunity?

HALS
Incomplete letter.
1.   Alexander Pope, 'To Mr John Moore, Author of the Celebrated Worm-Powder' (1716), l. 32. 'This is where the worm never dies and the fire never goes out' (Mark 9:48), a biblical description of hell.

To Rebecca Ryves

Sunday February 13ᵗʰ 1853

Many thanks my dearest Rebecca for your kind letter of yesterday – and its inclosed Bullet! – which Lady Hotham says "is most <u>cheering</u>! and it will be an ill wind in March if it don't blow you some good" but I have such faith in the Devil taking care of his own that even this accident and the bad blood it has to encounter gives me no hope of release, God forgive the wretched creature if he dies, – and turn his heart, and mend his ways if he lives since no miracle is beyond Gods power or Gods mercy. – I am very sorry to hear of Mr Lloyds sad accident; and also that poor Massy suffers from this bitter weather; I wish I <u>could</u> send him a little Madeira sun shine, but it was Mrs Tyler who sent him the last cake, and not I, for <u>very cogent reasons</u>. I am still "<u>spacheless wid de fluency</u>" but of all my sufferings, those of the <u>chest</u> continue the worst, and most mortal, and now my dearest Rebecca I am going to trouble you with a very disagreeable commission, and one I would fain spare you if I could – as you have had enough of that sort of thing already – but truly necessity <u>has</u> <u>no</u> law! – I will send, you by the first opportunity (as I don't like to risk it in a letter –) a little Diamond ring – of mine – if you could get me £2 upon it I should be greatly obliged to you; it cost £5 – only get a <u>common</u> Ticket for it as I hope to get it back in April – but dont tell <u>them this</u>! you may suppose how it pains me to trouble you with such a commission but what <u>can I do</u>? ...

HALS
The end of the letter is missing.

To Rebecca Ryves

Thursday February 17ᵗʰ 1853 In Bed

My dearest Rebecca I wrote in such a hurry yesterday, and in such pain I quite forgot to say that I must <u>insist</u> upon Tibs journey to Brighton being refunded to your brother with ten thousand thanks, it is bad enough for hims mud, to be a beggar, and on de Wideworld, but <u>de Dog</u> sall not be reduced to the same state, as long as hims mud has a breath left in her, which is to be hoped wont be very long – for when moral, and physical suffering goes on eternally with a hundred torture power life cannot resist for ever. We have been snowed up here for the last week – and the cold would transfix a Laplander and since its advent trebly have I regretted my poor warm little Kennel where I had more plenty, and more comfort, than I am ever likely to have again – but Gods will be done. I wrote you all my news of the Dinner yesterday, and hope I shall hear today that yours was equally agreeable. Did Willy send Emily[1] a Valentine? I suspect he did <u>The Honble</u>! Miss Tyler was so like his writing. De Dog is too Innocent! if you could see the Domiciliary Hunts of Moths, and shadows he gets up to amoose himseps, when mud cant take him out; – him desires hims bestest of loves to hims Aunt Rebecca I am glad Massy is in good spirits; as to be so is the shortest and surest road to getting quite well. – Good bye God Bless you with kindest regards to your Brothers, believe me Dearest Rebecca Ever your obliged & affect Rosina Bulwer Lytton.

HALS
1.   Emily Tyler, the daughter of Mrs Hardinge Tyler.

To Rebecca Ryves

Wednesday February 22nd 1853

My dearest Rebecca I am much disappointed at not having heard from you yesterday; or this morning – I hope however, that your cold is not worse, and that Massy was not worse; and that I shall get a letter from you by the 2 o'clock Post. I suppose you have seen by the Papers that in coming down the Rhône from Avignon to Lyon[1] in a steam Boat – the Boiler burst and that little reptile Henry Bulwer had to swim ashore for his life the paragraph concludes by saying "As the Humble gentleman is in a very precarious state of health, great fears are entertained for his recovery"[2] – verily it would appear that the Devil is collecting his dues, by the state of the Brothers Bulwer. Sir Liar <u>must</u> have a lie to the last, for Mrs Tyler heard from a person who can see into his very windows, that it was not his arm he hurt at all, but a far worse affair, a gathering in his hand – (from his evil courses –) which he is obliged to have probed, and lanced every day – and which the wise ones say portends a break up of nature in such a subject. – <u>Gorge</u> also, is indefaticable in his <u>kind</u> <u>bulletins</u> about him: – here is a passage from his letter to lady Hotham the day before yesterday –

"I met Bulwer again after I last wrote to you – he inquired <u>tenderly</u> after the state of his Wifes <u>health</u>? I said it was anything but <u>satisfactory</u>! as there was no chance of her making him a Widower, he did not look so much disappointed as I should have expected, and I thought to myself as I looked in his face, <u>you</u> are much more likely to leave her a Widow for any thing so <u>fearfully</u> aged, and wretched looking I never saw! The next day I heard he was taken dangerously ill; and allowed to see no one. – I yesterday met Lady Joderel[3] in the street she told me he was desperately ill and added I hope the wretch may die for his poor Wifes sake – for I know more of his infamy than most people <u>She</u> takes Lady Bulwers part warmly and asked very kindly after you."

Now this Lady Joderels Husband Sir Richard Joderel[4] is the Bulwers first cousin, I dont know either of them personally; so that her speech was all the more flattering to and Authentic of Sir Liar. Tonight we are going with Lady Hotham to a Lecture at the Albion rooms.[5] Grace Lady Webster lost no time in calling after she met me, and has asked me to an "at Home" tomorrow evening. I shall go for two reasons, first because she has always first rate music and next because I shall be sure to meet some of the <u>Clique,</u> and I happen as Cherubina de Willoughby <u>said of herself</u>! when she wore the white roses to be "<u>looking lovely</u>!"[6] just now, having become quite slight from my illness as you may suppose, when I tell you that all my dresses have had to be taken in 5 Inches! I dont know myself I look so youthful! which reminds me of Innocence, who desires hims bestest of loves to you, and begs I will tell you that him is de most popular dog in Brighton <u>even</u> among the Cats! both bi<u>ped</u> and quadruped. Mrs Tyler is very anxious to know whether Alice spent the day with you on Sunday? –

Pray forgive this abominable scrawl, but I am paperless and <u>penless</u> as well as <u>penniless</u>! so will release you from this <u>griffonage.</u> With kindest regards to your Brothers and best love to yourself. Believe me Dearest Rebecca Ever your Obliged And Affect Rosina Bulwer Lytton.

HALS
1. The River Rhône flows through the French towns of Avignon and Lyons.
2. In 1851, there was a steamship named after him called *Sir Henry L. Bulwer*.
3. Lady Jodrell (d. 1860) was the wife of EBL's relative, Sir Richard Jodrell. See below, n. 4.
4. Sir Richard Paul Jodrell (1781–1861) was a poet, who succeeded to the title of second Baronet Lombe of Great Melton, Norfolk. He was the first cousin of EBL, whose mother was a member of the Jodrell family from Norfolk.
5. These may be part of the Royal Albion Hotel in Brighton, built in 1826.
6. The heroine of Eaton Stannard Barrett's 1813 spoof of the Gothic novel. The line is 'so lovely', Barrett, *The Heroine* (1909), p. 61. See RBL, 24 December 1836.

To Rebecca Ryves

Brighton
Wednesday February 23rd 1853

As I before said, I am indeed grieved dearest Rebecca that you should have to go out for me in such weather! and particularly on such an Embassy!! – but oh! how selfish that same stern <u>necessity</u> makes us I suppose – Mrs Tyler or Emily – will write and thank you about Alice.[1] I am writing to you in the greatest haste, having so many letters, of <u>congratulation</u>! to answer, about the state of that wretched man, but I must not tell you from whom, as with the usual English <u>caution</u> they begged their sympathising effusions might be burnt, one person who was at Lady Dorothy Campbells on Monday Evening – and met a good number of the disreputable Legion from Mrs Milner Gibson down to that old Hell Hag Lady Morgan, gives the following Bulletin – "they say he is so dangerously ill; that there is no chance of his recovery" – as I said before may God blot out his sins, and forgive him, as I <u>do now</u>. – The lecture last night (on the duality of the brain) was too stupid; the Lecturer being the <u>facsimile</u> of an old Ourangoutang – with a broad Scotch twang – in one part of it – he said "I <u>dont</u> know if I make myself <u>plain</u>!?" "Oh! Heavens! said I that <u>would</u> be a work of supererogation" whereupon Lady Hotham laughed her laugh, and <u>winked her wink</u>! till she brought the eyes of the whole room upon me. I am very glad Massy has been out for a drive, and hope he is all the better for it; with kindest regards to him, and your brother William and de Dogs bestest of loves Believe me Ever My dearest Rebecca your obliged and affect Rosina Bulwer Lytton.

HALS
1.   Mrs Hardinge Tyler's daughter.

To Rebecca Ryves

Thursday February 24ᵗʰ 1853

No, my dearest Rebecca Tib says hims Aunt Faisey's picture has never been sent, and a lucky thing too, for I should not have had a penny to pay for it; as for Mr Moore he turns out to be what I very soon thought him to wit, a Humbug. What to do; I'm sure I know not, or what is to become of me I cannot imagine; for exclusive of my being thoroughly wretched, and out of my element here; – my affairs seem to be in a state of complete stagnation, and I am tied, hand and foot and cannot move, an inch. – and even if I <u>get</u> the cap of Liberty I know I shall be left a beggar, – still I say may God forgive the wretch as I do <u>now</u>, notwithstanding the thousand torturing deaths he has inflicted upon me during my miserable existence. Again I must repeat my dear Rebecca – how <u>sorry</u> I am that you should again be bored, by such a commission as that ring – for me – but what <u>am</u> I to do? – the <u>most</u> terrible part of my most terrible lot is: that I am <u>always</u> in <u>a false</u> position, – and one that compels me to <u>pay</u> money, without even having the pleasure of spending it, and between worry, illness, and eating nothing; having got so thin, – and being obliged to get all my dresses altered will cost me at least another £1. Poor Mrs Barclay who is a very nice amiable unselfish person; – is I am sorry to say ill in bed from this dreadful weather. I try to keep the House as quiet as I can for her; – but there is no stopping that eternal screaming against time, tune, and taste, which English young ladies call singing! – When I wrote to you yesterday it was a warm thaw, but before 6 o'clock the ground (after a deluge of rain) was a quarter of a yard deep in snow; and it blew one of the most fearful Hurricanes, I ever felt, or heard, in which about 11 at night I sallied out like one of the "weird sisters"[1] to go to Grace Lady Websters – who ...

HALS
Incomplete letter.
1.   A popular description of the witches in Shakespeare's play, *Macbeth*.

To Rebecca Ryves

Sunday February 27th 1853

Thank you a thousand times, my dearest Rebecca for all the trouble you so kindly took about the poor ring; – I almost wish now it had been one of the Eternal bracelets, for I dont see how I am to eke out this £1"7 – for six weeks. – If it be true that the darkest hour is before the dawn, I should almost think the dawn was at hand for never were things – so dark – so desolate – and so repugnant in all ways – as they are now – but then I <u>feel</u> that there <u>is</u> <u>no</u> <u>dawn</u> – no release for me! On Friday night I went to the play with Lady Hotham in one of the front Boxes sat the elegant Mrs Fonblanque[1] bedizened at all points going away – Mr Turner (for vulgar people are always free & easy and ill bred) said "Do you know Sir Edward Lytton is in Brighton I rather think not said I – "oh there is no doubt of it for Mrs Fonblanque – met, and spoke to him two days ago" – by this it would appear then that all his illness was a Hun[2] like everything else about him; – for if he is able to travel this weather! he cannot be so ill as he pretended but what is equally probable, Mrs Fonblanque may have also told a lie – she was grinning, and nodding to me like a Mandarin the whole Evening and I never took the least notice of her. – De Birard writes Lady Hotham a miraculous account of her <u>lake</u> at Hereford House[3] being colonized by snipes! it shews how severe the season must be for them to venture so near a human habitation; – this is certainly a <u>long bill</u> so it is to be hoped it is a <u>true bill</u> of the Preux Chevaliers.[4] – I will write to you more at length in a day or two, when I am less ill, and if possible less wretched. – De dog goes to school every day next door with poor little Cassy who is very fond of him; and as him is de especial favorite of the French Governess at this Miss Martins him now barks French with de true Poodle accent and without the slightest English twang – which is a comfort when one is always hearing of the <u>Tooler – rees</u>!!! commonly called Tuileries – addio – God Bless you My Dearest Rebecca and with kindest regards to your Brothers believe me Ever your Obliged and Affect Rosina Bulwer Lytton

HALS
1.   The wife of Albany Fonblanque. See RBL, 5 February 1838.
2.   A nomadic tribe, originally from the Middle East, who invaded the Roman Empire.

3. Situated in Earl's Court, Brompton, this was the London home of Lady Hotham.
4. Valiant Knight (French).

To Rebecca Ryves

Brighton
Tuesday March 1st! 1853

I have but a quarter of a minute to thank you my dearest Rebecca to thank you for your kind note, for yesterday being one of the loveliest days that ever came out of the Heavens – deep blue cloudless sky, Neapolitan sun, – and soft west wind, with all the balm of Araby[1] on its wings, I took advantage of it to pay a colony of visits and take Innocence [for] a long walk – so all my Monday's stitching and mending was driven into this mornings when the Paper that should come at latest on Monday morning also arrived – so that altogether I am in arrears; – I yesterday found "Grace Lady Webster" on the wing for London and on calling at Mrs Wheelers heard that "she was as well as could be expected"! which does not mean that a new member has been added to the family but <u>au</u> <u>contraire</u>[2] that an old one, has been removed from it; as poor Mr Wheelers brother aged 75 died suddenly of apoplexy on Friday – so the Dinner (of course) is put off – for which I am very thankful. You are indeed right my dear Rebecca, things may and do, become too bad to mend – and even for omnipotence, I do believe it would be easier to make a thousand glorious destinies every second – than in ten thousand ages – to mend so untoward – and entangled a one as mine! but you are young and where there is youth there is always <u>Hope</u> however bad things may be. I had horrid Dinner!?? since so it is by courtesy called so I must say good bye – with de Dogs love and my kindest regards to your Brothers Ever your Obliged and Affect. RB Lytton.

HALS
1. An archaic, poetic form for Arabia.
2. On the contrary (French).

To Rebecca Ryves

Brighton
Wednesday march 2nd 1853

I was very sorry my Dearest Rebecca to write to you in such a hurry yesterday but had I had three hours, at my disposal, I had not one scrap of news to tell you, on anything – but worries to dilate upon, and as no doubt you have enough of those of your own; there is no need of my adding mine to them; and <u>now</u> here are two more troublesome commissions – if you will kindly execute them, one is to write to Gates, and say that I would do so myself – but am not well (which is as true, as gospel) and that I am sorry to hear she has been ill, and equally sorry that I cannot send her the £2 she <u>says</u> I owe her (for I can find no memorandum of anything among my accounts – so of course it is the finale of the system of fleecing to which I was subjected –) that is I cannot send it her before the 14th or 15th of April, – I would not give <u>you</u> the trouble but I do not like to write myself and say I cannot pay such a sum! – but your writing and saying I am ill and will settle it when I settle my April accounts does not <u>look </u>quite so bad: – although it amounts to the same thing in reality! – be sure you put chapel St <u>West</u> or she wont get the letter. What is the use of having a <u>Mousequetaire à Genoux</u>! (anglice[1] an apothecary's Boy) for a Lover – if he cant guard her against inflammation of the side, but although Edwards affects the "gemmen" I suppose he hasn't '<u>haved as sick</u>" though the blue pull paper is evidently his selection, be <u>sure</u> you say I am sorry to hear the poor girl has been ill. You never told me if you were good enough to shew Elton the mistake he had made in his bill, about charging me <u>twice</u> over for Calendering my buff chair covers? for if not; it will be Mrs Allens History over again when I come to pay his bill. –

Now here is the other commission, would you kindly go to Blackburns, (wind and weather permitting?) and get – that is tell him to send me down by the 7th – Instant at latest as the Birthday is on the 8th an emerald green, or else a violet, or if that is not to be had (which it <u>is</u>) a royal purple velvet Common Prayer book lined with white watered silk – with gilt corners and clasp, – and on the escutcheon plate in the centre (if 'Common Prayer" is not already engraved on it, as it sometimes is) to have the name "Kate Long"[2] in Gothic letters engraved on it. I don't want a very small Prayer Book but a good sized one, like the pattern piece of paper I inclose; and pray take this opportunity of blowing up Blackburn about my Sunday paper which never arrives till Tuesday – and to be sure I have the prayer book at <u>latest</u> on the 7th though as much before as he likes, and whether – Green – violet or purple to take care that it is <u>a beautiful color</u>. Mr Yellow plush objects to living in families "where fainting is always going on"[3] where Birthdays are always going on! is equally arduous but this poor little Kate Long is a poor gentle cowed little thing and being in the humble dependent line – like myself: I feel for her. Mrs Barclay was very much obliged for your enquiries, and desired to be kindly remembered to you: yesterday while I was at Dinner Lady Hotham <u>swam</u> here – for she and the Ducks always luxuriate in the same puddle dock weather. In "Georges" last letter he says there is nothing the matter with Sir Liars hand – or arm (<u>so much for reports</u>) but that he is dying of Atrophy – Lady H brought me "The Spectator"[4] saying that in it was a terrible mauling on "my novel"[5] and castigation of Sir Liar. But from the quantity of critical cayenne she had lead me to expect, I found it mild and mawkish as a

Timbal of Maccaroni – as the Jeffrey or Gifford(?)[6] of "The Spectator" seems to bear in mind that the author of "my novel" like his own semi – Jewish Baron[7] – "has mixed with the first society! and called the cabinet Minister "My dear fellow!" – and therefore that his nerves are <u>of</u> too kid glove a texture, to bear any Iron grasp of critical handling, however, he <u>does </u>wind up by saying that the author of "my novel" <u>is worthy of the highest Gibbet</u>"! – I hope Massy did not get cold from his walk? forgive this most stupid scrawl but I am ill, wretched and frozen. I am glad you are going to Mrs Ripons[8] – as I have no doubt you will hear good music, Good bye. God Bless you, with kindest regards to your Brothers and de Dogs best love. Believe me Ever My Dearest Rebecca your obliged and affect Rosina Bulwer Lytton

---

HALS
1. Abbreviation for anglicize.
2. A young woman whom RBL befriended, who is dependent on relatives.
3. Thackeray parodied EBL in 'The Yellow Plush Papers', which began publication in *Fraser's Magazine* in 1838.
4. A literary journal. See RBL, 10 January 1832.
5. EBL's novel *My Novel by Pisistratus Caxton, or Varieties in English Life* is the second in the Caxton series and completed its serialization in *Blackwood's* (September 1850–January 1853). The hero is Lenny Fairfield, who eventually becomes a successful novelist in London and marries his childhood sweetheart.
6. More likely to be Francis Lord Jeffrey (1773–1850).
7. Baron Levy is a Jewish moneylender, who is the illegitimate son of a rich English grand seigneur by a Hebrew lady of distinction in EBL's *My Novel*. The actual quotation from the review is: 'Dandy literature and superfine sensibilities are tokens and causes of a degenerate art and an emasculate morality; and among offenders in this way none has sinned more, or is of higher mark for a gibbet, than the author of *My Novel*', *Spectator*, 26 (19 February 1853), p. 179.
8. Louisa Anne Ripon is a widowed friend of Hugh Massy Ryves, who marries Rebecca Ryves's brother William at the end of October 1853. See RBL, 23 October 1853.

To Rebecca Ryves

Friday 4 o'clock March 4th 1853

My Dearest Rebecca just 5 minutes after I had despatched my last scrawl to you – I got your kind letter, and now write to say that <u>if</u> Blackburn cannot get a green – or violet velvet Church service (which is all fudge as there are Oceans of them) the Royal purple one he has will do – <u>provided</u> it is a <u>bright</u> <u>good</u> <u>color</u> – <u>not faded</u> and the <u>lining</u> not tarnished or <u>soiled</u> – for it is always my fate to pay more dearly for bad, ugly – and damaged things than other people do for good and pretty ones. – (I am writing like Lady Hotham, I only wish I could sign my name to what she can or even to a less miraculous draught (draft). I know Kate Long has £200 a year in money – but I call – every one a dependant who has no natural Home, and is dependant upon <u>relations</u>! for a shelter – and people who spoil, and pamper their own children have seldom any kindness to spare for other peoples. Pray forgive and burn this scrawl but I am iller – than ill and hope soon to be "Where the wicked cease from troubling and the weary are at rest" Till then Believe Me Dearest Rebecca Ever your obliged and affect RB Lytton

---

HALS

To Rebecca Ryves

Brighton
Friday March 4th 1853

I am glad on your account but sorry on my own to hear My dearest Rebecca that you are going to Ireland and doubly sorry – to think that I cannot settle my debts with you before you go; but indeed, when I think of that, and all the rest, added to being without a Home! a Hope or a Chance! thrown on the wide world – I am almost out of my senses, and despair being now Chronic with me; I labour without intermission under the oppression of a sort of permanent presentiment – that some terrible Catastrophe is about to happen; – at this minute I feel doubly weak, and ill, having suffered for the last three days with Lady Hothams Commercial Mans – or Jones's <u>Diary</u> you did quite right to tell Mrs Greene[1] what you did, I cannot possibly pay her, her remaining £5 before the 15th or 16th of April, would to Heaven I had no other care. – I am hunting for some Piggery to <u>Board</u>! in – where they will take me for £100 a year – without a maid – for Wales, – the Isle of Man – and all other Theoretically cheap places are all very well – and <u>would</u> be much <u>pleasanter</u>; but where am I to get the money to go to them and so long – a journey alone, I could not undertake oh, if it would but please God – to take me – and save me from all these horrors, for – I am too old now to buffet with the nether worlds – vicious vulgarities, and vulgar vices. – I have not seen Mrs Wheeler since, so cannot tell whether Mr Wheelers Coffers, have sustained any influx, by his brothers death. What you tell me of the Antique Cheeses, is no news to me; for when I found that with so <u>few</u> Bridesmaids, they did not give you a Bracelet or anything, I came to the conclusion (aided by the Homeopathic globule of cake) that they added stinginess to their other snobbish attributes. I am ashamed to send you such a scrawl – but I am too ill to continue it further than to give you Innocences best love, my kind regards to your Brothers, and to assure you that I am ever my Dearest Rebecca your obliged and affect R Bulwer Lytton.

HALS
1.   A livery stable woman.

To Rebecca Ryves

Brighton
March 6th 1853

If I write to day my dearest Rebecca it is merely to ask you how you are? For I have nothing to say – except that I am as ill, and as miserable as I can be; which intelligence is neither new – nor pleasant –

I Envy you going to Mrs Lloyd – as you say she is such a nice Lady-like person, besides – I dont think Irish people ever think so much of crumbs of bread, and grains of salt as English people do, because they are never so innately vulgar minded – and even when outwardly vulgar, their vulgarity is of a less offensive, because less stuck up – and of a more original kind. Perhaps you had better write to Mr Moore, saying you are about to leave England, – and as the commission was left in your charge – you dont like to send me back the Picture without having ascertained from a competant Judge – whether it is or is not a Wooverman.[1] This poor little Picture is now my only hope! if that can be called a hope which does not amount even to a shadow! but if it should turn out to be an original I would myself have it raffled for – for I plainly – see no one else – will <u>do</u> any thing – English people if they make a great parade of pulling <u>one</u> foot out of the mire for you always leave the other sticking in farther than ever, – and think they have done wonders – taking it out of you in every way with the Irish curse of bad manners (vile bad ones truly!)

My prospects are charming – having in April (with out Brownes bill) about £120 to pay and £47 to pay it with <u>this</u> and other millstones round my neck to recommence the world – in some new Piggery – where of course I shall as usual be fleeced – at every turn, – and so get deeper into the mess; – when my kind friends – will no doubt as usual grin in my face, and wonder that – having been dismembered of House and Home and all I possess in the world I am not <u>yet</u>! out of my difficulties! – Mr Elton is quite wrong I <u>never</u> sent any spr[ig]s of Furniture to him to be cleaned – when I went to Thurloe Cottage save the pieces of White Cashmere of the Curtain draperies. – I am so ill I can write no more, than to say good bye and God Bless you – with de Dogs best love, and my kindest regards to your Brothers ever my dearest Rebecca your grateful & affect

R B Lytton

HUNT
1.   A painting by a member of the Wouverman family. See RBL, 32 December 1852.

To Rebecca Ryves

Brighton
Tuesday March 8 1853

Thanks, much and many my dearest Rebecca for your kind letter of yesterday. – As for my side! the whole Homoeopathic, or any other Pharmacopia would not do it the slightest good, for they cannot "Minister to a mind diseased!"[1] – besides – Medicine is the least part of all remedies – and a cup of Broth, or gruel, that was eatable, would be quite unattainable here, and I cannot swallow pepper, and grease by the Cart load, to say nothing of that detestable – maids verjuice[2] looks, giving me a sort of permanent Cholera. Alas! my dear Rebecca up to the present moment you know as much of where I am going in April as I do! for I have not yet heard any thing more about it from Mrs St George[3] – whom I asked to look out for such a place for me – and as <u>she</u> lives at Kemp Town, my journeys to see her cost me 4s – which as you may suppose – I cannot afford, – oh! could I have only fallen into English ways – and Beareries – & divested myself of the foolish Arab notions of Hospitality – with which I was brought up – I should not now be in quite the destitute state I am; and yet I fear it wont be live, and learn, for the more I see of English ways the more they revolt, and disgust me. – The Book came from Blackburnes last night (Many thanks to you for kindly taking so much trouble about it) I think it Handsome – but not very fresh, nor is the <u>color</u> of the velvet very good – he sent it in some foolish way by which I had 1"2d to pay for it! whereas for a large box of Boots and shoes from Mrs Framptons some time ago I only paid 6d. – I never saw such weather! yesterday I went out to drive with Lady Hotham it was so brilliantly fine – the Sun like gold, the sea like silver …

HALS

Incomplete letter.

1. Shakespeare, *Macbeth*, V.iii.40.
2. Derived from the French *verjus* (green juice), this is a very acidic juice made by pressing unripe crab apples or grapes.
3. In 1848, RBL, who had been living in apartments at East Ham, left to stay with Mrs St George and her husband, the assistant chaplain at the Tower of London.

To Rebecca Ryves

Brighton
Friday March 11th 1853

Thank you My dearest Rebecca for your kind letter recieved at 3 P:M: yesterday: All you say is very true, and very kind; I never for a moment doubt, the justice, goodness, and mercy of God; but with the very strongest conviction, and trust in

all three, poor human nature, is such a frail miserable rickety misbegotten thing
– that it cannot but totter, and groan under its sometimes unsupportable burden
that is when the nails in its cross – are more than usually rusty and so fester the
wounds – they make. However – all has been Halcyon[1] amiability for the last
three days and so I try to take theoretical draughts of Lethe,[2] – and strengthen
my conviction – that the <u>good</u> is <u>real</u>, and the scum only on the surface, and at
all events it is a proof of a good disposition – the turning over a new leaf – as
soon as the discovery that the former conduct inflicted serious pain and this I
feel I owe to the never varying amiability of the <u>other</u>. – From Mrs St George
I have yet heard nothing for you know English people – never care; how long
they keep you in suspense, but every day feel my heart withering – and my spirits
flagging more – however Gods will be done, and although "To bear is (<u>not</u>) to
conquer ones fate" yet what cant be cured, must be endured. – I am very sorry to
hear that Mrs Kitchener has got a swelled face and dare say it <u>may</u> jeopard[ise]
her likeness to Venus[3] – as you know it was <u>Adonis</u>[4] who was " <u>the Swell</u>"! and
not Venus. – Strange enough I was reading "Lewis Arundel"[5] only last week,
and read out all about Faust[6] to Tibby – who said as it is the <u>coat</u> that makes the
gentleman now a day's – <u>him</u> is a much finer canine Gentleman than Mr Faust
– it is <u>well</u> written, but nothing original in it Rose Arundel being the ditto of
Ruth Pinch in "Martin Chuzzlewit"[7] Frere,[8] the facsimile of Tom Pinch,[9] – and
Jemima the Daguerrotype of Mrs Gampe.[10] – I am going to read "Villette" by
the Jane Eyre Woman.[11] – Mrs Tyler says "The Deans Daughter" by Mrs Gore,[12]
is great rubbish. I wonder how a book called "The Devils Darling" would take?
I have the Hero all ready <u>Cut</u> – and <u>dry</u>! (if he drinks as he used to do?) Forgive
this stupidest of scrawls but I have not one scrap of news – but will send you any
I may kick up in the course of to day or tomorrow. – So now good bye, and God
Bless you, and with kindest regards to your Brothers believe Me Ever My dearest
Rebecca Ever Your Grateful & Affect Rosina Bulwer Lytton

HALS
1. The halcyon is a kingfisher type of bird which, according to classical legends, would calm
   the sea in order to nest on it.
2. Meaning 'forgetfulness' in Classical Greek, this was the name of one of the rivers of
   Hades. Anyone drinking from it would experience complete forgetfulness or oblivion.
3. In Roman mythology, the goddess of love.
4. Adonis was the mortal lover of the goddess Venus. See above, n. 3.
5. Frank E. Smedley, *Lewis Arundel: or, The Railroad of Life* with illustrations by 'Phiz'
   (1852).
6. The protagonist of the classic German legend in which a medieval scholar makes a pact
   with the Devil.
7. The governess in Charles Dickens's, *Martin Chuzzlewit* (1844).
8. Brother (French).
9. The brother of Ruth. See above, n. 7.

10. Mrs Gampe is a nurse in Dickens's, *Martin Chuzzlewit* (see above, n. 7), who deals with birth and death, the lying in and the laying out.
11. *Jane Eyre* (1847) was Charlotte Brontë's first published novel and *Villette* (1849) her third. See RBL, 27 March 1858.
12. Catherine Gore, *The Dean's Daughter, or The Days We Live In* (1853).

To Rebecca Ryves

Brighton
Sunday March 13th 1853

My dearest Rebecca I am so ill in bed with a violent sick Headache from the glare of the lights at the Play last night, and laughing, and crying at that pretty Louisa Howard[1] in the Zingara[2] and Jack Sheppard,[3] that I can scarcely keep my eyes open long enough to scrawl you these few lines, and tell you that I am very glad you had such an agreeable Evening at Mrs Ripons– I have had another bother with the inclosed letter from Mr Scarnell[4] you know you paid them that Bill of £1"18"3 – for spoiling a Dressing gown for me (which I have never been able to wear) and six petticoat bodies – in January – when you paid Greene the Livery Stable woman £5 – on account of her bill of £9"19"6 and Mrs Rogers her Bill of £14"16"0 – you sent me the memorandum of these monies – on a slip of paper – but I dont think you sent me the receipts – though you said you would do so – however I cannot get up – to look to day I am sorry to trouble you to go to Scarnells– again but will you do so and make them understand this bill of £1"18"3 was paid, and tell them to send me the shift they altered in a parcel by rail, as there seems no chance of your Brother Williams coming would you also have the goodness – to send me Eltons <u>two</u> bills that I sent you or I shall have some bother about them when I pay them. Browne has never sent me down Fairy's Picture I hope he has not spoiled it in the cleaning! perhaps some day you would have the kindness to see about it? – nothing have I heard yet from Mrs St George – and suppose I shall have to hunt myself for some hole of the sort but how I am to exist there even if I <u>do</u> find it I know not! Lady Hotham is for ever telling me to remember that there is always a room at Hereford House for me when ever I want to go to London on Business – or pleasure!!! In vain I tell her I have no money for either – so hard is it to make millionnaires comprehend the <u>literal</u> meaning of those <u>bare</u> simple words <u>I have not a sou</u>![5] Forgive this scrawl I am in such terrible pain and with Upsy Pupsy love and kind regards to your Brothers Believe me Ever My Dearest Rebecca your grateful and affect Rosina Bulwer Lytton.

HALS
1. Louisa Howard was an actress, who had played leading roles at the Haymarket Theatre, London.

2. *La Zingara* (Italian for *The Gypsy Girl*) is an opera by Gaetano Donizetti, first performed in Naples in 1822.
3. Jack Sheppard (1702–24), the thief and prison-breaker, was eventually executed at Tyburn. *Jack Sheppard the House-breaker* (1825) was written by W. T. Moncrieff, who had pirated EBL's *Eugene Aram*. See RBL, 26 February 1832. A few years later, William Harrison Ainsworth's best-selling romance, *Jack Sheppard* (1839), illustrated by some of George Cruikshank's best woodcuts, inspired many imitative romances and a large number of stage plays.
4. Dressmaker.
5. French coin of little value, worth five centimes.

To Rebecca Ryves

Brighton
Wednesday March 22nd 1853

My dearest Rebecca Although your letter was dated "Monday Mng" I only got it late, in the day yesterday. – Thank you very much for going to Brownes; I hope there will be no further dawdling in his at length! Sending down my poor little Fairy's Picture as the Raffle is already opened for it by 3 subscribers at a guinea each I would rather have parted with one of my hands, than that poor little picture but Starvation has no law! – and as nothing has ever been done, or ever will be done about the other, it needs must be; – and a few drops of gall, more or less in the Cup of affliction, when one has drained it to the dregs matters little. Are you or your Brothers, sufficiently intimate with the gentleman who has been staying at Langothlan[1] to ask him to have the goodness to write to the Inn keeper there and ask him what he would Board, and lodge, a Lady – her maid, and a little dog for; – a week? – for six months, – or perhaps longer; – but it must be something very <u>reasonable</u>, or she could not afford to go: – if you – are not intimate enough with this gentleman to do this; perhaps you would at all events have the goodness to ascertain for me as <u>soon</u> as <u>possible</u> – the price of the first and second class fare on the Holy head line[2] as <u>far</u> as Langothlen; for <u>it</u> seems to me far <u>cheaper</u> than any thing I have as yet heard of – Mrs Tyler wrote to a Captain and Mrs Somebody in the Isle of Man[3] – for me to board with them; as House keeping – with what I have, or rather with what I <u>have not</u>, on any scale is out of the question; they have only an 8 roomed cottage, of which they could give me but one room, (a small one) and for which they ask (without a maid) £100 a year, which I think considering the cheapness of every thing in the Island, extremely dear; as in <u>London</u> people can get <u>good</u> Board and Lodging for £70 – besides I am sick of <u>soi-disant</u>[4] English Ladies(??) and gentlemen! who murder the Queens English in the most remorseless manner and give one <u>low</u> life <u>above</u> stairs both as to <u>manner</u>, and <u>matter</u> at every turn, till a trip to the Bay of Biscay,[5] would be pleasant compared to ones sensations. No, I would far rather be with some good honestly vulgar people. No one knows that the Picture to be raffled for – for £100 is mine; so pray say nothing about it to <u>any one</u>; as I should be very sorry it got to Landseers[6] ears, the whole affair is quite galling, and painful enough as it is, without any embellishments, or additions to the skinning, and torturing process. – If your brother William is good enough to bring those things for me on the 30th – have the goodness to make a <u>separate</u> parcel of the sugar bason; for unless they were <u>very</u> carefully packed indeed – if together, it might – and would cut the linen to pieces. – Sir John Eustace called upon me yesterday – his <u>Bulletin</u> of Sir Liar was that he is too ill to go out; his legs being frightfully swollen; this they say is the, last, and fatal stage of atrophy – again I say God forgive the wretched man, much all his unimaginable wickedness; and his worldly triumphs – through such crooked means have availed him to come to such an untimely end! Yesterday we had the heaviest fall of snow that we have yet had; it pelting down, in the midst of a brilliant, and <u>warm</u> sun! The ground is still covered. I suppose you saw by the papers, that 3 men were killed last Week, by the boiler bursting at the Brighton Station. – Forgive this stupid and Egotistical scrawl and with kind regards to your Brothers, and best wishes for you all, Believe Me Ever My Dearest Rebecca your Obliged and Affectionate Rosina Bulwer Lytton.

HALS
1. Llangollen is the correct spelling. This is a town in north-east Wales in the Dee valley.
2. The railway line on the way to Holyhead, a town in the county of Anglesey, north-west Wales.
3. An island, located in the Irish Sea off the west coast of England.
4. So-called (French).
5. Named after the Spanish province of Biscay, this bay is a gulf of the North Atlantic Ocean, lying along the western coast of France and the northern coast of Spain.
6. Edwin Henry Landseer (1802–73) was a well known painter of nature and animals, particularly dogs. He painted the portrait of RBL's spaniel Fairy, which he gave to her as a gift. She wanted to conceal from him that she was trying to sell the picture, to help pay off her debts.

To Rebecca Ryves

Brighton
Thursday March 24th 1853

My Dearest Rebecca I did not get your Tuesday's letter till late in the day yesterday, I herewith send you the reciept for <u>Chapped</u> hands – but the best way to get <u>Chaps</u> off your hands is to tell them as I do that "All man is <u>BEAST</u>!! with a very big B!! this I have found infallible as it hurts the vanity, selfishness, and self love, of which they are wholly, and solely composed; – that it drives them off instantly – and the Noble science of self-defence" – (for <u>women</u>) that of ridding oneself of those most troublesome and mischievous Ephemera men, and mosquitoes – I acquired great proficiency in, in Italy: would to Heaven! I had only learnt it a little earlier in life. – Thank you very much for going to Brownes, and Gregory's – July! July! well it is to be hoped I shall be dead and buried before that time; – as I am on the same <u>regime</u> – as the Horse that was fed on an Oat a day and just as <u>he</u> was getting accustomed to it he died! I can now fully appreciate the old Joe Miller story of the man asking another who had been staying with a mutual friend, that was just married "Well Jack – and what sort of a wife – has he got? and what sort of table do they keep?" Jack – "Well the wife is like a cow in Everything but her breath, and everything is sour in the House <u>but</u> the vinegar" – but such must always be the case when every thing is left to servants – and very common vulgar servants too, and the mistress – can devour anything and everything set before her from rancid butter down to flour and water kneaded with tallow candle tasted dripping which she calls Pastry! – and is quite satisfied that every thing belonging to her!!!!!! is the best in the world! and as bad has a <u>supremacy</u> as well as good. So it is – ...

HALS
Incomplete letter.

To Rebecca Ryves

Brighton
Easter Sunday March 27th 1853

My dearest Rebecca I have only 5 minutes before Church to thank you (which I do very sincerely) for your kindness in writing to Llangollen they ought of the two take a woman much cheaper; as men Eat, and drink so much more, and I have now for some time past forsworn my favorite beverage – the Woden[1] nectar beer, only taking it on very rare occasions. – There is no fear of my going to the Isle of Man – as the people wrote after to try and screw another £20 a year making it a £120! – Pray beg of your Brothers to be <u>very</u> particular in <u>never</u> Enlightening Gorge, as to any of my <u>real</u> movements, but always to put him on as many wrong scents as they please, as I more than ever believe him to be a Jesuitical double-dealing knave – Lady Hotham has had another letter from him in which he says he thinks Sir Liar is – cracked it seems, it is not a House in Hereford St, that he has bought, but has returned to our old house; in Hertford St (May Fair) an additional proof of his beastliness, and total want of human feeling were any wanting. – That insufferable dawdle Browne has not <u>yet</u> sent the Picture it is a charming position to be in – not to know on earth where I am to go and not (up to this time) to have one sou in the world to go any where with but I have long ceased to look forward, and only look upward – to remind me that God's will must be done. I shall feel very sorry when you are gone to Ireland – but if I begin to think of all I have to feel sorry for I shall not be able even to pray for this thought always stuns, and stupefies me, – it is quite true and by no means new, that Every one is afflicted in some way or other, but poverty is a concrete of all other afflictions! the Carbuncle in Sir Liars hand; does not much tally with Gorges assurances to Lady Hotham that he had nothing whatever the matter with his hands. – It was this day two years that my poor Innocent Tib if you remember, was taken out of the House of Bondage, would that some good Samaritan[2] would walk behind you and I to day and render us the same service! Good Bye, and God Bless you with kind regards to your Brothers. Believe me in Great Haste my dearest Rebecca Ever Gratefully and affectly yours Rosina Bulwer Lytton.

HALS
1. Anglo-Saxon name for the Germanic pagan god Wodan, more commonly known as the Norse god Odin.
2. The parable of the 'Good Samaritan' (Luke 10:34) in which a stranger helps a man, who had been attacked, even though the Jewish victim was his traditional enemy. See RBL, 22 April 1881.

To Rebecca Ryves

Brighton
Friday April 1ˢᵗ! 1853

My dearest Rebecca I am really sorry to be such a constant bother to you "But who is bored himself must be himself a bore!" I have had a dun from Mrs Beedle pleading a Drs bill of £45 – for which I am very sorry poor woman but repeat, what I have told her, that I am going – because I would not be in the way of their going to Paris in May. And be sure not to be taken of unawares should she launch out – as she will be sure to do – about the imprudence of my taking that [ill]ge – but say that it was no imprudence at all, but quite the contrary – a very economical plan – only that every one is liable to be cheated once in their lives if not oftener – even she herself! as she told me having once been cheated out of £1,500 – with this difference that that was a drop in the sea to her whereas half the sum would have been more than my all – it will be better for all our sakes that you try and dun into her head, that I am a good manager – as indeed I am, but such a long process of fleecing as I have undergone Croesus[1] himself could not bear up against.

I can say – verily Zoroaster[2] was right in his doctrine of duality – or the mystical relation of the principles of good and ill – and so I identify his twin spirits Jezden – the benign influence or a well filled coff[er] Ahriman[3] – the Devil! ie an Empty purse! God knows I have proved the latter, in every way that a poor wretch can. –

Lady Hotham returns to Town on Monday – but dont go and see her for a week or some days till she is settled in her house while I think of it let me put you on your guard to say <u>nothing to her</u> (or indeed to any one else) of how wretched I have been here, but merely will you kindly call upon her – and tell her what is the truth, that I am ill in bed, and much grieved [tha]t I cannot settle her [acco]unt (or even a part of it now – and dont even say that I will do so in July but say I will do so the moment I can get my affairs a little straight but that I was so skinned before I left Town – that it will take me some little time to recover it; every one, and every thing seems to conspire against me – Browne has not <u>yet</u> sent the Picture! & until it is here a shilling cannot be got upon it, and that is my last faint hope – it is really too bad of him – and I am more worried, and annoyed than ...

If you see her besure you tell her what is true, that I am very fond of her, and always speak most gratefully of her kindness to me. – To add to my comfort I have managed to hurt my right foot dreadfully – and cannot put it to the ground without screaming.

Llangollen is no[w] [my] last hope every other place I have sought after, (and they are many) being much too dear. – I hope your Brother William wont come to day as I shall not be able to see him. <u>March</u>! you see has come and gone! hang that false varlet of an Astrologer! God Bless you My dearest Rebecca – and help us both – and with kind regards to Massy – and Innocences best love to you Believe me Ever

      your grateful and affect

      Rosina Bulwer Lytton

HUNT

Section missing.

1.   Croesus (595–*c.* 546 BC) was the King of Lydia and renowned for his wealth. His name has became a synonym for a wealthy man.

2.   Manicheanism is a doctrine, which incorporates this belief and elements of the teachings of Zoroaster, an ancient Persian prophet and religious poet.

3.   Ahura Mazda is the spirit of the divine within Manicheanism; its opposite is Ahriman, the personification of the devil in Manichean belief.

To Rebecca Ryves

Brighton
Wednesday Mg April 6th 1853

My dearest Rebecca I am indeed truly grieved to learn by your letter just received that poor Massy has had a relapse! he ought to be more careful – than I fear he is. Tincture of Arnica[1] – about 5 drops in a wineglass full of water – is the best styptic he could take; but of course Dr Williams knows what is best for him; – this indeed must be a sad addition to all your worries, and sincerely do I feel for you – but alas! <u>that</u> can do you no good, – Thank you very much for Mrs Phillips'[2] letter which is as you say very satisfactory will you kindly write her a line to say the Lady hopes to be with her by the end of the month, but will of course write to her before naming the day, and all particulars, I cannot at present state anything more specific, as till I can scrape at least a £10 note clear – I cannot of course set out upon so long a journey – would that it would please God to have mercy upon me and take me the last long journey before that, as truly I am weary of this fearfully long unequal struggle single handed – against such a world. – Thank you also very much for your kindness in going to Mrs Beadle I am sorry poor woman I cannot pay her now, and a good many more just at this time; but as you truly say want of money is "the most prevalent complaint going – and <u>never gone</u>"! like Jonases literary production which I am again afflicted with and which quite wears me out, I cannot think what your Brothers ideas of looking well! can be, for I think I look badly enough to frighten the D—l[3] himself – I hurt my foot through my own folly – kind little Mrs Barclay gave me a solution of Ivy for a hard corn. I like an ass put it also to a soft corn, which skinned my whole foot. The dinner at the Suttons[4] was only ourselves (they being in Lodgings). I like her very much – and Mr Sutton is a charming gentlemanlike old man. I dont know when Emily is going to Town – or whether she is going at all; – however, she may safely go as far as Massy is concerned, – as she has had half a dozen Hobbledyhoy flirtations since then. I was disgusted at her total want of feeling when he broke that blood vessel she then being all flutter and twitter about a Mr Atkinson <u>anything</u> in the shape of a <u>man</u>! does; – as a more thoroughly empty headed empty hearted, <u>ignorant</u>!!!! English Miss I never saw thinking of nothing else but "<u>getting</u> married" as in servant maid Phraseology she elegantly expresses it; she is now all flutter and twitter about young Sutton, a mere brat of a boy – oh! of all the disgusting things under the Sun – that running after – adulation – and adoration of men, is <u>the</u> most disgusting – and she has the complaint most confluently (pray burn this as I should not say it to anyone but you so pray don't repeat it to your brothers) – Poor Kate Lloyd is laid up with the measles, <u>à propos</u>[5] – Blackburne could not have charged 11"6d for engraving the name on that Prayer book, as they generally engrave it for nothing – or at the outside charge 6d a letter, which would be 7 letters – which is all the for[e] names contain 3"6d perhaps if you are passing some day you would kindly inquire about this? I am so ill, I can scarcely hold up my head to write it we have had 3 days of dense Fog, or rather Scotch mist which always knocks me up – and brings on Jonas's literary production when I feel the re-action of Jonas's lost in a fog style. I do hope your next will bring a better account of poor Massy – with kindest regards to him, and Willy, and Innocences best love, Believe me Ever My Dearest Rebecca your grateful and affect Rosina Bulwer Lytton

Be sure you send me back the paragraph from the Yorkshire paper about Sir Liar – they copied it from a London Paper.

HALS
1. A homeopathic remedy which RBL is recommending as a styptic, which contracts the blood vessels to stem bleeding.
2. Mrs Amey [*sic*] Phillips (1791–1857) was the innkeeper of the Hand Hotel, Bridge Street, Llangollen, where RBL stayed in 1854.
3. Devil.
4. This is probably at 79 Hamilton Terrace, St Johns Wood, London.
5. In connection with (French).

To Rebecca Ryves

Brighton
Thursday April 7th 1853

My dearest Rebecca We earnestly hope this may find poor Massy better; and your anxiety about him a little abated; – if I had no worries of my own – it would be quite fretting enough to think of the way you are all in and to be able to do nothing but add to your misery by so selfishly bothering you as I am always doing with my troublesome commissions but at all events pray believe me I will do as much for you, whenever an opportunity offers. I write now in great haste as a <u>ray</u> of hope has beamed which may save my poor little Fairy's Picture – Just after it had gone to the jewellers yesterday where it is to be raffled for Mrs Sutton came in the kindest manner (Mrs Tyler having asked her to take a ticket) and said she did not like the idea – of its been raffled for and that if I would send her the Wooverman (or whose ever it is) she knew that good kind clergyman Mr Baker – would not only get the best judge in England to decide upon the master but get the Picture adequately disposed of – so never mind Mr Moores having any thing to do with it <u>even</u> if he now offers – but have the goodness to direct it forthwith

"To Mrs Sutton
79 Hailton Terrace
St Johns Wood

With care this <u>side uppermost</u>, and to be <u>kept dry</u> carriage Paid and Booked. The Parcels Delivery Office is close to you at Turners my milk mans next the church Mrs Sutton goes to Town on Friday, so I should like if possible, it should be there when she arrives. – If your brother could conveniently call at Herries on Monday for my Parish allowance (for which I inclose a cheque I should be greatly obliged to him, and then you can take for the Parcels delivery of the Picture, and also the list of things I inclose – but don't <u>pay anymore</u>. – I am aware Pierson Till Elton and others are owing – but they <u>must</u> wait, as I have about £24 of <u>borrowed</u> money to pay here and this £19 to pay it with – but I <u>now</u> do feel something like a hope in Mrs Sutton; God grant it may not be frustrated – for your sake as well as mine. When you are good enough to pay those bills be <u>sure</u> you get me <u>stamped</u> receipts for all the £5 £7 & £8 and simple acknowledgements for the others. God Bless you and help us all My dearest Rebecca – all unite in best love to you kindest regards to your brothers, and best wishes for poor Massy pray let me know how he is going on? and Believe me Ever your Grateful and Affect Rosina Bulwer Lytton.

Lady Hotham don't go to Town till Saturday

HALS

To Rebecca Ryves

Brighton
Friday April 8th 1853

My dearest Rebecca I sincerely hope that poor Massy is better and going on favourably – that is taking care of himself and attending to the Dr's orders in keeping as quiet as possible for he cannot be too quiet; or too careful in his present state; and the more care he takes, the sooner he will get over it, and be able to go out I was sorry to trouble you but I hope you <u>lost no time</u> <u>in</u> sending off the Picture to Mrs Sutton; <u>even</u> if you had made any previous arrangements with Mr Moore; as we have had long, and repeated proof that there is no reliance to be placed upon <u>him</u> – and Mrs S is my last, and only chance, not that I allow myself to <u>hope</u> – but if my poor Fairy's Picture could be saved, it would be a <u>great</u> relief – and reprieve, how Providential, that Mrs Sutton should have intervened – for only fancy Edwin Landseer is now down here the Duke of Devonshire having lent! him his House at Kemptown,[1] and it would have been very distressing if he had known the fate of his gift – as he most assuredly <u>would</u>, had it been raffled for here – as the subscribers were flocking in fast, and one man offered to Purchase it for £60gs for which I would not sell it. Mrs Sutton thinks it would bring more than £100 – sold privately in London – and so has taken it with her, but Heaven grant it be not sold at all, but the poor fat white Horse instead.[2] Mrs Sutton also very kindly went to a Mr Deans[3] a Clergyman here where that wretched son[4] of Sir Liars was (Mr D being his private Tutor) just before he went to his infamous Uncle at Florence[5] the account was horrible in the extreme – ie that he had ran through as great a rig of vice as a man of 60

– smoked 20 cigars a day – till the Dr said he would kill himself and limited, him to two he complained bitterly of having no home, and seemed utterly wretched, and reckless – but somewhat reformed before he left there but Mr & Mrs Dean fear, that in the infamous school,[6] he is now in, – he has gone back, as they cannot get an answer from him to any of their letters – it is evident to me the final aim of the two Fiend Brothers, the father and uncle is to <u>kill</u> him out of <u>their way</u>, by premature dissipation, and vice, so as to leave my cup of misery – undrugged by no single – drop of gall strange to say Mr Dean had never had the slightest communication with either Sir Liar! or the reptile Henry– so I suppose the Boy went there of his own accord. – Mr Deans version – of Sir Liars bad arm is, that he has privately fought a Duel, but I defended him from <u>that</u> suspicion, by assuring Mrs Sutton that he was <u>far</u> too great a coward for anything of that sort, and had slunk out of too many – not certainly that duelling is any proof of courage – quite the contrary, but still he has not even the vulgar animal courage of a bully – or a Blackguard – though he is <u>both</u>, to the uttermost extreme. I had a long letter from Mme Alphonse last night and some unreadable hieroglyphics from the poor Poodle – they were very sorry to hear of Massys accident and desire all kinds of kind messages, and good wishes to you. the Poodle told my fortune on the 29th of March – strange to say here is the result "you have been much worried about this time from recieving a letter from a man – trying to extort money from you – and threatening to go to Law with you" (so I had from that wretch Allen) "but you will get the better of him through a friend – you are meditating a long journey and have a great many fears about it but you need not you will soon recieve an unexpected sum of money but will have a struggle with yourself – about accepting it; – you have had horrible torments about money – you have also been robbed, and betrayed (though you are not yet aware of it) by a person – in whom you have long placed implicit confidence" (this must be Byrne – for I can think of no one else – as I never placed implicit confidence in Jonas, or any confidence at all – or else <u>he</u> is quite capable of both robbing and betraying his own mother let alone me – for 2 halfpenny)

"But be of good cheer your miseries – at this very moment are about to end, and you will enter into the road of fortune in a surprising and unexpected manner and <u>always</u> through this yet unknown <u>Ace of Spades</u>! who appears to be a man of High rank – a widower – and a Foreigner that is not an Englishman – through him you will become as rich, as you have been poor – you will also soon see a person that is dear to you – and whom you have not seen for many years – and never hoped to see again – after this unexpected interview, your whole fate will change already friends have stepped forward that you did not expect to help you in a matter of traffic – or negotiation which will be a great relief to you" – <u>strange</u> is it not? to say the least of it. –

Here is the Post man and it is raining <u>gallon drops</u>!! so with kindest regards to your brothers and best wishes for Massy – Believe me in great haste my dearest Rebecca Ever gratefully yrs Rosina Bulwer Lytton

---

HALS
1. 1 Lewes Crescent in Kemp Town, Brighton, was built for the sixth Duke of Devonshire in 1828, who wanted a regal home near the Royal Pavilion.
2. This is *Favorite Pony and Spaniels* (*c.* 1841), a painting by Edwin Landseer and engraved by William Giller, depicting a plumpish horse with a white tail and mane called Belle, a black-and-tan spaniel called Cora and RBL's Blenheim Spaniel, Fairy. When Landseer retouched the painting several years later, he remarked that the horse 'needed grooming'.
3. RBL's son Robert lived with the Revd Mr Deane and his wife in the rectory at the village of Wyck Ripington, Stow-in-Gloucestershire.
4. Robert Bulwer Lytton.
5. Henry Bulwer was posted minister plenipotentiary at the court of the Grand Duke of Tuscany in Florence in 1852. His retirement from that post in January of 1855 was due to ill health.
6. Harrow School in north-west London. See RBL, 4 July 1849.

To Rebecca Ryves

Brighton
Sunday April 10th 1853

I was truly sorry My dearest Rebecca to find by your – two last kind letters, that poor Massy had again had a return of the hemorrhage; there is nothing for it, but to submit, that is for some time to keep in One temperature; not even going from one room to Another, as even that much Atmospheric change is bad, and a little patience at first, would get him well much sooner – well can I enter into your feelings – about these Church yard walls; for I envy none <u>living</u> not even the happiest, and the greatest, but only the quiet dead to whom no further change can come for they are where "the weary are at rest, and the wicked cease from troubling"[1] but you are too young for such thoughts the world is all before and with youth there is every thing to hope. – I know very well what you allude to about Emily – for we were not two hours in the house before that detestable maid of Mrs Ts[2] told it to Byrne which shews what wretches servants are; – but <u>that</u> I would never hint to mortal for, for the irremediable afflictions which God sends, I have the greatest commiseration and respect; but for the detestable faults of scarlet and yellow vulgarity and sickening Vanity self conceit, and cretin ignorance, which being of our own making – is in our power to alter, I have not perhaps as much toleration as I ought; at least the ignorance and vulgarity, one might pity were it not propt up on all sides into a rampant, and offensive perpendicular by the sturdy poles of arrogance and insufferable conceit. You will shudder at seeing the yellow card return! but if you could get it out I should be greatly obliged to you, as upon some future emergency – I could sell it outright for something nearer its value, there will be about 36 I believe to pay for the 5 weeks Interest; if you would then make it up into a paper parcel, about the size of a book (an old pen box would do – as it is too small to send without increasing its bulk) and have the goodness to forward it to me by rail – I begin to get into a nervous fever about the poor picture! least after all Mrs Sutton should not be able to sell it for any thing like its value – that is for any thing – that would at all go <u>near</u> to meet, all I have hanging over me; – still hopes, fears, sufferings, – and all else, resolve themselves into Gods will be done"! for the fact that in all one's aggravated miseries one would not be those who do the wrong; – brings the consolitary conviction, that if it is not the Almighty's will to save us <u>from</u> the storm – he perhaps does better, and <u>saves us in it</u> – would one could attain to this frame of mind, – <u>before</u> one had undergone as much laceration, for as Jeremy Taylor truly says – "It is the tossing to, and fro, and the struggling, and striving – that inflames and irritates ones wounds."³ – I have great faith however in that good Mr Baker– he has such an excellent countenance and is so fond of de dogs – speaks de Dog language perfectly and told Tib dat with such eyes and such a Nose! him! could well dispense with having hims Ears more fluffy since the Poodles announcement of my having been robbed and betrayed – I feel afraid to have Byrne down to pack up my things – and indeed like all English people I think her both selfish and ungrateful – for though she always costs me more than any other maid would do she always seems to think she is doing me a great favor! – even for the fortnight she was with me here I gave her three guineas, and a half – but if I thought her capable of treachery of course I should not like her even to know where I was going much less to take her with me as far as my place of destination but all this must be over till the fate of the picture is decided, but I am in an agony – till I get away from this – not that I have worn out the welcome (for one cannot wear out what one never had) but the whole thing is painful and repugnant to me – and therefore every hour past here, seems a Century (or as Mrs T – pronounces it a <u>Sentry</u>!!! A Lady living here went to Town on Friday to see her brother who lives next door to Sir Liar – the latter is living in Hertford St Mayfair and at no 36 – but not at the no 36 that I lived at as there are two 36s in Hertford St, or it may be that it is 34 he lives at, as the Lady only said he lived next door to her brother and her brother lives at 35 Hertford St. Nothing could she find out as to what is the matter with his hand, only that it, like himself had been very bad. I have just had another dun from Mme de Blarer! which makes 2 in 3 days – pray tell her when you pay her that after spoiling all ones things – she ought not to go on in this way. – Forgive this stupid scrawl – and with Tibbianas best love, kindest regards to your Brothers, and best wishes for poor Massy

Believe Me My Dearest Rebecca Ever your grateful and affect Rosina Bulwer Lytton

---

HALS
1.   'There the wicked cease from troubling; and there the weary be at rest', Job 3:17.
2.   Mrs Hardinge Tyler.
3.   Jeremy Taylor (1613–67) was a Church of England clergyman, who became a well known writer. His most popular works were *The Rules and Exercises of Holy Living* (1650) and *The Rules and Exercises of Holy Dying* (1651).

To Rebecca Ryves

Brighton
Tuesday April 12 1853

My dearest Rebecca I have cut my right hand so badly that I can scarcely hold a pen – but must scratch you one line to say how grieved I was to learn by your note of last night that you had been obliged to sit up with poor Massy. I earnestly hope both for his sake and yours that your next Bulletin will be more favourable pray don't bore yourself about my troublesome commissions till you are quite able to do so. – Did you go to? or hear any thing more of, or from the Moores? I hope to morrow to be able to write to you more legibly and with less pain. If the Dinner at the Hudsons was as bad and vulgar as their servants – I pity your brother – with kindest regards to them both and best wishes

Believe me Ever gratefully & affectly yrs R Bulwer Lytton

HALS

To Rebecca Ryves

Brighton
Wednesday April 13th 1853

My dearest Rebecca least you should think I am following Sir Liars Example, and am laid up with my hand I scribble one line to you to say how sincerely [I] hope both Massy and you, are better? and that you have not been obliged to sit up with him since; – I am rather disappointed at not having heard from you this morning – but perhaps I may do so by the 2 o'clock Post, to which it wants 5 minutes. – My hand is still painful but as you percieve much better. – You asked me in your last if I owed Turner the milkman – anything I thought not; but upon referring to his book I find that instead of his being paid up to the 11th of December makes it just 2 weeks and 4 days – that he is owing for – get his bill from him, and send it to me; but on <u>no account</u> pay him, till I see it. – The Post is just in – but no letter from you, which makes me rather uneasy – I hope poor Massy is not worse – or that you are not ill? – nothing from Mrs Sutton yet either; which keeps me in a fever; for I am weary of always being suspended over a Precipice by a single hair, and that of the very slightest. The Post man cant wait so good bye your grateful and affect Rosina Bulwer Lytton.

HALS

_____

To Rebecca Ryves

Brighton
Thursday April 14th 1853

My dearest Rebecca I am delighted to hear that Massy is so much better, and that you are able to go out. Thank you for doing my troublesome commissions – there was only <u>One</u> Brougham[1] owing to Mrs Greene after her bill was sent in, as the one to the Hodgsons that night is down in the bill – the whole bill in fact with that exception being for Mrs Tylers Broughams when I have lived longer in England I shall not be so silly – but be as vulgar, selfish ill bred, and grinding as the rest of the world – for <u>Heavens</u> <u>Sake</u> dont go and pay Mrs Greene this additional £1"5"0 as I am in desperate want of every <u>farthing</u> of the balance of that pittance but tell her I shall be in Town the beginning of next month and will then settle it, <u>dont</u> pay the milk man either – (of whom I wrote to you about yesterday) nor indeed any one else another <u>sou</u> as I must wait for the chance of the picture. – I warned Lady Hotham when I told her where I was going, on <u>no</u> account to tell <u>Gorge</u> – but I wish you would reiterate this to her, and take that opportunity of telling her, that the reason I have no opinion of him is from the toadying and violent love letters he used to write to Mrs Disraeli[2] during the life of her first Husband some times two a day! although he saw her every day![3] – hoping no doubt thereby to step into Wyndham Lewis's shoes when he died[4] – but Disraeli being the cleverer rascal of the two distanced him at this honorable game, these letters this vain ass of a woman used to shew me, and laugh over, as did I many a time, and ...

_____

HALS
The end of the letter is missing.
1. A hard-topped town carriage.
2. 'Gorge' George Beauclerk was regarded by society as the lover of Mary Anne Wyndham, while she was married to her first husband.
3. Beauclerk was living at 23A Governor Street during the 1830s, very near the home of the Wyndham Lewises.
4. Mary Anne Evans's first husband, Lewis, died in March 1838. She married Benjamin Disraeli the following year.

To Rebecca Ryves

Brighton Thursday April 14ᵗʰ 1853

My dearest Rebecca upon referring to Mrs Greens Bill I find the Brougham for the 7ᵗʰ and 9ᵗʰ of December 1852 is <u>not</u> included in it – therefore that £1,5″6 I will pay her next month, but pray have the goodness to get me a proper stamped receipt for the £10″0′0 she has already received ie £5 in January and £5 12ᵗʰ of April – 1853 – and as her bill is only £9″19″6 I shall owe her £1″5″0 for which let her make out a fresh, and separate bill. In great Haste affectly yours R B Lytton

for at present I have <u>no</u> receipt at all for this £10

———

HALS

To Rebecca Ryves

Brighton
Sunday April 17ᵗʰ 1853

Thank you a thousand times My dearest Rebecca for executing all my troublesome commissions, and for the Homeopathic globule of money which arrived safely yesterday, but too late to acknowledge by return of Post. I am very glad that you are going to be <u>Churned</u> into a larger house, as no doubt you can all be together there, which will be much more agreeable to you. Poor innocent Tib has – got such an awful cough, and cold, that it is quite pitious to see, and hear him, no doubt, from not being properly dried when he was last washed, for it would not be consistant if anything was done here as it ought to be but it is the conceit and self praise that goes on from mng till night that is so disgusting it is a terrible and cruel position to be in, to be where one is not wanted, where every thing is repugnant, and distasteful to one, – and from which one has not the means of getting away – my heart begins to sink down into my shoes about Mrs Sutton, and the picture, for tomorrow will be a week since she was to have busied herself about it, and as yet I have heard nothing; and fatal, and frequent experience has taught me that when those sort of things are not done at once, they are not done at all. – but Gods will be done what cant be cured, must be endured. – That Miss P (not "B") Horton that you heard at Mrs Edgeworths, was some sixteen years ago (despite her red hair) a very fine girl, and sang charmingly, – I dare say having become Mrs Reade has not improved her; – though of course she is not much <u>shaken</u> by the <u>wind</u> she has always contrived so successfully to raise. I am still very ill, and good for nothing, for indeed my health is completely broken by incessant worry.

Would you kindly some morning call at – poor Thurloe Cottage and request (very civilly of course) that they will take the <u>greatest</u> care of my poor carved looking glass in the dining room – and not stick lighted cigars in the birds beak, as the morning I was turned out – the man who was there, was smoking away at a terrible rate, and I should not like to get back my Glass all charred and spoilt, don't forget also to inquire particularly after the poor Cat? The 8 more that you gave Gates I have entered to your account. – Brighton as you may suppose is now quite deserted, and I am panting for the time when I can contribute to its emptiness – truly I am weary unto death, of my lacerated, and impeded existence, – for mine is a sort of <u>Garotte</u> life, as I am always bound hand and foot, and therefore unable to resist, or escape from any amount of annoyance, or persecution I may be subjected to. – Earnestly hoping that poor Massy may continue to improve. Believe me with kindest regards to your Brothers Ever my dearest Rebecca your Grateful and Affect

Rosina Bulwer Lytton.

How was Gates[1] looking? and is she going to be married to Edwards?

HALS
1.   A female servant. See RBL, 12 December 1852.

To Rebecca Ryves

Brighton
Tuesday April 19th 1853

My dearest Rebecca I write you one line in a great hurry as I am going down by appointment to see Mrs Wheeler – who goes to Town on Thursday – I hope you are well and Massy going on well? and that you have accomplished your flitting comfortably. I send you Mrs Suttons letter which is as you may suppose a deathblow to me! and yet it is only what I expected. My poor Tib has been so ill, these 3 days that I have been obliged to have the Dog Dr to him, he is a little better to day – I have also been such a martyr with my side – that to my great annoyance Mrs Tyler went and wrote to Dr Laurie I don't want to get better and have no guineas to spare – and I don't chuse to be put under obligations to those sort of people, which always costs one more in the end. You will smile at Lady Hothams letter, which send me back oh! Friendship oh Fiddlestick! what a fudge thou art! I think you will own there <u>is no</u> end to my good luck, when I tell you that Mr Wheeler called upon me on Sunday to say good bye in the course of conversation he said. – "I suppose you will be quite glad to return to your pretty house?" I then told him, I <u>had</u> no house, to return to – "God Bless my soul!" cried he – when I had told him the history of <u>that</u> sacrifice "how very provoking, two friends of mine sisters last November were in want of a furnished cottage – and said it <u>must</u> be Elegantly furnished and at the Piccadilly end of London – I instantly thought of yours, as the very thing for them – and wanted Mrs Wheeler to write and ask you if you would let it? as you were coming to Brighton – but she said she was sure you would not!" now this £200 – a year that these old maids would have given me for it – would have just saved that terrible sacrifice of my poor furniture! and me much past, present and future misery! the month is drawing to a close! and I have not the means of moving – so should not wonder if I even lost the power of going to Mrs Phillips. My God! My God! have mercy on me. – I hope I shall hear from you to day Good bye God Bless you, and with kindest regards to your Brothers believe me Ever my Dearest Rebecca your Grateful and affect Rosina Bulwer Lytton.

The weather here is atrocious, foggy cold, and damp. –

HALS

To Rebecca Ryves

Brighton
Wednesday Night April 20th 1853

My dearest Rebecca I am still confined to my bed with the addition of a bad sore throat – it was a relief to me to hear from you as I am so nervous about every one, and every thing that instead of no news being good news to me, it always makes me anticipate <u>Evil</u>, the only one of my anticipations that are sure to be fulfilled. – I was sorry to hear by your note that Massy had been out walking, as I really think after such an attack, this is no weather for him to try any experiments of the sort. I am glad you are going to Mrs Ripons[1] – and envy you not a little meeting that lovely charming little Lady Jane[2] – with regard to her poor mother you may take my word for it you will meet many <u>infinitely</u> <u>worse</u> <u>women</u> – in every way, amid the <u>soi-disant</u>[3] <u>Elite</u> of English society. – I enclose you a very kind note I had today from poor Mrs Wheeler, it <u>is</u> very kind still it humiliates and degrades one to be under those sort of obligations to any one but relations; especially when they only humble without helping one. The inclosure was £10 the <u>gem</u> I shall purchase with it, will <u>be to pay</u> Mr Sandby's[4] Interest! If you see Mrs Wheeler in Town (she will be at 48 Dover St Piccadilly) you may say that I had told you how kind she had been, and how gratefully I appreciated her kindness. Will you my dearest Rebecca have the kindness to send me my stamped receipts, as you have no idea what inconvenience and confusion it subjects me not getting my receipts at the same time I pay my bills – for having so many things to worry and distress me! I am apt to mislay or forget them, if I don't get them regularly can you also forward the ring as I can sell it here to a <u>real</u> Jeweller. – would I were in Heaven where there is no buying or selling, – or above all marrying! that root of all Evil. – I shall not go to Lady Hothams even if I can manage to get to Wales (which I sometimes begin to despair of) for I <u>cannot</u> afford those fortnights in the gay world – which are far more onerous to a poor wretch like me, than months would be, as the same outlay would suffice. – I wish it could be managed that I could go at the same time you go to Ireland as it would be pleasant to go together – as far as Llangollen – but you will see by Mrs Suttons last which I enclose you what a brilliant chance I have even of selling my poor Fairy. I scribble this tonight as I may be too ill to do so tomorrow. – Good night God Bless you. Poor Innocence is better – pray take care of your chest, and with kindest regards to your brothers Believe Me My Dearest Rebecca – Ever your grateful & affect Rosina Bulwer Lytton.

HALS
1. Louisa Anne Ripon is being courted by Rebecca Ryves's brother William. See RBL, 23 October 1853.
2. Lady Jane Seymour Stanhope (1833–1907) became Lady Mount Charles and Marchioness Conyngham in 1876. See RBL, 7 April 1854. She was the daughter of Major-General Charles Stanhope, the fourth Duke of Harrington.
3. So-called (French).
4. Revd Mr Sandby of Flixton, Suffolk.

To Rebecca Ryves

Brighton
Thursday April 21ˢᵗ 1853

My dearest Rebecca In reply – to your <u>Nasal</u> Aphorism – of "no one knows what may turn up"! (no truly) I in great haste inclose you a very kind note just received from Lady Hotham (which send me back) Mrs Tyler strongly urges me to accept the proposition and not <u>reject</u> her kindness so I have done so – and written to Byrne to be in readiness – Perhaps perhaps – something may really turn up at Paris! who knows? Pray when you see Lady Hotham tell her how grateful I am for her kindness to me, which (in <u>her</u> way) has been great – Perhaps after all I may see you in London before I, and you go – the time for this trip to come off – is not yet settled of course I will let you know the moment it is. – I am still in bed with my desperate sore throat – and it is raining cats and dogs. Mrs Tyler has kindly asked poor Innocence[1] to remain here, while I am in Paris – so that will be a <u>Patte à terre</u>[2] for him poor fellow, – How I wish you were to be of the party to Paris too – but since what I certainly never expected in my wildest dreams has come to pass in <u>my</u> going to Paris! who knows what other things may come to pass too and I may yet be able to take you for God <u>is</u> very good to us in the midst of tribulation. God Bless you with kindest regards to your Brothers, and hoping Massy wont go walking out such weather Believe me Ever My Dearest Rebecca your grateful and affect Rosina Bulwer Lytton

---

HALS
1.   A dog.
2.   Literally: 'paw on the ground' (French), word-play on *pied-à-terre*. See RBL, 10 December 1837.

To Rebecca Ryves

Tuesday April 26th 1853

My dearest Rebecca I write you one line in great haste to thank you for your kind note received late yesterday, with the packet of return letters, and the suspicious looking Epistles from Thurloe Cottage; which looked like Duns but thank Heaven turned out to be only circulars from shops. – I am very sorry to hear that poor Mrs Hodgson has been ill, what is the matter with her? I also have been suffering martyrdoms as it appears my spine is a little affected as well as my liver, and the weather here has been atrocious – till today, which is lovely. – the German <u>Bouquet</u> being now gone the House is a little sweeter, and Byrne thank Heaven will have her room. – I shall be most sincerely glad to see you again; – my dear Rebecca and only wish, it could be, in a House of my own – however we must only try, and hope against hope and see what the turn of the Wheel at Paris – will bring forth, I have told Lady Hotham I would not go without Byrne, as my general health is far too bad for any such discomfort, for I really am as weak as water, whereas she is as strong as a little Shetland Pony. I think you had better pack up my ring in a little box of some kind, and send it to me by rail. – God Bless you, and with kindest regards to your Brothers, believe me, in desperate Haste Ever your grateful and affect Rosina Bulwer Lytton.

Dont forget to call at Thurloe Cottage about the looking glass.

HALS

To Rebecca Ryves

Brighton
Thursday April 28th 1853

Thanks much and many My dearest Rebecca for your kind letter just received; I am more distressed, and grieved than I can say at what you tell me of Mr I Lloyds[1]

not having paid your brothers as it was one of the very, or rather <u>the</u> very first debt he should have paid, surely if Mr Lloyd <u>Père</u>[2] knew it, he would not leave it unpaid – this does not give me a very favourable opinion of Mr I.L. – and grieved am I to the soul that I should (mais avec <u>circumstances attenuantes</u>[3] that is from a complication of impossibilities over which I have no control up to the <u>present time</u>) so far resemble him. Poor Lady Hotham! "Still harping on my daughter! alias my House! it is a good excuse however for doing nothing – but as you say – and as the Scotch parson said "We must be thankful for [small] mercies" and therefore I hope you told her how grateful I am (as I really <u>am</u>) for what <u>she has done</u>. I hope you <u>will</u> walk over spend a long day – and dine with her. I am very glad you are going to Mrs Ripons, and envy you meeting that dear little Lady Jane. Byrne will not be able to stay a moment when she passes through Town, as I shall not have her till the last minute, on account of hampering the Tylers, but <u>mind</u> you don't say this to Lady Hotham as I would rather <u>she</u> thought she <u>was</u> actually here. I am still labouring under "the toothache of the mind" and should not be surprised if my journey to Paris was stopped altogether, for want of the essential – I hope Lady Hotham wont start before the 15th or 16th of May – as it will be very inconvenient to me if she does considering how my movements are always brought to a stand still for want of money! I wish Willy would marry Miss Holford– the £1000 a year is not to be sneezed at; and her <u>expectations</u> from so rich an Uncle, must be great. Yes old Mrs Carey is in Town my love to her and Alice– tell Carey I miss her much. Innocence (now better known by the name of Upsy! Pupsy!) is very much obliged to you for your kind wishes about him which wag with hims own exactly – as the odds are poor fellow him will be left with the servants (as they are going as well as me) and dat like an Aristocratic Pup dog as him is – him detests God Bless you my dearest Rebecca with kindest regards to your Brothers and best wishes Believe me Ever your grateful and affect Rosina Bulwer Lytton

you must broach the subject of <u>Gorge</u> by telling her not to tell him of my going to <u>Wales</u> & then say why I have no opinion of him about his love making to Mrs Dizzy during her Husbands life time
  you had better send the ring by rail.

HALS
1. The son of Mr Lloyd, probably the brother of Rebecca Ryves's friend Miss Lloyd.
2. Father (French).
3. But with extenuating circumstances [*circonstances attenuantes*] (French).

To Rebecca Ryves

Brighton
Tuesday Night May 3rd 1853

My dearest Rebecca I am ill, and feverish and am going to bed having had a fainting fit this Evening – but Innocence, wont let me do so – without Wagging hims aunt Rebecca hims best thanks for her kind invitation, which him accepts, with him biggest and Blenheimest of pleasure. – Neither could I go to bed without telling you that I have just had a letter by express – from dear kind Mrs Sutton announcing to me the sale of my poor darling little Fairys Picture for the enormous sum of £195! Still it is a sore heart ache to me to be obliged to part with it, I know not yet who is the purchaser I am reconciled to dear good Mr Wheelers not getting it from the conviction that he has no <u>gusto</u> for modern Pictures and merely came forward as a good Samaritan device to render me a service. – I am much grieved but not surprised at Massys Cough it was so very imprudent of him to go to Mrs Ripons the other night. Poor Lady John Somerset, I am very sorry for <u>her</u>, but <u>cannot</u> be sorry for any one who is so happy as to die. – I see Sir Liar has been flaring up about the Income Tax,[1] "What a pity a man of such Exquisite notions"![2] should deduct it from the Parish allowance he makes his wife! Oh Humbug! Oh! balderdash! Oh! Bulwer! <u>when</u>? and where will ye end? – Hoping to see you about the End of next week with kindest regards to your Brothers Believe me Dearest Rebecca. Ever your grateful and affect Rosina Bulwer Lytton

---

HALS

1. The Tory Chancellor of the Exchequer William Gladstone holds the record of four hours and forty-five minutes for the longest budget speech, which took place on 18 April. He suggested a sliding scale for income tax with the view to its abolition in 1860. On 25 April, EBL spoke on Gladstone's first budget and opposed him by defending the principle of differentiating between earned and unearned income. EBL argued, however, that income tax should not be 'a habitual feature of our taxation'. The attack on income tax was lost by the opposition and the government won by a majority of seventy-one. The Income Tax Act was passed in 1853.
2. RBL, *Cheveley; or The Man of Honour (1839)*, ed. Marie Mulvey-Roberts (London: Pickering & Chatto, 2005), p. 233 and p. 502, n. 75. The quotation refers to Jean-Jacques Rousseau, who had five illegitimate children, whom he sent to a foundling hospital in Paris.

To Rebecca Ryves

Brighton
Thursday Night May 6th 1853

My dearest Rebecca I was truly grieved to learn by your kind letter of tonight, that you are laid up with the "<u>Fluency</u>" <u>pray</u> keep in bed, and take care of yourself; for this is the most treacherous, and cold catching month in the whole year, – I hope the change of air may do poor Massy good, and only wish you could try the same remedy. I am very sorry you cannot dine at Lady Hothams tomorrow I am scribbling this to you at one in the morning – tired as an old Post Horse, after a hard days Packing for though Byrne comes to me tomorrow yet not being constantly with me – I of course must sort – divide, and arrange my things ready for her partly to put away and partly to take with us to Paris. – So I will say all my say when we meet, so pray get well by that time, and now good night (or rather Morning) and God Bless you – and with Innocences Love, and kindest regards to your Brothers Believe Me Ever your Grateful And Affect Rosina Bulwer Lytton

HALS

To Rebecca Ryves

Brighton
Sunday May 8th 1853

My dearest Rebecca By not having heard from you again I fear your cold is no better; and I was very much grieved to hear in one of Lady Hotham's letters, that she had called at your door and the servant said you were very unwell. Pray take care of yourself – and get well by Saturday next, when I hope to see you about 2 o'clock as I shall call upon you on that day en route to Hereford House. I also have been laid up with a bad sore throat, but thanks to Bella Donna and Aconite,[1] am a little better to day – which is surprising considering we had a snow storm yesterday – and I am much worried, and inconvenienced, by Mrs Suttons not having yet sent me a cheque for the money – which keeps me in a fever about Essentials, – however Byrne is a great comfort to me, and a good nurse – I only wish you had as good a one to take care of you – and that we were not both adrift au grè des vents[2] without a Harbour – we can call our own, – but courage! God is good as well as great. – Dat Dog is getting too Innocent poor fellow, just as him is about to be left. – Good bye God bless you with kindest regards to your brothers – and best wishes Believe me Ever – My dearest Rebecca Gratefully and Affectly yours Rosina Bulwer Lytton

As I shall be in Town so soon, of course you need not send my ring now

HALS
1. Homeopathic herbal remedies.
2. At the mercy of the winds (French).

To Rebecca Ryves

Brighton
Wednesday May 11th 1853

My dearest Rebecca I am so hurried that I have scarcely time to thank you for your kind letter, and say how glad I am that you are even a <u>little</u> better and I am looking forward with real pleasure to see you on Saturday. Davis has just been down here with Lady Hothams love, as she expects me on Saturday as we start for Paris on Monday – Mrs Sutton[1] has just sent the money but minus £23"11"0 for Commission – and auction fees which is a <u>terrible</u> diminution with all the pulls I have upon me. – Would you kindly write one line to Blackburne, and tell him to discontinue sending Punch,[2] and the Bells messenger[3] as I am going on a visit where they will be taken (you need not say to Paris) and that I will be in Town in July and settle his account – good Bye – God Bless you and with Innocence's best love, and kind regards to your Brother Believe me in whirlwind Haste Ever Gratefully & Affectly Rosina Bulwer Lytton

HALS
1. A member of the auction house.
2. See RBL, 6 February 1850.
3. RBL had some of her poetry published in *Bell's Weekly Messenger*, which was founded by Richard Dighton as a Sunday newspaper in 1796 and ran for 100 years.

To Rebecca Ryves

Hotel de Rivoli 24 Rue de Rivoli Paris
Friday May 20th 1853

My dearest Rebecca, I should have written to you before this, but for a serious misfortune that befell us through the carelessness of Lady H's[1] servants, who lost her Jewel Box! <u>en route</u> containing her Diamonds – about £40 in money – and Papers of importance to her, and it was only yesterday morning after unheard of exertions that we <u>miraculously</u> succeeded in recovering it; I must say she bore the loss most heroically – saying it might have been much worse, had any accident happened to any of us by the Railway – but as you may suppose this <u>contretemps</u> so upset me, and I had such innumerable letters to write about it; that I have not literally had time to breathe till this moment, what made it worse was that she kept saying that for 50 years she had travelled with that box, and no accident had ever happened to it before, <u>ergo,</u>[2] the deduction to be drawn from this , was that it was <u>my</u> usual ill luck that had prevailed – she also reiterated that she had £4 in the box which Lady Harrington[3] had given her for troublesome commissions which she certainly should not repay her!!!! <u>entre nous,</u>[4] my dear Rebecca up to the present time I never had so miserable a <u>sejour</u>[5] at Paris! the one fault marring all and the incessant <u>waggling</u>, and screaming about every <u>sou</u>, quite wearing me out, and the discomfort which is the natural consequence of such intense "<u>prudence</u>"! (since that is the new word for fabulous meanness) causing irrational low spirits to one who is accustomed to every creature comfort, and who with her <u>more</u>, than ample means, could and should command them Every where and as mme de Pompadou complained of Louis Quinze[6] she is beginning to be "<u>unanswerable</u>" – and I to feel, that I have been unpardonable in incurring such an expense for <u>nothing</u>! for if we go on as we are <u>now</u> doing, we shall go no where, nor see any one; indeed though still <u>here</u>, the Empress[7] continues so ill that there are no receptions, she has drove out for the first time the day before yesterday for the first time, and was so exhausted after it as to be much worse. Lady H dined with <u>me</u> yesterday at the Hôtel de Paris, and as the dinner was, as it always is there <u>first rate</u> and the wine a little less <u>stinged</u> I being the Hostess – she for the first time since ...

HALS

Incomplete letter.

1. Lady Hotham.
2. Therefore (Latin).
3. The Honourable Mrs Leicester Stanhope (*née* Elizabeth Green) (1816–98) became Lady Harrington. Her husband was Leicester Fitzgerald Charles Stanhope, fifth Earl of Harrington (1784–1862), and Lady Jane Seymour was her niece. RBL stayed with Lady Harrington at Ashburton House, after her return to England in 1847.
4. Between us (French).
5. An abode (French).
6. Jeanne-Antionette Poisson (1721–64) married Charles Guillaume le Normant d'Etoiles in 1741. On 15 September 1745, she was legally separated from her husband and pronounced the Marquise de Pompadour, the official mistress of Louis XV (1710–74).
7. Eugenie, Empress of the French (1826–1920), was Empress Consort of France (1853–71), the wife of Napoleon III, Emperor of the French. See RBL, 28 May 1853. She had been recovering from a miscarriage. See RBL, 23 May 1853.

To Rebecca Ryves

Hotel de rivoli Rue de Rivoli, no 24 Paris
Monday May 23rd 1853

I was delighted my dearest Rebecca to receive your letter yesterday, as it was like seeing an old friend and god knows I wanted something to cheer me for I am worried to death with the <u>incessant</u> worry and <u>screwing</u> (Grandity![1] by comparison was a Princess so you may <u>guess</u> what it is!) and an obstinacy and self will about everything that amounts to perfect monomania insisting that every thing must be just the same as it was 40 years ago when first she came to France

– her heart failed her about coming properly with her own carriage and Horses consequently you can have no conception of the fighting and haggling about every thing which combined with the mad frenzy and the long rambling rigmarole so confuses the people that she never gets a single thing she orders, then too she always begins in the most magnificent style as if she wanted the finest wines – and finest dishes – when lo! it inevitably dwindles down to the very commonest and the very fewest then about the carriage – the man thought at least she was going to have a carriage and four – and when she had agreed for a carriage and Horses – then it dwindles down to a <u>one horse</u>! affair and when the bargain was concluded for 12 francs a day then she wanted to beat him down to 10 – the consequence was the man turned on his heel, and sent no conveyance at all, so I was for two days ill in bed from sheer worry (with Jones's literary production) and she trolling all over the Town on foot which she is strong enough to do, but I am not; another of her crotchets was that there was no fish! to be had in Paris and that was another source of ill temper, it was also high treason because the carriage she had the first day which was very shabby and very dear was complained of by me, for it jumbled me nearly to death, and was so small there was not room for 2 people, costing just 8 franks a day more than the beautiful one I used to have from Mitchell – <u>she</u> did not care for appearances and it was a very <u>good</u> carriage for Paris as the Harness was generally tied with ropes. (yes 40 years ago) till at length yesterday fairly worn out with the fruits of her own obstinacy and confusion she came slinging to me, and said she would give me <u>carte</u> <u>blanche</u> if I would order Dinner and get a carriage – consequently she had a very nice and very hot dinner at 5 o'clock with excellent <u>fresh</u> Turbot epigrammes d'argeau au petits poix – coquille de volaille – Bechamele au Truffles[2] – Charlotte Russe[3] and asparagus – she was both surprised, and delighted with the dinner, and could not tell how I managed it, simply I said by writing a <u>menu</u> of the dinner, in the <u>morning</u> and <u>specifically</u> stating the dishes I wanted. I also succeeded in getting her a <u>decent</u> Brougham, and took her after dinner to the Jardin d'Hiver & the Chateau des Fleurs[4] with which she was both surprised and Enchanted! and drove home by the Bois de Boulogne through Passy[5] – so that she is in a little better humour. She was all surprise that the Comtesse de Melfort[6] to whom she had not called had a letter from Lady Harrington containing £4 for a commission upon inquiry I found, that instead of sending the note civilly by her servant with a card she had flung it very rudely into the post without one word from herself stating her address! So I had to write a long note of apology to Mme de Melfort – and this is a sample of the way she does every thing; but you are wise, in making no <u>comment</u> about any thing I tell you in your letters, as yesterday she asked out of idle curiousity to see your letter!! and desired her love to you. – I am very glad Mrs Ripon[7] takes you out to drive – but more sorry than I can say that I shall not see you on my return and mine poorest of Tibs! how him will miss you poor Innocent fellow for like hims mud him dreads the things. The matter with the Empress[8] is that she has had a bad miscarriage brought on by taking too long a walk with Mme de Montbello,[9] and getting into an over heated Bath after. – Lady H[10] has evidently a Hankering to go to court with the Eternal shilly shally – and <u>Bother</u> the odds are even I shall not. Write soon, and <u>pray</u> <u>don't</u> <u>pay</u> your letters with many kisses to my poor Tib and kindest regards to your Brothers Believe me in great Haste and Worry Ever My dearest Rebecca your grateful and affect Rosina Bulwer Lytton

---

HALS
1. RBL's nickname for Lady Hotham.
2. This may be *agneau* (lamb) with peas and truffles in a béchamel sauce, served in eggshells (French).
3. Charlotte Russe is a cold dessert, invented by the French chef Marie Antoine Carême (1784–1833), consisting of Bavarian cream set in a mould lined with ladyfingers.
4. Winter Garden and Castle of Flowers (French).
5. Situated on the Right Bank, Passy was a commune until 1860 when it was annexed to Paris.
6. The wife of the sixth Duke of Melfort, George Drummond, who, in 1853, by Act of Parliament was raised to Earl of Perth.
7. Louisa Anne Ripon, William Ryves's future wife. See RBL, October 1853.
8. In 1856, Eugenie, Empress of the French, gave birth to the heir, Napoleon Eugene Louis. See RBL, 20 May 1853.
9. The Duchesse de Montebello was a lady-in-waiting to Empress Eugenie.
10. Lady Hotham.

To Rebecca Ryves

[27? May 1853]

... me have been here, was in high good humour. Paris looks more beautiful than ever, and the delicious Garden of the Tuileries & the Luxembourg[1] in high beauty – being one blush of roses, lilacs and accacias, Every thing at least a month forwarder than with us – peas – magnificent strawberries moss roses and lilies of the valley in profusion – but all this affluence of beauty, and of pleasure only makes one <u>more</u> wretched when <u>one</u> feels ones <u>own</u> fate to be <u>so</u> ugly and so destitute but in all this there is only one point to vere to that of <u>Gods will be done</u>. Tell my poor innocent Tib with 20 kisses on hims nutmegs dat all de poor Puppy dogs here, are muzzled, and me saw 3 poor Doatskin Blenheims in de same category yesterday and de latest fashion among de Dogs – for de hot weather is to wear de left ear turned back To night I hope to see Rachel[2] in Mme Emile Girondins new Play "Lady Tartufe"[3] as I have sent to secure Places at the Théâtre Français our journey upon the whole was a pretty fair one, we sailed from Folkstone[4] at

2 o'clock on Monday but about half past 3 the most fearful storm of Thunder, lightening and rain I ever witnessed came on without a moments warning – and as there were a great many Horses on board, who screamed, and kicked most horribly poor things – the scene was a frightful one and the Cabin of a Boulogne Steam Boat in a storm! the floor heaped with sea sick wretches – of all sizes, countries, and appearance was as you may suppose <u>anything</u> but <u>agreeable</u>! we slept at Boulogne that night, started for Amiens[5] at 6 the next morning and on reaching Paris at 3 the same day found every Hotel, full to over flowing and poor Michel in despair at not being able to recieve us; but that young Booby Lord Talbot, and Lord Harry Vane,[6] were just driving away from the door – turned away as we drove up – After being refused at <u>nearly</u> every Hotel in Paris – we had the singular good fortune to get an apartment <u>au</u> <u>premier</u>[7] here, this being a new Hotel, not quite finished looking of course on the Tuileries Gardens – a Handsome and very Civil Hostess, and our only crowding being that Byrne is obliged to have a <u>lit de sangle</u>,[8] in my room and Farmer in Lady Hothams dressing room ... .

... .I know not if there are any letters from you, or from any one else for me at the <u>Poste Restante</u>[9] as Lady <u>H</u> not wanting letters of course we have not sent there but I shall ask when I take this I hope Massy was not the worse for our disagreeable trot on Sunday. Forgive this hurried scrawl which I am scribbling before Breakfast now good bye, and God Bless you my dearest Rebecca and with a Kenel full of kisses to my poor innocent Tib and kindest regards to your Brothers Believe me Ever your grateful & affect

   Rosina Bulwer Lytton

HALS

Incomplete letter.

1. The gardens within the grounds of the seventeenth-century Luxemburg Palace were opened to the public during the nineteenth century
2. The French actress. See RBL, 17 September 1839.
3. Delphine de Girardin (*née* Gay), known as Mme Emile de Girardin (1804–55), was a French writer, who wrote a number of acclaimed plays. See RBL, 28 May 1853.
4. Town in Kent.
5. A city in northern France, north of Paris.
6. Charles John Chetwynd-Talbot, nineteenth Earl of Shrewsbury, fourth Earl Talbot (1830–77), would have been about twenty-two years old. Lord Harry George Vane (1803–91), the future fourth Duke of Cleveland, had held posts in Paris in the Foreign Service before entering the House of Commons in 1841.
7. First class (French).
8. Camp bed (French).
9. Post office (French).

To Rebecca Ryves

Hotel du Rivoli Paris
Friday May 28th 1853

I am indeed very sorry my dearest Rebecca to hear that poor Massy has had a return of the bleeding that the arnica did not achieve the wonders for which Mrs Tyler stood sponsor. I am afraid, Massy – walks, and exerts himself more than he ought after so severe an accident; but also know that it is next to an impossibility to make men succumb with a good grace to any necessity or bear patiently the slightest restraint. – I feel truly grieved to think that you leave London, the very day that we shall return there (next Monday) after the most miserable <u>arduous</u> fortnight I ever passed in my life. So Chained to the Oar have I been that for the first time on coming to Paris, I have not even been able to go to Pere La Chaise[1] to visit the grave of my poor sister,[2] where I would gladly have laid down the too heavy burden of my miserable existence. To give you some idea of the <u>sort</u> of <u>pleasure</u> I have had here Lady H has done <u>literally</u> nothing but trot <u>on foot</u>! to old curiosity shops, – <u>she</u> like a human steam engine as she is, can walk through crowded streets under a vertical sun – from this as far as Notre Dame! and back! about 6 miles – and I like Panting Time am expected to trot after her, – which as you may suppose makes me really ill and increases the pain in my side to an unbearable degree, and then she is so dreadfully ill tempered, and unreasonable when through her own fabulous stinginess and <u>obstinacy</u>! she has made Every thing wrong and uncomfortable to the last degree; not a Theatre (the only thing I care for here) have I entered since I came – I had sent to the Theatre Français[3] to take two places when I would have gone with Byrne – rather than miss seeing Rachel[4] in "Lady Tartuffe"[5] but all the places had been retained for 3 weeks before we <u>could</u> have got a box for <u>40</u> Francs – about 32 shillings – but of course <u>poor</u> Lady H could not afford so stupendous a sum! on Wednesday she nearly killed me for we went to Versailles[6] by Rail, and to save <u>One Frank</u>! we <u>walked</u> under a tropical sun, from the station to the Chateau! (about a mile and a half) and then in <u>doing</u> the Palace had to traverse about 5 miles of rooms and galleries without counting innumerable flights of stairs – and then last night while rumbling through the Champs Elysée,[7] in an old Hackney[8] coach she says in the most provoking voice "Well this would have been very pleasant if I had brought my own carriage and Horses, and I wish I had now, and then We could have gone to the Tuileries"[9] – whereupon I told her that my dream in coming to Paris had been the idea of seeing the Emperor,[10] and finding or making an opportunity of asking him for apartments in one of the Palaces – but this had no effect upon her, for even the most forcible appeal to the <u>absence</u> of all feeling in a very selfish person, is turned aside – like hail stones falling on an armadillo's back the substance it falls upon being too hard for it to make any impression. That this visit to Paris might lack no crowning horror – yesterday on going to the Exhibition of Modern Artists– who should I see but that Fiend Mrs <u>Sandby</u>![11] who looked at me like a Demon, which verified my mornings dream of a huge cat trying to scratch me. After I suppose 3 or 4 stupid days at Hereford House I shall head for Wales – with about £10 in my pocket to begin the world with! and renew this terribly unequal struggle in the Battle of life with neither health nor strength, or a single hope – If you Pass through Llangollen perhaps you would kindly ask Mrs Phillips if she can recommend me a place where I can be boarded cheaply till I can go on to her, that is till she can take me in October and write me word (to Hereford House) what she says? for it is terrible to go to a far strange place, and not know <u>where</u> to go to – Byrne will go there with <u>me</u> but not remain. Tell my poor Innocent Tib with a sack of kisses – dat last night me saw four Ladies in an open carriage, and <u>each</u> lady had a Blenheim on her lap! dis Harvest of Puppy Dogs – was de finest sight me has seen in Paris – send your answer to this letter to Hereford House God Bless you my dearest Rebecca and send you a good journey and with kind regards to your Brothers a Happier fate than your Ever affect and grateful R Bulwer Lytton.

HALS

1. A cemetery, east of Paris.
2. RBL's elder sister Henrietta Wheeler died of consumption in Paris in May 1826.
3. The Comédie-Française or Théâtre Français, situated in Paris, is the French national theatre, associated with Molière.
5. A prose comedy by Emile de Girardin, first performed in Paris in 1853. See RBL, 27 May 1853.
6. The palace of Louis XIV, located just over 16 km from the centre of Paris.
7. Avenue des Champs-Élysées is the broadest avenue in Paris.
8. 'A four-wheeled coach, drawn by two horses, and seated for six persons, kept for hire' (*OED*).
9. The Tuileries Palace, which had been Napoleon's chief residence, stood on the Right Bank of the River Seine until 1871, when it was destroyed. The building had been started in 1564 by Catherine de'Medici (1519–89), the widow of Henry II, King of France (1519–59).
10. Napoleon III, Emperor of the French (Charles Louis Napoleon Bonaparte) (1808–73), was President of France from 1849 to 1852, and then Emperor of the French under the name Napoleon III from 1852 to 1870. He was the last monarch to rule France.
11. Mrs Sandby is the wife of the Revd George Sandy. On returning to England from Switzerland in 1847, RBL was given refuge by Mrs Sandby at her home, Flixton Vicarage in Suffolk.

To Rebecca Ryves

Hand Hotel[1] Llangollen North Wales
Friday June 3d 1853

My dearest Rebecca I hope you arrived safely at your journeys End, as I did at mine. "Willey" (as Mrs Wheeler called him) very kindly stayed and saw me off and Tib having put on one of his most innocent faces, and biggened hims Eyes to de uttermost extent made a conquest of the three old Fogeys in the Carriage (for I had smuggled him in with me) so that on arriving at Shrewsbury[2] their coats were as white as his – from his liberal cadeaux[3] to them of the latter – Nothing can exceed as I suppose you know the exquisite beauty of this vale of Llangollen I quite agree with Puckler Muskau[4] – that it far exceeds that of the much bepuffed Rhine-land. Amy Phillips[5] mine Hostess is a dear nice old woman but there is still some difficulty about her taking me before October which however I hope will be solved to day – as I should prefer remaining here to turning out, and coming back in October even if she gave me the worst room in her house till then. How I wished for you at dinner yesterday – such delicious Trout, small welsh mutton gooseberry fool – cream – custard – Sir Watkin Puddings[6] – [ill] Llangollen all!!!! which must be the nectar that Wodin[7] is now quaffing in his druidical Elysium,[8] and though last – not least a Huge fine fellow of a black cat with a red collar on – who dined with us (invited by Tib). I offered him some cream but he turned away disdainfully which made me suspect he was a Temperance Cat, a suspicion that was confirmed on leaving the room for a minute, by finding this abstemious Grimalkin[9] who could not even look at plain cream before me stealing and devouring Custard! This piece of Feline hypocrisy reminds me of that reptile Jonas whom your brother said had pretended, he was looking for and could not find your House as he had a Box for you at the Lyceum! don't you wish you may get it? – I do hope – I shall not have to turn out of this – I have such a terrible quantity of Luggage yet that said Luggage is by no means the heaviest thing I travel with. – I shall not write to Mrs Kitchener to congratulate her prematurely, as so many did to me. I shall write to Lady Hotham in a day or two – and tell her I bear her no malice – indeed although there is nothing the matter with me – I feel too near the little Church yard upon which my Bedroom window looks out to do so to any one. I will write to you again when my fate is decided. Pray let me hear from you soon and how you got on, and over and sincerely hoping that you are as well as I wish you (and you could not be better) Believe me

Ever My Dearest Rebecca your grateful and affectionate Rosina Bulwer Lytton Him Dogs best love.

HALS
1. A seventeenth-century coach-house, situated in Bridge Street, Llangollen, Denbighshire, north Wales.

2.   A market town in the county of Shropshire, which borders north Wales.
3.   Gifts (French).
4.   Prince Hermann, Fürst von Pückler-Muskau, was a travel writer, who wrote about his adventures in England, Wales and Ireland in *Puckler's Progress: The Adventures of Prince Puckler-Muskau in England, Wales and Ireland as told in letters to his former wife, 1826–9.*
5.   After the death of her husband Jos, Mrs Amey [*sic*] Phillips became the innkeeper of the Hand Inn in Llangollen until her death in 1857.
6.   Named after the Welsh politician Sir Watkin Williams Wynn of Wynnstay, Denbighshire, north Wales. He attended Jesus College, Oxford, early in the eighteenth century, and every St David's Day, the pudding is served in his memory. The pudding is also associated with Shropshire, where he was born.
7.   Woden is an Anglo-Saxon pagen deity corresponding in certain respects to the Roman god Mercury and the Norse god Odin. He was the leader of the wild hunt and the one who carried off the dead.
8.   The Greeks believed that, after death, the souls of the heroic and virtuous would rest in a paradisiacal Elysium. The Druids were a pagan priesthood and, according to the historian Tacitus, were first sighted by the ancient Romans in Wales.
9.   Name of the witches' cat in Shakespeare's *Macbeth*.

To Rebecca Ryves

Hand Hotel Llangollen North Wales
Sunday June 5th 1853

Many thanks My dearest Rebecca for your affectionate letter which I received this morning with the Post mark of "Put in too late" upon it. I am glad to hear that your passage though rough was ready – ie that you were not long getting over. I try as much as possible to submit myself to gods will, and truly may I say that "the spirit is willing but the flesh is weak"[1] and blow, after blow, of every description, has so shattered my health that the body buffets the mind and wont always let it keep its equilibrium. – Even since I have been here, I have had another pull down, for my dream of being able to have you here, is now at an end, for Mrs Phillips wont take me a sou[2] less than the £2"2"0 – a week or 6s a day – and something extra for attendance and even this, as a mighty favor, at this time of the year, I tried several other places, about here, including Farm Houses, and Pokey Lodgings – over a Haberdashers, and next door to a Butchers! and for two rooms alone they ask £1"10 a week; nowhere for the £2"2"0 not only is fire and light included, and the food plentiful and excellent, but I have wax lights – and a clean Tablecloth and napkin every day which is to me a great desideratum, as the piggery of poverty, is its worst part, unfortunately she cannot leave me in these nice old <u>large</u> rooms, looking out upon the quiet village Church yard, where I hope soon also to be at rest; but tomorrow I am to be moved into two little new vulgar Pokey rooms in a new remote added to Australia part of the House, where there is not room to swing a Cat, at least not such an Elephantic one as Major the black cat of the Inn. Byrne will stay to stow away my things (for to settle them will be impossible) and then returns to Town on Thursday, when my "abomination of desolation"!³ will begin. As "Pardon to the injured doth belong"⁴ I wrote to Lady H⁵ yesterday and told her, I had no feeling of resentment towards her. Poor Massy I wish he could get over to Ireland to see Dr Stokes for I was both shocked, and grieved to see him looking so shadowy. – I forgot to tell you in my last, that when I arrived at Llangollen Road – a pretty little bird, perched upon one of the wires of the Electric Telegraph, and looking me full in the face, as if especially addressing himself to me, began turning his head from side, to side; and chirping most vociforously – I don't know – whether <u>this</u> was the bird as Byron wrote, and therefore of <u>course</u> as Massy would quote "in my solitude singing which speaks to my spirit of thee"⁶ The walks about here are lovely if I could take them but I can scarcely drag one foot after the other – I never saw such lovely scenery – all the wild bold outlines of the Uberland⁷ with the cultivated garden richness of Devonshire salmon leaps – and little silvery babbling bounding rivulets such as one sees near the Mont D'Or, in the Pyrenees⁸– In short I wish you were here, and that I had where with all to Harness one of my fellow creatures of the long eared and long suffering genus – to a car and take nice drives – but there is no use in wishing! Except that this may find you well, and happy and that you will write soon my dearest Rebecca to your grateful & affect Rosina Bulwer Lytton

---

HALS
1. 'The spirit indeed is willing, but the flesh is weak', Matthew 26:41.
2. French coin of little value, worth five centimes.
3. Matthew 24:15.
4. 'Forgiveness to the injured doth belong. But they ne'er pardon who have done the wrong', John Dryden, *Conquest of Granada* (1672), Part 2, I.ii.1670–1.
5. Lady Hotham.
6. 'And a bird in the solitude singing, / Which speaks to my spirit of *Thee*', Byron, 'Stanzas to Augusta' (1816), l. 48.
7. Part of the island of Helgoland, situated in the south-east corner of the North Sea.
8. A small spa town in the mountain range in south-west Europe, which forms a natural border between France and Spain.

To Rebecca Ryves

Phillips's Hotel¹ Llangollen
Thursday June 10ᵗʰ 1853

My dearest Rebecca I have not written to you for the last few days, because I have been very ill, and very busy – and had a great many letters to answer (amongst others a long one from Mrs Tyler with of course nothing in it, but hoping I should long be Established at Hereford House!!!) to day I have just received your kind one of Tuesday for as all letters trot to London first, it takes two days to get a letter at this place and the Post only comes in once a day; – I am indeed very sorry for poor Massy that Mr Munsell[2] has resigned – but there is no end to ones causes of sorrow and vexation in this world – mine at least fall thick as leaves at Val Ombrösa[3] and I am now – in more trouble, and hot water, after having taken every precaution to prevent it – but in this beastly kingdom they must cheat, and over reach you in some way or other; Mrs Phillips, when first I came here, made a great many speeches about her fears, of not being able to make me comfortable, as she should be obliged to give me such very pokey rooms for the summer, I said I would put up with anything till October – rather, than have the trouble, of moving, and all was settled well yesterday I paid her my first weeks bill, – and the only attempt at extortion, was charging me separately for Byrnes, and my Beer, this I remonstrated against but in vain – as beer is always included in board, – she said Captain (?) and Mrs Lloyd paid the same a day that I did but, that "they drank very well!! as their bill for wine && – was as much again as their food" – I suppose she included Mrs Tom,[4] on the principle of man and wife being one, when they are not two, as is more generally the case. – Well nothing did Mrs Phillips say yesterday – which makes her conduct worse but this morning she comes, to me, and says I must go into Lodgings as it did not at all answer – her purpose to give up two rooms at this time of year – here was a pretty blow for me! as you will Easily believe, when I tell you that I had to borrow £10 – from Byrne – to pay my way here till July – and she being thoroughly English, and doing nothing for nothing or never thinking herself paid do what one will, I have to give her £3 – with this £10 in July – besides £2 for her months wages – and that's the way my wretched pittance goes! – now £3"15 went to pay Phillips's bill yesterday – out of this £10! – and now I am to have the trouble of hunting for, and far worse the expense of moving into a dirty lodging and unsettling all my things which Byrne has been quite cross and disagreeable enough about having to settle, in so small a compass – besides the expense of keeping Byrne two additional days to do it – what makes Mrs Phillips's conduct the more disgusting is, that she tried, to get off, upon the Hypocritical cant, that she was sure I was so uncomfortable when I had not made a single complaint, but on the contrary praised everything up to the skies – God help me for I am well nigh out of my senses – with all these never ending – great, and petty worries – and fruitless struggles – Byrne with that tadé, and good feeling! that all English people possess has just as if it was the pleasantest news in the world! brought me a newspaper with an account of a Dinner party Sir Liar had on Wednesday week, consisting of all the Blackguards in London from the present Duke of Wellington[5] down to Ben Disraeli: The Drama in Wilton Place[6] will not be complete, unless Georgina goes off with Polly Hopkins!– forgive this stupid and egotistical scrawl, but I am <u>so</u> worried I can scarcely write at all, continue to direct to me at this Hotel till you hear again – I have had no answer from Lady Hotham so suppose she is at Dover but it is very little matter. Your brother William forwarded me 3 letters yesterday but without a word, one of them was an Invitation to a Ball from Mrs <u>Bell</u>! the fat Woman at Princes Gate[7] for the 17th of June – good bye and God Bless you my dearest Rebecca Ever your gratefully and affecty yrs Rosina Bulwer Lytton.

HALS

1. This is the Hand Hotel, Llangollen, run by Mrs Phillips.
2. In 1850, Lord Massy purchased Milford House on the banks of the Shannon at Castletroy, County Limerick, from the Maunsell family, a few kilometers from his home, the Hermitage.
3. 'Thick as autumnal leaves that strew the brooks in Vallombrosa', John Milton, *Paradise Lost* (1667), I.302. Vallombrosa (*vallis umbrosa* (Latin), shady valley) is a village situated 32 km from Florence.
4. The wife of Captain Tom. Both are guests at the Hand Hotel, Llangollen.
5. In 1848, EBL's brother Henry married the Duke of Wellington's niece. See RBL, 17 November 1854.
6. Situated in the City of Westminster in south-west London.
7. Prince's Gate in South Kensington, London, was named after the Prince of Wales.

To Rebecca Ryves

Dee Villa Llangollen
Wednesday June 15th [1853]

I am delighted My dearest Rebecca, that you are now with your kind friend, Mrs Eyre Lloyd, as from all you have told me of her agreeability and amiability, I am sure that must be a great delight to you; I am also very glad to hear such good accts of poor Massy – and only hope he wont undo the efforts nature is making for him, - by going into hot rooms – Will you ask him to send me my Gil Blas[1] by rail, and not on any acct to pay it; - What on Earth can that Smith the upholsterer want with me? Surely he is paid – as for Mrs Beedle and all the other Duns – they are awful and worry my life out, - add to which this desperately wet weather makes my side so bad that I could almost scream with the pain, of it, and my back, and think it must be a protracted gestation of my creditors! from which I never shall be be [*sic*] safely delivered, either by chloroform,[2] or any other form! – I send you Lady Hothams letter, no 1 – and will send you 2 more, in a day or two; in reply to this one, I said I <u>was</u> wrong – however goaded, or irritated to tell her I would send her a cheque for the Paris expenses; but that as for dining with her at Folkstone, I cried for mercy. I could not have done it had she been the arch angel Michael, so torn, and exhausted, was I by the sea sickness, and by the hurry, flurry, scurry – of that awful journey – that luckily for herself, but, very unluckily for others – <u>she</u> had the strength of a steam Engine, with which no one else could cope – and which prevented her having a human feeling for any one else, with regard, to my irritability at <u>contretems</u>[3] I said, no one could bear better, and without murmuring the disagreeables of <u>necessity</u> than I could, having long carried off all the prises, in that hard school, but the constant, pitched battles, and haggling about every <u>centime</u>,[4] and not trusting to her servants even to pay a rail way fare, where they could not cheat her; and then calling this aggravated high pressure case, of hot water a party of pleasure!!! was enough to have irritated the combined tempers of the army of martyrs, – and I concluded with the following little home thrust, "do for Heavens sake my dear Lady Hotham believe, that there is a wide difference between, the holy, and God – the attribute of <u>Truth</u> properly so called, and saying wantonly, and gratuitously rude things to every one – for instance a person might have a hump upon their back, and the said hump being a fact, <u>would</u> in one sense be a <u>truth</u>, but to announce this fact to the owner of the Hump, - would not exactly come under the head of <u>truth</u>, but of gross bad feeling, and that people fond of hurling such facts! at their neighbours heads, might chance to find themselves in the same category as Mr Moses Mundungus,[5] who when he said to his wife – "Facts – Mrs M: Facts Madam! I say are <u>stubborn</u> <u>things</u>" – the wife replied – "Then bless me Mr Mundungus – what a <u>great</u> <u>fact</u> you must be!" – I also told her, that if her Husband had had had [*sic*] the power of turning her out of House, and home, to make way for his mistresses, kicking her through the world, from post to pillar and bribing that Infernal machine the Press to assail her with their cowardly Parthian[6] Weapons – perhaps – her great Leviathan "<u>The World</u>"! might have kept <u>eveven</u> [*sic*] more out of her way – than it does out of mine. – In her growl of yesterday with her usual good breeding she seems to doubt the fact of my having Eaten green peas here a fortnight ago –and having full blown Damask and cabbage roses above the drawing room windows (<u>as there are none yet at Hereford House</u>!)[7] and I mentioned the cold weather and Hurricane[8] of four nights ago which uprooted a Patriarchal rose accacia tree,[9] which now measures its length on the ground, while its beautiful branches are bathing in the rushing, racing – roaring river, in reply to this – I sent her two magnificent roses – one damask, and the other cabbage – with a parcel of Peapods! in a letter (what extravagance! for it cost me 6 stamps – and leaves me minus for my packet to you to day) she ends this charming Epistle by saying with her usual <u>good feeling</u>! "now that you are settled down <u>with Every Comfort</u> I hope you will soon be better." In reply to this I said "Even so my dear Lady Hotham I did not make either the bad weather – or the Peas! – with regard to the former, there is no accounting – for the contradictions it pleases God, to make both nature, and human feelings guilty of – with regard to the latter, the peas I eat, a fortnight ago, I understand came from Chester, as most of the vegetables do here – there being plenty of peas there as there were, as well as strawberries a month ago – at Paris, where you were very positive there was no good fish to be had, <u>because</u> there was none 40 years ago! – forgetting that steam has annihilated distance though it may have increased vapouring! but as I don't like to be accused of lying even <u>sub rosa</u>[10] – I send you some of my really magnificent roses. – As for my "being settled down <u>with every Comfort</u>"! they must be of a new description, when on £160 a year! and without even a maid, at my age! for the first time in my life! but as I verily believe that our being well in this world depends more upon the largeness of our heart, than of ones means, perhaps in one sense I may be better off than many who have an indigestion of wealth, at all events, at all events I try hourly to remember – that our whole fate down to the <u>minutest</u> <u>circumstance</u> that befalls us, is all preordained, by the unerring wisdom, of a Covenant God – and however bitter the ingredients of our cup of life may be, when we submit ourselves – more, and more implicitly to the Omnipotant will that mingled them, we shall gradually become, less irritated against the <u>secondary</u> <u>causes</u>, He employs as Whips, and scourges, in our discipline. – Two days ago brought me the most outrageously insolent, and lying letter, from that old wretch Steinberg[11] – accusing <u>me</u>!! of having set Lady Hotham at her! – and <u>that</u> I had gone all over, Bayswater[12] with Lady H – to defame – and persecute, a poor defenceless woman! While de Birard had called and abused her violently then she goes on to say "Lady <u>Lytton</u>! I had expected better things of you – though you had the bad taste never to answer any of <u>me</u> letters – often have I defended you when I have heard you called "a most vindictive and unfeeling woman" & & - you may guess if my blood boiled – I replied to the old wretch –

"Madam never having answered any of your former letters, I had hoped to escape further insult and persecution from, you I could not take any notice of your letters, as I have made it a rule never to hold <u>any</u> sort of communication with any of the reptiles who crawl around Sir Edward Bulwer Lytton. I know nothing of Lady Hotham or the Chevalier de Birards movements – but I would have you remember that I ...

HALS
Incomplete letter.
1. *Gil Blas* is a novel by Alain-Rene LeSage. See RBL, 23 November 1833.
2. In 1847, the Edinburgh obstetrician James Young Simpson first used chloroform for general anesthesia during childbirth, which was popularized by Queen Victoria to whom it was administered in 1850 for her seventh delivery, when she gave birth to Arthur, the future Duke of Connaught.
3. Contretemps; hitches.
4. French coin of very little value.

5. Mundungus is a rank-smelling tobacco and the name of a character who, with Smelfungus, appears in Laurence Sterne's *A Sentimental Journey through France and Italy by Mr Yorick* (1768).
6. In ancient Parthia, in Asia, it was customary to discharge an arrow at the enemy while retreating; hence the expression, a parting shot.
7. Lady Hotham's London home. See RBL, 5 December 1855.
8. The Meteorological Office was founded in 1854 to provide maritime forecasts for shipping.
9. A shrub with bristly brittle branches and clusters of pale purple or rose flowers.
10. In secret (Latin).
11. See RBL, 0D274RR21.
12. Bayswater is an area in the west of London.

To Rebecca Ryves

Llangollen Friday June 24th 1853

My dearest Rebecca I can scarcely hold up my head to scrawl you these few lines – as I have been in bed with a raging fever of some sort since Sunday it is to be hoped it is the <u>last</u> stage and that I am nearly at my journeys end – Poor Massy! I am very sorry but going on as he does is nothing more or less than committing suicide. You will see by Mrs Tylers letter that Emily lost no time in "<u>encouraging</u>" them – but I fear they wont "<u>prepuz</u>"! for all that – is this weedy news about your brother William true? – I wrote some days ago to calm Mrs Wheelers fears! saying that I did not believe it, as I think I should have heard of it if true; – but it seems by this second edition as if it was true, I do hope you have got rid of your cold by this time? it does nothing but rain here – Poor Innocence seems to know that he is all I have got in the world, him has grown – so very affectionate – if I die; poor fellow dont leave him here, for common people especially English people have no feeling – but pray send for him. God Bless you my dearest Rebecca Ever your grateful and affect R B Lytton.

HALS

To Rebecca Ryves

Dee Villa Llangollen[1]
July 6th 1853

My dearest Rebecca I am more grieved than I can tell you to hear such bad accounts of poor Massy but such I feared would be the case when I last saw him, if he persisted in going out, Mrs Tyler writes me word that he is going to the South of France, God grant this may be of service to him – she also writes me

word that Willy[2] is considered the handsomest man in London – and that those
<u>Elegant</u> <u>British females</u> the Lewises[3] dont believe his denial of his engagement
to Mrs Ripon[4] – great matter indeed whether they do, or not, but Mrs Tyler says
<u>she</u> does. – I was so desperately ill after I last wrote to you, that I was obliged to
have medical advice, as it was basins full of nothing but <u>green</u> bile I used to bring
up – the Dr said it was almost incredible – and I must have had a most extraordinary degree of mental annoyance and bodily fatigue to bring me to such a
state, the quinine I have been taking – has got the fever under, but makes my
head dreadfully bad, as you truly quote from Tom Carmudgeons friend Jean
Paul – this is a perfect winter painted green – only I must add in <u>water colours</u>,
as the rain has never ceased till yesterday – and to day when the sun like a poor
wit, is endeavouring to shine – under difficulties – no my dear Rebecca I don't
think there is a chance of Lady H – leaving me a <u>sou</u>,[5] when I was in the height of
favour – she might perhaps have left me £50!!! since she thinks so much of that
sum, lent on her return from Paris – I have no doubt Mr <u>Goo</u>lding[6] was ordered
to deduct the 5 and leave the cipher – she substituting her <u>good</u> <u>wishes</u> instead
which indeed is about the extent of the outlay that English friendship ever makes
– not so the "<u>go a head</u>" yankees! as you shall hear presently I see by the Morning
<u>Paper</u> (which Mrs Wheeler sends me) that that very detestable personage Miss
Cecily Gore[7] (Mrs Gore[8] the authoress' daughter) was married on Monday to
Lord Edward Thynne,[9] she must be <u>now</u> six or seven and thirty – so far she is well
matched that her Edward Thynne – is the greatest Blackguard extant, – after my
thin[10] Edward! – (who must always have the pas[11] – in all rascality) – he Lord E
Thynne killed his first wife[12] from sheer brutality – he is moreover very like Sir
Liar in person and looks like Moses in the burning bush,[13] looking out of those
red whiskers of his. – it is written that as I cannot go to America – America shall
come to me – last Thursday Evening I had crawled as far as the vicarage about
100 yards from this to thank Mrs Edwards the Rectors wife– for the good cream,
and butter she is always sending me, but which I must not yet touch by the bye
– I wish you could see the lovely grounds of that said Rectory – such an affluence of wood water – mill – dale – rich meadow land – luxuriant flowers – and
evergreens you never – saw – Capability Browne[14] with that great Omnipotence
unlimited gold at his command, could never have achieved what nature has done
here. – well as I was returning – I saw two ladies – a little boy about five years old
and his bootest, of little King Charles dogs – admiring the view – Tib showed
master puppy dog – hims favourite spring – and de dogs having struck up an
acquaintance – I presently heard – a voice at my Ear – which if the unmistakable
<u>twang</u> of which – had not given "the world assurance of a" <u>Yankee!</u> the "<u>madam</u>"
would have done so – well the voice said – "you seem fatigued <u>madam</u> – will
you accept of my arm?" this piece of good Samaritanship was so very <u>un</u>English
that I accepted the Courtesy as kindly as it was offered – on arriving at my own

– door – I could not but ask them in and indeed to tell you the truth, Robinson Crusoe could scarcely have been more surprised, and <u>delighted</u>! when he in <u>his</u> solitude discovered the print of the human foot in the sand,[15] than <u>I</u> was at again hearing a human voice to break the fearful silence of mine – well they remained and drank tea, or rather hot water with me – and made themselves so agreeable that they stayed till a quarter to 12 – they pressed me to go and dine with them the next day at the Inn – making my mouth water with a list of all the good things Mrs Phillips gave them – for <u>here</u> – the cooking is atrocious, except at Mrs Tylers, I never saw food so libelled – moreover a most profuse scarcity – but I told them I was quite unable to do so – and asked them to come here the next Evening instead – taking the wise precaution to be sure and eat a good dinner first – up to this time we were anonymous to each other, but the next day when they came – they had found out from my friend Sarah the maid, at the Inn – who I was more know Tom Fool[16] – than Tom Fool knows – and thereupon – Ensued a scene, that would have done for Sam Slick[17] – "Oh! madam we had no idea that the affable, agreeable lady we – had the pleasure of spending an Evening with – was the celebrated &&& then followed a long tirade about what the Yankees call their appreciation for Ginius! and the old story of my being so popular in America.[18] They were mother – and daughter (both handsome) the daughter a Mrs Wills – the mother a Mrs <u>Pike</u>![19] (a fish not often caught in the Dee!) in the course of conversation they asked me if this was true, and the other was true, about Sir Liars conduct to me – whereupon I told them the whole history – at which they cried much – they could hardly believe that he only allowed me £400 a year as they said they did not know how I could exist upon it but you should have seen their faces, and have heard their scream – when I told them that even from this beggarly pittance the mean brute deducted the Income Tax!!! The mother said she would like to practise gymnastics to the extent of breaking a Parasol stick across Sir Liars back. They after expressing their deep regret that Henry Bulwer had not been drowned during his dip in the Rhône said Sir Liars house was no 1 Park Lane, he had just bought it and it had been pointed out to them as his. – They went away to their son and Brothers wedding on Sunday (in London I believe) but the mother said she was so miserable – at the idea of my passing the long dreary winter here alone that if she could possibly manage it she would come down and pass it with me if I would go back to the Hotel – yesterday morning arrives a Hamper of wine, and huge packet of Tea! – I conclude from them, but I cannot write and thank them as I don't know their address – I may now "<u>do my drinking</u>"! as well as Captain and Mrs Tom but as my illness has made my skin, and complexion as delicate as a girl of fifteen and me beautifully thin to boot, I think it would be a pity to spoil it by any such orgies – so I will wait in the hope of <u>your</u> coming to take the part of the <u>Captain</u> for as you say she is a great fool – I feel quite competent to do justice to that of the Lady. Innocence desires hims love since the mountain air has blown through hims ears – you have no idea what much better kissing there is on him – God Bless you My dearest Rebecca and believe me Ever your grateful & affect Rosina Bulwer Lytton

---

HALS

1. RBL was staying in this boarding house, which overlooked the Dee River, on Mill Street. It was run by John Allen (b. *c.* 1815) and his wife, Helen (b. *c.* 1821).
2. William, the brother of Rebecca Ryves.
3. These may be relatives of Wyndham Lewis, the first husband of Mary Anne Disraeli.
4. Louisa Anne Ripon is William Ryves's future wife. See RBL, 2 March 1853.
5. French coin of little value, worth five centimes.
6. This is most likely to be a misspelling of Mr Golding, Lady Hotham's lawyer. See 0D274RR21
7. Cecilia Anne Mary (*c.* 1816–79) was the only daughter of Catherine Gore and Lieutenant Charles Arthur Gore.
8. Catherine Grace Frances Gore (1799/1800–61), novelist and playwright, was an exponent of the fashionable novel, starting with *Women as they Are, or, The Manners of the Day* (1830) and culminating with the highly acclaimed *Cecil, or, The Adventures of a Coxcomb* in 1841.
9. Lord Edward Thynne (1807–84) was the fifth son of Thomas Thynne, the eldest son of the third Viscount Weymouth, who became first Marquess of Bath. He was the MP for Weobly in Herefordshire in 1831–2 and MP for Frome between 1859 and 1865. He married his second wife, Cecilia Gore, on 4 July 1853.
10. RBL is punning here on EBL's physical thinness and the pronunciation of 'Thynne' as 'thin'.
11. Step or dance (French).
12. Edward Thynne's marriage to Elizabeth Mellish on 8 March 1830 ended in separation. The bride's father had taken steps to prevent him getting hold of her money through the marriage settlement since Thynne's reputation as a notorious debtor was well known. Thynne's father had to mortgage his Irish estate for £20,000 to pay off part of his debts.
13. A burning bush that does not burn is a miracle performed by God on Mount Horeb to convince his prophet Moses of his divine calling (Exodus 3:2).
14. Lancelot Brown (1715/16–83), known as Capability Brown, was a famous landscape gardener.
15. The footprint belongs to man Friday, the only other inhabitant of the desert island where the hero of Daniel Defoe's novel *The Life and Adventures of Robinson Crusoe* (1719) is stranded.
16. This may be Thomas Skelton, the 'Fool' or Jester of Muncaster Castle, who sometimes misdirected passing travellers towards the marshlands and quicksands. Tom Fool died around 1600 and his ghost is said to haunt the castle.
17. Sam Slick was the pseudonym of Thomas Chandler Haliburton (1796–1865), a Canadian judge and author of the best-selling *The Clockmaker, or the Sayings and Doings of Samuel Slick of Slicksville* (1836). These were satiric sketches of the colonial life of Nova Scotia, mocking both Canadians and Americans.
18. RBL's novels were published in America and included *Bianca Capello; An Historical Tale* (New York: J. Winchester, 1843) and *The School for Husbands* (Philadelphia, PA: A. Hart, 1852).
19. Mrs Pike is a misspelling of Mrs Pyke. See RBL, 7 September 1853.

To Rebecca Ryves

Llangollen
Tuesday July 12th 1853

I am indeed truly grieved my dearest Rebecca at the sad account of poor Massy though not surprised at them; for I was greatly shocked at his altered appearance even when I saw him in London; and not a little horrified to see him persist in going to parties in such a state of evident weakness, and exhaustion as he was in.

It is not I assure you the least heavy part of my too heavy burden – to think that I cannot yet send you the remainder of my debt to you, I am hard at work again at my Sysiphus[1] task – for thanks to that Fiends too successful machinations it is sickening to me to have to labour in vain – however perhaps "The Reverend Muster Smith"[2] will do me the service of getting a Book[3] published anonymously a sort of Railway – Shilling Affair that will sell by the Thousand if it sells at all. – Thank God (who tempers the wind to the fleeced traveller as to the shorn lamb) both my health, and strength are better, after my late severe attack. – I have not felt so well, and so active for years – I felt the being without a maid woefully at first – but there is nothing as poor Lady Mary Shepherd[4] would have said – and Grandity have echoed – like achieving "a triumph of mind over matter" – the doing my hair and lacing! my stays were awful impossibilities! at first, but I have at length conquered them; and get both my room and my self done – by half past ten every morning when I come down to breakfast; "à tout malheur quelque chose est bon"[5] – and the good of being without a maid is, that my room is now as neat as a new pin: – my things in perfect order, – and repair, – which was far from being the case when I had a maid – my worst corvée[6] is washing poor Tib as my back is still so weak I suppose from the heavy burden it has all its life had to carry. – I have heard that Lady Clonbrock[7] is a very nice person; – but if she is a grand daughter of the Duke of Graftons[8] – she must have been a Fitzroy[9] – unless it was on the mothers side and that she married a Churchill.[10] So Lord Ernest Vane Ld Londonderry's[11] youngest son has had a quarrel with his Private Tutor – ran away and inlisted. in an Irish Dragoon Regt[12] – Oh! the blessing of having Sons!! is it not great?

Thank Heaven that vau rien[13] Ld Edward Thynne – has met his match in the little viper[14] he has married; – among his other noble exploits – he was once in the Bench for Vestris's[15] debts; as Jonas would inform you had you the happiness of being near him – he not being an adept in driving Duns – he took to driving a Stage Coach. I did not see Mr Marlborough Fitzgeralds[16] Paris adventures – he ought to get a clerks place in some Commercial House as no one understands Book keeping – clearing out and making Entrys better than he does – his winking wife – was an equal horror they used to say that she intrigued with every one and any one, for neclaces and Bracelets – she certainly used to appear in new, and very costly sets of jewels every night when they said they had not £300 a year in the world – and their house was a sort of Aladdins garden transformed into furniture; but then I suppose he even at that time forestalled the revenues of his Chevalier d'Industrie-ship[17] – A propos[18] of Chevaliers[19] – I had a long letter from poor little de Birard yesterday, which made me laugh exceedingly in as much as that <u>he</u> therein gives me a pressing invitation to go and spend a couple of months with Lady Hotham!! assuring me of her intense regard for me! and the great interest she takes in me!! – I told him at all events, I would <u>wait</u> till <u>she</u> asked me; but that I could not go if she did, for when one is at the Gallies one must "finish ones time" – I drank Tea at The Rectory[20] last Evening – they are nice friendly hospitable people – and such a charming house! – I met there two of the very prettiest girls I have seen a long time two Miss Wynne Owens[21] – one dark hair, the other blonde, but <u>une blonde un peu hasardé</u>[22] but such lovely skins – and complexions – teeth, and eyes I have seldom seen, and those rare things in girls, beautiful moulded, and <u>very</u> <u>white</u> hands and arms – they were moreover exceedingly Lady like – so much repose ease, and quiet self possession of manner, – without the least forwardness – what a relief after and what a contrast to the terrible missyish and servant maidish vulgarity of poor Emily Tyler.– I never got my Gil Blas[23] – but it is of no consequence so dont bore poor Massy any more about it when you write.

I shall barely save the Post so good bye and God Bless you – and with Innocences best love – who makes an immense sensation here <u>him</u> being de only Blenheim in the place but I am sorry to say behaved very ill last night – snapped at Miss Wynne Owen – tore through Mrs Edwards Conservatory and decapitated three beautiful salvias![24] – there I told him I'd complain to hims Aunt Rebecca of him and so I have done

     Ever my dearest Rebecca
     your grateful and affect
     Rosina Bulwer Lytton

HUNT
1. In Greek mythology, Sisyphus, the founder and king of Corinth, was punished in the Tartarus, a region below heaven and earth, by having to roll a huge boulder up a hill then watch it roll down again for eternity.
2. James Elishama Smith. See RBL, 23 December 1852.
3. RBL, *Behind the Scenes.*
4. The philosopher, Lady Mary Primrose (1777–1847), later known as Lady Mary Shepherd, published *Essays on the Perception of an External Universe* (1827) and *An Essay upon the Relation of Cause and Effect, controverting the Doctrine of Mr. Hume, concerning the Nature of that Relation* (1824).
5. In every misfortune something is good (French).
6. Labour (French).

7. Caroline Elizabeth Spencer (1805–64) married Robert Dillon, third Baron Clonbrock, in 1830, with whom she had twelve children.
8. Her grandfather was Augustus Henry Fitzroy, third Duke of Grafton (1735–1811), who served as a Whig Prime Minister in the 1760s.
9. Lady Clonbrock's mother was Lady Frances Fitzroy (1780–1866).
10. Lady Frances Fitzroy, a younger daughter of the third Duke of Grafton, married Lord Francis Almeric Spencer (1779–1845), second son of the fourth Duke of Marlborough, who was raised to the peerage as first Baron Churchill, after retiring as a MP in 1815.
11. Lord Ernest Vane-Tempest (1836–85) was the fourth son of the fourth Marquess of Londonderry (1805–72). Three years hence, he was put on trial for spitting in the face of a cavalry officer.
12. Ernest's grandfather, Charles William Stewart, third Marquess of Londonderry (1778–1854), was created Earl Vane in 1823. He had been Lieutenant-Colonel of the 5th Royal Irish Dragoons.
13. Waster (French).
14. Cecilia Gore. See RBL, 6 July 1853.
15. Lucia Elizabeth Vestris (*née* Bartolozzi) (1797–1856) was an actress, who had been Edward Thynne's lover.
16. Edward Marlborough FitzGerald (1809–83) was a traveller and writer, best known as the poet of the first and most famous English translation of *The Rubáiyát of Omar Khayyám* (1859). FitzGerald had lived in Paris between 1816 and 1818.
17. The industrious knight (French).
18. In connection with (French).
19. Chevalier de Birard. See RBL, 9 January 1853.
20. The home of Rector Revd Edwards and his wife.
21. These may be relatives of Mrs Middleton Biddulph (*née* Owen).
22. But a slightly risky blonde (French).
23. A popular eighteenth-century novel by Alain-René LeSage. See RBL, 23 November 1833.
24. A herb belonging to the mint family.

To Rebecca Ryves

... Poor Mrs Pyke <u>did</u> give me a most cordial Invitation to new York – but alas! as you well know – <u>that</u> is not the <u>one thing needful</u>! I am sure Mrs Phillips must have been charmed at the way she and I "<u>did our drinking</u>"! as she gave me Claret, and Champagne every day while she stay'd I hope to see her back by the end of next week. My miseries are now beginning as the London season being over – "The Neighbourhood" have returned, and are flocking to call upon me, which is a sad bore to me, and dont suit my Book at all, as I had taken "a long farewell" of all my finery, and provided myself with workhouse looking stuff gowns – adapted to my present circumstances- and congenial to the mountains and molehills of the country, worse still it is an aristocratic neighbourhood too: Lord Mostyn Lord Dungannon The Watkyn Williams Wynnes – The Tottenhams (poor Lady Haywardens Father and mother) and the Myddleton

Biddulphs[1] – of that magnificent old Feudal Palace Chirk Castle, – the latter lead the way – (Col Biddulph being Lord Lieutenant of the County The Battlements are so wide at Chirk Castle, that two people can with ease walk abreast in them, and from them is a magnificent view extending over seventeen Counties! The damage Oliver Cromwells[2] cannon – did to this beautiful old place (which was built, in 1013) took £80, 000 to repair – the Moat and Portcullis, are among the finest remaining in the Kingdom but alas! visits! and dinners seven miles off! entail Post Horses! and you know how well they suit my finances! I had hoped to have remained quiet, in my insignificence – burried in my ruins for the rest of my miserable existence but I suppose it is all owing to Lord Dungannon, and that horrid Archaeological Society – who wont allow any <u>antiquity</u> to remain unexplored in this neighbourhood. Àpropos[3] of antiqueties – I see by the papers that Lord Seafield[4] died at Cullen House[5] on the 30th of last month so now I suppose "his <u>disconsolate</u> widow"![6] will marry[7] that Mr Stuart who appeared to be the Chisholm[8] of that ménage.[9] I have found a Treasure here, in the shape of a çi-devant[10] Ladies Maid a Miss Williams – who makes my dresses <u>beautifully</u> for 4s 6d (and such <u>pretty</u> caps – for 9d! I giving her the materials) she packed and unpacked and arranged all my things so nicely for me, – and comes and does all sorts of odd jobs for me. Addio God Bless you – my book goes briskly on, so heaven grant it may go off! ditto. – write soon and believe me ever gratefully and affectly yours Rosina Bulwer Lytton.

HALS

Incomplete letter.

1. The Mostyn family were Welsh landowners, who had originated from Pengwern, near Llangollen, Denbighshire. Sir Edward Pryce Lloyd (1768–1854) became Sir Baron Mostyn in 1831 and was succeeded by his son Edward Lloyd (1795–1884), who assumed the additional surname of Mostyn. For Dungannon and Watkins Williams Wynn, see RBL, 18 August 1853. Charles John Tottenham (1808–78) married Isabella Maude (c. 1814–92), daughter of Cornwallis Maude, third Viscount Hawarden, in 1839. They lived in Berwyn House, Plas Berwyn, Denbighshire. For Myddleton Biddulphs, see RBL, 4 February 1853.
2. Oliver Cromwell (1599–1658) was the republican and later Lord Protector of England. In 1659, his Parliamentary General John Lambert laid siege to the castle demolishing the western side and three of its towers. The estate was subsequently plundered to the amount of £80,000.
3. In connection with (French).
4. Colonel Sir Francis William Grant of Grant, Baronet and sixth Earl of Seafield (1778–1853), died on 30 July 1853.
5. Lord Seafield's mansion house lies outside the town of Cullen in Moray on the North Sea coast of Scotland.
6. Louisa Emma (c. 1818–84), a daughter of Robert George Maunsell of Limerick, was the second wife of Lord Seafield whom she married in 1843. See RBL, 7 February 1856.
7. Louisa married Major Godfrey Hugh Massy on 31 January 1856.
8. A Scottish clan.

9.   Domestic arrangement (French).
10. Former (French).

To Rebecca Ryves

Llangollen

Saturday August 6th 1853

My dearest Rebecca no doubt you have thought I was dead and buried! – but no such good luck I have only been as usual worried and bothered out of my life, first I was ten days in bed with the Influenza which has left me with a cough that tears my lungs out, next those wretches at Dee Villa, furious because I told them I should return to Mrs Phillips's in October took that opportunity of Annoying, and insulting me, in every possible manner the beast of a man being always dead drunk and frightening me to death, and the woman being the lowest Billings-gate[1] you can concieve [*sic*] – one part of their insolence consisted in writing to say I could not stay in their Lodgings after to day Saturday the 6th though by my <u>agreement</u> I had a right to remain there till October, but the Coup de Grâce[2] was last Wednesday in the morning before I was up – the great cart horse of a Welch maid who looks like a Drayman in petticoats – came creep mousing into the room whereupon Tib who was on my bed, began to bark at her – upon this she pretended to be so frightened that she ran down stairs and returned five minutes after with her scarlet haired wretch of a mistress – who rushed into my room with a great thick stick in her hand- screaming out "I'll do for that Dog!" at this as you may suppose I jumped out of bed and by main force pushed the wretch out of the room – this being a regular and most unwarrantable assault – I knew very well what to do – so as soon as I was dressed I set off to Mrs Phillips's to ask where a solicitor was to be found – she was horrified and so exasperated against those villainous Allens[3] that she vows she'll expose them and never recommend them any one else – the Lawyer soon settled them saying unfortunately I had been too good to them paying them a month in advance – but as a <u>pis aller</u>[4] of extortion they wanted to trump up a bill of 10" a week!!! for poor Tib which the attorney of course laughed to scorn – and but for my clemency the wretch of a woman could by law have been well finished.

But God is very good to me in the midst of all my awful and never ending worries for upon getting to the Hotel one of the servants met me and said – "Mrs Pyke(!) had arrived the night before, and was just sending up to know if I could recieve [*sic*] her?" I instantly went to her – she said she had been to Liverpool to see her daughter on board for New York and could not resist coming over to see me though she must return to Town for three weeks before she came here to stay ten minutes after I came into the room before I had told her anything about those beastly Allens she said "Now Madam you must not be offended – with me; before I saw you I always had the greatest esteem, and admiration for you, and having heard a great deal more of your persecutions since my return to London my heart literally aches for you – as I dont see how you are possibly to rub on upon the miserable pittance you now have, even had you a quarter of your beggarly £400 a year in advance you might be able to do so here and there my heart would be a little at rest – so pray – pray instead of a Trinket do me the favor of accepting this trifle as an Earnest of the true friendship of one American Woman" The trifle was two £50! notes – I need not tell you (though this was a sad temptation considering the plight we are all in) that <u>nothing</u> could induce me to accept such a sum, from an almost utter stranger but the tears were in my eyes – and my heart in my mouth to think of <u>such</u> kindness from a stranger! and how many hundred years it would be before <u>English</u> compassion if indeed that same ever exists?? would find an egress through its purse the only way I could pacify her was by promising that should I ever be in great distress for money (alas! is not that my normal state) I would write to her – For this flitting I had to borrow £5 from Mrs Tyler and I would rather have cut off my hand than have done so – As soon as my Energetic Yankee friend – heard of that wretch Mrs Allens outrageous conduct she went to her – and made her go down on her knees to beg pardon – I have dined with her Every day at the Hotel since and fared sumptuously – so that her arrival was quite a God send and I am sorry to say she goes on Monday – I moved into these Lodgings (the only ones to be had) on Friday night – over a Linen drapers shop – not very pleasant – but the woman civil and obliging and had been Bar maid to Mrs Phillips – I dont even know the name of the street but a letter directed to me Llangollen North Wales will be sufficient. Mrs Tyler wrote me word she had seen Massy "riding" in the Park but whether this means he was really on the outside of a Horse; or the Vulgar English mode of expressing that a person is inside a carriage driving – I cant tell you. Mrs Wheeler also writes me word that Willy told her Massy was much better – her good sposo[5] is really very kind in sending me divers Newspapers and but for them, I should be much in the same advanced state of civil, and political knowledge as the Derbyshire Landlady Temp – George the first; who had for her sign a grim looking Effigy of the King of Prussia, and being suddenly told by a Traveller one day, that his Majesty was just dead – Exclaimed

"Indeed Sir! Then may I make bold to ask <u>who</u> is <u>now</u> Lord Mayor of London?!!!" –

I cannot tell you what a relief it is to me to be out of that horrid place where every thing was bad – but as the schoolboys say – the <u>Tea</u>! flogged Every thing – and no wonder for it was all <u>Birch</u>, and therefore was only labouring in its vocation. As for my book thanks to "<u>me</u> <u>illness</u>!" I have only written 150 pages – but must set to work on Monday when my Yankee friend goes, and work like a Dragon. – Poor Innocence is Him <u>Seps</u> again – now he is out of that vile place – petted and admired by every one – for he as a Blenheim makes quite as as [*sic*] great a sensation among the village curs as him Muds Paris Bonnet does at Church among the village Golgothas.[6] – Forgive this scrawl – which I have written by Electric Telegraph – to save the post. Let me hear from you soon – and with Tibs best love to Hims aunt Rebecca – Believe Me Ever Dearest Rebecca

> Gratefully and
> Affectly yrs
> Rosina Bulwer Lytton

Did you go on the visit you intended?

HUNT
1. The famous London fish market, which in 1850 was moved from the dock at Billingsgate to a purpose-built market building on Lower Thames Street. Its name was a byword for coarse language.
2. Literally: 'blow of mercy' (French); death-blow.
3. John and Helen Allen ran Dee Villa boarding house in Llangollen where RBL had stayed. See RBL, 6 July 1853.
4. Last resort (French).
5. Husband (Italian).
6. The original of 'Golgotha' is 'place of the skull' in Hebrew, and here denotes being bareheaded.

To Mrs Pyke

Llangollen N: Wales
August 14th 1853

I am indeed truly sorry Dear Mrs Pyke to hear that you have not been well; but hope it is merely the result of fatigue, owing to your hurried journies. – And now before I forget it, I must protest against your <u>sending</u> me any Pears; it is true I gave you a <u>commission</u> to <u>bring</u> me some, but <u>sending</u> them would in the first place be worse than useless as they would only keep them at the station, as they do everything else, till they are as old as I am. I fear also by this, that you are not coming back; therefore it was <u>very cruel</u> of you to be so kind to me and make me so fond of you; as it was only creating for me a new affliction dont déjà j'ai l'embarass du choix![1] – but, I must let your kind heart know the great service you have rendered me, two days after you went, I had a pressing <u>dun</u> for £7 which but for <u>you</u>, would have worried me to death; so see that I shall <u>ever</u> be indebted to you in the way of kindness and in money till October – I congratulate you upon having your dear little Grandson with you again I hope <u>he</u> will persuade you to come back here, as the Donkeys, and more especially the <u>Donkey Boys</u> are anxiously awaiting his return – My miseries are now beginning for the London season being over – the County people have returned, and have flocked to call upon me; – which is to me in every way <u>a bore</u> as I am in no position to associate with my equals in birth, who are so much my unequals in wealth: and to tell you how I groan in spirit, at the guineas it costs me for Post Horses to return these visits (for they are all seven and eight miles off) is impossible!

I have been suffering a great deal with my heart, and side but no wonder the weather has been a mosaic of horrors! – perfect water spouts of rain, Hoar frosts the Gardeners say at night; -Fogs, mists, and other damperies, add to which, the bad dinners are telling upon me as I am becoming visibly thinner, and bid fair soon to re-become quite <u>svelte</u> but my hair comes off dreadfully, which is not so pleasant: you kindly said you would give me that receipt for an American Hair Wash, I hope you will <u>bring</u> it; but dont <u>send</u> it as that horrid station is a sort of deputy "Bourne from whence no traveller" (in the shape of a parcel at least) returns. Miss Williams has made me up the <u>Marie Stuart</u> cap, with the point, that <u>you</u> cut out, and it looks so pretty, I am sure you will have one like it when you see it; it is a great improvement upon mine. – A friend writes me word from Ireland great brags of the <u>warm</u> weather! and the <u>Comet</u>! which they see there, with what I suppose the Americans would call the <u>indelicate</u> Eye! as we call it the <u>naked</u> eye; I remember when I was a very little child there was a comet, with a beautiful star at one end of it, and a long tail of fire like a Harliquins sword at the other; the heat <u>then</u> was <u>intense</u>! as I well recollect all the Children and caterpillers being consumed by it, I <u>try</u> to <u>glow</u> with the remembrance of this heat <u>now</u>, – but my teeth chatter, and wont let me, so much for "The Pleasures of Memory"! and of "Imagination" which are null, and void! without those of "Hope"! – and there is little hope of fine weather now But I <u>will</u> still hope to see you soon again; and in that hope Believe me Dear Mrs Pyke Ever, your grateful tho' obliged

R Bulwer Lytton.

HALS
1. Of which I already have an embarrassment of choice! (French).

To Rebecca Ryves

Llangollen

August 18th 1853

[Engraving of Chirk Castle[1] at head of sheet]

This by no means does Chirk justice, – as <u>this</u> gives one the idea of its being <u>low</u>, and <u>Mesquin</u>[2] whereas it is high, and grandiose! – and the <u>finest</u> Timber I ever saw in any Park, some of the oaks being from 800 to a thousand years old.

– Dearest Rebecca I write in a whirlwind for I am very busy – but I wish to answer your question and tell you that I don't know Lady Wynne,[3] at first I attributed her not calling with the rest, to that little reptile Lady Doyle[4] whom you know was a daughter [of] Charles Wynnes (vide[5] Mrs Carlyles)[6] but Mrs Edwards says they are in the Isle of Wight[7] for her health, she being supposed to be in a consumption poor thing! – no good ever comes of cousins marrying[8] – so dont you go and get yourself <u>Insured at Lloyds</u>![9] unless you want to be <u>wrecked</u>, – but this I can tell you – that Wynstay though <u>manured</u> with <u>money</u>! is a new, and Peelish looking Place,[10] and in my humble opinion not to compare with Chirk Castle, or even to Lord Dungannons Place.[11] Not having time to transcribe it – I send you the Chevaliers letter which will amuse you about <u>Gorge</u> and his friend Sir Liar! send it back to me. – Tib says you must for de sake of him nerves learn to write <u>Canish</u> or de dog language correctly, and say vezy great <u>big</u> much and not "vezy great much" for he like hims mud, suffered so much at The Tylers from hearing the queens English murdered, "<u>Lizer</u>!" as they elegantly called her being head governess to Mother and daughters the fruits of which were that they talked of "Cooky!!!!" and "Coachman"! and Mrs T of "propo<u>sh</u>als" and doing things "<u>surrupshusly</u>"!!! vulgo[12] – surruptitiously till Tib, – and hims mud have had an Elocution fever ever since. – Poor Massy! I cannot think how his brother can bear to go to Harlyford;[13] but men <u>have</u> no feelings, and that is the truth of it. – I still wish Massy had the Claret, as unless you will come and help me to drink it, it is no use to me, as being alone I cannot open a bottle for myself as it spoils if not drunk directly if I could find any one going to London I would still send it to him. I don't know what you mean by your fine weather it is very fine weather here! for what "Punch" calls <u>making Hay</u>, as it does nothing but rain Pitch forks! – Forgive this scrawl, but all my pens are worn to the stump writing "the Doctors great work on Propagation!!" so with black Eyed Tibbianas best love Believe me ill, and in Haste Dearest Rebecca Ever gratefully and affectly yrs Rosina Bulwer Lytton.

HALS

1. Chirk Castle is a fortress of the Welsh Marches, built in the late thirteenth century by Roger Mortimer, Justice of north Wales, it is situated about 10 km from Llangollen.
2. Small (French).
3. Marie Emily Williams-Wynn (d. 1905) was the wife of Sir Watkin Williams Wynn (1820–85), sixth Baronet, MP for Denbighshire (1841–85). See below, n. 7.
4. Sidney Williams-Wynn (d. 1867) married, in 1844, Sir Francis Hastings Charles Doyle, Baronet (1810–88), a celebrated poet, the son of Sir Francis Doyle, RBL's mother's cousin. She is described by RBL as 'little, silly, selfish, squeaky' (*Unpublished Letters*, p. 271). Lady Doyle was the niece of Lady Grenville and the daughter of Charles Watkin Williams-Wynn (1775–1850), known in the House of Commons as Squeak, to distinguish him from his brother, Bubble. See ibid.
5. See (Latin).
6. Jane Carlylye and her husband Thomas, the famous historian, were RBL's staunch supporters. See RBL, 18 March 1851.

7. The Isle of Wight has a relatively clement climate, due to its southerly location off the English coast.
8. In 1852, Marie Emily, the daughter of Sir Henry Williams-Wynn of Llanfroda Hall, married her cousin Sir Watkin Williams Wynn.
9. Originally, Lloyd's Coffee House, London, was where merchants, ship owners, and underwriters met to transact business. By the end of the eighteenth century, Lloyd's had progressed into one of the first modern insurance companies.
10. Sir Watkin Williams Wynn, third Baronet, completed the building of this small, substantial house on the Wynnstay Estate, Denbighshire, north Wales, by the time of his death in 1749. Sir Watkin Williams Wynn, the fourth Baronet made extensions to the house in 1770 which, by 1858, was nearly completely burnt down. See RBL, 8 March 1858.
11. Arthur Hill-Trevor, third Viscount Dungannon (1798–1862), had his family seat at Brynkinalt in Chirk, Denbighshire, a fine Gothic edifice, much visited by the Duke of Wellington.
12. Commonly (Latin).
13. There was a Harleyford estate in south-west England, situated 1.5 km west of Marlow and located on the banks of the River Thames.

To Rebecca Ryves

Llangollen
Monday August 22d 1853

I am indeed truly grieved my dearest Rebecca at your terrible accounts of poor Massy – have they <u>no one</u> among their fine acquaintance <u>able</u> – and willing (though they seldom go together) to expedite his journey to Spain? for I consider remaining in England with such weather as there has been, quite equivalent to a bad winter, anywhere else – oh! dear – oh! dear! this poverty is indeed a legion curse! and it takes all ones faith, all ones powers of endurance, and constant prayer, to submit, oneself to, and bear up under the daily, and hourly torments, humiliations, – and anxieties it subjects one to; – nullifying our every good feeling, and rendering even virtue impossible! The billet (anything but <u>doux</u>)[1] that you enclosed me was a dun from Mrs Frampton for her £2"8 – don't you wish she may get it! – you cannot think what a strange feeling it is to me, to be liked and courted for myself as I am here being in a literary point of view more popular than Sir Liar – Mrs Myddleton Biddulph is such a nice, kind woman and rarer still, perfectly well bred, she apologised so nicely for what she called intruding on me, – but said from my Books and a great deal more of "<u>that</u> sort of thing"! She had such a wish to know me and thinking I must be moped to death in this place, they conceived it their bounden duty to try, and make it a little agreeable to me – I have refused all other invitations, but they are so pressing that I should go and spend a few days at Chirk, that I see no loophole of escape if I can only get a reprieve till October for till then I have not a sou! She comes and sees me very often and can do so having her nice Pony Phaeton and outriders – all well appointed like Lady Wiltons[2] turn she is going to show me, (which they have with the Title deeds) the Act of the Long Parliament[3] which they have for <u>demolishing</u> Chirk Castle altogether! but thank heaven they did not hatch long enough for that. – Tib and I are to have the state room, and bed in which poor Charles the first slept,[4] and after dat, me supposes him will fancy himself a King Charles dog! instead of a Blenheim. – To give you a laugh in the midst of your dismals – I send you the Rev Mister Smith! in a paroxysm of romance! floundering among the nettles!!! I told him I was sure the Heroine of the Parasol must have been <u>English</u>! Let me have his extraordinary Epistle back again – it is quite evident from it, that his Reverence has been thrown into a great state of commotion! by some fine women – <u>finely</u> <u>dressed</u>! lately. – you will know the name of my book when I send it to you – till then being rather an original sort of book and as I mean to publish it anonymously I mean to treat it like the Devil and not mention its name to "Ears polite."[5] There is a Cattle Fair here to day and the squeaking of the Pigs is such! (as all the Farmers are going the whole swine) that I know not what I write so will say good bye, and god Bless you. – Edwards and I, are going on a little excursion of 12 Miles on Thursday by the Canal Boat which is large and covered like a Gondola – and which trip only costs 9 pence! Hoping to hear better accounts of poor Massy in your next Believe me Ever My dearest Rebecca Gratefully and Affectly yrs. Rosina Bulwer Lytton

HALS
1. Letter ... love (French).
2. Possibly a relative of Thomas Grosvenor Egerton, second Earl of Wilton (1799–1882).
3. The Long Parliament is the name of the English Parliament called by Charles I, in 1640, following the Bishops' Wars. It was so called because it sat almost continuously during the English Civil War until 1653 and then again in 1649.
4. In 1651, two days before the battle of Worcestor, which was the final battle of the English Civil War, Charles II stayed at Chirk. The bed in which he slept has been preserved.
5. Alexander Pope, 'An Epistle to the Right Honourable Richard, Earl of Burlington' (1831), l. 149.

To Mrs Pyke

Llangollen
Monday August 22nd 1853

I am so very sorry my dear Mrs Pyke to hear that you are still suffering from the pain in your chest and side I hope you have advice for it? as being in London, you can have the best, if there <u>is</u> any thing in medicine? ce que j'en doute?[1] – I regret also to hear that your sons affairs, are not progressing as you could wish, but wherever Lawyers are concerned, you must not hope for expedition! as slow and sure – to empty <u>your</u> pockets and fill their <u>own</u>, is their motto. – I do not know Sir Watkyn William Wynne as he, and Lady Wynne are in the Isle of Wight; for her health as she poor thing is supposed to be in a Consumption, which is very melancholy as they were only married last year, so I suppose are still fond of each other; but no good ever comes of cousins marrying – or indeed of any one's marrying! that I can see. – I have no doubt that a few of the excursions you mention, and a little society would take me out of myself and do me good – but you forget the Bulwer "<u>Union</u>"! to which I alas! irrevocably belong and therefore must remain, till it shall please God to release me; in "<u>the Parish to which I have been passed on</u>!" for not having a <u>sou</u> I have refused all Invitations, for I have quite enough to do with my 47!!!! <u>pour tout potage</u>[2] in October – oh! if I could but get to your great, and <u>really</u> free, and enlightened country, where women are not ground down and treated like beasts of burden, as they are in England, I should soon make plenty of money, and be in that way at least <u>independant</u>, for the rest of my miserable and most cruel existence. This last week, I have had another of my terrible Bilious attacks, or I suppose I ought to call it a <u>Bill</u>-<u>you</u> <u>owe us</u> attack, as I have been worried to death in that way – Poor little Miss Williams[3] <u>is</u> very useful kind, and attentive to me, and not being <u>English</u>, is not grasping and over-reaching Jane with her serious solemn never smiling but with all honest face I continue to like; and master Tiber continues to <u>trample</u> upon me in the most <u>Husbandly</u> manner There is no fear dear Mrs Pyke of my ever forgetting one who has been so <u>very</u> kind to me as you have; were I to make all the new friends in the world; and I still live in the hope of having the great pleasure of seeing you, and your little Grandson back here, as I am sure this fine pure air would be much better for you than the London fog, and smoke

So hoping that your next will be to tell me that you <u>are</u> coming; Believe me with Compliments to your daughter Ever your grateful though obliged

R Bulwer Lytton

HALS
1. Though I have my doubts (French).
2. Literally: 'for all thick soup' (French).
3. A Llangollen dressmaker, who used to be a lady's maid.

To Mrs Pyke

Mrs Pyke Hôtel de Provence Leicester Square[1]

Llangollen
Monday August 29th 1853

My dear Mrs Pyke My <u>mud</u> who is not very well herself – having a sort of Church-yard Cough – is afraid you are still suffering from that tiresome pain in your side, and chest which you mentioned labouring under when you last wrote and she wishes me to ask you? which me has great pleasure in doing as it gives me the opportunity of thanking you for having advised my Mud to leave off giving me salt with my dinners; as since she has taken your advice my coat does not come off at all; and me should have been <u>vezy</u> sorry to have lost it <u>entirely</u> as me is <u>vezy</u> sure, there is not a Tailor in this village who could make a coat fit for a Blenheim Dog – or any <u>other</u> London <u>Puppy</u> to wear. – <u>Me</u> has become acquainted with several very great canine beauties since you were here; King Charles's Blenheims, and Poodles – but pray assure Miss Fanny that <u>her</u> charms have never been effaced from my heart which is still overshadowed by her magnificent Ears! to say nothing of her darling little hind paws – but thereby hangs a – tail! you must forgive this terrible scrawl – but there is a Cattle Fair here to day, and the din is perfectly deafening! as all the old Farmers are going <u>the whole swine</u>! and as the old women carry off their newly purchased little Pigs – the attempts of the said animals to squeek <u>under difficulties</u> is truly appalling. So I shall end by telling you how much my mud, and I both miss you – and wish you back, and how we hope at all events soon to hear that you are better? and with compts to your daughter, and my best wag of the tail to your pretty little grand son – et mille Baise<u>pattes</u> à la Charmante petite Fanny[2] – Believe me my dear Mrs Pyke your Faithful Dog (old style) Tibby Fine Eyes!

---

1.   This square in the West End of London contained several hotels.
2.   And a thousand kisses on the paw to the charming little Fanny (French).

To Rebecca Ryves

Llangollen
Wednesday August 31st 1853

I was very glad

My dearest Rebecca to get your letter this mng which I should have had yesterday. – The accounts of poor Massy are indeed very distressing, and I cant think how his brother can leave him, especially now that there is no one in London to go and see, and amuse him. That Mrs Churn is indeed a Miracle among Lodginghouse keepers the very <u>butter</u>! of human kindness, and I hope one may be able to do her a good turn yet. – Yes poor Norton![1] I do pity him – very different is he indeed from that concrete Brute Sir Liar – as <u>he</u> is only an ugly Christian! Whereas Sir Liar is a hideous Demon – or alas! not <u>Demon</u> as <u>that</u> means a <u>disembodied</u> spirit – but <u>fiend</u>. The Isle of Wight hero that Norton alluded to is Sidney Herbert[2] – and the £500 a year <u>pretended</u> to be left her by Mrs Sheridan is the money <u>he</u> gives her for poor Mrs Sheridan had not five hundred pence![3] – as for Mrs Norton! she would <u>be</u> (in more senses than one) with the Devil, or Sir Liar which is the same thing – her tirade about working as hard as any Lawyers clerk! was as fine a piece of acting as the rest, for producing 2 novels in 17 years![4] can hardly come under that denomination! – and it is not with her head she has worked but <u>wicey</u> <u>warsey</u> as Billy Lackaday[5] says. When she was living in Bolton St[6] with her uncle poor Charles Sheridan[7] she made such a regular bad house of it, that he was obliged to break up his ménage-<u>entre autres</u>,[8] Sir Liar was at that time intriguing with a Mrs Barton the wife of a Clergyman – and a cousin of Mrs Nortons – for it runs in the blood like the wooden leg!! as the Irishman said – some good <u>natured</u> friend told Mr Barton that if he would go on such a day – and such an hour, into the back Bedroom on the first floor at Mrs Nortons he would find Sir Liar with his wife; he did so, and I am happy to say gave him a good horse-whipping. Mrs Nortons <u>virtuous</u> and lady-like speech on the occasion was, – "Bulwer! if you are such a d—d fool that you cant manage a <u>little affair</u> of this sort without being found out you must carry it on else where." – But her own speech when she heard Lady Pembroke[9] had made up the marriage between Sidney Herbert, and Miss A Court[10] (which she did chiefly to break off his <u>liaison</u> with Mrs Norton) condemned her more than any body else could have done – "Ah!" said she "les menées de çes femmes <u>verteuses</u>![11] so she has triumphed at last! over a constancy of seven years!"

You will no doubt be glad to know at last (as I was) of <u>what</u> religion Sir Liar is? it was by the merest accident that I discovered it, coming out of church last Sunday I overheard the following dialogue between two of our dear Compatriots of the class Bricklayer from their appearance

1ˢᵗ Paddy

"Arrah <u>din</u> of what religion is he of itself?" –

2d Pat –

"Religion! cock him up wid a religion! what <u>wud</u> de <u>loikes</u> of him do <u>wid</u> a religion? <u>barring</u> it was de <u>Haythen</u> <u>Miss</u>-ology – or something of <u>dat</u> sort!"

Now there can be no doubt that Sir Liar is a <u>Haythen Missologyst</u>! Comets! indeed being in Ireland <u>you</u> may find it "the finest <u>divarshon</u> under the sun – to sit by the fire till the pratees are done but as we have no sun here, we have no comets – the amusements of our programme are very different, such as water spouts, Hoar frosts – fogs, and other damperies. I remember when I was a very little child there was a fine big comet, with a bright star at one end of it and a long tail like a Harliquins sword at the other which was also visible to the <u>indelicate</u> (as I suppose the Yankees would call the naked) Eye![12] but the heat was then so great that as I perfectly recollect (and <u>try</u> to <u>glow</u> <u>with</u> the <u>recollection</u> <u>now</u>! only my teeth chatter, and wont let my blood get up a boil -) all the children, and caterpillars were burnt up! and to this day in France the <u>Vin du Cométe</u>[13] is cited as the finest vintage that has been known for two centuries. – I have no news – of any importance to tell you except that yesterday Evening I bought

Eighteen penny worth of Terrier! the funniest thing you ever saw or heard of, next to the <u>price</u>! given for him – the <u>tan</u> on him alone is worth sixteen times the money – he is <u>very</u> ugly (but what can one expect for Eighteen pence!! – or even for Half a crown! which is the market price of Wives at Smithfield!) yes decidedly ugly – for he is the <u>image</u> of poor Mme <u>Alphonse</u>! now the Poodle would have been a better likeness for a dog – and on the top of his very small head – he has a great pair of Shuffling Shambling ears – which look as if he had dressed himself in the dark, and put on a mastiff's ears by mistake in consideration of his long nose – I call him <u>Trueneir</u> in contrary distinction to <u>Truensmoote</u> – who poor Innocence, after the new Blackamoor was scrubbed in a warm bath and fed – condescended to play with him, and is very fond of him – he – or she rather is the tiniest thing you ever saw like a dog out of a walnut, in a Fairy tail. – The <u>gentleman</u> from whom I bought him – <u>another</u> compatriot – who had evidently been <u>looking</u> at some Welshmen drinking! – in reply to all my animadversions – upon each – of this juvenile Canines bad points, – summed up with this quietus – "Oh well now you you [*sic*] may just abuse him till <u>yer</u> as black in <u>de fache</u> as he <u>ish</u> in de hide but I defy <u>ye</u> to <u>shay</u> he is <u>dear</u>!" Do you indeed? well then he <u>is</u> a dear little fright – so here, take your Eighteen pence! and vanish. – I should indeed be <u>very</u> glad to go to Chirk – <u>but</u> – <u>but</u>! – but for all the buts! and I need not tell you – that when the pockets are <u>light</u> the heart is invariably <u>heavy</u> – besides, when one is, as I am – it is a bad plan again to go among the luxuries, and elegancies of life, as despite ones firmest resolves, it <u>does</u> make one discontented with ones own miserable lot, and think how much better off are the Nortons of this world! though <u>only</u> in this world it is true. Good bye. God Bless you my dearest Rebecca

    Ever gratefully and affectly yrs
    Rosina Bulwer Lytton

HUNT

1. Hon. George Norton (1800–75) was the brother of Lord Grantley and the husband of Caroline Norton. See RBL, 24 December 1836.
2. In the early 1840s, the statesman Sidney Herbert, first Baron Herbert of Lea (1810–61), had an affair with Caroline Norton, who was unable to get a divorce. Their relationship ended when Herbert married. See below, n. 10.
3. Caroline Henrietta Sheridan (*née* Callander) (1779–1851) had written three successful novels. She secured £480 a year for her daughter Caroline under the laws of equity, to prevent her husband having access to the money. In 1851, Caroline Norton received this legacy.
4. Caroline Norton produced the novels, *The Wife, and Woman's Reward* (1835) and *Stuart of Dunleath* (1851). The gap between them was sixteen, not seventeen years.
5. A character from the comedy *Sweethearts and Wives* by Isaac Nathan (*c.* 1790–1864) was played at the Theatre Royal, Haymarket, in 1823.
6. Situated in the West End of London, near Mayfair.

7.   Charles Sheridan (b. 1773) was Caroline Norton's father's elder brother.
8.   Amongst others (French).
9.   Catherine Woronzow (1783–1856), the mother of Sidney Herbert (see RBL, 31 August 1853) and wife of George Augustus Herbert, the eleventh Earl of Pembroke.
10. The relationship between Sidney Herbert and Caroline Norton ended in 1846 when Herbert married Elizabeth Ashe A'Court, a philanthropist, author and translator, who was a relative of the barons Heytesbury and a friend of Benjamin Disraeli.
11. The intrigues of virtuous women (French).
12. RBL was about nine years old when she saw the dramatic and spectacular Great Comet of 1811, which was visible to the naked eye for around nine months. By day, it dimmed the sun since the Earth was enveloped within the comet's double tail, which by December extended to over 60 degrees in the sky. At the mid-point of the novel *War and Peace* (1865–9), Leo Tolstoy describes his character Pierre observing the comet.
13. The comet passed to the perihelion, the closest point to the sun in a planet's orbit, at the time of the French grape harvest.

To Rebecca Ryves

Aug 31 1853

My dearest Rebecca Yes poor Norton I do pity him very different is he from that concrete brute Sir Liar as he is only an ugly Christian, whereas Sir Liar is a hideous demon, or alas not demon as that means a disembodied spirit, but fiend The Isle of Wight hero that Norton attended to is Sidney Herbert and the £500 a year pretended to be left her by Mrs Sheridan is the money he gives her, for poor Mrs Sheridan had not five hundred pence. As for poor Mrs Norton she would lie (in more senses than one) with the Devil, or Sir Liar, which is the same thing, her tirade about working as hard as any lawyers clerk, was as fine a piece of acting as the rest, for producing 2 novels in 17 years can hardly come under that denomination, and it is not with her head she has worked but <u>wirey warcey</u>. Sir Liar was at that time intriguing with a Mrs Barton the wife of a clergyman, and a cousin of Mrs Nortons, for it runs in the blood like the wooden leg as the Irishman said. Some good natured friend told Mrs Barton that if he would go on such a day, and such an hour into the back bedroom on the first floor at Mrs Nortons, he would find Sir Liar with his wife, he did so & I am glad to say gave him a good horsewhipping. Mrs Nortons virtuous and ladylike speech on the occasion was "Bulwer! if you are such a d—d fool that you can't manage a little affair of this sort without being found out, you must carry it on elsewhere ...

    Ever gratefully and affectly yours
    Rosina Bulwer Lytton

HALS
Copy and incomplete letter.

To Mrs Pyke

Llangollen
Thursday September 1st [1853]

I am exceedingly sorry Dear Mrs Pyke that my fears about you have been verified; I thought such was the case, when I made Tib write the day before yesterday
and inquire how you were? – I am sure London dont agree with you – so <u>sur-
tous les rapports</u>[1] I wish you were here, but <u>dont</u> take me by surprise! as I hate
surprises even of a pleasurable nature and the Cuisine here is far too bad for any
<u>Dîners improvisés</u>[2] or even an ambign, and I should not like <u>quite</u> to starve you
in return for the Dive[r]s feast you used to give me as when you come and see
poor <u>Lazarus</u> he wishes to give you the best he can. But Mrs Davies is such a nice
kind, <u>good dispositioned</u> woman – that I shall be quite sorry to leave her and
even were she to give me Crocodile Cutlets! and Haunches of Hippopotamus! I
would <u>try</u> and eat them rather than hurt her feelings; – but she is too handsome
to be anything but good – I do detest ugly people, for they are always ugly within,
as well as without – and as for red hair! <u>that</u>! is my favorite aversion – even when
it is only in Homeopathic doses for men with fiery whiskers, have invariably fiery
tempers to match à propos – you say you had a horrid dream about me and your
letter is dated the 30th ergo, – you had this dream, on the <u>29th</u>!!!! no wonder it
was horrible! for there are strange mysterious sympathies, and affinities in the
interior world, and the 29th of August is the anniversary of my Execution! Vulgo[3]
Wedding day, – which has not been a <u>dream</u>! but a life-long nightmare to me
ever since. besides, I had bid "a long farewell to all my finery" and as you know
provided myself with re-lays of <u>workhouse</u> looking stuff dresses, suited to my
present circumstances, and congenial to the uphill and down dale work I have
daily to perform with poor innocent Master Tibby. Yesterday in returning from
paying a visit seven miles off I, and two ladies who were with me, were nearly
killed by one of the miserable Post horses falling – and the Postilion getting completely under him; we were all as you may suppose excessively frightened and
the fright increased my cough so much that I have been spitting blood all night,
– but the country we drove through – was lovely! oh! if my <u>prospects</u> were only
half as good as my <u>views</u>! I should have nothing to complain of; – it is ungracious
of me, but considering the miserable and false, position I am in, I wish the people would keep their visits to themselves; but I suppose I may thank that horrid
Archaeological Society for them which <u>wont</u> allow any <u>antiquities</u> in this neighbourhood (including Old Women!) to go unexplained. Jane, is very civil, and
attentive; gentle and quiet, and a great relief after that Cart Horse of a creature
at the Allens. – I beg give me <u>variety</u> enough in the dinners; but I cant say much
for the <u>Cuisine</u>, still I <u>wont</u> starve you if you come; and after all your repeated
promises to do so; – I should think myself very ill used, if you dont return, and

remember <u>no</u> Pears, unless you <u>bring</u> them, and <u>addio</u>[4] – and with Compliments to your daughter; and a kiss to your little grandson,[5] and pretty Fansy Pansy – Believe me Dear Mrs Pyke Ever your grateful <u>though</u> obliged

    R Bulwer Lytton

HALS
1. Above all the connections (French).
2. Improvised dinners (French).
3. Commonly (Latin).
4. Goodbye [*adios*] (Spanish).
5. Arthur Lowndes is five years old and an illegitimate son of EBL. His mother is Marion Wolstonecraft Godwin Lowndes, EBL's mistress, known as Mrs Lowndes, who bore three of his children. See RBL, 7 September 1853

To Rebecca Ryves

Llangollen
September 7th 1853

My dearest Rebecca I have only 2 minutes to thank you for your letter, and say how glad I am to hear a little better account of poor Massy taking the horrible discomforts of Spain into consideration – I think he will be much better in Devonshire poor fellow, de poorest of Pups is given away – his exploits being these; 2 pair of boots, and 3 gloves – made into minced meat like the reapers in Puss in Boots, in one night an India rubber sponge bag – gnawed open – and a packet of red Tooth powder carefully scattered all over the room and over Mrs Edwards's dress who was sitting by my bed side – but having I suppose an artistic eye for colour and not liking the <u>skulking</u> tone of the brick dust – he next brings a packet of white violet powder and mixes that up with the red! but the climax was the next morning him swinging himself to the bell rope – and ringing it as if the House was on fire which brought them all rushing up as they thought at <u>least</u> that I was in a fit. So him was given to a brother of Mrs Davies's a confectioner in this street,[1] five days ago; and yesterday as I was passing I felt something suddenly running and scrambling up my dress – which I in a great fright thought was a rat, but soon him poorest of pups was on my shoulder licking my face and whining in de most innocent manner – It seems the beast of a fellow from whom I bought him was on his way to the river to drown him! had I known <u>that</u>! I would not even have given him the Eighteen pence for him. – Mrs Norton did reply in "The Times"[2] of last Thursday – but all plausible Lies in the Sir Liar style – what a pity they were not married – but being a bold bad thoroughly heartless woman – and hand in glove with the Infernal Machine (The Press) – she has got on and will get on. you will be rejoiced to hear that Miss Aird![3] has written a novel!! I send you her letters – and as I really pity her poor thing gave her a letter for Skeet! (for which he will bless me! – I only hope she asked nothing "improper!" of that truly modest man – or that Horrocks[4] was there to protect him! The Evening before last – I got a box of grouse – and another of fine Pears (for which I have a foib-lesse)[5] with Mrs Pykes[6] kind regards – who had just arrived at "The Hand" and would be with me in the morning – she has now taken lodgings in this House for a month, and says she will pass the winter with me at the Hotel, her little grand-son a very pretty child of five years old is with her we mess (or Pig considering the cuisine, would be a more appropriate term) together which is a great relief to my dullness – she being thoroughly good natured, and genuinely American! very amusing – she has also brought the sun with her – for the weather is now glorious! – were you staying with Captain and Mrs Tom I should think you had been "doing your drinking!" as you date your letter August 5th so as we are now going to dinner – "I looks towards you"! and with Tibbianas best love – Believe me Ever my dearest Rebecca gratefully and affectly yrs Rosina Bulwer Lytton

For goodness sake don't let your Ink do its drinking! any more for such a dropsi-cally hieroglyphic as your last! I never saw

---

HALS

1. Jane Davies ran a bakery and confectioner's shop in Bridge Street, which turns into Church Street where the Hand Hotel is located, where RBL had been staying. See RBL, 11 February 1854.
2. There was no letter for a Thursday during this period written by Caroline Norton. RBL may be making an ironic reference to a letter in *The Times*, which appeared on Friday 2 September 1853, written by Lord Melbourne, which favours Mrs Norton in her disputes with her husband.
3. Marion Paul Aird (1815–88) was a Scottish poet, whose novel was *Heart Histories, Vio-lets from the Greenwood ... in Prose and Verse* (1853).
4. RBL's publisher Skeet's assistant. See RBL, 0D334RR21.
5. Weakness [*faiblesse*] (French).
6. Mrs T. Pyke is a disguised name for Mrs Waller, the mother of Marion Wolstonecraft Lowndes, the mistress of EBL, and his devoted amanuensis, who travelled with him to the Continent.

To Rebecca Ryves

Llangollen
Thursday October 6th 1853

Dearest Rebecca That you may not think my funeral has taken place I write one line to you to day – the first day of my being up – from the scarlatina[1] – the deaths here have been fearful averaging from 60 to 70 a week – but chiefly among the children. – Poor Massy very kindly sent me some delicious Guava Jelly[2] – would to heaven I had the means of sending him something that would be of use to him. Lady Minshalls[3] sister– (Lady M is one of my neighbours who has been particularly kind in supplying me with Peaches Hot house grapes and flowers) Mrs and Miss Lymes– a most beautiful and charming girl – have been lodging in this house and so kind to me – but have now gone back to Worcestershire[4] whither they have invited me, but Mrs Lymes having had a house at Leamington knew <u>Grandity</u>,[5] by <u>Tradition</u> and <u>recognized</u> her in Miriam Sedley,[6] about which she raves – and I really think <u>my</u> <u>illness</u> was brought on by their never letting me rest doing her Jack,[7] and the cosmetics && for who could do <u>her</u> nose without getting the scarlet fever! I promised Miss Lymes – that I could get from you one of the sticking plaster portraits of her – so if you have not got one you must do me another, and send it to me. – Poor Mrs Pyke who is still here – has been laid up with Bronchitis. – I have had (without my stirring!) thank Heaven an offer for my new book[8] – but the bargain is not yet concluded – and I must work very hard to get it done by Xmas as there is only a vol-and a half done. I send you a Hotham[9] I got to my surprise this morning – for I have not written to her these two months send it me back as I have no right to send poor Augustuses[10] secrets about the world – poor fellow! I feel for him. Tib is en <u>doodest</u> and en <u>bootsest</u>! And sends hims love to hims aunt Rebecca whom him is very glad to hear has been so gay. – I am so tired I must end this scrawl. God Bless you my dearest Rebecca Ever your Grateful and affect Rosina Bulwer Lytton

---

HALS

1. Scarlet fever (from the Italian *scarlattina*).
2. A jelly made from the guava fruit, which Spanish explorers of the 1550s discovered growing in America. It has many medicinal properties.
3. Mrs Margaret Minshall (b. *c*. 1781) was a widow who was counted among the local gentry and lived on London Road, Llangollen.
4. County situated in the west Midlands.
5. Lady Hotham.
6. Lady Laura O'Shindy in RBL's autobiographical novel, *Miriam Sedley*. See RBL, 23 January 1826.
7. This may be an abbreviation for 'Jack of all trades'.
8. *Behind the Scenes* is a three-volume novel, published by Skeet in 1854.
9. A letter written by Lady Hotham.
10. Lady Hotham's nephew, Augustus Shiel.

To Mrs Pyke

Mrs Pyke The Hand Hotel Llangollen
Friday October 21ˢᵗ [1853]

Dear Mrs Pyke I am sorry you have had no letter to put you out of suspence quant à moi[1] – I am so ill, I can scarcely lift my head from my pillow, – I grieve to hear that your pain still continues and that the day is so bad I have no chance of seeing you. – With a kiss to Arthur Ever your grateful & obliged R B L

HALS
1. As for me (French).

To Rebecca Ryves

Phillips's Hotel Llangollen
October 23d 53

My dearest Rebecca I have literally half a moment, as the Church bells are ringing – to thank you for, and acknowledge the safe arrival of Margracia Grandifudgia[1] I gummed her bumped the Cheek bone, and plummed the mouth a little more, which made the likeness a facsimile – and packed her off as the poor Dr would have been glad to have done many a time. I am so busy that I must drive off Chirk Castle till Xmas, – those good Chirkites must think my appetite as large as their magnificent Château as it is always 2 Hares – 3 brace! of Pheasants and 3 ditto of Parteridges – que ça![2] – The queen need not laugh at the Irish bill of fare, as I once saw a soi-disant[3] French letter of hers – to one of her relations – which for bad French – bad spelling and bad grammar might have carried off the prize, in any English Boarding school!! where all sorts of ignorance, and vulgarity, are taught, and learnt in perfection. – I saw Charley Humes[4] marriage in the Papers. Mr Long[5] – however rich, is a very long way off – from the Duke of Newcastle![6] however I sincerely hope that her dear mothers daughter may be happy – à propos[7] – Mrs Wheelers news is that your brother William is to be married in a few days to Mrs Ripon – and she not having much money they are to return to India. How is poor Massy? – In Haste Ever Gratefully and affectly yrs Rosina Bulwer Lytton.

HALS
1. A sticky plaster portrait of Lady Hotham. Spelt slightly differently below in RBL, 11 September 1855.
2. So many (French).
3. So-called (French).
4. Charles Hume may be a relative of RBL's friend Mr Hume. See RBL, 0D46MG8.

5.   Presumably, the father of Charles Hume's bride.
6.   See RBL, 30 December 1852.
7.   In connection with (French).

To Rebecca Ryves

Phillip's Hotel Llangollen
December 29th 1853

I was very glad My dearest Rebecca to see your hand writing once more; and sincerely wish you a merry Xmas, and many happy new years, – if there are such things? – but never having yet seen one, I must be pardoned for being a little sceptical on the matter. I wrote to you about a month or five weeks ago – telling you of "<u>me</u> illness" that horrid abscess on my arm but never having heard from you since, I was too ill, not to say totally unable to write to those who did not trouble their head about me, and an awful business! it was truly, having to be lanced daily – but the <u>most</u> awful part to me, is a surgeon's bill of £9"14"0 – and £3, for a nurse – rather a terrific slice out of my quarterly Parish allowance of £47!!! – but this was not enough – and now I am again laid up with an obstinate cough, and like my prototype Job 3 horrible boils – in my head! as big as pigeons eggs – not thin, that break, but great lumps – lifting up the hair and more <u>painful</u> than anything you can imagine – except a raging tooth ache in three different parts of my head – so that like Job I "sit in the Ashes"[1] and indulge in an extensive course of grumbling however, my comforters,[2] have not been like his – for nothing can have been kinder than my neighbours – Mrs Middleton Biddulph[3] coming over these dreary 12 miles to sit with me, and wanting me to go and be ill there; which I should be very happy to have done – he[4] is also a very nice person though not so handsome as his brother[5] who is about the queen. – Lady Marshall also – very kindly came over and stayed a week with me, but at that, (as you may suppose my <u>chest</u> rather groans!) more especially as I have had to ask Mrs Tyler to advance me my parish allowance (not due till the middle of January) in order to meet the Xmas bothers, which she has kindly done; but with Brown Pagett – Gosling – Blackburne Miss Dickenson,[6] in all about £80 of pressing worrying debts – and my quarter to pay here – you may guess – how <u>far</u> this £47 will go! – but it is a comfort to get such affect! letters from Lady Hotham. <u>So</u> anxious about my welfare!! (very) and to hear that I am off of the sick List – F.W. – d.g. E! I suppose you know that poor Lady Caroline Sanford[7] is dead – at last; – and so now you can look out for Mr Sanford – whom I think worth any three young men going. – I told you I had had, an offer for my book, well that has turned out only another bother, a flourish of de Birards[8] – who wrote me word, that a man of the name of Stiff the Editor of "The London Journal"[9] "had an exalted idea of my talents"&& and wished to buy my book"[10] but it turned out that he wanted me to write short tales for his journal at £7 – a week – which I could not possibly do till I had finished this book, here was a fresh bother being again at sea, and having a Publisher to seek for of course the more Sir Liar is gorged with gold, the more, he will think it necessary to starve me out of the market, and Routledge has just given him the fabulous sum of £20, 000[11] to publish (the copyrights) [of] his <u>old</u> books for the next ten years, upon which he has already made so much, by selling three times over – So I have been obliged to Employ "The Rev <u>Muster</u> Smith" not a very good diplomatist as you may suppose – he wants me to Publish of Boswort[12] a man of high character certainly but of no capital, and who therefore only publishes on the system of half profits, he is the man whom Mrs Stowe selected, as the Publisher of her own edition of "Uncle Toms Cabin" I have not yet closed with him and indeed owing to "<u>me</u> illness" I have still about 150 pages of the last vol to write. – I assure you my dear Rebecca, there are times when my joint load of body – and mind is <u>too</u> heavy – and the river[13] looks <u>very</u> tempting! but as poor Jenkins[14] says in her last letter, she has heard of the death of several <u>cats</u> lately, and can only account for it by supposing that each of their Eight supernumerary lives, have passed into me, and her. – I am very sorry to hear such continued bad accounts of poor Massy – and sincerely wish he was in the Pyrenees with his brother as the waters of the Mont D'Or[15] might do him good; I'm sorry to hear Mrs William Ryves has been so ill; but glad they are so happy, for it is a comfort to hear that any one is so. – Mr Darlingissimo Tibbiano is vezy well, and sends hims best love to hims aunt Rebecca – him has been writing to "The Family Herald"[16] something about the Rubicon;[17] – I am only astonished that so clever a dog – could ask so silly a question; – more worthy of the intense ignorance of a <u>British</u> <u>female</u>! than of a segacious Blenheim. Lady Marshall has given him a new, – and vezy darling name that of "<u>Pup</u> Innocent the Fifth" in allusion to hims being the fifth doatskin of his darling race that I have had. I am tired to death writing this, so again wishing you many happy new years Believe me Dearest Rebecca Ever your Grateful and affect Rosina Bulwer Lytton.

HALS
1. So great was Job's sorrow that all he could do was sit 'among the ashes' (Job 2:8).
2. Three friends of Job visited him during his suffering and told him that he was getting what he deserved. They insisted that God was punishing him for his sins even though Job was a good man. While appearing to offer consolation to Job, these 'comforters' actually make him feel worse.
3. In 1832, Fanny Owen (b. before 1817) married Colonel Robert Myddelton Biddulph, who became Lord Lieutenant of the county. She was an intimate friend of Charles Darwin and his sisters and loyal to RBL.
4. Fanny's husband, Colonel Robert Myddelton Biddulph.
5. General Right Honourable Sir Thomas Myddelton Biddulph (1809–78).
6. Miss Dickenson lent RBL the sum of £400, to cover her debts while she was in Geneva.

7. Lady Caroline Anne Sanford died on 25 November 1853. She was the daughter of General Charles Stanhope, third Earl of Harrington and Jane Fleming (a family known to RBL) and had married Edward Ayshford Sanford on 21 June 1841.

8. Chevalier de Birard. See RBL, 9 January 1853.

9. George Stiff (1807–73) owned the *London Journal* up to 1857. Even though its sales in 1852 approached half a million, Stiff died penniless.

10. RBL's novel *Behind the Scenes by Alciphron* was advertised in *The Times* on 15 March 1854 for publication at the end of March. Alciphron was a Greek writer (second century AD) who produced fictional letters.

11. Routledge actually paid EBL the even higher sum of £25,000 for the copyright to reprint thirty-five of his novels. It was a wise investment since 26,000 copies of EBL's *My Novel* were sold within the first year, with annual reprintings of 2,000 copies throughout the life of the contract. See RBL, 2 March 1853.

12. Thomas Bosworth of London was one of the publishers of Harriet Beecher Stowe's novel *Uncle Tom's Cabin or, Negro Life in the Slave States of America*. This edition appeared in July and August of 1852. This was a year after it began serial publication in 1851–2 in an abolitionist paper *The National Era*.

13. The River Dee runs across the road from Phillips Hotel.

14. Mrs Augusta Jenkins, who is a very old friend of RBL, is described by her as 'my poor pack horse'. See RBL, 28 May 1855.

15. A spa town. See RBL, 5 June 1853.

16. *The Family Herald: A Domestic Magazine of Useful Information & Amusement* (1842–1940) published a variety of items including fiction and by 1855 had a circulation of about 240,000 a week. It was founded by RBL's friend Revd James Elimalet Smith.

17. The Rubicon is an ancient Latin name for a small river in northern Italy.

To Rebecca Ryves

[1854?]

... that we got out to walk, but had not proceeded fifty yards – when such a sudden dense, and black fog – came on that we could not see each other – she (Lady H)[1] has asked to go to the Play on Saturday. Poor little de Birard – has been very nearly taking a Trip to the other world from a fit of indigestion similar to that by which the Duke of Wellington[2] died, all brought on by a Pork pie! with which he solaced himself during <u>madames</u> absence; – thus proving the fatal effects of a mans going the whole Hog! when he gets rid of his wife, it is only Sir Liar who is tough enough to resist this ordeal I had a long, and very kind letter from my dear friend Henriette d'Angeville[3] yesterday (the Lady who went to the very top of Mont Blanc[4] the only woman who ever did so[5] – she to whom I dedicated Miriam Sedley) she has taken Voltaires Château at Ferney[6] for six years; – she wants me to go and see her – would to heaven! that I could; for it is not the least of ones sufferings here, to have no earthly sympathy of heart, or <u>mind</u> for English <u>ignorance</u>; <u>is</u> something almost fabulous! – and vulgarity and ill breeding; is of course the natural consequence – The Dangeville says she sent me a pamphlet of 12 pages by <u>Mme</u> Tirard[7] who came to London last autumn – but also hunted, May Fair, and Brompton without being able to find my address the said Mme Tirard – adding, that the only thing that reconciled her to the disappointment of not seeing me, was the fear that I might think she was come to dun me! (for it is to her poor dear Woman hat I still owe that £100 at Geneva) fancy an English Trades person having such delicacy! and forbearance with regard to a debt, that has been owing 7 years – and which was promised to be paid 2 years ago. – I don't think the Mrs Boyes where little Miss Lloyd is at school is any rela-tion to those of Bath, as the latter spell their name Boys. – I have this moment got your very kind letter of yesterday – for which my dearest Rebecca I thank you sincerely it has caused me a good fit of crying – which has relieved me as I thought my heart was withering up – and my Brain burning to a cinder – you are mistaken however in supposing that Mrs Tyler would be annoyed, or care one bit at my seeking another shelter, even were I still poorer; on the contrary – since I announced my project of doing so from having been very rude and morose she is now all smiles and civility – I am not so dull as not to perceive, when I have worn out my welcome; and I know she wishes to go to Paris, or elsewhere this spring and my being here would be a burden to her; – besides I have invariably remarked – that whenever English people <u>promise</u> great things in the way of getting you out of any difficulty, and <u>fail</u> through <u>not trying</u>, they seem to owe you a grudge, and try to wash their hands of you, and I never require two hints; I shall be very sorry to leave poor little Mrs Barclay – who has been invariably kind, <u>gentle</u> – civil, <u>feeling</u> – and considerate towards me. – you are right that my having to pay for a shelter of any kind for the next year were it only £20 – will swamp and involve me still more but necessity not only has no law – but no pity! nor no justice! either, – my <u>only hope</u> is in natures giving way for I am rapidly sinking under all this tangled, accumulation of Tortures, and the more rapidly the better – the new dance of "Pop goes the Weasel"[8] is nothing to my old dance of Pop goes the Bracelet! I shall try and walk as far as Mrs St Georges, with one of those doomed ornaments to day – and get back as I can. – It is very selfish of me to bore you with all my miseries who have enough of your own, but it is not one of the least crimes of chronic misery that it <u>does</u> make one selfish and yet this crust, and wallet selfishness – is perhaps less offensive, than the puffed up well-to- do arrogant plethoric selfishness that oozes out of every pore, – and makes <u>self</u> the goal of every thought, and act.

     Poor Tib – even I think feels for hims poor mud, as he is much more affec-tionate than him ever was before he desires hims best love to you and hopes you will forgive this selfish, stupid scrawl – God Bless you my dearest Rebecca and with kindest regards to your Brothers, and best wishes for yourself Believe me Ever gratefully and affectly yours Rosina Bulwer Lytton

HALS
The beginning of the letter is missing.
1. Lady Hotham.
2. The Duke of Wellington died unexpectedly on 14 September 1852 after a series of sudden seizures.
3. In 1838, Henriette d'Angeville (1794–1871) climbed Mont Blanc at the age of 44, taking with her a feather boa, a black velvet mask and a parrot in a cage. She published *Extracts from My Journal, 1852*. This was later republished under the title *My Ascent of Mont Blanc*.
4. Situated in the French Alps, Mont Blanc is the highest peak in western Europe, rising to 4,731 m. Lying at the western end of the Alpine chain, it is vulnerable to changeable weather conditions, making it a dangerous mountain to climb.
5. The first woman to have made the ascent was actually Marie Paradis in 1808.
6. Voltaire's last home was at Ferney near the border of France and Switzerland, where he lived from 1759 to 1778.
7. In 1847, Henrietta d'Angeville obtained from two sisters of the Tirard family in the Carraterie street in Geneva, the sum of £100 to be loaned to RBL, and repaid within two years.
8. 'Pop goes the Weasel for Fun and Frolic', was published in 1850 by Messrs Miller and Beacham of Baltimore. The tune was published in *Gow's Repository* (1799–1820). The first British mention of the phrase dates from an advertisement by Boosey & Sons of 1854 which described 'the new country dance 'Pop goes the weasel' introduced by her Majesty Queen Victoria', which seems unlikely. The title is the catch line of the dance, sung or shouted by the dancers as one pair of them darts under the arms of the others.

To Rebecca Ryves

Llangollen In Bed
Sunday January 15th 1854

My dearest Rebecca I have been too ill with bronchitis to thank you for your last kind letter, but I did not feel its kindness the less – very different from that unfeeling lumps of Lead – The Rev Muster Smith; who with his scold caution – returned me the woman Pykes scrawl (which I now send you) without note or comment how I do hate such natures – and you may guess what <u>hopes</u> I have about my new book, since <u>he</u> is the negotiator, to add to my comfort my M:S: sent off more than a fortnight ago <u>only</u> arrived in London yesterday! so that I have been all this time thinking it was lost! and now I must be another fortnight in suspense to know its fate. Being quite unable to write Mrs Tyler the details of the Pyke conspiracy[1] – I told them to write to you for my letter containing them will you kindly send it to them, and the Pyke scrawl back to me. – Poor Massy! I often think and grieve over him this bitter weather – pray remember me most kindly to him when you write. – Though the triumphs and prosperity of the ungodly seem to increase, in proportion with ones own sufferings losses and crosses I never for one moment doubt the justice, wisdom and <u>mercy</u> of God – only being but human it is hard to bear and one groans under the burden accordingly just as if one had to lose a limb – all in acknowledging the necessity – and general efficacy of the amputation the flesh, would nevertheless quiver, and wince under the pain of the operation – but I must say that if anything could pervert the modern Britains back to Paganism it would be such Petrified Sticks, as the English Protestant clergy! – We have been quite snowed up here for 4 days last week, no Post, from any quarter, and man, horses <u>and</u> carriages, daily lost in the snow – and the largest of the two flannel Factories here burnt to the ground on new Years Eve! even to the wheel in the water, so those poor creatures began their new year out of work and starving about the roads with cold and hunger how was it possible to have the pleasure of being £27 – short of the sum I have to pay Mrs Phillips oh! if Mr Wheeler would only not take that £100 of his principle which is a drop in the sea to <u>him</u>, but an <u>ocean</u> to <u>me</u>. I might <u>exist</u> which now I cant hampered with a beggarly title married to a brute, wallowing in money and not having a placard on my back signed by the Parish Authorities to <u>convince</u> people that I <u>am</u> a <u>beggar</u> – and only Lady Bulwer Lytton by <u>name</u> for which however thank God! Mrs Biddulph is really most exceedingly kind to me – sending a servant over in a sledge with game, and things to me, now she cant get out herself – a letter from Lady Hotham to whom I have not written for ages full of the most affectionate <u>wishes</u> for the new year! – dont you think they'll do me a great deal of good? Addio[2] – and with Pup Innocents best love Believe me my dearest Rebecca Ever your grateful and affect Rosina Bulwer Lytton.

HALS
1.   RBL was convinced that the so-called Mrs Pyke was a spy in the pay of EBL, who had been sent by him to Llangollen, to poison her. See RBL, 31 January 1856.
2.   Goodbye [*adios*] (Spanish).

To Rebecca Ryves

Llangollen
Saturday January 20th 1854

My dearest Rebecca

You are quite right Sir Liars object is first, to worry me to death – by the mere act of <u>spying</u> which <u>would</u> wear any body's life out; – secondly never to lose sight of all my movements, that he <u>may</u> so torment me and last though not least to torture, and degrade me by bringing me in contact with such infamous wretches, – but thank God I am now prepared for them – Spy no 2 – arrived on Tuesday – with the self same black dog Tiney – <u>re</u>-christened Prince for the occasion Having told Mrs Phillips and Sarah – the head woman all about it, they are on the <u>qui vive</u> – from the view I got of the first arrival – a great Rawboned – gaunt woman I think it is Mrs Tate[1] his <u>House Keeper</u> – she said – she had come for her <u>young lady</u> (!) who was in deep mourning, and had lost her Mother and was to arrive the next day – Sarah[2] said "if you will tell me your young lady's name our men can attend to her at the station" whereupon she looked very much confused and said – "Oh – indeed I don't know her name, I'm only taken on a <u>job</u>" which last at all events was <u>true</u>! well no young Lady arrived the next day – nor the next – and Sarah asked her if she was not <u>frightened</u> about her <u>lady</u>! she said – "no – she did not think about it" – well on Thursday – Evening at 9 o'clock by the Omnibus alone! – the young lady arrives – Sarah – saw the meeting between the soi-disant[3] young lady (who asked if <u>a person</u> was here waiting for her) and the <u>soi-disant</u> maid! – the <u>latter</u> said nothing – but the former gave her one nod – and a wink!!!!

The <u>maid</u> never attended upon her in any way but took herself off to bed The next morning when they were going out Sarah ran to tell me a more vulgar – pert jaunty – impudent looking concern – than the <u>young lady</u>! I never saw – of the <u>Governess</u> cut – perhaps the one Sir Liar seduced in the Isle of Wight the year before last, that Byrne heard all about at the Hotel de Rivoli at Paris – which I think I wrote you word of at the time. – <u>This</u> morning the <u>maid</u>! (whom I suspect to be old mother Tate) was sent for in a great hurry and went off to London leaving the <u>young lady</u>! – whereupon Sarah – said – "I was surprised Ma'am that your maid – did not even know your name! when she came" Oh said the other growing very red – "I suppose she forgot (!!) my name is <u>Getting</u>!"[4] I suppose she has taken this name from <u>getting</u> well paid for her dirty work – Sarah then said – "that little dog is exceedingly like one that was here about six months ago – with a <u>woman</u> of the name of Pyke called Tiney" again she got very red, and said "Oh he is not my dog – he is one a <u>friend</u> lent me"!! did you ever know such a set of bunglers as they are in the midst of all their villainy? At all events old Pyke (whose conscience I really believe has smitten her) told the <u>truth</u>, in saying this spies name began with a <u>G</u>. – Yes the Myddleton Biddulphs, are most exceedingly kind – but alas Chirk Castle is 12 miles off! – I am so grieved to hear about poor Massy – but in our wretched climate – what can one expect. – You shall have a Copy of my Book the moment it is out – Old Bartletts letter was forwarded from Thurloe Cottage <u>how</u> or by whom I know not! The one from Massy was another dun – from Blackburne– <u>how</u> I am to weather it for the next six weeks till my Book is out I know not – and but for Mrs Tylers kindness in advancing me my Parish allowance – I should even <u>if</u> possible have been more tortured and worried than I am – Forgive this scrawl but I am in such a fever with this second Spy that I scarcely know what I write I forgot to tell you that the Dog keeps running in and out of my room – answers and wags his tail to the name of "Tiney" but takes no notice of that of "Prince" Old Pyke was reading

"Chevely" when she was last here and said she should Christen the next dog she
had "Prince"! so I suppose this is the result of it!

> God Bless you
> Ever Gratefully And Affectly
> Rosina Bulwer Lytton

HUNT
1. EBL's elderly housekeeper at Knebworth.
2. Sarah Brellisford, the waitress and head chambermaid at the Hand Hotel, Llangollen.
3. So-called (French).
4. Miss Getting is from Brighton and was an intimate of EBL, who had allegedly sent her to
   spy on RBL.

To Edward Bulwer Lytton

Llangollen
Wednesday January 26th 1854

The sooner the Spy no 1 calling herself Getting returns to town to her lawyer
(Loaden! no doubt) and her Blackguard Employer Sir Liar Coward – Bulwer
Lytton the better – no innocent person would have returned such a letter! as
Lady Lytton wrote the spy Getting last night – or remained in the place one
hour after having recieved it – but as she was fool enough to return it, Lady Lytton will make a point of keeping – it to produce in Court! with the other letters
from one of the gang since you dastardly Brute and too contemptible liar... with
such an unmitigated Blackguard as you are I give you fair notice that if ever you
again attempt to send any of...

...of a daughter to hunt and spy me or that hidious brute calling herself Getting. – contemptible reptile will you be tired of your dirty work? and does it
never strike you – the fearful account you will have to settle...

> RBL

HALS
Letter partly destroyed.

To Edward Bulwer Lytton

January 29th 1854

So you loathsome Brute you are at your dirty work again! not content with being
steeped to your hidious eyes in the most unnatural vice you must be plunged
equally deep in Blackguardism and send your infamous Spy the woman Waller[1]

calling herself Pyke[2] – and her trull of a daughter no doubt your strumpet of a mistress to hunt and spy me all the summer – and now replace her with the wretch Getting – of whom however old Pyke turning queen's evidence warned me Truly might you tell me you cowardly brute that I had neither Father nor Brother! and so was completely in your power – no truly for had I either, you would have been Horse-whipped down St Jame's St[3] and kicked after, the only way to deal with such an unmitigated, and dastardly Blackguard as you are – but as often as you renew your dirty work (having no father or brother to kick you) so often will I direct to you by your well <u>merited</u> titles through every club – hotel and publishers in England including the <u>DCL</u> which of course means d—d confounded liar

  Rosina Bulwer Lytton

HALS
1. See RBL, 1 September 1853.
2. Sometimes spelt Pike or Pykes.
3. St James Street, central London.

To Edward Bulwer Lytton

To be forwarded to the Reptile Sir Liar Coward Bulwer Lytton
Knebworth Park Stevenage Herts England

Same letter at 3 : 201

       Llangollen
       [January 29 1854]

Beware! Fiend – And pause in your unmitigated Blackguardism for one of your Infamous gang of spies has turned queen's evidence.

HALS

To Edward Bulwer Lytton

Coward Bulwer Lytton Athaeneum Club[1] London

       Llangollen
       [January 30 1854]

Beware Fiend! And pause in your career of unnatural vice and of unmitigated Blackguardism – for one of your gang of infamous spies has turned queen's evidence

---

HALS
1. The Athenaeum Club is a gentlemen's club at 107 Pall Mall, London.

To Chevalier de Birard

Phillips's Hotel Llangollen N Wales
January 30th 1854

My dear Chevalier – I am now going to ask you to do me a service that you really can render me, without giving yourself much trouble, but after this perhaps somewhat formidable Proem[1] I should tell you that it is neither to fight a duel! nor to get you into any sort of hot water çela posé[2] – I will now proceed to lay before you Sir Liar Coward Bulwer Lyttons last infamy and blackguardism towards me – of which like his hidious self there is no end – and I think he will at last gain his point and worry me into my grave, the dastardly brute, having bade me years ago – remember "that I had neither father nor brother that he had got all my money out of me and that <u>therefore</u> I was completely in his power!" – adding (and I repeat it as the solitary truth of his iniquitous life) "and my conduct shall be so infamous to you that I promise you, you will get no one to believe it!" Acting upon this noble! manly! and high minded plan! he has for the last 14 years beset me with spies, in what ever part of the world I have been in, not from the motive of finding out any thing wrong in my moral conduct for <u>there</u> thank Heaven I could always defy him – but from the still more infamous and inexcusable motive of setting these spies under the guise of friendship! to me to defame and stab me in the back – by telling people that all the fault was on my side!!! and that he poor dear man! bore with <u>my</u> misconduct!!!!! for the sake of his children! <u>his</u> children! one of whom he murdered, slaving the poor child to death at his beastly German translations the vile charlatan! and the other whom he has perverted into almost as much infamy as his own – and whose mother the loathsome reptile through the agency of his equally villainous brother the reptile kicked out Chargé d'affaires[3] – he tried to entrap by a diabolical plot into a public bad House in Paris! – but I have a protector of which he never dreams – <u>God</u>! while I was staying in the house of friends, the cowardly brute was <u>afraid</u> to continue his dirty work, but the instant I came to this out of the way place – ill, unfriended, and alone! – to work hard for my daily bread, the Fiend not content with having tampered with every Publisher – by bribing all those <u>shiri</u> of the press against me, – so as to prevent my making myself independant as I used to do; – and getting out of the difficulties his infamous plots have got me into, – he begins his infamous <u>Espionnage</u> – and conspiracies <u>again</u> voici toute la trâme[4] Last July I was walking by the canal side when two very vulgar looking women a young and an old one – with a little boy of five years old – and a little King Charles dog past; Tiber stopped to speak to the dog – whereupon the old wretch in a strong yankee twang said to me "Oh! what a butiful dog you have <u>madam</u>" from that she began admiring the scenery – <u>et ainsi de suite</u>[5] for two or three evenings – when she affected at length to have discovered my name expressed her delight at having made my acquaintance! telling me how popular I I [*sic*] was in America, and gave me a great deal of what the Yankees call "bottled thunder and greased lightening about my books and expressed one of those sudden and eternal friendships! for me which the Americans are so fond of going a head with, – <u>bref</u>[6] her indignation against Sir Liar was so violent and her <u>sympathy</u> for me so great! that she begged I would anti date our friendship and if a few hundreds would be of any use to me to consider her purse as mine! <u>this</u> of course, I resolutely declined – nevertheless thinking how different hearts were made in every part of the world but England – where like gun locks they are all propped with flint. Her <u>darter</u> as she called her always seemed uncomfortable and ashamed to look me in the face (as well she might) in a few days they went away – but to my surprize, in less than three weeks the old woman with the child returned she called herself <u>Mrs Pyke</u>! (though I have since discovered that her real name is <u>Waller</u>) I expressed my surprise! at her returning here; she said she had taken such a fancy to <u>me</u>! – and liked <u>Llangossling</u>!! as she called this place so much that having been to Liverpool to see her "<u>darter</u>" off to America she could not resist coming here, she called the child <u>Arthur</u> (I suppose Sir Liar had him christened after his blackguard friend the present <u>dis</u>-grace of Wellington) I asked what his other name was? she said he has no other name! this I thought very odd! so I told her, and what with her intense and fabulous vulgarity , from that out, I began to suspect her. – to my great annoyance she came and lodged in the same House with me and with true American <u>sans gêne</u>,[7] used to march into my room before I was up in the morning, – after she had been "<u>located</u>" as she herself would say with me, about a fortnight, – a friend who sends me the papers, – sent me the "Morning Post" the first thing I saw in it was "Sir E Bulwer Lytton has left Park lane for Harrogate" about ten minutes after, old Pyke came in, and said – "I've had a letter from my "<u>darter</u>" and she's gone to Harrogate with a friend" – at this I bounded up in the bed – and said "Why Mrs Pyke -you told me your daughter had gone to America"! "Oh! she changed her mind" said the old wretch, "my firm belief is" rejoined I, looking into the very centre of her conscience – if she had had one? – "that your daughter is his mistress!" this she never in the least <u>resented</u>! but said quietly –"Oh we dont even know him" – I replied – bursting into tears – "Oh I'm so sorry that I allowed you to pay that £6 for me the other day – for although I have given you above £25 worth of things – I cannot repay you the money till October, – she then said she should be quite offended if I ever thought of repaying her that when she was so much in my debt. – The plot now began to thicken – <u>that day</u> the woman Waller alias Pyke, – was taken seriously ill, as I am <u>not</u> <u>English</u> – I could not let her be and die so for a fortnight I had incessant slavery night, and day nursing her, and one night that I had strained my side getting her a bath by instalments! when she had got back to bed she burst into tears and looking me for the first time full in the face she exclaimed à propos de botte[8] "no! – no! I never <u>can</u> injure you" – "I hope you have not been thinking of doing so?" said I coldly – she sobbed on and said nothing. – Well the next day I was standing at the drawing room window – and the child Arthur whose <u>head</u> is the facsimile of Sir Liars – though he has his mothers black eyes – was standing beside me, when a man from <u>this</u> Hotel came down the street <u>so</u> like my Brute, that it gave me a dreadful turn – while this thought was passing through my mind – the child exclaimed pointing at him "Oh! there's a man so like my Papa! like <u>one</u> of my Papas – like my rich Papa" – "Why pray how many Papas! have you?" "I've two, or three" Indeed! and do they <u>all</u> live with your mamma?" "Oh no, none of them, but they come and sleep sometimes, but never at the same time but the one like that man is my rich papa he has <u>such</u> a fine! house in the country – and one in London – but we dont live with him – but he sends us <u>Deers</u> (venison I suppose he meant) and pheasants – and Pineapples, and peaches – and things –" "And are you very fond of him?" – "No I dont care for either him or mamma I love you much better for you are always kind to me, and they never are" – My brain was now working to know – how I could tax the old wretch with all this villainy, without committing the child – whom I was afraid she would half murder if she knew what he had said. – After this I was as you may suppose colder than Tee to her, and and [*sic*] got away as soon as I could to this Hotel and it has since come out that while the old crocodile was affecting to cry over my persecutions (of which she was one!) <u>she was</u> telling Mrs Phillips that <u>I</u>! should be too glad to go back to Sir Liar!! – the vile old Hypocrite and a letter she wrote to Mrs Davies after she left (the woman where we had lodged – ostensibly to inquire after my health! but in <u>reality</u> to discover if I had yet found her out – this was written on the Envelope outside which letter Mrs Davies gave me to day "this letter has been sent from Brighton to be posted in London – the gentleman who now posts it dont know the writer" – so that old Pyke had gone to Brighton where Sir Liar <u>then</u> was to report progress to him – and wanted to make it appear that she was in London! – this letter I have also got safe, and sound. – Before the old wretch went away the last time she said her son before Xmas was to marry a Lady of large fortune(???) and that he, she, and the Bride would come and spend the Xmas at this Hotel, then said I – I must decline their acquaintance, as I dont want to know any <u>more</u> of your family. Well Xmas came, but thank God no Pykes – (or rather Wallers – but instead the following letter of which I give you an exact copy –

"Hôtel de Provence Leicester Sqre December 27th 1853

Dear Lady Lytton (impertinent wretch)
     Pity me – I have lost my son – and my daughter her baby – <u>pray</u> be on your guard – a person will be sent down – with a dog to attract your attention – her name will begin with a G: for God's sake be on your guard – I am off to Paris

– but could not go without warning you <u>pray</u> be on your guard your <u>friend</u> M J Pyke"

Now unless the wretches mean to give me slow poison as I suspected old Pyke had done I was so awfully ill with constant wretchings while she was here, or to forcibly abduct me, and shut me up where I'd never be heard of more, I dont know what I have to be on my guard about – but upon this I shewed old Pykes letter to Mrs Phillips and all the servants who were accordingly prepared for Spy no 2 and 3 weeks after old Pykes letter an other old wretch arrived one morning who I strongly suspect to be Mrs Tate Sir Liars Housekeeper with the identical black dog – <u>Tiney</u> re-christened Prince for the occasion but <u>only</u> answering to the name of Tiney! She said she had come to take apartments for her young lady(!?) who was in deep mourning having just lost her mother (this no doubt was act the first of the plot to excite my compassion the Infernal wretches) well the next and the next day passed and no young lady came – at length Sarah the head Chamber maid said to the <u>soi-disant</u>⁹ maid – if you will tell me your ladys name our men shall inquire at the station about her" "well really" said the old oaf looking dreadfully confused "I – I – I – dont know her name as I am only taken on a <u>job</u> (<u>that</u> at all events was true) The next <u>night</u> the young <u>lady</u>! a most hidious black beast of about 30 – who looks like one of old Jerdans bye blows – by Letitia Landon – arrived and as soon as she did so the <u>maid</u> decamped, – though upon Sarah saying how strange it was that her <u>maid</u>! should not know her name! she said "Oh! she was only leant to me as my friends do not like me to travel alone"! "But that is just what you <u>did</u> do, and at night too! ma'am" said Sarah very sharply – feeling she said desperately inclined to kick her – the young <u>lady</u> then informed her that her name was <u>Getting</u>! which name I suppose she took from getting well paid for her dirty work well for the 10 days this wretch remained here, I was too ill from indignation and worry of every sort to stir out but she kept pacing up and down the garden, and looking up at the windows, in the most brazen and <u>effrontée</u>¹⁰ manner – at last tired of not being able to catch a glimpse of me she began asking questions about me "what <u>could</u> keep me here?" Sarah told her "a long tissue of my husbands villainy and that he was always besetting me with Spies." "Spies! but what can he have to spy on in an Hotel?" "The <u>very</u> place if there <u>was</u> anything" replied Sarah – "but thank good-ness Lady Lytton can bear spying from morning till night if it was not for the insult and degradation of the thing." "<u>He</u> I have always understood said Getting, is a very profligate man, – I suppose it would not do for me to ask Lady Lytton to take a drive with me?" – no certainly not" said Sarah "for I should think it was her ladyships place to ask <u>you</u> if she wished it" when Sarah repeated this to me. it was in the dark of the evening about five o'clock – I could contain no longer – so calling for my blotting book I wrote the wretch a note telling her that the whole plot had been denounced to me by one of the gang – who not having done her work to Sir Liars satisfaction in as much as that her conscience had smitten her, had been sent off – and had turned queens Evidence – and so the sooner she Getting Spy no 2 returned to her infamous employer the better" – the wretch was furious, but refused to go, – however Mrs Phillips insisted upon her taking herself off the next morning (Saturday) and I'd give something to see the fight between Sir Liar and his myrmidons! before she went the insolent wretch wrote me a letter directed "To Lady Bulwer Lytton (misnomered)" which I sent back unopened through the Post Office – the address the wretch left to have her letters forwarded to (which of course is not where she lives) is Miss S Getting Westbourne Terrace North Westbourne Green London – wherever that is? Now, as I <u>have</u> neither father, nor brother to kick him down St James's Street the only way to deal with such an unmitigated scoundrel steeped as deep in Blackguardism – as he is in unnatural vice of every sort, – I yesterday wrote the wretch about 18 letters – Through every <u>Club</u> he belongs to – every Publisher, – also the House of Commons, – his House in Town, and to Knebworth directed in full in a large round hand to Sir Liar Coward Bulwer Lytton in which I told him that as there <u>was</u> no legal protection, or appeal for gentlewomen in "Moral England" and he had reduced me to begging by his ceaseless and most dastardly persecution and his villainous conspiracies – to prevent my having a fair sale for my books – the <u>only</u> way in which I could meet the awful legal, and other expenses his atrocity has entailed upon me I should the very next time I caught him at his dirty work – take the benefit of my pauper position and denounce him not to <u>one</u> magistrate, but at Every Police Office in London and then his villainy must be made <u>public</u> – what makes this latest plot of his with the wretch Getting the more inhuman is that he must have heard from his Spy Pyke (whom from all I have suffered I verily believe gave me slow poison) how seriously ill I am – but no doubt the monster wanted to lash, and spur me into my grave, as he did my poor murdered Child – if I had one farthing in the world which at this moment I have not I would to day set off to Town ill as I am – with an incessant <u>mal de mer</u>[11] and at <u>once</u> appeal to a magistrate against his deadly persecution – <u>pray</u> make no secret of <u>this</u> letter but shew it to every one you can. – One of these 18 letters to Sir Liar I inclosed to him as follows To Sir Liar Coward Bulwer Lytton care of his infamous Spy no 1 The Woman Waller calling herself Pyke – Hôtel de Provence Leicester Square London" – for although the wretch acknowledged she did not live there with their usual under hand double dealing – she had her letters directed there. Now my dear Chevalier what I want you to do is to go there and find out as much as you can about this woman Waller calling herself Pyke – from the landlady who is a Frenchwoman – and you will greatly oblige me – I am sure it is all a lie about her son being dead – but <u>this</u> you could also ascertain there – and as <u>soon</u> as you can if you please. – Again I beg you to make the contents of this letter as public as possible, you need not tell me that English people have no feeling I know it to my sorrow, far better than you, and I have no doubt that the conventional Icebergs round their left sides will crackle again! at the notion of a <u>wife</u>! directing in such Epethets to her Husband! but they will never be the least horrified at that Husbands having violated every law human and divine towards her, first taking her out of her home to make way for one of his mistresses – and then for 14 years – hunting her as with Bloodhounds through the wood – up to the present hour when he will not even let her starve or die in peace – doing nothing openly the disgusting coward as there is nothing that he can openly accuse her of neither will their frigidities revolt at his ultra Blackguardism – nor regret that their Country is disgraced by not having a single law to protect a woman from such dastardly villainy when she becomes a legal slave; <u>I know all this beforehand</u>, still make the facts contained in this letter as public as you can

Forgive this volume and with Compts to Mme de Birard and hoping it may find you both quite well? Believe Me My dear Chevalier your much obliged Rosina Bulwer Lytton

A Pleasant! opening of Parliament to Sir Liar, when he gets my letter at the House of Commons tomorrow

---

HALS
1. Prelude.
2. Having established that (French).
3. In charge of business (French).
4. Literally: 'here is the totality of the threads' (French).
5. And so on (French).
6. In brief (French).
7. Without discomfort (French).
8. Turning to quite another subject (French).
9. So-called (French).
10. Impudent (French).
11. Seasickness (French).

To Rebecca Ryves

Llangollen
Monday February 6th 1854

My dearest Rebecca I am very uneasy at not hearing from you, and hope that you are not ill? or that poor Massy is not worse? as soon as I hear from you I will tell you how I put the spy Getting to flight, and what I have done to her infamous Employer Sir Liar – but I am too ill to day to write a long letter indeed for the last 3 months I have been suffering from <u>incessant</u> sickness at the stomach a violent dysentery which absolutely refuses to yield to all remedies although I have taken chalk drafts enough to turn me into one of Dovers cliffs[1] – which makes me think that wretch Pyke alias Waller must have given me slow poison the more so that she took such pains to impress upon Sarah how ill I was – saying – "I tell you Sarah Lady Lytton is <u>much</u> worse than you have any idea of" and to Mrs Phillips – "Mind if anything happens to Lady Lytton that you get every nurse, and Dr in the place, I'll take care you are paid – <u>and well paid</u>!! – you will not be the least surprised to hear that that Boethian[2] old ass the Rev <u>Muster</u> Smith completely bungled the negotiation of my book, and <u>Husbands Bosworth</u>[3] (I dont mean the <u>market</u> town so called in Leicestershire) but the Judas Scotch Publisher in Regent St,[4] after solemnly promising to keep the MS: only 4 days – kept it 5 weeks – no doubt shewing it to Sir Liar * that he may get all the abusive reviews – ready by the time the book is out – so as I could not afford to lose any more time, I went back to poor Skeet, who was delighted to publish it – if you can fancy <u>Skeet</u> in an ecstasy!! but as usual we had a <u>set to</u> about the <u>title</u> of the book – Skeet writing to me with inky tears gushing from his pen "Good Heavens! does your Ladyship suppose that the circulating libraries will ever subscribe to a book with such a title![5] for how can <u>they</u> possibly divine that under it is the sparkling ore! the brilliant mine there is?" – !!!!!!! from which metaphorical and poetical flight I conclude that poor Skeet will some fine morning be fished out of the Thames and that <u>Horrocks</u> is by this time in a strait waistcoat! propped up like a stuffed alligator with chess boards and old Tomes in that dark corner of the shop leading into the den where you and I used to frighten him so when we used to make our descents upon him in Skeets absence. However I wrote Skeet word that rather than frighten him out of his senses <u>also</u> (<u>pre</u> supposing <u>Horrocks</u> to be already non compos)[6] and the Circulating Libraries into a state of Catalepsy I would rather alter the title, have done so, and the book is only gone to press to day. Dr Price who has just left said had he known me then he would have given the world to warn me when old Pyke was here as he is convinced she is the keeper of a Badhouse – I have something to tell you of <u>Gorge</u> that will put you in as great a rage as it did me – but have only time now to say God Bless you write soon and with innocences love Believe me Ever your grateful and affect Rosina Bulwer Lytton.

* and then returned it to me saying he found it would not suit his <u>engagements</u> (to Sir Liar no doubt) to publish it. –

HALS

1. The white cliffs of Dover are made out of chalk, a substance used as an antedote to poison.

2.   A side-stepping of an argument, a description deriving from the Roman philosopher Anicius Manlius Severinus Boethius (b. *c.* AD 80), who wrote *The Consolation of Philosophy* in prison while awaiting execution for disloyalty to King Theodoric the Great.
3.   Two London-based publishers, Joseph and Thomas Bosworth.
4.   Thomas Bosworth was based in Regent Street, London.
5.   *Behind the Scenes, A Novel.*
6.   An abbreviation of *non compos mentis* (Latin), not of sound mind.

To Rebecca Ryves

Llangollen
Saturday February 11th 1854

I am very sorry to hear my dearest Rebecca that you have been <u>spacheless</u> with the fluency – but hope you will now begin to be <u>fluent</u> after the <u>spachelessness.</u> – I am very glad to hear such good accounts of poor Massy – as I think he <u>must</u> by this time have past the Rubicon, and will do now : – As for Mrs Willey's[1] little ailments – I suppose like <u>me</u>, – she is only troubled with a <u>little Bill</u>! but unlike me, she may look forward to being safely delivered! which in my case I see no chance of! – Dr Price[2] (not Rice!) has at length hit upon something to relieve me – but he says though quite capable of giving me slow poison for he firmly believes Pyke to be the infamous old keeper of a bad House! (this was like their Paris plot of trying to get me into that one about the character of a servant where luckily Sir Henry Webster[3] & Monsieur Le Dru went for me and saw the reptile Henry Bulwer walking up and down with Mr Howard,[4] and looking in all directions to see whether I should arrive!) yet Dr Price thinks it is only superhuman worry anxiety, and over work. I will now explain to you the <u>cause</u> of the earth sinking under Sir Liar. When the spy Getting had been here about ten days – walking up and down opposite my windows and looking up at them in the most brazen manner during which time I never stirred out – she at length in despair at losing her time said to Sarah "I suppose it would not do for me to ask Lady Lytton to take a drive with me?" certainly not said Sarah very savagely – it would be Lady Lyttons place to ask you if she wanted your acquaintance – but she has been so spied by her infamous Husband – that she is now determined never more to make any <u>chance</u> acquaintance – indeed one of the gang have peached and written to warn her about another spy's coming down first with a black dog as you have" – "Spies!" cried Getting in mock astonishment "what could <u>he</u> have to spy <u>her</u> about? – <u>he</u> indeed is I have always heard a very profligate man – and in an Hotel! too what could he hope to spy"? – "The very Place said Sarah if there <u>was</u> anything to spy – but beyond the irritation and the insult of it, Lady Lytton of course don't care if she was spied from morning till night." When Sarah repeated this to me it was about 6 o'clock in the Evening I was ill in bed –

but wrote to the wretch Getting – telling her that that infamous old Pyke had betrayed them and warned me of the whole conspiracy – and that they must be fools indeed if they thought that the <u>same</u> dog – and the same trap would do twice and that if she did not instantly quit Llangollen I would take summary means to expose her, and her infamous employer Sir Liar Coward Bulwer Lytton who had much better spend some of his ill gotten wealth in giving his wife enough to live on instead of paying such a set of low spies to hunt her to death. – I then put on my dressing gown sprang out of bed – and going to the wretches sitting room – opened the door and without going in flung the letter upon the table saying – "There – when you have read that take it back to your infamous Employer" – she wrote me a most insolent note saying my attempts at intimidation should not get her out of the place. I wrote her back word that if she did not instantly go I'd apply to a magistrate – that I had used no intimidation on the contrary – that <u>if</u> <u>I</u> had said <u>one</u> word of <u>her</u> – her infamous employer Sir Liar the woman Waller– her daughter his mistress or his Bastard Arthur – that was <u>not true</u> I challenged them one, and <u>all</u> to put it into a Lawyers hands, and instantly proceed against – and expose <u>me</u>. – Mrs Phillips then told her she <u>must</u> go – or that I should go and she most certainly would not have me, annoyed and insulted – Getting then swore by all the (Infernal) Gods she was respectable! and could prove it by a letter she had, had that day from her sister – "Then" said Mrs Phillips "perhaps you will have no objection to let Lady Lytton see that letter?" "none whatever" said she but at the same time taking good care to plunge it securely back into her pocket – <u>Bref</u>[5] the next morning she was bundled off – writing me a letter insolently directed To Lady Bulwer Lytton (Misnomered!) which I did not even open – but returned to her through the post. I then sat down and wrote to her dastardly employer Sir Liar – through <u>every</u> one of his publishers – every one of his clubs – to his house in Park Lane and at Knebworth – directed in full To Sir Liar Coward Bulwer Lytton – To be forwarded to the Reptile – and on the one directed to the Conservative club, I also added "Doer of dirty work – politically and <u>privately</u>" and I sent him one letter under cover to old Pyke directed – "for Sir Liar Coward Bulwer Lytton care of his infamous spy the woman Waller calling herself Pyke – Hôtel de Provence Leicester Square". In these letters I told him that as he had told me I had neither father not brother – that he had got all my money out of me – and that I was completely in his power I would for the future prove to him – that so dastardly a villain was in <u>my</u> power, and that of fearless truth, and honesty to <u>expose</u>: <u>fear</u>, being the only weapon to wield against such a low mean nature, – and that the <u>next</u> time I caught him at his dirty work, as there was no redress for a gentlewoman in moral <u>England</u>! I would take the benefit of my Pauper position, and denounce him not only to one magistrate, but at <u>Every</u> Police office in London – and <u>then</u> his villainy must be made Public" – now all this was a fortnight ago and <u>he</u> and all his gang have been as mute as stones ever since – and as for Lady Hothams nonsense – why the wretch has not left <u>one</u> villainy unacted towards <u>me</u>; – and this fear of <u>exposure</u>! as I have no brother to kick or horse whip him down St James's St is the <u>only</u> defence I have against his <u>ceaseless</u> persecutions and unimaginable Blackguard-ism. – I also sent him one letter so directed to the House of Commons – so he must have had a <u>pleasant</u> opening of Parliament and <u>this</u> is the reason he feels the world crumbling under him! as I told Lady Hotham if his friend <u>Gorge</u> don't divulge the secret <u>he'll</u> take care to pocket the affront of these letters directed in his true titles. – As for his spy Pyke through her <u>over cunning</u> as you will see by one of de Birards letters – we have got a clue to her – as all her letters though directed London or Hampstead whether to me – Dr Price, or Mrs Davies;[6] – were written <u>from</u> Brighton where she had gone to report Progress to Sir Liar who was then there, and then sent these letters under cover, to the Assistant Commissary Genl Price[7] – a relation of <u>my</u> Dr Prices with whom the latter had quarrelled, from his also – having swindled him! but upon the Envelope of all these – letters the said Commissary Genl had written "I think it right to warn you against the writer of these letters who ever it may be? as they should have been posted at Brighton; – and they have been sent under cover to me, to be posted in London and such a round about proceeding can mean no good." – See how villainy always over leaps itself. As for Gorges kind efforts (<u>soi disant</u>)[8] of getting Sir Liar – to increase my allowance! as I told de Birard I did not believe one word of it! as in the first place I was very certain that Sir Liar would not allow any one even to Broach the subject to him, – but that as Mr G Beauclerc had past his life in Legacy hunting, and toadying rich people – no doubt he thought this boast would make him appear amiable in Lady Hothams Eyes. – at all events that <u>I</u> should consider a beggarly hundred a year only as an additional insult after all the outrages, and persecutions I had unremittingly endured for the last 12 years but that he could now give his <u>Fides Achates</u>[9] Sir Liar a helping hand by saying that that dear amiable man! was just going to increase my allow-ance, when I knocked it all in the head by those outrageous letters! only I advised them when they were about it to make it £500 a year as the story would tell bet-ter, as for Lady Hothams scepticism as to his motives! – I told her she forgot that I had <u>twice</u> had the wretch in a court of Justice for similar conspiracies – once for a gross Libel, and once for catching his spies – as the Gens D'armes[10] at Paris did in the <u>act</u> of stealing my Papers – his own letters that he had denied on oath! and as for his motives, I referred her to Sir Frederick Pollocks and M. Berryers[11] speeches on both those occasions, and as to the <u>violence</u> of my language – that when speaking of Sir liar – I always resorted to on <u>Oratorical principles</u> those of suiting the <u>language</u> to the <u>subject</u>, and therefore in speaking of <u>him</u>, I always selected the most violent, most brutal, and most coarse, – not to say blackguard-edly, with which I was acquainted.

Be sure, and let me have both de Birards letters back as he is now in London I hope to hear that he has succeeded in Capturing what Isaac Walton calls "The river shark"[12] alias the Pike! – Plots, mysteries, and romances seem to thicken round me – you must know that one of the Heroes of my new book is a most benevolent and high-minded Jew[13] – I took the <u>facts</u> about him from a newspaper and give them as my authority least people should think such noble high mindedness only existed in the brain of a novelist, well here is what Skeet says in his letter to day and you will own the coincidence is an extraordinary one as the circumstances upon which I have founded my story as far as the Jew is concerned happened four years ago –

"I have the pleasure (and it is a real one) of being intimately acquainted with Mr Benjamins[14] whom your Ladyship has so flatteringly (though no more than he deserves) immortalized in your new work – and with your permission – I will gratify him – by letting him know the ample justice you have done to his noble conduct. – with regard to the work your Ladyship was kind enough to recommend to my consideration of Miss Airds![15] it was an impossibility! – and I am sure had you seen it your judgement of its de-merits, would have gone beyond mine – I think the very type would have laughed! till they could not have been set for such a production!" – now as "great wit to madness nearly is allied" – you may guess how this ever increasing Epistolary brilliancy and vivacity! Of Skeets alarms me! – But is it not <u>odd</u> about my heroic Jew? I begged he would have a copy of the book handsomely bound for him, and presented to him with my most sincere Esteem. I think you and I – and even Horrocks! would be ready to take our "<u>Davies</u>" to Skeets critique on Miss Airds! little production! Poor Innocence sends hims best love to you it is very odd – that the whole time that wretch Getting was here Tib did nothing but keep up a continual growling and snapping while she was here. My kindest regards to Massy – and best wishes when you write; forgive this scrawl but I am still so weak, and I have had so much writing to do lately that my hand feels ready to drop off Ever your grateful and affect Rosina Bulwer Lytton.

HALS
1. A society fund-raiser for charity.
2. RBL's physician in Llangollen, who was a Fellow of the Royal College of Physicians at Edinburgh. She dedicated her novel *Very Successful!* to him in 1856.
3. Sir Henry Webster had been staying next door to RBL at Hôtel de Brighton. Charles Dru was one of the best lawyers in France, who was one of RBL's legal team. See below, n. 11.
4. A diplomat based in Paris. See RBL, 17 September 1839.
5. Briefly (French).
6. RBL lodged with Mrs Davies. This may be Jane Davies, who ran a bakery and confectioner's shop on Bridge Street, Llangollen. See RBL, 7 September 1853.
7. A relative of Dr Price.

8. So-called (French).
9. Loyal Achates (Latin). In Virgil's *Aeneid*, Aeneas's best friend, Achates, is referred to as '*fides* Achates'.
10. Literally: 'Men of Arms' (French).
11. The legal counsel engaged for RBL at her trial in Paris for 22 March 1840, in which she took action against Mr Lawson, an attorney and his clerk Mr Tom Thackeray for stealing papers from her house at 30 bis, Rue de Rivoli in Paris, bribing witnesses and defaming her character.
12. Izaak Walton (1593–1683) was the author of *The Compleat Angler* (1653), where there is no mention of a 'river shark', and a number of biographies. See RBL, 22 June 1858.
13. RBL's Jewish character, Jacob Jacobs, in her novel *Behind the Scenes* favourably contrasts with EBL's half-Jewish character, Baron Levy, in his *My Novel*. See RBL, 2 March 1853.
14. Thomas Macknight published a venomous literary and political biography, *The Right Hon. Benjamin Disraeli*, in 1854.
15. Marion Paul Aird was the author of *Heart Histories, Violets from the Greenwood … in Prose and Verse*, published in 1853. See RBL, 7 September 1853.

To Rebecca Ryves

Llangollen
Tuesday February 21ˢᵗ 1854

Many thanks My dearest Rebecca for your kind letter, I am very glad indeed to hear such an improved account of poor Massy – and as I said before, I think now he has turned the corner – and past all danger only he must be very careful. I send you a long yarn of N. P. Willis's[1] on the subject and if true??? – his recovery seems most miraculous! I only wish that I could send a Horse – groom saddle bridle – wages for the biped, and provender[2] with the Quadruped with it not to use you, as my dear <u>friends</u>(?) do me, and lapidate[3] you with those hardest of all stones to the wretched empty "<u>good wishes</u>!" not that some of them trouble me even with them. That beast Getting did <u>not</u> see me, when I took the note, she only saw me for half a second, one morning, when coming out of my bedroom I came full upon her and looking at the hideous beast – I said – "So – that's spy no 2; – and she looks well worthy of her office" – I don't know whether I told you – that when Sarah – told her that I had been warned against her as a spy she said – "Oh dear, I am not in a sphere of life to know Sir E Bulwer Lytton as an <u>Acquaintance</u>, and I …

HALS
Incomplete letter.
1. Nathaniel Parker Willis (1806–67) was an American author and editor, who visited Europe in 1831, recording his observations in *Pencilings by the Way*, first published in *The New York Mirror* in 1835 and published as a book in 1844.
2. 'Food, provisions *esp.* dry food, as corn or hay, for horses, etc; fodder, forage' (*OED*).
3. 'To throw stones at, to pelt with stones; also, to stone to death' (*OED*).

To Rebecca Ryves

March 1ˢᵗ 1854

The <u>Only</u> Mutual aid, ever seen or heard of in <u>moral</u> England [above printed cartoon of two drunk men leaning against each other]

I do not send you the above <u>charming</u>! tableau My Dearest Rebecca as typical of <u>my</u> proceedings, as I am only taking <u>bitters</u> leaving the <u>gin</u> to Sir Liar, who has always so literally supplied me with the <u>former</u>. I know the "Greek phrase" well as I have it at Geneva among my poor books – which I now never hope to see Again; – it is not what is called a very rare book among Bibliopholes – but I quite agree with you as to its merits, – I hope you <u>wont</u> write to the Rev <u>Master</u> Ursa Major[1] Smith;[2] – for he wrote me such an unwarrantably brutal letter – saying – that if Sir Liar did – spy me – it must be to prove that I was mad – as none <u>but</u> a mad woman would believe – in plots – or talk of spies – in the 19ᵗʰ century this precious epistle I sent back to the brute without word – or comment – he then wrote a letter of apology of which I took not the slightest notice – as I never mean to do of him the vulgar wretch again. – Pup Innocent is vezy great big much obliged for de violets with which him says him is as fine, as a Gardeners dog with a nosegay tied to his tail. – I have had no Walpolean[3] epistles from Skeet since so cannot give you any Skeetiana – but of his <u>dementation</u> there can be no doubt, as you would have been convinced had you heard the Flourish of trumpets! with which he announces my Book in last Saturdays "Athenaeum" <u>Certes</u>[4] when a modest man <u>does</u> take to Brass! he dont do it by <u>halves</u>. De Birard writes me word to day that all the Booksellers say Routledge will be quite ruined by his <u>bargain</u> with Sir Liar and that he begins to fear so himself. – <u>Gorge</u> being still in Ireland he says he can give me no news of the Enemy – but that he had a letter from Lady Hotham that morning who desired her best love and <u>earnest wishes</u>! that my book[5] might be a great <u>succés</u>[6] I fear that like <u>witch</u> wishes hers are so <u>sterile</u>! that they produce a contrary effect. I get very wretched as the spring approaches – as of course Mrs Phillips wont let me remain here at what I can afford to pay her – . however come what come may [*sic*]; I must only <u>submit</u> to God which is sometimes harder than to trust in Him which I do at <u>all</u> times – however fierce the storm, and black the clouds, – I hope you continue to get good accounts of poor Massy? pray remember me kindly to him when you write. The weather here is the most lovely you can imagine, quite Neapolitan[7] – but the Gardeners are croaking and say we shall pay for it in sharp frosts and spring blights. – addio[8] – and with Tibs best love Believe Me Ever My dearest Rebecca your Grateful and affect
      Rosina Bulwer Lytton

HALS
1.   Great bear (Latin).

2. Revd James Elimalet Smith.
3. Horace Walpole. See RBL, 28 May 1834.
4. Certainly (French).
5. *Behind the Scenes*, published by Skeet.
6. Success (French).
7. Appertaining to Naples, Italy.
8. Goodbye [*adios*] (Spanish).

To Rebecca Ryves

Llangollen
Monday March 6th 1854

My dearest Rebecca I have such a cart load of letters to write that I scribble you a few lines at a hand gallop to thank you for your kind one just received ; – I am very glad to hear that you are leading Lord Massy[1] such a dance! and hope you will teach him the matrimonial <u>valse à deux temps</u>[2] – for if one must marry I think a fool – is by far the best material for a husband. In a letter I had from Mrs Tyler yesterday she tells me that Kate Long (who is staying with Dr <u>Laurie</u>! for all that family like Kneb and her mother with regard to Dr Pennington seem to think it necessary always to be without reach that Dr Laurie may see that the medicine has <u>had the desired effect</u>!) met Massy a day or two ago in the Pantechnicon[3] and said he was looking the <u>"picture of health"</u> tell him with my kind regards – if he goes to Ireland this summer – and I am still at this Hotel – I hope he will break his journey by coming to stay a week with me? you see I am learning the <u>prudent</u> <u>limitations</u> of "English <u>hospitality</u>"?? but alas! you know the reason why – Truly as you say would that Mrs Willey had included <u>us</u> in the Charity! for never were there fitter subjects for it; and as it <u>wont</u> begin <u>at</u> home! I wish it would abroad; could she not get up another Concert, and change her magnificent <u>notes</u>, for <u>cash</u> on our behalf. I forget <u>Moores</u> story about the italics! – but <u>sure</u> enough the Italics! have been at it again! a whole week have I been kept without a single proof – and on Saturday I get a vol and a half!! all at one fell swoop! and so vilely printed that it …

HALS
Incomplete letter.

1. This is RBL's cousin Hugh Hamon Ingoldsby Massy, fifth Baron Massy (1827–74), of Hermitage, Castleconnell, Limerick. He succeeded his father as Baron when he was only nine years old. The estate was managed by his mother, Mathilda, until he was twenty-one. See RBL, 20 August 1850.
2. A two-step waltz (French).
3. An imitation Greek word for a bazaar in Moncomb Street, Belgrave Square, London around 1830, intended to convey all aspects of the arts.

To Rebecca Ryves

Llangollen
Monday March 13th 1854

My dearest Rebecca – whatever honours! I may attain to, or whatever honour (?) may be "thrust upon me" – I am not proud! and although I did recieve the enclosed last week from Corporal Humbug! You see I write to you just the same as ever! – as for Massy as I never say what I don't mean; if still at this Hotel, I shall be delighted to see him the arnica he must use for bathing his ankles, is the Mother Tincture of Arnica only to be got good at a Homoeopathic Chemists; the proportions 15 drops to a wineglassful of water – but what I found strengthen my ankles much more – and is 90 times as cheap for 1day's worth will last 3 months is about a Tablespoonful of powdered alum– to about a tumbler, and a half of cold water, to bathe his ankles with this night, and morning – he would soon find them stronger – not of course wetting the soles of his feet and rubbing them dry with a coarse bath towel. – I am sorry to hear such bad accounts of Mrs Willeys health my kind regards to her sposo,¹ and compliments to her when you write, and tell your brother I wish he would remember me most kindly to Lord, and Lady Gough,² who will better remember me as that naughty little girl Rosina Wheeler, whom they used to be so kind to in Guernsey long ago – when my poor darling Uncle was Governor there, and his, and (afterwards) Lord Goughs Regt the 87^{th3} was quartered there. –

Mrs Tyler kindly sent me £5 yesterday – (a volunteer) that I might pay my long promised visit at Chirk Castle – but as I told Mrs Biddulph when she was here on Saturday that I could not go till April, and I would then try and go for a few days at Easter before they went to Town. – But this will do to stop Mrs Framptons Mouth, who has dunned me incessantly for her £2"10 – so that I put my foot in it when I dealt with her Oh! this horrid! horrid! want of money! what a worm that never dies! – what a debasing curse it is! – De Birard writes me word that Sir Liar is "very shaky – and breaking fast, his intellects quite failing him except when under the influence of excitement and does not know which way to turn for a shilling"! No wonder – for there is nothing so costly as ubiquitous vice – for although first and last he cannot have made less than £80, 000 by his writings (as he got £1000 for each of his Plays alone) yet what with dirty work, and its sine, que non,⁴ hush money and his drabs of mistresses in all directions, with the 155 natural children, which they tell him are his – even if he only allowed them 2d a week each (and I have no doubt he screws them to the uttermost) yet for such an expenditure, the coffers of a Rothschild⁵ would not suffice – and as a set off to all his outlay, he has only one poor wretch of a wife, to pinch, screw – cheat, and economise upon. As for my book I don't see how it can be out under 10 days for on Saturday my proofs were only up to page 52 of 3rd vol – yesterday I had none, and to day I <u>could</u> not have any – so there are 2 days lost, and I wrote to Skeet positively forbidding – him to have it hurried through the Press without my seeing, and revising – every line of it, which is quite necessary from the specimen I have already had of the printing! as for the confusion of the genders, and the tenses! in the French, and the Latin ! I defy Babel[6] to have matched them. Skeet concludes his gentle <u>Emollient</u> his emulsion of Almonds of a letter of Saturdays – Post, in these very cheering – words – if they will but come to pass! – "I have an impression" (I did not think any thing of <u>that</u> as publishers must have a great many Impressions!) "that your Ladyship will reap a harvest that you little expect from this work – as the inquiries about, and orders for it, are already great – and certainly the book will fully bear out the expectations of it." I try to believe him sincere, as he seems to be "going a head" as the Yankees say and laying out a little fortune, in the extensive manner, in which he is advertizing it. If there <u>is</u> ...

HALS
The end of the letter is missing.

1. Husband (Italian).
2. Hugh Gough, first Viscount Gough (1779–1869), was an Irish-born field marshal. He was appointed Commander-in-Chief of British India in 1843 and, in 1854, he was appointed Colonel of the Royal Horse Guards. In 1807, he married Frances Maria Stephens (1788–1863).
3. The 87th Royal Irish Fusiliers (the Prince of Wales's Irish Regiment) were also known as the 'Faugh a Ballaghs' (Clear the Way), named after their ancient Gaelic battle-cry. This battalion was headed by RBL's uncle General Sir John Doyle. Lord Gough served in the regiment after 1796 and, in 1805, he was promoted to the rank of major.
4. Without which (it is) not (possible) (Latin).
5. A wealthy banking family. See RBL, 17 July 1835.
6. A word, which originates from a Hebrew word for confusion, being also the name of a biblical tower and a city (Genesis 11:1–9).

To Rebecca Ryves

Llangollen
Monday March 27th 1854

The original intention of the Authoress was merely to have appeared as Editor of this work[1] but circumstances have occurred during its progress through the press, which render the acknowledgement of the Authorship necessary desirable

[printed paragraph, "necessary" crossed through "desirable" added by hand]

My dearest Rebecca – being still under the influence of Bronchitis Influenza and Co – though one O'clock – I am only just up – and just as I came out of my room – that Rascally Harper strikes up "The rising of the lark!"[2] I suppose to pay me off for Foxes Book of Martyrs[3] – Before this reaches you you will no doubt have recieved "Behind The Scenes" Skeets letters! would kill you if you could read them – and no wonder he thinks so much of what he calls my "rapid(!) and brilliant talents" when I tell you that he has been just 3 weeks, in labour of the production I have appended to the top of the opposite page, and has only safely delivered of it last Wednesday but I am happy to say that he, and Horrocks! are both doing well, and Skeet continues as well as can be expected; – The letter that accompanied this brilliant effusion began – "After many struggles I have ventured to take this step without your Ladyship – I hope you will not consider it a false one?" – as if I should own it! if Skeet had committed a faux pas![4] with me! and according to the English tariff of morality(?) what matter? as long as it was "Behind the Scenes" He ends – by begging I would excuse "this scrawl, but I write in great haste, and agitation (!) at a Confectioners shop in the vicinity of Myers's Printing office"– now cannot you fancy Skeet, – after all was said and done, – and he had actually ventured upon the strong – not to say desperate! measure of concocting this affiche[5] – printing and publishing it all on his own responsibility!! – rushing into a confectioners, and indulging in a penny bun as a sedative? On Saturday I received a letter from the manager, and Lessee of the Southampton Theatre,[6] asking me if I would, dramatise or if I did not like trouble, – allow him to dramatise my novel of Molière when he would give – me a good, and he hoped adequate remuneration as he had no doubt of its great success as there was a Mr Somebody whose name I could not make out; whose wonderful histrionic powers – only wanted a suitable original part of gnawing jealousy – struggling with deep love – and high feeling – like that of Molière, to stamp him as one of the first – or rather the first actor of the age" – I declined dramatising it knowing as I told him nothing of stage business – as it is called, but that he was welcome to do so – as you may guess how glad I was of the promised remuneration! Which God grant may come, P.S. De Dog left hims love for you but is gone to the diggings as they have discovered an immense mine of gold! at Dolgelly[7] 12 miles from this. Lady Hotham writes me word that Gorge has not yet returned from Ireland – I had a great mind to write her back word, that no doubt he soon would to pay his legacy duty! to her . – I shall be very much obliged to you if you will inquire about those poor Miss Doyles – poor things or rather poor thing – for the one that is gone has had a happy release. My dear old Dr Price who quite spoils me has just sent me such a magnificent cake, and what is much sweeter a delicious bouquet of white violets and Heartsease[8] a propos[9] Chalon writes me word of some wonderful exotic he bought at the Duchess of Bedfords sale (Georgina Duchess of Bedford)[10] which he says perfumes his whole conservatory – and that he wishes he could send me a string of the beautiful pink hearts that hang from it I told him I wish he could also as I have had such a string of <u>black</u> hearts to contend with that it would be an agreeable change. As you may perceive this is a steel pen – and I cannot write with it – so thanking you for your kind letter just recieved – I will say good bye – and with kind regards to your Brothers when you write. – Believe me My dearest Rebecca Ever your grateful and affect Rosina Bulwer Lytton.

HALS
1. *Behind the Scenes.*
2. Possibly a servant, who was singing this traditional song, composed by Elizabeth Grant (1745–1814). The lyrics are written by Lesley Nelson-Burns.
3. Known as Foxe's *Book of Martyrs*, the full title is *Actes and Monuments of these Latter and Perillous Days, touching Matters of the Church* (1563). Illustrated with woodcuts, this work on the persecution of Protestants was written by John Foxe (1516–87).
4. Social blunder (French).
5. Public notice (French).
6. Mr. Leighton, purported to be a theatrical manager.
7. Dolgellau is a town in north-west Wales.
8. A common perennial wild flower, also known as wild pansy.
9. In connection with (French).
10. Lady Georgiana Gordon became the second wife of John Russell, sixth Duke of Bedford (1766–1839). She was a great patroness of the arts and had a long-standing relationship with the painter Edwin Landseer, despite having a happy marriage.

To Mr Leyton

Mr Leyton Esqre Theatre Royal Southampton[1] England

Phillips's Hotel Llangollen
March 30th 1854

Sir I regret to say that all my set being changed at Paris – The Hôtel Castalan, where I used to meet so many literary – and Theatrical persons – being no longer open But I do know two persons formerly connected with L'Odéon[2] – and L'Opéra Comique,[3] only unfortunately they are no longer in Paris, but at Marseilles however to them I will write, and I know if they can do any thing they will. – I have no doubt of Mr Robsons[4] being able as the French call it to <u>create</u> the <u>rôle</u> of Molière,[5] and that it in his hands it will make a great sensation – if produced at one of the London Theatres, but allow me to suggest that the Playgoing public of the present day have been so pampered with magnificent scenic effects – and <u>spectacles</u>, that the very perfection of acting without it; I fear would fail to attract them, now in the gorgeous court of Louis quatorze[6] there is ample scope for all this – and I think – one scene of a theatre within a Theatre – (as in "The Corsican Brothers[7] –) that is Molières <u>own</u> Theatre of the <u>Petit Bourbon</u>[8] with all the celebreties of the day in <u>correct</u> costume, as I have described them in the novel – in the side boxes of the mimes stage so as to be seen by the <u>audience</u> would be very telling; – but as I communicated your proposition to Mr Skeet my Publisher – I also requested him to have the goodness to write to you on the subject, as he understands these matters better than I do –

> Wishing you every success in your undertaking I Have the Honor to Be Sir your obedient servant
> Rosina Bulwer Lytton.

HALS

1. A town, now a city, on the south coast of England.
2. L'Odéon theatre in Paris was inaugurated in 1782 by Queen Marie-Antoinette.
3. The Opéra-Comique is an opera company and opera house in Place Boieldieu, Paris. It is housed in the second *Salle Favart* (the first burnt down) which accommodated the Opéra-Comique between 1840 and 1887.
4. Thomas Robson Brownhill, whose theatrical name was Frederick Robson (1822–64), was an actor in burlesque and comedy, who worked with J. R. Planché. In notes to his *Extravaganzas*, Planché observes that Robson proved there was but 'one step from the ridiculous to the sublime'. James Robinson Planché, *Recollections and Reflections: A Professional Autobiography* (London: S. Low, Marston, 1901), p. 183.
5. French playwright and actor Jean-Baptiste Poquelin, whose stage name was Molière (1622–73). He is the hero of the proposed stage version of RBL's novel *The School for Husbands*.
6. Louis XIV (1638–1715), known as the Sun King, ruled as King of France and of Navarre from 1643 until his death.
7. *The Corsican Brothers; or, The Fatal Duel* is a three-act drama by Dion Boucicault (1820–*c*. 90), who adapted Alexander Dumas's French original while he was dramatist in residence at the Princess's Theatre, Oxford Street, London. The play was first shown there in February 1852 and staged by Charles Kean.
8. Molière's company joined a famous Italian Commedia dell'arte company where he became firmly established at their theatre, Le Petit-Bourbon, where in 1659, he performed the première of *Les Précieuses Ridicules* (*The Affected Young Ladies*), one of his masterpieces.

To Rebecca Ryves

Phillips's Hotel Llangollen
Saturday April 1ˢᵗ 1854

Dearest Rebecca I have such avalanches of letters to answer – containing obituaries from the Bousefield[1] Epidemic! that I have only time, to thank you for your very kind letter just received– and tell you what you will be glad to hear i.e. that Skeet! has at length had – <u>an idea</u>!!! it is to be hoped that it is an Idea and Heir! and will inherit, all its sires, <u>mild</u> effulgence! – I hope you have by this time got "Behind the Scenes" which is much better printed than usual, with the exception of the French! which <u>as</u> <u>usual</u> is a disgraceful hash, and they have quite spoilt that very good story of the Jerninghams about "mes très chers frères, – et vous autres canaille chretiens!" by making bad French of it with their canaille <u>de</u> Chretiens![2] – Skeet who really seems to know every one, and every thing – it appears – knows <u>who</u> this Mr Robson[3] is whom he says has quite genius enough to <u>create</u> the rôle of Molière. The Managers idea is if possible to get it brought out in Paris – at the same time it appears in London – and to have a magnificent spectacle – of the gorgeous Court of Louis Quatorze[4] – and one scene – of Molières own Theatre of Le Petit Bourbon[5] – with all the celebrities, and Sommetes Aristocratiques,[6] of the day assisting at one of his – plays, – in Paris I know it would have a great run, as Molière is still, and ever will be the idol of the French. I'll get "Mordaunt Hall"[7] after what you say but ever since "Emilia Wyndham"[8] I have had a horror! of Mrs Marshes books.[9] Least you should not believe <u>me</u> I send you the official announcement! of the birth of Skeets Idea! and with Gold Paws's best love – am in Flash of lightening Haste – Ever my dearest Rebecca Gratefully and affectly yrs Rosina Bulwer Lytton

---

HALS

1. Illness has struck Mrs Bousefield's household. See RBL, 9 May 1854.
2. 'My very dear brothers and the rest of you Christian rabble!' ... rabble of Christians! (French).
3. See RBL, 30 March 1854.
4. Louis XIV. See RBL, 30 March 1854.
5. See RBL, 30 March 1854.
6. The highest point [*sommets*] of the aristocracy (French).
7. *Mordaunt Hall or A September Night*, a novel by Anne Marsh Caldwell was first published in 1849 and reprinted twice in 1853.
8. Anne Marsh Caldwell's novel *Emilia Wyndham* was first published in 1846 and went through a number of reprints including in 1853 and 1854.
9. Mrs Anne Marsh Caldwell (1791–1874) of Linley Wood, Staffordshire, published a large number of novels. See above, notes 7 and 8.

To Mr Leyton[1]

Mr Leyton Esqre 23 Park Street Camberwell[2] Surry England

Phillips's Hotel Llangollen
April 6th 1854

Sir I lose no time in forwarding to you the accompanying letters, which this mornings Post, brought me from Marseilles from writing in such haste Mme Gérard writes in rather a confused way – however I glean from her letter that there are three or four openings for having your Piece produced on the Paris Boards – (The <u>Théâtre Français</u> would if attainable be by far the <u>best</u>;) but as I suspected nothing can be done at the other side of the water without the <u>trans-</u>

lation being remitted. – I also see by Mme Gérards letter that if you do not avail yourself of the letter to Monsieur Jarry of Her Majesty's Theatre[3] it is to be returned to her – I suppose her motive for thrusting me so much more <u>en avant</u>[4] in the business than I have any right to be, is that she knows in London my name (out of curiosity) would draw an audience for the Play. Have the goodness to let me know which of the places proposed by Mme Gérard you decide upon? <u>as soon</u> as possible; that as she requests I may lose no time in answering her letter. I Have the Honor to be Sir your obedient servant

      Rosina Bulwer Lytton

HALS
1.   Mr M. Leyton professed to be a theatrical manager.
2.   Camberwell was originally a village, south-east of London.
3.   Situated in the Haymarket, West End of London, the theatre was renamed in 1837 when Queen Victoria ascended the throne.
4.   Forward (French).

To Rebecca Ryves

        Llangollen
      Saturday April 7th 1854

My dearest Rebecca I have but a quarter of a minute to acknowledge your letter, and say how annoyed, and vexed I am to hear that you have not <u>yet</u> received the Books and will write Skeet a jobation[1] that will require a bottle of <u>Brandy</u>! instead of a <u>penny bun</u>! to recover him from. I was just going to fire you off a line to tell you of Lady Janes[2] marriage Lady Hotham having written to announce it to me – to my congratulations I <u>amiably</u> added – that it was not the least of my joy – the wormwood this good (in a worldly point of view) match would be to the <u>Parvenue</u>[3] "Juvenile Countess" as Chandos Pole[4] – undutifully calls his mother in law – Poor little thing I sincerely hope she may be happy but I should tremble for the sort of Husband – <u>his</u> fathers son would make- it is a love match (not the better for that) on both sides <u>her</u> poor mother is in great delight. – What you say of people passing sentence on books they have never read, and would not understand if they had, is so true that I wish you would have it placarded about in large four feet Blue and red letter sandwiches – with a man between to do the progression and circulation part of the <u>fact</u>. In a flash of lightening Ever your grateful and affect R Bulwer Lytton.

HALS
1.   'A reproof' (*OED*).
2.   Lady Jane Seymour Stanhope (see RBL, 20 April 1853) married George Henry Conyngham, third Marquess Conyngham (1825–82), on 17 June 1854.

3. Upstart (French).
4. This may be Edward Sacheverell Chandos-Pole (b. before 1834–73), who married into Lady Jane's family in 1850. His wife was Lady Anna Caroline Stanhope, daughter of Leicester Fitzgerald Charles Stanhope, fifth Earl of Harrington. His mother-in-law was Lady Elizabeth Stanhope, *née* Green (b. before 1816–98), Lady Jane's aunt. Parvenu literally means 'arrived' in French and may allude to the fact that Elizabeth Green had recently come from Jamaica where she had been brought up. Her name of 'Juvenile Countess' may refer to having been married in 1831 at the age of fifteen.

To Rebecca Ryves

Llangollen
Wednesday April 12th 1854

My dearest Rebecca One line in the greatest haste to say that I have just heard from Skeet – who says the reason (stupid why he did not say so at first) that he did not forward your copy sooner was – that as I had ordered him to pay the carriage – he found it so very expensive – that he wanted to get it conveyed free as far as Dublin – and that it was now on its way; but you had better ask for it as the Circulatory Library in Limerick,[1] than wait for this slow coach copy. My worries are again beginning – if that which never ends, can be said to re-commence, – Mrs Phillips whose soul – like most of the natives of the British Isles is made out of an old farthing – could not think of letting me remain here the summer as she thinks she could make or scrape so many more Two pence half pennies – by having a succession of occupants for my room – so on the 1st of May I have to turn out God knows where? for the Lodging houses here, are so wretched but the worst part of it to me is, that having paid her her quarter without a sou, to do it with, unless – I am paid by a periodical – which has no right to pay before the end of May – and I dont like to pester Skeet for an Instalment least <u>he</u> should make it a pretext for prematurely winding up the accounts of the book. Poor Mrs Tyler is very ill at Dr Lawries! that beast Eliza![2] having given her a wrench in dressing about 6 weeks ago – which makes her fear a rapture. – Good bye God Bless you – In haste and high pressure worry of every kind Your grateful and affect Rosina Bulwer Lytton

HALS
1. Limerick city is situated on the River Shannon in the mid-west of Ireland. Rebecca and RBL's relatives, the Massy family, are associated with Limerick.
2. Mrs Hardinge Tyler's lady's maid.

To Rebecca Ryves

Llangollen
Easter Monday April 16th 1854

My dearest Rebecca – I am so ill – coughing my lungs out, and spitting blood and worried in every way – that I can only thank you for your kind letter of the other day and tell you that you cannot long half as earnestly as I do – that at all events Skeet may be honest enough to give me where with all to liquidate some of those debts – which press the most heavily upon me – as I dont wish to figure in the same schedule as Mr Tom Lloyd.[1] – But I see and you will see by the <u>Assinarum</u>[2] which I send you – that the Press gang Juggernaut is at work to crush my poor book, with every lie they can invent. – It is easy to know <u>who</u> wrote <u>that</u> attack in the Ass – the <u>conscience</u> stricken – <u>àpropos de bottes</u>[3] dragging the scheme to prevent my getting my books published – into court – though I have never even <u>alluded</u> to <u>that</u> fact in this book, then the pains taken to assure "the pensive" or pe<u>nce</u>-give public that the book is so horribly dull – and so vulgar and that the characters are <u>unnaturally</u> drawn! though

"The head and frame of my offending" is, that the likenesses are so startling as to bring down all this <u>manly</u> and gentlemanlike abuse – on my devoted heart – you'll <u>see</u> the scene that is <u>not</u> <u>fit</u> for publication!!!! and this from men who be-praised and be-puffed that revoltingly coarse – and improper book "Jane Eyre" written by a <u>miss</u>[4] too – that equally coarse, and offensively vulgar book "Shirley"[5] and that revoltingly blasphemous book "The Wuthering heights!"[6] but then to besure the Bills as they call themselves

. – but the Miss Brontés – like genuine ...

... Happy Grandity! whose "maternal love" never got noticed at all except by <u>one</u> paper – which said the only sensible thing they could find in the book to quote was where Catherine said to some one "Do you chuse any Luncheon?" and certainly, it was Grandity's idea of <u>fiction</u> – as in <u>real</u> life <u>she</u> never asked any one such a question!

HALS
Incomplete letter.
1. A family friend of Rebecca Ryes, whose wedding is mentioned in RBL's letter of 4 January 1852.
2. RBL's mock pronunciation of the journal, the *Athenaeum*.
3. Turning to quite another subject (French).
4. Charlotte Brontë, who at this time was unmarried, had received favourable reviews for her first novel, *Jane Eyre*. See RBL, 11 March 1853.
5. Charlotte Brontë's second published novel was *Shirley* (1849).
6. *Wuthering Heights* (1847) was written by Charlotte Brontë's sister Emily.

To Rebecca Ryves

Llangollen
Tuesday 18ᵗʰ April 1854

My dearest Rebecca I have only this moment recieved your letter of the 15ᵗʰ
I assure you need not have asked me – as my first intention was – to send you
all I could the moment I got it; before as I need not tell you I cannot; – I
know too well from daily and hourly experience what your worries are; and
all this added to my own – nearly drove me mad – poverty is nothing – it is
debt that is the D—l¹ – though it is almost impossible to have the extreme of
the former – without being plunged nolens, volens² into a good eddy of the
latter – I am so ill to day I can scarcely hold up my head and am waiting for
Dr Price who however I feel can do me no good – beyond his extreme kindness in every way poor dear old man each little fan or trinket that he stumbles
upon of his poor wifes – who died two years ago – he sends to me – and a
fresh bouquet of flowers every morning. – Skeet though he owes me several
letters on business – does not write me a line – had I not lost the <u>power</u> of
hoping – I should augur from this, that the book <u>is</u> selling like wildfire for on
the least fillip of that sort Skeet is always in such a state of nervous exultation
– that he cannot put pen to paper – or even give a lucid order to Horrocks!
– I send you my Grandmothers Gazette the literary³ – one of Sir Liars <u>special</u>
tools – in which I am as grossly abused as usual, and all this! in return for my
extreme kindness to that infamous old Jerdan⁴ for years – and for my protection and generous defence of his mistress (and Sir Liar) that poor wretched
Letitia Landon⁵ whom I shielded against the whole world till her [ill] <u>proofs</u>
of her vicious career – became indisputable the <u>hint</u> at the end of the abuse
– that my Book is a fitter subject for <u>Lawyers and Doctors</u> – is a carrying out of
the Getting conspiracy – of my being perfectly <u>insane</u> that unredeemed ruffian
Sir Liar – has certainly aided by his infamous clique – done enough to make
me so; – but alas! I have not even that blessing – for in my case it <u>would</u> be one.
Dr Price writes me word that he has got a glorious! review of my book which
he will bring with him that will be something <u>new</u> at all events! – does not
Massy tell you that it is greatly abused? but <u>that</u> troubles me very little seeing
the <u>profound</u> contempt I have for the opinion of that concrete Ass the British
Public! provided it only <u>sells</u>: – you do not say whether you got the book? and
reading all those garbled reviews I will quite spoil it for you. Alas! you know
little of the granite grained with adamant of whic[h] Mrs Philips is made, if
you think that she, any more than Shylock⁶ will bate one <u>atom</u> of her pound of
flesh, or let me leave her house, without paying her to the uttermost <u>farthing</u>.
I think <u>even</u> Sir Liar would be severely punished for all this infamy could he
be only for <u>one</u> week racked with the complete torture he has doomed me to

for life – God forgive the wretch – and those who support him in his inhuman villainy ...

———————

HALS
Incomplete letter.
1. Devil.
2. Whether willing or unwilling (Latin).
3. RBL's mock name for the former editor of the *Literary Gazette*. See below, n. 4. On 15 April, RBL's novel *Behind the Scenes* received a hostile review in the *Literary Gazette and Journal of Science and Art*, pp. 347–9. The review opens: 'Previous works by this writer, and other antecedents, unhappily too well known to the public, render it unnecessasry to say more of this novel than that it is the most extraordinary that has yet appeared from the pen even of Lady Bulwer Lytton' (p. 347). It ends: 'What we have quoted will enable our readers to form some idea of a work, which may more fitly become subject of consultation for doctors and lawyers than for critics and reviewers' (p. 349).
4. William Jerdan was seventy-six years old at this time and had been editor of the *Literary Gazette* for thirty-four years until his retirement in 1850. See RBL, 29 April 1830.
5. Letitia Elizabeth Landon, the poet who published under the name of LEL, had been Jerdan's protégée. Her work had been much admired by EBL. See RBL, 23 January 1826.
6. In Shakespeare's play *The Merchant of Venice*, Shylock demands a pound of flesh from Antonio, who is in his debt.

To Rebecca Ryves

Llangollen
Wednesday April 26th 1854

My dearest Rebecca
    The first Bell is ringing for Church – so I have only time to say how annoyed I am at your not having yet got your Copy of the Book – and I have again written to Skeet – to dun him for an instalment for the beginning of next week – when I hope to let you have what you want – he <u>says</u> that he will do his <u>uttermost</u> to realise as much as he can for me – as my "cruel position – and honorable and indefatigable exertions – fill him(!) with respectful admiration and commiseration for me"! but that still I must bear in mind the widely organised and ever active conspiracy against me. – Vanquished by de Birards persuasions and the Editors <u>gold</u>! I have begun – writing – for the London Journal for little Tales[1] – of about 80 pages of my writing he pays me £25 – and says he will take as many tales as I can send him – as he is delighted with the one I have just sent him – and Paid away the £25 for me as an instalment yesterday – to one of my London Duns – this is miraculous pay for a Penny Paper – still alas! I have but one head, and one pair of hands – and when I think of <u>all</u> I have to pay and live besides – it is very like trying to empty the Sea with a Thimble. I don't suppose this Tale will appear for a fortnight – though the Editor has honorably paid for it, it is called "The Bromelia or Pensey Playfairs Pineapple Gown"[2] – I'm surprised he

should think it so good as I wrote it in two days – if you see it; you will percieve that I have stolen your pretty story about the "cohabiting"! and that it has lost nothing.

De Birard writes me word that he heard from a personage about a high quarter (The Duchess of Bedford[3] I suppose) that Sir Liar was furious – because the Queen had sent for my Book the moment it came out, and neither she nor Prince Albert think <u>me</u> such a monster! There goes the last church Bell so good bye, and God Bless you

Ever gratefully and affectly yours
Rosina Bulwer Lytton

HUNT

1. The *London Journal and Weekly Record of Literature, Science and Art* (1845–1912) was founded by George Stiff (see RBL, 29 December 1853) at a penny for thirty-two pages. It pioneered a deluge of popular illustrated journals.
2. RBL had insisted that the story be published anonymously, but to her dismay her initials appeared with the published version.
3. The Duchess of Bedford (*née* Lady Anna Maria Stanhope) (1783–1857) had been Queen Victoria's Lady of the Bedchamber between 1837 and 1841. She was married to Francis Russell, seventh Duke of Bedford (1788–1861).

To Rebecca Ryves

[29? April? 1854]

... in Town – says she will go to Fulham some day – and try and sift the matter. Only think of that infamous old Sternberg – whom I ordered last year – never to presume to write to me again; – after her expidition to Knebworth, and her insolent note to me upon Lady Hothams affair – writes to me the other day – (through Skeet) to say that if "My <u>Ladyship</u> would <u>honor</u> her with an interview – she had something of the highest! importance to communicate which she thinks I ought to know" – of this I need not tell you I shall not take the slightest notice, but it only shews how that contemptible Reptile Sir Liar – is trying it on, in all directions. I also send you Parkers[1] last (the old storey in which honorable mention is made of the brothers Bulwer when <u>will</u> the devil call in his mortgage upon those two Fiends? I was startled yesterday by seeing in The Times – "Death of the Member for Hertfordshire" – but it was Mr Halsey[2] – the other county member and not Sir Liar! – who perished with his wife, and children coming from Genoa[3] – but then to be sure even had Sir Liar been in the same boat, there would according to the Proverb, have been no chance as those who are born to be Hanged, are never drowned. – The Biddulphs before they went to Town the week before last, made a large dinner for me, and not <u>always</u> to refuse I accepted, but at the eleventh hour was obliged to send an excuse on account of my usual <u>chest</u> complaint, – as I had promised to stay a week there, – incessant hard labour without adequate remuniration worries – disappointments – and against ones <u>graineries</u> of every kind – does indeed make life so <u>bitter,</u> and heavy to bear, that I doubt if the Infernal regions can have any worse torments. – Dr Price is indeed a dear kind old man, and I dont know what poor Tibbie fine Eyes; and hims Mud would do without him. Remember me kindly to poor Massy when you write; What are the Kitcheners about? Has Georgina – gone off with Polly Hopkins yet? God Bless you my dearest Rebecca and with de Dogs innocent love Believe me Ever your grateful and affect

   Rosina Bulwer Lytton.

HALS
Incomplete letter.
1.   Godfrey Parker is claiming to be the son of General Bulwer's niece and the cousin of EBL. See RBL, 31 July 1857.
2.   Thomas Plumer Halsey (1815–54), heir to Great Gaddesden Place in Hertfordshire, along with his wife Frederica and their youngest son Ethelbert, was drowned on 24 April 1854 on the passage from Genoa to Marseille. Along with EBL and Sir Henry Meux, Halsey had been elected as a Tory MP for Hertfordshire in 1852.
3.   A city and a seaport in northern Italy.

To Mr Leyton

"Mr Barnes Alias Leyton M Mr Judas Iscariot New Road Llangollen"
[on envelope]

[May? 1854]

... but one of the most intensely interesting things I ever saw on any stage had little, or no Plot, being too long and intricate to have any – which was Eugéne Sues Mystères de Paris[1] – but what made it so thrillingly not to say breathlessly interesting next to the inimitable acting! which was nature itself – was the <u>dramatic effects</u> and constant <u>Coups de Théâtre</u>;[2] – the same as in a piece brought out at the Lyceum about two winters ago called "A Chain of Events" in which the author had done little in the way of plot and Charles Matthews[3] did every thing – by his perfect acting – and the stirring dramatic effect – and <u>well filled up</u> incidents of each scene But as you intend making Molière only a three act Drama I would suggest that you reserve the two scenes at page 107 – 8 – 9 –10 – 11 – 12 – 13 15 16 and 18 of the 3d vol of the novel where Molière discovers the Duc de Laugun[4] with his wife – and his scene with <u>her after</u>, – as the culminating point of the interest, – <u>and the conclusion of the play</u> having – for the filling up and comic portions of the drama – the scene at Louis quatorzes[5] "<u>En Cas de Nuit</u>"[6] where Molière and <u>Colbert</u>[7] sup with him: – The arrival of the Hawthorn

Family[8] at Paris where Mme de Sévigné[9] meets them at the "Golden Porringer" the scene in the <u>Près du clercs</u> between Rupert Singleton, and the man in the wax mask (Cartouche) and also the robbery of Courtin the Miser;[10] for the rest Molières <u>own</u> <u>soliloquys</u> – as in the novel, had best be made to tell the unsuspected Tragedy of the great comic actor, and authors own Life – which is where the <u>real</u> scope lies – for the genius of the Actor – who can at once concieve create and <u>represent</u> the character. I wish I could suggest anything better, but I cannot. I Have the Honor to be Sir your obedient servant

> Rosina Bulwer Lytton.

HALS

Incomplete letter.

1. Eugene Sue's *Les Mystères de Paris* (1842–3) is a novel set in the Paris slums.
2. Histrionic climaxes (French).
3. See RBL, 28 January 1853.
4. The plot of RBL's novel *The School for Husbands*. The title is taken from Molière's play, *L'École des maris* (*The School for Husbands*) first performed in 1661. The original title had been *Molière's Tragedy: His Life and Times* but RBL had to change it for marketing reasons.
5. Louis XIV's (French).
6. Literally: 'the affair of the night' (French), the name of an incident when food was brought to the bedside of Louis XIV in the presence of Molière and Colbert.
7. Jean-Baptiste Colbert (1619–83) served as the French Minister of Finance from 1665 to 1683 under the rule of King Louis XIV.
8. The family of Lucy Hawthorne. See RBL, 30 January 1853.
9. Marquise de Sévigné was a French aristocrat. See RBL, 30 January 1853.
10. Characters in RBL's novel *The School for Husbands*.

To Rebecca Ryves

> New Kennel Llangollen
> Tuesday May 2d 1854

My dearest Rebecca I write one line in great haste; to say that as I am tired of waiting for Skeet – and know by long <u>experience</u> the state you must be in – I have borrowed £10 to send you till I hear from him and now wish I had done so sooner – but the reason I do not like either to <u>hurry</u>, or to dun him is, that he might make my doing so a pretext for winding up accounts prematurely – and so mulct[1] me out of my lawful dues. – Pray let me know by <u>return of post</u> whether this reaches you safely? and Believe me with Innocences best love – in Electric flow and Haste Ever gratefully and affectly yours

> Rosina Bulwer Lytton.

HALS

1. Defraud.

To Rebecca Ryves

Llangollen
Tuesday May 9th 1854

My dearest Rebecca

Like Mrs Bousefield I have been <u>that</u> low![1] and <u>that</u> nervous! that any one might have knocked me down with a feather but nothing about my new kennel which is exceedingly nice, and comfortable, and moreover the only clean one I have been in here – the people are remarkably kind, and attentive – and my Landlord (the poor man whose large Factory was burnt down Xmas Eve (being a sort of genius – and man of taste had had made a most beautiful Book case (really in excellent taste) for himself – in his study below – but I having cast my affections upon it – found it transported (books and all though very large) into my sitting room the next day so that I feel a little more like home here; -but my worries are never to end; – for that loathsome reptile Sir Liar is again at his dirty work – and since my book came out, I have recieved the most scurrilous <u>anonymous</u> letters – purporting to be written by a <u>Reviewer</u>! and though blackguards as they mostly are – no reviewer would have penned such things! and from certain phrases in them they are evidently written by Sir Liar himself: – and in continuation of this dirty work The proprietor of The Weekly Times[2] – who is also that of the London Journal – was going to the Isle of Wight – and ordered that there should be – a flattering or as he was pleased to call it a just review of my book when lo! to his honor on his return he found the most abusive and unjust that had yet been! he instantly sent for the Reporter a man of the name of Ross and dismissed him from his service – when it came out that <u>he</u> (Ross) – had been bought over by the Morning Post – one of Sir Liars special tools – I'll send you the letter when I get them back – but I have sent them to Skeet for he ought if he was worth a farthing – make this officially authenticated piece of dirty work – <u>public</u> as it is – a sample of the manner in which nearly all the reviews of my books are <u>honorably</u> conducted. – But what has so completely upset me is a piece of villainy of a far deeper dye – at least I am morally certain, that such it will turn out to be – on Sunday morning I got a letter dated "Auckland Cottage North End Fulham"[3] and signed "Judith Blaine[4] Evidently not the note of a gentlewoman and the hand without any attempt at <u>disguise</u> the facsimile of Miss Gettings! – this note began by saying that the writer was the one seeking pecuniary assistance – but that the "writer had known my dear Emily[5] intimately and that from the tender manner she had often heard her speak of her mother she (Miss Blaine) had the greatest desire to know me – and if I was in or any where near London – she hoped I would grant her an interview if only for the sake of my child who had loved her the writer well" – this was sent through Skeet – and I think is merely a <u>ruse</u> of these infamous wretches – to find out if I am still here – as they do not even stop at desecrating my poor murdered childs grave to torture and insult me – so I replied – that although nothing would give me greater pleasure than to know any one whom my poor martyred child had loved – yet from the system of Espionnage – persecution – and guet – à-pens[6] her infamous father pursued towards me – I was very cautious of making acquaintances out of the regular routine and whose identity was not authenticated – and antecedents certified to me, and that I must be permitted to say it was <u>rather</u> strange she should never <u>before</u> all these years been seized with a desire to know me! but only at <u>this</u> particular <u>juncture</u> coming on the heels of all the recent spying and anonymous letters I had had, and that moreover her writing was most suspiciously like Sir Liars last spies Miss Getting. – this answer I did not put my address to but sent it to de Birard telling him to <u>take</u> it himself to Fulham – and find out – who? and what this person was – if indeed any such person lives there? When I get the letter back I will send it to you with one of Gettings – to shew you how like they are; – but Mr Ponsonby Ferrars[7] – is greatly Caricatured! is he not? as if any villainy but Sir Liars own <u>could</u> be its parallel. –

HUNT

1. See RBL, 1 April 1854.
2. The *Weekly Times*, a London newspaper of history, politics, literature, science and art (1847–85). George Stiff had been its proprietor along with the *London Journal*. See RBL, 29 December 1853.
3. The home of Judith Blaine. Fulham is an area in south-west London.
4. The governess of Emily Bulwer Lytton, while she was living with Mary Greene.
5. RBL's daughter Emily, who died in 1848.
6. Ambush [*guet apens*] (French).
7. The EBL character in RBL's novel *Behind the Scenes*.

To Rebecca Ryves

Llangollen
Saturday May 20th 1854

My dearest Rebecca – I am so ill from this Postscript of Winter and incessant worry that I can scarcely hold up my head to scribble you these few lines – and thank you for your kind letter received this morning. – It seems, that letter was not from the wretch Getting, or any of the gang but from a poor woman who had been governess to my poor Children when they were starved at that infamous Miss Greenes – I will send you her letters when I get them back from a person to whom I sent them as they contain a few additional traits of Sir Liar's infamy. – I send you <u>one</u> (not her first or her last) of that Mrs Wellington Boate's[1] letters – and 3 of her songs that she sent me, her first letter was thanking me cordially for having shown up that infamous clique her <u>last</u> (which I will send you next week) is full of the infamies of that Dunghill divinity Mr Charles Dickens– and the <u>Guilt</u> of Literature.[2] She says she is coming out with a Thunderer in 3 vols – in a few months" – wherein she will not deal with that infamous gang as tenderly as I have – God speed her undertaking say I. – I also send you a very kind note from dear old Mrs Hodgson. – Mrs Tyler had written to Mr Wheeler – asking him not to take that £100 of the principal each year – which he kindly agreed not to do – but I find that the Policies of Insurance being taken out only for one year <u>each</u> – <u>this</u> would only hamper me <u>more</u>- had it been but <u>One</u> policy for the whole ten years of the Principal! – but every thing seems to conspire to laden and hamper me as heavily as possible. No news from Skeet yet. – To be sure I know – that Miss Edwards,[3] she was that beast Mrs Sandby's governess – I am very sorry to hear she has turned out badly – I never knew any bad of her, except that like <u>all</u> English governesses – she spoke <u>bad</u> grammar – and vile bad English – such as the Dickens School of Literature(???) has now made patent she told me that girl she was governess to in Portland Place[4] was an Heiress, but a perfect <u>idiot</u> ...

HALS
Incomplete letter.
1. Mrs Edward Wellington Boate was a celebrated Irish songwriter. She published a collection of poems called *Nugae Canorae* (1847) and a novella, *The Maid of Avoca: or, the Maniacs Prophecy with Songs of the Camp* (1851) under her maiden name, Henrietta O'Neil. Two of her song lyrics that were published separately include: 'Come oh! come to me' (1852) and 'On! to the battle on!' (1852).
2. RBL's parodic name for the Guild of Literature and Art. See RBL, 5 October 1851.
3. Governess to the Sandy family of Flixton Vicarage in Suffolk. See RBL, 28 May 1853.
4. West End, London.

To Mr Leyton

M: Leyton Esqre Theatre Royal Reading Berks

Llangollen Denbighshire
May 21st 1854

Lady Bulwer Lytton Begs to inform Mr Leyton in reply to his letter of the 19th Instant: – that she intends remaining the summer at Llangollen. As for the difficulties which have sprung up with regard regard [*sic*] to Mr Leytons dramatising any novel of Lady Lytton's, <u>of course</u> they are the <u>usual</u> ones, ie – the dastardly underhand machinations of Sir Liar Coward Bulwer Lytton – that other Dunghill Divinity Mr Charles Dickens, and the rest of the votaries of Brandy and Blackguardism composing the Guild – or rather <u>Guilt</u> – for a most iniquitous <u>swindle</u> it is!) of "Literature, and Art" – of the <u>Art</u> there can be no doubt; – and doubtless Mr Robson does not deem it <u>politic</u> – to offend this gang by personating any character adapted from a work of Lady Lyttons; – otherwise, setting aside even his name, and fame, it is impossible to concieve, and certainly to <u>create</u>, a character of more intense – dramatic, and domestic interest than that of Molière. Lady Lytton is only sorry that Mr Leyton had not the fear of this iniquitous Gang – more properly before his Eyes – before he lead her into writing to Mme Gérard, and giving herself, and others so much useless trouble.

HALS

To Mr Leyton

M: Leyton Esqre Theatre Royal Reading Berks England

Llangollen Denbyshire
May 28th 1854

Sir I am sorry if any thing in my last note; annoyed you but considering the continual and <u>Occult</u> infamy I am enduring – from the Infamous **gang** comprising that most nefarious of modern swindles "The Guild of Literature"! I can only solve every enigma into <u>them</u>; untill my solution is proved to be erroneous, when I am always ready to apologise most humbly to those whom I have so grossly insulted as to have supposed them to have had directly – or indirectly, any communication with such a set of unprincipled Disreputables. I am well aware, that there being neither taste, feeling, nor instruction in "The British Public"! but an almost incredible amount of apathy, and ignorance! a great deal of coarse daubing <u>untrue</u> to nature is required on the English stage: – Witness that in the <u>Original</u> <u>French</u> <u>Piece</u> charming Play "The Lady of Lyons"[1] – wherein Claude Melnotte is <u>not</u> a dishonorable rascal – but writes a letter to Pauline,[2] frankly confessing his subterfuge; – but which letter for the sake of the plot of the play – is suppressed by the Mother, but at the <u>end</u> quite exonerates the Lover; – but witness into what a Rascal this honorable, and noble minded young man is changed for the English stage! – but then to besure, with regard to Rascality "They best can paint it who have practised it most"![3]

With regard to what you say of the passion of jealousy in general, – and Molières jealousy in particular I can only answer you as Shakespear would have answered Ben Jonson[4] – or Greene;[5] – had they told him that jealousy was either Comic; or Tragic, and that <u>therefore</u> he must make Othello's![6] jealousy have a dash of the comic in it! – he would have replied – "you are right, jealousy <u>is</u> either comic or tragic, – but Othello's jealousy was tragic, and therefore I cannot make it comic." –

I have no doubt that were you to make Molière a perfect Buffoon, it would suit the English stage and come up to English ideas of him (if they have any? –) much better; – but it would not be Molière the French Comic <u>Author</u>, and <u>Actor</u>, but intensely melancholy man. – And yet as Molière in society was the Prince of good Fellows, – and boon companions; – it appears to me, – that there is a fine scope, and nothing easier, than for a dramatic <u>Artist</u> to combine both attributes – by subtile, and delicate touches, – drawing a <u>connecting link</u>, – between the <u>surface</u>, and the <u>soul</u> of the man; fine masterly touches, so easy for an actor (who <u>is</u> an actor) to <u>embody</u> – or as the French say <u>create</u> – so difficult for an Author to <u>convey</u>. – I have nothing more to say on the subject. And Have the Honor to Be Sir your obedient servant

      Rosina Bulwer Lytton.

HALS
1.   EBL claims that the source of his romantic drama *The Lady of Lyons, or Love and Pride* (1838) is a tale by Helen Maria Williams, *The History of Perourou; or, The Bellows-Maker* (1801).
2.   Pauline Deschapelles.
3.   Alexander Pope, 'He best can paint 'em, who shall feel 'em most', *Eloisa to Abelard* (1717), l. 366.
4.   Shakespeare would have known Jonson as it seems likely that he played the part of Old Knowell in Jonson's *Every Man in His Humour* (1599).
5.   Robert Greene (*c.* 1560–92), one of the so-called 'University Wits', was a playwright and polemicist.
6.   The jealous Moor in Shakespeare's play *Othello*.

To Rebecca Ryves

Llangollen
Monday June 5th 1854

Many thanks My Dearest Rebecca for your very kind letter, for one feels doubly grateful for kindness in the midst of not exactly a magic – but a <u>black art</u> circle of the most unscrupulous villainy diabolical treachery – and fiendish persecution. I told you, or at least I intended to tell you – that Skeet had of course – sent me his statement of the number of the Edition he <u>pretended</u> to have published which <u>he</u> reported to be 375!! Copies – now as Bull[1] never published an Edition of less than 3000 of my Books, – and as we <u>know</u> that 375!!! would not supply the London libraries alone, much less Scotland, Ireland, the Provinces, India, and America – I wrote to de Birard– who knows a man acquainted with Skeets printer – to get out of him, the number – published now – Printers are always in league with the publishers – but Nugres not having been crammed for the Occasion – said being taken unawares, – and thinking to do it <u>thoroughly under the mark</u> in <u>Skeets Interest</u>; 500 – already a <u>considerable difference</u> as to

<u>profit</u> – for Skeets evident intention – in starting this ridiculous number of 375 – was to give me next to nothing – by making out that the expenses of printing and advertizing (which he <u>don't do</u>) had with his own percentage swallowed up the proceeds, – Now as I was hearing right and left that he had sold <u>me</u> as well as my book (the <u>whole</u> Edition of which he sold the first day of publication) and as every one said he would have been only <u>too glad for his own sake</u> to have gone instantly into a second Edition – had he not been bought over; – I wrote to him – a most kind, confiding and complimentary letter – telling him of these injurious reports, but adding – that notwithstanding – that they appeared to be confirmed – by his strange conduct in totally suppressing the book – after his so sanguinely expressed opinion of its success – and although his Printer owned to 500 copies which was rather different from his statement of 375 – yet nothing would make me believe him capable of such inhuman conduct (as this would be considering all the circumstances of the case, and the implicit confidence I had placed in him) unless it was confirmed by himself; and therefore I hoped <u>he</u> would give me the power of refuting this report every where ...

HALS

1. Edward Bull published RBL's first three novels: *Cheveley: or, The Man of Honour* (1839), *Budget of the Bubble Family* (1840) and *Bianca Cappello: An Historical Romance* (1843).

To Mrs R K Barnes[1]

Llangollen
Monday June 12th 1854

Lady Bulwer Lytton Presents her Compliments to Mrs R: K: Barnes and begs she will accept her best thanks for the "Galop"[2] which she has so kindly sent her and which <u>looks</u> exceedingly pretty. Lady Lytton is also exceedingly obliged to Mr Barnes for the Trout he was good enough to send her – and which were excellent

---

HALS

1. A guest at the Hand Hotel in Llangollen.
2. *Le galop* (an abbreviation of the original French term *galoppade*) is a lively country dance. It was introduced in the late 1820s to Parisian society by the Duchesse de Berry and became popular in Vienna, Berlin and London.

To Unknown

Llangollen
Friday June 16ᵗʰ 1854

Sir It would be very difficult (without you were there to show you the <u>many written authentic proofs of it</u>) to make you – or any other honest, honorable or gentlemanlike minded man, – <u>understand</u> the tangled web – and <u>occult</u> arcana of <u>widely</u> organized and <u>deeply planned</u> low – Blackguardism, and unscrupulous villainy – in which Sir Edward Bulwer Lytton indulges; – being not only a contemptible profligate, who has left no vice unexhausted, but what is <u>infinitely worse</u>, – a slimey Hypocrite, who has left no virtue <u>unassumed</u>! – therefore you are greatly mistaken in thinking – that <u>he is too far removed</u>! from the practical business part of the Green room to influence its decisions, or its proceedings – he is no – clumsy Tyro[1] in the black art of every villainy – and there would be no use in his having a <u>Gang</u> – if he were such a <u>bungler</u> as ever to be <u>seen</u> – or <u>detected in doing his own dirty work</u>. – That ineffable Blackguard and Charlatan Mr Charles Dickens,[2] – as well as Douglas Jerold[3] – are members of this gang – with again a numerous Legion – of subordinate <u>Shiri</u> – or hired Literary Assassins <u>under them</u>, and in <u>their</u> pay; – the system is to crush all rivals – in the fields of Literature, whether Dramatic or otherwise, – who are not <u>in</u> and of the clique, and to persuade that concrete Ass the British Public – by dint of incessant steam Engine puffery – and projectiles of cheap publications (which fill <u>their</u> pockets, and Brandy Bottles – but ruin literature as a profession)that the said public should confine itself exclusively to Sir E: B: Lyttons "brothel Philosophy" as a contemporary critic most justly calls it; – and Mr Dickens's Pothouse Philanthropy. –

Of Mr Douglas Jerold I know nothing – but was a great admirer of his works, – till my admiration was allay'd by being told that <u>he</u> solaced himself with the <u>manly</u> passtime of kicking his mother – which convinced me that the old Proverb was true of "Tell me your <u>company</u>; and I'll tell you who you are". – As for Mr Dickens – only that I am not at Liberty to divulge other persons – affairs I could shew you a long document wherein is circumstantially detailed step, by step, the Ruffianly – and cold blooded manner in which he effected a a [*sic*] poor authors ruin, and how – he manoeuvred till he contrived to get him turned out of house, and home, with the vain endeavour to re-possess himself – of a threat[e]ning letter he had had the cowardly rascality and folly! (in one of his drunken fits I suppose) to write him. – With regard to myself individually – there has been if possible rather more dirty work than usual done – about my last Book "Behind the Scenes" – <u>one</u> reporter was dismissed – from a paper – from having in open defiance to the Editors orders to write a favorable review of that book – written a most scurrilous attack upon it – and upon me – when it came out that he had been bought over by the "Guilt" – and that there is a low Pothouse in The Strand called "The Cheshire Cheese"[4] where these myrmidons of that infamous clique meet once a week the said Guilt, not only finding the supper and gin ad libitum but when any of them get dismissed for doing their dirty work, (as this man was) supporting them, till – they can get other employment. – One of the gang having peached to a literary friend of mine for there is no end to the Double Janus[5] black treachery of all these wretches – it also came out that about a fortnight ago forty of these Literary <u>Shiri</u> met; – to decide upon (<u>for their principals of course</u>) how they could more effectively and expeditiously <u>Crush me</u> those were the words on the minutes, and after sitting in committee for four hours, – upon this <u>important</u>! subject – the <u>Forty Thieves</u>![6] Could resolve upon no better plan than continuing – the long organized conspiracy – of giving out, in all directions that I was <u>quite insane</u>! – But to give you a better idea of the <u>pains</u> which the Captain of this Gang Sir E: B: Lytton takes – not to have his infamy brought home to him – and the fiend – like astuteness with which he carries on his plots here is "a taste of his quality" his <u>maitresse en Titre</u>[7] the infamous Miss Laura Deacon now calling herself Mrs Beaumont, the wretch – for whom I and my poor children – were turned out of our home, and made to submit to every species of privation, while she, and her vile Paramour, are wallowing in luxury. – <u>This</u> woman who had lived with half a dozen other men – the late Colonel King amongst the rest – by whom as well as by Sir E Lytton she has several children – this creature he sends about the world – gulling respectable people as a Virtuous Widow!!! and <u>she</u> passing her villainous keeper Sir Liar off – as the <u>Guardian</u> of her children!! – and this wretch is actually on a visit to the Yelvertons in Carnarvonshire[8] in her <u>rôle</u> of virtuous widow!! nor does the infamy end <u>here</u> for what is infinitely more iniquitous – is that her equally vicious sister Miss Caroline Deacon – who carries on the same <u>philanthropic</u> trade he has pensioned off by setting up in a young ladies school!! at Kensington – where she is patronized by all the <u>clergy</u>!! and where poor unfortunate parents are gulled, by the <u>highest</u> <u>testimonials</u> to Miss Deacons <u>respectability</u>!!!!! into sending their poor children Now there is a two fold motive in this unparalleled villainy which is to get himself puffed by these wretches – and his poor victim wife calumniated – and when these calumnies get about then comes the iced cucumber cant, which <u>he</u> unsuspected has so astutely organized of "Oh I did not hear it from Sir Edward, or from any of <u>his</u> set, or from any one <u>he</u> could possibly know; – I heard it from a lady on a visit to my friends the so as so's, or from Mrs this who has a daughter at school, at Kensington or from Mr That the Clergyman of such a place – and so on <u>ad infinitum</u>,[9] and <u>wheel</u> within wheel: and the infamous way the monster takes to spy me, and find out all I am doing – or intending to do -) so as to lay fresh snares for me – as he did through a <u>pretended</u> stock jobber who so cheated me – that the moment I had furnished my cottage at Old Brompton I had to sell every thing! and come and starve down here) is by sending his infamous mistresses and his bastards – to scrape acquaintance with me, under false pretences – as he did only last Autumn – when a vulgar old wretch and her daughter with his natural son <u>Arthur</u>[10] a child of five years old, called I suppose after his friend that other Patent Ruffian the present Duke of Wellington – came here and scraped acquaintance with me, under the pretext of being <u>Americans</u> – the daughter who to do her justice, could not look me in the face – soon took herself off (I believe <u>her</u> the person from what I have since heard – who is now living with Sir Liar in Park Lane) the old woman calling herself Mrs Pyke – but whose real name is Waller – remained with the child – and very soon after I became dreadfully ill, constant retching – and excruciating cramp in my stomach – and Dr Price, says – there can be <u>no</u> doubt she began by giving me small doses of slow poison – more especially as she said to Mrs Phillips – "Mind – if anything should happen to Lady Lytton – you get all the Drs, and nurses in the place – <u>I'll</u> take care you are well paid" – while to Brelisfort the head waitress she was always saying – "remember I <u>tell</u> you Lady Lytton is in a worse way – than you have any idea of – for with her skin and complexion it will be some time before it shews" – (what shews?!!!) In the midst of this, the old wretch got a severe illness herself – I little dreaming, who, or what she was nursed her through it; – and one night, after I had got her back to bed, after taking a Bath, she for the first time looking me straight in the face burst into tears, and clasping her hands said "Oh! no – no – I never can injure you!" – I hope you had no intention of doing so? said I – but I could get no more out of her – and the next day the child Arthur – let out that he had <u>three</u> Papapas!! (que ça!)[11] but that Sir Liar – was his <u>rich</u> papa I was determined the moment the old wretch was well to tax her with this infamy – but before I could do so she had lost her son (which I believe to be all a lie) and she was off to Paris to his funeral ...

HUNT

1. 'A novice' (*OED*).
2. Charles Dickens (1812–70) was a leading novelist and a vigorous social campaigner. He was a close friend of EBL who, as a novelist, proved himself to be a best-selling rival of Dickens during his lifetime.
3. Douglas Jerrold (1803–57) was a very successful playwright, who was close to Dickens and acted in his amateur acting troupe. His plays included *Black-Ey'd Susan* (1829) and *The Rent Day* (1832). He was also a leading journalist, being the lead writer for *Punch* in the first half of the 1840s and the owner of a couple of newspapers.
4. A seventeenth-century tavern, situated in Fleet Street, London, frequented by Charles Dickens and before him by Oliver Goldsmith and Dr Johnson.
5. Two-faced.
6. 'Ali Baba and the Forty Thieves' is a tale in *Arabian Nights*. See RBL, 14 October 1833.
7. Official mistress (French).
8. Hon. Mrs Yelverton lived at Whitland Abbey in Pembrokshire, south Wales.

9.　Endlessly.
10.　Arthur Lowndes. See RBL, 1 September 1853.
11.　How about that (French).

To Rebecca Ryves

Llangollen
Friday June 16th 1854

My dearest Rebecca

I am so ill, and so worn out with <u>incessant</u> writing which each mornings Post entails upon me that I have <u>literally</u> scarcely time or strength to thank you for your very kind letter between <u>treachery</u> and infamy of every kind I am really bowed to the earth – that rascal Skeet – after telling me and every body else that he had not a copy of my book left at the end of 4 months – the moment I demand my acct and say – I will myself bring out a 2d Edition sets to and advertises <u>one</u> (but obstinately persists in not advertising it in "<u>The Times</u>" the <u>only</u> paper it is the least use to advertise in) – and pretends to me that this 2d Edition is a few copies he has got back from agents! a <u>likely story</u> – my acct or the <u>printers</u> affidavit as to the number of copies printed – I <u>cannot</u> get from him though I have repeatedly asked for it – the wretch has paid £80 for me for stop gaps – but Mrs Boate[1] says by <u>his</u> <u>own</u> statement even he should have given me £200 redress I have none – for poor Mr Hyde is too ill to do any thing and Hodgson – would be the worst person in the world – to apply to as – he would advise me to submit to Skeets Cheating as he did to Allens from whom I have never heard more – because I was <u>firm</u> in <u>not</u> submitting to his imposition. – I <u>did</u> write to Harper[2] the great New York Publisher a week ago – but have no earthly hope from <u>that</u> or any other quarter as I have no doubt the dirty work has extended to <u>there</u> by this time. You will see that I am also plagued by Mr Leyton– it is so hard to make people understand that the iniquity against me is an organized – <u>widely organized and deeply rooted conspiracy</u> and <u>not</u> a mere tampering with this or that individual as they start up – but is all well planned and anticipated – all this I had to write him a voluminous explanation of yesterday – shewing him that Dickens and Jerold were the very pivots of the Clique

There is no use in my repeating to you my dearest Rebecca how doubly grieved I am at all this on your acct my only hope now being from the Play – and America if Hope it can be called??? – where hope there is none. – But what is chiefly worrying me to death at this moment is that paragraph at the end of Mrs Braines[3] last letter about the "<u>Pensioned Authoress</u>" I have written to her to say that I do not ask or want to know the authority or <u>how</u> she came by the information? but <u>imploring</u> her to let me know by return of post <u>exactly</u> what he passes relative to the Pensioned Authoress in conjunction with my name – and then

I shall be able to <u>judge</u> whether the clique were merely wreaking their spite on her for having tried to serve me? or whether she is <u>their</u> tool – employed to get me into a fresh snare – such as securing my papers under the pretext of writing my life – and so in true Literary fashion <u>betraying</u> <u>both</u> parties – <u>such</u> infamy would be incredible – with any wretches – save the scum of the earth connected with – that Infernal Machine the Press! When you read her last letters, I know you will say it is impossible, but then <u>you</u> Believed in Rathbone[4] long after I saw through his villainy As for me I have been so surfeited with gratuitous treachery – that I begin to doubt even my own shadow, which seems only to stalk beside me to betray me. De Birard would, or could do nothing with Sharpes,[5] or any other mag – he is the abject <u>tool</u> – of the Judas[6] of the "London Journal" – and is very angry that I will not be his <u>fool</u> – besides he is all brag and no stability. Send me back the two Irish Papers I send you – I wish I could send you some of the fine Peas, cucumbers and strawberries the Biddulphs kindly order to be sent to me while they are in Town God Bless you my dearest Rebecca and Grant He may soon have mercy on us all Ever your Grateful and affect

    Rosina Bulwer Lytton

HUNT
1.   Mrs E. Wellington Boate. See RBL, 20 May 1854 and 22 December 1857.
2.   Founded by James Harper (1795–1869) with his brother John, the publishing company's first great success was *Awful Disclosures by Maria Monk* (1836) by Theodore Dwight, which sold 300,000 copies.
3.   Miss Phillips was the governess of RBL's children at Cheltenham, while they were being looked after by Mary Greene. She discontinued when she married Mr Braine. By May 1854, she was living at Auckland Cottage, North End, Fulham Road, London.
4.   See RBL, 23 January 1856.
5.   *Sharpe's London Magazine of Entertainment and Instruction* (1852–70) had been a weekly periodical, which moved to being monthly in 1848. By the late 1850s, it had become more of a women's magazine.
6.   The proprietor was George Stiff. See RBL, 9 May 1854.

To Rebecca Ryves

Llangollen Union[1]
Monday July 3d 1854 Vide Almamack January Vide[2] Fire

My dearest Rebecca the kinder you are the more my regrets increase – but even regrets – however profound cannot kill! – or I should not have the misfortune of still being on this side of the grave to tell mine but I am really <u>far</u> on my way I hope to "The Land of the Lile" being <u>really</u> ill from all my worries – so ill – that I have neither heart nor strength to write and so send you my letters if you can make anything out of them which I cannot. – I shall be sincerely glad to see Mr and Mrs Wheeler – and have of course written to say that they must be my guests – as not being Lady Hotham I have not the fear of being ruined before my eyes – indeed there is that solitary advantage in being so – that one no longer fears the Advent of him – God grant however that that villainous fellow of The London Journal[3] may pay – me – or I shall be even a little more worried than usual. – after the Wheelers visit Dr Price has written a very sharp letter to de Birard to get me paid[4] as he got me into this insulting contract with this fellow – and I am determined not to write to either of them again – so he will have all the more leisure for toadying George and Lady Hotham. I have written to Mrs Boate to set the London Mr Norris[5] at Skeet – but don't expect any thing – to come of it but additional expense for me. – The longer one lives the more disgusted one is at the great difference people make between themselves and other people! When I sent her some time ago a statement of my terrible and unparalleled outrages – she sent me back some cold blooded twaddle, about her never making use of violent language! but always calling and treating men as Gentlemen! – however it seems she varies her rules when her pocket is touched! – I wrote her back word on that occasion that I never profaned the socially sacred title of gentleman – by applying it to Blackguards – I confess I have no opinion of her, as she seems all caprice, and Irish braggadocio: some time ago – she sent me a vulgar printed puff – stating – "A Life of Lady Bulwer Lyton will shortly appear – with a Portrait – written by a Peeress – with copious annotations written by a distinguished statesman" I wrote to implore that she would not publish any thing of the sort, as I did not want my stern truths invalidated by such barefaced falsehoods. As Sir Liar does go to the Zoological Gardens would to Heaven one of the Keepers would cage him with the other Tigers. It is some slight consolation to think that that wretch Mrs Beaumont is likely to be unmasked in Yorkshire,[6] – I suppose it is on the strength of her being a Queen that she passes herself off as the widow of a King![7] – And now with Innocences best love – good bye and God bless you my dearest Rebecca – and between a flash of lightening a clap of thunder – and a dun!!! (by far the worst of the three) Believe me ever your grateful and affect Rosina Bulwer Lytton

---

HALS

1. This may be a reference to the canal system since the Llangollen Canal leaves the Shropshire Union Canal, north of Nantwich in Cheshire, and proceeds through Shropshire farmlands, crossing the border into Wales near Chirk.
2. See … see (Latin). The entry on 'fire' in this annual book of ephemerae is probably from the *Illustrated London Almanack* for 1854.
3. The proprietor, George Stiff. See RBL to Rebecca Ryves, 16 June 1854.
4. RBL demanded payment of £21 for a second tale that was published in the *London Journal*. This was called 'The Soldier's Wife' and appeared in the issue for 25 November 1854, pp. 187–9. In the end, RBL recovered only £9.
5. He is probably connected to Robert Norris, who was the head of the Liverpool-based firm of solicitors, Norris and Sons. See RBL, 5 July 1854.

6. EBL was giving a talk at the Mechanics Institute in Leeds, a town in the county of York-shire. Mechanics institutes were educational establishments formed to provide education for working men and were used as 'libraries' for the adult working classes. In his speech delivered on 25 January, EBL expressed support for the institute and advocated adding classes for women. He indicated that he favoured local state-aided initiatives rather than a centralized free education available to all.

7. EBL's mistress Laura Deacon (alias Miss Beaumont) had lived with Colonel King as his mistress but had never been married to him.

To Rebecca Ryves

Llangollen Denbighshire
Wednesday July 5th 1854

My dearest Rebecca

As usual I have but a quarter of a minute, to thank you for your last kind letter and send Mrs Boates last Weathercock – for if you remember when I told her I had fared no better for having had a most stringent stamped agreement with that other swindler Shoberl, but on the contrary a great deal worse; she wrote me back word, that it was all the better that I had borne with Skeet, as I now came under the protection of the law between author, and Publisher, and that put Skeet from his conduct completely in my power! but now she wheels round again because Mr Norris of Liverpool – (who as a country solicitor knows no more than the Cow in the opposite field about the ins, & outs of publish-ing) said he feared I laboured under a disadvantage from not having a written agreement as long as I thought she was going to place the matter in the hands of some London solicitor I had some faint hope – now I confess I have none as she seems so terribly en l'air[1] like her talking of Skeet purchasing the Copyright of my book! even had he the capital to do so; which he has not: she forgets that I have no right to sell it to him , or any one else, till I get Harper's[2] answer from America, having given him the refusal of it: but all this is nothing new for I generally find when my volunteer advisers have stirred me up and made me thoroughly uncomfortable by pointing out, and aggravating all the evils of my position, and telling me how much more cleverly they would have acted under the circumstances they usually conclude by giving me the neither novel, nor sat-isfactory intelligence that nothing possibly can be done, but what I have already done: – and that I am precisely where I was – barring a little additional worry, waste of time, and waste of money. I think you will own that De Birards con-duct is even! more honorable and gentlemanlike at the end, than it was at the beginning – when I tell you that he has never even answered Dr Prices letter! – In one way I dread Mrs Wheelers visit, my ménage being monté[3] on the same unextensive plan as that of the maids of Honor in Harry the Eights[4] time; and consisting solely of a maid servant, and a spaniel! À propos[5] – I have not time to tell you of Mr Tibs profligate conduct, and how him went yesterday with hims mud to pay a visit at a Girls school – and how him lagged behind, and how after a long search him was found not <u>on</u>, nor <u>under</u>, but <u>in</u> one of the very prettiest of the girls beds! and how she defended him, <u>pour l'amour de ses beaux yeux</u>![6] nevertheless with hims capacious Puppy heart him unites hims love to that of your Grateful and affectionate Rosina Bulwer Lytton

---

HUNT

1.   Aloft (French).
2.   The New York publisher. See RBL to Rebecca Ryves, 16 June 1854.
3.   Household ... assembled (French).
4.   King Henry VIII (1491–1547).
5.   In connection with (French).
6.   For the love of his beautiful eyes (French).

To Rebecca Ryves

Llangollen
Wednesday July 12th 1854

My dearest Rebecca – I am so ill, in body and mind, and in such a state of dilapidation! that I only feel fit for Dogs meat, but Tib says <u>no</u> – de dogs are not cannibals, and therefore never eat their muds. – I send you Mrs Boates last rigmarole – and you will but wonder that I should be worried and annoyed, seeing that I never <u>can</u> get people to do <u>what</u> I ask them, and if they would but believe it I really know my own affairs best – and the Boates – pottering saves me nothing – as I shall of course have to pay them far more than a solicitor (for doing <u>nothing</u>) but worrying and keeping me in suspense I have <u>refused</u> to write that very silly letter they enclosed for me to copy – as that would put me completely at Skeets mercy by seeming totally to waive all claims save to what <u>he</u> chose to give me – so I have ordered Mr Norris to write to him a most sharp, and stringent letter saying that if he did not <u>instantly</u> comply with my most <u>moderate</u> and merciful demands – or rather <u>compromise</u> (for I only ask £10 more than the wretch offered to give me ie £110"0 and <u>that</u> to pay poor Miss Dickenson) I should instantly commence an action against him – and produce a file of the "Times" in court since February last to prove his lie!! about the advertisements and for his other barefaced falsehood!!! about my saying I would be content with £70!!! if I had ever said any thing so improbable! I must have made the statement in <u>writing</u> – as I had never stirred from Llangollen or he from King William St[1] since first the negotiation for the Publication of "Behind The Scenes" was mooted – and therefore I challenged him to produce every line I had ever written to him on the subject in open court when I on the other hand would produce the letter I had in my possession stating the Printers account to be 500 copies and should

subpoena two witnesses to swear to that fact: – I further instructed Mr Norris to warn him (Skeet) of what a sorry figure he would cut, not only in a court of justice – but with "The Trade" when it came out publicly that he had taken that notorious he had told me [*sic*] – I would not invest him with any discretionary power, and that nothing should be altered till it was first submitted to me, for curtailing a book, was one thing and mutilating it another – and the brilliant critique about the stale sprats! and of Bob Bunfus[2] not being a Ragamuffin when he is essentially so till redeemed – and of comparing him to that very mediocre piece of Mountebankry Sam Weller![3] to whom he, is as superior as the Koh-i-noor,[4] is to a Bristol stone![5] convinces, me, – how wide of the mark Skeets Critic! is of
"Reading in the spirit that the author writ."[6]
But the real English of the matter is; that Skeet wants to scrape as many pounds (L.S.D) off my bones in the printing as he can and this is what he has been driving at from the first. Be so good as to return me the wretches letters, and the Critique by return of Post. Yesterday little Helen Hyde,[7] came and paid me a long visit (with violets) by my bed side her father, was to return to Aller[8] to day: – she made me promise if I was able, I would drive over on Wednesday to have a long talk with Mr Hyde. – She is engaged to be married to "a friend of my brother Clarences" a Dr Dixon,[9] – who must be a very clever man, though only four & twenty; as he it was, who wrote that admirable work "The Fallacies of the Faculty"[10] but as the poor man is now at Cawnpoor – the execution is not to take place for 3 years. Just after she went, Miss Comer[11] came; so I asked her to go with me to Aller on Wednesday– if I am able to go – as I should be afraid to go all that way alone. She poor girl, is to be Executed on Wednesday week and came with an entreaty that I would do her a great favor neither more, nor less, than to go to the Dejûner![12] but I told her the exact truth, that I had no clothes to my back, and no back to put them on if I had – would I then drink her health, in a bottle of champagne if she sent it? "yes, that, I would! in two if she liked, and to break the disappointment; I promised faithfully to ask her to my next wedding when I meant to wear what I think instead of orange blossoms Brussels lace and all that rubbish ought to be the standard Execution costume; to wit, a wreath of nettles, surmounted by an Extinguisher – yrs affectly R B Lytton

---

HALS
1.   21 King William Street, Charing Cross, London.
2.   Bob Bumpus is a character in RBL's novel *The World and His Wife* (1858). See RBL, 17 June 1858.
3.   A fictional character in Charles Dickens's first novel, *The Pickwick Papers*, first serialized in 1836–7. Sam is Mr Pickwick's humerous Cockney servant.
4.   The Koh-i-noor was once the largest diamond in the world, originating in India. In 1877, it was seized to form part of the British Crown Jewels of England when the Prime Minister, Benjamin Disraeli, proclaimed Queen Victoria 'Empress of India' in 1877.

5. Bristol stone (rock crystal or brilliant crystals of quartz) was found in the mountain lime-stone near Bristol, and used to make ornaments and vases, etc. When polished, it was known as Bristol diamond.

6. 'A perfect judge will read each work of wit/ With the same spirit that its author writ;' Pope, *An Essay on Criticism* (1709), ll. 235–6.

7. Possibly, the daughter of Charles Hyde, RBL's lawyer.

8. A parish in the hundred of Somerton, in the county of Somerset, two miles north-west of Langport.

9. This is a misspelling for Samuel Dickson, M.D. (1802–69), a London doctor, who campaigned against blood-letting.

10. Samuel Dickson, *Fallacies of the Faculty being the Spirit of the Chrono-Thermal System. In a series of Lectures* (1839).

11. See RBL, 16 April 1857.

12. Dinner (French).

To Rebecca Ryves

Llangollen Denbeighshire
Monday July17th 1854

a <u>real</u> July day at last!

My dearest Rebecca

You will not wonder at my being worried to death when you read the inclosed rubbish from that disgusting false weathercock of a woman[1] with her eternal parade! of all she does! when in reality she does nothing but worry, and annoy one and tell lies – one contradicting each other in the most idiotic manner: – I wrote her back word, that had she said all this at <u>first</u> my laziness – and my ill health might have yielded to it against my judgement; but as on the <u>contrary</u> she took – such pains to point out how completely Skeet from his frauds was at my mercy – and <u>urged</u> me so strenuously to expose him – I could not after having followed this advice – put myself so <u>completely</u> in Skeets power as to <u>return</u> to a paper war with him, in my own person! there by proving to him my utter destitution of all decision – and all help – by shewing him that I had not even the felons resource, of an appeal to a Lawyer – that she was <u>quite</u> <u>wrong</u> about a stringent Lawyers letter to him entailing upon me, the enevitable necessity of bringing an action against him – and <u>more</u> wrong still in saying that I could do nothing! as I had not his account!! – as my motive for getting that Lawyers letter written to him was to peremptorily <u>demand</u> that account, which all <u>fair</u> means had failed to elicit from him – and to shew him the pretty figure his complex frauds would cut in a court of justice – where I was determined to see him for the <u>full</u> amount of what he owed me – if he – did not immediately close with the very moderate and merciful compromise I had offered him: – I also told her ...

HUNT
Incomplete letter.
1. Mrs Boate.

To Rebecca Ryves

Llangollen
Tuesday August 29th 1854 My St Bartholomew![1]
Alias the anniversary of my Wedding day!

You have no doubt been thinking my dearest Rebecca that I have at length! succeeded in achieving two of my wishes – ie – dying – and being buried – but no – I cannot manage even that – I have only had a mountain of additional worry – these beastly people – according to the usual practise of Lodging house keepers – who never can impose upon one enough in every way the moment Mrs Wheeler was gone on account of the little additional trouble they had had (although they were well paid for it) were so insolent nothing could be like it, broke through their agreement said I couldnt have Mrs Braine here – and that I must leave the 4th of September – instead of in November when my quarter would be up – There was I as usual without a sou![2] or knowing where to get one – and a fine trumpy[3] bill to pay on account of Mrs Wheelers visit – and Mrs Phillips not able to take me till the middle of October – and every Lodging full to the Eaves – but Mrs Phillips wonderful to say – (and if you knew how stingy – and what grasping wretches the Welsh are in general – and she is in particular) you would think it wonderful! sent me a very kind message through her daughter to say that if these peoples shameful conduct plunged me in any pecuniary embarrassment, as she feared it would to call upon her for any sum I wanted – The Wheelers too – very kindly wanted to come to my assistance but that I would have starved sooner than have accepted – it would have been so like making them pay for their visit: so at last poor Dr Price got me £30 from his Barber to be repaid in October, at only the rate of 5 percent interest, which will be but a few shillings – still it is this for ever forestalling my beggarly Parish allowance from unavoidable contretemps– that so completely crushes and swamps me – beyond the power of ever getting my head above water – combined with being swindled and cheated by every wretch whose pockets I work to fill – because from my miserable, and unparalleled position they know I am at their mercy to swindle and betray as they please I have at length succeeded in getting two miserable Pokey dirty rooms – higher ...

HALS
Incomplete letter.
1. St Bartholomew's Massacre, the mass murder of French Huguenots, began on St Bartholomew's Day, 24 August 1572.
2. French coin of little value, worth five centimes.
3. An abbreviation of trumpery meaning 'deceit, fraud, imposture, trickery' (*OED*).

To Rebecca Ryves

Llangollen
Wednesday August 30th 1854

My dearest Rebecca When I wrote yesterday I meant also to have enclosed you the accompanying letter from Mrs Braine: – the <u>last</u>, which I said I could not send you; – was merely again stating the history of Sir Liars wanting to get the Woman Beaumont married the same as in Mrs Braines other letter only more explicitly than it is stated in the letter I sent you which paragraph I copied out for you but the letter itself I got her to write with fuller details that I might send it into Yorkshire. As I told Mrs Braine I think it must be one of William Bulwers[1] sons who is going to be married – for Sir liar is by far too much of a Bashaw to allow his poor fool of a son to marry first, for fear of its making him (Sir Liar) appear too old! 2dly because his doing so, would establish him independently as a man: and lastly and <u>above all</u> if he married a <u>Christian</u> woman, she might put some touch of human feeling into him and remind him of his duty towards God which would considerably endanger the pestiferous influence of his patent ruffian of a father: – things come strange about in this world – Dr Price had been to Valle Crucis Abbey[2] the other day with one of the members of the Archaeological society – when he returned he told me that Miss Lloyd (the person who shows it) after asking after "that poor dear <u>h</u>injured <u>h</u>angel Lady Lytton" said she had heard enough of Sir E's villainy the other day – from a young man of the name of Fitzgerald[3] who when he saw my name in the visitors book at the Abbey – burst out into a paroxysm of indignation at the treatment I had had from my monster Husband – & said he had been at Harrow with that poor wretched boy of mine – and was his most intimate friend there – that one day about 4 years ago he (my boy) had locked himself into his room which he was pacing like a maniac and sobbing as if his heart would break – as he would not let Fitzgerald in the latter broke open the door, and said "good God! Lytton what on earth is the matter with you?" he was a long time before he would tell him – at length he said "Oh! Fitzgerald I adore my mother, and I had written to her telling her so, – but my Father who watches, and finds out everything – has found it out – intercepted the letter and has been here playing the very D—l"[4] I as you may suppose went over to Valle Crucis the next day and saw Miss Lloyd who confirmed this statement (how strange! that the boy himself <u>never has though</u>! or even shown one human feeling towards his poor outraged mother) she also told me much more about his being so clever (faugh!) and writing beautiful Poetry – but his father never allowing him to feature in any of the Harrow speeches – Oh! no the same crushing system that has been exercised so brutally and effectually towards the mother, is of course extended to her son however – thank Heaven it <u>must</u> soon end now, for I cannot bear much more crushing – and this being <u>alone</u> from morning till night with such a world of misery on my shoulders – and so ill in body, as well as mind, without even a maid! – is really more than I can bear up under much longer: – nevertheless, I do not feel at all tempted to accept Mrs Braines proposition of living with them; as to tell you the truth I am tired of being made use – of – and hate the fetter, and false position of being with those sort of <u>soi disant</u>[5] Ladies and Gentlemen, – besides with such a tribe of children as she has, I should be distracted with noise, and ruined in presents. – as you may like to know how Chalon and <u>John</u>[6] are going on; I <u>t</u>hend you <u>hit</u>h last very impertinent of him talking of <u>his</u> Dogs eyes! when he has seen mine – which out Topaz those of bright Canis![7] Itself! God Bless you my dearest Rebecca Ever your grateful and affect Rosina Bulwer Lytton

---

HALS
1. The first of William Bulwer's sons to marry was William, the eldest, who married Mary-Anne Dering Lee-Warner on 5 July 1855. They were engaged on 8 March 1855 after William, who had been fighting in the Crimean War, had been repatriated after being wounded in his hand on 20 August 1854.
2. This thirteenth-century ruined Cistercian Abbey, is situated beneath Llangollen's steep – sided mountain.
3. This is likely to be Robert Allan Fitzgerald (1834–81), a cricketer, who wrote books on cricket. He was educated at Harrow School from 1847 to 1852. RBL's son, Robert, started at Harrow in 1846, where he remained for at least the following three years. Both boys were in the same house called The Park.
4. Devil.
5. So-called (French).
6. John James Chalon (1778–1854) is the brother of Alfred. He was also a painter and elected a Royal Academician in 1841.The brothers were co-founders of the Sketching Society.
7. Dog (Latin).

To Rebecca Ryves

Llangollen
Thursday September 7th 1854

I cannot tell you

My dearest Rebecca how your letters add to my misery – to think I can do <u>nothing</u> to help you, or lighten your burden in any way but God knows (who has packed it) my own is <u>so</u> heavy – so daily getting heavier that I really do not think I can cumber the earth much longer. – As for me I don't believe a word of that beautiful <u>myth</u> – about Sir Liars <u>worthy</u> sons affection for his mother as for that Mrs Fitzgeralds[1] not coming to see me – as you grow older you will daily find the <u>truth</u> of what I have so often told you ie that there is not <u>one</u> touch of human feeling in the natives of the United Kingdoms from one end to the other – <u>Any</u>

Foreigner not excepting a South Sea Savage – would have <u>even</u> gone 20 miles out of his way to see me under the circumstances – much less have inhabited the same Town for a week <u>without</u> doing so. – I was also at first much mystified with Mrs Braines version of Miss Laura Deacon – alias Beaumont[2] too – but this is what it means – Col King[3] the man who formerly kept her – and from whom Sir Liar took her, is <u>not</u> dead (but even <u>his</u> real name is not King – and <u>he</u> had also deserted <u>his</u> wife) so it is vice upon vice, and lie upon lie – the taking the <u>name</u> of Beaumont was only to swamp the name of Deacon and put me on a wrong scent – of course there <u>never</u> was any Mr Beaumont – and the story about him and his death is only got up to palm Sir Liar off on the sapient! and <u>virtuous</u>!!! British Public as Guardian to his own and other mens Bastards it appears by her letter of to day which I send you that her informant (I mean Mrs Braines) is some servant companion – or hanger on of that vile old Hell hag Lady Morgans. – Yes thank you send me back all the letters quite safely. – Forgive this scrawl – but I write in bed with a nervous fever from an accumulation of worries – and utter hopelessness about all the things – I put that Stiff affair into good Mr Hodgsons hands to try and get me my money – the wretch wants to Cheat me out of £10 – and make out that I agreed to give me name for £25 – but as Mr Hodgson says – there are all his and his much more infamous doer of dirty work that ungrateful old de Birards letters to prove to the Contrary – but no doubt as usual they will succeed in cheating me – as for the Skeet affair it is also dawdling on – for of course the more letters there are about nothing the more 6s 8d I shall have to pay. I am sorry to still hear such indifferent accts about poor Massy – but what have the poor to do <u>but suffer</u> in <u>every way</u>? <u>he</u> would be horrified at the desecration of Byron! in this house – where there is the full length portrait of him in the sailors dress with the boat – hung up all smoke dried, and fly blown! in the Kitchen!!! but he is in good company as on the Chimney piece are busts of Shakespear! and Milton[4] – the old woman – who is quite an original – and moreover a good old fashioned body spinning her own sheets – and many a long yarn besides – speaking of these busts the other day which are now painted oak color – said "Ah! they <u>wur</u> plaister, – but I went to wash un, – and the shoulder of that <u>ere fur chap</u> (pointing with her thumb over her shoulder to Milton) <u>come</u> clean off." Her figure is the <u>facsimile</u> of Lady Hothams only she has a very pretty old face – speaking of the finery and over dress of my late stuck up Landlady – and the rest of that class here she said "Ah my Lady – I cant afford it – for such doings rubs all the <u>goold</u> off the gingerbread!" She always wears a good black stuff gown and a snow white lawn handkerchief pinned corner ways – with one of Lady Hothams <u>Betty</u> caps. The <u>cooking</u> – which this good old fashioned body does herself – and knows how to do is excellent and the food <u>plentiful</u>, and <u>varied</u> not always mutton! My bedroom is large, and airy which reconciles me to the Pokery of the rest of the house. – poor Innocence! was stung with a wasp yesterday and he <u>did</u> pity himseps! even more den hims mud pitied him though that was great big much –.

> With his best love Believe me
> Ever my dearest Rebecca
> your grateful and affect
> R B Lytton

<u>No</u> of course I never hear from the Tylers

HALS
1.   Possibly a relative of Mr Fitzgerald. See RBL, 8 June 1836.
2.   EBL's mistress Laura Deacon was also known as Mrs Beaumont.
3.   Colonel King. See 0DO73RR21.
4.   Both William Shakespeare (bap. 1564–1616), the pre-eminent playwright, and the poet John Milton (1608–74) were popular icons.

To Rebecca Ryves

Llangollen
Saturday September 30th 1854

My dearest Rebecca I was very glad to hear from you again, – though alas! you like myself are always dans les tristes – à pattes du désespoir![1] and I am truly grieved to hear such continued bad accounts of poor Massy – with that heaviest of all Mill-stones round his neck – poverty! to prevent his finding even suitable <u>air</u> to live upon – God – help us – for no one else will. – Long ere this you have got my dismal honour of a letter; well since I wrote it "The Town ladies"[2] or vice versa have taken their departure I suppose finding the place too hot for them as every one was open mouthed at their goings on. It is very odd – I who never used to dream the wretch have the most horrible! and Characteristic dreams of Sir Liar which I have now been tormented with for nine nights running – and Miss Williams[3] – my little factotum[4] – dreamt the other night that <u>I</u> was going to be married – and dressed in the most exquisitely pure & dazzling white which the old women wise in the mystery of dreams – say, is a sure sign that he – or I will die soon:- Brellesford[5] the waitress of "The Hand" told William that an old lady who had been staying at the Hotel this summer said she had seen him lately, and never saw such an object in her life! – that he looked <u>90</u>! and was literally bent <u>double</u> I asked Mrs Biddulph if she had seen him in Town. She confirmed this account by saying yes. – that she had seen him at a State Ball, and such an object of premature decrepitude & decay she had never beheld. – I have...

HALS
Incomplete letter.
1.   In the midst of sadness – and on the brink of despair (French).

2.   This may be a reference to Mrs Barnes and her maid.
3.   She became RBL's lady's maid.
4.   'Jack of all trades' (*OED*).
5.   Sarah Brellesford was a waitress at the Hand Hotel in Llangollen.

To Rebecca Ryves

Llangollen
Monday October 9th 1854

My dearest Rebecca The reason that you have not heard from me before is that I have again been ill, very ill, and giving poor Dr Price a great deal of trouble, without getting much better, the fact is, I am daily dying a lingering moral death and have no hope of release – or relief from any quarter, not even from the only sure one – Heaven – which seems to have abandoned me – in order (for no doubt some <u>ultimately</u> wise purpose) to let villainy reign triumphant. What frets me next to you more than anything – is that I am now £15 in arrear to poor Miss Dickenson – Mr Norris's bill for doing <u>worse</u> than nothing injuring me in every possible way – is £8"3"6 – ! the £35 I borrowed to pay those infamous people to come here – and my six weeks here about £13 – nor does the drag end <u>there</u> – for Byrne to whom I <u>owe</u> £3 – sent me in with a civil dun – a fang bill of £11!! – <u>luckily</u> I have my account book here with me – and in it every separate item of this bill <u>paid</u> with <u>her own receipt to it</u> at Hans Place in 1851 – <u>this</u> I sent her "she was extremely sorry such a <u>mistake</u>! should have occurred – but left it entirely to my Ladyship" which of course is only a clever way of getting the money out of me – really that woman (like most tipplers is a Horse leech – for after having like a fool left myself without a farthing – to help that ungrateful worthless de Birard – I was obliged to borrow £10 from Byrne to come down here – for which I gave her when I <u>repaid it</u> at the end of a <u>fortnight</u> £3 – far more than Jews interest and "only one Halfpenny worth of bread to all this sack!" – or in other words – only my parish allowance of £47! to pay this £67 – with, – besides other innumerable duns! – but it is a wonder as Lady Hotham would say and the unfeeling Legion of her class, – that in this cheap place – I don't save a fortune! is it not? with such a necklace of millstones – oh! verily I am sick – sick to death of it all – I send you poor Hydes last kind letter which will show you what a forlorn hope Skeets affair is – the Stiff business I put into good Mr Hodgsons hands promising that I must <u>insist</u> upon paying him for it – here is the way in which that ineffable Blackguard Stiff contrived to cheat me – his decoy letter told me to state my <u>own</u> terms I asked as I think I told you £25 <u>without</u> my name which he sent me by return of post <u>before</u> the Tale[1] was printed – this Tale consisted of 5 chapters – the 2d I sent him had only <u>3</u> – therefore I only asked £15 what does the Jew do? – but condense them into 2 – and though by the original stipulation of £25 a tale I had a right to that sum the Chevaliers[2] Humbugging letters – that he (Stiff) would pay me more in proportion for shorter Tales – on the strength of the 2 chapters the fellow only pays me £10! and as but for Mr Hodgson I should not even have got that out of the swindler – I sent Mr H £5 – which he would not accept saying his conscience would not allow him to take more than £2 – so the other £8 went to pay a pressing London Dun To add to all this, – I am just now particularly sick – like every body else – at that loathsome Hypocrite – and ridiculous mountebank Sir Liars Crocodile tears! about Mr Halsey![3] (whose death mind you puts him at the head of the Pole so you may guess how sincere! they are) at the Hertford Agricultural Dinner – it is universally considered with unmitigated disgust that this piece of funereal humbug out Richards that of Richard the third.[4] dear! sweet! amiable soul that he is! (moral! above all) it is now ascertained without a doubt, that the soi-disant[5] Mrs Barnes and her maid(?) were street walkers[6] – and the people here are furious about it I am very glad you have better accounts of poor Massy – and not sorry to hear that the Tylers are abroad as the £25 I still owe Mrs Tyler for the redemption of my Bracelets – is another, and by no means the least of my Mill stones – Oh! why! why! when one has nothing to live on – or for! – cannot one die? I cannot tell you what a nervous – morbid dread I have of that Mrs Braine being a continuation of the plot – it seems so strange that in all these years – she never sought me out before – and every one that comes near me seems only to do so – to injure, to defraud, or to betray me, but I ought not to add to your sorrows by boring you with all these horrors! and yet if I don't write about them what have I to write about? God Bless you my dearest Rebecca – send you better days, and End mine soon – and with darkling starry Eyes best love – and a snap of the fingers for Cupid! Believe me Ever your grateful and affect Rosina Bulwer Lytton.

I suppose about the 15th I shall go back to the Inn and then that Mrs Braine will come, which I can very ill afford

---

HALS
1. See RBL, 26 April 1854.
2. Chevalier de Birard.
3. The death of the Herfordshire MP. See RBL, 29 April 1854.
4. This may be the scene in Shakespeare's play *Richard III*, when Richard woos Lady Anne over the coffin of her dead husband, Edward, Prince of Wales, whose death he had instigated. The expression to 'out-Richard Richard III' echoes Shakespeare's 'out-Herods Herod' in *Hamlet*, III.ii.14.
5. So-called (French).
6. RBL is slurring the woman and her maid as prostitutes, who she claims were spying on her for EBL. She described them in unflattering terms in her memoir, *A Blighted Life: A True Story*, 2nd edn, ed. Marie Mulvey-Roberts (Bristol: Thoemmes Press, 1994), p. 13.

To Rebecca Ryves

Llangollen Workhouse
Monday October 16th 1854

My dearest Rebecca Your letter had pained me more than I have any words to express – from my total inability to help you being precisely in the same penniless state – with the addition of a mill-stone of debts which are killing – and crushing me – and no hope of chance – or hope of ever being able to pay. Gladly would I send you more – but on Saturday every <u>sou</u>[1] of the Parish allowance was paid away and poor Miss Dickenson still unpaid! which of course will be productive of serious annoyance to me – I was ashamed to go to Dr Price again just after having paid him the £35 he lent me to meet the conspiracy that haunted me out of my last shelter – so I have borrowed £2 from Miss Williams – the little woman works for me – and wanted to borrow £5 – to send you – but she had not got it – men indeed are to be envied! under <u>all</u> circumstances – for they <u>can</u> go and be killed which is called glory which <u>we</u> cannot. I for one would rather be shot than have to go back to that hard unfeeling grasping Mrs Phillips – whom – I feel convinced – would sell me body and soul – for Half a crown if any fresh villainy happens there – and who has insulted me twice by turning me out of her Inn when it suited her pocket to do so – so that altogether it is a great gulp to be <u>compelled</u> by the Tyrant <u>necessity</u>! to return to her – but such are some of the grinding delights of Beggary! I am more over laid up with a severe cold – unable to move without screaming from this vault like bedroom in which I cannot have a fire on account of the smoke – and in this state I have the pleasure of packing up – and returning to the Hand; – and as my cup of <u>delights</u> is never full enough – poor Mr Hodgson like all people who do business for me has <u>bungled</u> the <u>giving away</u> of my furniture so much – that – that grasping Scotch shark Mr Campbell – wants to cheat Mr Chew my Landlord out of his fixtures – ie – the dresser!! in the kitchen – the <u>double</u> doors! which I put up between the drawing rooms – and the <u>fixed</u> Venetian blinds <u>outside</u> the windows which Chew put – up. My French blinds that cost me £10 the Jew Campbell had with all the rest of my beautiful furniture for <u>nothing</u>! and poor Mr Hodgsons <u>advice</u>! would be to pay this gross extortion (£20) rather than dispute it – but where in Gods name am I to get all the £20 – £30 – and £10 – I am so ceaselessly and remorselessly cheated out of? if it does not please God to end my life and misery soon I really shall go mad under the never ending persecution and ever increasing difficulties I have to encounter – with strength of body – and mind daily failing me – but what kind creatures rich friends are! are they not? – The two to me most touching incidents of the war[2] are the poor young Russian officer found dead on the battle-field – with his calm happy face – and his hands clasped in prayer – and the other poor dead Russian with his poor innocent little dog – sitting between his feet – whom no entreaties could lure away from his dead master! this I read out to Innocence and me thinks him understood it as de tears welled up in hims big booty eyes. – Poor Massy! I am very sorry for him – and yet envy him his chance. – A friend of that vulgar heartless Mrs Disraeli, and a Toady of Dizzy's[3] – who has of <u>course</u> forgotten my existence for the last 14 years – coolly writes me a flummerising letter on Saturday (her husband is member for Bedford[4] and being a conservative most likely a toady of Sir Liars!) asking me to Edit a novel for her niece![5] I told her if she wanted the book well, and effectually crushed by paid for abuse – I would, – truly this <u>is</u> a disgusting world! but till I am out of it Believe me my dearest Rebecca with sincere prayers and every good wish though no single hope! your grateful and affect Rosina Bulwer Lytton

---

HALS
1. French coin of little value, worth five centimes.
2. The Crimean War (1854–6) was fought between Imperial Russia and an alliance of France, Britain and the Ottoman Empire.
3. Benjamin Disraeli.
4. William Stuart was the Tory MP for Bedford in 1854 and 1859.
5. RBL worked on a novel with Emma Robinson (1814–90), entitled *Mauleverer's Divorce: A Story of Woman's Wrongs* (1857).

To Rebecca Ryves

Phillip's Hotel Langollen <u>Cemetery</u>
Friday November 17th 1854

My dearest Rebecca I have indeed been ill and so bowed down in mind – that I had not the least wish to add to your miseries – by telling you mine. Your letter of the 13th which I have only this moment received– made my heart stand still with joy when I read about the £700 a year – however it soon began to beat again – when I came to the sedative £100! Still even a crumb when one is starving – one is thankful for – moreover – good fortune like ill – when once it makes to itself an opening however small – is apt to be followed by more, which I sincerely hope may be the case with you and yours – if ever I hear from the Tylers again I shall be sure to say what you wish respecting this windfall – but I hear they are abroad, and never hear from them – neither have I heard from Mrs Wheeler since she left this but twice – while she was here – I tried hard to get her to ask Mr Wheeler – to speculate as far as £20 went for me as my <u>last</u> and only hopes of ever getting my head above water – but the answer was that he never speculated! though we know people on the stock exchange must do something of the kind. I don't know whether I told you that – that skinflint Mrs Campbell wanted – to claim all Mr Chews fixtures – and has pounced upon my poor handsome old

carved glass (the only thing I reserved from the wreck!) till he is indemnified
for them and poor Mr Hodgson as usual is letting me go to the wall – not a line
from Mr Hyde! so whether he is doing anything with Cheat I know not – I see
the latter has got another victim to publish with him a Mrs Hubback[1] who has
brought out a book called "May and December".[2] 3 weeks ago I had another letter from that Mr Leyton from the Theatre Royal Aberdeen[3] saying that a press
of business had prevented him completing his task sooner – but that in another
week the Play would be fit to submit to a manager & that then he might require
to have an interview with me – since then I have heard no more – and cannot
divest myself of the idea that the whole affair is one of that Fiend Sir Liars iniquities. However things being now at the worst with me – without one ray of hope
from any quarter I am spiritually speaking resigned to Gods will – be it what it
may; but the human phase of this resignation is very little despair as I have ceased
even to pray with Olianna.
"Tho' but a shadow, but a sliding
Let me know some little joy,
We that suffer long annoy
Are contented with a thought
Through an idle fancy wrought,
Oh! let my joys have some abiding"![4]
When Xmas comes what I <u>am</u> to do; God only knows – for I know not. – I hope
Pan may be of service to poor Massy added to the <u>moral</u> ray of sunshine of the
£100 a year. – I suppose your brother William has given up the idea of going to
the Crimea,[5] as you say nothing further about it; pray magnify by <u>implication</u>
the £100 to £1000 a year that Grandity may sit down and sulk – not indeed
under the shadow of her own Fig tree, but under that of her own nose! which
far exceeds in dimensions any fig tree I ever saw – though no one would give a
fig for it. I had a long letter from poor Mme Alphonse yesterday in which she
desires many remembrances to Miss <u>Reeves</u> as she always <u>spells</u> you she wrote to
consult me touching a plan with which the Poodle is big – i.e. that of coming to
England to sell Lithographic[6] Portraits of Napoleon the 3rd with his autograph
attached to them by which she thinks she would make a fortune! I wrote and
dissuaded her from it, unless she wanted to be in the same state they were before
– as the Anglo Saxons of the present day – unless they can get it trumpeted in
"The Times" are by no means fond of parting with their pence. – Yes – Mrs
Braine paid me a visit of three weeks – and it might have lasted 3 weeks longer
but that she was threatened with an execution[7] in her House – which I think
was the real reason of her coming down – as no one has any mercy upon me
and now that I have <u>but</u> my skin, they even try to get that off my bones – she is
very handsome but intensely <u>selfish</u> and <u>unfeeling</u> like all the Welsh – one day
she modestly asked me to give her the only warm dressing – gown I had – so

that I am now without one – I had sent her in the summer – (which I need not tell you how ill I could afford) £5 to come down here and return – which was £2"10" more than she needed had she come by the 2nd Class – well instead of having the honesty to keep the money for that purpose she has – the inhumanity (considering my own utter de<u>stitution</u>) and indelicacy to ask me for £2 to go back which I had to <u>also </u>borrow from Dr Price – nor was this enough when I told her my utter inability to lend(?) her the £16 for which she said her furniture would be seized – she modestly asked me to give her that jewelled Sevré[8] cup of mine to <u>pawn</u>, this so disgusted me that I flatly refused – saying at Xmas I should probably be obliged to sell all I possessed myself to meet my own necessities – since her return her landlord has settled the matter for her and she affects to write me the most grateful letters! though she never showed any symptoms of gratitude while here – and I confess her inhuman manner of spurring a free horse to death – gave me a great disgust to her neither did she spare me a single agony about my poor child – telling me that her Fiend of a Father about two months – before her death (when she was in reality dying -) used to say to his mistress the woman Beaumont "That ugly wretch of a girl – I wish she was dead! I cannot get her up of a morning – she that ought to be <u>too</u> happy to have the <u>honour</u> of <u>looking</u> even at such a father!!" and it was because the Monster got his inhuman wish so soon – that the Loathsome Hypocrite of <u>course</u> had puffs put in all the papers – at her death – about his intense grief! the too disgusting Hypocrite – I understand that one of the woman Beaumonts Bastards is attaché with Henry Bulwer![9] – so in such a school; and sewer of iniquity! and complicated vice – no wonder my son should have turned out such an unnatural – wretch. Here is a charming little sample of Satan reproving Sin – Sir Liar makes sad complaints to his trull[10] Beaumont of the shameful way – in which <u>Henry</u> Bulwer <u>Beats</u>, and ill uses <u>his</u> wife!!![11] – is not this good? he also told her that the poor Duchess of Wellington[12] wanted to separate from her brute – but our little selfish sensual idiotic wretch of a queen – that there might be no <u>esclandre</u>[13] at <u>her</u> court – intreated the poor victim to remain at the stake. I understand Sir Liar – leaves his <u>old</u> mistress the woman Beaumont so destitute of money that she is often obliged to sell her <u>clothes</u> to pay her Baker – but she solaces herself with the idea – that I am dying – and that then she will be at Knebworth as Lady Bulwer Lytton – where <u>she</u> and that infamous L.E.L.[14] used to visit my Satanic old Mother in Law the moment I was turned out of my home, it appears Sir Liar only got ten thousand pounds from Routledge <u>one</u> of which he has spent in puffing, and placarding himself all over the rail ways.[15] Here is a pithy colloquy Mrs Braine over heard one evening in an Omnibus between two Footmen –

"So, James never got that situation at Sir E Lyttons after all – and lost 2 places by waiting for it" – 2nd Flunky Loquator[16] "Ah! – he's a sad Humbug is that Bul-

wer and a sad Blackguard too and the public will find it out one of these days"
– First Flunky – "Not far out there, – but I <u>spose</u> the reason he <u>would</u> not take
James – was he's too good looking a <u>feller</u> and he was <u>afeared</u> as – he'd cut his
master out with that ere Swiss <u>gal</u>[17] as he's got with him in Park Lane"– Poor
Chalon is in great grief as poor <u>John</u>[18] is dead. – I have barely time to save the
Post – so Believe me ever my dearest Rebecca yours affectly Rosina Bulwer Lyt-
ton. Write soon and let me know if Massy has started for Pau

HALS

At the top of the first sheet is written 'starry eyes Best love'.

1. Catherine-Anne Hubback (1818–77) was a novelist and the niece of Jane Austen. She started writing fiction to support herself and her three sons after her husband, the bar-rister John Hubback, had been committed to an asylum after a breakdown.
2. *May and December. A Tale of Wedded Life* (1854).
3. The Theatre Royal was built in 1789 and demolished in 1877 in Aberdeen, a city in north-east Scotland.
4. 'Sleep' from *Five Elizabethan Songs* by John Fletcher (1579–1625).
5. Most of the action of the Crimean War (see RBL, 16 October 1854) took place on the Crimean peninsula, with additional actions occurring in western Turkey, the Baltic Sea region and the Russian Far East.
6. An early form of printing using chemicals, which by the middle of the nineteenth cen-tury could be in colour.
7. RBL's way of referring to a wedding. See RBL, 1 September 1853.
8. Sèvres is a town on the outskirts of Paris, renowned for its manufacture of porcelain.
9. Since 1862, Henry Bulwer had been minister plenipotentiary at the court of the Grand Duke of Tuscany at Florence.
10. 'A low prostitute or concubine; a drab, strumpet, trollop' (*OED*).
11. In 1847, Henry Bulwer married the Hon. Georgiana Charlotte Mary Wellesley (1817–78) at Hatfield House. She was the youngest daughter of Henry Wellesley, first Baron Cowley (1773–1847), and a niece of the Duke of Wellington. See RBL, 10 June 1853.
12. Lieutenant-General Arthur Richard Wellesley, second Duke of Wellington (1807–84), married Lady Lady Elizabeth Hay in 1839.
13. 'Unpleasant notoriety' (*OED*).
14. Letitia Elizabeth Landon. See RBL, 18 April 1854.
15. Routledge's Railway Library thrived during the 1850s and 1860s, when 120 authors were represented in the series. These were known as yellowbacks on account of their cover design. In 1876, Routledge purchased all of EBL's copyrights from his son Robert, and his entire oeuvre went yellowback.
16. Speaker (Latin).
17. Miss Pion, EBL's mistress. See RBL, 6 May 1851.
18. John James Chalon, the brother of Alfred, died in London on 14 November. Alfred had accumulated an extensive collection of pictures, sketches and drawings by himself and his brother. In May 1855, he arranged an exhibition of the work of both brothers at the Society of Arts in the Adelphi, which attracted little public attention.

To Rebecca Ryves

Llangollen Cemetery Where however – one has
only the gloom – without the repose of the grave –
November 23rd 1854

My dearest Rebecca – Though I am almost blinded by a severe cold – and my eyes
– are streaming – I will thank you for your kind letter to day least I should get
worse and be quite unable to do so – for the snow has now begun and to describe
the atmospheric influences – in a style more <u>Carlylean</u>[1] than Ossianic[2] hurricanes of cutting razor-like winds rush down the <u>Backside</u>(!) of the mountains
– imitating in the <u>awfullest</u> manner the roar – of thunder, Cannon, Squeek-
ing– Pigs – Panting Steam Engines – Scolding Husbands!! – <u>and the like</u>! Mrs
Braines last bulletin is that Sir Liar is very ill at Knebworth – I have heard that
story so often that it has become a case of the shepherds boy and the Wolf[3] to me;
– though she told me – when here that Furgisson had told that infamous old cat
Lady Morgan – as a profound secret! At the time they all wanted to amputate
Sir Liars hand – that it would in reality be of no use – even if they took off the
arm above the shoulder – as the virus was in the blood, and he could not possibly
live longer than a year or two – time will tell, – but my own opinion is – that
he will again have the pleasure of wiping his eyes – on the Public in the <u>rôle</u> of
<u>disconsolate</u> widower! – for every day the iron seems to enter more into my soul
– and this abomination of desolation – of <u>solitary</u> confinement from morning
till night, would crush the spirit of an Angel and tame that of a Devil. I try hard
to dilute my own intense misery – by merging it in the ocean of bitter tears now
shedding by the poor broken hearts – caused by this horrid war! – but find <u>that</u>
only adds to it instead of diminishing it – and every day I feel more exhausted
from the too fearfully prolonged struggle – of always trying to cast <u>secondary</u>
causes behind me and look steadily forward and upward – to that "great <u>first</u>
cause – <u>least understood</u>"[4] <u>God's Will</u> – or I could <u>not</u> bear it a single hour – if I
remember rightly – Euripides[5] makes Polynices[6] in his conference with Jocasta[7]
reckon up – <u>five</u> miseries of an exile! – the <u>least</u> of which he adds would be quite
sufficient to deject and crush, a pusillanimous spirit – while he was about it, he
had better have enumerated five thousand, and then he would have been somewhat nearer – though still wide of the mark. – I enclose you Mr Leytons last
letter received this morning – about that unhappy Play! (let me have it back) I
begin to think it <u>may</u> be bonâ fide as it pretends to be – and <u>not</u> the plot continued still I <u>hope</u> nothing – for Hope with me was dead, and buried long ago – and
I am not yet nor never shall be – out of mourning for her – for though she <u>always</u>
deceived me still she was the best & kindest friend I ever had. – I must not forget
to tell you that last Monday Mr Tom Lloyd – whom I understand is staying at
Oswestry[8] – sent up the enclosed beautiful scrawl wishing to see me – as I had

no wish to see him – I sent down word I was too ill – I hear he is the shadow of his former self – and has left his wife – who has gone back to her parents – the description of her – when she was here was – that she had a wretchedly bad and vulgar figure – which she made still worse by wearing a wrap rascal – and wide awake – and was always laughing and talking loudly in the streets – and switching a great stick, in most masculine fashion, against <u>her thigh</u>! I see that Skeet is just Barking his new victim's book as he did mine – by never advertising it after it is out – how any one – <u>not driven</u> to it <u>like me</u> – ever publishes with these sort of fifth rate publishers, I cant understand. My eyes – <u>wont</u> let me write any more – so I must say good bye and God Bless you – de Dog vezy great big much offenced at your never mentioning him in your last – not a line yet – either from Mr Hyde or Mr Hodgson – so God only knows what they are at? Ever your grateful & affect Rosina Bulwer Lytton R

HALS
1. To Thomas Carlyle (1795–1881), the essayist and historian, RBL dedicated her novel *The School for Husbands*.
2. A romantic style of writing based on the Ossian poet. See RBL, 12 September 1829.
3. Aesop's fable about a bored shepherd boy who entertained himself by calling out 'wolf'. Nearby villagers who came to his rescue found that the alarms were false, so when the boy was actually confronted by a wolf, the villagers ignored his cries for help and his flock perished.
4. Alexander Pope, 'Thou great First Cause, least understood' in 'The Universal Prayer' (1730), usually appended to *Essay on Man*.
5. Euripides (*c.* 480–406 BC) was a great tragedian of ancient Greece.
6. Son of King Oedipus of Thebes and his wife Jocasta.
7. The wife of Oedipus (see above, n. 6), who at the start of Euripides's play *The Phoenician Women* (*c.* 409 BC) tells the story of Oedipus and its aftermath.
8. A town in Shropshire, very close to the Welsh border.

To Mr Leyton

Phillips's Hotel Llangollen
November 23d 1854

Sir, I beg to acknowledge the reciept of your second letter from Aberdeen (without date) by this mornings Post. – I have no knowledge what ever of the gentlemen whose names you mention as Dramatic critics – and have no doubts that they are all highly honorable, and loyal:– still as we are all, more or less – (though <u>ignoring</u> the fact <u>ourselves</u>) <u>Marrionettes</u> in the hands of others – and are not always aware whose forbidden power is that pulls the wires of our opinions – to this side; or that; but as <u>I</u> am <u>perfectly</u> <u>aware</u> from long and bitter experience of the cunningly devised and widely organised plot there is for crushing effectually every sort of literary production, with which I am in any way connected – and where by dint of money – and <u>back</u> <u>stair</u> influence – has so well succeeded as to have driven me into publishing with fifth rate Publishers – who not only cheat one with a fifty Publisher power! by the strong warrant of impunity! – but burke ones books, – by the most disgraceful typographical errors – finally destroying them by filling their own Pockets with a creeping sale of the two first Editions and then never more advertising them. – I should for your <u>own</u> sake recommend your not mentioning – <u>even</u> to the Umpires – to whom you submit your Play – that you have dramatised it from <u>my novel</u>; – I would only mention that fact (in the event of its being accepted) in the Play <u>Bills</u> – when I know it would help to draw Houses, – more especially were it brought out by Christmas, – unfortunately being so far from London I can do nothing to render you any very effectual service towards <u>pronéeing</u>[1] it; – if I remember rightly; Euripides[2] makes Polynices[3] – in his conference with Jocasta[4] – reckon up <u>five</u> miseries of an Exile the least of which he adds were enough to deject, and crush, a pusillanimous nature; – had he reckoned up five thousand! while he was about it, – he would have seen some what nearer – though still wide of the mark, and it is not one of the least trying that the aforesaid exile must tamely submit to the barbaric hoards of their Enemy – doing their murderous work – unchecked by the tardy reinforcements of their supine friends(?) Being therefore unable to render you any more active assistance in your undertaking I must only beg of you to accept my good wishes – that it may succeed on its own merits – and I have the Honor to be Sir your obedient servant

  Rosina Bulwer Lytton

HALS
1. Advising (French).
2. See RBL to Rebecca Ryves, 23 November 1854.
3. See ibid.
4. See ibid.

To Rebecca Ryves

Llangollen Cemetery
Decr 6th 1854

I was very glad to hear

 My dearest Rebecca that poor Massy had at length got off to the Pyrenees – although I have been so long in telling you so, but the fact is, I have been so <u>démoralisée</u>[1] in mind, and body – that I might as well, have sent you the concentrated croakings of a whole pond of frogs, or of a whole Rookery of Ravens

– as have written to you, – and that would have been paying rather too dearly for good Company as the crow said, when he got into a Pigeon pie. –

I am rejoiced to hear that the report of poor young Lord Fitzgibbons[2] death is contradicted – and that he is only taken prisoner – Ainsi qu'il est quitte pour la peur![3] – as the Czar treats all prisoners, more especially all prisoners of Mark[4] well; the only good I can foresee of this too – too horrible! war is, – that the English by freyering with the French[5] may be infected with a little humanity no one ever doubted their animal courage – or even their being able on a great emergency to find their way to their pockets! provided – the extracts therefrom – were duely chronicled, and Emblazoned in "The Times" – but of all the nicer, and nobler élans[6] of human sympathy or of taking the initiative in any generous or self-sacrificing feeling they are up to the present time – quite incapable We might have waited long enough before we should have heard of an English Field Officer – in the heat, and onslaught of such! a mêlée[7] – or rather Brutinery as that of Inkermann[8] stopping to pick up a common soldier! galloping off with him to a place of safety on his own horse – and then kissing his rough – but brave hand! – before he left him, as that fine fellow of a French general did that poor English sergeant whom he found with unequal odds of five Russians upon him! – but still, – it is fearful only to learn the Humanities of life! in the Slaughterhouse of Death!! – The Biddulphs do not go to Town till the 10th as Parliament is to be re-rogued on the 12th – they are very kind in supplying me with game & & but in this terrible weather – and these awful! Hurricanes – what Carlyle would doubtless designate, as the flatulentest atmospheric influences that ever – could be concieved – much less – brought forth! – I cannot of course expect to hear the exhilarating sound of her Poneys feet beneath my windows – so am left alone in the abomination of desolation! – to add to which – I had this day a most melancholy letter from poor Mr Hodgson saying that his poor dear wife is sinking fast! and has been given over by Dr Latham and a consultation of Physicians at which I am most sincerely and unaffectedly grieved – as a better, and kinder creature than poor good Mrs Hodgson – I think never lived – God comfort him and his poor children for He alone can. – I will now say good bye, and God bless you my dearest Rebecca and wish you a happy Xmas, and many of them, as I know I shall not have the heart to do so from my living Tomb when that Merry! (very!) time arrives. – De Dog is appeased and joins hims innocent love! with that of yours Ever

    Affectly

    Rosina Bulwer Lytton

HUNT

1. Demoralized (French).
2. In the battle of Alma (20 September 1854–23 November 1854), the first victory over the Russians, Lieutenant J. C. Viscount Fitzgibbon of the 11th Hussars was first thought to have been killed.

3.   There is no longer any need for fear (French).
4.   Rank.
5.   In January 1854, the Anglo-French fleet sailed into the Black Sea. After that France, England and Turkey made a formal alliance against the Russians.
6.   Outbreak of feeling (French).
7.   Conflict (French)
8.   Inkermann, a small Tartar village, east of Sebastopol harbour, was the scene of a battle between the Russians and allied forces. After a prolonged struggle on 5 November 1854, the Russians were defeated.

To Rebecca Ryves

Llangollen Cemetery
December 11th 1854

My dearest Rebecca I am indeed very glad to hear that poor Massy has arrived safely at his journeys end, but his account of his travelling disagrémens[1] – only confirms what I have already said i.e. that those said bare discomforts – to poor Invalids – more than counterbalance any thing they may gain in climate; – however I sincerely hope his next bulletin may be to the credit of the Pyrenees – is he going to the Mont d'Or? The fate of that poor young Lord Fitzgibbon – is indeed melancholy, or rather that of his poor bereaved parents! – and the false reprieve of his reported capture – makes the blow of the fatal truth! fall all the heavier, – God comfort them! poor people: – in one sense, poor wretches like me – who have neither Husband nor Children, House nor home! and who are bound to existence by no single tie save the hard knot of misery – are better off in as much as that they are ready – at any moment – having no encumbrances – in the way of earthly affections, and therefore being always in light marching order for the other world, still the Champagne in this one, is weary work! however deeply one may feel convinced that afflictions and tribulation – are Gods great training school for immortality; – however steadily we may trust the unerring wisdom which we cannot always discern ; – and none can become profoundly imbued with the truth of the former fact or can rely more implicitly on the latter, than I do: – yet humanly speaking, – the most elastic spirit will snap at last, – for there is a point of tension – beyond which neither hope – nor endurance can extend; – and worse still, – even ones spiritual vision at length grows so dim with ceaseless tears, – that look upward as intensely as one will – one fails athwart the gloom to discern one glimpse of Heaven! – And though ones heart may be a Goliath – of long standing – yet the stripling David[2] delegated by the inscrutable decrees of Omnipotence can effectually annihilate it.

HALS

1.   Annoyances [*Désagréments*] (French).
2.   Goliath was a Philistine warrior, who was defeated in battle by David, the young Israelite boy, who had been chosen by God to be the next king of Israel.

CHAPTER 8 (1855–7) TAUNTON

I am, as you may suppose nearly in pieces with all this writing ...

RBL to Louisa Devey, 28 April, 1881

To Rebecca Ryves

Llangollen Cemetery
Monday January 8th 1855

I am indeed very glad to hear such improved accounts of poor Massy My dearest Rebecca and it is certain that with youth, and a good constitution on his side – that a pure <u>dry</u> – and soft air like that of the Pyrenees can do wonders; – if he were only within reach of a sugar factory – where they bake sugar – and could for 2, or 3 hours a day inhale the fumes – he would be quite cured in six weeks. With regard to my lungs – as they know now to do nothing about a sick room or any other in this place except to deck themselves out in all sorts of finery beyond their station I think I injured them by attending the wife of the man who keeps the Post Office, who was in a galloping consumption but who poor creature began the year, well and wisely, by dying at 10 o'clock on New Years morning. – Were not Lady Hotham superannuated, and moreover besotted with Poet Snuff and Toadies– one might fairly call her a <u>very</u> great beast: for although besides the Chevalier d'Industries[1] letters I also sent her a note of Dr Prices to me at the time – saying after de Birards most ungrateful conduct to me – he thought I was quite right not to write to him and I moreover said to Lady Hotham that as she <u>was</u> a gentlewoman by birth I wondered she was not revolted at de Birards dishonourable meanness – and paltry spite in violating the sacredness of a private letter[2] – for the sole purpose of trying to injure a woman who had long done all she could, and a great deal more than she ought to try and serve him. She merely returned me these <u>proofs</u> of his double dealing baseness – and scrawled on a dirty scrap of paper "Really Lady Lytton I have neither time spirits or inclination to read all the letters you have sent me – my <u>good</u> <u>opinion</u> of the poor dear Chevalier remains unaltered it is too bad such <u>coarse</u> language calling him a liar and a Toady – your pen has been your Enemy – pray write no more – it is that that irritates your husband"(!!!!!(is not this rather too much?) "I wish you happiness dear Lady Lytton which you cannot have while your mind is <u>so</u> <u>disturbed</u>". The old Hyena! but all this is only part and parcel of my brutally unjust fate ...

HALS
Incomplete letter.
1.　Chevalier de Birard. RBL has nicknamed him the Knight of Industry (French) as he had produced translations, which she had tried to sell around London to raise money for him, as he was so impoverished.
2.　Birard read out to Lady Hotham an extract of RBL's letter to him referring to her 'cast-iron constitution and an iced cucumber heart'. See RBL to A. E Chalon, 24 March 1855 (*Unpublished Letters*), p. 187.

To Rebecca Ryves

Llangollen Cemetery
Monday March 26th 1855

Dearest Rebecca I have only one minute to thank you for your letter, and to <u>implore that you will not go</u> and put it into Chalon's head to apply to Mr Long[1] – for that picture of mine,[2] or even tell him <u>where</u> the picture is, as I do not choose for <u>it to be exhibited</u>, still <u>less</u>, to be <u>applied for</u> to a person who behaved so shamefully to me, – and from whom after his poor wife's death I failed to get it back by fair means:- As no one seems to have the least human feeling or <u>common sense</u> for me, on <u>any</u> occasion (the latter deficit arising out of the former) I am obliged to write in this downright sledge hammer fashion – as my dear friends (?) one half from sheer folly – and heartless indifference, and 'the other half from black treachery and premeditated villainy – are always – getting me into whirlpools of hot water humiliations, and <u>degoûts</u>[3] which render my miserable existence a sort of high pressure hell to me. I can well enter into your annoyance at being obliged to stay so long at Mr Lloyds but is there one single torture and humiliation – ever omitted from the <u>repertoire</u> of Poverty!! no verily – not <u>one</u>. For God's sake don't mention to Mrs Lloyd – or any one else my intention of going to Taunton – if I can get there?? – for I wish it possible to have a little reprieve from the inhuman persecutions of that Fiend – I am to pay the <u>same</u> at the hotel there if I can go – as I do here, and send you Augustas[4] last letter on the subject which return to me. Poor Mme Alphonse has written me another pressing letter to go and live with them; without paying them a <u>sou</u>! a likely thing I would! however its well to find a little heat and a little gratitude any where; if indeed it is not a bait for some fresh trap! – which all the <u>seeming</u> gratitude I meet with generally proves to be. – Here is Mrs Biddulph with another carriage load of "British Females!" I get quite cross – under these repeated invasions to stare at the Wild Beast – and if I am compelled to remain here – shall do as Lady Mary Wortley Montague[5] used at Venice, when ever she was importuned with visits of curiosity (for it is nothing else) from ill mannered ill bred English women) viz – receive them in a Mask and Domino.[6] Good Bye – and with love from silver paws and diamond eyes, Believe me ever affectly yours Rosina Bulwer Lytton

HALS
1. Probably a relative of Kate Long.
2. In the 1840s, A. E. Chalon sketched RBL for Countess Blessington's annual literary magazine *Book of Beauty* in which the portrait never appeared. RBL gave the portrait to Lady Harrington and it disappeared after her death. In 1852, Chalon did a drawing of RBL, which was engraved by J. Jewell Penstone. See frontispiece to this volume.
3. Loathings (French).
4. Augusta Boys.
5. Lady Mary Wortley Montagu (1689–1762) settled at Venice around 1758, where she resided until the death of her husband in 1761.
6. 'A kind of loose cloak, app. of Venetian origin, chiefly worn at masquerades, with a small mask covering the upper part of the face, by persons not personating a character' (*OED*).

To Herries Farquhar & Co

To Messrs Herries Farquhar & Co. Bankers 16 St James's St London

London
April 11th 1855

Gentlemen Please to pay Bearer the ninety four pounds, three shillings and four pence – £94"3" 4" due to me by Sir Edward Bulwer Lytton Bart on the 10th Instant
Rosina Bulwer Lytton

HALS

To Rebecca Ryves

Llangollen
Saturday April 28th 1855

My dearest Rebecca

I begin to be uneasy at not hearing from you; I hope you have had no bad accounts of poor Massy? let me know how, and where you are? and then I will let

you know all my never ending still beginning miseries which have culminated! within the last month. In great Haste with best wishes – Ever your affect
Rosina Bulwer Lytton

HARV

To Mr Barnes

May 6th 1855

To Mr Barnes – signing himself "The Gipsy King" Though only Chargé d'affaires[1] to The King of the Blackguards

If Sir Liar Coward Bulwer Lyttons infamous spy the waiter out of place looking fellow, – calling himself Mr Barnes, alias Mr Leyton the Strolling Player – who comes 20 miles out of his way to go to the Chester Races!! presumes to send any more of his drunken letters, either from <u>himself</u>, or any of the rest of his Blackguard gang – composing "the <u>Guilt</u> of Literature" or the infamous <u>lower detachments of it stationed in the village of Llangollen</u> – as the writing can be <u>proved</u> he, and they will find it the <u>worse for them</u>, as well as their too despicable employer Sir Reptile Bulwer Lytton, as a magistrate has been appealed to, who is <u>determined</u> to <u>expose</u> this infamous system of anonymous letters – Espionnage and dastardly persecution

HALS
1.   Head of business (French).

To Rebecca Ryves

Llangollen
May 10th 1855

How very extraordinary! – really a passing strange coincidence! my dearest Rebecca that <u>the</u> very passage you cite – and comparison you make in your last letter between the infamous Lord Leicester![1] and the still more infamous Sir Liar, – I made in <u>the</u> Book,[2] – and wrote down between 2 and 3 this morning! – only I added <u>another instance</u> – of the patronage and protection, which <u>unbounded</u> vice receives from <u>virtuous</u> <u>monarchs</u>! in the instance of the infamous Rochester and lady Essex[3] – and James the first[4] – and the Posthumous conviction of poor Sir Thomas Overbury's[5] murderers (the apothecary[6] who at that infamous couples instigation poisoned him in the Tower, was little consolation to his manes!) As for the persons who wonder! at the conduct of Sir Liars son! they are about as <u>wise</u>! who kindly offer to write and inform him of the distress I am in!! when he has done, and is doing everything possible, and almost impossible! to achieve this state of things – as the twig is bent so will it grow – that wretched boy was <u>first</u> carefully trained to be the unnatural monster he is – to serve his vile father's purposes – and then plunged into a sea of equal vice – to complete the work – so what could he be? but what <u>he is</u>. I will send you Mr Hyde's letter when I get it back from Jenkins, but in the meantime send you the Spy Barnes's last Blackguardism which you will perceive is just the same hand writing scarcely disguised (except in Liquor!) as the pretended Mr Leyton! and the wise acres who cannot see the <u>motive</u> of such inane trash! are dull indeed, since the motive is so glaring to insult to annoy and to outrage me in every possible way – only about the Play there was a more diabolical malice, as it was to give me a hope that I was about to earn money – which that mean and dastardly Blackguard Sir Liar – prevents my doing in what ever way I attempt it – But there is a day of vengeance still linger it may, but come it <u>will</u>! Let me have this packet of letters back by return of Post as I want to send them to Hyde – I shall barely catch the Post – so good bye – and God Bless you with Doatskins love. Ever your Affect Rosina – Bulwer Lytton

---

HALS
1. Robert Dudley, Earl of Leicester (1532/3–88), was a favourite of Queen Elizabeth I.
2. RBL compares her husband to Lord Leicester in her first novel, *Cheveley*, ed. Mulvey-Roberts, p. 209.
3. Robert Carr, first Earl of Somerset (*c.* 1590–1645), who was created Viscount Rochester in 1611, was a Scottish politician. He became the lover of Frances Howard, Lady Essex (1591–1632), who was married. Because Rochester was a favourite of King James I, Essex managed to get her marriage annulled. Her subsequent remarriage to Somerset was opposed by the poet Thomas Overbury.
4. James I (1566–1625) offered Thomas Overbury the ambassadorship of Russia, which he declined. Overbury's refusal so displeased the King that he imprisoned him in the Tower in 1613.
5. Sir Thomas Overbury (1581–1613) was a poet and essayist. He circulated his manuscript poem *His Wife* about the virtues required in a wife. This, Rochester believed, implied a criticism of Lady Essex and so she succeeded in discrediting Overbury in the eyes of James I, who had him imprisoned in the Tower. Overbury was later poisoned through the machinations of Lady Essex. She and her husband were convicted of murder, but spared execution, though four accomplices were hanged.
6. An apothecary called Franklin poisoned Overbury. He was assisted by a gaoler, known as Weston, and later by a Mrs Turner, the widow of a physician.

To Rebecca Ryves

Llangollen
Tuesday May 15th 1855

My dearest Rebecca I am <u>so</u> bothered and worried and so ill with the worry that I am scarcely able to thank you for your kind letter; and tell you that <u>at</u> <u>last</u>! on Saturday I got my Parish allowance so that poor Hydes letter frightened the wretches it would seem – be sure and let me have it back by <u>return</u> <u>of Post</u>, as I want to show it to Mr Whalley[1] the magistrate whose letter I send you, and dont know what day he may return; but I am now <u>determined</u> to expose the whole gang[2] as far as possible. To show you how hard Sir Liar died (alas! that this should be only figurative!) finding the money did not come the day it had been so faithfully <u>promised</u>! Mr Hodgson sent his son up to Loaden to know the meaning of this? when he said that Sir Liar had sent a cheque but so villainously and incorrectly drawn that he was obliged to return it, when at length the precious document returned for £94"3"4! being the double Income tax carefully and fractionally deducted! the last news of the village is that Judas Iscariot Jones,[3] is gone to Malvern![4] where Sir Liar is, or was. – I forget whether I ever told you that Old <u>Hotham</u> had sent me back all the things I had ever given her (except my books which I should have been very glad to have had back) but the worst part of the affair was, at least the part <u>I</u> felt most keenly, was my having to pay 4"6d! for the Parcel – for like Sir Liar true to her pocket, though to nothing else, of <u>course</u> she did not pay it. Though I wrote, as I told you to Mr Hodgson to find out about it, and pay Browne[5] for your China – never have I been able to extort a word from him either about it, or my doomed looking glass – which that Scotch shark[6] has of course swindled me out of. The Clifton advertisement, which you kindly sent me, I sent Jenkins to see about, she wrote me word, it was a part of the Town alone which no respectable person could live in: you ask me what <u>I</u> mean to do?! rather ask what God means to do with <u>me</u>, as my munificent £43 a quarter – barely sufficient to pay Mrs Phillips now 3 months and six weeks bill as my Laundress – so to fret the heat out, in this odious hole – is my only alternative – and literally a <u>sorry</u>! one. Silver paws, writes with me, in best love, and Believe me my dearest Rebecca Ever your grateful and affect Rosina Bulwer Lytton

---

HALS
1. Maynooth Whalley, MP for Peterborough.
2. This includes Mr Barnes and Mr Jones. See RBL, 17 August 1857.
3. The disciple, who handed Jesus over to his enemies, and Mr. Jones from the tavern in Llangollen.
4. See RBL, 16 August 1851.
5. In April 1855, RBL was informed by her lawyer Robert Hodgson that Browne had become a bankrupt. RBL had left her china and household linen in his charge.
6. Mr Campbell. See RBL, 16 October 1854.

To Rebecca Ryves

Llangollen
Monday May 21ˢᵗ 1855

My dearest Rebecca I have barely half a minute to save the Post and thank you for your kind letter. Mr Whalley came down here on Saturday – and nothing <u>could</u> be more <u>actively</u>, and zealously kind than he was: – he went to a little dirty rascal of an attorney here of the name of Richards[1] – a great Crony of that Blackguard Jaques;[2] – and also to a Mr Cooper[3] the <u>respectable</u> <u>rich</u> man! of the village and said he had now traced the conspiracy through that Barnes's infamous anonymous letter – and that from this out he as a magistrate, and Col Biddulph as the Lord Lieutenant of the County were determined to keep a sharp look out to prevent my having the slightest molestation or annoyance and to thoroughly expose the Perpetrators – and as for that Blackguard Jaques he should next year refuse him his licence, and that if they had the slightest respect for themselves or their Parish – they would <u>Physically</u> throw the fellow out of the place – and that they ought to feel themselves only too honoured at having "such a Lady in it &&" with a great deal more that neither my time, nor my modesty will allow me to repeat. Mr W:[4] also very kindly pressed me to go and stay with them for some months, as that old shark Mrs Phillips has told me that I cannot have my rooms longer than the 12ᵗʰ of next month! so you may guess the fever this has put me, – in as more especially poor August[a] 3 weeks after she had so kindly offered me that £80 wrote to abuse me for not having taken it as they had just had to pay a Chancery bill of £110! which they could not have done if I had: – I have however written to her to say if she cannot beg borrow or steal the £50 by June – half to be repaid when my Parish allowance comes in July – and the remainder in the following October, and January – what I am to do God only knows. – Old <u>Hotham</u> did not send me back the Chevalier Piqueassiettes[5] letters, as she delights in tormenting people, and no doubt has kept them to torment him. Hoping you will soon hear from Poor Massy Believe me in Flash of Lightning Haste Ever your grateful & affect Rosina Bulwer Lytton

---

HALS

1. Charles Richards was the head of a Llangollen firm of solicitors of this name, which had been founded in 1770.
2. Jones from the tavern. See RBL, 17 August 1857.
3. This is Ebenezer Cooper (b. *c.* 1800), who was involved in setting up the local school and building the railway. He was a master currier by trade and lived in Chapel Street, Llangollen.
4. Mr Maynooth Whalley.
5. RBL had sent Lady Hotham copies of her letters from Chevalier de Birard, criticizing her ladyship. This was in retaliation for Birard reading out extracts from RBL's private letter

to him to Lady Hotham (see RBL, 8 January 1855). Her nickname for him is based on the French words 'Pique assiette' for a style of mosaic that incorporates pieces of broken ceramics. Picassiette is also the name of a character in RBL's novel *Very Successful!*, who is based on Augustus Shiel, Lady Hotham's heir.

To Rebecca Ryves

Llangollen Treadmill
Monday May 28th 1855

My dearest Rebecca Between illness, business and worry of every kind I have but half a minute to thank you for your kind letter just received – I have had a narrow escape of a Bilious fever, but Dr Price has dosed it off for the nonse, but his wonder is, that I am alive! and mine too. – I send you a <u>most</u> kind letter from my poor Pack horse Jenkins, but after the other slip between the cup, and the lip – I shall be in a fever till the money arrives: – if it does? D:V:[1] I hope to get out of this Inferno[2] the 12th of Next month. As soon as I get it back from Mr Hyde I will send you a volume I got the other day from Mrs Braine detailing the visit of another spy to her! parts of the description would do for Sternberg! in her best <u>Cognovat</u>[3] attire and parts for Pyke– having the long black ringlets! and roman nose! – but then to besure, the ringlets might have been false Ibid[4] the nose! as we know the woman is: – Every one says Sir Liar is mad; and I really think he must be to put himself in the power of such infamous wretches. I am very glad poor Massy is getting his teeth arranged by Brewster,[5] who is not to say the best dentist in Europe, but in the whole world, he has performed some almost fabulous <u>Tours de force</u>,[6] in the way of Dental surgery: – and has made (Yankee like)[7] an enormous fortune, which he deserves – seeing how long he has gone to work <u>Tooth</u> and <u>nail</u>! If me did not mention de Dog – it was because it would take an Encyclopaedia to contain all hims Doatskinries and darlingries, so what was de use of craming in only de tip of hims ear, at de tail of a letter; and as for taking Sebastapol[8] – if any thing could do it dose paws of his would, there is a green mountain in Dr Prices garden <u>covered</u> with Primroses, and to see dat fellow on de top of it in de midst of dem barking at hims mud to look up at him is <u>too</u> innocent! him desires hims love to be stuck like a plum in de midst of mine – In Whirlwind haste ever your grateful and affect Rosina Bulwer Lytton

I suppose Lord Massy's Bride[9] died of it? that you have never mentioned her

---

HALS

1. *Diis Volentibus* (Latin), if the Gods want.
2. Hell (Italian).
3. A cognovit is 'an acknowledgement by a defendant that the plaintiff's cause is just; in which case the defendant, to save expense, suffers judgement to be entered against him without trial' (*OED*).

4. The same (Latin).
5. Christopher Starr Brewster (1799–1870) was a celebrated dental surgeon, who had worked in the United States and Canada before settling in Paris. He became the dentist of Louis Philippe and the Emperor of Russia.
6. A masterly feat (French).
7. Brewster was an American who was born in Hartford, Connecticut.
8. The Siege of Sebastopol (1854–5) was a major siege during the Crimean War when allied troops besieged the city of Sebastopol, home of the Tsar's Black Sea Fleet, which threatened the Mediterranean.
9. On 5 June 1855, RBL's cousin Lord Hugh Hamon Ingoldsby, fifth Baron Massy, married Isabella, the daughter of George More Nesbitt of Cairnhill, County Lanark, Ireland, at Charlotte Square, Edinburgh.

To Rebecca Ryves

Llangollen
Saturday June 2d 1855

Snowing! and freezing as far as the cold goes.

Many thanks my dearest Rebecca for your kind letter just received– only fancy in all my worry having left the letter to you enclosing Mrs Baines in my blotting book for 3 days! and never discovering it till yesterday – when I sent it off dont send it back to me now but send it to "Miss Boys 63 High St Taunton Somersetshire England"[1] – and write her a line with it telling her what I really have no words to say how grateful I am to her for her really unexampled kindness – <u>her</u> letter to me dont return till I arrive and write to you for it, Augusta sent the money all safely this morning like a Trump as she is. – For God's sake dont tell Massy or any one where I am going, or else it will be all over London directly – and the Blood hounds after me, as soon as they were at this place:- let him think I am still here I hope the <u>ice</u> jaw! may succeed; but it is the <u>first</u> time I ever heard of an <u>ice</u> jaw with a Dentist! poor fellow I am very sorry to hear he is so thin, remember me kindly to him. I must now tell you of the excessive dissipation! of this place; yesterday a large Equestrian Troop arrived here it was what Mr Pepys[2] would have called "a mighty pretty sight!"[3] The vans were all driven <u>ten</u> in hand! darling fat Pie balled horse – then came the ladies of the Troop – on Isabelle coloured horses with <u>scarlet</u>! Hunt Habits and black sombreros with black plumes, and gaily dressed Monkeys! on Doatskin little Pony's bringing up the rear: as some of these darling Horses were tied to the inn yard wall, and being groomed – and the rest of this Picturesque Cavalcade was winding down the hill – it really made a beautiful Tableau, a perfect living Wouvermans.[4] Dr Price came and carried me off to this Circus, in the Evening – and you will be glad to hear of a public, and well merited compliment paid to Sir Liar, on the Occasion the Clown was <u>justifying</u> on logical! principles(?) his having picked a pocket – when he wound up with "For – as Sir Edward Bulwer Lytton says – with plenty of money and a little caution you may <u>do anything</u>! and as thats his dodge, he ought to know!" at which sally there was roars of laughter, and thunders of applause. Dont expect to hear from me again till I get to the other side of the Styx[5] but I shall hope to hear from you before then and that you have got the "The <u>Turkish</u> Spy"[6] safely? as Sir Liar <u>is</u> the greatest <u>Turk</u> that ever existed. With him doodest of Dogs best love Believe me in – Presto begone Haste Ever gratefully & affectly yrs

      Rosina   Bulwer Lytton

Would I could separate they twain more completely

HALS
1. This is destined for Augusta Boys at Taunton, a small market town.
2. Samuel Pepys (1633–1703), a naval administrator and MP, is best known for his diaries that he kept between 1660 and 1669, which were not published until the nineteenth century.
3. Samuel Pepys had an affair with his wife's friend Deborah Willet, whom he described in his diary (1666–7) as a 'mighty pretty' girl.
4. A family of Dutch painters, who painted small landscapes, hunting pieces and battle pieces. See RBL, 23 December 1852.
5. One of the rivers of Hell in Greek mythology, which forms a boundary between earth and the underworld, Hades.
6. *Letters Writ by a Turkish Spy who lived Five and Forty years undiscovered at Paris* (1691–4) by Giovanni Paolo Marana (vol. 1) and Roger Manley, William Bradshaw and Robert Midgeley (vols 2–8)

To Rebecca Ryves

Phillip's Hotel Llangollen
Saturday Night June 9th 1855

My dearest Rebecca I thank Heaven this will be the last print of my paw, that you will get from this place and yet now that it has come to the last, I am really, and seriously grieved at leaving Dr Price, who has been, so uniformly and ceaselessly kind to me, in all my manifold miseries, and worries: direct your first letter, under cover to Augusta and I shall hope to hear by it that poor Massy passed well through the Chloroform ordeal.[1] What Mrs Braine meant about Mr Layard[2] is this; she writes in rather a confused style and just after telling me of that infamous Mrs Gurwood[3] having had a dinner party of Sir Liar, and that other disgusting Blackguard The Duke of Wellington she said "What do you think of Layard – who hates him (Sir Liar!) personally and politically"? and I thought she meant Layard had been of this party! – to which she replied "Oh! no you must not suppose good Layard, was among such a set." I am so dead beat, that I have scarcely strength to say good night, and god Bless you, and with master Koh-i-noor Eyes's best love Believe me ever gratefully, and affectly yrs Rosina Bulwer Lytton. I am curious to hear the history of Jenkins's split with The Stuartdina

---

HALS

1. Massy's dentist, Mr Brewster, was a pioneer in the field of anaesthesia. In 1847, he successfully administered ether to his patients.
2. Chief Commissioner of the domestic police in 1868–70.
3. Fanny Mayer (*née* Kreilsamner) married Colonel John Gurwood (1790–1845). Her daughter Eugenie (aged ten at the time) is now believed to have been the illegitimate daughter of Napoleon Bonaparte. Her husband edited the *Dispatches of the Duke of Wellington* in thirteen volumes from 1837 up to the time when he committed suicide on Christmas day 1845 by cutting his own throat. In 1889, Gurwood supposedly communicated from beyond the grave by planchette, parodying the famous phrase from EBL's play *Richelieu; or The Conspiracy* (1839), 'The pen is mightier than the sword' (II.ii.308), with the words 'It was the pen did for me, not the sword'. Quoted by Rufus Osgood Mason, *Telepathy and the Subliminal Self* (New York: H. Holt & Company, 1897), p. 70.

To Rebecca Ryves

Friday June 22nd 1855

In my other letter I forgot to tell you of poor Mr Goldings[1] sudden death! so herewith send you Mr Hodgsons letter telling me of it which be sure and send me back. No doubt old Hothams <u>selfishness</u> will be greatly affected at this Catastrophe: one cannot feel sorry that so hard selfish – and utterly unfeeling a person should at last have a <u>slight</u> portion of this worlds annoyances. This is a very ugly view of Taunton – I'll try and get one of this Hotel. Ever affectly yours RBL

HALS
1. Lady Hotham's lawyer.

To Rebecca Ryves

Giles's Castle Hotel[1]
Friday June 22nd 1855

My dearest Rebecca I have only two minutes to thank you for your kind letter of yesterday having mountains of needle, and other work to do – to make up for my week of idleness. Augusta and Fanny I am sorry to say are gone to Frome[2] till the 2d of August, they went yesterday, but Augusta desired me to thank you for your kind letter, which she said she would answer when she got to her brother in laws: – I'm sure I dont know how I shall get through the next six weeks without them they have been so very kind to me, in <u>every</u> way so unlike ones <u>rich</u> friends

(?) The Crowder affair[3] was the cause of the split between Mrs H[4] and them – he (the Judge) I understand is a very handsome man and she (the Divorcée) has an enormous brooch of a miniature! of him as an <u>Amateur</u> <u>Brigand</u>! which she wears at the very <u>end</u> of the stomacher of her dress! so that it looks like a march of intellect improvement on Eves primitive brooch of the Fig leaf. – Mrs Wilson (<u>not</u> Grandity's defunct friend) met her racing through Westbourne Terrace[5] last Sunday with an open <u>Bible</u>! in her hand (so no doubt she has flown <u>out</u> of the <u>Crows</u> nest!). I suppose it was open at the Book of Judges; that all who ran might read! I like this place better, and better and my Phoenix[6] of a landlady[7] kills me with kindness and attentions of every sort – and she has two little girls, such dear little things who bring me fresh flowers every day – what a contrast to the old Hyena of the shark Hotel Llangollen! By moonlight this Hotel is really a beautiful pile of Castellated building – and the old arched Gateway is very handsome being the original one of 1269.[8] – You must be very glad to have that pretty little girl back; I hope Mrs Lloyd is better? and am glad you have such good accounts of Massy. Be sure you return me the 2 enclosed letters of Messrs Hyde and Hodgson – and the Envelopes they are in, as they are endorsed which saves me trouble. There is a charming park of Lord Wiltons[9] 5 minutes walk from this to the great delight of Master Koh-I-noor[10] Eyes – but alas! to the infinite despair of hims mud – the people are beginning to call upon her. – with hims love in great Haste Ever your grateful & affect Rosina Bulwer Lytton.

---

1. A medieval castellated building, located by the Castle Green in Taunton, Somerset.
2. A town in Somerset.
3. This may refer to Mr Crowder MP, who had been debating the Common Law Procedure Bill.
4. Possibly Mrs Hyde.
5. A handsome line of houses near Little Venice in London. Leases for thirteen houses in Westbourne Terrace Road were taken in 1847 by G. L. Taylor, an architect of grand houses.
6. A mythological fire-bird that at the end of its life burns to death in its nest from which a young phoenix rises.
7. Mrs Charlotte Clarke was born sometime between 1818 and 1821. She married a draper, with whom she was no longer living. In 1850, Robert Mattock (*c.* 1787–1859), an ex-servant, had been left Taunton Deane Manor by the eccentric owner, Thomas Southwood. Mattock offered the hotel to Clarke, who was then the barmaid. As she had insufficient funds to buy it outright, he agreed that she could pay rent until she had saved enough to purchase it, which she did in 1866.
8. The hotel was once a Norman fortress.
9. The Kinglake family were the owners of Vivary Park. They lived in Wilton House, situated behind the lake in the park. Since 1851, the park has been used as a venue for public events.
10. Once the largest diamond in the world. See RBL, 12 July 1854.

To Edward Bulwer Lytton

Saturday Evening July 4th 1855

Having now for eight years recieved from you every species, & variation of ill-usage – that, that privileged – Brute – an English Husband is authorized to bestow upon a wife – from the Plebeian blow up to the aristocratic zero of the most profound neglect – I have come to the resolution of enduring it no longer – <u>you</u> seem to have ordained that I should be a human spider extracting poison from everything the mingled yarn of <u>good</u> and evil that is spun out for all other mortals you have cancelled for me – in a Husband <u>I</u> am to have a Tyrant and a –jailer – but – never – a companion or a friend – or even a <u>conventional</u> Protector – the world has eyes – therefore you accuse <u>me</u> of maligning you! Injured shade of Henry the Eighth! It was your wives severed heads that maligned <u>you</u> – had not their rebellious blood dared to flow – who could have breathed a word against <u>you</u> – apostle of Thugs - Martyr of Husbands!! Farther still do I reap the destiny you have made for me – for while <u>you</u> wince at the least breath of public censure – you cannot assume the prudence that would give me the benefit of a little kind <u>conduct</u>. To Mrs Wyndham Lewis (a person whom you say you despise – and have reviled and abused incessantly! You go to complain – and hold out your favorite threat of repudiating me! She told you – you had not a single accusation against me – and therefore <u>could</u> <u>not</u> do so <u>legally</u> – but I will still be, as I have always been, your <u>only</u> friend – and save you that trouble – Henceforth you shall not be doomed to the <u>hourly</u> trouble of telling me <u>how much</u> I have cost you – of reminding me – that when you tore a piece out of my cheek – your amiable – and Christian – like mother withdrew her good offices from you because her prophecy was verified that <u>I</u> was not good enough for her paragon of a Son! – but softly – softly I am not <u>quite</u> mad yet – as Platonism is I believe the Doctrine you profess (if you profess any) – no wonder you despise me – for if souls in their present bodys are indeed punished according to their crimes in a former state – what must <u>I</u> have been? – even the Mrs Bulwer Lytton of some former sphere – do not however mistake me – I am perfectly aware of the <u>great</u> sacrifices you made in marrying <u>me</u> of the <u>very</u> little money I had – yet as it was you thought it worthwhile to take it from me do not think I shrink from going out alone upon the world because I am a Beggar beggary with freedom is bearable every other woman that is grossly ill-used or <u>neglected</u> by her Husband, has some <u>earthly</u> redress – <u>I</u> have <u>none</u> – and you know it – or I should not now be the miserable wretch I now am – but there <u>is</u> a <u>God</u> in Heaven for <u>me</u> as well as for everyone else – you have the satisfaction of thinking that you have twined a serpent round my Heart, but <u>recollect</u> that while it crushes me it also poisons every feeling against <u>you</u> - and the distruction may be <u>infectious</u> <u>you</u> write for fame – <u>I</u> may be obliged to write for <u>Bread</u> – it is easy for <u>you</u> to be the elegant Ring adorning <u>soi dissant</u>[1] History with all the exulcresences of fiction but take care that I am not to homely Polskins - <u>believed</u> in preference, despite the hardness of my style – you have left me but one wish – but one goal the grave – therefore do not think that those poor and shadowy scarecrows of this world – <u>appearances</u>! can frighten me from it. £50 a year and a separation are all that is asked by your poor victim

	Rosina Bulwer

By a separation I would be clearly understood to mean – a legal one – not such as the late Dwarf and Giant compact I had lately all the evil of, and – you all the Benefit, of at Gloucester where my words – were always to give the lie to your actions – and think myself highly honored – by Mr Bulwer Lytton's occasional sop to cerberus donations of fruit and game accompanied by a "Dear Madam" epistle written with all the sincerity of a Jesuit & all the kindness of a Stepmother – or the still greater honor of having my existence remembered by your brother Henry when he with the servility of a pauper – set me to ask alms of the Literary Gazette[2] in the shape of praise for his most Beggarly Trash – from your Elder Brother's tender Mercies I am safe as I have now nothing which by virtue of his <u>Trusteeship</u>! he could defraud me out of – of a separation at least I <u>will</u> have the benefit – you have accused me <u>most falsely</u> of having published your conduct – but henceforth the seal shall be off my lips – that is, I will not as hitherto deny any statement I may hear against you <u>if true</u> – if <u>false</u> I shall be the first to do so.

HALS
1.	So-called (*French*).
2.	The *Literary Gazette and journal of belles lettres, arts, sciences &c* (1817–60) was a weekly journal whose proprietor had been Henry Colburn and whose editor had been William Jerdan. See RBL, 18 April 1854.

To Rebecca Ryves

[*c*. 15 August 1855]

… taken or the queen – the way of it was this, Augusta always kindly takes me a drive, when she goes to pay any visits; and some days ago – as she was going to call upon the Esdales[1] who have a most lovely place 5 miles from this, she took me, but as she had the carriage from this Hotel, I was to call, and take her up – now you must know, that they have not only exceedingly nice open Carriages here quite like – private ones in excellent taste but what is not equally so – are the Postilions, who are dressed in [t]he royal livery! but quite <u>new</u> and bright – scarlet jackets – the royal badge on the left arm, snow white Buck skins – new-market[2] Boots – black velvet Jockey caps – with silver Tufts and powder! – so as

I of course was "dressed all in my best" to match so fine a turn out; two men who – were standing under the old arch way as I got in – said "<u>Lawr</u>! if there aint the Queen – she's a deal handsomer nor her pictures" – now Tib, and I got a much better compliment 3 days after – when there were great doings here – with Triumphal arches bands of music, Fire works dinners Dejûners,[3] and heaven knows what, when Lord Portman[4] came to lay the foundation stone of a new Town Hall:[5] – like the rest of the world, Tib, and I, went out to Breakfast, to see the Procession; and as we were getting out at the House where we were going to, – a man in the crowd – exceedingly drunk hiccoughed out: – "well! – you <u>air</u> the <u>puttiest</u> dog as ever I see, and as for your <u>missus</u> – why she's a stunner!" – and now I must tell you of <u>the</u> most doatskin things in the annals of darlingry which Master Tib, and a friend of <u>hims</u>, – did about six weeks ago; you must know that there is a vezy boots little black dog – of Mrs Clarkes called Jerry , – <u>not</u> a King Charles; but smooth as satin, – with little funsests of Ears, like tufts on a Clowns cap, very fine eyes, would fit in a gravy spoon and has de most charming manners, which are at once authenticated, and accounted for, by the fact of him having been pupped in France, well, – I never go out to walk without this dog as well as Tib, and it is the prettiest thing possible to see Day, and night, as I call them, together. One Evening I went to walk in some beautiful meadows near this called The Priory fields[6] – at the entrance of which on the left hand is a deep ditch covered with nettles; from which ditch, on the Evening in question proceeded the most feeble little moan of infant cats down went the "<u>twa</u> dogs" – and up they came the next minute, with a poor little just born kitten, in Each of their mouths (which some wretches had thrown there) and laid them on the grass, in the sun at my feet, it was impossible not to respond to such an appeal! so I dried the poor shivering little things in my handkerchief rolled them up, in the corner of my shawl, and brought them home, to poor Mrs Pussy here, who had, had kittens about a fortnight; and as two of them had been taken from her the day before she was delighted to recieve the poor little Foundlings; – Three nights ...

HALS
Incomplete letter.
1. The Esdales were landed gentry, who lived in Cothelstone Manor, in Cothelstone, Somerset, north-west of Taunton.
2. The race track in East Anglia.
3. Dinners (French).
4. Lord Portman (1799–1888) was Lord Lieutenant of the county. The family had lived at Orchard Portman, a Tudor manor house, now demolished, about 3 km south of Taunton.
5. This took place on Tuesday 14 August 1855. The building was completed in 1858 and became the law courts.
6. East of Taunton's town centre.

To Rebecca Ryves

August 30 1855

It is indeed a long time since I have written to you my dearest Rebecca but the truth is, I have been so ill, and cast down, with all my ceaseless worries, that I have been unwilling to add to yours, by sending you a packet of blue devils, which is all I could have sent you. Alas! poor Mr Hyde has been so ill, that he has done nothing; – and though at Aller,[1] only six miles from this, wrote me word two days ago, that he had made four ineffectual attempts to come over and see me: but even if he were well poor man, I have long known that when one is compelled to have recourse to law, in formâ pauperis,[2] one must relinquish all hopes of justice! – Mrs Tyler returned me my packet of letters safely, but without a word: however one is never surprised at any thing ill bred or unfeeling from English people in a much higher sphere than hers. – I saw poor Sir Richard Bourkes[3] sudden death in the paper, – and felt grieved at it, from all you had told me of him, though he, and such men as my poor dear uncle, are much fitter for Heaven, than Earth, and do a great deal of harm in this Millennium of Meanness, by spoiling one, for all the rest of the world. This horrible paper on which I am writing, is called the <u>Alliance</u>[4] paper! – trust the English when they <u>do</u> attempt, anything like taste! or sentiment for achieving a triumph of vulgarity. No doubt that little selfish, sensual wretch of a queen has as usual disgraced the Country well with her disgusting meanness at Paris; – as it is not Every day, that an English Monarch goes to France, or receives such Arabian nights Entertainments[5] she ought to have left at <u>least</u> £30, 000 for the poor of Paris – which she might well have afforded out of the five hundred thousand she so iniquitously accepted from that old mad Miser Neal[6] away from his starving relations; but of course she has not exceeded her usual Twopence halfpenny Homoeopathies. – I think the best Mob? <u>Mot</u>[7] – I've heard was the people spelling over daily programme – of the royal movements, and being always posed at the Eternal "lunch à une heure aux Tuileries – on à L'Elysée[8] till one more versed in English "Fashionable arrangements" as the Morning Post[9] calls them – than the rest – suddenly exclaimed "fiche nous le camp! – c'est une erreur d'imprimerie, – çela veut dire le <u>punche</u>!!!! les anglais ne faut rien sans Pouche et la reine le prend toujours à une heure"[10] – and as the lure of her majesty's nose, seems to corroborate this statement no doubt the solution was thought most satisfactory. – My pride and my vanity – both received a sad blow the other day in being ...

... After, I had a Childs – Party, in honour of the little cats Christening which came off with great splendour! Tibby being Dog father to his own little cat, which is most beautifully masked like a little Tiger, and Jerry being Dog-father to his – which is black like himself, with one little white star on its forehead – but what is quite new in grimalkin archives is, that I gave them a <u>surname</u> and as most distinguished! families owe theirs, to some remarkable circumstance connected with their origin – I called these young heroes by the name of Catfield! – Tibs being Christened in rose water "Tibby Alma -Catfield – and Jerry – Jerry Inkerman Catfield. At first when they began to open their eyes – owing to their nearly watery grave the poor little Eyes were very weak but now, that they are progressing towards Cathood – Tibby Alma has the most darling little face you ever saw – every one really raves about his beauty – and it is too doatskin to see the two Dogfathers – playing and rolling on the rug with their dog children: – Mrs Garland (Augustas sister)[11] who arrived from Jamaica last week – laden with Yams, and Pineapples, – has begged so hard for Tibby Alma, that as a great favour – I have let her have him – he is so fluffy, and boots, with that most innocent little cats face of his. I hope you saw that Baron Rothschild[12] has a horse called "Little Tibby" which won at Goodwood.[13] Fleas being now in season! here is a conundrum <u>my</u> Tib made the other morning while I was com[b]ing him – "Why are the fleas that you get out of mud, like the Jews at Rome?" "Give it up?" – "Because they live at the back of the Tiber"[14] Oh! I instantly sent for the Dog Dr but he said de dog was not mad, only talking fool, as hims mud does so often to him. And so, me only sent him off, with a flea in hims ear. Here ends all I have to tell you except horrors, and worries, – I got your letter yesterday, but besides, its being my Execution day I mean the anniversary of my fatal marriage: – I had more than my usual quantum of crying to do, – for as my quarter here becomes due the 5th of September – full six weeks – before my Parish allowance is <u>due</u>; and God knows how many before it will be screwed out of that ineffable Blackguard; – and as poor Mrs Clarke[15] has been so very kind, and liberal to me; I could not bear the idea of keeping her out of her money so long, to say nothing of the shame, and disgrace to myself – so I packed up the <u>last</u>! things I have now to sell, – ie Lord Byrons picture! and that old Jewelled Sévres Ecuelle[16] with the portraits of Louis Quinze, and The Duchesse de Châteauroux[17] on it and poor Jenkins is kindly gone to Bath to day to see what she can do with them; but I dont expect even to succeed in this miserable <u>pis aller</u>:[18] it is this cursed being <u>compelled</u> to move so constantly out of the routine of my Treadmill quarter that so completely skins me; – and <u>that</u> is the motive of that fiends incessant persecution – and hunting for I think if he could succeed in <u>literally</u> getting the skin off my bones as he has figuratively; he would not then rest till he had ground the bones themselves to powder. I dont think the Brute has <u>yet</u> succeeded in tracking me; – by the people whom he sets to ...

HALS
Incomplete letter.
1.   Aller is a village and parish in Somerset.
2.   As a pauper (Latin).

3.   Richard Bourke (1777–1855) was a general and colonial governor, renowned for his humanity. In 1839, Bourke was appointed high sheriff for County Limerick, and then declined the offer to stand for Limerick in the parliamentary elections of 1841. He died suddenly on 13 August.

4.   It would appear that the proceeds of this notepaper went towards supporting the war effort of the military alliance of France, Britain and the Ottoman Empire against the Russians during the Crimean War.

5.   See RBL, 14 October 1833. On 23 August, a magnificent fete and ball was given by the municipality of Paris in honour of Queen Victoria's first visit to the capital. She was entertained at an imperial ball at the Palace at Versailles, the gardens of which were illuminated with impressive fireworks.

6.   John Camden Neild (1780–1852) had bequeathed £500,000 to 'Her Most Gracious Majesty, Queen Victoria, begging Her Majesty's most gracious acceptance ... for her sole use and benefit, and her heirs, &c'. Neild was a miser, who sometimes slept on a bare board and dressed in old, worn-out clothes. The Queen increased the £100 left to his executors by ten-fold and also provided a legacy for his housekeeper of twenty-six years who had been left no provision.

7.   Word (French).

8.   'Lunch at one o'clock at the Tuileries – to the Elysée ...' (French).

9.   See RBL, 30 September 1845.

10. Literally: 'get out of here! (don't be silly) – this is a printing error – what it means is punch!!!! The English don't do anything without Pouche and the queen always takes it at one o'clock' (French).

11. A sister of Fanny and Augusta Boys, who had been living in Jamaica.

12. Sir Anthony Nathan de Rothschild (1810–76) was a member of the Rothschild banking family. During the early 1850s, he bought Aston Clinton House, near Aylesbury in Buckinghamshire, where he bred thoroughbred racehorses, producing a number of successful winners on the track.

13. Set on top of the Sussex Downs, the race course was started on the Goodwood Estate of the third Duke of Richmond in 1802.

14. The main watercourse that flows through Rome. The city was founded on the east bank of the river.

15. Charlotte Clarke is the owner of Giles's Castle Hotel, Taunton.

16. A shallow, flat-bottomed bowl with vertical sides and two handles, made out of porcelain, and typically used for serving soup. See RBL, 17 November 1854. This artefact was given by Louis XV to Marie Antoinette and then passed down to Philippe d'Auvergne, Duke of Bouillon, who gave it to RBL's mother in 1813.

17. Marie-Anne of Mailly-Nesle, Duchess of Châteauroux (1717–44), was a mistress of Louis XV and the youngest of four sisters, who served as courtesans in the royal court of France.

18. Last resort (French).

To Rebecca Ryves

Tuesday September 11th 1855

Many thanks my dearest Rebecca for the Three not indeed <u>Graces</u>![1] nor even Holbeins[2] – but <u>old</u> <u>beans</u> of Grandity! – which like Sampson[3] have already slain their thousands and with the self <u>same weapon</u> too! the convulsions of laughter they excited are really fearful! – especially with one young lady who having been in Dublin this summer, – had my orders to prowl about Merrion Square till she succeeded in catching a glimpse of the inconceivable <u>Original</u>, but alas! without success; you will not be surprised to hear – that the flourish of Trumpets, about the house in Merrion Square, is a sham, and a brag, like every thing – that quintessence of brummagem Grandity – alias Margracia Grandifudgea[4] ever did, as Dr Somebodys name is on the door, – so that she has only Lodgings there. I am sorry to hear that Massy has gone into the Middlesex militia (or become a <u>Malicious</u> man! as the common people call it here) as not only do I fear, that the drills, and Lark – like risings will be too much for him, but also that it will lead him in to terrible expenses; far exceeding any emoluments it may bring him. – Alas! for the Bath expedition that Augusta so kindly took – it only partially succeeded; but even <u>that</u> was more than I had hoped or expected: the poor Cup, sold for £21 – and – the dealer in <u>Vértu</u>[5] who bought it said if he had, only had the Byron miniature a month ago – he was sure he could have got £50 for it from a Mr Bryner (Byron mad) who is now abroad he knows not where; but Raing (the dealer) kept it to see what he could do with it: – I cannot bear to think of it, so will now end the subject. – Yesterday I went over to Bridgewater[6] with Augusta Fanny and Louisa to spend the day with Mrs Forde[7] a cousin of theirs, who has a pretty place near it: the day being lovely young Forde[8] her son drove us all over to see The Agapemone (The Abode of Love!)[9] – Mr Price[10] the originator of this Blasphemous Humbug – is called <u>The Lord</u>! and asserts himself to be our saviour![11] he had been curate to a Mr Starkey[12]– whose sister he married, and whose self he perverted – he allows none but very rich people to join this impious community, and they are all obliged to make over their whole property to him by Deed for <u>ever</u>, so that if they leave the Agapemone they have not a <u>sou</u>! <u>he</u> Prince, has always <u>two</u> favourite sultanas who are dressed in white and called (while in favor!) the Queens of Heaven – the favourite par <u>excellence</u> at this moment was a Laundress! but, an exceedingly handsome woman, his <u>real</u> wife is set aside, and called Sister Julia! During the Queens visit to Paris he went over, and took his <u>2</u> favourite Odalisques – and Mr Thomas[13] – another ci-devant[14] Parson! of the gang was allowed to take <u>one</u> of his! but – if ever any of the husbands are detected kissing, their own wives, while they are the <u>Lords</u>! Favorites, they are instantly condemned to the most menial, hard labour for days, as a punishment – all this iniquity began under the cloak of religion! but now they say they are in Heaven!

and require no more prayers – so the Chapel a most gorgeous one has now been converted into a Billiard and music room – in which there is the most splendid Grand Piano – (a Broadwood)[15] actually a mass of wrought gold – on the outside, and all other instruments and amongst them a most wonderful one made by a man in the Black Forest[16] (now dead) which is called the Uturpeon[17] made to imitate – which it does to perfection a full opera Orchestra – violins – Flutes Harps – pianos, Hautboys,[18] Clarionets – Cornets à Pistons – Bassoons Drums – Trumpets Violincellos Piccolos &&& – it played while we were there most exquisitely the overtures to William Tell,[19] and the Semeramide[20] – it has 12 Enormous boards and the inventor was 7 years making it which I thought a very short time seeing what a Herculean achievement it is; – but I thought considering its present locale – it should have been called the YouTurkean This music room with its big Groined Cathedral ceiling, and windows, is most gorgeously! furnished, with Crimson Velvet divans, Ottomans – && luxuriously springed, and stuffed, with carpet to match, and a Dais at the upper End. The Agapemone itself, is a long low range of Gothic cottage orné[21] buildings – looking very like – a set of modern Elizabethan Alms Houses[22] – but covered with the richest possible foliage of beautiful wisterias and other creepers going over the roof:- the grounds – which are the beauty of the place, are exquisitely laid out, with Terraces && – forming a perfect Paradise of flowers, – as the parterres in the velvet lawns, are arranged in mosaics of the most vivid and lovely flowers, – so as to look exactly like a carpet of growing flowers – from the pattern – I'm not quite sure that I admired the exterior of the Green-houses, Hot-houses and Conservatories – being a little too chinois[23] but the roofs certainly were pretty, and novel being Dome shaped – and painted so as to resemble, a rainbow which had broken into beams around them. – In the Banqueting hall, the tables ascend through large trap doors, from the kitchen ready served – and descend at the end of the repast in the same Theatrical and Mysterious manner re-mounting with the Dessert. – But next to the grounds, the thing best worth seeing there was the stud! for a finer one of thorough bred Horses I never saw – and all such tame, well mannered darlings – rubbing their fine, small beautiful heads, against one and lifting up their delicate hoofs – to shake hands. There were "Morning Star" "Evening Star" – "Eothen" "Early dew" – "Sun beam" "Lightening Foot" "Arabian Godolphin"[24] and "Elgin" whose acquaintance I especially made – the names of the others I forget. The Harness room was also well worth seeing – they never go out without four Horses and out riders, – ridden by gentlemen not grooms who as long as "The Lord" is in sight remain uncovered! – and are always Chapeau bas[25] the moment he appears; – they often come into this Town to make purchases – as the ladies dress most magnificently; but they left off dealing at the Howell, and James's[26] of this Ilk – because the man refused to direct the parcels to "The Lord! – we did not see "The Lord"! yesterday – but I understand he is a fair, very handsome aristocratic, but with all dissipated looking man (and no wonder!) on state occasions – he always wears a long velvet robe, trimmed with Ermine; in which costume he announced his departure to Heaven some time ago – from a large field! but it is to be presumed he had a return Ticket, as he was again at the Agapemone the next day. It would be only charitable to suppose Mr Prince mad; instead of wholly so very bad; but the chief wonder is, how he found so many parsons – and chiefly Clergymen! to go mad at the same time; – I understand sometimes they walk about the grounds <u>en costume de Paradis</u>!27 even minus the fig leaf! – one of the members hung himself in the wood near the Agapemone a Fortnight ago – and I'll swear that one of the men – who showed us over the place yesterday a hideous fellow of the name of Rouse was melancholy mad:- and now I've told you all I know about the Agapemone; – except that whenever they go out, their very splendid <u>Cortége</u>28 is preceded by four magnificent black Blood hounds. – Last night before we left Bridgewater, while at Dessert, we were startled by the firing of Cannon, and Blazing of Bonfires and heard that Sebastapol29 had at length really fallen and on our return here, thought we should be killed driving from the station the horses were so frightened at the ignited Tar barrels rolling about in all directions squibs – fire – works – and – crackers, – and as Mrs Clarke had sent an open carriage for us, it was anything but agreeable – and I thought of all the aching hearts, and desolate hearths there were that night for truly as the late Duke of Wellington said, and it was the only right thing he ever <u>did</u> say, – "There is nothing more terrible! than a victory – except a defeat" I shall be late for the Post – so with Tibby fine Eyes – best love – Believe Me Ever

Gratefully and Affectly yours Rosina Bulwer Lytton.

HALS

1. In Roman mythology, the Three Graces (the *Gratiae*) – Aglaea ('Beauty'), Euphrosyne ('Mirth') and Thalia ('Good Cheer') – were attendants to the goddesses. In art, they were often the handmaidens of Venus as in *The Three Graces* (*c.* 1501–5) by Raphael.

2. Hans Holbein the Younger (*c.* 1497–1543) was a German artist who painted in a Northern Renaissance style. He is best known for his numerous portraits.

3. Samson killed a thousand Philistines single-handedly with the jawbone of an ass. See RBL, 26 October 1835.

4. Nickname for Lady Hotham's plaster portrait. See RBL, 23 October 1853.

5. A specialist in 'objects of vertu', high-quality art objects.

6. A town in Somerset.

7. A cousin to Fanny and Augusta Boys.

8. Mrs Forde's son is a second cousin to the Boys sisters.

9. A religious cult set up in 1846, situated in the Somerset village of Spaxton.

10. The founding father of the community was a defrocked clergyman, the Revd Henry James Prince (1811–99).

11. Revd Prince believed himself to be an embodiment of the Holy Ghost.

12. Revd Samuel Starkey's sister Julia became Prince's second wife. Like his first wife, Martha (*née* Freeman), she was an older woman with her own income.
13. Revd George Robinson Thomas had been a member of the Lampeter Brethren and was with Revd Prince from the earliest days of the cult.
14. Former (French).
15. John Broadwood & Sons were the producers of this make of piano that had been popularized in England by Queen Victoria, Mendelssohn and Chopin.
16. The Black Forest is a wooded mountain range in Baden-Württemberg, south-west Germany, bordered by the Rhine valley.
17. This sounds like an early version of the orchestrian, which is essentially an organ, run on electricity, which plays by means of perforated rolls.
18. An oboe.
19. The overture to Gioachino Rossini's opera *William Tell*, first performed in Paris in 1829.
20. *Semiramide* is an opera by Gioacchino Rossini. The libretto was written by Gaetano Rossi, based on Voltaire's tragedy *Semiramis* (derived from the legend of Semiramis of Babylon). It was first performed in Venice in 1823.
21. Ornate (French).
22. Charitable houses for poor, old and distressed folk.
23. In the Chinese style (French).
24. *Godolphin* (1833) is also the title of EBL's novel.
25. Hats off (French).
26. Howell, James & Co. were retailers of jewellery and silver merchandise. See RBL, 22 March 1837.
27. Literally: 'in the costume of Paradise' (French); in the nude.
28. Procession (French).
29. The French seizure of Malakoff Tower in the Crimea concluded the Siege of Sebastopol, marking a victory for the allies in the Crimean War. See RBL, 28 May 1855.

To Frederick Hodgson

Wednesday October 10th 1855

My dear Mr Hodgson I hearby authorise you to recieve my quarterly pittance due to day; and if it is not immediately paid – give yourself no further trouble about it, but instantly let me know; – and I shall proceed accordingly. – Yours sincerely Rosina Bulwer Lytton

Tuesday April the 14th 1857

I Hereby Authorise Frederick Hodgson Esqre of 32 Great Broad Street Buildings – Bank of England London – to recieve for me, in lieu of his late excellent, universally respected, and much lamented Father, Robert Hodgson Esqr of the above place. – on the 10th of April 10th of July – 10th of October and tenth of January of Each ensuing year – untill it shall please God in His Mercy – Either to remove me from this world, or confer upon me the equal blessing of making me a widow – the beggarly Parish allowance of One Hundred pounds £100 quarterly minus the Income Tax!! doled out to me by Sir Edward George Earl Bulwer Lytton Bart M.P. (for the last time) and [ill] many other titles not fit to write. – Rosina Bulwer Lytton (alas!)

HALS

To Rebecca Ryves

Tuesday November 6th 1855

My dearest Rebecca I was very glad to see the print of your paw once more, as Innocence would say if him condescended to speak the Biped jargon but I was truly sorry – and shocked to hear of the poor Lady's death! what a shocking thing for Mrs Lloyd, and you, its having taken place during her visit, – but poor soul – she has now reached her eternal home, and like all who do is to be envied. You say you wish your brother Williams child, were born to better prospects; alas! in <u>some</u> instances and <u>luckily</u> in others; <u>few</u> are born <u>to</u> the prospects they are born <u>with</u>; moreover I never pity a <u>man</u> born into the world, as <u>they</u> can always kick, crawl, or climb through it; it is only we poor wretched women who are for the most part doomed to a sort of moral macadamization. – I am glad to hear such a good bulletin of Massy, but no wonder, since according to his hydropathic description of Aldershot[1] he is what the Cockneys would call <u>well wet</u>, meaning <u>vel vet</u>. I really have a sample in writing to you never having any thing to tell you but the same Treadmill worry! worry! worry! – humanly speaking it really lasts too long – and I am quite worn out – not having one ray of hope, or a loophole through which I can creep to help myself. I have been much annoyed by poor kind well meaning but perfectly passive and therefore awfully compromising Mr Hodgson – having obeyed a mandate of Sir Liars – to call upon him in his Den in Park Lane to receive my parish allowance – that wretch Loaden having gone abroad – and Mr Hodgson – having said that after the Blackguardism of his conduct on the last occasion – and total breach of faith with him; nothing would induce him to meet Loaden again: – I couldnt help asking Mr Hodgson if it was possible he could be such a dove! as to suppose that Loaden acted as he did out of his own head! and not according to his infamous Clients instructions? – at all events I have forbidden Mr Hodgson for the future to have any personal communication with Sir Liar, as I consider any <u>nominal</u> agent of mine doing so on civil terms – is a gross insult to me, – I have begged that he may always merely enclose my order for the money – and if the contemptible Reptile refuses to send a cheque without his going for it – just to let me know; and he shall never repent it but once. To add to my comfort I have every chance of losing my things – Linen – Books and China – with the few Pictures left in Brownes care – as there is still £26 owing to him, on that abominable £55 Inventory! And he has trumped up a bill of £10 for the standing – that is Warehouse room of them – and the Bankrupt Assignees have now removed them to the Pantechnicon where they are further eating themselves up – and even had I the means – (which I have not) of removing them from thence – of course the Assignees would not allow me to do so till Brownes £36 was paid: As for my poor old glass in the clutches of that Scotch shark Mr Campbell– poor Mr Hodgson has let him so unmolestedly keep possession of it for the last year that I have now neither hope, nor chance of recovering it. Truly may they say that a rolling stone gathers no moss; last week I got from Brighton the 8 trunks left at Mrs Tylers, and which Mrs Tyler took care of when she left Brighton – the locks of the two Boot Imperials[2] – were forced open – and out of one was taken that little silver convolvus[3] shaped candle stick – a miniature and several books: but I have said nothing to Mrs Wheeler about it, not knowing whether this was done at her house; – or at Mrs Tylers; but I should rather think at the latters as I know – that horrid Eliza used to rob her in every way. As for <u>my</u> working! toil as I will; it is only the wheel of Sisyphus or the tub of the Danaieds;[4] – I have a book[5] ready – that live, or die I am determined <u>shall</u> be published and I dont hesitate to say it will make a fortune for whoever does publish it, not from its literary merits but from its subject – but that very subject requires such secrecy in getting a Publisher that down in this ditch – and with <u>no</u> one I can trust to negotiate such a matter, with fidelity to me or common intelligence – as to the business part of the matter there it lies a dead letter – had I but £200 I would publish it on my own account as I know by publishing it in <u>One</u> thick vol – uniform with Russell The Times correspondents letters from the Crimea[6] – I should clear thousands by it – but <u>without</u> money it is impossible to make money; or even to stave off ruin. I have been reading Mrs Nortons letter to the Queen[7] – it is exceedingly well written – <u>so well</u> – and containing such incontrovertible truths, that I wish some more injured and more unblemished woman had written it; however be what she may – that does not alter the force of her statements, or palliate Nortons marital Blackguardism – a copy printed in gold ought to be presented to every woman about to marry – to tell them how the Ecclesiastical laws of England are!!![8] and what they have to <u>expect</u> if a Husband <u>chuses</u> to avail himself of their barbarous iniquity – but Lord save us! As far as any hope of human sympathy – and redress goes – she had far better have addressed her letter, to the statue of Queen Anne in St Pauls Churchyard[9] – for <u>she</u> used from Marlborough to Masham[10] always take the womens part whereas that little dumpy heartless marionette queen Victoria – not only boasts – that <u>she</u> always takes the mens part! but proves it by surrounding herself with all the most notoriously profligate men and infamous husbands she can collect. À propos[11] – of both – dont you remember – how Carlyle used to abuse that brute Foster and the Dickens gang and quote whole pages of "Chevely"[12] saying "you bit off his brummagem enthusiasm and the like! capitally"– well now it appears on the plan of union being strength he's joined that infamous clique – as you will see by that disgusting piece of humbug in The Times of the 2d Instant – where they (the gang of <u>course</u> including Sir Liar – for no humbug is complete without <u>him</u>!) want to get £400!! to buy an annuity for Dr Johnsons God daughter and her sister the two Miss Lowes who are the happy possessors of the old Fir desk upon which "the great moralist"! wrote his Dictionary![13] now if it be true that Routledge gave Sir Liar?? £20, 000 for his old Copy rights; and; that almost equally loathsome Hypocrite Dickens cleared £10, 000 by "Bleak House"[14] alone – I think it would have been more decent for them to have put their hands in their own pockets for this £400: – but then to besure their great virtue! benevolence! And Charity!! would have been as much ignored by the public at large as if they did not possess these attributes!!! – this balderdashtic appeal, is evidently written by Carlyle – and signed

"Thomas Carlyle"

"Charles Dickens"

"John Foster"

The Times will put in any thing as an advertisement – and had I money enough to pay for it I certainly would Parody this appeal – in behalf of the great greatgrand daughter of a God daughter of Dr Bushy's who had in her possession (well authenticated) the identical hat which the Dr did <u>not</u> take off before the King! and two things used to flagellate the boys even in the presence! when ever that operation was required to establish his own supremacy! and sign this letter

Thomas Marstyle

Charles Trickens

John Fudgester. –

Talking of the <u>fundamental</u> manner in which learning was inculcated in the days of the merry monarch under the auspices of the great Bushy! reminds me of a charming <u>mot</u>[15] of a young gentleman of 14 at a Picnic I was at about six weeks ago: – having for three long hours preserved a profound silence never once opening his mouth but to eat; he all at once made an appeal to the whole company without reserve ladies included, to the following effect. "Why is it that a steam engine can never sit down?" – "give it up" we did: – "Because it has a tender – <u>behind</u>!" We were so far like steam engines after this! that we could not sit any longer – but took to our heels as fast as possible to laugh at this tender speech

– and as it is all I have to make you laugh – I'll say good bye and with Tibs best love Believe me Ever gratefully and affectly yrs. Rosina Bulwer Lytton

you never told me if Lady Massy (the Bride) was as handsome as she was reported to be?

HALS

1. In 1854, the heathland around Aldershot, a town in Hampshire was established as an army base, due to the Crimean War. At one of the four gates of the camp lies Farnham, which is where Dr Edward Lane's hydropathic establishment at Moor Park was located.
2. Imperials were large flat trunks fitted to the top of coaches. Boot imperials were probably large trunks that were placed in a carriage's enclosed area, used for carrying goods.
3. *Convolvus* is a Latin generic name usually related to plants, meaning to twist or twine.
4. The Danaids were fifty daughters of Danaus I, who married the sons of Aegyptus I, and murdered their husbands on their wedding night, except one, because he had respected the virginity of his bride. The other Danaids buried the heads of their husbands and were punished in the underworld for their deeds by having to carry water to fill a leaky jar.
5. *Very Successful!* See note to RBL, 10 May 1855. This novel is the story of Mary Penrhyn, a widow looking for a position as a governess, who is befriended by Phillip Phippen (see RBL, 5 May 1857). She finds a position in the household of Sir Gregory Kempenfelt (see RBL, 4 November 1856). The novel is a roman à clef satirizing EBL as Sir Janus Allpuff (see RBL, 22 June 1858) and Benjamin Disraeli as Jericho Jabber.
6. William Howard Russell (1820–1907) was an Irish reporter with the London *Times*, who spent twenty-two months covering the Crimean War.
7. Caroline Norton's *A Letter to the Queen on Lord Chancellor Cranford's Marriage and Divorce Bill* (1855).
8. English laws concerning the Church of England, relating to the ecclesiastical court. See RBL, 17 August 1857.
9. Queen Anne (1665–1714) reigned from 1702 to 1714.
10. Sarah Churchill, Duchess of Marlborough (1660–1744), and Abigail, Baroness Masham (d. 1734), were close friends of Queen Anne. The Duchess of Marlborough wielded enormous political influence due to her friendship with Queen Anne. This was undermined during 1707 by her cousin Abigail Masham, who was related to Anne's Whig minister Robert Harley. It was through Masham that Harley exerted influence over the Queen.
11. Connected with (French).
12. RBL's novel is spelt *Cheveley*. See RBL to Mr Leyton, 27 January 1853.
13. Between 1746 and 1755, Samuel Johnson wrote *A Dictionary of the English Language*, which was published in 1755. See RBL, 23 January 1826.
14. Charles Dickens's *Bleak House* was his ninth novel; it was published in nineteen monthly parts between March 1852 and September 1853. The first complete edition appeared in 1853.
15. Word (French).

To Rebecca Ryves

Monday November 19th 1855

My dearest Rebecca as you expressed a wish to see Mrs Nortons "Letter to the Queen"[1] I send you mine though it is so filthy I am ashamed to do so. – I having made a point of cramming Every British <u>female</u> with this digest, and exposée[2] of our iniquitous Ecclesiastical laws – among others Mrs Clarke who kept it so long down in the <u>Bar</u> – that it became as dirty as if it had been bred to it! I must trouble you to return it to me at your leisure as this the 4th Edition is again out of print so you see how it has <u>sold</u> though the Press has preserved such a discreet silence about it, – I see the gist of the matter exactly – there is no <u>doubt</u> of what Mrs Norton is – but Norton like a mean wretch connived at it for years – as long as he found it lined his pockets; – and furious at her having a retiring(??!) Pension of £500 from Sydney Herbert as well as the one of £600 from old Melbourne whom every one knows was not addicted to Platonics – and she having accounted for Sydney Herberts £500 a year – by making out that her <u>mother</u> had left it to her – when every one knew – and more especially Norton, that Mrs Sheridan had not 500 pence to leave – he in a fury stops the £600 a year alimony that he allowed her; but instead of honestly saying why he did so; he entraps her into one of these disgraceful swindles which our charming Laws give an English Husband full and irresponsible powers to Exercise upon his legal victim. I see Skeet has got another ...

HALS

The end of the letter is missing.

1. Caroline Norton, *A Letter to the Queen*. See RBL, 6 November 1855.
2. Exposure (French).

To Rebecca Ryves

Tuesday December 4th 1855

My dearest Rebecca In order that I may not forget to answer your questions, the best way is to do so immediately first promising that in January as soon as I have paid my "liabilities" (which alas! are anything but "<u>limited</u>" the limitation being confined to my means) I will get a clean copy of Mrs Nortons letter, and send it to you – sincerely wishing I could send you something more useful to you for a New Years gift, – The Lady she alludes to in the reign of William the 4th[1] – was Lady Westmeath and the reason of the Duke of Wellingtons[2] surprising! because very unusual tender hearted benevolence on her behalf, – was because he was – or at least was <u>said</u> to be intriguing with her, and it was upon <u>his</u> account – that Lord Westmeath[3] (at all times an ill tempered brute) turned restive: – she was an exceedingly pretty, and agreeable person – and the only woman of that stamp I was ever guilty of liking how ever <u>elle chassait bien de race</u>[4] for her mother old Lady Salisbury was also a <u>femme</u> <u>gallante</u>![5] I remember years ago – before I was turned out of my home I was sitting with Lady Westmeath – who had then apartments in St James's Palace[6] – and Sir Henry Halford[7] who was attending her came in – among other things he prescribed for her <u>counter irritation</u> "What nonsense, – said I when you know <u>Polygamy</u> is not allowed in this country – this was a jest we could both appreciate the Bitter reality being no joke! to us. I am convinced that had old Melbourne[8] lived – to go on telling her blessed majesty queen Victoria smutty stories, and continued Premier Mrs Norton <u>would</u> have been one of her Bed chamber women; – for <u>after</u> that disgraceful Trial – she received her at court! Lord Melbourne being then living; – but since his death – Mrs Nortons immorality – has of course assumed – a more heinous and indefensible character – I know it <u>well</u> – and remember I tell it to you – the atmosphere of English society (I mean the <u>haute vole</u>)[9] is profligacy, and its dry <u>rot, selfishness</u> and <u>without</u> these two pales a poor conscientious fool has no chance; as that Infernal Machine the Press – has carried out <u>one</u> half of Bagots[10] injunction with regard to Mrs Nortons Pamphlet – ie that of making it "<u>Private</u> and <u>confidential</u>" I am glad you are going to fulfil the <u>pendant</u> – of this incompatible fiat – by <u>disseminating it everywhere</u>!! – your Idea of a "<u>self supporting</u>" Printing office for poor Authors to be their own Publishers and <u>reapers</u>, is a capital one and quite original – and alas! likely to remain so – as that disgraceful swindle The <u>Guilt</u> of Literature– was an attempt – of course under the pretence of Charity! to fetter the Press and crush – and cripple poor Authors – God help them more than they already are, but however it is quite on the "<u>Elevating principle</u>"! as the beastly gang belonging to it Sir Liar – Dickens and that ugly noseless Ruffian Forster[11] – are always drunk, as for my poor book – I have no earthly chance in the present generation of finding a Publisher – though were I dead tomorrow – I have no doubt with my usual good luck! it would be a fortune to any Publisher it is not as I told you a novel in short – I'll tell you the title, but <u>really</u> <u>Privately</u> <u>and confidentially</u> – and <u>not</u> with bigots clause to be disseminated every where! I call it "The Nemesis of Humbug – or letters from the Shade of Lord Byron To the rising – and risen Generation of Great Britain" it contains my whole History with all Sir Liars infamy laid bare including the letters of his infamous spies which I should have facsimiled but as you may suppose these letters, are not <u>confined</u> ...

HALS

Incomplete letter.

1.   King William IV (1765–1837) ruled from 1830 until his death.
2.   The first Duke of Wellington. See RBL, 13 March 1825.
3.   See RBL, 7 January 1836.
4.   She is such a chip off the old block (French).

5.   A female gallant (French).
6.   Up to 1837, St James's Palace, situated in The Mall, London, was the official royal residence and was where the Royal Court was based.
7.   Sir Henry Halford, first Baronet (1766–1844), was President of the Royal College of Physicians from 1820 to 1844. He had also been physician to George III, George IV and William IV, and attended all the royal dukes and princesses at that time.
8.   Lord Melbourne died in 1848. See RBL, 23 January 1826.
9.   Literally: 'high flown' (French).
10. William Bagot, third Baron Bagot (1811–87), was a Tory MP for Denbighshire and after entering the House of Lords served as a government whip under the Earl of Derby and Benjamin Disraeli.
11. John Forster. See RBL, 17 September 1839.

To Rebecca Ryves

Wednesday Decr 5th 1855

My dearest Rebecca

You will say that there is no end to my scribbledoms today but I have just read in The Times -the following and confess it gave me a greater shock – than I am sure it has done most of her dear <u>friends</u> and Toadies

"On the 30th Instant at her marine residence Western House Brighton Lady Hotham in the 80th year of age – of Great Finborough Hall Suffolk[1] and Hereford House Brompton"[2] – I wish you would write a line to Davis (Mr John Davis Western House Brighton) which you might do by saying you had seen her death[3] in the Paper and wished to know if she had been long ill? and that you hoped she had left him and all her old servants well provided for – and that you also hoped her nephew had the bulk of her property – and not her Toadies like that little despicable Chevalier – which will be nuts to Davis – as he always detested him – and used to tell me in Paris he was far from worthy of all the kindness wasted upon him – being a low mean reptile, which God knows he fully proved himself to me. –

> In Haste to save Post
> Ever your affect
> R B Lytton

HUNT
1.   Great Finborough Hall is located near Stowmarket in the county of Suffolk. It was built on the site of a medieval manor house in the sixteenth century. Lady Hotham's first husband, Roger Pettiward, transformed the house into a neo-classical structure.
2.   Hereford House, Earls Court, Brompton in London was built around 1815 by Philip Gilbert. The house was demolished between 1901 and 1904.
3.   Lady Hotham died of bronchitis.

To Rebecca Ryves

Thursday Decr 6th 1855

My dearest Rebecca when I asked you to write to Davis yesterday I quite forgot to tell you to be sure and enclose him a stamped envelope for his answer as I am sure he has lived too long with poor lady Hotham not to think a great deal of a penny. – I have written what you had better say; in great haste, as I am just going down to the Court to hear Mr Cole[1] open the case against a wretch by the name of Tutton[2] – the son of an auctioneer[3] in Bath who attempted to poison his poor old Father – who had always been a most indulgent one to him – the poor mother, and sisters are perfect living skeletons with agony of mind but the wretch himself brazens it out and has got as fat as a porpoise since he has been in jail, as Mr Cole said last night it requires the greatest possible interest in these days of mock sentiment for crime to get a real villain hanged – so he has no doubt this one will get off – and so be let loose to finish work another time and perhaps poison his sisters out of revenge for being witnesses against him. Ever gratefully and affectly yrs RB Lytton.

HALS
1. RBL's friend Mr Henry T. Cole QC was a barrister. RBL went to hear his speech for the prosecution at the Taunton Assizes. Mr Wilton, a solicitor, defended the accused, who later took on some of the defence himself.
2. Thomas Tutton (b. *c.* 1832) was accused of deliberately administering arsenic to his father.
3. Charles Tutton.

To Rebecca Ryves

Monday Dcr 10th 1855

My dearest Rebecca – I send you the first private intimation I have had of Lady Hothams death – which is not much, but I have written for further particulars – and to know whether she was buried at Finborough,[1] or at Brighton – but I suppose the former. – I told Mrs Wheeler that I could only inform her whom she had <u>not</u> left anything to – but of course as the will would not be read till after the funeral no particulars of it are yet known. I am writing to you under the greatest difficulties of Pillows and bandages having met with a serious accident on Friday by slipping on a frosty stone, which cut and sprained my back terribly and I am still faint from the loss of blood – and I fear it will be many weeks before I can get about. Oh! it is when I am laid on a sick bed that I doubly feel the cruel injustice of my miserable, and unparalleled position; and to read puffs in the papers about that Fiends large fortune – and the good taste and brilliancy of his Equipages at Paris – while his legal victim is without even a maid – or the commonest necessaries according to her sphere of life, is more than a human being can well bear, added <u>to all the rest</u> of course the other villain[2] was let off the other day because he <u>was</u> a villain – never was evidence <u>so</u> strong against any culprit, and never did I see so hardened and villainous a countenance, – among other things it was proved that he had been trying experiments on poisoning Cats, and had spent the money his poor Father had given him to set up business on bad women – the only touch of human feeling he evinced during the long 12 hours Trial was when his poor wretched mother could <u>not</u> give her evidence against him and her shrieks filled the court as she was carried out – then <u>he</u> actually wept too! so that it seems even Felons, and murderers have some touch of natural feeling for their mothers, <u>all</u> except the arch Fiends son. While his poor sisters were giving their extorted evidence he looked at them like a very demon if a word dropped from them that could compromise him and had they been <u>properly</u> cross examined, he <u>must</u> have been hung – as Rosa Tutton[3] owned to Augusta <u>after</u> the trial – that she had seen him hurry the paper the arsenic had been in into his pocket when he had mixed it with the Potatoes and they all owned he had attempted to Poison the poor old man <u>several</u> times before, – he said wringing his hands poor man "See what comes of spoiling a child!" – When the wretch was acquitted by a jury as villainous looking as himself at 9 at night – he rushed out of court – in the most hardened manner; – and it appears a Legion of Prostitutes were waiting for him – who escorted him in triumph to some Tavern.

P.S. It was very interesting but revolting to hear – the minute and scientific Evidence – of the two Herepaths[4] Father, and son as to finding the Arsenic – in the food – by all the different tests and more than 20 grains were found and all produced in court – under different phases – young Herepath is the wildest German nightmare, Monster in Frankenstein[5] looking animal you can imagine, and gives one the idea of having been like Mithredates[6] fed on Poisons; – or at least, weaned on Arsenic, – and drammed with Prussic acid and old Herepaths sly twinkle of the Eye, in contempt of the judges <u>un</u> scientific ignorance and his "not <u>exactly</u> my Lud" every time his Lordship betrayed it were worth going any distance to see, and hear though indeed I would rather be hanged myself than ever pass such another 12 hours. –

HALS

1. Lady Hotham's home, Great Finborough Hall, Suffolk. See RBL, 5 December 1855.
2. Thomas Tutton.
3. One of Thomas Tutton's four sisters.
4. A father and son, who were both analytical chemists in Bristol.
5. The monster created by Mary Shelley in her novel *Frankenstein* (1818).
6. Mithridates VI of Pontus (132–63 BC) was the King of Pontus in Asia Minor and an enemy of Rome. Mithridates sought to harden himself against poisoning by taking

increasingly sub-lethal doses of certain poisons until he could tolerate lethal doses. When Mithridates was at last defeated by Pompey and in danger of capture by Rome, he tried to commit suicide by taking poison. Because he was unable to take a sufficient amount, he fell on his sword instead.

To Rebecca Ryves

Tuesday Night Decr 11th 1855

Many thanks My dearest Rebecca for your kind letter just received; which is about as much as I can say seeing that I am so unexpectedly verifying in my own person – the young gentlemans charming conundrum, of the whys and where-fores; Steam Engines are incapacitated by indulging in s<u>edentary</u> habits and therefore I must stand upon the ceremony of answering your letter when I am better able to do so; merely by this post forwarding you the memoir of young Massy[1] – which some day or other I should like back not having a second. – I also to save the trouble of copying it, send you a letter with a strange <u>on</u> <u>dit</u>[2] – about Miss Murray;[3] – I wrote back word that I could easily account for it, for as we always judge of things, more or less by our <u>own</u> <u>twinges</u> doubtless after a comparative analogy, and <u>anatomy</u> of her own, and her fellow maidens slavery at Buckingham Palace,[4] she very naturally gave the preference to the <u>Nigger</u> sys-tem[5] over the <u>niggard</u> one, under which she had graduated – I told Mrs Wheeler to call upon Davis– and find out as many particulars as she could; – and when I hear any thing further I'll let you know. – Master Fine Eyes says do him is a great votary of Terpsichore[6] and dances most bootley – woe be to the dog who ever presumes to call him Terps! It would be a fine stroke of meanness – worthy of the clique – and of the rest of her conduct towards me if Lady Hotham – had left Sir Liar – the legacy she originally intended leaving me – what ever that was; – and I should not be the least surprised that such was the culminating point of the plot. Though she let him almost starve – I hope poor Carew[7] will now get his £700 for her own monument which she so long superintended! Felice notte[8] – Ever affectly yrs RBL.

HALS
1. Dawson Massy, *Footprints of a Faithful Shepherd: A Memoir of the Revd Godfrey Massy* (1855).
2. Gossip (French).
3. Amelia Matilda Murray (1795–1884), the daughter of Lord George Murray, was cho-sen to be Maid of Honour to Queen Victoria in 1837. She continued in that post until 1853.
4. As a result of her tour of North America (1854–5), Murray became an advocate for the abolition of slavery. She was warned by court officials not to publish her account of her travels, so she resigned from her position in the Queen's household.

5. Murray writes about the plight of negroes in her *Letters from the United Sates, Cuba, and Canada* (1856).
6. In Greek, literally means 'delight of dancing'. In Greek mythology, Terpsichore was one of the nine Muses ruling over dance and the dramatic chorus.
7. RBL dined with John Edward Carew (*c.* 1782–1868), the well-known Irish sculptor, or his son F. Carew, at Lady Hotham's home, Hereford House, in 1853. See RBL, 4 March 1858.
8. Good night (Italian).

To Rebecca Ryves

Miss Massy Ryves at Eyre Lloyds Esqr Prospect Castle Connell Limerick Ireland[1]
[Dec 12 1855]

So now the wretch[2] is again at large to resume his poisonings I think he had better offer his services to Sir Liar – who no doubt would be happy to employ him Mr Cole, was really Eloquent, but that Baron Parke[3] the Judge is a complete old woman – and a most ridiculous looking one too – while Saunders who defended the Parricide – was a most vulgar looking fellow – with a short Hatchet manner like Loaden– and a voice of equal vulgarity of inflection as Albert Smiths:[4] – his <u>sobriquet</u> on Circuit is <u>Terps</u>, – Terpsichore[5] – being too long and his Father having been a Dancing Master. I am in such pain I can write no more – and you must forgive this <u>broken backed</u> scrawl – let me have back Mrs Wheelers letter, and with Master Fine Eyes best love believe me Ever your grateful and affect RBL

HALS
1. A landowner in Castleconnell, a village on the banks of the Shannon River, 11 km from the town of Limerick.
2. Mr Tutton.
3. Sir James Parke, Baron Wensleydale (1782–1868), was a conservative judge who, in 1834, was transferred from the King's Bench to the Court of Exchequer, where for some twenty years he exercised considerable influence. After finding that the changes introduced by the Common Law Procedure Acts of 1854 and 1855 conflicted with his legal conservatism, he resigned in December 1855.
4. This sounds like Albert Richard Smith (1816–60), author of *The Pottleton Legacy: A Story of Town and Country* (1849). See RBL, 11 February 1858.
5. See RBL, 11 December 1851.

To Rebecca Ryves

Bed, and Bolster Lodge
Sunday Night Decr 16th 55

Many thanks for your kind letter: – with regard to your "hope that I have a good Dr?" I must Quaker like reply with a query "Where would I get the money?" though indeed had I plenty I am so weary of my too miserable existence and false position – that I would not spend one <u>sou</u> of it upon Drs – as I am too anxious to give myself every legitimate chance of getting out of the world – I only wish I could do so – without suffering quite so much; besides Drs – cannot "minister to a mind diseased"[1] – neither could they rid me of the Arch Fiend who is the cause of all my miseries – and certainly for villainy that has neither parallel, nor prototype in History sacred or profane old chronicler speaking of Memprick King of the Britains says "<u>no</u> good thing is remembered of him, except that he begat an honest son." – a mode of authorship that cannot even be awarded to Sir Liar. I am very sorry to hear of Massys troublesome companions the Chilblains if they are <u>not</u> broken and he will get (which he could have done at a Chemists) an ounce and a half of nutgales[2] boiled in half a pint of water – and then apply this decoction by steeping linen rags in it, and laying them on the chilblains – the burning, and irritation will be allayed in a day or two. – <u>You</u> think because up to a point I unmasked that miserable little reptile de Birard Lady Hotham will leave him nothing – but I'd lay you anything you please – except an egg! that to what ever she originally intended to leave him she has added what she meant to leave me, for he was on the spot to fool her, and persuade her black was white, and so concentrate and confirm all her spite against me: however the way I console myself is – that under <u>any</u> circumstances <u>I</u> should never have benefited by her good <u>intentions</u>! towards me for <u>had</u> she left me her House at Brighton, and £5, 000 a year to live in it, <u>then</u> she would have been <u>sure</u> to have lived 20 years longer and I to have died within the next six months. All I know is that Xmas arrives with its usual happy! and cheering prospects for me as I have an imperative £50 that <u>must</u> be paid and not one penny to pay it with. God knows when I shall hear from Mrs Wheeler touching her visit to [ill] as it always takes 3 or 4 months to achieve a letter, but I'll let you know as soon as I do. Had I not met with this terrible accident; – I could not as you may suppose have accepted any of the Xmas invitations I have had in this County as I am not fond of visiting in <u>Formâ pauperus</u>[3] "<u>clever</u>" Sir Liar! how completely his noble honorable – and manly calculations have answered in crushing his victim – as effectually as if the Tomb Stone were already over her and the daisy quilt spread. Sir James Parke is greatly redeemed in my opinion – since I heard that he brought his black cap into court ready to pass sentence on that vile Tutton – and had prepared a most severe speech for the occasion, – not seeing how any Jury on earth could acquit him and he said he was perfectly dumb with Horror! and surprise! – when he heard their verdict of "not guilty" – I am in such torture from writing this much that I must with Doatskins best love, say good night and God bless you – and wishing you many happier returns of the season.

Believe me my dearest Rebecca Ever your grateful & affect Rosina Bulwer Lytton

I hope you got the "Illustrated Times"[4] containing the memoir of young Massy safely?

HALS
1.   Shakespeare, *Macbeth*, V.iii.40.
2.   A nutlike swelling produced on an oak or other tree by certain parasitic wasps, also called gallnut.
3.   As a pauper (Latin).

To Rebecca Ryves

Monday Night Dec 17th 1855

My dearest Rebecca you will think there is no end to my scribbledom but though I wrote to you last night, I got another letter from you this morning which (as they phrase it in this nation of shop-keepers)[1] I wish to "acknowledge due course" – I quite agree in what you say of young Massy's unspoilability, for the worlds Harpy contact can only spoil the characters it makes, or that are made for it; fine and noble natures, it neither influences, nor comprehends. – With regard to what you say of poor Lady Hotham – I do <u>not</u> concur; – for like all infinitely suspicious people more especially rich old women her suspicions – though ever falling thick and sharp like Parthian[2] arrows – also like them generally fall wide of the mark – from being aimed in a flying cowardly retreating fashion – you know I have strange – and it may be unorthodox theories – touching the progression, and transmigration of human souls – in order for the working out of retributive justice – so that I have no doubt that her keen punishment now is poor woman to feel the most <u>ardent</u> desire to do good to all, and <u>not</u> to have the power to do it to any, – as a per contra account to her having for 80 years possessed ample power of doing so, without once having done it, or even felt the inclination to do it: – and it is by such – a summing up and the <u>like</u> – that the Devil concocts the <u>chiefest</u> ingredients – for forming, what Poets, and Theologians, are alike agreed for want of better <u>excerpts</u> from a more Catholic meaning to call Hell. – Such being my creed; – I dare affirm – that in <u>mockage</u> of all mere <u>verbal</u> virtue, and <u>printed</u> Philanthropy (which is as – widely inferior to true Christian that is <u>active</u> benevolence as the adventures of Don Quixote[3] are to the glorious achievements of the Cid)[4] that Mr Thomas Carlyle himself as one of the <u>chiefest</u> of Modern Humbugs will find <u>his</u> future mission, to be that of Lazarillo de Tormes[5] realized; – I mean the hero of Hurtado de Mendozas[6] amusing novel, – who after numerous short commons situations, subsequently became <u>Footman</u>! to seven Tradesmans wives – <u>fancy</u> Carlyle! in a state of silk stockings Flunkeyism and Servility! reduced to the beery beatitude of Board wages and doomed to powder <u>without</u> – puffs! – I regret for your sake that my "Nemesis of Humbug" is likely to be dormant a generation; – as Carlyle is served up in several of the letters. – in his own stiff jointed – obsolete jargon. I think I told you that Fanny and Augusta were to pass the Xmas with a rich cousin in Cheshire so that I shall be more solitary than ever: that Mr Garland[7] <u>is</u> a very good sort of man I only wish, that as he is one of the few men who lead a good life that he had a good living. Dr Price who though in London has written me a budget of Llangollen news – says "the gang there have began to have their visitations – as that old shark Mrs Phillips has lost her hopeful son by Delirium Tremens[8] – and is herself very ill, and the King of the Blackguards that fellow Jacques of the Gin Shop – has had the Bailiffs in his den" Gin, and drunkenness as forming its chief portions naturally reminded me of the History of England[9] – and Macaulay[10] is at length safely delivered of two more vols of his, – which thanks to my horrible leprosy of poverty Heaven only knows when I shall see. I am still in terrible pain – I bear it as well as I can, but I do not <u>grin</u> – as even that bastard relation to a laugh I can command no longer. No language can convey an idea of de bootsness of dat

Dog with de diamond eyes, and velvet ears

And silver paws as bright as spears

And his only fault when him was Parish dog of being a little rough, and harsh coated has now thanks to four years good petting been kissed quite smoothly so dat hims ears are now most fluffy, and bootsest, and him desires hims innocent love to hims Aunt Rebecca in which hims much joins. So now good night

      Ever your grateful and affect. Rosina Bulwer Lytton.

No news from Miss Wheeler yet. –

HALS

1.   A disparaging remark about Great Britain supposedly made by Napoleon. It was used earlier by Adam Smith in *The Wealth of Nations* (1776).

2.   In ancient Parthia in Asia, it was customary to discharge an arrow at the enemy while retreating; hence the expression, a parting shot.

3.   The hero of Miguel de Cervantes's picaresque novel, *Don Quixote*, Part 1 (1605) and Part 2 (1615).

4.   Rodrigo Díaz de Vivar (*c.* 1044–99), known as El Cid Campeador, was a Castilian nobleman, who conquered and governed the city of Valencia.

5.   *The Life of Lazarillo de Tormes and of His Fortunes and Adversities* is a Spanish novella, published anonymously in 1554, credited with founding the literary genre of the picaresque novel.

6.   In 1607, the novel was attributed by Valère André to Diego Hurtado de Mendoza (1503–75), Spanish novelist, poet, diplomat and historian. In 1888, Alfred Paul Victor Morel-Fatio demonstrated that this attribution was not tenable.

7.   Augusta Boys's brother-in-law from Taunton, Somerset. See RBL, 30 August 1855.

8.   Trembling delirium (Latin) caused by alcohol withdrawal.

9.   Volumes 3 and 4 of *The History of England* by Thomas Macaulay (see below, n. 10) were published in 1855. The first two volumes appeared in 1848. He died at the end of 1859, before completing his fifth volume.

10.   Thomas Babington Macaulay, first Baron Macaulay (1800–59), was a poet, historian and Whig politician. In a letter to A. E. Chalon, 23 February 1856, RBL wrote of Macaulay: 'I know nothing of him *personally*, but admire him hugely as a writer, as I think he is indisputably *the* Master Spirit of the Age in Literature. It was his misfortune and not his fault that he have been at Cambridge with Sir Liar' (*Unpublished Letters*, p. 246).

To Rebecca Ryves

Wednesday Night Dcr 19th 1855

My dearest Rebecca – to save the Post, I send you the inclosed (just recieved) without note or comment – except that I am very glad about Mr Shiel[1] both for his own sake, and mine as it is the first time in my life I ever succeeded in any thing I tried to achieve. What a shame! about poor Davis and Bradly.[2] Ever your affect R Bulwer Lytton.

HALS
1.   Augustus Shiel was Lady Hotham's nephew and heir.
2.   Servants of Lady Hotham.

To Rebecca Ryves

9 at Night Dec 26 1855

From "The Times" of to day Wednesday December 26th although this will has figured in all the Provincial Papers for the last Fortnight *[clipping missing from top of first sheet]*

My dearest Rebecca Although I am ill – and more than ill, in mind, body, and soul, I must thank you for your kind letters just received, and Massy for his kind and <u>very acceptable</u> remembrance of me, in his, intended present of a Pâte de foie gras[1] – for which I plead guilty to having a <u>foiblesse</u>[2] – although well aware that it is a species of Cannibalism for a goose like me, to indulge in foie gras

– however, as I never can enjoy, any sort of good thing by myself – and Augusta and Fanny, are now away and these Pâtes de Strasbourg³ will keep any given time if Massy will add to his kind remembrance of me – for which pray assure him; I am very grateful – and will keep it for me till the <u>first week</u> in <u>February</u> and then send it to me (when you can give him my address) I shall be <u>doubly</u> obliged to him, and only wish that you, and he, could be here, to help to discuss it, and that some of my millionaire friends, would open their hearts – no their chests and send some Champagne to baptise it which is almost a <u>sine qua non</u>⁴ with <u>Foie gras</u> I have heard nothing more yet from Brighton, as soon as I do – I'll let you know. Poor Dr Price is very anxious to go and rummage Lady Hothams Will, at Doctors Commons⁵ thinking that she <u>may</u> have repented of her brutality to me, and felt a proper disgust at the Chevaliers Blackguardism, treachery and ingratitude, but I tell him <u>no</u>, not to waste his shilling, as those are precisely the <u>virtues</u> requisite for succeeding in the world, and which act as magnets to Legacies, and all other largesses. Dr Price also tells me that that insolent old shark Mrs Phillips – has lost her hopeful son, who dies of Delirium Tremens from being always drunk – and that the other chief Ruffian of Sir Liars Llangollen gang, that Blackguard Jacques of the Gin shop, has had the Bailiffs in his den, from which poor Dr Price, somewhat illogically concludes that the wicked are <u>always</u>! visited in this world; whereas it is the old story of the spiderweb, through which the large delinquents break, while the lesser ones are snared, and entangled in it. I said in my last that I would tell you another charming trait of the House of Bulwer well it appears, that Sir Liar Coward Bulwer Lyttons craven, unnatural and therefore <u>worthy</u> son – has turned Poetaster, under the <u>Nom de Plume</u>⁶ of "Owen Meredith"⁷ and the subject he has chosen for his <u>début</u> is the old Classically worn threadbare one of Clytemnestra⁸ now though every one is aware, that there is not the slightest similitude between either my history, or my individuality with that of Clytemnestra; and that there is still less analogy between the noble minded chivalric Agamemnon⁹ and the cowardly Liar, low debauchee, and ridiculous political mountebank Sir Edward Bulwer Lytton! – yet under the <u>circumstances</u> considering – that in the <u>reality</u> <u>his</u> poor Mother was turned out of her Home, to make room for the adulteries of his Father and had had every outrage, and injustice heaped upon her and that in the <u>Myth</u> Clytemnestras own son Orestes¹⁰ – is made to murder his Mother, to avenge his Father! I think it was both good taste! and good feeling!! to select such a subject – and still more to go <u>out of his way</u> to deviate from all history and falsify his text – by making Clytemnestra the <u>seducer</u>!!!¹¹ Of AEgisthus!¹² a violent fury to boot and the cause of all the Evils which befell the race of Agamemnon when – Sophocles, AEschylus, and Euripides¹³ – are all unanimous that her conniving at the murder of Agamemnon was to avenge his murder of her daughter: but of course the meaning of all this distortion is – to convey to the world <u>without</u> – that is the world

at large – who ignore the real facts, how poor dear Sir E Lytton and his <u>amiable</u>
sons <u>existence</u> have been blighted! by their horrible wife! and mother!! and the
<u>moral</u> English Press are neither scandalised nor revolted at <u>this</u>, any more, than
they were at one of Sir Liars Brothel Biographys opening with a father taking
his young son to see his mother hanged!!¹⁴ oh! dear no – their only pious horror
is if this too foully outraged wife and mother is suspected of writing at such a
monster of a <u>Husband</u>! in both instances the <u>moral</u> English Press have not steam
engines enough to puff the Brothel Philosophy of the Father or the tame trash
of the son – for these <u>Extracts</u>, which are all I have seen of his production (and
which be <u>sure</u> you send me <u>back</u>) appear to me a weak and very muddy infu-
sion of Tennyson¹⁵ dregs, and water, and as for the piety! <u>all things</u> <u>considered</u>!
I think it is perfectly blasphemous! but <u>that</u> of course is <u>another</u> <u>clever</u> <u>dodge</u>!
of his clever and consummately villainous Fathers . With all this! you may think
how <u>doubly</u> happy My Xmas is! – now do you not think it a difficult matter to
pray for such a Fiend? – at least beyond the castrated curse – of God forgive
him! God Bless you My dearest Rebecca and send you many happy, and happier
New Years, and with Poor Fine Eyes's innocent love Believe me Ever your grateful & affect Rosina Bulwer Lytton

The Paper came quite safely on Monday: one stamp was quite enough
　　It is blowing a Hurricane! and raining gallon drops!

HALS
1.　Goose liver pâté (French).
2.　Weakness [*faiblesse*] (French).
3.　Pâté from Strasbourg, a town in France, until it was annexed to the German Empire in
　　1871.
4.　Something that is absolutely essential (Latin).
5.　Doctors Commons were a society of ecclesiastical lawyers in London, forming a distinct
　　profession for the practice of the civil and canon laws.
6.　Pen-name (French).
7.　Robert Bulwer Lytton took his pseudonym, Owen Meredith, from the names of two of
　　his ancestors on his mother's side: Owen Gwynned ap. Griffith, King of North Wales,
　　and ap. Meredith ap. Tudor, great-grandfather of Henry VI of England.
8.　*Clytemnestra; The Earl's Return; The Artist, and Other Poems* (1855) published by
　　his father's publishers was Robert Lytton's first volume of verse. In Greek mythology,
　　Clytemnestra is the wife of King Agamemnon.
9.　King Agamemnon who goes to fight in the Trojan Wars to avenge his brother, Mene-
　　laus.
10.　Orestes, with his sister Electra, avenged the death of his father, Agamemnon, who had
　　been killed by his mother Clytemnestra, by slaying her.
11.　In the Homeric version, Aegisthus plotted to seduce Clytemnestra and murder Agam-
　　emnon once he returned from the Trojan War. Aeschylus, in his series of plays called
　　Oresteia, portrays Clytemnestra as plotting with her lover to murder her husband, infuri-

ated by him for having killed their daughter Iphigenia, and bringing home another wife, Cassandra.

12. The son of an incestuous union between father and daughter, he helped Clytemnestra kill her husband upon his return from Troy. Together with the queen, Aegisthus then ruled Mycenae for seven years. He was later murdered by Agamemnon's son Orestes.

13. Ancient Greek playwrights, who dramatized Clytemnestra: Sophocles in *Electra*, Aeschylus in *The Oresteia*, a trilogy of tragedies, and Euripides in *Electra*.

14. At the beginning of EBL's novel *Lucretia*, an English dancer is beheaded for adultery, along with her noble French lover. At the end of chapter 1, the father of her child Oliver Dalibard ominously utters: 'Learn how they perish who betray me'.

15. Alfred Lord Tennyson (1809–92) was the Poet Laureate from 1850 until his death. EBL had publicly quarrelled with Tennyson, regarding his poetry as effeminate doodle.

To Rebecca Ryves

January 10th 1856

True Copy
Copy of my order for my Parish allowance with 1 letter of Mr Hydes – <u>2</u> from Mr Hodgson– and the spy no 7 the <u>soi-disant</u>[1] Miss <u>Hennas</u>!??[2] Missive

Dear Mr Hodgson – I hereby authorize you to receive that disgraceful quarterly swindle, which Sir Edward Bulwer Lytton calls an allowance! Should there be any fresh attempts at dirty work – to delay the payment of it, – through that very <u>appropriate</u> <u>Channel</u> for all such – Mr Loaden, give yourself no further trouble about it; but let me know <u>instantly</u>; as all my measures are taken – in order to expose the long tissue of villainy, and <u>almost fabulous</u>! Blackguardism to which I have been subjected, a villainy, and a blackguardism in proof of which I can luckily adduce reams of documents, and bring forwards clouds of witnesses, and I cannot have a more suitable occasion for doing so than on the Eve of a General Election.[3] I Remain Dear Mr Hodgson yours && Rosina Bulwer Lytton

---

HALS

1. So-called (French).
2. In a letter to A. E. Chalon, dated June 1855, RBL claims that 'a creature calling herself Miss Henna (why not Henbane at once?)', claimed to be a governess staying near Trinity Church (3 km from RBL in Taunton), with a doctor who could not be traced. See RBL, *Unpublished Letters*, p. 212.
3. A general election did not take place until April 1857 when Lord Palmerston led the Whigs to their biggest election win since 1832.

To Rebecca Ryves

January 23rd 1856

My dearest Rebecca It is certainly very hard to understand; and still more so to make any one else understand such intense Blackguardism as Sir Edward Bulwer Lyttons but as I have often explained to you, and as I should have thought you had seen enough of my affairs to know, the wretch's motive is to find out everything I do, and every one I know, to frustrate the one, and embroil, or injure me with the other; or as far as his spying goes – thank God since the hour he turned me out of my Home, I should not care if he could have converted my very shadow, into a spy – it would have been all the better for me, unless indeed he could also have converted it into an unscrupulous Perjurer like himself; – but even that swindler Rathbone[1] who has since been in gaol turned out to have been an Emissary of his – since he was lié[2] with that reptile Henry Bulwer, in what is called the Clayton Bulwer Treaty.[3] – you see I was right – Poor Mr Hodgson thought no man, would or could – tamely swallow the aspersions thrown upon him in that order of mine! – but cruel villains as Sir Edward Bulwer Lytton – who has not even a villainous virtue – the courage of his vices, must swallow that, and much more, and it had the desired effect, as I knew it would be extracting the money instantar[4] but I will say, – that no man in, or out of Newgate;[5] who would make even a show of disproving such specific and damnatory allegations would tamely pocket them by calling them "characteristic and amusing" – ! I doubt his finding them quite so amusing in the sequel! – I think you will be amused at his little beggarly – blackguardly note to Mr Hodgson which is just such a one as old Fagan[6] scrawled with a trembling hand to the "Artful Dodger"[7] in a "Finish" in St Giles's[8] while under the Basilisk eye[9] of a Bailiff – with a fine Hanging Wood (vulgo[10] Gallows) in the vista, as cowardly fear and impotent rage trembles in its every scratch, – as for the too contemptible quibble of my dating the orders the 10th instead of the 7th or 8th! why if one is at St Petersburg[11] and writes a cheque on a London Banker why one dates it London, and the day the money is payable which is never considered either commercially, or conscientiously as "falsifying"! the transaction but then to be sure, to a man of such vestal purity! of principle! such scrupulous delicacy! of feeling and such exaggerated probity! as Sir Edward Bulwer Lytton! the wholesale perjurer, retail liar, and would be poisoner! – the nicest punctilio[12] of honour – can scarcely be fine enough – However I send you a copy of my answer to him upon this matter which with his scrawl – be sure you let me have safely back but be sure you read them both, first to as many persons as will take the trouble of listening to them: The more immediate cause of my sending him this Earthquake of a letter, was that terrible old woman Mr Hodgson – (who ought too have been commander in Chief in the Crimea!)[13] writing me word that I had better in future, date my orders the 7th or 8th – now really this was <u>too</u> much from <u>my</u> <u>nominal</u> Lawyer, so I wrote him back word, that to deal, with that wretch, I wanted a granite pillar, and not an Elastic belt, yielding at every point; and that what <u>he</u> ought to do, instead of in the flush of so signal a victory – as I had just gained – hurling <u>me</u> from my vantage ground to throw <u>me</u>, under that monsters Chariot wheels, would be if he wanted to insure the future punctual payment of my disgraceful pittance; – to turn the tables upon him, by writing to him to say – that "in future it would save trouble to all parties if Sir Liar, would always give him a cheque in advance, so as to insure <u>my</u> having the <u>money</u> always punctually on the 10th as he must be aware, that being kept one hour out of so <u>very small</u> a sum – occasioned me the greatest possible inconvenience; besides there would be another advantage or rather <u>two</u> in his forwarding him <u>my receipts</u> for the money – instead of my orders ie – that they would not only be a guarantee that I was actually alive! (and kicking as he shall yet find to his cost) a whole 48! hours <u>after</u> the portentous 10th!! but also that he (Mr Hodgson however much he might be tempted to do so – had not abstracted a single coin of that <u>valuable</u>! deposit and thereby risked the cumbering Estates of Knebworth, and Wood Dalling[14] perhaps to the immense extent of half a Farthing!!!" – three Lawyers, have seen my letter to Sir Liar, and approve of it hugely, being like myself quite convinced, that though "the action wont lie" – the man it is written to <u>will</u>! – Have you seen that resumé of the Palmer Poisonings[15] in "The Leader"?[16] if not I will send it to you – as they say "the amiable Mr William Palmer seems to have derived his code of Domestic morality from Bulwers Lucretia.[17] – how delightful it would be if it turned out that the Palmer was a "Pal" – of Sir Liar! Like myself, I don't think you want anything to increase your disgust, and bad opinion – of that brute "Gorge"! but if anything <u>can</u> do so – I think it will be his letter (the wretch) to poor Mrs Davis[18] – the <u>fact</u> of the accusations, against Mr Shiel about influencing Lady Hotham in her Testamentary behests coming from <u>him</u> are quite sufficient to my mind to disprove them; but still I am truly disgusted surprised and disappointed to think that with her prophecy Mr Shiel should also have inherited so much of his aunts flinty parsimony – as to refuse to to [*sic*] do an act of common <u>justice</u> (for it does not amount to generosity) by providing for poor Davis, – and by so doing erase a foul blot from his aunts memory. – I have begged of Davis – to send Mr Shiel Gorges – <u>letter</u> (not a copy) as I have no doubt though the wretch abuses him so to the Davises, – he for <u>Dinners sake</u> would toady the nephew, as he did the aunt, only a minor degree, as <u>he</u> has no legacies to leave: I also said to Davis what a pity it was he (Gorge) could not cajole Lady Hotham into leaving <u>him</u> <u>Everything</u>! and <u>then</u> there would have been no one but the man in the moon! to lay the treachery towards poor Davis upon: – he is as I said to the Davises, – but a bungler after all to get but £2, 000 – considering that he has devoted his whole life – to plastering casts for laughing stocks, and old women for Legacies,

– with the pretty little interludes of violating Children (the loathsome wretch!)
but there was <u>one</u> of the many lies of his letter I begged leave most explicitly
to refute, ie the one of his never having flattered Lady Hotham!!! when he did
<u>nothing else</u>, not only by his diurnal and voluminous, almost love letters – but
upon what do you think? – her figure? <u>no</u> for <u>that</u> really was marvellous, her
taste in Pictures? – China? Furniture? <u>no</u>, – for <u>all these</u> would have been <u>truths</u>,
so of course did not come in <u>his</u> way: but I may as well tell you, – as you will
never guess, – her <u>perfect</u> taste in dress!!!! – I confess that I am sorry that, that
vile little cross breed, between Judas Iscariot, and Jeremy Diddler,[19] the Chevalier should for doing Gorges, and Sir Liars dirty work so effectually have had
his villainy rewarded with £300, which will be an El Dorado[20] to <u>him</u>! – but
Everything proves that vice and vice only, prospers in this world. Me's vezy sorry
to tell oo that Master Fine eyes, has been so vezy great big insolent to a brown
Pup – belonging to the Boots, that I have threatened to alter my will! and leave
Every thing to the Cat except a pair of iron rimmed nose pinchers like Jonas's!
which I mean to leave to <u>Gorge</u>! to go with Lady Hothams "<u>goold</u>" ones and
"goold warming pan! – I wonder whether he wears it? it would be a beautiful
addition to that odious Flowerpot hat! and those disgusting washed out blue
and white trousers! which always alarmed one – thinking that the wretch would
burst through them – and that poor Lady Hotham would see more of him than
ever! – Addio[21] God Bless you – My kind regards to Massy when you write Ever
your grateful and affect Rosina Bulwer Lytton

HALS
1. This may be Theodore Woolman Rathbone (1798–1863), a member of the philan-
    thropic Rathbone family from Liverpool. See RBL, 0D421RR21.
2. Linked (French).
3. Sir Henry Bulwer and US Secretary of State John Clayton signed the Clayton–Bulwer
    Treaty on 19 April 1850, which involved a proposal to build what became the Panama
    Canal across Central America. Its importance was the pledge to respect its neutrality by
    contracting governments.
4. Pressingly [*instanter*] (Latin).
5. In the first half of the nineteenth century, Newgate Prison was London's chief prison,
    where prisoners were held before execution.
6. A fictional criminal, who teaches a group of children pick-pocketing and other crimes in
    Dickens's novel *Oliver Twist*.
7. Jack Dawkins, known as the Artful Dodger, is a fictional character, who is the leader of
    the gang of pick-pockets trained by Fagin in *Oliver Twist*. See above, n. 6.
8. St Giles had been an impoverished area of London since the seventeenth century.
9. The basilisk was a mythological snake-like creature, upon which it was impossible to gaze
    and survive. The golden basilisk poisoned everything by his mere look.
10. Commonly (Latin).
11. Capital of the Russian Empire until 1917.
12. 'The highest point' (*OED*).

13. The progress of the Crimean War was marred by inadequate commanders on all sides.
14. Knebworth is the Hertfordshire family seat of EBL. It had been the property of the Lyttons since the reign of Henry VII. Wood Dalling Hall, Norfolk, was the home of his brother Henry, and had been in the Bulwer family since the days of William the Conqueror. Henry was given the title Baron Dalling in 1871.
15. Dr William Palmer (1824–56) was tried for one poisoning on circumstantial evidence and prosecuted by Alexander Cockburn (see RBL, 3 December 1857). He was found guilty and hanged at Stafford on 14 June 1856. The newspapers called him 'The Rugeley Poisoner' and 'The Prince of Poisoners' and printed numerous rumours and accusations gathered from local gossips. These alleged that Palmer had poisoned at least a dozen others, including four of his five children, his wife, mother-in-law and his brother.
16. *Leader* was a progressive and liberal national newspaper. See RBL, 6 April 1851.
17. EBL's novel *Lucretia* (1853) concerns Lucretia Clavering, who murders her first husband, Oliver Dalibard and poisons her second. In 1854, Palmer's wife Ann died, apparently of cholera after he had taken out a £13,000 insurance policy on her life.
18. The wife of John Davis, Lady Hotham's butler.
19. Jeremy Diddler, who excelled in raising money on false pretences, is a character in James Kenney's farce *Raising the Wind*, which was first performed in 1803. The name is synonymous with a trickster; a confidence man or a continual borrower.
20. A legendary South American city containing immense wealth.
21. Goodbye [*adiós*] (Spanish).

To Rebecca Ryves

Thursday Night January 31st 1856

Many thanks My dearest Rebecca for your kind letter, but I am sorry you did not return me Mrs Davises; as I particularly wanted it. You are quite mistaken about Mr Shiel having £500 a year – he has nearer £6, 000 and hence Gorges fury! and surprise! as dont you see he says in his letter to Mrs Davis; – that Lady Hotham had told him she only meant to leave "Augustus £500 a year – and therefore that he (Gorge) was never more astonished than when he heard what she had left him, and hence accuses <u>him</u> of influencing her in the altering of her Will. But I <u>do hope</u> the Davises have sent Mr Shiel Gorges letter as I begged them to do. – Mrs Davis so far keeps a Lodging house, that she lets the Drawing, and Dining rooms of this house – and I believe cooks for the persons who take them. Mr Shiels conduct in not providing for poor Davis, is truly disgusting, and savours strongly of the Beggar on Horseback[1] <u>Manége</u> (not <u>ménage</u>![2] as the English newspapers generally print it) but you need not be surprised at Mrs Riddle – as do you not by this time know – that English sympathy for misfortune, never extends farther – than wishing somebody <u>else</u> would assist, or relieve it; but they are never so egotistical, as to think of doing anything <u>themselves</u>! Tell Massy with my best thanks that I shall <u>Joi d'honnête femme</u>,[3] gratefully receive his kind present of <u>foie gras</u> as <u>soon</u> next week, as he likes to send it; but on <u>no</u> account to think of paying the carriage as that I will gladly do: Fanny and Augusta return on Saturday so Massy's Pâté will be a sort of "Cheer (Chear) Boys! Cheer! for them. I am very sorry I cannot send you the Paper with Walkendens[4] Evidence, as I take no Paper what ever – which is a great saving to me here – as they take nearly all from "The Times" down to "Punch" and "Bells Life"[5] at the Hotel: I cannot Even send you "The Leader" but I send you the long Extract from it about the Palmers which I told you of. I am delighted that they got up a Testimonial of a gold sword, at Trinity College Dublin to that young Redan Massy.[6] They swear my letter was not tampered with at the Post Office here; but as far as the contents of the last went, I wish it had been opened, and read at every Town village, and Borough – through Europe, Asia, Africa and America. I have such an awful cold – which I caught by opening a window, to throw some chicken bones out to a poor starved dog – that I cannot see to tell you of the super dogskin darlingry of that Tib – this time, but send you a scribbledom of poor Williams full of hims innocent paws. The spy has never been seen, or heard of, since the night she got the sack here. You say you wonder if old Pyke did dose me? Neither I nor Dr Price have the least doubt of it. – Good night God Bless you and with a Kennel full of love from Tib – believe me Ever your grateful and affect R Bulwer Lytton

---

HALS

1. An expression meaning a person, originally poor, who has become arrogant after achieving wealth. This is also the title of a play by Robert Sullivan, performed in 1833.
2. Horsemanship (French).
3. Joy of an honest woman (French).
4. Lucy Walkenden's deposition related to the death of Walter Palmer, the brother of Dr William Palmer, the so-called 'Rugely Poisoner'. See RBL, 23 January 1856.
5. *Bell's Life in London* (1822–86) was a colourful journal, founded by John Bell, which covered London low life to high society, as well as publishing some of Dickens's shorter fiction.
6. Lieutenant Dunham Massey of the 19th Regiment had distinguished himself as a young hero at the Redan, which was a Russian stronghold attacked by the British during the Siege of Sebastopol.

To Rebecca Ryves

Thursday February 1st 1856

My dearest Rebecca when I wrote to you last night I quite forgot to ask you, if in that large packet I sent you with Mrs Davis's letters there was not also a letter from Mr Hyde telling me of poor Mrs Hydes[1] upset? if so? let me have it back. Sir Liar must have got my letter the morning of Sir Robert Peels Wedding[2] the Breakfast of which was given at his present disgrace of Wellingtons, the next (to

Sir Liar) greatest Blackguard and Ruffian in England – so I hope the said letter was an addition to his felicity! – you say Napoleon[3] must have had Sir Liar in his minds Eye, when he described the Russian character; but I rather think Mirabeau[4] must have had a prophetic vision of him in his description of Necker[5] where he says "he had not <u>even</u> a series of political principles xxxxxx he seeks <u>applause</u>, and does not think of securing <u>esteem</u>. He understands neither the present, nor the future with just so much intellectual face as goads him to sapire[6] after the first offices of state, he is totally destitute of the talents that should give them <u>Utility</u> and <u>fame</u>

xxxxxxxxxxxxxxxx

Esteemed by no man, loved by no woman, he trusted he should find in the ostentation of wealth, an equivalent for every other enjoyment." –

But really in this age of Testimonials I think Messieurs Wooler, Tutton Monaghan and Palmer![7] should present him with a golden Gallows for having brought them so near it with his <u>charming</u> works of "Lucretia"!!! <u>and</u> "Eugene Aram"![8] By the bye, thanks to "The Poisonings at <u>Manchester</u>" I find they have a street there, called <u>Tib</u> Street[9] which greatly redeems – its cotton commonality in my opinion. I suppose a letter addressed to massy Aldershot Camp[10] will find him? as Tib says I must write and thank him for the <u>Paté</u>, which the said Tib is anxiously expecting; – having like <u>hims</u> mud a <u>foible</u> for truffles and <u>Foie gras</u>; to say nothing of Plum Pudding! which him danced on hims <u>hind</u> paws – <u>all</u> round the room after yesterday like little Tommy Tucker[11] dancing for his supper; him now joins hims mud in best love to hims Aunt Rebecca Ever your grateful and affect Rosina Bulwer Lytton.

HALS
1. For a description of Mr Hyde's wife, see RBL, 28 March 1856.
2. Emily Hay (1831–1924) married Sir Robert Peel, third Baronet (1822–95), on 17 January 1856.
3. In June of 1812, Napoleon began his fatal Russian campaign, which brought about his own downfall.
4. Honoré Gabriel Riqueti, Marquis and Count Mirabeau (1749–91), was a writer, popular orator and statesman.
5. Jacques Necker (1732–1804) was the finance minister of Louis XVI whose financial policy Mirabeau disagreed with. See above, n. 4.
6. To know (Latin).
7. This is intended to be a list of murderers. In 1855, Joseph Smith Wooler was charged with poisoning his wife and was acquitted by the jury. Tutton was tried and acquitted for poisoning his father (see RBL, 6 December 1855). Monaghan is a misspelling of James Monaghan (b. *c.* 1831), who was tried with George Barry and Thomas Bull Holland for attempting to poison Monaghan's father, John, to recover £300 from a life insurance policy. Palmer was the poisoner, who was actually hanged on 14 June 1856. See RBL, 23 January 1856).
8. The protagonists of these two novels by EBL are both murderers.

9. Tib Street, in which large textile warehouses had been built, is located in central Manchester, the capital of Lancashire, which had expanded with the cotton industry.
10. Lieutenant Dunham Massey of the 19th Regiment. See RBL, 31 January 1856.
11. The title of a nursery rhyme for children, first published in 1829. The name of the hero was commonly used to describe an orphan.

To William Spurrell[1]

Mr W Spurrell Carmathen S. Wales

Giles' Castle Hotel Taunton Somerset
February 6th 1856

Lady Bulwer Lytton

Having seen Mr Spurrell's Advertizement in to days "Times" of "Old, and rare Books to be sold a bargain; a list of which will be sent free for 1dy Stamp" Incloses the Stamp, and will be much obliged to Mr Spurrell to forward her the list – with the prices – to the undersigned address

---

NLW
1. William Spurrell (1813–89) founded Messrs W. Spurrell & Son (House of Spurrell), a firm of printers and publishers in 1840.

To Rebecca Ryves

Thursday February 7th 1856

My dearest Rebecca I must write you one line in great haste to acknowledge the safe arrival of Mrs Davises – Mr Hydes, and Williams's letters, with a kind one from yourself for which, many thanks. I am surprized! at Lady Seafield's[1] marriage, not at her marrying, – what has become of Mr Stuart? [2] as I, and every body else thought he would be the happy man. I think her an exceedingly Ladylike and agreeable person. – Now that I have taken to my hair again! I am sorry to hear that Widows marry in Bonnets! but your humorous description of the Orange blossoms for the Present, the Forget me not for the dear departed, and the flower of Hope for the dearest future! rather consoles me, though should such a shocking accident ever happen to me! again, I'll vary the Parterre,[3] by substituting Rue, and nettles for the dear d—d[4] departed Bachelors buttons for the dear — alive and a sprig of thyme! for the Donkey of a Future. –

HALS
The end of the letter in missing.

1. Louisa Emma Maunsell (*c.* 1818–84), the daughter of Robert George Maunsell from County Limerick, Ireland, married sixth Earl of Seafield, the Scottish nobleman and MP in 1843. After the death of her husband in 1853, she remarried Major Godfrey Hugh Massy (1779–1862) on 31 January 1856.
2. William Stuart.
3. 'A level space in a garden occupied by an ornamental arrangement of flower beds' (*OED*).
4. Dead or damned.

To Rebecca Ryves

Wednesday February 13th 1856

[Newspaper clipping]

– GIFTS FROM HER MAJESTY TO THE CRIMEAN SOLDIERS
    The thoughtful manner in which the Queen evinces her sympathy for her gallant army shows how kindly and skilfully she can touch the chord of the soldier's heart. A few days before Christmas, amongst other gifts, two or three silk handkerchiefs for each division, hemmed by her own fair fingers, arrived in the Crimea for distribution amongst the bravest and most deserving of the wounded soldiers. In the Light Division, by universal consent, the first handkerchief was awarded to the distinguished young hero of the Redan, Lieut Denham Massey,[1] of the 19th Regiment, as facile preceps[2] amongst the brave and deserving sufferers. He is stated to have been delighted and comforted beyond measure when handed the precious gift in his bed (where he has lain since the 8th of September) by the Assistant Adjutant General. Such is the homely and touching manner in which our good Sovereign attaches to her those gallant men who freely bleed for her on the battlefield]

My dearest Rebecca Though much hurried and worried – I must write you one line to tell you that the Champagne was excellent! And the Foie gras super excellent!! Which pray tell Massey with my reiterated thanks – by repeatedly drinking your health I assure you the judgement we formed of the Champagne, was by no means superficial. – As for its being so hard to make people understand Sir Liars Villainy it is not so much that as upon the Universal principle of worshipping the powers that be. They think it more prudent to affect not to do so, as that dispenses with the necessity of any compromising act of credence. To me the most revolting phase of his hideous character after his inhuman conduct to my children and myself – is his loathsome printed Pro bono publico[3] hypocrisy – about his vile old Mother, whom he used alternately [to] court, and bully for her unentailed Estate, and I remember when the brute kicked me till I was nearly dead about a month before my poor murdered first child was born, his charming speech on the occasion was "Da—n[4] your soul Madam you can bear nothing; – I've often felled my mother to the Earth!" There is a man in Gaol <u>here</u> now under sentence of death for having kicked, and <u>killed </u>his wife under similar circumstances; – what bunglers! Common people are – Now the "Enlightened and all accomplished Sir Edward Lytton!" can always manage to drive <u>his </u>Infernal Machine, whether Murder, perjury or forgery within half a hairs breadth of the <u>safe</u> side of the <u>Law</u>! however like Mr William Palmer he may overshoot the mark at last! – you said in a former letter what a pity I did not bring it <u>home to him</u> at the time old Pyke dosed me – and so I would had I known at the <u>time</u> – all I was told some <u>months</u> after when her letter warning me against the other spy Getting came, – <u>then</u> it was for the <u>first</u> time I was told – all the things she had been saying to different people which first lead me to suspect what Dr Price is sure she <u>did</u>. I think I once told you that when that vulgar old wretch Sir Liars mother came into possession of Knebworth, which really <u>is</u> a fine old Henry the Seventh[5] place – she took down the old oak stair case, and stuck up a <u>modern</u> <u>stone</u>! London House one – she also ploughed up the oak floors, in the bedrooms, and replaced them with deal!! and tore down the fine old Bugle Tapestry putting up white dimity!! hangings to the Windows and beds! and she not only took every spear and shield out of the great Hall under the Music gallery and <u>sold them</u>! but she actually painted the old carved oak wainscoat blue!! and white!!! well in one of this years Pocketbooks there is a view of Knebworth, of course with Elaborate puffs – and after being told that the most "<u>touching</u>" thing! amid so many gems, is Sir Liars filial affection in keeping his <u>Mothers</u> room intact! with an appeal to her posterity hoping they will preserve it inviolate!!! – Next comes a flourish about the <u>armour</u>!! which makes me conclude – that Sir Liar must have expended vast sums in the purchase of <u>Heirlooms</u>!! and <u>Ancestors</u>!! in Wardour Street[6] which coupled with those requisite for his innumerable vices, hush money – and ceaseless puffs you can Easily understand how the poor dear man is compelled to deduct the Income tax from the £400! a year, he with such Princely munificence! allows his legal encumbrance? – I am sorry to hear your poor friend has been obliged to submit to a surgical operation. – As you mean to go to Dublin in the Spring – I don't see why you should not come on to Taunton? Yes the English papers rang with that iniquity about poor Haydn[7] – no wonder he died of it! that little odious wretch of a queen is too disgusting with her meanness and the beastly Press for over plastering her – though I verily believe they mean it for satire in disguise – the enclosed pocket handkerchief affair put me in a great rage they should give her a wipe with those handkerchiefs. They say Lover has just got a pension – of £100 a year. I have a heart rending Episode to relate about Master Innocence but I cannot do it now – being much harried and worried – so addio[8] and Believe me Ever with Doatskins love your grateful and affect Rosina Bulwer Lytton

HALS

1.   See RBL, 1 February, 1856.

2.   Easily the first [*facile princes*] (Latin).
3.   For the public good (Latin).
4.   Damn.
5.   In 1490, Sir Robert Lytton, who had fought with Henry VII at Bosworth and became Under Treasurer to the Household and a close confidant, purchased Knebworth. Ten years later, Sir Robert started building onto the existing gatehouse, a new four-sided house enclosing a central courtyard.
6.   During the second half of the nineteenth century, Wardour Street in the West End of London housed many antique shops, brokers and furniture makers.
7.   Benjamin Robert Haydon (1786–1846) was a painter in the Grand Style, who opened himself to public censor through his autobiographical writings. He fell in love with the writer Mrs Norton, who had sat as his model for *Cassandra* (1834). See RBL, 4 March 1856. He was fearful of being cited in her divorce case as was Lord Melbourne. Prone to making enemies, he became a bankrupt and eventually committed suicide.
8.   Goodbye [*adiós*] (Spanish).

To Rebecca Ryves

Wednesday February 13th 1856

My dearest Rebecca

I have only a moment to thank you for your kind letter, and to say – that you must at least be my guest for a month – and if I resort to this niggardly <u>Limited Liability</u> which the English misnomer Hospitality! you know it is "my poverty, and not my will consents"[1] – I am full of worries, as I wrote a day, or two ago – to Mr Hodgson saying that although I am very grateful to him for his kindness yet it would be more profitable to me, even in a pecuniary point of view, to pay, for having my business attended to, than to be laid under an obligation for having it neglected; and that I must beg that he would instantly write a letter to Sir Liar, saying that he must send a cheque Every quarter for the Parish Allowance when Mr Hodgson would forward him my receipt for the same, which was the only guarantee he should have from me of my existence; and this he Mr Hodgson must do, or let some one else do, as really it was more than my life was worth, to have such a battle for this beggarly swindle every 3 months.

Well "a soft answer turneth away wrath"[2] and I send you his; but to shew you what he is! I send you 2 letters he <u>should have</u> sent me five months ago! from that shark Mr Campbell; poor Mr Hodgson like a coward as he is, saying he <u>fears</u>! he will force me to pay it – I wrote to him a letter to send Mr Campbell saying that what ever Errors there might be in Mr Browns hastily written, and very useless inventory that as I could be <u>upon Oath</u>, that the morning I went myself over Thurloe Cottage with Mr Campbell, and that he modestly asked me if House Linen was not included! in the beggarly £350 he had given for what had just cost me £983 – I then, and there most explicitly told him, that the Venetian outside blinds – The Linen Press on the Landing, and the black china door and bell knobs and plates belonged to Mr Chew, and that had Mr Campbell paid Mr Chew £100, instead of £14"17"0 for these things that he had no earthly right to take away, any more than he had to carry off the lead from the roof, the Pump from the yard, or the Hall door from Mr Chews House still, after having had the want of conscience to take at one fell swoop £983 worth for £350! – none but those 3 synonyms – a Shark, a Scotchman, or a Swindler, would have the effrontery to attempt this additional Extortion and as I certainly should <u>not yield to it</u> Mr Hodgson must insist on taking possession of my Glass. – You may guess how all these extortions, not only skin but worry me and poor Innocence is gone for a week to de Dog Doctors – who luckily is a very dood man – but me's very miserable without him. I'd walk as far as Brighton to shake hands with that sensible man who so <u>thoroughly</u> appreciates the English

God Bless you my dearest Rebecca and hoping to see you after the Ides of March – Believe me Ever your grateful and affect

Rosina Bulwer Lytton

HUNT
1.   'My poverty, not my will consents', Shakespeare, *Romeo and Juliet*, V.i.75.
2.   Proverbs 15:1.

To Rebecca Ryves

Tuesday March 4th 1856

<u>No</u> my dearest Rebecca I did <u>not</u> misunderstand your meaning; on the contrary, it was because I understood, and <u>fully appreciated</u> your kindness that I feel so additionally worried; and I think <u>you are</u> quite capable of understanding why I <u>should</u>. – indeed I feel that if <u>some</u> turn in my fate does not <u>soon</u> come, I can<u>not</u> bear up under it much longer, it is easy – if not pleasant to economise, and retrench when one has enough to <u>live</u> upon; but when has not enough even to <u>exist</u> upon – it is a cruel, and impossible struggle, to have to pay back large arrears out of what even unmortgaged would be with difficulty made to meet ones current pinchings. – I would have answered your letter yesterday when I received it but was waiting for Mrs Clarkes answer, – which I have only this <u>moment</u> got – and though I screwed her down to the very lowest figure, I think it is too much, but she says – the war has made every thing so dreadfully dear, that she could not do it for less; – and to give you up a sitting room <u>entirely</u> she could not do either having no small rooms – the ones I am in, being the only moderate sized ones she has; – and yet without a permanent sitting room she says she could not do it less than £1"15"0" a week So now I think you will have to accept my <u>limited liability</u> invitation, for a month which nevertheless is a very <u>sincere</u> one, and as you may

naturally wonder <u>how</u> I can afford even this; since I cannot pay my just debts? – I will tell you, that I am <u>never</u> able to settle Mrs Clarkes bill in full, but while I remain she kindly allows me always to be in this arrear till I can get my book out, and so pay it all off: – The Easter King offered a reward for anyone who could invent a new pleasure![1] I would give my hands, the only things I now possess of any value, if any one would discover <u>how</u> Beggars <u>can</u> avoid debt? without committing suicide? for the mere <u>act</u> of existing, without ever s<u>pending</u> money which one cant do, when one has not got it; <u>incurs</u> expense. Cassandra![2] will be believed at last! There is a capital critique on Sir Liar in Frasier[3] this morning echoing what I have so long been saying – to wit – that "The Caxtons[4] is only a re-stuffed Tristram Shandy"[5] and we have only to go across the Channel to find out where all his other stolen goods came from. If you do not come I shall be <u>exceedingly</u> dis<u>appointed</u> – and your not doing so will save me <u>nothing</u> as I must do something to <u>keep</u> Mrs Clarke in good humour by letting her make a little more, than she now does by me and my cold water I shall lose the Post so with the dogs best love who says him will put all the Fleas him can catch, in a letter and send them to you if you don't come? Believe me Ever your Grateful & affect Rosina Bulwer Lytton

---

HALS
1. This is the Eastern king. According to Athenaeus (end of 2nd century–beginning of 3rd century AD), in *Deipnosophistae* (*The Banquet of the Philosophers* or *The Philosophy of Banquets*), the Persian kings 'rewarded anyone who invented a new pleasure', 12.545–6.
2. Cassandra was the daughter of King Priam and Queen Hecuba of Troy. Her beauty prompted Apollo to grant her the gift of prophecy. When she would not return his love, Apollo placed a curse on her so that no one would ever believe her predictions.
3. *Fraser's Magazine* was a general and literary Tory journal, founded by Hugh Fraser and William Maginn in 1830. A devasting anonymous review accusing EBL of plagiarism and comparing his novel *The Caxtons* (see below, n. 4) with Laurence Sterne's *Tristram Shandy* (see below, n. 5) appeared in *Fraser's Magazine*, 53 (January–June 1856), pp. 253–67.
4. EBL's novel *The Caxtons. A Family Picture* was first published in 1844.
5. *The Life and Opinions of Tristram Shandy, Gentleman* is a novel by Laurence Sterne published in nine volumes from 1759 to 1767.

To Rebecca Ryves

Monday Night March 17th 1856

My dearest Rebecca I have been so full of worries these last two, or three days, that I have been quite unable to thank you for your kind letter and good story about Sir Liar I'd have given any thing to have seen his hideous face, when fishing for compliments, he fished up those great sea serpents of <u>truths</u>! did the lady say

<u>where</u> it was he was travelling? and how long ago since this occurred? – My Eyes are streaming – and my head aching so terribly that I can scarcely see to write this; but would not let another Post pass without sending you a line I did not at first tell you the irresistible inducement to you to come here, fearing that if I had you would have set off in some demented manner, not waiting for money or Massy; or any thing else – but it is this, I have on my chimney piece two Chinese monsters <u>so</u> <u>like</u>! or rather such facsimiles of "Jonas"! That they might pass for <u>casts</u> of him. I forget if I ever told you that, I saw the marriage in the paper, some time ago, as having taken place at Paris of the unfortunate individual whom as you wittily observed Steinberg[1] took <u>as</u> – prey! "<u>Misther</u> Frederick Asprey,"[2] whom she tried to "Cognovant"[3] out of House, and Home. I do indeed hope you may soon see Massy and be able to arrange with him to bring you down here as nothing truly is so wearing as that constant incertitude – as to what <u>is</u> to become of one! I know it well from long, and bitter experience. De dog says him will keep all hims news till you come. So with best love and all good wishes, which alas! are neither loaves! nor fishes![4] Believe me Ever your grateful and affect Rosina Bulwer Lytton.

HALS
1. This may be the female friend of Lady Hotham mentioned in 0D133RR21.
2. The Aspreys were famous jewellers at 167 New Bond Street, London, who received a royal warrant from Queen Victoria.
3. A cognovit is 'an acknowledgement by a defendant that the plaintiff's cause is just; in which case the defendant, to save expense, suffers judgement to be entered against him without trial' (*OED*).
4. A reference to the miracle of Jesus feeding loaves and fishes to 5,000 followers on the shore of the Sea of Galilee (Mark 6:41).

To Rebecca Ryves

Thursday Night, or Rather Friday Mng March 28th 1856

My dearest Rebecca – it is now 99 o'clock! but I cannot put out my candle till I have thanked you for your kind letter; – though I am so tired, I can scarcely hold the pen any longer, having been obliged to make up for my illness and my idleness of the last three days, and scribble till now (4 in the Morning. I began by getting a violent cold in Church last Sunday and tried to bully it, as I had asked my dear good old Bulldog Hyde, and his wife over to spend the day on Tuesday and go to the Madrigal Concert in the Evening, music being the only thing he cares for and this being the only little attention I have it in my power to show them. Mrs Hyde is a very clever, well educated woman and <u>sans çela</u>[1] she would have won my heart by the perfect Forest, of magnificent red and white Camelias she brought me, which have made of my rooms a perfect Chateau des Fleurs[2] – I wish you could have been here to meet them; Hyde enjoyed your historiette[3] of Sir Liars "traits of Travel" quite as much as I did; he says how he is in fighting order again and is itching to have a set to at Sir Liar again – and as I fully expect Mr Hodgson will recommence his creep mouse inanities when my Parish allowance becomes due – I've no doubt good honest Hyde will have the opportunity he wishes: – they were very kindly pressing for me to go and stay with them and said they would drive over for me; but as I told her having no maid I really could not go and stay any where and as soon as they were gone the next day I was obliged to take to my bed, where I have been ever since; but obliged to work all the same. I am very sorry you could not go to the St Patricks ball;[4] still well do I know the misery of having to go out, when one has nothing fit to go in, and no means of getting any thing. Only fancy! There is a Dr Viner who was Tutor to George Willoughby[5] and is <u>now</u> tutor to the sons of Eisenberg the corn Dr![6] (I should say chiropodist!) I wanted some boots from Mrs Frampton Augusta got this Dr Viner to order them and have them sent to him to forward to me, he had just received the said Boots on Saturday and was hurrying with them down to the Train, when in Eisenbergs passage as he was going out, with the parcel directed to me in full who should he nearly tumble over but Sir Liar! how I regret that my feet were not in the boots, that I might have given him a good kicking. I hear that Blackguard Forster of the Examiner[7] who would say or swear <u>any</u> thing has answered the exposée in Fraser[8] – I <u>said</u> he would be the only one with brass enough to do so – I have not seen it yet – the only tack that they can go on – will be to say that Sir Liar did it for a wager – to see how much the ignorance of the "British Public" could, or would swallow – The Assizes begin to day and as I lay in bed, from my Window – there being a Fair on the Castle Green – which is the way down to what are called the Judges Lodgings – I had the full benefit of the ridiculous pageant of the Judges <u>entrée</u>[9] with the Clarions and Trumpets – and men on Horseback with white wands decked with ribbons preceding their carriages one might have fancied one self back in old Besses[10] days. – As <u>Crowder</u>![11] is on the Circuit, and puts up at this Hotel, I hope I shall see him as they all say he is so wonderfully handsome. De Dog and de day light say I must not write any more so with hims innocent love and hoping soon to see you Believe Me Ever My dearest Rebecca your Grateful And Affect Rosina Bulwer Lytton

HALS
1. Without that (French).
2. Castle of Flowers (French).
3. Little story (French).
4. This traditionally takes place on 17 March, the Feast Day of St Patrick, the patron saint of Ireland.
5. George Dobson Willoughby (1829–57) was related to Rebecca Ryves.

6.   This is EBL's chiropodist, who lives in the Haymarket, London. RBL accused him of being a quack, and her lawyer Mr Hyde took a successful legal action against him for overcharging A. E. Chalon. See RBL, 18 November 1856. He may be the Mr Eisenberg, who is a chiropodist in William Thackeray's *The Book of Snobs* (1848).
7.   John Forster was editor of *The Examiner* (1847–56). See RBL, 17 September 1839.
8.   *Fraser's Magazine*. See RBL, 4 March 1856.
9.   Enter (French).
10. Queen Elizabeth I.
11. Judge Crowder. See RBL, 22 June 1855.

To Rebecca Ryves

Tuesday April 2nd 1856 Cold, rainy and Novemberish

Many thanks my dearest Rebecca for your kind letter, and good story about the Archbishop what he said of one Colonel of Dragoons, is <u>generic</u> as to most, I am writing as fast as I can to try and finish my book that we may have the more time for walking, and talking when you come; – I think I will get poor dear good Hyde to hunt me out a Publisher I send you such a nice letter I had from him the day before yesterday – which let me have back: I also send you a much ado about nothing from Mrs Wheeler; as there is a message to you in it: as she took 5 months to answer my letter which <u>did</u> require an answer I shall take at least as many to answer <u>hers</u> which does <u>not</u>. I also send you "The Examiner" you'll see as I said the tack Fudgester[1] goes upon – as I said is to say the plagiary was <u>intended</u>! and the upshot of his mendacious trade is to impress upon that <u>uncrossed</u> – because <u>thoroughbred</u> Ass the British Public! that the more his friend Sir Liar plagiarises the more strikingly original!! he is! – but I'll <u>swear</u> by the appeal to <u>generous</u>!! and liberal criticism!! at the end of that most ridiculously barefaced effusion; – that Sir Liar according to his wont wrote it <u>himself</u>. I forgot to tell you that Dr Viner, who tumbled over him, added "I had no idea he was such a <u>very</u> old man"! this is what <u>every</u> one says so much for vice, as he is barely 50. – Full, and busy as I am, I forced my way into the Crown Court, on Monday to see Crowder! Making every allowance for that disfiguring <u>assemblement</u> the judges scarlet window curtains trimmed with white cats skin, he is <u>frightful</u>! a sort of bloated George the 4th looking[2] person and then he is fair! and I detest fair men, – with those horrible scarlet runner whiskers they always have; there is not a shadow of excuse that I can see for the Stuartdina,[3] – Crowder is another of your Profligates, – with a Chevaux de prise[4] of natural Children and as we have the flower of English Profligacy, for judges – Chancellors, Chief Justices, – attorney and solicitor generals, – and for our Legislation!! no wonder our Ecclesiastical laws are the barbaric and iniquitous national disgraces they are.

With him doatskins best love Believe me my dearest Rebecca Ever your grateful and affect Rosina Bulwer Lytton.

HALS
1.   John Forster.
2.   George IV was nicknamed 'The Fat Adonis of fifty'.
3.   This may be connected with Mrs Stuart Hayes.
4.   Prize horses (French).

To Edward Bulwer Lytton

To that Loathsome old Ruffian Sir E B Lytton

April the 12th 1856

Recieved through Robert Hodgson Esqre Solicitor of 32 Broad St Buildings London ineffable Blackguard Sir Liar Coward Janus Plagiary Allpuff Edward Bulwer Lytton the disgraceful swindle of £94"3'4 !!!!!! which he doles out to me his legal victim as out pauper of those Sodom and Gomorrah[1] Sinks of iniquity the Park Lane and Knebworth[2] Unions!
Rosina Bulwer Lytton

Alas!

HALS
1.   For the sins of their inhabitants, the two cities Sodom and Gomorrah were destroyed by brimstone and fire from Jehova. See Genesis 19:24–5. The names are also used as metaphors for sinfulness and sexual deviation.
2.   EBL's homes.

To Rebecca Ryves

Thursday April 24th 1856

My dearest Rebecca I was indeed very glad to get your letter (which I did by the 3d Post last night too late to answer it) for I was beginning to be uneasy at not hearing from you, – I shall live in hopes, that now you have got so far, you will come farther without I hope faring worse, though the Cuisine here is execrable! as apparently the D—l[1] does not send any cooks to this part of the world. I am suffering very much from dysentery just now, and what is worse de dog, had been vezy exceeding ill, and hims poor innocent left fore paw; is so lame, dat hims mud is going to get him a crutch nevertheless him desires hims best love to hims Aunt Rebecca (whom him hopes soon to see to tell her all about it) and to degrass in de poor little square as it was as you say de first place him Idled in when him was taken out of de land of Egypt and de House of Bondage[2] – I am ill from worry, which I think you will not wonder at when you read the enclosed, and see the way in which not only my interests are compromised – but my feelings, outraged, and disregarded upon all occasions; – as I wrote you word Mr Hodgson <u>was</u> to have written to that Brute 3 months ago – enforcing the punctual payment of my Parish allowance to <u>him</u> – with his usual supineness he never did so, and when the time came round – just look at the cringing pusillanimous – ridiculous thing he did write! and much good he did by it for it put me in such a rage, that instead of forwarding the receipt to him I send you a copy of what I sent to Sir Liar, Mr Wheeler kindly lent me £25 at Llangollen upon the Bracelet worth £80 which I never yet have been able to get back and perhaps my things from Brownes might share the same fate – saddling me with an obligation! besides; – so I begged of Mr Hodgson not to get me deeper in Mr Wheelers debt till I had paid off that £25, – and that I thought the best thing they could do – would be to open a Penny Subscription at the Stock Exchange for Sir Edward Bulwer Lyttons Pauper wife – with the name in full; as without something of the sort – with this eternal pay back, pay back – of £20 & £30 every minute and £2 –30 a year interest money – it was not very clear – at least to me; how I was to exist besides – for <u>living</u> it was not. I have never heard from Mr Hodgson since, and never shall for the next three months, so that you know as much about my affairs as I do – you will see my poor dear Hydes letter; that I have not much hope of his being able to help me to a Publisher, but he mistakes about my book it is not <u>merely</u> what is called an amusing book – but I flatter myself it is a very interesting one, and for a wonder! (with <u>me</u>) a good plot. I took your kind, and kindly meant advice and wrote to Mrs Wheeler, but Heaven help me! used as I have been by almost every body – I sometimes think are they and Mr Hodgson bought over, under the pretext of serving me, to strip, and swamp me more? at all events I don't at all like the way Mr Hodgson manages – alias mismanages my affairs – more especially as regards Sir Liar – Who do you think I am going to meet to night? Mrs Bennet the wife of <u>the</u> Mr Bennet late of St Pauls Wilton Place,[3] and now Rector of Frome; – they said at the time it had a letter too much and that he should have been sent to Rome I'll keep all I have to say till we meet which I hope will be very soon. – so with my kind regards to Massy – whom I'm glad to hear such improved accounts of – and again thanking him (and <u>you</u>) for his magnificent <u>Festa</u>.[4] Believe me my dearest Rebecca with 75 Innocent fictions from de lame dog, who says you must make haste to come and help him over the style Believe me Ever your grateful &affect Rosina Bulwer Lytton

HALS
1. Devil.
2. God's prophet addressed the Israelites thus: 'Moses said unto the people, Remember this day, in which ye came out from Egypt, out of the house of bondage' (Exodus 13:15).

3.   St Paul is a church in Knightsbridge, London.
4.   Feast (Latin).

To Rebecca Ryves

April 26th 1856

Many thanks my dearest Rebecca for your kind letter, and enclosures which reached me quite safely. You rather mistake about this being an out of the way place, for no Assize Towns[1] are so; and all such are comparatively dear, here they ask 30 a week, for a beggarly lodging over a shop – without fire or any single thing – and the rule is to turn out twice a year while the Judges are here, and Mrs Clarke makes it a great favour to me not to exact the same as they are at those times full to overflowing:- but as I before told you the £2 a week that I pay her is 5 less – (and certainly worth 10 more for what I get) than what I paid that old shark at Llangollen who <u>swore</u> to me she never took Mr and Mrs Lloyd – for what they told you. This £2 does <u>not</u>, include Beer – so I drink nothing but water; but it includes fire in the bedroom and sitting room – and candles so that really for the rooms and three meals a day clean sheets once a weekend Towels ad libitum[2] I do not think it dear one could not possibly bring ones expenses – including food, fire and washing (House linen) with <u>that</u> even in beggarly lodgings of s10 a week; – but the servants cost me about £5 a quarter extra. I have seen Mrs Clarke again, and said all I could to urge her to make it s30 and give you a permanent sitting room; but she says <u>that</u> if you gave her £5 a week she could not promise to do; – and makes such a favour of it to me to do it for £1"15 that I see she does not care to conclude the bargain, – except to oblige me; but as I said before my sitting room is at your service, with the one restriction of not taking away, or disarranging my books, or papers; – as when ever the servants here do so, my whole time is taken up hunting, and looking for them and having no maid (which I <u>cannot</u> get used to-) and from growing every day older instead of younger – the slavery of mending my things – and keeping my rooms neat, and having to write – not for bread but for stones! besides, is at times almost more than I <u>can</u> bear, and if it were not for the pleasure it would give that Fiend God forgive me – but there are times when I should throw myself into the river – for my burden <u>is</u> <u>too</u> heavy, and not a single hope to lighten it. But as I before said my dearest Rebecca before you conclude, any bargain with Mrs Clarke you must come for a month to me, to see how you would like the Place; the <u>reason</u> of this English limitation! irritation! you know alas! too well, but should I by a miracle get any thing like a fair price for my book I shall then insist upon your being my guest for all the months that you can remain here; – if Mr Hyde does <u>not</u> do something for me about this book, what I <u>am</u> to do! – God only knows

– for this last quarter having an arrear of £37 to pay Miss Dickenson– I was unable to pay Mrs Clarke a farthing – so that the next I shall have to pay her six months- and £10 to Mr Sandby and £10 to Miss Dickenson – and so I go on or rather stick fast in such a Slough of Despond[3] as no poor wretch ever was plunged in! and you cannot wonder at my writhing under Mr Hodgsons supine, apathetic stupidity putting me more and more in the monsters power who has made my wretched existence such a perfect Hell. For Heaven's sake dont tell Mrs Kitchener – or any of that hollow heartless set where I am – or indeed <u>any</u> one. When? and where? did that poor silly Mrs Browne[4] die? – I ought to condole with <u>you</u> about poor Kingsford! and will do so, in flowers, <u>not</u> weeds when I and de dog – have de pleasure of seeing you – which we hope will be soon; – you see you pay £5 a week for Lodgings alone, so 10 more – is not Exorbitant for food, and firing.

Did you see in the Police reports yesterday – that a "Mr <u>Jones</u>" was picked out of the Kennel near Bedford Square[5] hopelessly <u>drunk</u>! so far the description would do for our friend – but it appears he was covered with costly jewellery – having been lately unexpectedly left a legacy – which from having been in a state of extreme indigence had (with gin) turned his brain though the stomach Pumps was applied, they failed to recover the poor wretch. Above all! should you meet that little Reptile Jones,[6] in your neighbourhood <u>on</u> <u>no</u> <u>account</u> tell him where I am. As I shall lose the Post in three minutes more I must say good bye. Forgive this scrawl and with kind regards to Massy. Hoping to see you soon, and de Dogs best love. Believe me Ever my Dearest Rebecca your grateful & affec Rosina Bulwer Lytton.

Is no 13 Inhabited?

HALS
1. Towns where periodic criminal courts visited to try the most serious cases.
2. At one's pleasure (Latin).
3. Christian in Bunyan's *The Pilgrim's Progress* sinks into the Slough of Despond under the weight of his sins. See RBL, 6 October 1831.
4. The wife of the china and curiosities shopkeeper of 48 Sloane Street, London.
5. Bedford Square is in central London.
6. George Jones, sometimes nicknamed Jonas by RBL. See RBL, 12 January 1853.

To Rebecca Ryves

Tuesday April 29th 1856

My dearest Rebecca De dog – and de dogs mud, have only a quarter of a minute to save the post; and tell you that we shall look forward to Monday to have the pleasure not of welcoming you home! for alas! we have no home; but of welcoming you as well as we can – and at all events as sincerely as if we had a Castle of our own to welcome you to. In Electric Telegraph haste – with kind regards to Massy – believe me – Ever Gratefully & affectly yours Rosina Bulwer Lytton

---

HALS

To Rebecca Ryves

[1856?]

My dearest Rebecca I have only a quarter of a minute to thank you for your letter – for in this millennium of meanness as every thing is managed in the most economical manner possible in <u>cluding Heavenly</u>(?) as well as mundane matters they have crammed the thanksgiving for the Peace into the Sunday work not to take them from their adored L.S.D.[1] – on a week day and the <u>real</u> Established Religion of England which is Mammon worship alas! the reason I have not written to Mrs Tyler which pray tell her with my love – is not having yet been able to pay her – and if God does not have mercy and open some way for me soon – I <u>cannot</u> not bear up under it much longer. – I wish for many reasons (that I will explain to you) that you would <u>not</u> fail to call on Mrs Wheeler 48 Dover St Piccadilly. – I'll order dinner then as usual at 7 on Wednesday as I never dine before. – De dog says – him can get grass enough here rather better than the Devonshire brown grass of London – and so should prefer a Daisy Cain. – With kind regards to Massy Ever affectly yrs RBL

HALS
1.   Pounds, shillings and pence.

To Rebecca Ryves

Friday 5 0 clock October 31ˢᵗ 1856

I was very glad to hear My dearest Rebecca that you arrived safely at your journeys end; but sorry that you were (as I feared you would be) so cold. I assure you Maboots and I, miss you very much – more especially at, and after dinner, but try to console ourselves by hoping that you have a better one. I can well understand your not liking Torquay[1] just yet for I do not think one would like Paradise itself till one got used to it; as one always feels in a strange place (at least I do) as if one had left ones skin behind, and was reduced to going about in ones bones; but independent of the beautiful scenery – I hope the gaiety and sociability will soon make you feel much happier than you were in the dull Slough of Despond. I have been twice to Days[2] – and Miss Dyke[3] has not yet got your dress from London but has promised it by the end of the week when I will instantly consign it to "Extremely much obliged" of all Miss Dykes importations I only covet one – a gem of an Opera Hat from Baudrons (only five guineas) black velvet with a black feather round the crown put on! as only Parisian fingers <u>can</u> place feathers and a bunch of full blown roses (3) at the side looking as if the leaves would fall about and as if the flowers themselves had been blown coquettishly on the side of the hat by some stray zephyrs[4] – but never touched by human hands however I did <u>not</u> buy it for two reasons, one of which might suffice imprimis[5] I had not the five guineas – secondly Taunton has not an Opera. I was afraid yesterday you had carried off all the fine weather with you, and meant to ask you to send us back a sun beam or two by return of Post – but today has been a perfect fine day – and I have just returned from the poor old walk past the Wesleyan College[6] with Fanny Boys – who with Augusta desire their love to you, and Maboots and hims mud wished vezy much you had been with us to see the glorious sunset! Maboots desires me to tell you with hims love that him has quite got rid of hims Cough – but as there is no such thing as being well on <u>all</u> sides in this world – de rascally Tax gatherer has found him out, so him has to fork out 12 tomorrow (where? or how? deponent sayeth not) Elliot has not yet been seen! or even heard of so that <u>now</u> the book is waiting for him, and Fred has at <u>length</u>! made the wonderful discovery! that he would have printed it faster himself at his own house than Woodley[7] has done – he sent me the Title Page last night which really looks very nice. Recollect if it ever comes out! and I ever pay you my debt that I also owe you a month of Mrs Clarkes Bill and I hope if you find nothing more agreeable that you will come over, and starve with Me and Maboots at Xmas? – you ask what Massy would say if you were to appear in so costly a costume as his? I fear he would act as well as dress like a Turk, as you know, or ought to know by this time, that there is a great difference between "a fellow" and a "Female". I sent Mrs Clarke down your message about the bread. I had my Aegean stable[8] to clean out yesterday, and Fred never sent the proofs till 11 at night, I was not in bed till 5 this morning – with close hard work – and being Maid of all work all day, and ill I really think is hastening the consummation Sir Liar so devoutly wishes – for as poor [Kirk ... ?] says in one of his letters [ill] stole, and distaste of my [ill] seem to be playing at ball – the stake my life – Provided the game would only end soon I should not care however now that I "spot the <u>oak</u>" like a fading Barrister – I find it a great comfort. God Bless you My dearest Rebecca and with kind regards to Massy Believe Me Ever Gratefully and affectly yours Rosina Bulwer Lytton.

I have got such bootsest of boo buttons for the dresses you so kindly gave me

---

HALS
1. A fashionable seaside resort on the Devonshire coast of south-west England.
2. Draper's shop in Taunton.

3.   Local seamstress.
4.   Greek god of the west wind.
5.   In the first place (Latin).
6.   This Tudor-style, Wesleyan college, located on the Trull Road in Taunton, was built in 1847.
7.   William Augustus Woodley was a West Country newspaper proprietor.
8.   As one of his twelve labours, the mythological hero Hercules had to clean out the Augean stables, which housed thousands of animals, in one day. The stables were owned by King Augeas who owned more cattle than anyone else in Greece.

To Rebecca Ryves

Saturday Night November 1ˢᵗ 1856

My dearest Rebecca Having had the proofs two hours sooner! and Fred[1] having got himself converted from a snail into an Electric Telegraph! by giving me <u>since</u> this morning at 2o'clock a revise in red – of the Preface another of the Dedication and <u>26</u>!!!! Pages of proofs besides, – and I having recovered my astonishment! and got over my work; – I sit down to tell you that Miss Dyke having got back the sold dress and I, to my infinite surprise! <u>finding</u> that by night they were both the <u>same</u> – took the one we saw the other morning; having begged Miss Dyke to make me a very pretty French sleeve that I saw – there, and which I thought rather beyond "Extremely much obliged" the latter will begin your dress on Monday. Miss Dyke, and she, both expressed their regret, at your departure. To day, Doatskin, and I, having been to Dinah's to thank her for a <u>cadeau</u>[2] of [chintery?] she sent me; I put in, at the Boys, from stress of weather when they forced two glasses of Blewetts[3] sherry down my throat – and as I was very tired, and it very good with the red Borracha[4] twang I was nothing loathe, – on my return home – (drunk and disorderly!) while I was taking off my things Dr Edwards[5] was announced and as he was <u>solo</u> I was very glad to see him, – as in the course of conversation he said his father in law, had so far behaved honourably to him, that he wrote to him before his marriage saying she was a natural daughter – but that her mother was dead(!!!) "and indeed" added Dr E till lately I never knew, who her mother was" – "But you know now?" said I? " – Oh yes, but Anna does not and yet I think I ought to tell her – but scarcely know how to do so." – I then said "her son (Mrs Mc's)[6] is a Methodist Preacher is he not?" Oh the very antipodes of <u>that</u>!" he replied with a groan!!! "he is an Omnibus driver"!!! So you see every <u>fresh</u> discovery one makes in this horrid history – is worse, and worse poor Dr E. then told me that the £2, 000 his <u>Beau père</u>[7] had promised him on the day of his marriage, had never been paid from that day to this so that his (Dr E's) mothers jointure had to be mortgaged to start them in life.

As I had him all to myself I thought I'd take courage and <u>Pop the question</u> I was so anxious to have elucidated, so, I said "where was your wife so fortunate as to meet with you? for when one thinks of <u>what</u> her lot might have been, with such a father! she really was <u>most</u> fortunate." – "Well – I first met her at Sir Richard Bethels,[8] whose daughters[9] had been school fellows of hers, – and she was young then, and foreign, and – and – in short I married in haste – " sighed the poor man, – as if he were adding in his own mind – "and repented at leisure" – while we were speaking Frizzledom[10] came up to say Mr Somebody was below, who wanted to see him, and though it wanted only 5 minutes to 7 I could not prevail on him to stay for dinner, but he said he would come in, some other day by himself as he should like to talk it over: it seems that Dr Howel was the Town crier who told him about Mrs McDonald when he went to Windsor.[11] – Dr Edwards asked very kindly after you and said he was very sorry you were gone. Poor man he seemed dreadfully out of spirits. Day returned yesterday and was good enough to take the picture himself to Kensington, but "My friend Chelong"[12] was at Richmond. I sent you to day the Snails Gazette Woodley's[13] paper – with the continuation of the Agapemone[14] history in it – as it is now very late and I must mend my rags before I go to bed I'll not finish my letter till tomorrow. –

Sunday November 2nd many thanks for your kind letter just received the Sprig of Myrtle and poor Mr Healds which I return and think it of course a very sensible letter, as it perfectly coincides with my own opinion of the murderous martyrdom of continental privations for Invalids. The letter to Mr Lloyd I will post, being alas! well able to understand Massy's reasons. I find your generous present of stockings a great comfort, and if I don't thank you as I ought; why when you gave them to me, you must have expected that I would put my foot in it. "My friend <u>Chelong</u>" in a letter I had from him this morning <u>ith</u> very <u>thorry</u> I have <u>lotht</u> my agreeable companion – he repudiates the Duchess – and says it is only an old Engraving <u>pasted</u> on Plaster of Paris, as it <u>could</u> <u>not</u> be engraved <u>on</u> it.[15] Is there no Miss Bonnar[16] that Massy could convert into Mrs Ryves? – I can well imagine Frizzledoms gratitude at your having baited a fresh <u>gin</u> for him, of which I assure you I had the <u>full</u> benefit. I think the history of Mr Princes[17] loathsome blasphemies in this weeks Paper is really too revolting. – Having come to the end of my tether I must with Maboots's best love and my kind regards to Massy say good bye and Believe me my dearest Rebecca Ever your Grateful & Affect Rosina Bulwer Lytton alas!

HALS
1. Frederick Clarke of the Caxton Head Press, Taunton, is printing RBL's novel *Very Successful!* See RBL, 11 January 1857.
2. Gift (French).

3. Sherry from the publican who is courting Miss Comer. He is probably Benjamin G. Bluett (b. *c.* 1803).
4. Crude rubber or the rubber tree.
5. Dr Edwards of Wiveliscombe married the illegitimate daughter of RBL's uncle. See RBL, 29 and 15 June 1858.
6. Mrs MacDonald.
7. Father-in-law (French).
8. Richard Bethell, first Baron Westbury (1800–73), was an MP and judge, who became Lord Chancellor (1861–5). He had been instrumental in the passing of the Divorce Act 1857.
9. Bethell had seven surviving children with his first wife.
10. A male servant at the Giles Castle Hotel, Taunton.
11. West of London.
12. Alfred Edward Chalon.
13. William Augustus Woodley was the proprietor of the *Somerset County Gazette* at Taunton.
14. The Abode of Love cult. See RBL, 11 September 1855.
15. In a letter to Chalon of 2 November 1856, RBL writes: 'I much doubted the fact of that horror being engraved *on* plaster of Paris, but, having great faith in the fallibility of my own ignorance, I am never positive about anything of which I am not sure; however, la belle Louisa (or according to plaster libel ...) having been well plastered ... can afford to be ill-plastered in effigy (see RBL, *Unpublished Letters*, p. 277).
16. A wistful reference to Rebecca Ryves friend Mrs Bonar.
17. Revd Henry James Prince was the leader of the religious cult, Agapemone. See RBL, 11 September 1855.

To Rebecca Ryves

Tuesday Evening November 4th 1856

My dearest Rebecca

I have only time (by two minutes) to save the Post and tell you how sorry I am to hear of poor Mr Dangerfields illness, but glad he is out of danger – you are all indeed lucky to have such a kind friend in <u>need</u> as Mrs Bonnar,[1] as rare as friends of any kind are now a days – <u>those</u> are the rarest of all. I went on the reciept of your letter to "Extremely much obliged" who says your dress will not be home from Jessets[2] till <u>next</u> Saturday consequently all your things will not be done till Saturday week, so that it would be useless to incur the expense of sending the new dress till the others are finished. I am also sorry to tell you that Day says the Furrier said the Chinchili is worth nothing – being discolored from lying by – and though it could be done up so as to look well for a week, it would not be worth the expense at it would forthwith relapse into its brown study again – moreover the moth, is slightly in it. From all I hear Blewett is not likely to come to the <u>pint</u> as long as poor Miss C[3] is content to be a <u>gill</u> to his Jack. I had a visit from the Bride and Bridegroom yesterday – a more ugly vulgar

Country Townish nonentity than she is I never saw poor Miss Comer looks like an Empress compared to her, but men <u>have no</u> taste. – I am happy to tell you that I have at length got a good looking, and gentlemanlike Sir Gregory Kempenfelt[4] – and the 2d vol, was finished yesterday. Here is Tib's last – What is the difference between Fred and his brother? – give it up? one is Alfred,[5] and the other All-Fred!! (Oh! with a big O!) I have <u>not</u> heard from poor dear Dr Price, and am always fidgety when I don't, fearing the poor old man is ill. I hope Massy wont leave you long by yourself and that Mr Dangerfield will soon be well. – With de Dogs best ove – who is better den dood, and has quite lost hims cough – Believe me in whirlwind haste Ever

My dearest Rebecca your grateful & affect

Rosina Bulwer Lytton

By the Bride, and Bridegroom I mean Mr & Mrs John Ford[6]

HUNT
1.   Rebecca Ryves's friend, who is presently in Torquay.
2.   Dressmaker.
3.   Miss Comer.
4.   General Sir Gregory Kempenfelt of Baron's Court, 3 km from Mold, Flintshire, north Wales, is a fictional character in RBL's novel *Very Successful!*.
5.   Alfred Clarke, brother to Frederick of Caxton Head, Taunton, a publishing company, who brought out RBL's novel *Very Successful!* with the London publisher Whittaker & Co. in 1856.
6.   John Ford is probably a second cousin to Fanny and Augusta Boys.

To Rebecca Ryves

Thursday Evening November 6th 1856

"Brief time had Conrad now to greet Gulnare"[1] as Byron sang, and Massy would say – but having been kept in from two till 5 by a visit from Mrs Hyde and her fair daughter Helen whose carriage had gone astray at the other Castle and if [?] they could not look for it at this! I have only a ... *[2 pages illegible]*

... half cotton Bournouse[2] – not half as pretty or as good as mine and not even lined, for which he asks six guineas. – I don't think it is Jessets fault about your dress as when I went last Monday Extremely much obliged was only <u>then</u> wrapping it to send to him.

Many thanks for your kind thought about the cream but pray don't send it as I am so bilious I am far better without it. I send you a letter from poor old Dr Price that I had yesterday so you see the meeting of the Shingles! don't kill. The cold here is <u>Siberian</u> and I have not got my shelter yet. With Maboot's best love to you kind regards to Massy – and hoping to hear better accounts of poor Mr Dangerfield

    Believe me in flash of lightening haste – Ever gratefully and affectly yrs
       Rosina Bulwer Lytton

HUNT
1.   Byron, *The Corsair* (1863–4), II.vi.
2.   A fringed, knee-length mantle with a hood.

To Rebecca Ryves

Saturday November 8th 1856

I am very sorry My dearest Rebecca to hear that your cousin has had a relapse but it is only what I feared would be the case – he is indeed most fortunate in having such triply kind friends, I mean friends who have the will, the <u>power</u>, and who <u>know</u> <u>how</u> to be kind, for the latter is not the least rare of the three, – I have no doubt you find any rooms without <u>portieres</u>[1] cold, after mine; I have at length got my shutter which is a great comfort and I need have <u>some</u>! as not having Housemaids work enough already – I have now of a morning to light my own fire – and gather up the ashes into an empty coal scuttle which additional piece of drudgery I prefer doing – to being kept for four hours without a fire and sustained with dust when it is lit, after my already having had the trouble of dusting the room but the worst of all this Treadmill slavery is, that when I sit down to write I am <u>so</u> tired I should much prefer laying down to die. – Mrs Edwards[2] arrived about 3o'clock to day – it was to ask me if I knew any of the East India[3] directors as "Frank[4] has a claim on the Kingdom of Oude[5] of £90, 000 lent by his father Colonel Edwards to the late King of Oude." – I said I did not; but recommended him to first take Counsel's opinion write to Lord Dalhousey[6] giving him a synopsis of his claims and then Memorialise the East India Company – and if that don't avail I told him I would then get "The Times" to take it up, for him as he luckily has a friend at Court by having an intimate friend who is one of the chief writers for "The Times" he came for his wife about 4 and she insisted on the strength of his Doctorship on dragging into my room he greatly admired my old Oak Chest as I saw his knowledge of anatomy much puzzled by my "<u>Blowd out bag</u>" which was hanging up and which I saw him stealing an enquiring look at now and then. Augusta is off to her beloved Bridgewater to day till Monday. – I have no means of any sort so send you a continuation of the Agapemone[7] blasphemy. It was not to be supposed that Fred could keep up his steak to any extent last night the proofs had again dwindled down to two. With Maboots ever kind regards to Massy and hoping poor Mr Dangerfield will show his gratitude for his good nursing by soon being quite well. Believe me tired to death. Ever my dearest Rebecca, your grateful & affect Rosina Bulwer Lytton

---

HALS
1. Porters (French).
2. RBL's cousin.
3. The British East India Company had monopoly trading interests in India. By 1856, it had become the effective ruler of the country until 1858 when the administration of India became the responsibility of the Crown.
4. A relative of Mrs Edwards and RBL.
5. The East India Company moved its troops to the borders of Awadh (Oude) in north-east India, which eventually led to the annexation of the region, justified on the grounds that the native prince had been guilty of 'disorder and misrule'. These actions led to the Indian Mutiny of 1857.
6. Lord Dalhousie (1812–60) was Governor-General of India whose notorious doctrine of lapse enabled a native state to became part of British India if there was no male heir at the death of the ruler.
7. The Abode of Love cult. See RBL, 11 September 1855.

To Rebecca Ryves

Tuesday November 11th 1851 6

On the River <u>Plate</u> Vulgo[1] purifying the Plates for Dinner!

My dearest Rebecca

I almost feared from you yesterday that poor Mr Dangerfield had been worse, but am very glad to find my fears were groundless – and sincerely hope that he will now weather the storm, and make the best return he can make to such very kind friends – that of soon getting quite well. – The £90, 000 <u>has</u> truly a "pleasant" <u>sound</u>, even if it never has more – though if got it has to be divided among 8 still Eleven thousand some odd hundreds a piece is <u>not</u> to be despised, and I only wish we had – or even had a <u>chance</u> of half of it! – the Boys's too have had a small windfall of £150 – Each, – from that Mrs Twentyman of Liverpool[2] whom you may remember "The Times" mentioned some time ago as <u>really</u> being "The Oldest Inhabitant" so you see the wheel goes round and the wind blows off golden pippens for every one but <u>me</u>! En revanche[3] Mrs Edwards I understand does me the honor of giving out every where that I am her Cousin!! indignantly <u>y mette ordre</u>[4] by telling the people that I should have enough to do if I acknowledged all such cousins! which I suppose would amount to a sort of Encyclopedia of natural History. Poor Miss Comer though wearing a necklace of <u>blisters</u> – <u>looks</u> exceedingly well. Fanny and Augusta made me go there to supper last night the consequence is, that unaccustomed as I am to Either public, or private Eating, I have been ill all day. – I am sorry your cold continues so bad, and that you find

Torquay so cold; I envy you your good milk and meat; and you need not envy me the <u>bread</u> – which of course has become as bad, as anything else in the house. I should think any Farm House you would go to; they would be glad to supply you with home made bread; I have always understood that Torquay was famed for its good bread. – I hope to send off your box on Saturday. The Boys's desire their love as does itty Maboots, and with kind regards to Massy – and hoping to hear better accounts of your poor cousin

> Believe me in Whirlwind Haste Ever
> your grateful & affect
> Rosina Bulwer Lytton

Lionel Massy[5] – the <u>late</u> Lord Clarina's youngest son is dead. –

HUNT
1. Commonly (Latin).
2. Mrs Elizabeth Twentyman of Duke Street, Liverpool, died in September 1856 at the age of ninety-six.
3. In return (French).
4. I am putting things straight (French).
5. George Lionel Massy (1805–56) was the third son of Eyre Massy, first Lord Clarina (1719–1804), who was Governor of Limerick.

To Rebecca Ryves

Tuesday November 18th 1856

I am very glad My dearest Rebecca that your Box arrived safely and that you like your dress. I have no doubt that the yellow spot was done at "Extremely much obliged" as there is no end to the dirt disorder, and carelessness of the people here, and once they get you into their clutches, they have neither conscience, nor honesty so as <u>they</u> get the money <u>that</u> is all they care for – I have really been worried almost to death within the last five days – but the worst of all was yesterday – when poor Innocence was so ill, I thought I should lose him – could scarcely crawl when him went out – began to shiver when him came in would not look at hims dinner, could not even do hims growling – and kept making such a piteous little moan – that it broke ones heart to hear him – I sent off for Channing[1] – who on feeling him said hims poor little Tummy was crammed till he was in perfect <u>agony</u> – and this is all the wretches will do – as they are too lazy even to put him out of a morning – Channing took him away with him to give him some castor oil last night and syrup of Buckthorn[2] this morning – I have just come from there and him is much better and coming home in an hour. As soon as the <u>paper</u> had at length arrived, of course there was some <u>fresh</u> bother and bungle, and so last night I had another note from that half Ass half Bear Clarke[3] apologising for there being no proofs <u>again</u>!! last night as when he had gone down to the Office he found they had broken up all the type!!!! Why not that Mr Woodley[4] had sold the Copyright of the book at once? – the one would have been just as warrantable and justifiable a proceeding as the other – Augusta says that rogue Woodley has done Clarke out of the whole £100 and the latter not having the scratch of a pen to bind him is completely at this Sharks mercy were I not as usual the victim I should be too glad that pig headed fellow suffered for the insolent, and obstinate manner he <u>would</u> go counter to Augustas caution, and my wishes. – The frightful [Anastelic?] affair arrived <u>only</u> last night! and after my <u>repeated</u> orders to have the letter press – done in nice small copper plate – like my visiting cards which I even sent as a <u>pattern</u> they are still in the same vulgar type! and instead of 'painted from memory" they have put "<u>printed</u> from memory! – I just now met the fellow in Hunts Court[5] who turned as white as a sheet – and took off his hat – I passed on, without taking the slightest notice of him – Augusta has just been here saying he is in such a state and says he could hang himself – and does she think I <u>would</u> add to all my other goodness by receiving an apology from him – which he would write on his knees(!) if he thought I would but forgive him? – "<u>That</u> Mr Clarke is what you should have began by doing days ago for if the letter you presumed to write Lady Lytton was shown you might leave Taunton within the next hour for it would ruin you for ever and setting aside its gross and intense insolence except Sir Edward Bulwer Lytton I should not think there was another man in England brute enough to write such a letter to a woman." – Fred in tears! Which must have been a Hydraulic – if not a beautiful sight! – "Oh ma'am pray don't say <u>that</u>, – for if I thought I could be like such a ruffian – as that in any way – I would end myself at once" – this certainly evinced a knowledge of right and wrong, – in sober sadness – which in some degree extenuated the drunken letter, I cant send you Hydes letter till I get it back from poor Dr Price whom I know takes such a kind interest in all my ceaseless worries that I sent it to him today – <u>Mais en revanche</u>[6] I send you the <u>copy</u> of one just received from my friend <u>Chalon</u> – having despatched the charming original to "The Brothers Hyde"[7] – I am very glad your cousin is so much better, and that Massy is so well. – I have no message to Captain King – except my kind regards – and that I hope her Majesty has come <u>right</u> <u>royally</u> into possession of his Claude[8] – à propos[9] – not of the beautiful picture, but of the ugly queen – Miss Comers story is that the queen has written a book!!![10] and is going to publish it – !!! I only hope she will do so at "the Caxtons Head"![11] <u>that's all</u> Augusta desired her love to you, and with my kind regards to Massy – Believe me in Whirlwind Haste – Ever Gratefully, and affectly yrs. Rosina Bulwer Lytton

HALS
1.   Possibly, a Taunton veterinary surgeon.

2.   Up to 1867, syrup of the medicinal plant buckthorn was used as a purgative medicine, being a favourite rustic remedy for children.
3.   Frederick Clarke, RBL's Taunton publisher.
4.   See RBL, 31 October 1856.
5.   Situated near Castle Green in Taunton.
6.   More in return (French).
7.   Henry and Charles Hyde were solicitors, business partners and brothers.
8.   Claude Lorrain (1600–82) was a French Baroque artist, renowned for his landscape painting, who was active in Italy.
9.   In connection with (French).
10. Queen Victoria published two books during her lifetime, *Leaves from the Journal of Our Life in the Highlands: From 1848 to 1861* (1868) and *More Leaves from the Journal of a Life in the Highlands from 1862 to 1882* (1884).
11. The publisher in Taunton. See above, n. 3.

To Rebecca Ryves

[c. 19 November 1856]

... write to me, and whose letters are forwarded to me from Llangollen through Mr Hyde – his being the only address I left them there:- letters too, from persons – who could not possibly know I had been at Llangollen unless they recieved their orders – and the full address of Phillips's Hotel from <u>him</u>; – for instance, the other day I recicieve [*sic*] a letter from Brunswick[1] – from a person I have neither seen nor heard of for five and twenty years!!! a Miss Richardson[2] who when I was a girl staying at Brocket[3] (Lord Melbournes) where I first met that loathsome brute Sir Liar, – was a companion and Toady of poor Lady Carolines;[4] – a person whom I never could bear; – but whom I know has all these years kept up a correspondence with Sir Liar – she now writes to me ostensibly to borrow money – but imploring that I will <u>at least answer her letter</u> – and that is the burden of her song – even if I send her nothing – it is so likely that a person who for 25! years has never written to me should all of a sudden be so very anxious to hear from me! – and last week I get a letter from Brighton (the stronghold of Sir Liars spies and doers of dirty work) from that vulgar mad woman Mrs Wellington Boate! affecting to be sorry for her former insolence to me – and saying the fellow connected with the Guilt – for whom her Husband used to work for Thirty shillings a Week!! is a wretch of the name of Bell[5] – who is Editor of a Paper called "The Home News"[6] and is also Editing a new Edition of the British Poets[7] – he is she says a chum of Dickens's – and a bosom friend of Sir Liars[8] – for which <u>honors</u> he is qualefied by being always drunk – and living with another man's Wife; and that he it was, when "Behind The Scenes" came out, that went about London – by Sir Liars orders, – proclaiming by sound of Trumpet that I was mad – and most probably wrote me those anonymous letters. – Now as I think notwithstanding her affected abuse of this Bell, and the Clique; that it is more than probable that Mrs Boat may have been offered a £10 – or even a £5 note to find out <u>where I am</u>; and that, that is the <u>real</u> motive of her letter; I need not tell you, that I have not taken the slightest notice either of her, or that Miss Richardsons <u>feeler</u>: he must think me a precious fool – if he supposes, that I can be taken in by such bunglers as he employs. Would you kindly do me Instanter <u>two</u> more sticking Plaster portraits of Grandity! as nothing but herself can be her parallel and two ladies through Lady Laura O'Shindy are dying to see her effigy. I am very sorry to hear such continued bad accounts of poor Massy; pray give him my kind regards when you see him, and Believe me Ever with Innocences best love your grateful and affect

    Rosina Bulwer Lytton

[Newspaper cutting]

Fig 3 THE HON. MRS NORTON has addressed a letter to the Scotsman, in answer to some criticisms upon her late pamphlet addressed to the Queen, which have appeared in that journal. "The power," she writes, "these attacks (and I must expect many such) have over me is limited. The person over whom they have real power for vexation and heavy regret is one who is much sympathised with by those who know him – a gentle, kindly young man, in delicate health, who has the misfortune to be son to the warring couple alternately attacked and defended in the public papers. He is also the one person who has power over me; and the effect of personal and cruel attacks upon me only draw us closer together, and daily alienates him more and more from the fierce, false group who think their own vindication depends on slandering his mother. His letter lies before me, begging me to be comforted always by the conviction that he loves and reveres me 'more than thousands of sons in houses where no question was ever raised'; which does comfort me always, as he most truly thinks it ought. His life began with a blight and sadness, such as these home quarrels must leave, and those who strike at me now only wound him, for I am past the wounding, and superstitiously, if you please – convinced that I am a martyr to a particular cause, and that the cause must prosper."

HALS

1. A town in Lower Saxony, Germany.
2. Fanny Richardson was an acquaintance of Caroline Lamb and her husband. Caroline Lamb alludes to her in her correspondence between 1821 and 1826, mentioning her singing voice.
3. EBL proposed to RBL at Brocket Hall, Hertfordshire. See RBL, 27 August 1826.
4. Lady Caroline Lamb.
5. Robert Bell (1800–67).

6.   *The Home News* for the Australasian and other colonies was a monthly London journal, which circulated among English residents. Bell took up the editorship in his later years.

7.   He never completed his twenty-nine volumes of the *Annotated Edition of the English Poets* (1854–7).

8.   Bell assisted EBL in establishing the London *Monthly Chronicle*, a national journal of politics, literature, science and art (1838–41), and eventually became its editor.

To Rebecca Ryves

Friday November 21ˢᵗ 1856

My dearest Rebecca I am very glad to hear your cousin is so far recovered as to be able to go out; but hope he will not as men generally are be imprudent on the strength of it. Innocence thank Heaven and Channing; is him seps again. I'll blow up "Extremely Much obliged" about your Jacket but doubtless she thought you wished to make it a present to Grandity and so made roomy quarters for a hump in it. Augusta made that extremely disgusting personage Mr Fred Clarke[1] write me a most humble apology for his unpardonable insolence and ingratitude – but I am convinced by the extraordinary! corrections in some of the proofs that he is in the habit of getting drunk; in confirmation of which, he stuck a wet! postage stamp on the packet he sent me last night! but the snail and Tortoise press; having again gone to work, they have actually arrived at the 170ᵗʰ page of the 3ʳᵈ vol. and the book is announced for early in December. I send you Mr Hydes letters and shall be glad of them back by return: the only one of the letters forwarded from Llangollen that I had to send him was that Feeler of Miss Fanny Richardsons[2] from Brunswick,[3] when Sir Liar put all his irons in the fire to find out my place of refuge, when I had escaped from Llangollen. In reply to Mr Hydes letter of to day I told him I could perfectly see through the game the wretches were playing – finding that I was determined to sift this last infamy – that beast the Duke of Argyll[4] was all of a sudden seized with great dissatisfaction at the amiable Mr George Davies – for whose <u>respectability</u>! he was so <u>empressé</u>[5] to stand sponsor for a few months ago; all of which being interpreted – means that Davies – under the pretext of being dismissed – is in reality to be bribed with a sum of money by Sir Liar, and <u>promised</u> a better appointment by his <u>dis</u> grace, for fear he should peach and expose the whole affair; – but I have begged of Mr Hyde <u>coûte q'uil coûte</u>[6] – to circumvent this, and above all, to impress upon Mr Rowland Hill,[7] and Mr South, that <u>such</u> is my <u>firm</u> conviction, touching the duke of Argylls – <u>sudden</u> dissatisfaction at the conduct of the "highly respectable" (<u>his own words</u>) Mr George Davies, and his <u>hurry</u> to dismiss him. – I am like the continually Influenzad Jane Collier,[8] sneezing and freezing, by my Bed room fire side with the additional embellishment of a swelled face, which did not however prevent my receiving Fanny and <u>Garland</u>![9]

with little Jerry – who stayed two hours, thank Heaven – Mrs Edwards <u>cannot</u> favour me with her – anti-delightful society as often as she would like, I have <u>not</u> seen him since poor man: Do you think Massy could get me from Mr Garland <u>all</u> the words of "old Rosin – the Bow"[10] <u>soon</u>? the music I suppose would be out of the question. – With kind regards to him – and Doatskins love to you – Believe me in great Haste, and worry my dearest Rebecca Ever your grateful & affect Rosina Bulwer Lytton

---

HALS

1. Frederick Clarke, RBL's Taunton publisher. See RBL, 18 November 1856.
2. A companion of Caroline Lamb. See RBL, 19 November 1856.
3. A town in Germany. See RBL, 19 November 1856.
4. George Douglas Campbell, eighth Duke of Argyll (1823–1900), was a Liberal politician, who was Postmaster-General in Lord Palmerston's first Cabinet (1855–8).
5. Impressed [*impressionné*] (French).
6. Cost what it will (French).
7. Rowland Hill (1795–1879) introduced a system of uniform penny postage, which was implemented in 1849, putting an end to the MP's frank.
8. A character in Albert Smith's *The Pottleton Legacy: A Story of Town and Country* (1849). See RBL, 11 February 1858.
9. Fanny Boys and her brother-in-law Mr Garland with the dog, christened Jerry Inkerman Catfield by RBL. See RBL, 30 August 1855.
10. A traditional Irish song.

To Rebecca Ryves

Monday November 24th 1856

My dearest Rebecca This is via the Irish Post merely to tell you that I really am too ill to write, being in agony from head to foot with bronchitis swelled face, and violent cough – and a twist! that makes me feel as if Africa and the Nubian Desert[1] [were] tightly packed up in my unhappy throat & Chest – and being too ill to make myself any Barley water – and being able to get nothing here – you may guess how <u>comfortable</u> I am still the "wicked flourish and are in great prosperity" amen – Poor Augusta too is I am sorry to say confined to her bed with the same sort of attack – but luckily she has some one to get her a glass of water. Fanny tells me she is better to day. I would have sent you the continuation of the Agapemone[2] blasphemy yesterday – or rather Saturday but that lazy, forgetful dawdling, bungling free and Easy – pig headed fellow never sent it – and this morning when I wrote to complain of his neglect, he never even vouchsafed the slightest apology Mr Garland said he looked so stupid and maudlin in the middle of the day on Friday that he was sure he was drunk then – <u>pleasant</u> look out for me! with all the rest. Thank massy for promising to get me "old Roisin – the – Bow" and with kind regards to him, and poor Innocences love – Believe me

My dearest Rebecca Ever yr grateful and affect Rosina Bulwer Lytton.

HALS
1.	The Nubian Desert is in the eastern region of the Sahara Desert, north-east Africa.
2.	See RBL, 1 November 1856.

To Rebecca Ryves

November 25th 1856

My dearest Rebecca I am so far better, that my cold has shifted its quarters, from my throat, and face, to all my limbs; but to day I have been able to put on my stays which is a great comfort; though of course I shall not be able to go with Fanny and "dear Garland"! to the Madrigals tomorrow night. Poor Augusta, being a little better, was obliged to go to her Tread-Mill to day. I am sorry you were prevented by so disagreeable a cause from going – to the musical soirée,[1] but think when one has every thing to do for oneself being confined to the Hulks is pleasant easy relaxation, compared to going out. Every thing I hear about that Fred[2] makes me fear I have got into a Hornets nest, for where his unlimited ignorance, and free, and Easy insolence does not wreck one; his – extortionate mode of doing every thing – will; it seems, that he had the modesty to charge Mr Comer – only a guinea more, than any one else in the Town asked for printing a few Programmes, and when Mr Comer told him so, – said coolly "oh then I suppose I must do them for £1"10'0 instead of £2"10, as I had charged you" and when I reflect that my all is risked in such a leaky, rudderless – craft – no wonder I feel low, and wretched and ready to hang myself. I send you a very clever, wittily written pamphlet sent to me the other day by some Publishers of the name of cash[3] (what a delightful! thing if cash and Publisher were always synonymous) "respectfully requesting I would honour them with my confidence and Publish with them" I told them it was too late (alas!) for this book – but I would bear them in mind – how exceedingly cheap their charge for drawing – and engraving is; and I wonder what that fellow will have the conscience to charge for those vulgar, and beastly aesthetic things – you see with his 10 for common cloth binding – he already charges 4 more than the London prices as they gild, and letter, for 10 – be sure you send me this pamphlet back as I should keep it as a check upon him. What a formidable! looking woman that Mrs Sherman;[4] such an awfully strong minded Nose! – After that sullen sulky stuck up Bear Fred, what a comfort it is to have to do with civil, businesslike – London Tradesmen. Last Saturday I saw Mr Dolby[5] of Regent Sts advertisement to send 48 Postage Stamps and one would receive by return of post a 100 Envelopes, and a quarter of a ream of note paper with ones crest on it a quarter of a ream is about 2 of those 2"6d packets pf paper: on Monday morning I get a very civil note from him saying he regretted not having a die of the crest ready cut, which would delay the paper a day or two; and this morning I receive the quarter ream, and 100 Envelopes post free, of which this sheet is a specimen– cheap enough goodness knows. If you have no news; I have not even the ghost of news so with kind regards to "a fellow" – and de doodest of all fellows best love to you Believe me My dearest Rebecca – Ever Gratefully, and affectly yrs Rosina Bulwer Lytton

HALS
1. Evening (French).
2. Frederick Clarke, the Taunton printer.
3. W. & F. G. Cash, 5 Bishopgate Street, London, was a publishing house, which produced books on worthy impecunious causes such as impoverished juvenile delinquents and a penny emigrant's guide.
4. London tradeswoman.
5. This is probably the radical cheap publisher and bookseller Thomas Dolby (1782–1856).

To Rebecca Ryves

Sunday November 30th 1856

Many thanks My dearest Rebecca for the <u>last</u> which as you know, is always acceptable. Only think of my forgetting to answer your query about Mrs Fred![1] – but I have been so hampered, harassed, and overworked this week that I seem rather to have shot through it, than got through it. – Last Tuesday, I said at the end of my growlery to that Lusus Naturar[2] – partly snail partly Tortoise but chiefly sloth Fred, that I hoped Mrs Clarke's cold was better? whereupon he writes to thank me for my kind inquiries; and that he was happy to say that both Mrs Clarke and the Baby! (with a big B) were doing exceedingly well; which was the first intimation I had that Mrs Fred had at length! produced her Epitome of natural History – but <u>when</u>? or <u>what</u>? deponent sayeth not, and last night Fred favoured me with the astounding intelligence! (astounding to <u>my</u> old slow coach experience in these matters) that she intended reappearing down stairs to day! would that he, would take a leaf out of her book, for the despatch of business – but although there are now only 60 pages to print, this disgusting dawdle informs me that the work, wont be completed till the 10th of December! So that in reality, it will not be actually published till tomorrow (Monday) Fortnight the 14th – I am vezy unhappy about my poor Innocences cough; which is vezy great big bad, again – <u>exsqueeze</u> but it is hims autograph – de black letter Edition of de Doatskin Archives. Augusta very foolishly came down in a chair here yesterday Evening

– she begged her love to you – As Sunday "shines no day of rest to me"[3] I have a hundred letters to write; so with de King of de darlings love, believe me in Post haste my dearest Rebecca – Ever your grateful and affect R Bulwer Lytton

The Papers announce the death of the Crocodile[4] – but I have not heard the report confirmed by hearing of Sir Liars death. –

I would order a copy of my Book to be sent to Mrs King;[5] but that I always dread doing anything Civil by English people

---

HALS
1. Mrs Frederick Clarke.
2. Freak of nature [*lusus naturae*] (Latin).
3. Alexander Pope, *Epistle to Dr. Arbuthnot, Prologue to the Satires*, l. 12.
4. It was reported in *The Times* on 26 November 1856 that George Grenvill Fortescue died while cruising in the yacht of his cousins Lord and Lady Drogheda. On the same day, there was also an announcement of the death of Mr Lockhart, the MP for Lanark.
5. Queen Victoria.

To Rebecca Ryves

Tuesday December 2d 1856

My dearest Rebecca you frightened me to death with your black Edged Envelope, and seal, but as you say nothing I suppose it means nothing. I have just paid Mrs Foreacre the 14"6d you sent, who of course is "extremely much obliged to you", I wrote a note to the Post master asking him to pay it to her for me; but had it back twice, and to write two more notes, – owing to your having mulcted me of half my name, and called me Lady Lytton, – whereas everywhere out of Taunton I go by – and therefore always sign the name of Bulwer Lytton. However she has got the money, which was very acceptable as poor wretched woman with a terrible swelled face and sore throat, she is to be deported to Gloucester tomorrow on that Trial for Bigamy – as the principal witness in it. I could not send you the Agapemone paper on Saturday as that lazy – apathetic – careless – dawdling brute Fred[1] never sent it, and now I have ordered him not to do so. – I really think I shall go mad before I get out of his clutches last night, I had only half of one slip by way of proof!! – the excuse being that 3 of his men were drunk, and the other ill. – Having asked to see the tail piece of the 2d vol – I see the pig headed beast has insisted upon making me answerable for a most terrible provincial vulgarism, which in my whole life, I never was guilty of, either in speaking, or writing, to wit, "awhile ago!! for while ago; the latter, (as I have told him) being alone English. – I have again to be extremely much obliged to you as last night for the first time I inducted myself into one of the night-caps, you were good enough to give me; and thought at first like the Engineers who laid down the tubes of the sub-marine telegraph I was sadly perplexed by the vast depth, and <u>breadth</u> before me, having once mastered (or I suppose I should say mistressed) them – I found the coiffure exceedingly comfortable; and moreover rendering me such a facsimile of Mrs Gamp![2] (minus the umbrella) that <u>should</u> any House breakers come, I'm sure I shall frighten them into a precipitate retreat, and compulsory honesty: but I farther owe it to the cap to say, that I had a better night and pleasanter dreams, than I have had for a long time; and Zadkiel[3] says – "The dreamer will soon send money to relatives or friends." which I am <u>delighted</u> to hear as I <u>must</u> have it before I can send it! –

I am sorry for your loneliness; – but hope the "fellow" will soon be back. Augusta who has just left me; begged her love to you – and Mr Innocence who has not been out these 10 days! scampered off with her in great delight, I do hope it wont make hims cough worse; – In ultra haste and Extra worry! Believe me Ever your Grateful, and affect Rosina Bulwer Lytton

HALS
1.   Frederick R. Clarke, publisher at the Caxton Head, Taunton.
2.   A fictional character in *Martin Chuzzlewit*, a novel by Charles Dickens. See RBL, 11 March 1853.
3.   Zadkiel is the archangel of benevolence as well as of mercy, freedom and forgiveness.

To Rebecca Ryves

Saturday December 6th 1856 6p:m. -

My dearest Rebecca I have <u>this moment</u> recieved a note from Massy saying he should pass through Taunton – to day by the 4-50 express Train and would leave a basket of Champagne! at the station for me, I really am <u>so</u> hurt, and angry – at this, - that it goes against my grain to <u>thank</u> him – for what all things considered annoys me so much; pray tell him with my <u>deepest growl</u>, that when he <u>has</u> the Celler – (which I sincerely hope he may one of these days) I will take, and be "extremely much obliged" for as many cases, as he likes to give me – but <u>till then</u> – I think it a very <u>hard case</u> that he should do such things, and that I should be the cause of them, moreover <u>Paupers</u> drinking Champagne is sure to remind one of Dr Johnsons regret that a "girl wanting a Flannel petticoat, should get a present of a pair of diamond Ear-rings" – as I have only this <u>moment</u> got Massy's note I suppose he must have left this 2 hours ago – I have sent down to the station; - for his most unwarrantable present – and if I am choked in drinking it, it will only serve him, and me right – I'll write again to morrow, so with kind regards (and many scoldings) to him and Maboots's love to you whom I am thankful to say is better. – Believe me in great Haste, and ditto pain – Ever your grateful & affect

Rosina Bulwer Lytton.

———————

HALS

To Rebecca Ryves

Sunday December 7th 1856

My dearest Rebecca If I was grieved, and hurt, when I got Massy's note announcing the Champagne – (which was quite <u>bad</u> <u>enough</u> of him and you to do) what do you suppose – was the amount of my <u>real and unaffected</u> distress! – on opening the box to find added to this Original Sin – a Térine de Foie gras! and a case of real Grauves![1] – now really this is <u>too bad</u> because – considering your position and my own you cannot suppose that I can take my pleasure in such luxuries ground out of you and Massy, - Unfortunately too the Boys's were here when they arrived – otherwise I should have kept them till Xmas, in the hope of your, and Massy being here to share them; which is the only thing – that could have lessened the Enormity; – I <u>solemnly</u> <u>swear</u> that if ever he, or you do such a thing again (unless you grow rich) I will send <u>them</u> <u>back</u>; but if you would but get rich – I should be safe – for <u>rich</u> people never do such things. I was grieved to hear the Boots's Bulletin that Massy's cold was very bad, - and what a fearful! night to travel in, this great house rocked again – and I was up the whole night, with the most excruciating <u>cramp</u> in my stomach which not even brandy and Cayenne pepper could master – <u>nothing</u> of my old complaint, which thanks to your prescription of the clove tea, which I take regularly every morning I have not had one single return of – and feel in heaven as far as bodily ills go – but of course – have ceaseless worries of every kind to fill up this vacuum of physical ill for it <u>would</u> crush a Giant, to have every thing against one, and nothing for one – and single handed it is impossible to struggle out of such a Slough of Despond, or make head against such fearful, and brutal Odds – and I have a heavy presentiment, that my all which is in the hands of that disgusting dawdle, drone, dolt, and bear "Fred" will be wrecked through hid pig-headed ignorance, indolence, obstinacy and imbecility; - he told Augusta yesterday morning that he had sent off the 1st and 2d vols of my book to London – which must have been a lie, as last night at 11 0'clock! the lazy dawdling bungler writes to me to know if <u>I</u> could tell him <u>where</u> the Portraits and views were to come in?!!! I could not help writing him back word – that if ever he got hold of another victim, (though he must not suppose that anyone else would Ever behave so foolishly liberally to him as I had done to be tormented at every point) yet it would be well for him to know

that one of the most simple and ordinary routine duties of a printer, composi-
tor, or Publisher, was in every work where Plates occurred, to make a note of
their whereabout previous to distributing or [portioning] off the M:S: and that
a little common attention to business accompanied by ordinary civility did not
inculpate any great zeal, or <u>exertion</u> – all this coupled – with the superhuman
blunders, and delays – that have already occurred, you will own – is a pleasant,
and cheering! look out for me. I see by the papers that the Bristol Athenaeum[2]
is to have a grand soirée soon, at which all the Literary Ruffianocracy including
Sir Liar are to be invited – <u>pleasant</u> to know the brute so near one! I also see
that Judas Iscariot Disraeli is in Paris, and is to have an audience of the Emperor
which coupled with my Lord Derby's civilities to Monsieur de Persigny[3] – and
the latters visit to Knowlsey[4] means I suppose that the Darbyites are heating all
their irons in order to forge some fresh Humbug. To go from one extreme to
another me is vezy happy to see that Innocence is much better and says <u>him</u> is
great big much obliged to Massy for the Foie gras, and never will spoil hims toat
again – him desires hims love to you. – I will let you know when Massy's banquet
comes off – meanwhile – reiterate my scoldings to him – and to <u>yourself</u> – and
with all good wishes to both; Believe me dearest Rebecca Ever your Grateful
affect, but <u>much</u> <u>grieved</u>

   Rosina Bulwer Lytton – alas!

HALS
1. Grauves is a village south of Epernay in France producing white and black grapes for the
  manufacture of champagne in vineyards owned by Moet & Chandon and Pol Roger.
2. The Bristol Athenaeum was founded in 1845.
3. Jean Gilbert Victor Fialin, the Duke of Persigny (1808–72), was a French senator, privy
  counsellor and minister, who was highly respected even though he was often in disgrace
  with the emperor.
4. Knowsley, a village near Liverpool.

To Rebecca Ryves

Thursday December 11th 1856

"When the hurly burly's <u>not</u> done"[1]
It is all nonsense my Dearest Rebecca your talking of the winds at Torquay! –
which by your account, <u>only</u> blow the womens petticoats over their heads – but
<u>here</u> they are quite capable of blowing <u>down</u> the "Leathers" off of Board! were he
not luckily confined to his room with lumbago – which prevents him <u>leathering</u>
away after the Hounds.- I am glad Massy is no worse for his journey – but do
hope – he will not (not from any fear of <u>exposure</u>!) be so imprudent, as to brave
the winds – and waves for "Hero's" or for any body's "sake", I am very glad your
cousin is so much recovered – <u>of course</u> <u>I</u> think him an <u>exceedingly</u> clever, sen-

sible young man – from his critique, on the Literary Morcana, and the Political Cagliostro.[2] To give you an idea how that stolid stagnant brute Fred, (whom I now call Dred) has worried and tortured me to the last, without a single apology, or expression of regret – after mulcting me the two last nights – of only <u>half</u> the usual quantity of snail work he stops short on Tuesday night within a <u>half a page</u>!! of the conclusion – and for this half page, – he keeps me waiting till 11 o'clock last night – however at <u>last</u>! by the 1 o'clock express this morning a.m. the whole Edition was at length! Forwarded to Whittaker[3] – In a letter I had from poor dear Dr Price to day, he says "Miss Heathcote who is staying here, had a letter from her brother Sir Charles Heathcote who is at Exeter – and says there is already a great demand there at all the libraries for your new book" – If it was not <u>too</u> selfish, I should <u>insist</u> upon you and Massy coming over here for the Xmas, but I know you will have pleasant parties, and good dinners, where you are; neither of which could I give you. – I had a letter from poor Williams[4] this morning – who has had a dreadful Rheumatic fever of several weeks duration – and for three weeks was quite blind! but adds she is quite well enough to come to me if I would but let her, but alas! thanks to that dawdling wretch! my purse is far from well enough <u>to</u> let her. – She also tells me with great grief and consternation as well she may – for he attended her indefatigably and gave her medicines gratis – that poor Dr Webb died nearby suddenly on Monday after only two days illness! he was only nine, and twenty – and his poor young wife is nearly frantic as Williams says – he was an excellent husband, and father, and so he was snatched away Mr Fitz Doodboots desires hims respectful <u>tompliments</u>, since him has taken de name and quartered de armorial <u>Paws</u> of Fitz Doodboots Him tant condescend to send hims love to any one. – As for <u>Bounces</u> one hears nothing else here – but alas! The General has very sensibly cut the connexion – for he is not to be had With kind regards to Massy and all good wishes – Believe me my dearest Rebecca Ever your Grateful & affect Rosina Bulwer Lytton.

HALS
1. Parody of 'When the hurly-burly's done', Shakespeare, *Macbeth*, I.i.3.
2. Morgana is Italian for Morgan Le Fay, the half-sister of King Arthur, who in some versions of British myth is represented as his enemy, often plotting his downfall. Giuseppe Balsamo, who became Alessandro, Count of Cagliostro (1743–95), was an occultist who was involved in the Affair of the Necklace, a scandal surrounding Marie Antoinette in 1785. He is said to have cheated an alchemist and was believed by many to be a charlatan.
3. Whittaker & Co. of Pater Noster Row are the London publishers of *The World and his Wife* (1858) and *Very Successful!* (1856).
4. RBL's lady's maid.

To Rebecca Ryves

Sunday December 14th 1856

Many thanks My dearest Rebecca for "Bentley"[1] – like all pretended criticisms on Sir Liar, it merely amounts to an additional Puff, but this is easily accounted for – like all those who have sold themselves to the Devil for a certain lease of unfailing success – every one while the bond <u>holds</u> are afraid of such persons – but no sooner is the breath out of them than the truth flourishes and their reputations stink, worse than their remains; – now you need not laugh at this Devil sealing hypothesis, for it has been done, and <u>is done</u> every day, – and that, without witches, wizards – incantations or even delving deep – into the Archidoxis, or Paramirum of Paracelcus[2] or dabbling with the rest of the Cabbalists,[3] but simply by totally setting God and his laws aside and devoting soul and body indefatigably to this world which world so far from being an ungrateful one as it is so called, <u>always</u> takes care of its <u>own</u>, and pays back its staunch votaries, in their and its coin – to wit, successful villainy. I think Massy's paper better than mine, then he has <u>two</u> crests, and even de effigy of a pup dog, is worth a guinea any day, – but still I hope he wrote to remonstrate about the charge? Of course, as <u>usual</u> one always hears every thing the day <u>after the Fair</u>, – Bragg,[4] who is most indignant at that Saracen's Head[5] of a Fred's treatment of me and says in the Trade, it amounts to what would be called a breach of faith and positive swindle – adds that <u>he</u> would have been <u>delighted</u> to have printed my book – would have brought it out, through Whittaker or Longman[6] which ever I preferred would at the <u>longest</u> have <u>not</u> been more than a month printing it, and would not have asked a <u>shilling</u> in advance; and does hope I will let him have the next. Whittaker Telegraphed the safe arrival of the work on Friday so I suppose it was subscribed by "The Row" yesterday – and will actually be <u>out</u> to morrow and right glad will its poor mother be to "know its out" – after the hard labour and <u>shocking time</u>! Sir Liars had with it. When ever you are good enough to do the [Tatters?] – you must take <u>great</u> care not to give [Boh?] an <u>idiotic</u> – but merely a maudlin drinker look – neither must the <u>features</u> be ugly – as he comes out strong in the book after – as a jewel rescued from a dunghill. <u>The Portugueses Los Empecinadas</u>[7] I'm in great hopes – finding there can be nothing got out of me; ... has deserted me – as I have seen – or heard nothing of her – and of course as usual she never sent the book of Emile Souvenestres that she promised me. As it is Sunday Mr Tibz Doodboots says – "him will condescend to send you half a speckle of love – and half a bushel of <u>hair</u> for Massys <u>best</u> loaf. With kind regards to him and best wishes to both, Believe me my dearest Rebecca Ever your grateful and affect Rosina Bulwer Lytton.

I return Bently with this. Braggs communication was to Augusta, not to me

HALS

1. *Bentley's Miscellany* was a literary magazine (1836–68), started by Richard Bentley, whose first editor was EBL's friend Charles Dickens.

2.   Paracelsus (1493–1541) was an alchemist, astrologer and physician. In his *Archidoxes of Medicine* (1524), he explains how astrological talismans can be used for curing disease and in *Paramirum* (*c*. 1525), he discusses the importance of alchemy.

3.   A branch of Jewish mysticism.

4.   William Bragg. See RBL to Rebecca Ryves, first letter of 13 October 1857.

5.   A mock reference to the Caxton's Head printing press in Taunton. Charles Dickens mentions a Saracen's Head Inn in his novel *Pickwick Papers*.

6.   Thomas Longman was a leading London publisher.

7.   Empecinado was the nickname of Don Juan Martin Diaz (1775–1823), a Spanish patriot and guerrilla, who distinguished himself during the Peninsular War.

To Rebecca Ryves

Wednesday December 17th 1856

My dearest Rebecca I hope ere you receive this you will have got "Very Successful"[1] which was despatched to you 2 hours ago. To give you some idea of how that vile Skeet[2] must have cheated me <u>wholesale</u> Mudie[3] <u>alone</u> – (and in London there are six libraries of Mudies calibre) has taken 100 copies of "Very Successful" – Skeet telling me he never took more than <u>10</u>! but like a canny Scot he wanted to get these hundred copies £3 less than the Trade price, and therefore would not subscribe them from Whittaker[4] but writes to Clarke for them – whereat Whittaker appeals to me – as to whether <u>he</u> is not to be <u>sole</u> London agent for the work? – I say <u>yes</u> – and I suppose the reason the advertisements in "The Times"[5] have not yet appeared – is that they are fighting it out between them – all of which is a marvellous good sign for the <u>sale</u> of the Book and how <u>less</u> than 900 copies can supply the London Trade <u>alone</u> I am at a loss to understand – still <u>I</u> shiver, and tremble on the brink of the fearful precipice I am on quaking least my usual good luck should prevail and that Whittaker alone will reap the golden Harvest as I cannot but suspect that his great anxiety that <u>he</u> should be the <u>sole</u> <u>source</u> from whence the work issues, is that <u>I</u> may not know the amount of <u>each</u> <u>separate</u> subscription – which can ...

... you seem to forget that nothing at all article in Beatty is 3 years back

---

HALS

Incomplete letter.

1.   RBL's novel.

2.   Charles Skeet, RBL's previous publisher.

3.   The lending library of Charles Edward Mudie (1818–90). By 1852, his library was situated at New Oxford Street, London.

4.   The publishers of *Very Successful!*

5.   By 27 January 1858, Whittakers will have placed an advertisement in *The Times* refusing to publish RBL's novel.

To Rebecca Ryves

Wednesday December 18th 1856

My dearest Rebecca I am very anxious to hear how Massys cold is; and do hope he will keep quiet & not go out while it lasts. I should have written you a line yesterday to tell you how his, and your munificent! Festa[1] went off; but that I was so ill from such a Balshazzar-like[2] feast; after such long starvation, that I could not hold up my head – and so like old Pyke[3] vowed "I'd never do so <u>no</u> more"! – all was excellent and the Pâté, and Guava Jelly super-excellent; and we drank your and Massy's health only too often for we injured our own. It would have done you good to see poor honest Fanny Boys <u>set in</u> for the work, for you know what an <u>Arnest</u> woman she is in the Eating way Augusta being more in Grandity's way – not caring <u>verbally</u> for Champagne, but still in <u>deeds</u>, heroically doing far more than could be expected. I am sure you will pity me, when I tell you, that the two last nights that Brute Fred, has only sent me <u>2</u> strips of proof – and last night when the book at the end of 14 long weeks dawdling ought to have been finished he stops short of one miserable half page!! which is to keep it dawdling out, <u>another</u> day and night! instead of its being in London to day – and last night the fellow coolly wrote to me to know if I could tell him what the Heading of the 9th Chapter of 3d vol was? as he had mislaid it!! so that I fully expect that <u>all</u> the headings will be wrong – or some other awful mess. Miss Gower has just been here, inquired very kindly after you, and spoke with great admiration of your figure, for there is no English Envy, or detraction about her …

HALS
Incomplete letter.
1. Feast (Latin).
2. King Belshazzar provided a feast for a thousand of his lords in which he profaned the sacred vessels of the enslaved Jews and, as prophesied by the writing on the wall, was slain (Daniel 7:1–3).
3. Mrs T. Pyke, the mother of Marion Lowndes.

To Rebecca Ryves

Xmas Day 1856

My dearest Rebecca I have been and am fearfully ill – but cannot let this day pass without scrawling one line, to wish you and Massy – very sincerely very happy, and happier returns of the day. I am truly grieved to hear he is again so ill but glad – he is going to try the Arnica[1] – if you remember I begged him to do so at York Cottage. – Besides my bodily ills mine I think is a spirit fever of utter despair – as I see these beastly Whittakers[2] are <u>completely</u> strangling my book at its birth only <u>one</u> advertisement (and such a thing as it was!) in The Times in a fortnight! it must be bad indeed when that fellow Skeet wrote to me saying that notwithstanding my bad opinion of him <u>he</u> was quite ready even now to take it in hand – as it "was cruel to see such a book! and one so beautifully brought out so mismanaged" and with only that noodle of a stagnant pool Fred here what I am to do God only knows! For those beastly Whittakers have only interfered with the sale by preventing the large orders of Mudie and the other libraries being executed by that ass Clarke. I send you what I am really pleased at, and proud of a letter I had this morning from Judge Haliburton[3] – "Sam Slick"[4] I told him how glad I should be to see him – ah! if I could get a clever <u>honest</u> man like that, – to give me a helping hand, – I might yet be saved Let me have the letter back by return of post. I don't know whether Mrs King got the books, as she never acknowledged them. I think as I have told him Judge Haliburts paraphrase of Lord Palmerstons[5] motto at the Manchester Athenaeum[6] delicious! With de King of de darlings regards and best wishes to Massy Believe me ever your grateful affect Rosina Bulwer Lytton

---

HALS
1. See RBL, 6 April 1853.
2. RBL's publisher. See RBL, 11 December 1856.
3. Thomas Chandler Haliburton (Judge Haliburton) of Nova Scotia. See RBL, 6 July 1853.
4. Sam Slick is the pen-name of Haliburton, see above n. 2.
5. Henry John Temple, Viscount Palmerston (1784–1865), was Prime Minister (1855–8).
6. The Manchester Athenaeum was founded on 28 October 1835 as an institution dedicated to bringing culture and education to the cotton town.

To Rebecca Ryves

Saturday December 27th 1856

I am indeed sorry my dear Rebecca to hear such bad accounts of poor Massy and your cousin, they <u>must</u> (if men can be so?) be patient and <u>careful</u>, and however indoor boredom may abound, not brave these keen winds, which are enough to bechamele[1] the toughest lungs – I was in hopes you would have had a Merrier Xmas than all this; but "man proposes" (and in truth now a days not even <u>that</u> if they can possibly avoid it,) "and God disposes"[2] you ask me what has been the matter with me? Physically I believe it is called Bronchitis but my real and I hope at length mortal malady is a <u>Desespoir</u> <u>rentrée</u>[3] for I find myself in the lowest depths of an abyss, without a single hope – or hand stretched out to help me but it must be Gods will or else it could not be; – so <u>Amen</u>. I have sat up to day for the first time in seven days – and poor good Mr Hyde has been sitting with me all the morning he says that he is so enraged, and disgusted that he could dash his head against the wall, as it is quite Evident that, that assified Prig the duke of Argyll[4] <u>fearing</u> to make a political Enemy of Sir Liar, has been squashing, – mystifying – retarding and <u>impossibling</u> every search into the Llangollen infamy with all my heart, as I am determined to expose the whole thing in a Pamphlet which will do the whole gang more harm than Sir Liars <u>villainy</u> will do them good – <u>all this</u> I told Mr Hyde 4 months ago but I am Cassandra[5] the 2d the very truth of my predictions prevents them being believed. Poor Mr Hyde did all he could to press me to go and stay with them at [ill] for 2 months (fancy my going any where for 2 months! or even for 2 days!) and Even said that he would carry me in my old oak chest on his back! but I told him that I had now lived in England too long, not to know how to interpret an <u>apparent</u> kindness; – and therefore saw through his base design which was from the extacies he was in with it, evidently to possess himself of my old chest and in order to prevent an action – lying – make me privy to the theft. The only Xmas festivities I have heard of – is a poor young Farmer at Wivelscombe[6] on Xmas Eve who had his head cut <u>off</u>! And was sent home that is his headless trunk! in his cart; to his poor parents! and all this for £5! Which shows that the <u>distinguished murderer</u>! (for we are fast coming to this sort of distinction!) was not mercenary his name is Nation – but he will soon be ennobled(!) and have a d before his name; – <u>pro tem</u>,[7] he is lodged in the Taunton jail so poor Mr Oakley[8] will have to get the Gallows ready at last. Mr Hyde said they are so infested with Ticket of Leave[9] Heroes at Highgate,[10] that his daughter (the <u>strong-minded</u> woman!) practices shooting with a revolver daily – and sleeps with two loaded by her Bed Side.

Anne[11] gives me great hopes! for you have no idea how suddenly my room became infested with mice, – and this she says is "a <u>sure</u> sign of long <u>illness</u> <u>hend</u>ing in death." you will I suppose laugh at me when I tell you that the first that was caught in the trap – looked so frightened, so cold – and so innocent with hims bright round black Eyes – and hims poor little paws squeezed up under him that like a fool as me is, me let him go; – The next gentleman I presume had been in the Crimea as he had only three legs – and this morning there was a poor little baby thing no bigger than a large moth stark dead, from the cold, with its poor little glazed Eyes – wide open; – truly if one had no miseries of one's own, it would be quite a sufficient one, to see how the Economy of this world seems to consist, in all things – torturing – hunting and destroying each other – but I especially pity these poor little mice, their fate is <u>so</u> like my own – their hard and indefatigable struggles to obtain a precarious, and miserable Existence, – only rewarded by having Traps baited, and springes laid for them in all directions! <u>So</u>! and <u>so</u>! the world goes round. – Mrs Clarke who has not troubled herself to know whether I lived, or died, or wanted a glass of water – last night sent me up a deliciously sweet, and large bouquet of violets!! as I have not seen such a thing at Xmas since I was in Naples – I send you some and with Doatskins love, and my kind regards to poor Massy – hoping soon to hear better accounts of him and your cousin Believe me my dearest Rebecca Ever your grateful and affect Rosina Bulwer Lytton

There has been no time for Reviews yet

————————

HALS

The last line of the letter is written at the top of the sheet.

1. A French sauce.
2. Thomas à Kempis, *The Imitation of Christ* (1420).
3. Despair returned [*rentré*] (French).
4. George Douglas Campbell, eighth Duke of Argyll (1823–1900). He was considered an excellent debater and was Postmaster-General in 1855–8.
5. See RBL, 4 March 1856.
6. A market town in Somerset, west of Taunton.
7. For the time being [*pro tempore*] (Latin).
8. William Oakley (1818–80) was the prison governor.
9. Convicts, who have been given a document or pass for having completed the second stage of their sentences. They have been granted a conditional freedom in which to earn their living as independent members of the community.
10. A north London suburb on the north-eastern corner of Hampstead Heath.
11. Servant at the Giles Castle Hotel.

To Rebecca Ryves

Tuesday December The 30th 1856

My dearest Rebecca I fear by my not hearing from you that Massy may be still ill – pray write me one line – I hope the Violets I sent you in my last, arrived fresh? – <u>Fancy</u>! the çi-devant[1] Mrs Hayes[2] having the impertinence to write to me! – I send you the letter to amuse you – even were I inclined to answer her; I could not write to an anonymous person – if she is really divorced – (which she is <u>not</u>, any more than I am) she ought to call herself Miss Boyd – unless she has to take any other <u>nom de pavé</u>.[3] – I am ill and worried to death – with that beastly stagnant Pool Fred – one might as well attempt to make an impression on the ice of the North Pole – as try to move him out of his stolid dogged routine. I am sorry to tell you that poor Dunham Massy[4] does <u>not</u> write a nice <u>hand</u> – that is a gentleman like one, for his letter frightened me to death thinking it was a bill! – his crest I see is a <u>Bulls</u> head through a Ducal[5] coronet – I suppose owing to his having made the bull of being a natural son (if he is one?) poor fellow as he says – the only professional recompense he has received for services in the <u>English</u> army, has been a <u>French Croix de la Legion d'Honneur</u>[6] I suppose that you saw in "The Times" of yesterday that Louisa Countess of Seafield[7] – wife of Major Godfrey

Massy[8] – had had a son on Xmas Eve?- <u>if</u> wigs <u>have</u> ghosts? I should think the shade of Lord Seafields must have stood on End! at this additional <u>hair</u>! (Heir) Pray let me hear from you soon? and with kind regards and best wishes to Massy and de doodest and doatskinnest of dogs love (who keeps two mutton-bone pistols always beside him, him is so afraid of does Ticket of leave dogs) Believe me Ever my dearest Rebecca your grateful & obliged Rosina Bulwer Lytton

---

HALS
1.   Formerly (French).
2.   Presumably, Mrs Stuart Hayes.
3.   Street-name (French).
4.   The usual spelling is Dunham Massey.
5.   A ducal coronet may be worn by a duke or a duchess or head of the family. It consists of a set of three strawberry leaves at the four points (front, back and both sides).
6.   French Cross of the Legion of Honour (French).
7.   Louisa Emma's first husband had been the sixth Earl of Seafield. See RBL, 7 February 1856.
8.   The son of Godfrey Massy appears not to have survived.

To Rebecca Ryves

Sunday January 11th 1857

My dearest Rebecca – I am indeed grieved – to hear such indifferent accounts of poor Massy – and can well understand your anxiety about him – though really think – Hercules himself would if he had the wealth of Cresus[1] – beside feel low, and out of sorts this wretched weather. – As for me – I cannot say that I am <u>now</u> writhing – as I feel positively stunned, and stupefied with the <u>weight</u> of my misery – you know perfectly well 3 weeks ago seeing perfectly the game Messieurs Judas – and Do nothing were playing with my book I told that stolid ass Clarke to take it out of their hands – but in vain – well of course the abuse came strong – and <u>thick</u> as I <u>knew it would</u> from the gang – for in this lip-moral country you had better talk Blasphemy than breathe a compromising truth of a Husband! – but as they all praised the book – I told that ass Clarke[2] to write to those infamous Whittakers[3] to adopt Colburns[4] old plan of extracting puffs from this very abuse – to publish with the advertizements – whereupon these wretches yesterday write back word that as the work has been so abused by the press (which is not true for it's only the <u>Author</u>) they must decline continuing to publish it! – now I fully expected that they <u>would</u> object to publish that "notice" – and <u>that</u> would have been all honest and fair – but to get me into the trap – and keep me in it for 5 weeks – till they got as much <u>injury</u> done to the book was perfectly <u>villainous</u> – you <u>mistake</u> – these vile Whittakers had <u>little</u> or no interest in the book – and <u>that</u> is the reason they of course were glad to swell their profits by selling me to Sir Liar – that brute Clarke it is who has a very great interest in it, but from first to last has been too great a fool to avail himself of it. My last poor Ghost of a chance now is this – I had a letter from Mudie[5] this morning – with this printed Circular – on which he has placed my Book at the head of the list – he says as my agents these Whittakers were bound to obey my orders which they have <u>never</u> done he then says – "would it not be better to cancel the notice – so as to give the <u>Book</u> a fair chance – for it is a pity such a book should not have one" I am sorry to tell you Mr Clarke sent the sheets – <u>without</u> the plates – and several sheets missing to complete the set – which is a type of the way that lazy stolid bungling brute – [h]as wrecked the thing by dawdles and delays from first to last! I wrote – to Mudie to day asking him – if <u>he</u> would undertake the London agency of the book? or kindly find me a Publisher that would and I told him also that I consented to withdraw the heterodox notice! provided he would then insure my Book a fair field – to urge this I threw myself on his compassion – and did not conceal from him that my all depended on the sale of that poor book, as to add to my millstone – I had had to borrow £100 to give that Noodle Clarke – you may guess the fearful state I shall be in till Tuesday's post brings me his answer – though I think the poor book is so <u>thoroughly</u> wrecked – by this, that it has no chance though Mudie seems to think otherwise – and as if all this were not enough I told Mr Hodgson on no account to pay that shark Campbell his extortion of £6"2"! if my poor glass were not in as good order as when I left it whereas in his usual way of driving <u>me</u> to the wall – he goes and pays it! – and then writes me word I shall find the glass much broken! and with the expense of all these battered things for which I have not even standing room only! My Parish <u>allowance</u> is reduced to £39!! this quarter out of which I have sent poor Dr Price his £35 – I that had been in a fools Paradise hoping that at <u>least</u> your money, and Augusta's[6] £100 would have been paid by this time! instead of which there is Mrs Clarke![7] and all my Xmas bills – to meet with this £4!!! oh! decidedly if <u>Mudie</u> does <u>not</u> help me – Sir Liar will have <u>prophetically</u> spoken the truth and I <u>shall</u> go mad – for more I <u>cannot</u> bear, – and you would pity me if you knew how really ill I am in body – I think my friend Chalon really <u>is</u> mad – for he sends me the other morning by <u>post</u> a wooden bowl! in which was a fragrant Effigy of Louis Napoleon[8] off of a Twelfth cake covered over like the babes in the wood – with all those fiddle faddle of leaves and withered flowers that my friend Chalon is so fond of – but as I wrote him word un Napoléon c'est un Providence quand on n'a pas le sou![9] – I had a letter from Mrs King on Thursday telling me she had been from home. Poor little Star of de Desert sends you hims best love – I am sorry to send you such a Jeremiad – but as you may suppose I feel as if an Elephant had trodden, on my heart and crushed it – with kind regards to

Massy – and these Empty things! best wishes to you Both – believe me Ever my dearest Rebecca your Grateful and affect

Rosina Bulwer Lytton.

HALS
1. Croesus is a synonym for a wealthy man. See RBL, 1 April 1853.
2. Probably Frederick Clarke, the Taunton publisher who brought out *Very Successful!* with Whittakers (see below, n. 3)
3. Whittakers are the London publishers who published two of RBL's novels, including *Very Successful!* See RBL, 11 December 1856.
4. Henry Colburn, the publisher.
5. Charles Edward Mudie, dated 17 December 1856.
6. Augusta Boys.
7. Charlotte Clarke, RBL's landlady at Giles Castle Hotel, Taunton.
8. Louis Napoleon was Emperor of France. See RBL, 28 May 1853.
9. 'A Napoleon is a god-send when one does not have a sou' (French). The Napoleon is the colloquial term for a former French gold coin.

To Rebecca Ryves

Tuesday – January 13th 1857

My dearest Rebecca I am too ill – too crushed to write – my last hope has failed me! Mudie cannot undertake the Agency of my Book not being – a Publisher but will be glad to take another 100 copies (which is odd! for a book which that infamous clique have given out is not to be published! and indeed truths of them scarcely are) – and then Mudie coolly recommends my returning to Skeet! whom he says he's sure will deal fairly by me – no doubt of it particularly now after the justly merited compliments I have paid him – but as this would be the worst sort of Financial suicide I have written to Dr Price to implore him to get up a Public subscription for me at Brighton stating all the circumstances that have necessitated it; there is poor Miss Dickenson pressing and poor Augusta's £100 given to that brute Clarke Mrs Clarkes 6 months bill! and because this is not enough Mr Hodgson sends down those things which besides the £25 bor-rowed from Mr Wheeler alone – the carriage amounts to £7"16"0! and I have not even standing room for them! – a man would have recourse to pistols or prussic acid I have recourse – or can have recourse to but one thing submitting to God's will –it is not even that blessed anchorage of trusting in Him – for it is Evident He will not help me that is let me help myself. The blood is now spout-ing out like a fountain Every cough I give- which makes me hope death will have mercy on me – but it is not pleasant to leave the world as a swindler, when one is not such from intention. I send you "The News of the World[1] – which poor kind Dr Price sent me this mng I am pleased at the Review of "Very Successful" in it

<u>not</u> from its praise but from its <u>honesty</u>. – Let me have it back. – The only New Years gift I have to send you is Jessets reciept – he dunned so for it that I paid it – I wish I could die – but I cannot even do <u>that</u>! I hope poor Massy is better but this black bitter weather is against every one – give him my kind regards and best wishes – and with poor itty Star of the Deserts best love – Believe me Ever My dearest Rebecca your grateful & affect

    R B Lytton.

HALS

1. The *News of the World* was a weekly newspaper with a large circulation of just under 10,000.

To Rebecca Ryves

Wednesday January 14th 1857

My dearest Rebecca I am very glad to hear poor Massy is better. I am too ill to write being hopeless – helpless ruined! strong iron villainy and clenching deeds <u>against</u> me – and nothing but Empty words and placid patience for me! how little does <u>any</u> one understand the <u>utter</u> desolation and ruin of my position! poor kind old Dr Price even in his letter this morning says he only takes back the £35 because I have no immediate use for it!! and this when I have told him that that [*sic*] the crushing of that book has been my utter <u>ruin</u>! he sends me the slip of paper I inclose you by which it would appear that those Whittakers have been even <u>more</u> infamous than I suspected <u>suppressing</u> the book while they disseminated the "notice" let me have this thing back again it is from a Plymouth Paper.[1] – Mudies recommending me to return to Skeet I consider a perfect heartless cold-blooded insult – and there can be no doubt that even <u>now</u> (from the very abuse it has had and the curiosity excited thereby) in the hands of a commonly honest publisher – the sale of that book would float me out of all my difficulty – but I have no human being to do any thing for me nothing but Fools like that brute Clarke – to injure me even more than the Knaves and I am now as prostrate with this hemorrhage as a felled ox. So things must only take their course – and let the people put me in jail if they like – no poor wretch can have struggled or worked harder than I have – I send you a letter I had from Captain King – I wish him joy making the acquaintance of that socinian[2] Pothouse Plutarch Mr Dickens[3] – with kind regards to Massy Ever your grateful and affect

    R B Lytton

HALS

1. There was the *Plymouth Mail* (1852–62) and *Plymouth, Devon and Stonehouse Herald* (1831–69), which published articles on literature, poetry and the fine arts.

2. An anti-Trinitarian sect, founded on rational principles during the sixteenth-century, which flourished in Poland, Transylvania and in the Netherlands.
3. Charles Dickens.

To Rebecca Ryves

Thursday January 15th 1857

My dearest Rebecca I send you on the other side the reciept and return the post office order which I certainly wont take. I am too ill to write – there is nothing but ruin for me compassed with snares and villainy on every side and no single help or counteracting power – from all that I have gone to I am quick at percieving villainy and treachery but never can get others to do so – partly from insolence and partly from supposing every one honest and honorable being a cheap way of appearing quite amiable and then when it turns out that I am right and that people are even greater villains than I suspected them to be – my soi-disant¹ friends(?) get frightened at the astute and stop at nothing infamy of my enemies – and leave me to struggle out of it, or sink under it as I can – That brute Clarke deserves a good kicking – [as] do those very infamous Whittakers, but even were I to employ Mr Hyde he would only as usual get me deeper into the mire – and so give the chief Fiend an additional triumph – I have not heard from Dr Price yet – but unless he would do as I asked him, set on foot a Public subscription stating the causes of it he would, or could – do me no good. To shew you the beautiful way my business is managed in every way – Brown² makes a very expensive packing case for that poor old carved glass (which by the bye that shark Campbell has broken to pieces) but makes it 5 inches too short – so to remedy this defect what does he do but coolly cut off the carved ornament at the top!! and instead of having sent off all the things together by the luggage train they keep dropping in separately and costing God knows what – when I am able to open them I fully expect to find them all in smash – depend upon it from Mudies advising me to return to Skeet he is a rogue like the rest – I ought to have some man to make those vile Whittakers and Clarke deliver up their accounts – I have not a human being or a farthing! – but I really feel my brain going for it is too much to be alone with such misery from morning till night – and such a Butchery going on totally unopposed against me without. I am very glad Massy is better, with kind regards to him ever affectly yrs.

    R B L.

HALS
1. So-called (French).
2. Brown has a china shop in London and has been storing RBL's possessions for her.

To Unknown

January 17th 1857

<u>Public and unconfidential</u>

Sir,

Though generally most grateful for even the <u>word</u> "sympathy"! yet verily the Editorial Adulteration of that paradiseical plant, as I have experienced it from yourself, and others, has such a sharp twang of trading Butchery in it, that the only feeling it excites in me is that of a violent and exhausting hemoerhage gushing from a mortally lacerated heart - But I was not aware of the <u>full</u> extent of the <u>literary</u> infamy that had been exercised towards me, till I read the enclosed extract from a Plymouth paper, which I must also beg of you to read <u>not</u> to excite any <u>more</u> Editorial "Sympathy" which considering its braco – like attitudes I would rather be without, but to shew you that I am <u>now</u> perfectly aware of the diabolical manner in which the <u>Literary</u> Springes – I beg pardon "Sympathies" have been laid for me. – As I before said – those infamous Swindlers and Traitors the Whittakers were at perfect liberty to <u>refuse</u> to publish that "notice" or even the Book, and I fully expected that they would do so – knowing as I do that in this highly moral country (very!) there is no amount of vice not only tolerated but adulated in men; it being <u>only</u> considered horrible for a woman! and more especially a victim wife, to allude to such things, especially when like Boileau[1] Elles "appellent un chat un chat"[2] that is, have a vulgar trick of calling things by their right names, or <u>worse</u>, as in my case by their <u>broad</u> <u>names</u> – for it is the idiosyncrasy of overwhelming and <u>unredressed</u> wrongs – to reflect the extreme vigour of <u>verbal</u> penalty on <u>their</u> <u>outrages</u> – therefore, had I even hinted at the vice for which that Loathsome old ruffian Sir Liar Coward Bulwer Lytton was drummed out of Nice some years ago – (at least so the Comtesses Marie de Waronzow[3] told me, and she heard it from Lady Pembroke)[4] as that vice is not yet publicly bartered among English gentlemen – though like all others it exists to a fearful extent) – then indeed, the <u>Scribes</u> who are all to a man <u>Pharisees</u> in England – might have elected to be scandalized at me! from the same intense and <u>ink like</u> purity that caused that disgusting old Satyr Jerdan[5] of the Literary Gazette, when my first book came out – at the end of much good unscrupulous paid for abuse – in "sympathy"! to indite the following <u>creditable</u> paragraphs "Lady Bulwer inveighs amain at Lord De Clifford[6] for intriguing with a poor French Governess, but forgets that she makes Lady De Clifford[7] guilty of a much more heinous sin the <u>adultery of the heart</u>" – certainly a <u>new</u> – and very <u>original</u> definition of resisted sin! though rather a work of supererogation – for him, and his Employer Sir Liar Coward Bulwer Lytton, as every one acquainted with the <u>intense</u> infamy and crapule of both their lives, are well aware, that <u>they</u> by no means patronized "the adultery of the heart"! not only from the slightly organic impediment of having no hearts – but from infinitely preferring the aboriginal style of that sin, which nine times out of ten, has nothing to do with the heart, being sheer vice in the superior sex, and mere vanity in the inferior one. – And now Sir, having written all these horrible! things (doing them is highly moral and beneficial to society at large) and again "unsexed" myself, whose Opinion do you think I am to – or can care for – Certainly not that of an idiotic Court which receives such a mosaic of every immured vice as Sir Edward Bulwer Lytton a society which tolerates him – nor still less that of a Venal and profligate press which puffs him, and by screening such infamy propagates it. No verily! Therefore I will rest content with the approval of the select minority of every honest man and Virtuous Woman in England – and leave him his paid and prudent majority of the Ruffianocracy and the Press that pulls the Wires of that Fantoccini[8] "The Public"!

    I have the honour to be Sir,
    your obedient servant
    Rosina Bulwer Lytton
    To the Sympathetic!
    Editor of "The   ".

Now cognizant as I am of the intense rascality and Blackguardism of every thing connected with the Literacy! and Publishing world of England, I could not have believed that those infamous Blackguards the Whittakers would have been guilty of such gratuitous treachery – and complex Swindling as while they were carefully suppressing my Book, and making it a dead letter to the public – they presumed to strike off garbled extracts from it and circulate them in all the "Literary Circles"! alias the foulest and most corrupt social sewers – in the world – and get the work carefully abused – and falsified by an infamous clique – while they effectually suppressed the Sale – to starve out its too grossly outraged Author but doubtless such fabulous infamy is more Editorial "Sympathy and forbearance"!!! Decidedly Hell must be over populated and the Devil has drafted off his superfluous Imps into an English Colony of Authors, Editors, and Publishers – in a word those potent scoundrels "literary men"!!

KNEB
This letter is a copy.
1.   Nicholas Boileau-Despréaux (1636–1711) was a French poet and critic.
2.   They 'call a cat a cat' (French). *'J'appelle un chat un chat'*, Nicholas Boileau-Despréaux, *Satires* (1716), I.146.
3.   A member of one of the great aristocratic families of Russia, she was the sister of Simon Romanovitch Woronzow, third Count Woronzow (1744–1832), Russian Ambassador to England (1796–1806). Woronzow Road in St John's Wood, London, where he resided, was named after him.

4. Catherine Woronzow, the daughter of Simon, Count Romanovitch Woronzow, who was brother to Marie, had married the eleventh Earl of Pembroke.
5. William Jerdan, the editor of the *Literary Gazette*, had extra-marital affairs.
6. Lord de Clifford was the villainous husband, modelled on EBL, in RBL's first novel, *Cheveley*.
7. Lady de Clifford is the wife of Lord de Clifford, who falls in love with Cheveley, Lord Mowbray, and appears to have much in common with RBL.
8. A puppet [*fantoccio*] (Italian).

To Rebecca Ryves

[17 January 1857]

I open my letter to beg of you to have the kindness to write to Captain King – and intreat him never to mention that unnatural monster Sir Liars son to me, as his name blisters my ears. It would seem by that extract from the Plymouth paper that, the conduct of those Whittakers and that brute Clarke is even more infamous than I suspected – and that while they were carefully suppressing the <u>Book</u> – they were distributing the <u>notice</u> about separately! But how comes it that if my characters are such libellous exaggerations! that the whole press gang without the slightest <u>clue</u> <u>instantly</u> recognize the <u>Originals</u> and fit on the cap – the likeness's must be at least faithful and if infamy there is it must be in the <u>originals</u> and not the portraits like Boileau[1] "I call a cat a cat"[2] and it is impossible even to allude to certain vices without using bad language had I even <u>hinted</u> at the Vice for which that loathsome old Puff adder Sir Liar was drummed out of Nice– I should indeed have polluted my paper. Let me have back the Extract from the Plymouth Paper by return of Post.

———————

HALS
This letter appears to be a note added to the letter above.
1. See RBL, 17 January 1857.
2. See RBL, 17 January 1857.

To Rebecca Ryves

Thursday February 12th 1857

My dearest Rebecca

I have indeed and still am with business – which I am always compelled to do in flash of lightening haste, that I literally have not had one minute to write to you, but thank God! I begin to see day-light at last! but oh! what <u>superhuman</u> <u>worry</u> I have had – with that loathsome brute Clarke – of Taunton who as usual has caused me Endless delays and of course proportionate expense, – but my poor book will be re-launched at last! or rather <u>published</u> for the <u>first</u> time, again next week by a Paternoster row[1] Publisher with a preface explaining the infamies resorted to, to suppress it. The judge has been very kind, – but that young Easton[2] whom I thought such a stone at first, has turned out a tramp and warmed into a perfect Dragon! he said he heard things of Sir Liar in London – (not from any one connected with me) which convinced him that nothing I could ever say of Sir Liar – could ever come up to what his infamy deserved and finding that all I had told him of that brute Fred was true to the letter, he has effectually taken him in hand, and not only got his iniquitous bill, but sent it to London to be taxed as it <u>only</u> amounts to £342"14"11!!

Every other Printers Estimate amounting for printing and paper – to £106 – or £104 – and even Skeets Estimate <u>including advertizing</u> to £150! – not withstanding the infamous suppression of the book it has realized more than enough to pay this, but of course I want to pay Augusta the £100, and do not want it ingulfed by that Shark Clarke who has so completely wrecked my book and tortured me in every way. Meanwhile a most fearless able and judicious Champion has started up for me – a Mr Walter Weldon[3] (well done! Mr Walter say I) who has gloriously defended "Very Successful" unmasked Sir Liar and shown up the villainous Press conspiracy existing against me – I will send you the review when I get it back from my London Publisher – meanwhile I send you "Master Walters" letter – which will pretty clearly prove the Press gang conspiracy against me, – however the wretches have overshot the mark, – the re-action has now commenced and the perfect furor in London – and through the Country to get the book ought if I am not as usual most cruelly and villainously cheated – to bring me in a golden Harvest – Even Mr Hyde writes me word of the excitement about the book and says the Press itself are actually unanimous in condemning the infamous conduct of those Whittakers. Let me have Mr Weldon's letter back by return of Post?

I am indeed grieved to hear of your brother Williams miseries for all your sakes, there can be no doubt that he did a very silly thing – and I don't think even showed much taste to excuse it; but poor fellow there is no use in reproaching him with this irrevocable folly – which he has already paid so dearly [for] – The tariff of the Fates appears to be that the worst vices, may be indulged in to any excess – and the blackest crimes perpetrated with impunity – but that even a moment! of folly is always to be expiated by a life-long punishment.

We must all only hope against hope for better days – and certainly I can speak from experience that when Gods hand is heaviest upon us, His arm is <u>not</u> shortened and He can, and will save when and where we least expect it. No poor hunted savage larded with poisoned arrows – could ever have suffered more than I have done in body, and mind for the last 3 months, in my miserable solitary confinement, – condemned to a mental Treadmill of hard and ineffectual labour – with all that money and power and unscrupulous infamy could do in one strong legion against me – and only my own poor weak hands to war against all this – pecuniary ruin compassing me on every side – and shutting out every ray of light with its cold dark shadow fear! for every day I dreaded that Mrs Clarke would insult me, and say I must leave the Hotel as I could not pay her – nor was this all – the wretches to torture me had got up a Cabal to try and deprive the poor Boys[4] of their bread by giving out, that they! had got me to ridicule Miss Prosser[5] in my book – and every thing I did – or tried to do failed – every thing but my prayers – which God had heard and answered – for suddenly and without any apparent cause the feeling of <u>every</u> one – Enemies, friends and neutrals becomes changed to me – my Enemies acknowledge that I <u>have</u> been <u>too</u> grossly outraged and persecuted – and have fought the fight nobly and triumphantly – though unaided my friends – instead of being verb neuters, becoming verb actives, the neutrals – growing zealous, Mrs Clarke never asking for her bill – but waxing very civil, and attentive – old Prosser better friends than ever with the Boys convinced though I took her name in vain – that I never meant to limn <u>her</u>! so that though I cannot like Massy's friend Byron say that "I got up one morning and found myself famous"[6] I did what I greatly prefer – got up one morning and found every one <u>believing</u> Sir Liar to be infamous the natural sequence of which is, that every one at length! begins to feel for me and tries to help me. I saw in The Times that the poor little Family Herald man "The Rev James Smith[7] A M of Palace New Road Lambeth" had died at Glasgow on the 29th of January aged 55 – I should have thought he was much older. This was the very night – and so the world goes round! – that Mrs Wheelers Fancy ball came off. Judging by the Brighton Paper which Dr Price sent me, she seems to have had a most vulgar set at it, and <u>entre autres</u>[8] that brazen drunken Mrs Fonblanque as Norma! <u>Miss</u> Fonblanque (my God daughter!) as "Flame"! which I consider as a Type of the Times – as according to the present aspect of things between the forwardness of the "British <u>Females</u>" and the backwardness of the British males – I think soon every Miss will have to be her own Flame – .

The Boys begged their love to you when I wrote so is archbishop Tib who is dooder den dood were him here, but having lapped some milk yesterday him not vezy well so is done to see hims Dr. With kind regards to Massy best wishes to you both, and better luck! to us all – Believe me my dearest Rebecca Ever your grateful and affect

Rosina Bulwer Lytton

HUNT
1. This is an area associated with publishing, situated near St Paul's Cathedral. The row was named after the rosary makers who worked there. The publisher's house which RBL is referring to is that of Messrs Whittaker of Ave Maria Lane.

2. This attorney acting for RBL may be Richard Easton (*c.* 1826).
3. Walter Weldon (1832–85) was a journalist, who started working for the *Dial* in 1854, which was later incorporated into the *Evening Star*.
4. Fanny and Augusta Boys.
5. In RBL's novel, there is a an unflattering description of a character called Miss Prosser, who is described as 'a teacher of modern slip-slop' and in appearance very broad and short resembling the 'moving panorama of a very large molehill, with a mushroom growing on the top of it': Bulwer Lytton, *Very Successful!*, 3 vols (London and Taunton: Whittaker & Co., Frederick R. Clarke at the Caxton Head, 1856), vol 1, p. 188. See RBL, 7 September 1857.
6. 'I awoke one morning and found myself famous', are Byron's words written in a memorandum in 1812, following the great success of the publication of the first two cantos of *Childe Harold's Pilgrimage* (1812–18). See *The Works of George, Gordon Byron* (London: John Murray, 1903), vol. 9, p. 106.
7. James Smith established, in 1843, his own weekly penny journal, the *Family Herald: A Domestic Magazine of Useful Information and Amusement*, which eventually had around half a million readers. He died in Glasgow, at the home of a friend.
8. Amongst others (French).

To Rebecca Ryves

March 15th 1857

My dearest Rebecca I <u>am</u> alive, and that's all. – pray say <u>nothing</u> of my Pamphlet[1] to any one till <u>you get it</u> which I hope will be the end of next week; – but this getting a thing printed <u>sub rosâ</u>[2] and out of the country is murderous work – as to <u>time</u> – worry, and <u>expense</u>! – I hope Massy – indeed both of you – will not brave these terrible Easterly winds – which cast iron lungs could not stand. – When I was able to open my things from Brownes I never saw such a scene of <u>wholesale</u> pillage and distruction! 2 doz pair of fine Holland sheets 2 doz fine Hamboro[3] damask Table cloths – 3 doz ditto dinner Napkins – 3 doz ditto Breakfast – gone <u>Every</u> <u>article</u> of silver abstracted and the <u>plated</u> <u>alone</u> left one whole <u>box of Books</u> 5 of my pictures gone – and the rest destroyed with <u>ounces</u> of dust upon them, and the beautiful frames, that <u>were</u> so bright and new all dim and dull with damp! – 14 of my Dresden[4] cups – and saucers gone and those 4 pretty little Dresden custard cups and covers – with the pheasants painted on them that I bought from Browne, and 2 little Dresden Plateaux[5] one you may remember a little woman in a green sacque,[6] and a fan painted on one of them – Browne lays it all on the Pantechnicon[7] and pretends to be making inquiries! about them – and then what ever was in – one box of mine – he has taken out, and crammed in that long set of India China of yours – which like all mine is disgracefully broken – but would you like me to send you on – what there is of it? – Innocence who really is dooder den dood – desires him ove as did the Boys'[8] when I wrote – and with kind regards to Massy and best wishes to you Both believe me worried to death Ever your grateful & affect

Rosina Bulwer Lytton.

HALS

1. *Lady Bulwer Lytton's Appeal to the Justice and Charity of the English Public* (1857) was a pamphlet where she complained about EBL and requested donations to make up for what she regarded as his miserly allowance.
2. In secret (Latin).
3. Cloth from Hamburg, the major trading port in Germany.
4. The town of Dresden in Germany was renowned for its manufacture of fine china.
5. 'An ornamental tray or flat dish' (*OED*).
6. 'A loose kind of gown worn by ladies' (*OED*).
7. A bazaar in Moncomb Street, Belgrave Square, London, containing space for storage. The word later applied to horse-drawn furniture removal vans.
8. Augusta and Fanny Boys.

To Isaac Ironside

[March 1857]

...and my mourning which for all I had, £10 would have covered, - poor Kate Planché[1] meaning no doubt very well – must needs order from Miss Baker the Court Dress maker in Piccadilly so that on coming to my senses – I had a pleasing little bill of £64 – for this alone to pay and other things – in proportion – since then I have only had <u>8</u> harum scarum hurried moves – like so may locomotive indigestions! And as I cannot very well drag – between Twenty and 30 large Packing cases and Trunks about <u>with</u> me, besides Carriage Imperials and Cap cases – the most inconvenient things in the whole world – when one has no carriage to put them on, and in; – besides a bill of £15 I had to pay for Warehouse room at the Pantechnicon[2] friends have given house room – to a great many of these things – and when they in their turn have had to move – I have had to take these things never less than £3 or £4 by the luggage Train – and generally minus a box or two, – of which no one can give any account, and last winter poor good old Mr Hodgson succeeded in rescuing some of my things that had been in charge of a man who had become Bankrupt – but when I got them through the <u>real</u> rubbish Trunks with old news papers and Pamphlets were all <u>intact</u> – there were only 5 Pictures, – 3 doz Fine Hamborough[3] Table cloths 5 doz napkins 3 doz very fine Holland pairs of sheets and ditto laced Pillow cases, - all of which I had been given with 13 doz Chamber Towels, several, valuable pieces of Sévres[4] and Dresden China, – the little plate I had not already sold in short – all I had calculated upon turning into money – was gone! – Poor Mr Hodgson did all he could to make the Rogue account for, or replace the value of these things- but in vain! – so all the <u>redress</u>! I got for <u>this</u> swindle was Mr Hodgsons <u>not</u> paying him his Bill of £7 – odd – for packing the wreck of my things to come down here. So that his £7!!!! actually went to swell my plethoric! coffers when I recieved my last April Parish allowance – <u>all</u> things considered – added to such a total prostration of bodily strength – that I am unequal – to the slightest exertion – beyond with some effort using my right hand – as I lie in the bed – or sofa – as I am writing to you now – all things I say considered – you cannot much wonder that I should be a <u>wee</u> bit weary; and not a wee bit <u>hopeless</u>!

You are very glib Sir with your £100! like poor Mrs Jernyn; - but pray Sir what is oo at now? promising to pay another £10 for me, before any of my ships of the Desart My Camels laden with gold! have arrived; - no, - not Even that £19 13 that I have been panting after "as the Hart panteth for the water brook"[5] and now – I hear that Mr Easton is gone to France! – "<u>purely</u>" to learn to danse I suppose? – Besides, you know Bull[6] said he would give up the Copyright for £20 – not £10 – you need not laugh – nor <u>doubt</u> my proselyting zeal – for of <u>course</u> I <u>would</u> have done my best, - to – have converted the Jew – into lending me money! on Christian principles would they only have sent me one! – but the nearest approach to it was a correspondence of flummerising letters I had some time after, with Mr Tomlin Baron Meyer de Rothschilds[7] secretary when I was in vain trying to do a little Pocket picking for two poor vilely used French women the victims of one of Mr Burns[8] "Blazes! of Triumphs"! though I must not be ungrateful – for at the end of 2 months hard seige – I <u>did</u> get £2 whole pounds!! out of Baron Rothschild – which would have gone a very little way to make up the sum I wanted, in fact it would have left it a perfect Jews disabilieties Bill! if pretty little Alice Tylers Birthday had not happened to fall – while she and her mother were staying with me, and instead of the watch her mother had promised her on her Birthday – she preferred giving the £15 to poor Mme Alphonse and <u>her</u> mother – which with the rest I had garrotted the people out of enabled the poor things to get back to Marseilles. I am very tired good bye God Bless oo – best loves to all from

     Rosina

HALS

1.   Katherine Frances Planché (1824–1900) was the daughter of the playwright J. R. Planché, who befriended RBL. See RBL, 31 July 1857.
2.   Moncomb Street, Belgrave Square, London. See RBL, 15 March 1857.
3.   A kind of cloth. See RBL, 15 March 1857.
4.   Porcelain made in Sèvres outside Paris.
5.   'As the hart panteth after the water brooks', Psalms 42:1.
6.   Edward Bull, RBL's publisher.
7.   A member of the famous banking family.
8.   Possibly J. W. Burns. See RBL, 1 July 1857.

To Rebecca Ryves

[28 March 1857?]

... does not destroy – those applications – for the appeal – he has it and could compare the writing with that Mrs Boate sent. – I am delighted to hear the wedding went off so well and have no doubt it was a very pretty one, – but regret the stupid and like all else of the present day stingy fashion of no longer sending Bride cake the only sensible part of a wedding, and also the only thing connected with marriage "<u>Cette invention mirifique !!</u>"[1] As Rabelais truly calls it – that one can swallow without difficulty À propos[2] of that British Slave Trade, – you can tell Mr Eyre Lloyd – that my poor little Fairy – who would have gone into a large walnut shell – or that big Chestnut box I gave I. I.[3] used to sleep in her own little blue velvet Berçaulette[4] – in my room, but never in the Procrustés bed,[5] – as I should have dreaded to bring so darling a little animal into the same den with so great & ferocious a Brute.

Pray do not write on those detached slips of Paper it is so impossible to find the context – more especially when you do your worst I used to tell the charming Mrs Dizzy[6] that her hieroglyphics were like a storm at sea, – but yours – are like a storm in the midst of the Jura,[7] – when as Byron (and of course Massy) says – "The big rack comes dancing to the earth" and one can literally distinguish nothing but long black columns of Nebulae and mist. The Town has been in an uproar to day – re seating Mr Mills whose Election[8] was petitioned against so Taunton will not become a rotten Borough[9] though rotten enough in every other respect. God knows such a darling thing has just happened in the middle of "this green"! so that I could see it perfectly from my bed. The hounds were coming in full cry – you remember the old Whipperman that we met out walking one Evening last summer with the Pup – he was taking to walk the Kennel? – well he had a fall from his pony – just this minute, and it was too boots to see all those Doatskins gathering round him – and licking his face till I thought like Acteon[10] the poor old fellow would be eaten up by his own hounds. I am not surprised at what you tell me about the brilliant display of Bugles when one is ones own <u>Trumpeter</u>! the more <u>Bugles</u> one has the better We have had 4 days of such bitter cold winds, and black skies here, that to add to my comfort, my chest is raw with coughing – though it is from its total Emptiness! – that I suffer the most – I would gladly compound even for <u>water</u> on it, if that could <u>liquidate</u> my debts! I am really alarmed at that Brownes[11] persisting in advertizing my Book and appeal in both his Papers – for I fear as I never gave him any <u>Encouragement</u>! that his "<u>intentions are not honorable!</u>"

HUNT
Incomplete letter.
1.   That wonderful invention (French).

2. In connection with (French).
3. Isaac Ironside (1808–70) was a Chartist, who was a wealthy local councillor, who helped found the radical weekly paper the *Sheffield Free Press*.
4. Miniature cradle [*berceau*] (French).
5. In Greek myth, Procrustes offered hospitality to strangers inviting them to sleep on a bed that matched the length of whoever lay on it. His method was to adjust the guest not the bed, by using a rack to stretch them if they were too short or chopping their legs if they were too long.
6. Mary Anne Disraeli.
7. A mountain range between France and Switzerland.
8. Arthur R. Mills (1816–98) contested Taunton on 30 July 1847. He became the MP for Taunton on 9 July 1852 but was unseated on petition in April 1853. He regained his seat at Taunton on 28 March 1857 until 6 July 1865.
9. A parliamentary constituency, which usually consisted of a small electorate, used to exert undue and unrepresentative influence within parliament.
10. In Greek mythology, the hunter Actaeon was turned into a stag by the goddess Artemis after he saw her bathing naked in the wood. He was subsequently torn to death by his own hounds.
11. Hablot Knight Browne (Phiz) (1815–82) was an illustrator. See RBL, 12 June 1857.

To Rebecca Ryves

March 31st 1857

[printed engraving of Chirk Castle at top of sheet]

What I am reduced to in the way of Paper

My dearest Rebecca – at last! I send you this poor miserable Pamphlet – which though I wrote it in two nights – and always sent the additions <u>back</u> with the proofs they have tortured me for five weeks, and after this protracted bungle have at length produced it with all these disgraceful blunders! and of <u>course</u> the day <u>after the Fair</u> – as to do me any good I of course wanted it for the Elections, and to put a spoke in Sir Liars wheel at Hertford – but slave as I will what chance have <u>I</u>, - driven by poverty, and isolation – to using in the way of tools – the dregs of apathy, imbecility and dawdling against the most unscrupulous go-a-head patent villainy machinery <u>ever</u> at work to injure me, however – I shall now with all its imperfections on its head, send it to all the Members of both houses of Humbug – all The Clubs – Publishers Mayors of Towns – Acquaintance among the <u>haute volée</u>[1] – London magistrates && and it is gone to America to be re-published – also with a request to Ricker and Thorn – to get me up throughout the States – a subscription – modestly beginning at a <u>cent</u>, and rising <u>à volonté</u>[2] to "the almighty dollar". I have sent one to Ursa Major[3] Clarke telling him that, as when he was sent down here as a scout, and was so anxious to know "<u>What I intended to do</u>?" that he now knew and the <u>fortuitous</u> coalition also – and that if I had not exposed the <u>pure</u> source, commensurate sincerity of "The Matrimonial

Causes Bill" it was he might rest assured from no conventional deference, to my Lord Sykes Norton Lyndhurst,[4] but because – age, like Infancy, had peculiar, and imperative claims upon our forbearance. Will you kindly send the 2 pamphlets I send <u>beside</u> yours – to Mrs Tyler, and <u>Dr Laurie</u>! for which I send the stamps; but on <u>no</u> account send them without one line to Mrs Tyler to say that of <u>course</u> I dont want her to buy my book as I had ordered a copy to be sent to her but <u>only</u> to read the statement – the one for Dr <u>L</u> you can send to <u>her</u> – and would you also <u>directly</u> write one line to Capt or Mrs King[5] – telling them the same that I only want them to read the statement. Do you think that any of the Libraries of Torquay would undertake to sell some copies of this appeal if it was sent to them? you can show it to them, and ask them. I wish the Fiend joy of the <u>exposée</u> he had brought upon himself – you may imagine the state of bodily, and mental torture – all this prolonged persecution from <u>every quarter</u> has brought on me when I tell you that poor Miss Dickenson – having at <u>length</u>! lost like myself all hope and all patience, <u>now</u> sends me a daily dun! – and wants me to renew my promissory note for a <u>fixed</u> time – which <u>not</u> being a swindler (at least a premeditated one) I wont so if this miserable <u>pis aller</u>[6] of an appeal to Public charity fails me – I have nothing for it but to beg my bread about the streets. That Mrs Mitchell <u>is</u> the <u>respectable</u> (not the <u>improper</u>) Mrs Mountjoy Martins sister they were Miss Elliotts – and most <u>lovely</u> girls, and perfect sylphes I remember them. Me is so more dan dood, dat me is to be canonized as Saint Silver Paws next week, but me's not proud so sends my <u>ove</u>. I hope poor Massy has got rid of his cough? With kind regards to him, and best wishes to you both Believe me Ever – my dearest Rebecca

>Your grateful & affect
>Rosina Bulwer Lytton – alas!

HALS
1. High flown (French).
2. At will (French).
3. Great bear (Latin), a constellation. RBL is probably referring to C. H. Clarke, her London publisher.
4. Lady Sykes, Mrs Norton and Lord Lyndhurst all had adulterous relationships.
5. Captain and Mrs King are friends of RBL. Sometimes she mockingly refers to Queen Victoria as Mrs King.
6. Last resort (French).

To Rebecca Ryves

Friday April 3rd 1857

My dearest Rebecca If I get them in <u>time</u> for tonights post I will send you 2 more Pamphlets[1] but I am tortured in <u>that</u> as in every thing else by only getting them in driblets; which is a considerable detriment to me in every way, as a thing of this kind to tell should be recieved simultaneously by <u>every one</u>: you may suppose I was pretty tired – the night I posted those to you – having <u>only</u> folded – pasted – directed and stamped 200 that day including my packet to America and to 9 millionaires, in New York – I have sent <u>one</u> to every club – Mayor of Every Town – Lord Mayor of London Metropolitan[2] Magistrates Heads of Colleges – <u>Students</u> of Glasgow![3] – Publishers – Lords Commons – my fine acquaintance of course – Dr Gully[4] – Dr Holland Dr Tweedie[5] – The Chief Baron (Sir F Pollack my old council in the libel case) – and the Lord Chief Justice (Cockburn) and the Barristers <u>now here</u>, at the Assizes – but my hope is from America. – Did I ever tell you – that last February in an account of one of Sir Liars dinner Party's I saw the name of that disgusting Ass – Sir F Doyle! – now really this was too contemptible for even such a fool – so of course having alluded to the disgraceful fact in it I sent him one of the Pamphlets – and this morning I get a note from the Booby – saying that I appear to think that <u>he</u> had joined in suppressing my last book which he begs leave explicitly to deny. This gave me the intense satisfaction of writing him back – a recapitulation of his own, and his Fathers heartless imbecility towards me from first to last and of pasting the printed acct of Sir Liars dinner party including his name at the head of my letter, which I began as follows

"Sir – being accused of Murder – you sapiently defend yourself against petty larceny! I never either suspected or accused <u>you</u> of being employed in the <u>active</u> dirty work of suppressing my last loaf of bread – for that would require astuteness, and <u>fine</u> <u>moucherie</u>[6] – and <u>you</u> must be content to remain in the mire of mediocrity in which nature placed you – only being made use of <u>unknown</u> to <u>yourself</u>! as one of those blunt tools – without which, clever Knaves could never weave their complex nets" and so I went on as you know I <u>can</u> go on! The whole county of Hertford have by this time got it – with kind regards to Massy and best wishes to both Believe me quite worn out and still starved to death. Ever your grateful & affect

  Rosina Bulwer Lytton

HALS

1. *Lady Bulwer Lytton's Appeal to the Justice and Charity of the English Public.* See RBL, 15 March 1857.

2.   Sir Robert Walter Carden, first Baronet (1801–88), was Lord Mayor of London from
      1857 to 1858.
3.   EBL was the Lord Rector of Glasgow University from 1856 to 1859.
4.   James Manby Gully (1808–83) was a physician and hydropath, who established a
      water-cure centre at Malvern, which was frequented by EBL. He was also a friend of the
      spiritualist medium Daniel Dunglas Home, who had visited Knebworth.
5.   Alexander Tweedie (1794–1884) was the eminent physician of the London Fever Hos-
      pital from 1824–61. He was sent by RBL to attend her daughter Emily during her final
      illness.
6.   Snubbery (French).

To Francis Doyle

Sir F:H: Doyle Receiver Genl of Customs (However infamous!) Lower
Thames St London

Clarkes Castle Hotel Taunton
April 3d 1857

Sir E Bulwer Lytton, bart., entertained at dinner on Wednesday, a select party,
among whom were – the American Minister,[1] Lord Burghley, M.P.,[2] Lord Robert Cecil, M.P.,[3] the Right Hon. Sir John Pakington,[4] the Right Hon. Spencer
Walpole,[5] Sir Francis Doyle,[6] Bart., Sir Henry Rawlinson,[7] Mr Cumming Bruce,
M.P.,[8] Mr Baile Cochrane, M.P.,[9] Mr Warren, M.P.,[10] Mr Varden, Mr Drummond Wolfe,[11] and Mr Munroe. [newspaper cutting]

From The Brighton Gazette of Thursday February 19th 1857
      Sir Accusé de Menitre! Vous vous excuser du Larcin![12] I never either suspected,
– or accused you of being made one of the agents for suppressing my last loaf of
bread; – being perfectly aware that you were by far too great a noodle to be entrusted
with any active dirty work of that sort, requiring <u>astuteness</u> and <u>fine</u> <u>moucherie</u>[13]
– no, you must ever remain content with the mirey mediocrity into which nature
has plunged you, and continue one of those passive tools, – <u>used</u> without <u>their own</u>
<u>knowledge</u>! – but for which, clever knaves could never accomplish the weaving of
their complex webs. – I so far acquit Mrs Carlyle[14] of any <u>intention</u> to add another
to my long list of unparalleled outrages, – by making over the wreck – the apathetic
imbecility of your poor Paralytic Father had commenced, – as an Heirloom to <u>you</u>!
as it certainly would be <u>difficult</u> for any one to <u>believe</u> that you <u>could be</u> as great an
ass as you look – still, when I begged as I would beg (not indeed for my life – but
to be rid of it;) that she would <u>not</u> let <u>you</u> injure me still more by sending <u>you</u>!
into the springs of that loathsome Ruffian whom I <u>knew</u> if he pleased it [could]
make a noodle of <u>your calibre</u>! commit a murder, – and never dream that you had
done any thing but what was most orthodox! conventional! and proper! Still, she
had no <u>right</u> to do it so expressly against my will, – my feelings, and my <u>judge-</u>

ment. – Sir Liar Coward S—e[15] Bulwer Lytton had boasted to me what a precious
fool your father was! as well he might! when after <u>my</u> finding Sir Liar with Miss
Laura Deacon at the Albany[16] – he not only after his hugger mugger interview with
Sir Liar – to which though <u>my</u> nominal relation!! he <u>never made me the slightest
party</u> but allowed me and my poor helpless children to be coolly turned out of our
house – but was actually such an incredible fool! as to <u>sign</u>!! a paper Sir Liar had
<u>brought ready drawn up in his pocket</u>!! stating that <u>he</u> (a fellow who at <u>that</u> time
had swindled me out of every shilling in the most <u>heartless</u> manner) had behaved
most honourably! to me in <u>money</u> matters!!! according to his <u>then</u> means!!! as was
amply borne out – by his fine Pompeian House in Hill Street – monté[17] with a
French Chef – that he took for himself, and old Kings[18] Mistress Miss Laura Deacon the moment he kicked off his legal encumbrances, – and by the bills for paid
Pianos which Dalmaine[19] unwittingly sent to me, as they had been ordered in the
<u>name of Lady Bulwer Lytton</u>! and also Dalmaines letter of apology – for having so
unintentionally insulted me – and 15 years after, – <u>vous</u> <u>Chassez</u> <u>si bien de race</u>![20]
– that after a two months torturing hugger mugger, – <u>you</u> also –are <u>honoured</u> with
an hermetically sealed! interview – with Sir S—e – one <u>particle</u> of what passed at
it though one would think <u>I</u> was the chief person concerned; you never favour me
with, – only the <u>result</u>, – which was your coming down to my beggarly lodging in
Sloane St,[21] – with a manner so brutally bearish that had I possessed a man servant I would have ordered him to <u>put you out</u>, – and when I indignantly alluded
to the manner in which your Father had wrecked me you said staring at me like
what you are, – the greatest and most heartless fool I ever knew "What could my
Father do? – when <u>he</u> said he would not live with you any longer!!!" a most valid!
and unanswerable argument truly! – and though no Jerry[22] sneak was ever so tied
as you are to your little silly selfish, squeaky wifes apron string – yet with such
exalted! notions of marital supremacy! – had Sir Liar thought fit to physically cut
my throat – doubtless you would have whetted the razor for him, and asked "what
else could you do? since <u>he</u> wished it!! God forgive your Father and God forgive
his son, – and as <u>your</u> children are innocent of it, I pray that such cold-blooded
unnatural and incredible imbecility be not visited upon them and their childrens,
children. Further – <u>you</u> next make a still greater ass of yourself by writing to Mr
Hyde – one of my solicitors – as the Champion of your dear friend Sir Liars morality! (but then to besure its in the Doyle family to be fond of sinecures) and are very
irate at my allegations against him now – my authority for <u>this phase</u> of the brutes
Bestiality was my friend the old Countess Marie de Warenzow[23] who came to see
me one day at Geneva – with a letter – saying "voyez ma chère çe que ma niece
Pembroke (The Late Lady P Sydney Herberts Mother)[24] vient de me mander de
votre Infâme! a Nice; – mais tant mieux pour vous; le miserable! finera par trop
faire – nonobstant ses sour des menées."[25] – And this was an account of the disgust
reigning at Nice – from Sir Liars infamies <u>not</u> with women; – and not being <u>you</u>! I

had not the slightest difficulty in believing it; – from not only <u>knowing</u> that there was no vice the brute had not exhausted! as there is no virtue he has not assumed; – but I also recollected how some years before, the loathsome monster had (the first day his confrère[26] Acrobat Disraeli returned from the East and came in – just as we were going to Dinner) dared to pollute my ears – when I asked him when he came up at three in the morning what had kept him so long below? by saying "By Jove! Dizzy has been making me wild to go to the East & & & and he says – one never would look at a woman again" But exclusive of all this – <u>I</u> have better reasons than any one for knowing that the Fiends vices – like his conduct are unnatural and revolting. – But what I think so <u>particularly</u> disgusting and contemptible in <u>your</u> conduct, and I am by no means singular in my opinion – is, that considering what an intense and heartless ass you are, and therefore framing every excuse for you – we will <u>suppose</u> that Sir Liar had told you that it was me whom he had found committing adultery – and had therefore turned me out of my home – adding (as he has always a virtue varnish for every vice) "and I did not on account of my children like the Ecslandre[27] of a Trial"!!! and had further added – that I had gone from bad to worse since, – as the way I have laboured! and the splendor! in which I have lived <u>proves</u>! all of which <u>you</u> were of <u>course</u> bound to believe! and act upon without even telling me of what he did accuse me which is at least the privilege of every felon in the Kingdom – still transposing the disgraceful facts in this way, you <u>are</u> a mean contemptible wretch to play Plagipatidi ! to that man at this time of day – when you never were once asked into his house! till he had exhausted <u>every outrage upon me</u>. – But notwithstanding the murder of Poor Lady Flora Hastings[28] and notwithstanding that the scandalous chronicle gave her father, as the father of yours! – you go! (when asked) to Buckingham Palace! for no doubt your little squeaking Wife – whose mind appears to be as vulgar – without being near as large as her handwriting – thinks it a fine thing to go to a Mob State Ball. The clever man, and his far from clever tools – have so terribly over shot their mark that they have no one to thank but <u>themselves</u> for the <u>more</u> than <u>European</u> Publicity I have now given to this too long endured, and ceaseless infamy – and I have told my Lord Sykes Norton Lyndhurst[29] that if I have <u>not</u> exposed the <u>pure</u> source, and the commensurate <u>sincerity</u>! of the power of "The Matrimonial Causes Bill"[30] it is not from any conventional deference to his Parchment Peerage – but that age – like Infamy – has peculiar and imperative claims upon our forbearance Rosina Bulwer Lytton alas! alas!

HALS

1. In 1856, President Franklin Pierce appointed George Mifflin Dallas (1792–1864), a US Senator from Pennsylvania, as Envoy Extraordinary and Minister Plenipotentiary to Britain, where he served until 1861.

2. Baron Burghely is the subsidiary title for William Alleyne Cecil, third Marquess of Exeter (1825–95), Tory MP for South Lincolnshire and North Northamptonshire.

3.   Robert Arthur Talbot Gascoyne-Cecil, third Marquess of Salisbury (1830–1903), known as Lord Robert Cecil, was Prime Minister on three occasions, for a total of over thirteen years.

4.   John Somerset Pakington, first Baron Hampton (1799–1880), was Tory MP for Droitwich in 1837. He was Secretary of State for War and Secretary for the Colonies in Derby's 1852 government; and First Lord of the Admiralty in Derby's 1858 and 1866 governments.

5.   Sir Spencer Walpole (1830–1907) was an historian and civil servant, inclining to the Whigs. His principal work was *History of England from 1815* (1878–86).

6.   Sir Francis Hastings Doyle, second Baronet (1810–88).

7.   Sir Henry Creswicke Rawlinson, first Baronet (1810–95), was a soldier, diplomat and orientalist. He is sometimes referred to as the 'Father of Assyriology'. He was MP for Reigate, Surrey, in 1858 and for Frome, Somerset (1865–8).

8.   Charles Lennox Cumming Bruce (1790–1875) was a Scottish Tory MP for the Inverness Burghs constituency (1831–7) and for Elginshire and Nairnshire (1840–68).

9.   Alexander Baillie Cochrane was a Tory MP for Lanarkshire who was interested in architecture.

10.   Samuel Warren (1807–77), barrister, author and MP for Midhurst in 1856–9.

11.   This may be Henry Drummond-Wolff (1830–1908), who started as a clerk in the Foreign Office. He was to become a well known English–Jewish diplomat and Tory politician for Christchurch (1874–80) and for Portsmouth (1880–5).

12.   Sir Accused of Lying [*mentir*] you make excuses for larceny (French).

13.   Snubbery [*sic*] (French).

14.   Jane Carlyle was the wife of Thomas Carlyle, Cheyne Row, London. See RBL, 18 March 1851.

15.   Sodomite.

16.   EBL's apartment rooms in Piccadilly, London. See RBL, 7 July 1835.

17.   Set up (French).

18.   Laura Deacon had been the mistress of a Colonel King.

19.   D'Almaine & Co. were London-based makers and sellers of musical instruments. Their bill of £300 was for a grand piano.

20.   You are such a chip off the old block (French).

21.   97 Sloane Street, Cadogan Place, Chelsea. See RBL, 11 April 1851.

22.   A henpecked husband, derived from a character in Samuel Foote's farce, *The Mayor of Garret* (1764).

23.   RBL's friend, the sister of the former Russian ambassador to England. See RBL, 17 January 1857.

24.   Catherine Woronzow, the wife of the eleventh Earl of Pembroke, was related to Marie de Waronzow. See RBL, 17 January 1857. Her son Sydney Herbert (see RBL, 31 August 1853) was the lover of Caroline Norton. See below, n. 28.

25.   See my dear what my niece Pembroke comes to inform me of, of your infamy in Nice; – but so much the better for you; the wretch! But she will finish – despite her scheming sisters (French).

26.   Colleague (French).

27.   'Unpleasant notoriety' (*OED*).

28.   Queen Victoria's lady-in-waiting. See RBL, 510DCD.

29.   John Singleton Copley, first Baron Lyndhurst (1772–1863), was a prominent politician who was Lord Chief Baron of the Exchequer and Lord Chancellor (See RBL, 3 Decem-

ber 1857). He was an advocate of women's rights in questions of divorce, and a friend and
chief supporter of Caroline Norton. For his affair with Henrietta, Lady Sykes, wife of Sir
Francis Sykes, see RBL, 3 December 1857.

30.   The Matrimonial Causes Bill was intended to made divorce more accesible by moving
litigation from the jurisdicion of the ecclesiastical courts to the civil courts.

To Rebecca Ryves

Saturday April 4th 1857

My dearest Rebecca I have just had another severe blow! – in a letter from young
Hodgson[1] – suddenly announcing the death of his poor Father! who was seized
with Paralysis on Monday – and expired on Thursday – I was always grateful to
poor Mr Hodgson for his kind feelings, and many kind acts towards me, but I
never knew the extent of my regard for him till – he was taken! when his many
sterling qualities rise up in bright array – and even his great fault as a lawyer a too
elastic easiness of disposition – now that all his account is summed up seems to
shine out only as an additional virtue. – I do feel sincerely for his poor bereaved
son, and daughter! I suppose that Fiend Sir Liar will make his death – an excuse
for not paying me my Parish allowance, but really I am now <u>so</u> starved out, and
broken on the wheel, that I dont care what happens. – America is my only shadowy hope, and God knows it is a forlorn one! but I am convinced, that what
between vanity – selfishness – apathy conventionality and mammon-worship
you might go from one end of England to the other without finding even a <u>dor-
mant</u> feeling to arouse. – I did not get any of those abominable things last night
– if any come to night, I will send you two more. With kind regards to Massy
– In great haste, – and superhuman worry – Ever your grateful and affect Rosina
Bulwer Lytton.

HALS
1.   Frederick Hodgson, the son of Robert Hodgson.

To Rebecca Ryves

April 12th 1857

My dearest Rebecca though laid up with what the common people here call the
<u>brown Titus</u>! anglice[1] Bronchitis – I write one line to tell you how sorry I am to
hear of poor Massy's attack but he really <u>must</u> take care of himself in this Judas[2]
of a climate – or he will get seriously ill. The only results as yet of my appeal
– is an enclosure of a post office order for the Book and a kind letter from poor
Lady Boynton at Brighton – but as I really feel I have <u>no</u> claims upon her as a

new acquaintance except great kindness while at Brighton – I returned her the order and sent her the Book – The other was a letter dated Junior United Service Club written on that paper inclosing 13 stamps and requesting – an appeal[3] might be sent to Mr Maxwell 40 Ladbroke Square Notting Hill but on looking in The Court Guide I see a Mr Burns lives at no 40 – My friend Chalon[4] I have not heard from as I did not send him one but to day I have sent one to Mrs Wabberts[5] and if I could only extract £1"11"6 from Dr Wabberts it would make me extremely happy! – I sent one to Mrs First Resurrectionist Cragie last week – but though she used to get so many pounds out of me for her Egyptian Spoilings – she has made no sign – nor of course wont, as I have invariably found that those "Exalted Christians"?? as they call themselves – have no Christian feeling. This morning's post brought me a Pamphlet called "An address on the Present Condition Resources and Prospects of British North America Delivered by special request at the City Hall Glasgow – on the 25th of March 1857. By The Honble Mr Justice Haliburton"[6] with "the authors kindest regards" written on it – so that I suppose he is not yet home and has not yet got My pamphlet I think between my "appeal" (of which I sent them several copies) and Justice Haliburtons visit the Glasgow Students will be a little enlightened as to their charming Lord Rector![7] – Have you heard from Captain King since? – Poor good Mr Hodgson! – it is easy to know he is no longer here – for here are 2 days past the time my Parish allowance is due & no sign of it! – You must forgive this very dirty paper – as it was Master Innocences Autograph dat did it – him or hims muds bed and do hims cough is very bad, him kicked so against taking hims squills that Anne could not catch him – so him jumped all hims Paws over my paper; for dis Easter Sunday being de anniversary of hims release from de House of bondage – him tinks him may do anything. – I'll send you Judge Haliburtons address when I have read it. With kindest regards and best wishes to you both. Believe me ever your grateful & affect Rosina Bulwer Lytton

---

HALS
1. Abbreviation for anglicize.
2. Judas Iscariot, who handed Jesus over to his enemies.
3. RBL's pamphlet. See RBL, 24 February 1838.
4. A. E. Chalon, the artist.
5. This may be a joke pronunciation of Dr and Mrs Roberts.
6. Thomas C. Haliburton had written a number of books on his native Nova Scotia before producing 'An Address on the Present Condition, Resources and Prospects of British North America' (1857). See RBL, 6 July 1853.
7. EBL was the Lord Rector of Glasgow University. See RBL, 3 April 1857.

To Rebecca Ryves

Thursday April 16th 1857

My dearest Rebecca I am indeed very glad to hear poor Massy is better, and hope he will do nothing imprudent to get a relapse. – I am ill at all points – mind body – heart and soul – the Boys are not yet returned – and poor Mrs Garland – accomplished the silly – (and considering their circumstances) unwarrantable wish of her life – being in the Family way! and died of it! as we generally do if we succeed in our wishes it is generally dogged with some puzzle of this kind – to prove to us that God will not have our dictation in any thing and that we must accept His fiats as he sends them. Poor creature she was taken ill on Good Friday and lingered till 4 on Easter Sunday morning – when she died. Miss Comer who was there wrote me word of it – by the bye Annes news is that she Miss Comer is engaged to Bluett[1] but I have not heard it from herself yet. – Poor Lady Boynton – like a good kind soul as she is returned the Post Office order and insisted upon my giving it to some poor deserving person – As I never swindle people out of obligations – I wrote her back word that I accepted it, for though I knew many – far more deserving I knew none so cruelly and hopelessly poor as myself. – I get heaps of orders for the Pamphlet for that only costs a shilling – and grati-fies curiosity of course my designs on Dr Wabberts will fail – you do not tell me whether you have heard from Captain King? The only good that appeal has done me as yet, is that that Blackguard Loaden called on young Hodgson 3 days before it was due! saying he had a cheque for my Parish allowance – for there is nothing but fear to act upon such degraded natures as his and his infamous employers. – I had such a nice letter from poor young Hodgson – saying if I would honour him with my confidence he should be most happy to continue to act for me as his poor Father had done. – I suppose you have heard nothing from Mrs Tyler? – Let me Have the Haliburton[2] speech back as soon as you have read it – I have heard nothing from him yet discretion being the wisest part of valour – and silence – the safest side of Charity! which latter people are mistaken about its being cold – as I know it keeps me in a high fever! God Bless you with kind regards and best wishes to Massy Believe me Ever your gratefully and affectly Rosina Bulwer Lytton.

HALS
1.   Bluett is a publican, who runs the Star and Garter tavern. See RBL, 1 November 1856.
2.   Thomas Haliburton. See RBL, 12 April 1857.

To Rebecca Ryves

Wednesday April 18th 1857

My dearest Rebecca I was so ill, so worried, and so <u>bothered</u> yesterday – that I had not a minute to thank you for you kind letter – but having got another drib-let of those abominable things I sent you one – also <u>18</u> to New York – to as many <u>millionaires</u> – whose names, I copied out of "The Times" some time ago – and one name and address is so thoroughly yankee! that it <u>ought</u> to produce me a few stars, after all the stripes I have had being nothing less – than "The <u>Honble</u> some-thing Steward – <u>Dry-goods</u> <u>Palace</u>!!! New York. – you will see by Mr Hydes letter – which I enclose, that like all English people – he suggests (when too late) some advisable impossibility for had I entered into circumstantial details of the infamies that have been practised upon me, I should have required an Encyclo-pedia – instead of a Pamphlet and it would have stretched to such a length, that no body would have read it – even as it is – I have not <u>one</u> solitary hope in this country – and America! will take such a time! even if it succeeds? that what may not happen before then – since independent of poor Miss Dickenson – here are my April liabilities

Mrs Clarke 3 quarters	£75"0"0
Day	50"0"0
Mr Eastons[1] bill which	<u>30"0"0</u>
I insisted upon having	<u>£155"0"0</u>
Parish quarters allowance	<u>£47"1"4!</u>

a <u>pleasing</u> position and still more pleasing prospects you will allow ? but of course with such <u>ample</u> <u>means</u> and never stirring beyond my two rooms I <u>ought</u> to keep out of debt! – Poor Mr Hodgson! I cannot tell you how much I feel his loss – and the wreck of all those things from Thurloe Cottage – recall his last kind-ness which ever way I turn – and the time approaching when I never failed to get one of his kind – punctual, methodical letters inclosing me my Parish allowance truly – "the heart knoweth its <u>own</u> bitterness!"[2] for I defy any one else to even guess at it. – Send me back Mr Hydes letter by return – as I want to send it to Dr Price to save the trouble of writing it all – I also send you Panizzis[3] receipt for my appeal – for you know the Law compels one (which in this instance I am very glad of) to send a copy of every thing Published to the British Museum – so that Sir Liars infamy will be preserved <u>there</u> at all events. – Some one this morning has sent me a Hertford Paper called "The County Press" containing a glorious acct of the County Election – Sir Liar it appears was received with hisses and groans – and upon his Proposer – beginning to talk of his <u>political</u> principles! cries from the crowd of "He has none"! I'll send you the paper – as soon as I have shown it to a few persons – but as it is was a new uncut paper I conclude it was the Editor who sent it to me so I have fired him off a Pamphlet – as indeed I did several to "The <u>free</u> and Independent Electors of Hertford" and to the Mayor – but <u>alas</u>! the day after the fair – as I am compelled to do everything in this abominable place; – but it will work against the next. – Meanwhile I must tell you the last <u>compliment</u> to Sir Liar that has reached me – which you may tell to Massy upon Bagots[4] principle of "disseminate this <u>every</u> where". An Old Colonel Del Host who is here – was looking at one of those hideous newspaper portraits of Sir Liar in a shop window the other day when to the great amusement of the passers by – he burst into the following soliloquy – "what a rascally looking ruffian! – gad! he ought to be eternally grateful for his wifes forbearance – as he only wants a pair of horns to make him a <u>perfect</u> Devil! – for so fiendish a countenance I never beheld." To go from one extreme to the other Doodboots King of de darlings – desires hims love – and with my kind regards to Massy & best wishes to you both Believe me Ever your Grateful affect and Worried to death R B Lytton.

Let me have back Panizzis reciept also –

Having been obliged to get a Court guide for my amateur Post office! I see that a Mrs Lennox has got poor Thurloe Cottage[5]

HALS
1. RBL's lawyer Mr R. Easton, see RBL, 12 February 1857.
2. Proverbs 14:10.
3. Sir Antonio Genesio Maria Panizzi (1797–1879) was responsible for the circular Reading Room of the British Library, which opened in May 1857.
4. Lord Bagot, after entering the House of Lords, served as a government whip under the Earl of Derby in 1858 and Benjamin Disraeli, who was Leader of the House of Commons.
5. Located on Thurloe Square, off Fulham Road, south-west London.

To Rebecca Ryves

Tuesday April 21st 1857

My dearest Rebecca I am very glad to hear Massy is better I can only so far relive his Byronic <u>Brown Titus</u>[1] – as to tell him – that the truths (like all truths alas! too late) about poor Byron were in the <u>last</u> February Number of "The Titan" which I saw by the merest accident – That advertisement was sent by poor Dr Price to "The Times" and returned with the money to him and I was glad of the opportunity exposing his venality of that <u>as</u> venal – and corrupt organ of the Press as any and no one of common sense would suppose from my statement of the fact that my book was selling at £3"3"0 – but that a Friend (as was literally the case) had sent that advertisement to The Times as a set off to the Enemies infamy – I never got your letter about Mrs Kings[2] having received the Pamphlet – and <u>more</u> than <u>suspect</u> – that half the letters that go from – and come to this abominable Post office – never reach their destinations – as I find that several Pamphlets that I sent to Brighton never arrived there. – Poor Augusta returned – very ill, and miserable yesterday and poor Fanny and Mr Garland[3] come next week. – Augusta had a letter from "Toosey" – Georgina Willoughby[4] this morning who was married to a Mr Willock (<u>not</u> an aristocratic name) on the 5th of March – and she, and her spouse – are to return to England in May which I am glad of – as this will be something to divert poor Fanny and Augustas thoughts. The Bride Elect drank tea with me last night – looking very pretty – and very happy I told her though by no means <u>despising</u> Wedding cake – I should prefer taking it out in Champagne – she asked very kindly after you – Me is in all the Maternal anxieties of expecting Doatskin home – him having been for the last 3 days at Channings[5] so with kind regards to Massy and best wishes to you both believe me Ever your grateful & affect Rosina Bulwer Lytton

HALS
1. *The Titan* (1856–9) was a literary monthly magazine.
2. The wife of Captain King.
3. The Boys sisters' brother-in-law.
4. Rebecca Ryves's relative.
5. Appears to be a Taunton veterinary surgeon.

To Rebecca Ryves

[*c.* 25 April 1857]

My dearest [Rebecca] I have only [a] minute to [thank you] for your kind [letter and to] say I am very glad to hear you are going to Clifton – which has the reputation of being a very genial climate and is only 2 hours [toiling] from this – but you must come and stay at least a week as you know I hate ... which only ... of breath, ... temper. – you 3 ... would you ... up one ... to that Sir ... – and one also to Baron Richards[1] to whom I dont know how to direct – and the 3rd to the Dublin Library the name of which I cant make out – I inclose the stamps for them, and would not give you this trouble if I knew how to do it myself. <u>I</u> am not at <u>all</u> surprised at getting such endless orders for the Pamphlet, and <u>none</u> for Very Successful – as you know, or ought to know by this time, that English Charity!? or Sympathy??? – never takes the vulgar turn of activity – or demonstrativeness and even poor good Mr Hodgson might have lived for ever, without my finding out he had any regard for me, so little intimation did he give me to that effect. I send you a letter from Norton I suppose there really <u>is</u> something in Graphology! for his servant is <u>so</u> like old Hothams – with regard to his <u>advice</u> I told him all he said was true with this difference that he was a man with £6, 000 a year and I an outraged hunted woman without a penny – I further told him that I never desired to hear the name of Sir Liar Coward Bulwer's son mentioned to me – but that he (Norton) was quite welcome to send my letter to his son Brinsley[2] – and let him shew it to his amiable friend if he liked. I dont know when I have been more disgusted than with the Extract in "The Times" from Mrs Gaskills memoir of Miss Brontë[3] I could not help parodying Falstaffs Tavern bill,[4] and exclaiming "Only one grain of talent to all this puffery!" the storey of the young lady her sister gouging the poor Bull dogs eyes with her fists!![5] is too disgusting – and it appears every soul she ever knew – in clucking her very ugly little self (who was always her Heroine) and her swearing sisters [ill] crammed into her books, but we hear nothing of their personalities her morose father and profligate brother[6] – appear to have been her he models – I wonder whether the Lady still living in May Fair – who seduces! her brother Bransley – is Messalina[7] Norton? – she, and all her sisters were governesses – and the seduced brother! a Tutor, (the Louis of "Shirley"!)[8] which accounts for the intense vulgarity of all her books. Doatskin will be quite beggared changing hims name so ... Royal assent as him is ... Tib with kind ... Believe me in gre[at haste ever] your grateful & [affectionate]

      Rosina

HUNT

Letter damaged by fire.

1. Chief Baron Richards was a judge, who resigned as Chief Commissioner of the Incumbered Estates Court in Ireland in 1857.
2. Caroline's second son, Thomas Brindsley Norton (1831–77), became fourth Baron Grantley.
3. There was a review article in *The Times* for 25 April 1857 on Elizabeth Gaskell's *The Life of Charlotte Brontë* (1857).
4. Sir John Falstaff, companion to Prince Hal, the future King Henry V, runs up a tavern bill at the Boar's Head tavern in Eastcheap, London, in Shakespeare's play *2 Henry IV*, II.i. See RBL, *c.* 26 April 1857.
5. Emily Brontë beat her fierce mastiff, called Keeper, for sleeping on her bed.
6. In July 1845, Branwell Brontë was abruptly dismissed from his post as a tutor in a private house, probably for having an affair with the lady of the house, an older woman.
7. Valeria Messalina (*c.* AD 17/20–48) was the third wife of Emperor Claudius, who was cruel, manipulative and sexually debauched. She was reputed to run a brothel, organize orgies and even challenged a notorious Roman prostitute named Scylla to an all-night sex competition.
8. Louis Moore is the romantic hero of Charlotte Brontë's novel *Shirley* (1848).

To Rebecca Ryves

[*c.* 26 April 1857]

... Messalina[1] Norton but as it is – I suppose it must be Mrs Fox Lane but I'll ask Mr Weldon[2] when I write – "My brother Bransley"[3] is of course the Louis of "Shirley"[4] if I had crammed part of my brothers amours into a novel! or in a Biography exposed the <u>living</u> infamy of an inhabitant of Mayfair! what an out-cry there would have been! at my <u>personalities</u> and <u>bad taste</u>!!! And if I had calumniated a school with the real name! more especially after a letter had been written to The Times stating there was not one syllable of <u>truth</u> in the picture – would there have been stones enough in England to lapidate me? and indeed when I read this extract I said to myself at the time as my Father – <u>only</u> allowed them potatoes <u>not</u> enough of them & <u>no</u> "flesh meat" as they disgustingly call it. I thought the school fare <u>must</u> have been <u>rather</u> traduced and as for that extract of "My Sister Emily"[5] gouging the poor dogs eyes! with her <u>naked fists</u>! it turned me positively sick with disgust – Miss Bronte is a person who does not interest me in the least – and her books from the intense vulgarity and Man-Worship – I positively dislike – and when I read the puffs about her "genius!" I cannot help parodying the comment on Falstaffs[6] tavern bill, and exclaiming "Only one half-penny worth of talent, to all this puffery."[7] "My Father"[8] and brother appear to have been great brutes – and as she crammed every one and every thing into her books, this accounts for all her nerves being ditto, you know – it is impossible to get any sort of book <u>here</u> and I should much like to <u>see</u> the ugly Portrait of Miss Bronte – so if you could put up the first vol (open at each end to show it is a book) for which I send the stamps – I would send it back by return of post. and be greatly – that is "extremely much obliged to you" with kind regards to Massy and all good wishes to you both Believe me Ever your Grateful & affect
    Rosina Bulwer Lytton

HALS
Incomplete letter.
1. A debauched Roman empress. See RBL, *c.* 25 April 1857.
2. Walter Weldon is a journalist, who writes for the *Dial*. See RBL, 12 February 1857.
3. Patrick Branwell Brontë (1817–48) was Charlotte Brontë's brother.
4. Louis Moore is the hero of Brontë's novel *Shirley* (1848). See RBL, *c.* 25 April 1857.
5. Emily Brontë (1818–48).
6. Shakespeare, *2 Henry IV*, II.i. See RBL, *c.* 25 April 1857.
7. 'O monstrous! but one half-penny-worth of bread to this intolerable deal of sack!', *1 Henry IV*, II.iv.540–1.
8. Patrick Brontë (1777–1861) was the father of Charlotte, Emily, Anne and Branwell Brontë.

To Rebecca Ryves

[*c.* 27 April? 1857]

... when Miss Brontë – puffed and adulated up to Olympus could be so indignant with G H Lewes;[1] – whom she did not know; – and who had gone out of his way to serve, and puff her in Every possible way, – winding up with an elaborate and exaggeratedly Eulogist Review in the Edinborough[2] merely because he had headed it "Mental Equality of the Sexes" and "Female Literature" and her intense vanity, – wished it to be supposed that that very vulgar and below par book "Shirley" was written by a man! – all the thanks he got was the following note

"I can be on my guard against my Enemies, but God deliver me from my friends! Currer Bell"[3]

and when the poor patient man in reply to this real piece of ingratitude (for she had not only something but every thing to be grateful to him, – for as he had served her effectually, – indefatigably and judiciously, in all the great lead-ing, and Fame making Reviews) wrote humbly asking her pardon for having unintentionally annoyed her; – she writes back "I know your nature it is not a bad, or unkind one, though you would often jar terribly on some feelings, with whose recoil, and quiver, you could not possibly sympathise I imagine you are both enthusiastic, and implacable you know much and discover much (now Mr Ironside knows nothing but en revanche,[4] he goes further than Mr Lewes, for he discovers what dont exist!) "But you are in such a hurry to tell it, – you never give yourself time to think how your reckless volubility will affect others, and what is more, if you knew how it did affect them; you would not much care."[5] Now this, of course was all very pardonable, and only shewed additional genius! in Miss Brontë, – But for me, to wince, and writhe under being insulted degraded and injured in every possible way, is of course unpardonable! now for Mr Ironsides opinion of my Books, or the opinions of 50, 000 such illiterate echoes as he is, I should not of course care one straw but unjustly and villainously as the press gang, themselves confess I have been treated, with regard to my writings when other trash is so bepuffed and when this injustice it is, that has beggared me; – I do care, writhe under, and resent, the wanton cruelty of any ones injuring me additionally; – more especially all in saddling me with an obligation!! in pre-tending to serve!!! me. Mr Ironside may say that he does think "Very Successful" such trash that he could not conscientiously say a word in its favor – very well, then he should not have written me such exaggerated praises of it: – and without compromising his opinion, there were plenty of extracts from other reviews that would have sold the book – like that for instance "we begin to think there is a conspiracy to suppress Lady Lyttons works" && But see how Drs differ; a Cler-gyman told us && At first I thought Mr Ironsides mode of advertizing my Book

– was only part and parcel of the extraordinary – exceptional and <u>marring</u> way he <u>does</u> everything! but since I have seen his ad "of the Squire of Beechwood"[6] I see he did it <u>on purpose</u>, and with <u>malice prepense</u>[7]

HALS

1. G. H. Lewes (1817–78), the philosopher, literary critic and extramarital partner of George Eliot, who had reviewed Brontë's novel *Shirley*. See below, n. 2.
2. See unsigned review of *Shirley: A Tale* by Charlotte Brontë, *Edinburgh Review*, 91 (1850), pp. 159–60.
3. Charlotte Brontë's pen-name was Currer Bell, under which she published a collection of poems with her sisters in 1846. She continued using it for her first two novels, *The Professor* (1857), published posthumously, and *Jane Eyre* (1847).
4. By return (French).
5. In a letter to G. H. Lewes, dated 9 January 1850, Charlotte Brontë writes: 'but you are in such a hurry to tell it all you never give yourself time to think how your reckless eloquence may affect others; and, what is more, if you knew how it did affect them, you would not much care'. Quoted by Elizabeth Gaskell, *The Life of Charlotte Brontë*, 2nd edn (New York: D. Appleton Co., 1858), p. 118.
6. *The Squire of Beechwood: A True Tale of Scrutator* [pseud.] by Knightley William Horlock is advertised as a three-volume novel, dedicated to the Duke of Beaufort.
7. Malice aforethought (Latin).

To Rebecca Ryves

Half Monday Half Tuesday all hour between Night & Morning May 5th 1857

My dearest Rebecca with all the good will in the world, I could not thank you for your kind letter this morning as it was as much as I could do to send you the two additional Pamphlets, which I did with many thanks. Those pamphlets, will avenge Sir Liar as well as me, for I think they will be the death of me – as the Labour which is really Herculean augments daily – and I am happy to say after Yorkshire and Lancashire, which are insatiable. <u>Scotland</u> and <u>Hertfordshire</u> are my chief customers but oh! the trouble <u>is</u> great, though I am always politely assuring myself that as it <u>is</u> for myself – I don't mind it in the least. I hope this time that wretch Dr Wilson will <u>pack</u> Sir Liar effectually – Even to the Infernal Regions. – I am very glad your Cousin went to the <u>respectable</u> Establishment Dr Gully's[1] – but he must take care, and not fall in love with Miss Gully (if she is still there; and still Miss Gully?) as she is an exceedingly pretty girl you know I met her at Mrs Carlyles I am very glad to hear you have a <u>female</u> Phippen[2] over head to lend you "The Times" and hope she may "<u>have as sich</u>" in other respects. Were ...

HALS

The end of the letter is missing.

1. Dr James Manby Gully (1808–83) was a physician, who specialized in hydrotherapy, or the 'water cure'.

2.   Philip Phippen is a kindly eccentric gentleman, who is a character in RBL's novel, *Very Successful!*.

To WGS Cavendish, Duke of Devonshire

13 Hans Place Chelsea
May 6th 1857

My Lord Duke I feel that some sort of apology is due from me to you for that liberty I am now taking in intruding upon your Grace; the more especially as I am well aware of the scandal and heinousness! [of] my present proceeding in this charming country where I am also aware from long, and bitter experience that a <u>man</u> if he only possesses a certain fortune, and makes himself unscrupulously useful to a party, is never censured however iniquitous his conduct may be; especially if it is <u>only</u> to his wife, and children, and that a wife is never pardoned, -if she is guilty of the emormety that is of the <u>manque de convenence</u>![1] of uttering a single complaint! no, – in <u>moral</u> England under such circumstances she may have relays of <u>lovers</u>, and then she is "poor thinged"! and "what wondered" and <u>pronéed</u>[2] and upheld right, and left; but she has no right to obtrude her private grievances on any one, we are a nomenally Christian people! but then of course individual oppression should never be interfered with, nor redressed, especially when as in my case it is the strong and the wicked against the poor, and the defenceless but being now <u>poussée à bout</u>[3] I really do not care one straw what the ever <u>just</u>! world says and still less what it thinks of me but as in the every slight intercourse I have ever had with your Grace I have always found you not only <u>très grand seignieur</u>[4] – but better still, a perfect gentleman – and an amiable, and courteous gentleman too, I should be sorry to do anything that might cause you the slightest annoyance without duly apprising you of it, I must beg of your Grace (little claim as I have upon your time) to read the inclosed letter, and then return it to me, – that I may forward it to its destination as being unable to get <u>any redress</u> – and having in vain tried every other means, and every other appeal – even to his common decency I am now determined being exasperated past further endurance to publicly expose that most contemptible wretch Sir E Bulwer Lytton, and see whether he prefers my selling oranges, and a brief memoir of him at the Gates of Devonshire House on the 16th or paying the paltry sum his reiterated infamies have compelled me to accept at different times from charitable mortals who did not like him wish to see me perish in the streets – for this sum amounting to £1,500 – my Parish allowance of £400!!! (from which Sir Liar deducts with his usual munificence the Income tax!!) is so diminished with interest – upon these monies – that indeed now that my health is failing I have too harsh a struggle to exist, especially as my mean Tyrant interferes (not indeed with the sale, but) with the price I get for my Books so that were the "Guilt of Literature and Art" really a charity, and not a sham! your Grace will percieve that the wife of the Charlatan who has originated it, for a probono publico[5] clap trap would be one of the most fitting objects to benefit by it. – Lest your Grace should doubt my statement about my poor martyred child I inclose you one letter from the nurse who attended her which I must beg you to return to me with the other. I Have the Honor to Be your Graces obedient servant Rosina Bulwer Lytton.

HALS
1. The lack of convenience (French).
2. Probably means advised as *proner* is 'to advocate' in French.
3. Pushed to the limit (French).
4. Very noble (French), sir (Italian).
5. For the public good (Latin).

To Rebecca Ryves

Saturday May 9th 1857

"Most Round and <u>appy</u>" as Tittlebat Titmouse[1] would say to see you on Tuesday let me know at what hour you will arrive? Mrs Clarke very sorry she can only give you the same room but it has been new-carpeted; and <u>washingstanded</u>. That Walter Weldon[2] is worth his weight in Koh-I-noors![3] – with kind regards to the <u>Fellow</u> Ever in lightning Haste yours R B L.

<u>Who</u> is Mrs Fitzgibbon of Sidney House Cork[4] – ? who directs to me as The Honble! Lady Bulwer Lytton! – which rather smacks of the <u>north</u> Cork – The <u>Parsons</u> are beginning to write me letters of sympathy

---

HALS
1. A character from Samuel Warren's novel, *10,000 a Year* (1841).
2. A journalist. See RBL, 12 February 1857.
3. Then the world's largest diamond.
4. Mrs Fitzgibbon, of Sidney House, Cork, in southern Ireland, was a painter and sculptor, who exhibited a painting entitled *Star Gazing*, and a sculpture group, *Venus and Cupid*.

To Rebecca Ryves

Friday June 12th 1857 12 – a.m.

My dearest Rebecca I have <u>just</u> received your kind letter for which <u>mille grâces</u>:[1] I am glad you arrived safely and found the <u>Fellah</u> well with the <u>ball</u> at his foot. – Your Trunks are just gone off – duly directed with the addresses you sent, and

I hope you will get them all right tomorrow. In sheer agony I was obliged – to write to Dr Price for advice the day before yesterday; he had kindly sent me (as is always the case when paupers seek medical advice an impossible prescription) I am not to stoop! or strain myself by lifting up my arms! – nor on any account to life heavy weights! I am to take gentle exercise carriage if possible? and to drink Claret!! dont you wish I may get it? however I have sent to Hitchcocks[2] for the physic part of the prescription which is all I can attempt; but the agony I suffer is indescribable, and insupportable, and I think it must be the gout – toothache and Tic douloureux[3] – which have been "taken in and done for" in my bed, and so are determined to return the compliment and do for me. – Our poor dear darling II[4] is certainly a human steam Engine for he never ceases night or day trying at something or other to serve me – he is improving also – as to his too stringent Economy of words – for he tells me to write to Boyd – to return me his letters – as he says he is determined to get his mine, and Boyds letters! published in the Glasgow papers!!! – I long to hear of your going in state to Fleet Street in the family coach, and also what Dent is like; my best love to all the Tylers – and excuse me about not writing – but verily every letter I write is a nail in my coffin – and you know how many I have to drive in daily. Poor dear Mr Hyde I am so sorry for him I wrote to his <u>worser</u> half yesterday. – Fitz best Boots sends hims love. – Poor Mrs Clarke was cast away at sea two nights she is not to be back till next week – Hoping you will come in for some of the Balls, Believe me with kind regards to the <u>Fellah</u> Ever affectly yours Rosina Bulwer Lytton

---

HALS
1.   A thousand thanks [*mille grazie*] (Italian).
2.   Pharmacist.
3.   Facial neuralgia (French).
4.   Isaac Ironside printed and published RBL's 'Lady Bulwer Lytton's Appeal to the Justice and Charity of the English Public' at the Free Press Office (FPO), Fargate, Sheffield.

To Rebecca Ryves

Friday 6 P.M: June 12th 1857

The enclosed curiosity of literature, or rather of illiterature just received from the admirable Mr Browne![1] this is his paltry spite because I would not answer his impertinent letter half love letter half bullying verily it is for exposing me to such insults as these that I hate Sir Liar with a Protocol of hatred for which I could not have believed there was room after the original matter – Do you not admire an Editor! and a critic!! beginning in the 3rd person and his rage lashing him back into the first person = I suppose what he means by its being too bad to quote and to abuse him! is that in my appeal I do quote one of his letters by saying "One Penny a liner, asserts that Sir E B Lytton assigns the vituperation of my books in justification of his conduct"! I then ask how many vituperative books I had written when he turned me out of my house and hunted me through the world? – you may send this Elegant Epistle to II[2] if you like, which will shew him the Editorial Blackguards my miserable position entails upon me.

Ever affectly yrs R B L.

HALS
1. Hablot Knight Browne (Phiz) was an illustrator, who designed plates for EBL but was most noted for his work on the novels of Charles Dickens.
2. Isaac Ironside.

To Rebecca Ryves

Saturday – June 13th 1857

"Boots"[1] assures me that you will receive your Trunks at 4 to day – alas! you cannot receive this assurance till Monday this being Saturday so I hope that ere that if you have not actually achieved the honours of the Family Coach! you will at least have had <u>de quoi</u>[2] to walk out like a respectable "<u>Female</u>" though not <u>British</u>! I send you Isaac's despatch of this morning – poor me! who cannot even take opium medicinally in the smallest quantities and the most modified form, no wonder one is so misjudged by one's Enemies, since it seems one fares no better at the hands of ones most devoted friends but what I am especially disgusted at as I have told him, is his not openly and honestly taxing me with the habit if he suspected it – strange that English people never <u>can</u> understand you being besotted with misery – or maddened with intense bodily pain – without attributing "the first great cause" to alcohol or opium. – My back retains a grateful recollection of your rub (would I had no others!) but the pain continues, an excruciating torture far beyond any in the <u>repertoire</u> of the Inquisition. But Mrs May's Balsam has worked a perfect miracle and quite cured my foot so that if I could only find a <u>fellah</u> to take me to one, I should be able to dance at a ball, which I have seen many old women do in England. Last Evening Fanny and "dear Garland" came in – I brandied, and soda watered them – the tea being as you know "Mr I how <u>do</u> you drink it?" this <u>spirited</u> arrangement seemed to be a great relief to Frizzledoms[3] mind – and maudlin also what between the Pump, and my persistence in dispensing with his attendance – began to look despondingly at his own pecuniary embarrassments at the Tap and the Winchester Arms.[4] The Boys and "dear Garland" – are going to Town for a week, and then I believe to Dieppe. Miss B's how <u>do</u> you get the money to do all these things? as my letters cannot go till tomorrow night – I will leave it yes – in case of having anything to communicate from this Evenings, and tomorrows Post. – Return me Isaacs strange Epistle – by your letter to me, I concluded he communicated his extraordinary suspicions to you, which mind he conceived before he tells me! – and they were confirmed afterwards!!!

Sunday

Many thanks for your kind letter just received I fear by it (though it may have been written early in the day) that you did <u>not</u> get your trunks after all; though "Boots" assured me you were to have them by <u>4</u> P. M yesterday – and that they were to cost 3"9" – You are quite mistaken about my <u>laughing</u> at I.I.'s[5] extraordinary accusations! I think it perfectly monstrous not that he should take such a thing into his head – but that he should <u>act</u> upon it as if it were a chronic and <u>proved fact</u>! Socrates was right – "God defend me from my friends!" – the punishment I have inflicted upon him – is to return him his letter (a disgraceful one for him ever to have written) for as I tell him, in my state of health I feel that I may die from one minute to another, and I should not like such a document to be found among my papers as there could be but <u>one</u> inference deduced from its <u>strong</u> and mysterious! language peremptory exhortation to leave off a vice – which I had never commenced! or confirmed! and solemn promise of <u>secrecy</u>!!! on his part respecting it ie – that to the despair of my best friends I was a confirmed and disgusting drunkard! "a vice" <u>decidedly</u> <u>not</u> "interesting in women"! and I may add, utterly revolting in men. – I have had no letter of apology from him, only the one – I enclose you <u>repeating</u> the charge! – I should like to see his letter to you on the subject! I suppose – it was that not going to bed – that made me so ill – and look so dilapidated which <u>confirmed</u> the charitable suspicions he had so glibly indulged in before he saw me I shall hope to hear on Tuesday that you recieved your Trunks in due time, on Saturday and are no longer a prisoner. <u>Nothing</u> seems – to alleviate the excruciating pain I suffer and having to exert my self corporeally as I do – under this total prostration of strength, – <u>must</u> end me soon, and that alone gives me courage to Endure it. Fitzzbestboots done out with the Marchioness, Anne[6] out for the day, so I am doubly miserable. With kind regards to the <u>Fellah</u> and all good wishes Believe Me Ever affectly yours Rosina Bulwer Lytton

I send the Pamphlet

The Easton, and Clarke[7] affair going on as usual, that is "<u>purely</u>" not at all

---

HALS

1. A servant called Hitchcock, whose brother was also called Boots. See RBL, [October? 1857].
2. The wherewithal (French).
3. A male servant at the Giles Castle Hotel, Taunton.

4. Taverns situated at Castle Green, Taunton, near RBL's hotel.
5. Isaac Ironside.
6. Anne is a chamber-maid at the Giles Castle Hotel.
7. RBL's lawyer Mr R. Easton and C. H. Clarke, the London publisher of the 1859 edition of RBL's *Very Successful!*.

To Rebecca Ryves

Tuesday June 17th 1857

My dearest Rebecca Thanks for your kind letter – I really am so fearfully ill, and depressed – that it is positive torture to me to put pen to paper, and every thing seems to add gloom to gloom – and trial to trial – with despair for the back and fore ground. – Such <u>Bosh</u> as Mr I's[1] Cottage advice to day – falls like vitriol upon a raw wound – Mr Hydes letter only confirms what I told him – and what I <u>knew</u> – that nothing will or can be done – and as usual I have only had all this plough-ing and harrowing work for nothing and verily I <u>am</u> weary unto death of it, – and as it is plain to me, that I shall soon lose even my poor Tib – would to Heaven it would please God to take me first. I cannot conceive what Mr I means – by saying he never suspected opium – till he saw me – when all his letters harp upon my having some besetting sin! which I was to leave off – and when in the one I sent him back occurs this sentence "I thought so before I saw you and this opinion is confirmed ten fold since I saw you" now it so happens that I have <u>not</u> discoloured teeth – I have two that are jet black at the roots from being badly stopped by two bungling Dentists – and what I put into my mouth was a bit of Orris root,[2] which I always Eat after medicine or any other disagreeable thing – and worn out from want of sleep and from violent pain – I had taken a rhubarb draught before din-ner that day – but when one is writing under such vital, and pressing miseries as I am – it does irritate one to have so much time, and patience wasted on chimerical nonsense. – Will you return Mr I Mr Hydes letter and tell him that I <u>have</u> asked at this Post Office to get the letters of a Sunday by sending for them and they <u>wont</u> give them. The Mrs Tibbs mentioned in that Jersey letter is the woman I mention in old Knebs imaginary letter on my death such a vulgar beast! She was the wife of an attorney and doer of dirty work and Toady in chief to my infamous old Mother in law. I thought Miss Brontes[3] mother was dead? it seems there <u>was</u> some scandal about her and Thackeray[4] <u>this</u> I had heard before – what an infamous set that lit-erary gang are, right and left! – I am glad you got your trunks at last – with kind regards to the Fellah Ever affectly yrs R B L

you may send the Jersey[5] letter on to Mr I.

HUNT
1. Isaac Ironside.

2. The root of a certain species of iris, used medicinally.
3. Maria Branwell (b. 1783) died on 15 September 1821.
4. Charlotte Brontë dedicated the second edition of her novel *Jane Eyre* to William Thackeray. At the time, she was unaware that his wife, Isabella Gethin Creagh (*née*) Shawe (1816–93), had been placed in a private asylum. Some readers made a connection with this and the fictional Bertha Mason, the insane wife of the hero, Mr Rochester, who had been confined by him in his house, Thornfield.
5. A letter from Mrs Wade, who lives in Jersey, the largest of the English Channel Isles.

To Rebecca Ryves

[17? June 1857]

... The Place where these Blackguard Reporters the mermydons of the <u>Guilt</u> meet is at a low Pot house in the Strand called "The Cheshire Cheese"[1] (not quite the cheese either!) the <u>Guilt</u> provides the supper – and gin – ad libitum[2] – and when the miscreants are discharged from any Paper for doing their dirty work endemnifies and keeps them till they get other employment, in short – it is a complete Inquisition of the Press and it was there that the <u>Forty Thieves</u>![3] met to decide upon some fresh conspiracy against me, but could decide upon nothing but a continuance of the old one, of giving out that I was mad!

Be sure and return me all these safely

R B L

HALS
1. A Fleet Street tavern, London. See RBL, 16 June 1854.
2. At one's pleasure (Latin).
3. From *Arabian Nights*. See RBL, 16 June 1854.

To Rebecca Ryves

Thursday June 18th 1857
In bed – not able to hold up my head

My dearest Rebecca It is very kind of you to write me such nice long letters and I would answer them in kind of course – were I able which I really am <u>not.</u> – Pray give my best love and thanks to dear Mrs Tyler and Mrs Barclay for all their kindness, – which I would do myself were I able; and tell Mrs Barclay that her Pishmina[1] or cashmere is the solitary comfort of my life, and that like the dandy who was obliged to lie in bed while his <u>one</u> shirt was washing – I am driven to the same expedient when my shawl pays a visit to the Laundress – I sincerely hope Emily may be happy and so tell her with my love. I send you Isaacs of to day – he is beginning to find the truth of what I say about the Publishers! and he will find I am equally true on all other points – he evidently does not understand – the technicalities of publishing – for that £10 per cent commission is the only just thing in Clarkes Bill – as it is always given when a Publisher does not buy the Copyright – I hope he will send you my letter of to day upon the "opium question" as I am quite unable to recapitulate it but I wound up by begging of him not to belie his own generous and like all generous gentle nature – by aping Mr Urquhart[2] in saying brutal things – and doing silly ones. – I also told him that I thought he often wasted words, as for instance in devoting a whole page to vindicating the intellectual superiority of the goose whose name had been taken in vain as an illustrative synonym for Mr Raymond Browne;[3] – for that every one acquainted with the slightest rudiments of natural History – was perfectly aware that far from being a silly – or even a stupid bird – the Goose was a remarkably shrewd astute diplomatic schemer but his name having for ages been unfairly used – as an illustration of imbecility – it would in all probability continue to be so as long as the world lasted; without the continual bévue[4] doing poor Goosey[5] any harm. The conclusion I came to upon reading the account of the martyrdom of poor little Urquhart was – "as this poor child – had not the good fortune to be born a Frog; what is the use of making him 'have as sick!? – I do follow poor dear Dr Prices Prescription as far as I can! but verily there is but one prescription on earth that would give me any chance of recovery to wit, the golden ointment of not owing a shilling & having £800 a year to live on. – which would enable me to keep a maid and a secretary both of which I want equally – and offer you a home independent of the Fellahs, – and yet if all of this arrived next week, I feel it would arrive too late. – Amen. I send you a Birmingham Paper that Isaac sent me – in which Sir Liar is well mauled though not half as much as he deserves – the loathsome brute let me have this paper back as I want to rejoice poor Dr Prices heart with it. I have written to Mrs Wade for an explanation of that strange history of Miss Bronte's mother,[6] being now living in Jersey,[7] and will let you know the result. Lady Westmeath (of course as my Ld Salisburys sister)[8] has taken no notice of my appeal that I sent her, so of course I shall not write to her for her Pamphlet. Poor Doatskins thank God seems better to day. – Ever affectly yr RBL

HALS
1. Pashmina is a type of high-quality mohair, obtained from a special breed of Himalayan goat.
2. Russophobe and eccentric, David Urquhart (1805–77) introduced the Turkish bath into Britain and was the owner of the *Free Press*, which was taken over by Isaac Ironside, author of the pamphlet, 'The Question is Mr Urquhart a Tory or a Radical?' (1856).
3. See RBL, 3 August 1857.
4. Blunder (French).
5. See RBL, 17 February 1830.

6. Maria Brontë (*née* Branwell) was born and spent her early life in Penzance, Cornwall. She met her future husband, Patrick, in Hartshead, Yorkshire, where she was helping her aunt with the domestic side of running a school.
7. See RBL, 17 June 1857.
8. Emily Anne Bennet Elizabeth Cecil (1789–1858) married George Thomas John Nugent, Marquess of Westmeath (1785–1871). Her brother was second Marquess of Salisbury. See RBL, 24 January 1858.

To Rebecca Ryves

Saturday June 20th 1857

My dearest Rebecca I am glad to hear the Dr's report of Massy's lungs – as there is nothing like leather! – Hope! you tell <u>me</u> to hope! – it would be cruel to make me do so if it were possible – but luckily it is <u>not</u>. A long life of cruel disappointments – is surely enough – and as we are told "blessed are they who do not expect" – I hope at least to leave the world one of the blessed. – And sorry am I that – that poor good man at Sheffield should give himself so much trouble – for what might have done some good 10 years ago – but which every painful breath I draw tells me is too late now. My poor Tibby is panting out his little life at one side – I at the other my fear is that he poor Innocent will reach the goal before me. This cannot go till tomorrow and I am unable to write more now.

Sunday –

Thanks for your kind letter my dearest Rebecca which I have a little more heart to answer to day – as I have some hope of my poor Doatskin, yesterday, – Channon thought it was chronic bronchitis – that he would not get over, – I implored him to try counter irritation, – give him <u>no</u> medicine, but blister hims poor innocent throat well, – all night I have been in an agony about him, – and had what doubtless the saints would call the wickedness – to pray God to spare him to me a little longer; moreover, I cast a Virgilian[1] lot – and said – it would be doubly sad if I lost my poor little star of the Desert of a Sunday! as it was as you know of an Easter Sunday me found him, – so I said if he dies tomorrow (Sunday) never will my fate change – if he gets better from the experiment; – <u>then</u> things will turn, and go well with me, – with fear and trembling I rang this morning, – when lo! Anne darted into the room like a sunbeam – crying out "Darling Tibby is <u>so</u> much better this morning, – Boots has seen him, he's not the same dog, and Mr Channing thinks he'll do now. So I feel as if Péleon and Ossa[2] had been taken off me. – Thanks to poor kind Dr Prices Prescription the excruciating pain in my back is much abated but my head – my head – no one can tell what I suffer with it or the feeling of <u>horrible</u> and <u>wicked</u> depression – under which I am labouring – and against which I do all I can to struggle – but the wish I have

to put an end to myself is almost insurmountable I have told Anne to leave no
knives in the room and to take away the Laudanum after it has been used – and
I have just enough reason left to feel how wrong all this is – and pray – against
it – may God hear my prayer, and grant the patience to the end but there is no
more preaching to me the Devils Expedient Hope! it is with that, he baits all his
springes, – and remember that exactly this time ten years, 1847 I had the same
Triumphant and sanguine letters from Mr Sandby[3] – that we must win! that the
case was a plain one that Sir Liar had got entangled in his own infamy, and could
not escape! and how did all this end? in my being fettered, and outraged ten fold!
– now I do not for a moment mean to insult our dear Isaac by comparing his
– noble Christianity of principle and chivalry of purpose, with the weak – vacil-
lating treacherous worldly Henpecked Mr Sandby! God forbid! – for I feel and
know, that Isaac well deserves his name – which in its Hebrew original means
love to our neighbour; and that the Day Star from on high of good will to men
has indeed risen in his heart – but still I do think – that he, nor no other human
being can undo the complex villainy that has been knotting, and hardening – to
strangle my existence for so many years past God alone can cut the Gordian
knot[4] by snapping mine – or Sir Liars thread of life – every thing short of this is
too late! and as I wrote to poor Walter Weldon[5] yesterday – it was a pity to waste
his life, and health in trying to serve me now! – moreover as I could logically
demonstrate to him – that I deserved to be hanged – at least according to those
spelling books now lost in the night of ages, under whose dogs ears, I graduated
when I first began my literary lamentations! for they set forth "To point a moral,
and adorn a tale"[6] that the Hero of the Horn book[7] "<u>DON'T CARE</u>"! was
hanged, – and I have become the very incarnation of don't care – therefore what
is the use of any one wasting their time on such gibier de Potence?[8] though I had
a letter yesterday from Rowland Hill[9] saying my request about getting my letters
by the north mail on Sunday morning should be attended to – upon my writing
to the Taunton Post master this morning he refused to give them, saying he had,
had no order from the Prig Master General – to that effect – so "Sunday shines
no Sabbath day to me"[10] since with regard to Isaac it is a <u>Dies non</u>.[11] – Fanny
went yesterday to Bath to meet "Dear Garland" Augusta came in here yesterday
Evening with her large family of small dogs – I begged off – Earl Percys Ears
from the shears – for so have I christened the prettiest of the Pups – as he has
been given away – to some one in Northumberland – and has already a whole
Chevey Chase[12] in those Electric Telegraph tan paws of his – Augusta went this
morning to Bath to join Fanny and Mr G. and tomorrow they all go to London,
having taken a house in Rochester Place Oxford Square[13] – which you know is
the other side of the Park to where you are, but they said they would go and see
you. I hope you will be able to read this, but from the dreadful pain I am in, I find
great difficulty in writing in bed. – my best love to all the Tylers and good little

Mrs Barclay – I wish Mrs Tyler could find out from Mrs Sutton – <u>what</u> became of my <u>soi-disant</u>[14] Woovermans;[15] in the Cathedral frame, you know the picture with the obligato[16] white horse – and cavaliers drinking at the Roadside inn – as I should like it sent down to me the Boys's could bring it. Did you take my sandal wood fan – to have made into a large green one? as I do not see it here. Addio[17] – and all good attend you my kind regards to the <u>Fellah</u> – Ever affectly yours R B Lytton.

How is poor dear Mrs Best? my love to her and Mrs Sutton. Have you seen Mrs Kitchener yet? – and is she still something between Venus and a Duchess as Gates used to call her – How is the Chisholm?[18] How did they all bear poor Sir James McDonnalds[19] death?

Have you seen Lady Mountcharles yet? and does she look as lovely as she used when little Lady Jane?[20]

HALS

1. A form of divination based on taking the first passage seen on opening a volume of Homer or Virgil.
2. The smaller mountains surrounding Mount Olympus. In *The Odyssey*, Homer tells of how the giant twins, Otus and Ephialtes (the Aloadae), made war upon the Olympian gods by piling Pelion upon Ossa to storm the heights of Mount Olympus.
3. Revd George Sandby. See RBL, 28 May 1853.
4. The Gordian Knot is a legend connected with Alexander the Great, which involves cutting through an intractable problem.
5. Journalist. See RBL, 12 February 1857.
6. Samuel Johnson, *The Vanity of Human Wishes* (1749).
7. The hornbook was used by children for several centuries; in law, a hornbook is a text that provides an overview of a particular area of law.
8. Prey for the gallows (French).
9. Rowland Hill introduced a system of uniform penny postage. See RBL, 21 November 1856.
10. Pope, *Epistle to Dr. Arbuthnot, Prologue to the Satires*, l. 12.
11. A Latinate legal expression for a day on which a court is not heard, such as a Sunday.
12. *The Ballad of Chevy Chase*, dating back to at least 1430 and existing in several versions, concerns a large hunting party ('chase') in the Cheviot Hills lying across the English Scottish border, hence 'the chevy chase'.
13. Located in Westminster.
14. So-called (French).
15. A painting by a member of the Wouverman family. See RBL, 23 December 1852.
16. Obligated (Italian).
17. Goodbye [*adiós*] (Spanish).
18. A Scottish clan. This may be a reference to Mr Stuart. See RBL, (nd) August 1853.
19. General Sir James MacDonald, who distinguished himself at the Battle of Waterloo, died 15 May 1857, being the last of his direct male line.
20. Her husband, Marquess Conyngham, also had the title Earl of Mount Charles in the peerage of Ireland. See RBL, 7 April 1854

To Rebecca Ryves

Monday June 23rd 1857

My dearest Rebecca Thank Heaven the Bulletin of poor darling Innocence is improving – not so hims mud, – whom as a certain class of British Females say is visibly "improving for the worse" – I send you Isaacs despatch of today. I told him that as I knew nothing of Mr Urquhart but his writings which I admired[1] – and his axioms to most of which I subscribed – the only data I had to go upon was – what he himself had told me when he said that when he first knew Mr Urquhart he had written him letters which made him (Isaac) "feel as if vitriol had been thrown over him." – and this I called saying brutal things – while as his poor little child was <u>not</u> a Frog, I considered bringing him up as such was doing a silly thing. I dont know if he (I I) sent you Mr Hydes letter about my iniquitous Deed of Separation? but it is as it has ever been – I mean the statement therein – <u>conclusive</u> of the irredeemable hopelessness of my position. But "Hope springs eternal in the"[2] Ironside breast; – but his great error is in supposing that he will get <u>others</u> – to even <u>reflect</u> a single ray of his own honesty – and right feeling, – Mr Wheeler[3] is <u>comme tous les Parvenus</u>[4] a sneak and a Tuft hunter, and he would as soon cut off his hand as sue Sir Liar – on the contrary – Sir Liar – would buy him and his better half – without haggling – in 5 minutes by getting them an Invitation to Devonshire[5] – or Stafford House[6] as sort of <u>Assignants</u>[7] – of which Sir Liar has always a large stock at his command – as that is part of the coin in which he himself has been paid for his own dirty work – for the last quarter of a century – and what ever Mr Wheeler might by such facile – means be got to do against me; he would certainly do nothing for me and least of all, would he jeopardy his £1000 by suing Sir Liar! – I did not tell Mr Ironside all this because I wrote to him in such pained haste to save the 3 o'clock Post but perhaps you will kindly do so? or to save yourself trouble can send him this. I did tell him why I had no faith what ever in Mr Neills[8] tender mercies! – I see by an article in the S.F.P[9] headed "The Father of English Journalism" copied from the "Shrewsbury Chronicle"[10] – that they speak of the <u>late</u> Captain Sterling[11] the Thunderer of The Times can this be the Captain Sterling – who would have served me but for that disgusting ass Sir Francis Doyle? – I mean Mrs Carlyles "Starling"[12] I'll leave this open till the 6 o'clock Post in case any thing comes to tell you of – for shame nothing but double leaded dullness – studded with despair – "Isaachar was a <u>strong</u> ass – crouching between <u>two</u> burdens"[13] but <u>I</u> am a weak one, crushed under <u>so many</u>! that never on this side the grave shall I be able to shake them off – and Bayard[14] Ironside had far better leave me quietly to die under them, than waste his time excavating my corse from under them – for while the grass grows the steed starves – that is, while he works so indefatigably poor darling, – the creditors worry – ditto.

Nothing by the last Post, but this letter from kind old Dr Price – I rather am inclined to believe that he is <u>right</u>; and that no letter ever was sent to Llangollen; but that the whole thing, was a juggle between Lord Lyndhurst[15] and Sir Liar, and of course, as a superannuated Debauchee of a Lord! is in the case, none of the Thompsons[16] are Johnsons will stir in it. I hope in reading that letter on the prevalence of Opium – dramming Isaac thought of my besetting Sin! which he tried so summarily to Urquhartise me out of; – well thank Heaven I am going where alone righteous Judgement can be hoped for – one thing is very certain – ie that Brutish Females of all ranks and grades, – <u>are</u> the greatest wine bibbers, dram-drinkers and Opiumisers under the sun – beating the <u>males</u> hollow – in those moral, and attractive little propensities: – and no doubt he judged me by that flattering standard – if he ever sees me again? I fear he will decide that the habit has sadly increased!! for decidedly I feel and look more hollow – eyed – and wretched than ever, for verily misery turned to a vulture by solitary confinement – is the most destructive sort of morphine possible. Kind regards to the <u>Fellah</u> whom I fear will never have the ball at his foot, as long as he has his foot at the Ball God Bless you Ever affectly yrs R B L

HALS

1. David Urquhart was the author of *The Pillars of Hercules, or A Narrative of Travels in Spain and Morocco in 1848* (1850). He also wrote for the *Sheffield Free Press*, where his writings cannot be easily distinguished from those of his wife, Harriet.
2. Pope, *An Essay on Man* (1733), I.91.
3. Samuel Wheeler.
4. Like all upstarts (French).
5. Devonshire House in London, home of the Dukes of Devonshire.
6. Stafford House was built in the 1820s by Frederick, second son of King George III. Frederick died before the house was finished and it was leased to the Marquess of Stafford and named Stafford House. In 1912, the lease was bought by Viscount Leverhulme, the house renamed Lancaster House and the lease given to the nation.
7. Parties to an assignation (French).
8. A journalist friend of Isaac Ironside.
9. The *Sheffield Free Press*.
10. The *Shrewsbury Chronicle* was a literary paper, which advocated agriculture and trade. Besides Shrewsbury, it was circulated throughout Wales and the English border counties.
11. Edward Sterling (1773–1847) was a journalist for *The Times*.
12. Thomas, the husband of Jane Carlyle. See RBL, 18 March 1851. RBL is punning on the title of his biography of Edward Sterling's father, *The Life of John Sterling* (1851).
13. This is how Issachar was described by his father Jacob (Genesis 49:14–15).
14. A man of great courage and honour, deriving from the knight Chevalier Bayard (*c.* 1473–1524).
15. RBL had sent a statement of her case concerning the Llangollen spies to Lord Lyndhurst in the hope that he would petition the House of Lords on her behalf. Her papers mysteri-

ously disappeared after having been collected by a young lady, claiming erroniously that she had been sent by RBL.

16. Major General T. Perronet Thompson (1783–1869), radical MP for Bradford from 1857 to 1859, had demanded an inquiry in the House of Commons into the mysterious disappearance of RBL's papers sent to Lord Lyndhurst. See above, n. 15.

To Rebecca Ryves

Saturday June 27th 1857

My dearest Rebecca This is the first day I have been able to sit up in bed long enough – since I last wrote to you – to attempt anything like a letter; the fact is, I am so weak – from the long course of starvation, and hard labour I have undergone here, that I have no strength to bear up against any fresh bodily ills that assail me, – and what I now chiefly suffer from after what Foreacre calls "the palpitations"!! are fainting fits, – upon the least exertion – even that of putting up and directing the few (very few now alas!) Pamphlets that are wanted , – it is a terrible state of things to be unable to do anything, and to be obliged to do every thing: – I could no more stand to take a shower bath, than I could fly! – for even after my sitz bath,[1] which I never can dispense with, while alive; I generally have a terrible fainting fit, and as I write every letter seems half a dozen dancing before me, – I of course did not tell him so poor dear old man, – but I would as soon think of dosing myself with Mr Ironsides Opium! as with Dr Prices Calomel[2] the only thing I have any faith in is Homoeopathy, – and what I want is, really good medical advice, – I must indeed write to Dr Epps;[3] – but it is about as reasonable to expect a Physician to prescribe – for, at least to make a cure of you from a written account of your symptoms without their seeing you, as it would be to expect a Painter to make a likeness of you from a written inventory of your feature, and complexion; – but enough of those very uninteresting subjects – myself, – and my miseries. – I am losing all my old Russian friends fast, – and truly I must say their kindness was of a very different fabric from the Anglo Saxon Article bearing that name, the poor Princess Bagration (Lord Howdens wife[4] –) died at Venice on the 2d of this month – poor soul, how she used to delight in worrying that little reptile Henry Bulwer[5] singing my praises, – and how invariably she took care to thrust me into the Post of honour – on all occasions, – I did not know her in Paris, it was at the Grand Duchess Anne's[6] I first met her, – with Marie de Warenzow – Princesses Galitzin[7] and Soltikoff[8] – alas! the two latter are now also gone – what has driven me back into this Montagne Russe,[9] – was getting a letter this morning nearly in rags! – and only 13 months old! From my old Florence friend the Comtesse Zagrowsky – (née Tolstoy) which letter had travelled from Moscow from Florence, – from Florence to the Baths of Lucca,[10] – thence to Pisa, Genoa,[11] – the Maremma,[12] Frankfurt, Geneva,[13] – Thurloe Cottage![14]

and ultimately "Try Taunton?" – ! her father Prince Tolstoy is governor of Moscow, – and this was a kind, if pressing invitation to the Coronation![15] in which she says "si votre Infâme vous traîte toujours de la même indigne façon – que cela ne vous arêtes pas chère amie; – <u>nous</u> vous arrengerons pour les diamens"[16] – what a good figure! my present wardrobe would cut at a coronation! and how a galaxy of Diamonds would Embellish it! but I confess – I was pleased to find that in 10 years – this at that time kind friend had not forgotten me; – moreover, it was refreshing to hear from any cold region – while the Comet is thus furiously wagging his tail, a gambol I for one, wish he would cease, – as not being St Lawrence,[17] I have no fancy for being boiled alive. As Mr Ironside ordered me to refrain from writing, – and as my letters – even to you! (because in <u>answer</u> to his question of what I thought of his plan about Mr Wheeler! I ventured to say that he was not exactly the person to entrust with the casting die of my whole fate) seems always to irritate him so much – I of course should <u>not</u> have written to him had I been able which I <u>literally</u> have not been. Sir Liar appears to be the only person – with whom he deals very gingerly, – and tenderly, and I have no doubt that amiable personage, thinks the game is equally in <u>his</u> hands, and that the "courtesy"! between them is likely to increase; – and the bargain be an Easy, – and cheap one, – if he only promises to write up Mr Urquhart; and write down Lord Palmerston. What ever my opinion may be upon this point; – Sir Liar may well feel sanguine; – as up to the present time, <u>invariably</u> the "Courtesy" he has met with from my <u>soi-disant</u>[18] Champions has ended in a fresh victory for him, and a fresh – and God knows supererogatory crushing for me. – "The Society for the recovery of Wrecked Vessels"! is now taking me up! – The secretary having written to me for my appeal; – very properly thinking no doubt; that such a terrible and utter wreck was quite in their line. – That rich old maid Miss Baldacquhu Lloyd of Ruthin,[19] – is also beginning to "affect me marvellously"! writes me very kind letters, – and has this morning <u>bought</u> "Very Successful", saying that although it is <u>not</u> fit for Ladies to read!! she is determined to run the risk. I began this beautiful scrawl at 12 to day, – I have returned to the charge Eight several times, and it is now 5 P. M. and I recollect it cannot go till tomorrow – so I will finish it then, – being quite exhausted now – only while I think of it – I did not write to the Boys – from not being able to write to any one – but their address is 10 Porchester Place – Oxford Square Hyde Park.– Miss Comer is also in London but I understand insists upon Blewett's remaining at the Star and Garter, – at Richmond[20] – I have heard of keeping a man at arms length, – which indeed is what all women ought to do; – but this keeping them at legs length! is an improvement on it, as it keeps them at a greater distance still. – Sunday

Oh! de wonderful man! dat Channing! dis morning – comes an innocent well known scratch at my bed room door – I get up as fast as I could – to open it, when who should rush into my arms – quite a new dog! but with de same heart,

and eyes – but Master Innocence – all perfumed after his bath (a delicate attention that Channing never omits) oh! how good it is to have some living thing
that loves one out – and out – seeing dis Doatskin so well, whom dis day week
me never hoped to see more ...

HALS
The end of the letter is missing.

1. A bathtub shaped like a chair in which one bathes in a sitting position, immersing only the hips and buttocks. A bath taken in such a tub was usually for therapeutic reasons.
2. A colourless, white or brown tasteless compound, sometimes used as a purgative, which had been prescribed by RBL's local physician.
3. Dr John Epps (1805–69) lectured at the London Homeopathic Hospital during the 1850s. He was a philanthropist, who championed liberal causes.
4. Ekaterina Pavlovna Skavronskya (1783–1857) had married General Prince Bagration. Her second marriage in 1830 was to Sir John Hobart Caradoc, second Baron Howden (1799–1873), from whom she separated.
5. RBL's brother-in-law.
6. See RBL, 30 September 1845, and below, n. 7.
7. This is probably Princess Bauris Galitzinm, whose portrait was painted in 1797 by Elisabeth Vigée-Lebrun (1755–1842), who also painted the portrait of Grand Duchess Anne in Russia sometime between 1795 and 1801.
8. Madame Soltikoff was a society hostess, whose husband was governor of Moscow.
9. Russian mountain (French).
10. Natural springs in Tuscany, Italy.
11. Italian cities.
12. An area in Italy, south-west of Florence and Chianti.
13. Cities in Germany and Switzerland.
14. RBL was living there off Fulham Road, south-west London, in 1852.
15. On 25 June 1857, Queen Victoria formally granted her husband, Prince Albert of Saxe-Coburg and Gotha, the title of Prince Consort.
16. If your Unspeakable always treats you in the same unworthy manner – don't let that stop you my dear friend; – we will arrange things for you for the diamonds [*diamants*] (French).
17. St Lawrence was martyred in 258 by being burnt on a red-hot gridiron. See RBL, 11 August 1857.
18. So-called (French).
19. A village in the Vale of Clwyd, north Wales.
20. Miss Comer's fiancé is spelt Bluett. See RBL, 16 April 1857. The Star and Garter was a well-known hostelry built above the terrace on Richmond Hill, where EBL retreated after his separation from RBL and where, by contrast, Dickens celebrated his wedding anniversary over a period of twenty years.

To Rebecca Ryves

Sunday June 28ᵗʰ 185[7?]

... you know their <u>prompt</u> <u>punctionality</u>! about every thing here – so the Gardener only brought these seeds of the Humea Elegantia[1] on Saturday Evening R

RBL

————————

HALS

Incomplete letter.

1. *Humea Elegans*, now known as *Calomeria amaranthoides*, whose common name is the incense plant, is a hot-house plant, which comes from Africa, Madagascar and Southern Australia.

To Rebecca Ryves

Monday June 29ᵗʰ 1857

My dearest Rebecca I inclose you the Sheffield despatch of to day which has annoyed me considerably – for I don't think either I, or Mr Ironside had any <u>right</u> (without asking her permission) to forward Mrs Wellington Boates[1] (not Miss Brontes's!!!!)[2] letter to the Loathsome – who of course will leave <u>no</u> infamy unresorted to, to vent his mean spite, and crush – and injure the poor womans book upon which her existence is depending – moreover I do think all this is an exceedingly puerile – and <u>Infra dig</u>[3] <u>guoad me</u> mode of proceeding – Sir Liar may – well enough, and take no notice – as long as Mr Ironside keeps firing Popguns at him of all the abusive letters people write to <u>me</u> about him – under similar circumstances I should do the same – and thank Satan, that no one had yet found – the uncharmed bullet – that could hit me in fact as I told you Mr Ironside for all the good such childs play will effect he might as well amuse himself throwing chaff into the sea – How right I was in seeing from the first – that there <u>was</u> nothing but despair for me, but I hope God has at last transmuted it into resignation. – At first I had a vague idea of Mr Ironsides infallibility – but the opium – chimera – and the headlong onslaught! on the strength of it, has quite dispelled <u>that</u> – and I do think he is quite too fond of rushing into print with every word that is said, – or written to him. I had a letter from the secretary of the Sheffield Committee of Inquiry this morning requesting more details of the Lyndhurst affair! as I wrote him word – I am really too ill to recapitulate them and referred – him to Mr Ironside who knows them all – or at least has been told them 20 times over – oh! <u>how</u> weary unto death I am of all this! – I have asked Mrs Boate the name of the man who set her at Sir Liar – which of course she <u>wont</u> give up. I must tell you as a matter of <u>secret</u> history – so pray <u>dont</u> telegraph it to Sheffield or any where <u>else</u> that old Mansfield brought Mrs

Clarke[4] home some plain work[5] – this morning – and came up to see me – her sibylline leaves[6] were that the <u>Loath</u>some – would very soon meet with a <u>fatal</u> accident, which would oblige me to remove from this; and that after <u>his</u> removal all would go well with me – and that at this juncture he was much worried by letters and the discovery of secret things. – <u>nous verrons</u>![7] I made too free yesterday – though neither with opium! nor brandy! and am again worse to day Darlings continues better – and sends hims love Ever affectly yrs Rosina Bulwer Lytton

---

HALS

1. The Irish author and songwriter. See RBL, 20 May 1854.
2. Charlotte Brontë was not an admirer of EBL's novels. See Introduction, n. 42.
3. An abbreviation of *infra dignitatem* (Latin), below (one's) dignity.
4. Charlotte Clarke was the proprietor of the Giles Castle Hotel, Taunton, where RBL is staying.
5. Plain needlework, used for purely utilitarian purposes.
6. In Greek mythology, the Cumaean Sibyl wrote her enigmatic prophecies on leaves, left at the mouth of her cave, and scattered by winds if no one came to collect them.
7. We will see (French).

To Rebecca Ryves

Tuesday last day of June 1857

My dearest Rebecca I am shocked! and grieved more than I can express, about poor George Willoughby![1] – poor Mrs Willoughby![2] God help her, and yet happy Mrs Willoughby! for I would rather have her one noble dead son – than a hundred living cravens – such as Sir Edward Bulwer Lyttons son I still try to hope – that by some miracle poor George may have escaped – and live to reap the reward of his heroism – do Fanny and Augusta know it yet? I believe they never see The Times. – Thank you for all your kind and affect letters – it seems ungracious not to be cheered by them – and yet I can only feel grateful for them, Galvanism you know can make a dead animal walk – but it cannot make it live – kindness may, and does cheer – but it cannot cure: I must screw my courage up to writing to dear little Mrs Tyler a congratulatory letter upon Emily's marriage – and yet to me congratulating any one on such a catastrophe is very like the <u>mauvaise plaisanterie</u>[3] of wishing a person joy upon them going to be hanged! however I sincerely hope poor child that all the happiness I missed she may find. I am glad Mr Eyre Lloyd[4] has corroborated what I have so often told you about the Loathsomes barefaced, and colossal plagiarisms from the French and German <u>contemporary</u> Literature – thefts which none – but such an ignorant press-ridden servile brute as the British Public would have tolerated for one moment. The precious <u>Morceaux</u>[5] I enclose – I cut from a Bath Paper last night – you can send them on to Sheffield, they did not, of course occur in the same order that I have pasted them – no one better calculated to <u>extinguish</u> a flame I should say than Sir Liar – and so much better is it (begging St Paul's[6] pardon) to <u>burn </u>than marry! that I deeply regret "The <u>Honorable</u>!! Bart" was not burnt to a cinder before he married I send you Mrs Wades letter about Thackeray's ill usage of <u>his</u> slave of the ring[7] – truly except at the old Bailey[8] or a state Ball – it is impossible to meet with such utterly infamous characters any where as in "The Literary World"! But it is the Augustan age[9] forsooth! and in one respect it certainly is, as far as complex, and unbridled infamy goes save that we may boast five hundred Fulvias,[10] without even one Octavia,[11] - Did you hear anything of this conflagration chivalry! of Sir Liars - ? it was last Wednesday week it was said to have happened ...

HALS

Incomplete letter.

1. George Willoughby was a British soldier, who was killed in action in Delhi on 11 May 1857, during the Indian Mutiny. See RBL, 1 July 1857.
2. The mother of George. See above, n. 1.
3. Bad joke (French).
4. Eyre Lloyd is from Prospect Castle Connell, Limerick in Ireland.
5. Gift (French).
6. St Paul said on the subject of women: 'But if they cannot contain, let them marry, for it is better to marry than to burn', 1 Corinthians 7:9.
7. William Thackeray placed his wife Isabella in a private asylum. See RBL, 17 June 1857.
8. The Old Bailey is a central criminal courthouse in London.
9. Fulvia (77–40 BC) was a Roman woman who had no interest in the traditional female role and is remembered for her political ambition and influence.
10. Octavia Thurina Minor (69–11 BC), also known as Octavia the Younger or simply Octavia, was the sister of the first Roman Emperor, Augustus (63 BC–AD 14), and fourth wife of the Roman politician and general Mark Antony (83–30 BC). She was renowned for maintaining traditional Roman feminine virtues.

To Rebecca Ryves

Wednesday July 1st 1857

My dearest Rebecca I have just had a letter from Jenkins,[1] in which she says – that every thing as yet remains in doubt as to poor George Willoughby's[2] fate, so that I cannot but still hope – that the poor boy is only smothered under his Laurels, and may yet live to wear them. As it is only a sister in Law! and all the "in Laws" are ones natural Enemies – I may tell you that Jenkins says your sister in law[3] is very much disliked in India. I have written to poor dear Mrs Tyler to congratulate her on the execution[4] tomorrow – I am grieved, and yet glad of what you tell me about poor Emily's neck – as it will save them the <u>embarrass</u>[5] of telling Dent "the secrets of the Rison house"[6] and yet it would have been shocking had he ignored them. – This being midsummer – to add to my comforts, which are already so great! the bills showering in <u>Dun</u> form – "To Bill delivered at Xmas!" God help me with <u>no</u> earthly <u>certainty</u> but that of <u>ruin</u>! to meet all this – and as an aggravation of my misery – I fear a popular fallacy prevails here – that my affairs are settled! or likely to be so! – from the innumerable delicate attentions I receive bouquets of Hothouse flowers – and fruit:- in France – I should receive them as mere courteous, and kindly evidences – of human sympathy, and unmotivated kindness – but here! – no, no – I know my Rule Britannia[7] too well for all <u>that</u>:- Old Mrs Stephen of the nursery garden, has just sent me an immense venison dish full of such enormous! Strawberries literally as big – as Eggs, – now I wish that you, and Isaac were here to eat them, or that I could send them to London or Sheffield, in any way that they could arrive in their present state of freshness, and beauty – as I should like even in imagination to see Jessie[8] & co "wacking into them" as the school boys say – though Mr Doatskin does dem every justice but is very angry dat him has no cream with them. – Poor dear Mr Ironside now finds that the Glasgow Editor will not print the Burns correspondence,[9] and so he will go on finding – that people will <u>not</u> do – any of the things which he makes <u>so sure</u> beforehand, that they will, and must do; otherwise it would be very easy with a dear head, and a sound heart to foil Knaves who had neither. Because I tell him it is dangerous for human beings to sleep <u>al fresco</u>[10] in this climate; he answers with where do the birds sleep? it is all these jumping to illogical conclusions that makes me despair of his doing any thing with Sir Liar. The birds are Emphatically called the birds <u>of the air</u> the beasts of the field – find a natural and congenial dormitory <u>in the fields</u>, – but the beasts of civilization – the human race require the artificial shelter of civilization. Your hieroglyphics under the seal were all torn, from the Envelope being too small for your letter, – so <u>make me sensible</u> in your next – what it was about? Ever affectly yours Rosina Bulwer Lytton.

HALS
1. Mrs Augusta Jenkins. See RBL, 29 December 1853.
2. Lieutenant George Dobson Willoughby, Bengal Artillery, was in command. He heroically defended his post, blowing up the magazine in Delhi on 11 May 1857 to prevent it being taken over by the mutineers and rebels. He was burnt and wounded when he fell into the hands of the insurgents. See RBL, 2 November 1857.
3. Louisa Anne, wife of William Ryves, Rebecca Ryves's younger brother.
4. RBL's way of referring to a wedding. See RBL, 1 September 1853.
5. Abbreviation of 'embarrassment'.
6. Unidentified.
7. A patriotic British song, deriving from the poem 'Rule, Britannia' by James Thomson, and set to music by Thomas Arne in 1740.
8. This may be Mr Ironside's wife since his daughters are called Fanny, Kate, Lilian and Una. See RBL, 0D39II and 13 July 1857.

9.   This is the correspondence between Major General T. Perronet Thompson, who cast
      doubt on RBL's version of events, and J. W. Burns, a member of the Sheffield Foreign
      Affairs Committee, who supported them. See RBL, 3 August 1857.
10.   In the fresh air (Italian).

To Rebecca Ryves

Friday July 3d 1857

My dearest Rebecca

I have had such a perfect Post Office of letters – to answer to day – that I am
nearly worn out and can only send you Mr Ironsides of which I cannot make
head or tail any more than of Mr Neills hieroglyphics, of which even <u>one</u> letter
I cannot decipher; – not being naturally brilliant, and from long and intense
suffering of mind, and body having become still more stupid the fact is I cannot understand Mr Ironsides Electric Telegraph breveties – but I am very sure
Bulls successor would not give up his interest in "Cheveley" at however low a
rate Mr Ironside and Mr Neill may rate it and sue for £5 or for anything like
£5! – Charles Surface[1] at the Sale of the Family Pictures was shocked at that
of "My Aunt Deborah[2] – a woman that set such a value! on herself going for
only five pounds!" and perhaps – I equally over rate myself – but so it is. – I am
now trying to look on, at this protracted game of Forfeit, for which my miserable existence is the stake – as an indifferent spectator. There is a new Piece at
the Haymarket,[3] in which Buckstone[4] personates a returned Husband, and is
described by the Theatrical Critic as presenting a strange compound of "injured
dignity and utter disreputability"! which I take it must be an exact Photograph
of Sir Liars appearance at the present crisis – Still I congratulate him upon my
champions(?) invariably pioneering away every obstacle for him; that he might
otherwise find insurmountable. I have had such a kind letter from a Mrs Jermyn
of Liverpool,[5] which I will send you as soon as I get it back from Sheffield inclosing the £5 for one copy of "Very Successful" and 6 more appeals.[6] I of course sent
her 3 copies of "Very Successful" which is the least I could do – but still feel more
grateful to her for the generous and womanly sympathy of her letter. – I long to
hear how the Execution went off yesterday – I'm sure my Carry cut them all out
including the Bride pretty as she is, and lovely Alice to boot. My best love and
wishes to them all. I must now send for some ice for my head for I can bear the
pain no longer Ever affectly yrs

Rosina Bulwer Lytton

Remember that <u>next Friday</u> the 10th Instant, is the day that my disgraceful Parish
Allowance is to be paid – and every thing on earth to insult, and annoy me – Mr
Hodgson "<u>waiting</u> on Mr Loaden"!! instead of <u>making</u> the wretches send the

Cheque to him – and Mr Ironsides Compliments! and Civilities on the other hand – well really if between them all I cut my throat no one can be surprised and in his delight! I hope Sir Liar will evince his gratitude to them all

Not a line from Mrs Boate! though I promised her another subscriber and from all General Thompson[7] hears!! nothing further can be done in the matter of course not!

HUNT

1. A character in R. B. Sheridan's play *The School for Scandal* (written and first performed in 1777), who auctions the family portraits in act IV, scene i.
2. 'Ah! poor Deborah! a woman who set such a value on herself! – [*Aloud.*] Five pounds ten – she's mine', Sheridan, *School for Scandal*, IV.i.18. This concerns the purchase of a portrait.
3. This may be Tom Taylor's *Victims: An Original Comedy in Three Acts*, performed on 8 July 1857 at the Theatre Royal, Haymarket in London under Buckstone's management.
4. John Baldwin Buckstone (1802–79) was an actor-manager.
5. RBL never met Mrs Jermyn (d. 1859), who was one of her most devoted supporters, donating money to her cause.
6. RBL requests subscriptions of £1 11s 6d in her 'Appeal' pamphlet.
7. Major General T. Perronet Thompson. See RBL, 23 June 1857.

To Rebecca Ryves

Tuesday July 6th 1857

Thanks My dearest Rebecca for your kind letter, God knows – I need kindness from some quarter, for I feel so bruised and lacerated body and soul – that I am one great wound – and the crowning torture of my despair is to remember – that even the solitary confinement – discomfort, and deprivation of every kind, that I was chafing under, – I am indebted to poor Mrs Clarkes charity – and forbearance for which charity, and forbearance like all earthly things – save my misery and outrages must have their limits – and then – and then – what am I to do? – So physically weak as I am that I lie for hours – in torture upon one side, because I literally have not strength to turn in bed; – and oh! those fearful Gethsemene Nights![1] when my agony is so great:- that I am surprised at not seeing the drops of blood fall from me. – "The Lord is a very present help in time of need"[2] – but He will not – help me – even so, – His will be done; – but it is harder to endure His will passively when he "writes such bitter things"[3] against us – than to do it actively in a healthy, – however arduous circle – of human duties; – but to have no part allotted one in the Drama of life but – hopeless, – helpless – heavy hot endurance – would wear down to stagnation the most vivid fervent spirit – that ever Emanated from God and sought to return to Him, – It is very kind of you to bear with my moaning if you were a man – without any reference to the cause

– you – would read the abstract moral Homilies denouncing the effect:- if one lazily fell asleep at ones post, -a sharp kick – to give one an impetus back into the fray may be a very salutary proceeding – but when a poor wretch has single handed defended the pass against legions – for so fabulously lengthened a period – and falls at last pierced with ten thousand wounds, and exhausted with loss of blood – there is no use in trying to bully them back into the battle, which is the course men invariably adopt. As you may suppose – it is neither the unfeeling conduct of, or my debt to, Mr Wheeler the millionaire that is felling me to the Earth – but the feeling that all the poor people who have been so kind, and for-bearing to me – are likely (as people generally do in this world) to suffer for their kindness – Then to go from great things to small the Endless correspondence that Pamphlet has entailed upon me – perfectly ruins me in postage stamps – for once beggary has set in every atom that falls upon it is added ruin. Last Friday – [I wrote of course immediately] to that kind Mrs Jermyn[4] – acknowledging the half of the £5 note – but have never heard from her since – so Heaven only knows if she ever got my letter; for every thing is confusion – disorder – and suspense in this place.

Another thing strikes me perhaps this <u>warning</u>!? of Mrs Boates may be the last order from Park Lane[5] – the result of <u>her letter</u> being sent to him for there is wheel, within wheel in this too infamous Press Gang.

HALS
1. RBL is comparing her sufferings to the Passion of Christ, while he was in the Garden of Gethsemene in Jerusalem (Luke 22:44). His sweat was compared to drops of blood.
2. This may be part of a prayer or sermon based on 'God is our refuge and strength, a very present help in trouble', Psalm 46:1.
3. The original quotation is 'For you write down bitter things against me', Job 13:26.
4. See RBL, 3 July 1857.
5. EBL lives at 1 Park Lane, London.

To Rebecca Ryves

Wednesday July 8th 1857

From the other side of The Bed which is a relief.

Thanks my dearest Rebecca for your kind Sibylline leaves[1] – from which I am glad to learn – that you have been to "The <u>Uproar</u>" and I am sorry I did not know you when I had a Box there, or you should have gone every night. I am indeed grieved to convert you into such a <u>souffre douleur</u>[2] by inflicting all my still beginning, never ending miseries upon you – but when one has a Niagara of wretchedness like its prototype down it dashes no matter on whom or what – I send you our dear Isaacs despatch of this morning and am only too glad – and too grateful to him to answer all my letters – à la[3] Wheeler – for getting one of that description is like shooting one through the head – I am so stunned – I know not what to say or do. – but as I have told Mr Ironside he will get nothing out of – or do any thing with Lady Cullum[4] who is a **FOOL** a brute, and a snake, and that ugly Impropriety her step daughter Mrs Milner Gibson[5] is one of Sir Liars —s – and of <u>course</u> tools – Lady Cullums address is "Hardwicke House Bury St Edmonds Suffolk"[6] I have also told Mr Ironside that I believe Parkinson Sir Thomas Cullums solicitor has, or <u>had</u> the duplicate original Parchment Deed[7] – though on second thoughts (which did not strike me when I wrote to Mr Ironside this morning –) Sir Liar – would have been sure to have pounced upon it at Sir <u>T</u> Cullums death, – though Mr Hyde had he any real care for my interest <u>ought</u> to have seized that opportunity of obtaining it; – or at all events, when Lady Cullum refused to act; – asking what had become of it? and insisting upon its being given up to <u>him</u> as my solicitor, whereas depend upon it, Sir Liar got it through his infamous She (and <u>he</u> for Milner Gibson is a most contemptible wretch) Milner Gibson tools – Mr Ironside will find the conspiracy <u>so</u> complex and <u>complete</u> that exposure is the only sword that <u>can</u> cut this Gordian knot (which to <u>untie</u> is <u>impossible</u>) and the sooner he sharpens and <u>uses</u> that Sheffield blade the <u>better</u>. No answer from Bull yet, who of course <u>wont</u> write till he receives his orders from the old Ruffian in Park Lane – but as you truly say the Publisher – or person negotiating the cheap Edition was the person to apply to him not me. – Such a kind letter as I have had from that Mrs Jermyn this morning with the other half of the note I told Mr I to send it to you – I only wish the indignation of the "military gentlemen" she mentions, would show itself by going <u>en masse</u>[8] to kick the old Park Lane satyr. I keep a book in which I every day put down the number of stamps I send to Sheffield – for the appeal as I receive them – and on referring to it I find that this <u>Benetts</u>[9] letter (that Mrs Boate affects to warn me against) was dated "Saxmundham Suffolk"[10] and I remember thinking at the time "Has Arethusa Milner Gibson anything to do with this?" But if Mr Ironside ...

HALS

Incomplete letter.

1. Prophetic letter. See RBL 29 June 1857.
2. Scapegoat (French).
3. In the manner of (French).
4. Lady Cullum was originally Miss Flood of Kingstown, County Dublin, becoming in 1832 the second wife of Revd Sir Thomas Gery Cullum, eighth Baronet (1777–1855), who was one of RBL's trustees for her deed of separation, dated 19 April 1836.
5. Arethusa Milner Gibson (see RBL, 1 January 1837) was married to a leading politician. Her salon was a great Liberal centre.
6. Lady Cullum's husband had embarked on a costly rebuilding project in the 1820s to improve the house.

7. The deed of separation dated 19 April 1836.
8. In one group (French).
9. RBL suspects this unknown person to be another of EBL's spies. See RBL, 0D421RR21.
10. A market town in Suffolk.

To Rebecca Ryves

Thursday July 9th 1857

My dearest Rebecca No letter from you to day at least by this mornings Post – I send you the Sheffield despatch – Alas! it is poor Mr Ironsides terrible sanguineness – that puts me in utter despair! Milner Gibson![1] a nice Hornets nest he would have got me into! the more I think of it and what else <u>can I think of</u>? the more I am convinced – that the only dignified – and <u>effectual</u> course for him to have taken both as regards himself, – and me; – would have been a <u>straightforward</u> and <u>point blank one</u>, – that is, for him to have written <u>sternly</u> to the monster, saying that <u>I</u> had appointed him my Trustee, – and as such, he demanded a sight of the <u>original Deed of Separation</u>? – as nothing short of <u>ocular</u> demonstration would make him <u>believe</u> that it was so ubiquitously one sided, – and unjustly oppressive as he had been told: – <u>this</u> would have effectually frightened – the ruffian and brought things to a <u>real crisis</u> of public arbitration, but all these little tortuous Impotent nibbles, – only serve to put the brute effectually on his guard, – and enable [him] to spring fresh mines under me at every turn like setting <u>me</u> to write to Bull!! who of course is consulting with the Park lane puff-adder; – and only fancy – the roars of laughter there would have been at the Amateur Brothel in Witton Place![2] if he had written to Milner Gibson! and how Sir Liar would have rubbed his skinny hands and chuckled – as well he may – and more creep mouse work with Mr Wheeler!! – will only rivet my chains – by <u>tangling</u> them more! – instead of attacking the cowardly brute <u>direct</u> and leaving him no loophole for evasion, – God help me! – God help me! – Then poor wretched Walter Weldon[3] ought to be delighted his Dial humbug – failed, though <u>he</u> dont see it! of <u>course</u> he dont! poor wretch, when his existence, and that of his family depended on its success, – I suppose <u>I</u> ought to be equally delighted ...

... not a word from that fellow Bull perhaps his orders are to treat me with contempt also as that – achieves the injury of preventing the reissue of my Book garnished with an insult beside – but perhaps Mr Ironside could <u>get at</u> Sir Liar through Forster!!!!!!![4]

HALS

The end of the letter is missing.

1. The Liberal politician. See RBL, 11 August 1857.

2.   This may be Wilton Place in south-west London.
3.   Walter Weldon was a journalist.
4.   John Forster. See RBL, 17 September 1839.

To Rebecca Ryves

Friday July 10th 1857

A thousand thanks My dearest Rebecca for your kind letters which are the only
rays of sunshine I get and Even graves, are all the better – for a little sunshine, as
we may see by that really lovely Cemetery here – where I so long and soon hope
to be – for
"Life is the Jordan[1] that divides
The spirit from its heavenly home;
And griefs they say – are angel guides
To worlds where sorrows never come
Bodies our weight, and hindrance seem;
Oh! for the hour to burst the clod!
Lay down the burthen; cross the stream
And be for ever with ones God!" –
Though I recapitulated in my letter to day to Mr Ironside all I said to you
yesterday – yet I hope – you took the initiative, and told it to him as he seems
to think all that comes from you oracular, – whereas whatever I say – he cav-
ils at and overwhelms me with sophistry – which wearies me in my present
deplorably weak state – I send you his <u>very</u> kind letter of this morning, – his
proffered hospitality – is like himself generous – and cordial, – but alas! always
– <u>always</u> – in the <u>vague</u>! while I am mutilated under the heavy clubs of realities so sharp – and stunning that they leave me powerless – yet now he talks!
poor man – one would think I had a pair of Eagles wings – to my shoulders,
and had only to open the window – and fly off to Sheffield – or elsewhere
with <u>only</u> my wings <u>leaving</u> my bill! behind me. – and even if poor Mrs Clarke
would let me do – this? – which perhaps <u>she</u> might? – what about all – these
"<u>little</u> accounts" which have now swelled into great ones? for what one cannot
pay in 3 months, – is sure to increase out of all proportion in nine! look at the
warehouse of chairs, – tables and wardrobes I am obliged to <u>hire</u>, – which it
would be far cheaper to buy had I the money; so that I owe Dinah alone, £10
where in the name of common sense – could Hope! find room to drop her
anchor, under all these shoals – of blue ruled unpaid paper? I believe I have
some of Thomases[2] letters in this house, but I might as well – have them in
New Zealand – Oh! the delights of being – so helplessly ill, without a maid –
or a human being to do anything for one; – yesterday all day, – and all night, I

was suffering so <u>dreadfully</u> – from excruciating cramp in my stomach && that I began to think Miss Madeleine Smith[3] had been paying me a visit – though I suppose it was only this cold damp weather – that caused this terrible attack – however of all nights in the year – Anne[4] in her usual disorderly way carried off the matches – so as you may suppose having fainted from getting out of bed and groping about in the dark I have got a fresh cold – but if all this <u>dont</u> kill me I am immortal!

Poor dear Mr Ironside! nothing will – open his Eyes or dampen that sanguine spirit of his as I told him – if anyone could thus pull the strings of <u>other people's volition</u>! wisdom would be at a discount, for every fool might play the game of Life, and win the stakes of Fortune. – I <u>have</u> pressed Mrs Boate only <u>4</u> times to give me the <u>name</u> of the mythological Peer – whom <u>she says</u> set her on at Sir Liar? – she <u>wont</u> answer, and I of course <u>cant force her</u>; – neither will that fellow Bull, – (<u>till at all events some fresh springe is baited</u>) neither will the Glasgow Papers insert, the Boyd correspondence, neither will General Thompson press my petition in the Commons neither will Mr Wheeler <u>do</u> anything but pounce upon the whole of my Parish allowance to pay himself – neither will the Trades people here without any definite period for payment, or <u>satisfactory</u> explanation – do anything but end by insulting – as well as tormenting me. – <u>without</u> all these "<u>neithers</u>" it would be plain sailing; and I should soon be out of troubled waters, – all you say about Mr Hyde, and the United Service Gazette[5] with many other things, has long struck me – more especially his backwardness in the Lyndhurst Affair – evident bowing down to the Lord! and jobbing me off with the chaff, and moonshine, of having interested the Post Office Officials in my behalf – But I have now explicitly told Mr Ironside – his <u>only</u> course; & if he wont pursue it; – I must only submit to my fate; – and finally perish on the rock, where so long I have lingered piecemeal, – and where the Song of the Siren[6] has but sounded like a bitter mockery above the howling of the storm; but it is too hard to pester you so eternally with all this; but as you plunged into "The Cruelty to animals act"[7] you must take the consequences. Massy is a good young man for understanding my wit about the Bugles – and tell him "The horn (whatever I wont say <u>where</u> ever that is?) of the righteous shall be exalted" I am glad it made <u>you</u> laugh as according to Cardinal de Rety "qui fait rire l'esprit, est maître du Coeur."[8] – of <u>course</u> I saw Corporal Humbugs Puff, – and of course <u>you</u> saw it contradicted; "By a relation?" I suppose Ben Willoughby; or Augusta;[9] – as it was not Sir Charles Napier[10] that got George and Edward,[11] their cadetships but an East India Director;[12] but no doubt Stocqueler[13] – thought "he'd been <u>and done it</u>" and as poor Mrs Willoughby is Jack Braggs own sister – I've no doubt she'll back this "<u>Art-Treasure</u>"! as an <u>original</u> <u>Carlo Dolce</u>![14] The 6 O'clock post in

<u>no</u> <u>answer</u> from Bull, till he has got the Fiends instructions how to gore me. – God Bless you – Ever affectly yrs Rosina Bulwer Lytton. –

HUNT
1. The River Jordan divides Jordan from Palestine.
2. William Thomas was the proprietor of the *Court Journal*, which published the libel against RBL on 19 October 1839.
3. Madeleine Hamilton Smith, the twenty-one-year-old daughter of a Glasgow architect, was tried for poisoning Pierre Emile L'Angelier, a poor Jerseyman of French extraction, in the summer of 1857.
4. Servant at the Giles Castle Hotel, Taunton.
5. The *United Service Gazette* was founded in 1833 as the first paper to advocate army and naval reform. J. H. Stocqueler had been one of the editors. See below, n. 13.
6. In Homer's *Odyssey*, the Sirens sing a song that is so irresistible it lures sailors to steer their boats onto the rocks.
7. The Cruelty to Animals Act was passed in 1835.
8. Cardinal of Bernis: 'Whatever amuses the spirit, dominates the heart' (French).
9. Augusta Boys.
10. General Sir Charles James Napier (1782–1853) was a British general and Commander-in-Chief in India.
11. George and Edward Willougby. See RBL, 18 September 1857.
12. A director of the British East India Company. See RBL, 8 November 1856.
13. Joachim Heyward Siddons Stocqueler (1801–86) was a journalist, government employee, entrepreneur and inventor. See RBL, 0D421RR21. He had also been editor of the *United Services Gazette*. See above, n. 5.
14. Carlo Dolce (1616–86) was an Italian painter, born in Florence, who painted religious subjects very delicately and laboriously.

To Rebecca Ryves

July 10 1857

LE CHAR L'ATTEND.[1] – Decimals. – Our swan is not a crow. See how proudly he rears his snow-white crest, distends his beautiful silvery wings, and spurns the wave, as he majestically strides forwards. – CYGNE[2] [newspaper cutting, top of first sheet]

I cant help having a suspicion that the above – which I have just cut out of "The Times" is a signal from some of Sir Liars myrmidons.[3] – Le Char L'attend – is a very good pun, and equivoque[4] on Le Charlatan[5] which <u>he</u> is – the "<u>decimals</u>" I take it alludes to day the 10th when my Parish allowance is due – and the meeting of poor noodle Hodgson (and perhaps Mr Wheeler retained on the <u>other</u> side) and the villain Loaden the signature of "Cygne" or swan – is doubtless to imply that all my geese are swans vide my friend Mr Wheeler I have just read with great disgust the acquittal of Miss Laffarge[6] Madeleine Smith[7] – and think by its flimsy sophistry and grandiloquent tinsel perorations – it must have been written by the Lord Rector of Glasgow[8] particularly that exquisite piece of Logic! – that her letters to the last breathing such devoted love for L'Angelier![9] she could have had no <u>motive</u>!!!! for poisoning him – ! forgetting the stubborn little fact of her having jilted him – and her Engagement to the other man[10] – she is now quite fit to become a great Literary character though her letters (beyond their profligacy) show anything but intellect; – mark my words – she will yet figure in another Dock for murder – for it is a well known fact in the statistics of crime – that Poisoners – <u>never</u> stop at their <u>Coup d'Essai</u>.[11] –

I hope you saw <u>me</u> stuck under Disraeli![12] in to days Times? the first time my appeal has been properly printed – I would rather they had put me <u>over</u> the devil and all his works higher up

Shall lose the Post

I. A. V. Rosina

HALS

1. The chariot awaits (French).
2. Swan (French).
3. Minions, who in Homer's *Iliad*, are the soldiers commanded by Achilles. In Ovid's *Metamorphoses*, the Myrmidons are worker ants on the island of Aegina.
4. Pun (French). This is a pun on the pronunciation of *Le char l'attend*. See above, n. 1.
5. The charlatan (French).
6. Marie-Fortunée Lafarge (*née* Capelle) (1816–52) was a Frenchwoman, who was convicted of murdering her husband by arsenic poisoning in 1840.
7. The acquittal of Madeleine Smith was upon an indictment in three counts: two for attempts to poison her lover, and a third for poisoning him. The jury acquitted her on the first count, and brought in a verdict of 'Not Proven' on the second and third.
8. EBL was the Lord Rector of Glasgow University between 1856 and 1859. Madeleine Smith was a native of Glasgow.
9. Pierre Emile L'Angelier was a poor Jerseyman of French extraction, who was the lover of Madeleine Smith. When he died in the summer of 1857, she was accused of poisoning him.
10. L'Angelier had expected to marry Smith, but she left him for William Minnoch, who was a more suitable match, in spite of being twenty years older.
11. First attempt (French).
12. Benjamin Disraeli.

To Rebecca Ryves

Remember that yesterday Friday July 10th was only the second time my "appeal" has appeared in "The Times" and the first time it was properly, that is <u>visibly</u> printed. [on envelope]

To Rebecca Ryves

Monday – July 13th 1857 2P.M.

My dearest Rebecca Mr Hydes letter to Mr Ironside – which I herewith send you is really my death warrant, and I have neither heart – nor strength to write – nothing can it is true equal Mr Ironsides generous kindness – but still we must come down to stubborn realities! and vulgar detail Putting Mrs Clarke and Day[1] – (who I suppose might be got – because they can afford – to wait) out of the question – and <u>supposing</u> that I had the strength to pack up the perfect warehouse of things – with which I am encumbered, and which I cannot afford to give away – and would get <u>nothing</u> for if I sold – and <u>want</u> wherever I may be – it would take me at least £60 of ready money to get with any credit out of this place – and since the poor creditors would have no chance of redress in the (now every day more probable) event of my death, suppose – I <u>could</u> make up my mind to go and live on Mr Ironside – does he think that I would – or could "with malice aforethought" go and swindle people who have shown me such kindness confidence, and forbearance? no – no – it is <u>bad</u> and bitter and murderous enough to be a compulsory swindler – but I never will be a voluntary one. – Nothing human could extricate me from this engulfing Slough of Despond[2] but a legacy of a couple of thousand pounds – which would give me breathing time to fight, and expose the monster thoroughly – but as no such God send is ever likely to fall to my share – I have now nothing for it but to die on the rack. – I.I. sent me a little golden lock of Jessies hair this morning I'll put it into my big golden heart with poor Emily's[3] – and Taffy's.– Under the exhilarating idea – that I am dying – the park Lane Satyr – allowed Bull[4] to write at last, so I got his hellow yesterday saying that he would give up the remainder of the Copyright for £20 – paid down – dont you wish he may get it? what poor dear kind sanguine Mr Ironside will not see is – what use is all the <u>right</u> in the world against the might of <u>money</u>? – except to sink one more, by making ones Enemies and aggressors more implacable, and inveterate, as it has always done more. I am so tired, I'll wait till the 6 o'clock post comes in, – you are to return the Deed, and Hydes letter to Mr Ironside. – 4 o'clock – I am in such a state of utter misery and perturbation – that I cannot wait for the second post – now what I mean is, that supposing I <u>could</u> order my wings, and fly off to Sheffield Mrs Ironside may be – and I am sure <u>is</u> – one of the kindest and best women in the world, in short worthy of her husband – but what right have I to come, and put her out of <u>her</u> ways? – and I am too old, and far too broken in health and spirit, to be put out of mine, – and as I now am, I <u>could</u> only be a nuisance – in any house less than Chatsworth,[5] – or Milton[6] where every one can do as they like: – <u>nothing</u> but perfect independence of circumstances <u>could</u> give me any ease of mind, <u>then</u> indeed, – it would be very easy, with all the appliances and means to boot, – to return to the habits of a gentlewoman rise at a reasonable hour and go to bed at ditto, – but having so long been and still being obliged to be – not only my own, maid of all work but my own Pack – horse, slaving early and late – that <u>so</u> <u>great</u> is the <u>one</u> redeeming point of being able in <u>perfect</u> liberty to work when, and how I can – without putting <u>any one</u> out of their way – or being put out of mine – that never would a single murmur escape my lips – at my condemned criminal solitary confinement had I <u>only</u> the means of continuing in it – I have suffered <u>so</u> much in other peoples – houses that I would rather go to the stake at once – than again lay myself under an obligation for what is for me the worst sort of martyrdom – and Even had I Williams here she is no packer like Byrne so that I should still have more trouble than I am equal to, though she would be invaluable to me in preventing the disgraceful rags – I am now in Flannels are as you know indispensable to me, and now – I have <u>literally</u> not a flannel gown, or petticoat, but what is in <u>unmendable</u> rags, they owe me nothing being now 7 years old, and patched over, and over again so that I am obliged to adopt the <u>real</u> Beggar woman fashion of substituting old shawls – and even going into debt – cant get one things in this odious place – a fortnight before you went, I gave 2 caps to Miss Dyke to get washed – and retrimmed – such as Williams used to do me up in 2 hours – I have <u>not</u> got them back yet – and when I do – they will be so vulgarly overladen with ribbon (to swell the bill) that I shall not be able to wear them. – But granting – I had all ready on the wing for Sheffield – the Creditors are still to be consulted; and when once apprised (as in common honesty they must be) of the state of their chances is it likely they would agree to any such arrangement, or rather <u>derangement</u> à propos[7] of Creditors – I dread seeing Augusta – would you kindly ask Mr Ironside to write to that Prig Easton to inquire what on earth he is doing about Clarke – and the 18 Copies of my Book <u>Cooke</u>[8] of London owes me for? – but <u>beg</u> of Mr Ironside to begin his letter to him "Dear Sir" and not "Sir" which always offends those little stuck up provincial nobodies and it is all vented upon poor wretched me. Fancy that ass young Hodgson writing to <u>me</u>! that "according to <u>Sir Edwards wishes</u>!!" he had applied to Mr Loaden for my Parish Allowance – but that <u>he</u> Loaden would not give it without a separate receipt for me- from me – as Sir Liar heard I was very ill! so he (Hodgson) sent me one begging I would sign, and return it immediately – but the very fact of its being "Sir Edwards wish"! was <u>quite</u> Enough – sign it I did'nt – nor answer his letter have'nt but sent both to Mr Ironside – now let them fight it out amongst them. – Of <u>course</u> the scoundrel Loaden's villain Client – will not <u>hear</u> of giving me enough to live on – for independence is safety – and how could – he grind me down as he has for 17 years – but for the maëlstrom of misery – and pecuniary whirlpools into which he has plunged me the Fiend! – Mr Ironside may write him letters filled with the most damning facts and blasting insults he will only snap his fingers at any thing short of public exposure – and even that – I have no doubt in this moral country money and perjury would get him out of with flying colours.

Thank you for your letter just come I am too ill and too hopeless to write more. Ever affectly yrs Rosina Bulwer Lytton

---

HALS

1. The owner of a draper's shop in Taunton.
2. A reference to Bunyan's *Pilgrim's Progress*. See RBL, 6 October 1831.
3. RBL's dead daughter, Emily, had blonde hair.
4. Edward Bull, RBL's publisher.
5. The ancestral mansion of the Duke of Devonshire situated in the Peak District of Derbyshire.
6. This may be Milton Abbey, Dorset, which was built as a mansion house by the Earl of Dorchester in 1771 who, determined not to spoil his view, demolished the neighbouring village and rebuilt it on the other side of a hill.
7. Trouble with regard to (French).
8. Nathaniel Cooke (1810–79) was a publisher at 198 Strand, London; he had been involved in the founding of the *Illustrated London News*.

To Rebecca Ryves

Wednesday 7 P.M. July 15th 1857

My dearest Rebecca I am so dead beat with this infernal letter hunt – which far exceeds any [Freichuts?] that ever was that I can only scrawl you one line – I have not yet come to Thomas's, and Mr Hartcups[1] letters about <u>my</u> consenting to the Divorce but have found that very important one from Melle George of Geneva[2] in 1852 detailing the visit to <u>her</u> and tampering with the people of the Hotel – of a spy calling herself Mme <u>Pianon</u>! and wanting to <u>bribe</u> her (Mlle George) to offer <u>me</u> the bribe of a sum of money – to consent to a divorce – that he Sir Liar might marry <u>her niece</u>!! – now this with some others I have just sent off to Sheffield, now remember the Malvern Trulls[3] name was <u>Pion</u> – but [from] Mlle Georges description of the soi disant[4] Mme <u>Pianon</u>[5] I am certain she is one and the same with old Pyke[6] of Llangollen Miss Pion was <u>not</u> governess in a <u>school</u> at Malvern but to an old maiden Lady of the name of Parsons – to whose niece she was governess. – you say in your letter of the day before yesterday you hope I have got my Parish allowance? – now if I had got it – that is if I had taken it; what earthly plea would Mr Ironside have had for attacking the monster, he is both word – and insult proof – <u>deeds</u> are the things and the only things to crush such a monster – and <u>deeds</u> he shall always have from <u>me</u>- when ever and wherever I am a free agent what a Fool! the brute is with all his cunning and all his villainy – had he been content with Mr Hodgsons receipt – without insisting upon <u>mine</u> – he would never have been caught in his own springe – but it is the retributive arrow of Gods arsenal that such wretches should overshoot their mark, and so be foiled at their own weapons. Dont <u>return</u> me any of the letters I send you – but keep them <u>safely</u> – one I found from poor dear Mrs Hare– of course her noodle was cross with her because <u>he</u> had caught cold! that horrid hemming in his throat that she mentions consoles me about poor Tib – as everyone then thought Mr H would die in six months of it – Pray take special care of that fragmentary gem of Puffery and Bombast of Corporal Humbugs to Mrs Willoughby! – a curiosity of <u>ill</u> – literature I also send you – from my infamous old mother in law. I drank your, and Massy's health, in a goblet of the white [wine] and water yesterday – and found it excellent – not so he or you for sending it – mind that I dont understand the allusion in I.I.'s[7] letter about Mrs Urquharts[8] mistake – and the Mayor of Gateshead[9] being the intermediary that set her right – made me <u>sensible</u>? a nice Herculean task for this hot weather God Bless you, Ever affectly yrs Rosina Bulwer Lytton

---

HALS
1. Mr William Hartcup of Bungay, Suffolk, is Revd Sandby's solicitor, who had been ready to proceed on RBL's behalf against EBL in the ecclesiastical court for his affair at Malvern with Miss Pion (also known as Mrs Lowndes). See below, n. 5.
2. RBL stayed at Mademoiselle George's home at Maison Duval in Geneva.
3. A trull is 'a low prostitute or concubine; a drab, strumpet, trollop' (*OED*).
4. So-called (French).
5. This is Miss Pion, a governess, who was the mistress of EBL. See above, n. 1.
6. Mrs T. Pyke is the mother of Miss Pion. See RBL, 7 September 1853.
7. Isaac Ironside.
8. Harriet was married to David Urquhart.
9. Gateshead is a town in County Durham in north-east England.

To Rebecca Ryves

Tuesday July 21st 1857

My dearest Rebecca I am so "Nobsquizzled" as Sam Slick[1] would say, with constant worry and constant writing that – the chief thing I feel upon the perusal of your letter this morning is a <u>sincere</u> commiseration for you (which said commiseration however, when as a noun substantive it stands alone, unfortunately never does any one, any good) – at the idea of your coming troubles – more especially those of your suddenly being Nephewed, and Nieced! – with squalling children; – I am of course sorry to hear of poor Mrs William Ryve's[2] illness, and all her other troubles – but can only say of her, as I never cease saying of myself – "<u>Sarve</u> her right, for marrying" – and I hope it will be a warning to you, not to go, and do likewise. – Then poor Massy's coats! – I fear he will find childrens – paws – even more detrimental to the gloss – and sheen of broad cloth – than those of

Puppy dogs. I send you poor dear Isaacs letter to Mrs Wheeler – and Lady Cullum – which send back to <u>me</u> as I want to send them to Dr Price – Mr Hydes letter you can return to Sheffield. I have warned I.I.[3] not to rush into the mistake – that Mr Wheelers is a congenial spirit to his! – or even that he has a single pip – of old Phippen[4] in him! <u>il sien faut bien</u>![5] – and therefore in his intercourse with him – to affect the practical rather than the Philanthropic – dwelling more on the <u>hard</u> <u>cash</u> (which is Mr W's:) than on the <u>hard</u> <u>case</u> (which is <u>mine</u>:) in short, I have warned him to keep – <u>more</u> on the <u>sunny side</u> of the <u>Stock Exchange</u> – than on the <u>shady</u> side of <u>Samaria</u>[6] I have also impressed upon him the veto of the <u>only</u> man who ever saw at <u>once</u> the <u>only</u> effectual method of dealing with such a monster as Sir Liar – I allude to Captain Sterlings[7] saying – he ought to be taken by surprise – as such a fellow ought <u>not</u> to be given 5 minutes notice to concoct a fresh plot and organize fresh villainy – had he been let to <u>act</u> by these loathsome fools – as he wanted to do, I should have had a very different Tale to tell now. – Augusta has just sent me Hawthornes (the author of the "Scarlet Letter", and "House of the Seven Gables" "Mosse from an old manse")[8] – in which the following immortal truth occurs at page 212 – speaking of English authors – "Bulwer nauseates me; he is the very pimple on the ages humbug. There is no hope of the public, as long <u>as he</u> retains an admirer, a reader, or a publisher."[9] – I have sent this gem off to Sheffield, hoping the "<u>Chiel</u> will <u>prent</u> it" in this weeks I.F.P.[10] – Addio[11] God bless you – kind regards to the "Fellah" and condolences to his <u>coats</u>; it would be improper to extend them <u>further</u> – Ever affectly yrs

     Rosina Bulwer Lytton

HALS
1. Pen-name of Thomas Chandler Haliburton. See RBL, 25 December 1856.
2. Rebecca Ryves's sister-in-law Louisa Anne is married to her brother William. They had a son, Hugh Massy Ryves, who was born on 20 August 1855 in Gwalior, West Bengal, India.
3. Isaac Ironside.
4. A kindly character in RBL's novel, *Very Successful!* See RBL, 5 May 1857.
5. Somebody's own [*sien*] is really necessary (French).
6. Samaria refers to the mountainous region between Galilee to the north and Judea to the south.
7. From Thomas Carlyle, *The Life of John Sterling*. See RBL, 23 June 1857.
8. The New England author Nathaniel Hawthorne (1804–64), published *Scarlet Letter* (1850) and *The House of the Seven Gables* (1851). See below, n. 9.
9. Correspondence from Hawthorne's *Mosses from an Old Manse* (New York: Putnam, 1851), p. 121. See above, n. 8.
10. The Free Press.
11. Goodbye [*adiós*] (Spanish).

To Rebecca Ryves

Thursday July 30th 1857

My dear Rebecca I am glad you are so far better as not to be worse – pray do not trouble yourself to write me such long letters – or any letters at all – as you are commander in Chief and I am a perfect cipher in my own affairs, – which require all the knowledge and experience I alone can bring to bear on them for God's sake – put <u>your</u> judgement – and Mr Ironsides want of it together, and do what you like, – for I really am past caring what's done – or what happens, but what is the use in my present almost helpless state, of bothering on at me, – to wade through a chaos of papers – when the shortest and easiest plan would be to put Mr Hartcup of Bungay[1] – the Suffolk lawyer – or his affidavit as to my statements – he knowing very well that I have <u>his letters</u> – but the conversation about Miss Parsons[2] denying Sir Liars statement – was not <u>written</u> but took place in Mr Sandbys drawing room. I have this moment received the enclosed boorish, and brutal – and foolish as brutal letter from Mr Ironside – who like all wholesale philanthropists has not a grain I begin to fear of real feeling – however as I told him not having yet mastered the judgement jargon, – having no Parrot wisdom, – and having had my foolish error of supposing I had any right to <u>feel</u> <u>anxious</u>, – and to know <u>all</u> the strong, and weak points of my own affairs better than a perfect stranger – pointed or rather stabbed out to me – I certainly never will from this out – trouble him with another line – and have peremptorily declined to receive any more of his brutal missives; – so now the sooner he goes over to my "gifted Husband" – and exchanges his cold civilities to him for warm ones the better. – Ever affectly yrs Rosina Bulwer Lytton

When poor old Mr Hodgson[3] said to me in giving me Mr Wheelers £1, 000 "But my dear Lady when £400 a year is too little for your station in life which it certainly <u>is</u>; how are you to live on less than half?" By writing hard said I – Of course neither this, nor the manner in which my only means of existence have been Burked is a matter of <u>no</u> importance and of course would have been divined by so clever a man as Mr Ironside! only they were <u>not</u>!

HALS
1.   Bungay is a market town in Suffolk, east England.
2.   See RBL, 15 July 1857.
3.   RBL's lawyer.

To Rebecca Ryves

Friday July 31ˢᵗ 1857

My dearest Rebecca – Pray don't think me ungrateful for all the trouble you and
Mr Ironside so kindly take in my affairs – which to tell you the truth I dont now
care one <u>Damson</u> about – no not if à la Mazeppa[1] I were tied to a wild horse,
and each of my creditors claiming and tearing a separate limb – I have suffered
<u>too</u> much, and <u>too long</u>, – and Mr Ironsides nutmeg grater letters seem to chafe
– and scrape me externally and internally – and always perform the supererogatory work of making me additionally ill for the whole day. – If I still had the least
care – what happened – I might well be alarmed! when I think that in all these
weeks of talk – not a thing has actually been <u>done</u> till at the 11ᵗʰ hour I suggested
and begged it – like the writing to poor Miss Dickenson and Mr Wheeler which
should have been the very first thing – but the chief source – of alarm is – at
Mr Ironsides more than penetration and clear – sightedness! for seeing things
that <u>dont</u> Exist; and his purblindness as to those that do and are glaring as the
sun at noon day – for instance he finds from Mr Weldons last letter that he is so
improved! (by Familiar words and nutmeggrater letters of course) as not only to
be able to stand upon his own legs – but also to be able to carry me!!!!! when it
would be plain to any one reading that letter – that after my having before decidedly negatived the ridiculous proposition from a man who had not the means
of supporting himself without eternally draining me that he was still trying to
<u>exploitée</u>[2] me – to go and live with them!! <u>En attendant;</u>[3] – I wish he had the
grace to acknowledge the Post office order I sent him 3 days ago – but as he is
improving perhaps he dont think that necessary as the paper knife <u>arrived</u> safely
– it was not very gracious of Mr Ironside to tell me it was in two – but these, are
the sort of underbred things – he is always doing that grate upon one so terribly
– when all ones nerves are out of tune, and unstrung as mine are. Pray <u>thank</u> Mr
Eyre Lloyd for his kindness in my behalf, all of which I know I owe to your kind
self – but why my dear Rebecca waste so much kindness, and trouble, on what is
as good as a dead Donkey. – I would not – and could <u>not</u> if I would to become
queen of <u>England</u> – and have the triune[4] fortune of the brothers Rothschild[5]
– copy <u>one line</u> of that infamous letter but if you like – I will send the whole
vipers nest – containing also that of the young viper as they returned from Sheffield – in a registered letter – which will be quite <u>safe</u> – and for Gods sake keep
them, or seal them up and send them to Mr Hyde – but dont return them to
me – for the very name much less the sight of them drives me mad and I want if
my friends will let me – to subside – that I may die quietly. I am again laid up in
bed – with one of my terrible floodings – from this accursed letter hunt, which
I cannot, and will not attempt again – nor is there the least necessity – if what I
now send is not decided slap dash to be of no use, – when if managed as I have

pointed out – it is quite as good as the original letters which I certainly cannot go up to the loft to look for the only remaining trunk of old letters I have – I have found a <u>copy</u> of a letter of mine to Hartcup[6] of the 24th of March 1848 in reply to a very irate one of his at the indignant letter I had written to him on his presuming to send me Beavans[7] infamous proposition of the Divorce now <u>this</u> gives the only due necessary i.E. – that that infamous proposition was made to me through Mr Hartcup on the 5th of January 1848 – and although every one is so clever that they <u>must</u> know my affairs and how to manage them better by intuition! than I can by a life long bitter experience – and I am such a fool that having so much spare time, and superfluous health I am always "scribbling yards of unnecessary letters" – I have with my usual folly – which comes at once to <u>facts</u> – written a copy of the sort of letter that ought to be written to Mr Hartcup – to obtain an attested copy – of this <u>5</u>th of January letter – and of Mrs Parsons to him. The only 3 letters of his I can find to me, and one from him to Mrs Sandby I also send – which will enable who ever writes to say as I have stated

"Lady Lytton having placed your correspondence with her of 1847 – and 1848 in my hands &&&" – I also – send in this packet – a letter of Kate Planchés[8] enclosing the receipts for the advertisements of my poor Child's death, – also my letter to that Infamous <u>Marshall Hall</u>[9] and to the Editor of The Lancet[10] for which mind you they never brought actions of <u>Libel</u>! against me – and of which moreover the Editor of The Lancet told Jones he did not at the least wonder at me as Marshall Hall <u>deserved</u> every syllable of it. – Next, I send a letter of Godfrey Parkers[11] in which he refers to the Firm of Forster and Co solicitors at Norwich[12] – to prove that <u>he</u> is the son of general Bulwers niece[13] – and Sir Liars cousin; – likewise I send a letter of poor kind old Mr Hodgson refusing the first fee I offered him – on receipt of Mr Wheelers £1,000 on the plea that my pecuniary circumstances did not enable me to offer it, which shows that good kind old man did <u>not</u> at the time consider that Mr Wheelers £1,000 in reducing my pittance to £180 a year had set me free! in the world from all pecuniary difficulties!!! – And "last, though certainly <u>not least</u>" – (though of course Mr Ironside – would at once decide it to be perfectly useless, without taking even the time to inquire <u>why</u> I had sent it?) I send you an anonymous letter I received from London – after the Paris Libel[14] the writer (an evident tool of the Bulwers –) affecting to admire the letters I had written to the Times – upon said Libel – and saying I <u>must</u> be mistaken in attributing the letter to any of my Husbands family! Now this letter is of course no use <u>per se</u>[15] <u>as</u> an anonymous letter – but of <u>great use</u> as pointing out the exact date of the libel which I had forgotten – as it appears by it – that my letter on the subject appeared in "The Times" of November the 1st 1839 – with this clue – any news Paper agent can procure – the paper containing it – also the number of the Court Journal[16] containing the Libel – which was probably a week or 10 days prior to my letter about it in The Times. – With regard to Thomases letters (the Proprietor of the Court Journal) to me it is just possible that Mr Hyde may have them, at all events – he has his <u>own</u> and in one of the <u>useless</u> letters I sent to Mr Ironside ...

HALS

Incomplete letter.

1. In the manner of (French); *Mazeppa* (1819) is an epic poem written by Lord Byron, whose hero is a Ukrainian page, who is tied naked to the back of a horse that is set loose.
2. Exploit me (French).
3. In attendance (French).
4. 'Three in one ... of the Godhead' (*OED*).
5. There were five brothers running the Rothschild empire in five European capitals: Amschel Mayer Rothschild (1773–1855), Salomon Mayer Rothschild (1774–1855), Nathan Mayer Rothschild (1777–1836), Calmann Mayer Rothschild (1788–1855) and James Mayer Rothschild (1792–1868).
6. Revd Sandby's solicitor.
7. Mr Beavan is an intermediatory acting for EBL. He was later forced to leave the country because of his involvement in fraudulent proceedings.
8. Katherine Planché was the daughter of the famous playwright J. R. Planché. In 1851, she married William Curteis Whelan (1820–69) of Heronden Hall, Tenterden, Kent. See RBL, [March 1857].
9. Marshall Hall was the physician attending Emily Lytton while she was dying from typhus fever. See RBL, 6 May 1851.
10. Thomas Wakley (1795–1862) was the first editor of *The Lancet*, a weekly radical medical journal, from 1823 to 1862.
11. Godfrey Parker was claiming to be EBL's cousin on his father's side of the family. See RBL, 29 April 1854.
12. A city in East Anglia, 18 km south-east of Heydon Hall, where EBL's father had lived.
13. General William Earle Bulwer (1757–1807) was EBL's father. He had six nieces. Godfrey Parker may have been named after the brother-in-law John Godfrey of 'The General', who had three daughters, Marian Julia, Harriet and Sarah Matilda.
14. This took place in October 1839. See RBL, 30 September 1845.
15. By itself (Latin).
16. For 18 October 1839.

To Rebecca Ryves

[August? 1857]

... and probably never even looked into by him – there is one from Mr Hyde in which he says "Thomas is very angry to think you should suspect him of puffing the Bulwers who had behaved so infamously to him" or words to that effect Mr Hyde also – is the person to give Chapter and verse of the said trial for Libel in London – which I gained costs and damages – Sir Frederick Pollack (the present chief Baron) being my council – prior to the Paris infamy and the news papers containing this Trial (once Mr Hyde gives the date) are easily obtained – Another useless letter that I pestered Mr Ironside with is that highly important one from Mlle George[1] of Geneva – detailing the visit of that infamous old Entremetteuse[2] Pyke – trying to <u>bribe</u> her to bribe me! to acceed to the same <u>honorable</u> terms of a divorce – that Sir Liar might marry her <u>niece</u>! as she said – and Mlle Georges Brother turning her out of the House. Now how it is possible to tell, and explain all these things <u>without</u> writing long letters I really dont know, – with all the orders to use my wits and other civil speeches now really were I in full health, and had not a single care – I should prefer spending my time in solving more interesting enigmas than those Mr I hurls at me like a diurnal box on the ear – of course after the letter I wrote him yesterday at length roused by the reiterated coarse rudeness of a man who has such an overwhelming deference for the superiority of Sir E B Lyttons position to his own! – I will not think it necessary to stir any more in this matter – nor do I want him to do so, – but as nothing shall ever induce me to write to him again I trouble <u>you</u> with all these documents which I should not – had you not so respectfully asked me for them; and it will be useless to echo the Sheffield hiss – and say they are of no use – for they <u>are</u>, but nothing is of use – to people who know better than the whole world – and everything by intuition! would you have the goodness to send me back that Leicester Paper – for not being <u>marked</u> – and I not putting "my wits" to it – which having been so long smothered in a pillow and nearly burnt out with fever I never saw one syllable about that Mrs Wigney[3] to whom Mr I alludes in his letter of to day, Mrs Roberts very kindly sent the £5 yesterday and Mr Easton having paid me for some stray copies of my book – enabled me to send £15 – of the £30 I owe Mr Ironside £10 Wednesday – and £5 yesterday – he sent back the £10 to day – and I have returned it and shall continue to do so till perhaps the notes get lost no earthly power will induce me to lay myself under a pecuniary as well as every other obligation to him like a true Englishman – with one thing or another he has contrived to make me <u>feel</u> the <u>weight</u> of it quite enough. Amen. God Bless you forgive all these "<u>yards</u>" of paper and if I am able to get up on <u>Monday</u> <u>let</u> me <u>know</u> if I shall send you the <u>other</u> letters registered as one cant get them registered on Sunday. Ever affectly yrs Rosina

---

HALS

Incomplete letter.

1.   Miss George had provided RBL with accommodation at the Maison Duval in Geneva.
2.   Go-between (French).
3.   Mrs Ann Wigfield (*c.* 1804). See RBL, 3 August 1857.

To Rebecca Ryves

Sunday August 2nd 1857

I am indeed grieved my dearest Rebecca at your incertitude about Willy[1] but in this Tempest tossed whirlpool called Life – we are continually driven to catch at these Buoys of wisdom Proverbs – to prevent our sinking – and you know the Proverb says "no news is good news" and so let us hope in this case though I know – it is far easier to preach hope than to practise it – and the state India is now in is of course a constant heartbreak to anyone who has friends there – I do indeed feel for his poor wretched wife – but what good can that do here – God help us it seems – to me as if some Fiend was shaking up the very dregs of Hell – and letting them out like a floodgate upon this doomed world – would to God one could without sin get out of it No my dear Rebecca it is not "a little temper" temper has nothing to do with it – it may be madness – and not a little for I am mad – and with good and ample – cause – the bodily pain alone – the fearful nights I have now agonized through for so many months – only again to find myself the butt and target – of another speculative caprice – the animal to be experimented upon – for more ruin! and an insupportable additional load of more suspense and more torture! – Here are the facts – Mr Ironside some months ago writes (most kindly but stringently, and with authority as he does every thing – which at that time inspired me only with the greater confidence and commensurate gratitude) for a schedule of my debts – he then comes to the house apparently perfectly sure of his plan (which pre-supposed that it was matured and organized but not – breathing a syllable of it to me – as appears to be the usual programme – and fatality of all who volunteer – to lift me out of one Abyss – only to hurl me into another, and a worse. – He being a perfect stranger to me – and having done so much in printing that pamphlet, I of course was tied in every way both by the laws of hospitality and the gratitude I owed him – and could not say to him roundly in so many words – "come – now tell me – what is it you mean to do?" because this to a man and to a stranger who had so kindly and authoritatively volunteered to ask for a list of my liabilities – would have been almost tantamount to saying – "Do you mean to pay them? No – Every thing should have come from him – and nothing did come from him – except an order – that I was on no account to write or answer any letter on business – but refer every one to him, which I thought still more kind – and which induced me – to set aside the strange way in which he had contrived to misunderstand me while he was here – and the coarse – and gross insult he thought fit to offer me as soon as he had left the house – and though I was still painfully floating in the Vague with this terrible Chevaux de frise[2] of sharp pencils – under me in Every direction where ever I might chance to fall – still my equally vague – reliance upon him – was so great – that it acted as a sustaining power – till one fine day I was rudely shaken down upon one – of the spikes – Mr Wheeler's kind and considerate <u>chum</u> then I <u>found</u> – that although so much had been <u>talked</u> not a single thing had been <u>done</u>! then came Mr I's first letter to Mr Wheeler – <u>so</u> vague – so wide of all tangibility – so inconsiderately ill-judged – to a <u>hard</u> narrow minded stock jobber – whom he might have judged to be such – from the <u>fact</u> of his cruelty in dunning me at such a crisis – and next to baiting the hook (as he <u>thought</u>) with imaginary virtues for Mr Wheeler – he sets forth rather more Emphatically – than good taste and Christian feeling would warrant – the facts of his not knowing of my existence 3 months before – his not yet knowing the case – and the immense – labour – and devotion it has required for him to wade through the Mass of documents – necessary to master it! – why of <u>course</u> no body could suppose – that undertaking such a case – would be no more trouble than plucking roses – and scattering the leaves and I for one – should have appreciated and magnified his labours more – had he done so less – and let me imagine that it was one of love – and not have accompanied his <u>system</u> of universal philanthropy with so many hard individual lashes, upon poor lacerated me, – next when young Hodgsons letter arrived – <u>I</u> did not even reply to <u>him</u> – but sent it on to Mr I – peremptorily refusing to sign the cheque (as <u>this</u> <u>I</u> <u>alone could do</u>) – and giving that Mr Ironside as his authority to <u>act</u> – it is true, that in my hurry and excitement I <u>did</u> foolishly say "perhaps leaving the money in young Hodgsons – hands – may calm <u>poor</u> Mr Wheeler's mind as to the safety of his interest" – But <u>then</u> <u>I</u> neither know – nor pretend to know anything about money but the want of it, – and surely having undertaken the business – and calling himself a man of business – Mr Ironside – should have done the business part when I entirely washed my hands of it – and said – "no, as you <u>refuse</u> to accept this dole – it should be instantly returned to Loaden – as on reflection – I see it ought to have been! I felt the more sure Ironside would do all <u>that</u> part of the affair systematically – as he is so very minute, about money matters – even telling me a month ago – that only 180 of the 3rd Edition – of the appeal had sold – which as at <u>that</u> time, I was still in his debt for publishing – I think would have been rather better taste – and more delicate not to have gone out of his way to do – when there was no earthly necessity for it. – Next, comes poor Mrs Dickenson like an avalanche upon me – showing more [ill] – and Mr Ironside writing me word – "if it were not for what you are suffering I should like the excitement of all this amazingly" – yes – <u>that's it</u>! But the greatest blow of all was, when at the Eleventh hour – Mr I – first launches a doubt – as to whether he is in a position of life to be authorized to deal with Sir E. Lytton? – and whether <u>he</u> might not lodge a criminal information against him (Mr I) for trying to make him break the peace!! And then every straw you (<u>very kindly</u>) throw out as a suggestion – is seized upon by him – as truly wonderful! and then ensue more <u>letters</u> to tell you so – all of which clearly proves that – (though <u>more</u> than my existence was

depending – on it; when he so vigorously snatched me out of the abyss – (as I
thought) and flung me on the high way – where he has left me) he to this <u>moment</u>
has no more <u>settled</u> – <u>organised or defined plan</u> – of <u>action</u> than the man in the
moon! and – <u>I</u>, who can alone possibly <u>know</u>, – the <u>carte du pays</u>³ to be observed
with the wretches whom <u>he</u> has never seen, – (and with one of whom he has
already made a fatal blunder with the <u>timely</u> working of his! Cold civil notes!! <u>I</u>,
am snubbed, and insulted at Every turn, – in the coarsest and sharpest manner,
if I presume in so cruelly vital – a matter to myself – to <u>impress</u> – that – which
from never receiving a coherent answer to any of my letters, – I have every reason
to believe has <u>not</u> been heeded – you say you see nothing offensive in Mr Ironsides – last letter to me: – I beg leave to differ from you; – I am neither Mr
Ironsides wife; – nor his concubine; – how dare he then, presume to write to me,
– or to <u>any woman</u> I will not even say gentlewoman in such a style "how you
nauseate with your repetition of common places spun out on yards of paper – as
if one had no brains ?? and the pen and ink and letter writing mania that is upon
you"!!! – <u>No</u>, – omnipotent as he thinks himself and still more omniscient! this
is <u>not</u> the Mania that is upon me but one of ruin and outrage – at every point,
– Mr Ironside told you my besetting sin! – I will now tell you his – egregious
<u>vanity</u> upon every particle – moral – physical and intellectual – that goes to the
composition of the aggregate called Isaac Ironside. – you spoke in your letter of
yesterday of the friends I had lost through writing that sort of letter – not so by
the Rood!⁴ I never had any <u>friends to</u> lose; -one and <u>all</u> had their own game to
play – or their own <u>Hobby to ride through me</u>; – then, as now, – <u>I</u> am but the
nine pin set up to receive the blows, and be eventually knocked down; – as the
up shot may decide. – Mrs Sandby's friendship was unbounded! as long as she
thought there was any chance of my getting an increased allowance, – which
would enable her to lead a merry life – at Paris with me; – for she could not but
remember that my notions of Hospitality are rather more Oriental – than English, – rather more princely than pauperish and that at all – events – I never
count the bits of bread, and cups of tea – my guests consume – Kate Planchés –
was an <u>enjoument</u>⁵ more like a mans mad, but short lived passion for a woman
and it was an excitement and a pastime – and a <u>mannière de se faire personage</u>⁶
in society to affect great devotion in my cause! And spend her time in the dull
country with me till – the Clique Harpoons were thrown out for Miss Matilda's⁷
Dickens and Ditchwater inanities – and <u>then I</u> was of course thrown over. The
<u>Carlyles</u>⁸ I certainly <u>asked not</u> to do anything with Sir Liar!! – but to find me a
<u>Publisher</u> a mighty service! which that cold clay pipe of an old Charlatan – might
have rendered me with Ease – Sir Donkey Doyle – I not only did <u>not</u> ask, but
positively <u>forbid</u> to make as I knew such an iced ass <u>would do</u> my position <u>worse</u>!
but here again, – I was totally set at naught; – in my own affairs! – you know the
mysterious hugger mugger, – that went on for 2 months between them and him!

you also know the result!! and therefore cannot be much surprised that I <u>should</u> <u>rather</u> <u>wince</u>, – at any <u>fresh</u> clever Cabinet councils, of my friends, from which I, the Cipher am excluded; – however, no doubt in this <u>obligation</u>! Sir F Doyle laid me under, – <u>he</u> gained his own noble ends! to wit, the <u>honor</u>!! of an invitation to dinner from Sir Edward Bulwer Lytton! at the end of 20 years! – whose doors he had never been allowed to darken before!!! No, no, my dear Rebecca – where <u>I</u> make Enemies, – of people who are certainly better fitted for the <u>rôle</u> than that of friends – is that what <u>does</u> exist, – I see so terribly clearly! – and what is worse – let them <u>see</u> that I do; – while for what does <u>not</u> exist, not all the sentimentality of <u>words</u> – throughout the universe, – can extract from me a profession of faith; – for instance, if a man tells you in a dozen letters that he has not even the penny to pay for the stamp – and is always – <u>à langlaise manoeuvering</u>[9] you out of money which – is their way of shirking an obligation in the matter, – and yet in a 13th letter which is written with the same financial designs; – they kindly patronize you by offering you a <u>gratuitous</u> Home in their yet to be built House!! – I call this not only Humbug – but Humbug of the most offensive because most bare faced, description, – which is very unamiable and of course very <u>ungrateful</u>! on my part; – while poor Mr Ironsides Philanthropic Acumen, – and comfortable self-esteem – can only see a miraculous! change brought by his <u>Bourreau bien faisait</u>[10] letters, – and "Familiar words"! and enabling – a hitherto helpless and Penniless man, – to spring to his own resources and grapple successfully with fortune! – but to lift with a vigorous arm another Equally miserable wretch out of penury into peaceful competency Faugh! – verily this – would make a sufficient emetic for all Germany – and relieve the national stomach – of "the perilous stuff" of vapid – vague sentimentality it has been so long ill of itself – and sickening the whole of Europe with. – For his <u>general</u> and <u>universal</u> Philanthropy – his <u>thoroughly</u> <u>honest</u> – and noble nature I give Mr Ironside the <u>fullest</u> and most admiring credit; I only wish – that to poor wounded – at <u>every</u> point dying gasping me – he had shown a little more individual kindness – a little more personal tenderness – and forbearance I only – regret – that before he <u>thrust</u> me as another iron – into Universal Benevolence – he did not more maturely weigh the terrible and complex trouble he would entail upon <u>himself</u>; – and the fearful <u>All</u> – and <u>more</u> than all I had at stake! – I am more grateful to <u>you</u>, – and to that other good Samaritan Mrs <u>Jermyn</u> for your kind anodyne words to me just now; – than for all your kind deeds – I know too, my dear Rebecca that there is nothing narrow, or dreggy – or vulgar – in your mind, or sordid and under currented in your heart and <u>that</u> is also a great boon at this miserable crisis for which I am duly grateful,- but you, nor no other Being save God and myself- <u>can</u> have any idea of the tortures of body and mind that I am suffering – I do – not think all the ice in Wenham lake[11] could cool the fever in my head alone; – I really feel as if there was but a sheet of silver paper – between me and raving – incurable insanity – you know I am not naturally a crying whimpering woman – I have had to dig and delve too hard for that – but my strength of body and mind – is now utterly prostrated – that I never get one of Mr Ironsides nutmeg grater letters that it does not throw me into violent Hysterics. Do in mercy to me try and convince him – that it is not only bad taste – but cruel bad feeling to try and force me to be under a pecuniary obligation to him against my will – I have again returned the £5 you sent this morning – which makes £20 – I have now sent and will send the other £10 as soon as I get it – and if they get lost by his so foolishly returning them it will be very hard – when I have received them on charity! which is the hardest of all things! I know not if there were any letters from Sheffield this morning as of course because particularly ordered (and I suppose like Mr Ironside "nauseated with my repetitions") they forgot to send to the post. You asked me the other day for an appeal but I have not one – you must get it from Sheffield. I'll send the vipers nest registered tomorrow. God Bless you. Ever Affectly yrs Rosina Bulwer Lytton.

HALS
1. Rebecca Ryves's brother William, who is serving in India.
2. Frizzy hair (French).
3. Lie of the land (French).
4. Cross.
5. Enjoining (French).
6. A manner to give the appearance in society (French).
7. Matilda Anne was Kate Planché's sister. See RBL, 24 December 1852.
8. Jane and Thomas Carlyle.
9. In the English way [*L'Anglaise*] (French).
10. Tortuous, well made (French).
11. The Wenham Lake Ice Company harvested ice from Wenham Lake in Wenham, Massachusetts, and exported it all around the world. It was highly prized and was awarded a royal warrant by Queen Victoria.

To Rebecca Ryves

Monday Morning August the 3d 1857

My dearest Rebecca I herewith send you the Vipers nest – which truly from so many years passing from hand to hand and from Post, to Post has become like the Common peoples "Papers" so dirty, as to be untouchable save with a pair of tongs. But for all the use they are, or good they will do, beyond eliciting a little more talk – I really might as well put them in the fire at once; for I feel – that my ruin is now completely, and irrevocably sealed – there is no law for me and fifty against me: and total want of tact, and want of judgement, in one who in his strange mania for schoolmastering the whole world, even misapplies the word, is not much to lean upon were it still there; but of course having stirred up the puddle, and splashed me a little more, – I shall as usual be left to struggle through it as I may. – I, know – all I say and see, and have experience of always goes in at one ear, and out at another with you – and that you invariably echo – as the Delphic wind did the Delphic Oracle[1] – everything the last newcomer says, you now assert that I generalize! you are mistaken I nauseate by the detail and precision of my re-iterations – it is your friend Mr Ironside who generalizes with a vengeance! I never should have been in debt had he been my admirer!!! so of course, were he in my present cruelly, and hopelessly miserable position, surrounded by a chevaux de fries[2] of complex difficulties – he could devise some method of procuring Postage stamps alone, without money to buy them, – without stealing them, and more immoral! than all, without going in debt!! but I am such a nauseous fool that I cannot. – perhaps I wince more than others at having my head broken by the precious balms, of my Patrons; from having passed my life, in making great sacrifices of my miserable, and insufficient means, and my scant personal comforts to serve utter strangers to me – giving my best of my abilities – and time to these efforts, – and I can safely say – so little have I thought – much less talked of them – that if ever I do reach Heaven – the recording Angel will have to show them to me before I remember them; – as I have always endeavoured – to confer any thing like an obligation as delicately as possible, knowing – that even the most hardened and professional Beggars like Godfrey Parker – have at least a feeling of annoyance at being obliged to beg if they have no other feeling – and though I am well aware that all delicacy is lost upon English people – still I have never doled out loans, with lectures to paupers – but have given – and give freely all I could, and more than I perhaps ought. Then see the kind friends my temper! has estranged from me lately!! There was Mr Raymond Browne who kindly began filering not exactly le parfait amour[3] – but a case with me – thinking like all brutes of English that an old woman of my age – must be much flattered! at an insult of this [s]ort– when in England even young Females are so; and when I with the coolest contempt, and the keenest satire slipped him off his hook – I of course incurred his vulgar enmity how very impudent! in my position as I ought to have been too glad to have had – even a fifth rate Literary Gent – at my beck and call – by being at his. – Then look at Mr Nortons kindness in sending me an order for Medical attendance on the Parish Doctor! which I had the ingratitude; and the imprudence to return to him – no doubt with a latent spice of that exigeance common to all Paupers thinking "The Worthy Magistrate might have sent me a soup ticket – and a trifle from the Poor box"! with it. – Then Mr Ironside who really did do me a great and noble service for which I was, and ever shall be greatly and nobly grateful, – thinks (like an Englishman!) that thereby he has paid the purchase money for me, and has a perfect right – to treat me as a plaything – or a foot ball – as the humour sets – and while, labouring under the most deferential difficulties – as to the mode of franchising – the awful gulf – between his position in life, and that of my "Gifted Husband"! permits himself to write to the repudiated wife of that gifted individual (she being at least born, and better still, <u>bred</u> a gentlewoman) – in a style of coarse free and easy brutality, – which no <u>man</u> <u>ought</u>, and no <u>gentleman</u> <u>would</u>, address a Kitchen maid. No, my dear Rebecca I dont "generalize" – when one is alone from morning till night, – year after year, and month after month – one has time to analyze – and that I do. – You did not send me back that Leicester Shire Paper with Mrs Wig-fields[4] meeting in it, which I should like to see. – No Sheffield Free Presses have come this morning – so I suppose Mr Ironside is very angry with me? Amen! – but oh! how paltry, and little – English people are. Pray let me know that the Vipers nest has arrived safely? and apologising for again making you the victim of "my Pen and ink" of which the innocent paper is only the surface. Believe me Ever affectly yr Rosina Bulwer Lytton.

HALS
1. Pythia was the ancient Greek prophetess known as the Delphic Oracle at Delphi, located on the slopes of Mount Parnassus.
2. Frizzy hair (French).
3. The perfect love (French).
4. The *Leicester Journal* reported on a women's meeting at the Town Hall on 23 July headed 'Woman's Voice on Women's Rights', over which, Mrs Wigfield presided. Other speakers were Mrs Cockayne and a Mr T. Emery. Mrs Wigfield delivered a lecture proving that 'woman is equal with man from the Word of God'.

To Rebecca Ryves

Monday Evening 8 O'Clock August 3d 1857

My dearest Rebecca As I wrote you word the T F P[1] had not come this morning – I lose no time in telling you that they have come by the last Post this Evening, which I am glad of – as it annoyed me to think that he could be so trumpery yea it has not only come – but sure enough he has Even served up the Porringer[2] of Lord Palmerstons[3] blood that I sent him – not exactly intending it for a public Banquet! not that I care; – as I despise Lord Palmerston so cordially that I'd spatchcock him <u>bodily</u> for a crown! – that is, to save the 3 United Kingdoms. – How kind and <u>Judicious</u>! it was of Mr Ironside to publish that letter of his friend Jenkinsons[4] about me, and there leave the matter, and the public with this nice flavour of the matter! but this is about the amount, of kindness, and <u>Judgement</u> – I generally do receive from my friends! from whom good Lord deliver me! – I have a notion that Mr Urquhart,[5] could better understand my position by analogy than any one – for <u>he</u> might be able to comprehend that what Russia & Lord Palmerston are to England,[6] Sir Liar, and Disraeli[7] are to me; and if my threads only snaps in working they are the remote but main cause of it, an hypothesis that would appear foolishness to the general mass. In haste Ever affectly yrs R B L

HALS

1. The *Sheffield Free Press*.
2. A shallow handled cup or bowl.
3. After Lord Palmerston's election as Prime Minister (1855–8), he was determined to get the Matrimonial Causes Bill passed, much to RBL's disapproval. In addition, he was a war hawk, who had been blamed for plunging Britain into the Crimean War. In a letter to the *Sheffield Free Press* for 8 August 1857, RBL attacked Britain's foreign policy and the conduct of the Crimean War, concluding: 'Lord Palmerston is the servant of Russia and the enemy of England'.
4. J. E. Jenkinson was the Chairman of the Bradford Foreign Affairs Committee. His letter supporting EBL, as opposed to RBL, appeared in the *Sheffield Free Press* for 18 July 1857 in a report of a meeting held by the Sheffield Foreign Affairs Committee. See RBL, 14 August 1857.
5. David Urquhart.
6. After Tsar Nicholas I died in 1855, the Russians wanted to make peace. Lord Palmerston decided that the peace terms were not harsh enough on Russia and so persuaded Napoleon III of France to break off negotiations.
7. Benjamin Disraeli.

To Rebecca Ryves

Tuesday August 4th 1857 2pm

My dearest Rebecca I congratulate you on poor Willy's safety – and pray God something may quell this wholesale Indian Butchery[1] and keep him safe; – God help us one and all. I thank you from my heart for your kind zeal in my behalf but don't you <u>see</u> – and <u>feel</u> my dearest Rebecca that as <u>usual</u> I am <u>utterly</u> and <u>hopelessly</u> wrecked with only the agreeable addition of an other and larger mountain of pecuniary difficulty – degradation and responsibility. Here is August – and of course Sir Liar will be off out of the Kingdom in a few days – and the question is – not what discussions will ensue – thereupon but what in God's name <u>I am</u> to do? – for talk may and will injure me more but cannot serve me. – you know that hampered as I already am – and dreading hourly expulsion – even from this miserable shelter – every breath I draw is a <u>costly</u> and additionally <u>involving one,</u> – <u>utter</u> destitution being about <u>the</u> most extravagant, and money sinking position any one can be in. – To give you some faint idea of the 50 per cent I pay for every thing from never having a farthing of ready money, – Hitchcock[2] charges in his Bill 9d for 2 ounces of Allum,[3] – I sent 6d to a shop the other day and got one pound for 3d! Day has mounted his 2 years Bill up to £78 – and I am in perfect <u>rags</u> – and not <u>literally</u> a thing to wear. Now no one, with a grain of human feeling – and only the commonest rudimentary knowledge of human nature, but must know – that Despondency is the natural consequence of <u>extreme</u> and hopeless <u>dependence</u>! and that while it gives us a true – and further a <u>prophetic</u> and painfully keen sense of the dangers around us – it at the same time totally inervates and deprives one of moral courage; and physical strength to bear up against them and above all against those humiliations which are the dark cold blighting shadows of the fell Fiend <u>Despair</u>! I will not apologise to you for the "nauseating reiteration of this common place-" as you I know have some human feeling – and therefore can understand when a poor wretch has been crushed with blow, after blow, as I have – and has been so many weeks stretched on a sick bed lonely and almost physically helpless – from intense bodily as well as mental suffering as I am – they cannot "use their brains"! and still less can they put their shoulder to the wheel of the juggernaut car that is [ill] if they had the good fortune to be a healthy young Ploughboy – it grieves me to grieve you with all this – but groans are the natural result of torture – God Bless you and take me – is the sincere prayer of yours gratefully and affectly Rosina Bulwer Lytton

---

HALS

1. At the end of June 1857 during the Siege of Cawnpore, British men, women and children were under attack for three weeks, culminating in a massacre. Harsh retaliations against the Indian population ensued.
2. Pharmacist.
3. Used medicinally as a topical astringent.

To Rebecca Ryves

Wednesday August 5th 1857

My dearest Rebecca – I am so cruelly ill with the too long mockery of all this fruitless talk that I can scarcely write another line, – I have answered Mr Ironsides – as usual vague and rigmarole note, – and told him that he, and you can discuss my faults as long as it pleases you so to do and the agreeable result is a mutual interflummerization but as I had the benefit of your "stupendous intellect" even before I had the benefit of his, and that nevertheless he found me in the position I was! it was a somewhat cruel proceeding to lift me out of the abyss – with a false hope – merely to fling me back on a former Chimera! – I also told him that as a gentlewoman and considering the obligations I was under to him – I never should have written to him – how doubly wrong it was in a man to permit himself to do so to a woman whom he had laid under these obligations – and that no gentleman would have allowed himself to write in such a strain to a Kitchen maid -Even had he constituted himself a deputy Lord God Almighty. – Well might Socrates say God defend me from my friends! – Even Mr Walter Weldon who had – or pretended to have a great esteem for me – by Mr Ironsides kindly pointing out to him my unpardonable crime in wincing under them in what he calls "dealing with my case!" – and you; having kindly pointed out – how I have lost all my former <u>friends</u>! (though I never lost one that was worth retaining – nor shall I now) Mr Isaac Ironside The Schoolmaster General, has now got this as an additional lash for his Cat o' nine tails to lay about me; – but he, or any one else – may now say – and do what they please – I am at last thank God – past their power to wound – or to injure more. I have had a letter from Boulogne this morning – full of the infamous strumpet Beaumont – and the old story of her having passed herself off as Lady Bulwer Lytton at the Petty German Courts – and requesting to know from me if she was the çi-devant[1] Miss Laura Deacon as every one said she was – I enclosed this letter, to Mr Ironside – who will of course "submit it to you" But for goodness sake give yourself no further trouble – I am injured – insulted, and wrecked <u>quite enough</u> – and dont want to be laid under further obligations for being still more so. – I am sorry to say a letter has come from a Major Abbott[2] – saying poor George Willoughby has been massacred God preserve poor Willy – Ever affectly yrs Rosina Bulwer Lytton

HALS
1. Formerly (French),
2. This is most probably James Abbott (1807–96), a British army officer in colonial India, after whom the Pakistani city of Abbottabad was named.

To Rebecca Ryves

Thursday August 6th 1857

My dearest Rebecca I am so knocked down with blow after blow that I really am <u>not</u> able to put pen to paper – the ruin is mounting like a tide around me and I have nothing to meet it but the certainty of further ruin – owing to all these accursed delays on Every side – that £100 borrowed from Augusta – for <u>six</u> <u>months</u>! will be a year due the end of this month and besides the premium – I shall have £5 interest to pay on it! where I am to get it God only knows . – but of course I <u>ought</u> to keep <u>out of debt</u>!!! £7"6 – I am also obliged to pay Mrs White of Bath in October, – thinking when I promised 6 months ago to do so, – that I was giving myself ample time! It is a thousand pities that as it now turns out, Mr Ironside had <u>no</u> fixed or definite plan, for extricating me from this hideous abyss! he should have volunteered to do so; – for if he had not your "giant intellect"! to fall back upon – what was to become of me? and as I told him though I had the benefit of that before I had the benefit of his yet strange to say I was still in the miserable plight he found me. I foresee the next avalanche of ruin I shall have will be a demand from Mr Hartcup[1] for £30 – or £40 – for though in my nauseating commonplaces I had <u>told</u> Mr Ironside that after Mr Sandbys Entrapping me to England by saying that his solicitor being Employed then in a largely paid Chancery suit should do the little business he had in London gratis – he nevertheless when they turned upon me sent me in the modest bill of £75! for six letters, and 3 visits – and that old ass Mr Hartley[2] went and <u>compounded</u> with him for £20 – or £30 – I forget which; while Mr Hyde said he would not have let me pay a farthing of it – yet now – Mr Ironside – instead of in a stringent, and business like way saying – "I shall of course pay your fees for these attested documents I now require" says in his usual loose shambling way – "on receipt of your letters I will remit you your charges," – whereupon the little attorney will of course make the profitable quibble of assuming – that a philanthropic millionaire has stepped forward to discharge my liabilities – and that I in a fit of very misplaced dignity am quite willing to liquidate the whole of his £75 Extortion. – I certainly have no earthly right to give Mr Ironside the trouble and expense (till I am able to reimburse him and <u>when</u>! will that be?) of coming up to London – to transact my business – nor do I see how any thing <u>can</u> possibly be done in a day! if he does. – But for Pity's Sake – ask me <u>now</u> no more questions; – I have nauseated Mr Ironside with the repetition of my common places, – which nevertheless, – I <u>knew</u> – and <u>felt</u> to be <u>vitally</u> necessary to even a <u>groping</u> through my miserable affairs, – he has found my folly a proof of a "giant intellect!" – when propounded by you; – surely then, nothing more <u>can</u> be required; – and I have nothing more to say – nor strength to say it if I had. – I thank you very sincerely for your most kind intention in writing to that Low Blackguard Jenkinson[3] – but am sorry you wasted so many words on him – and think Mr Ironsides mode of treating – would have in <u>this</u> instance been the most appropriate. Though my common places are so nauseating (as indeed <u>all</u> misery <u>is</u> – even at secondhand then what <u>must</u> it be to the poor wretch of a rightful owner! –) and though I certainly make no pretension – to "a giant intellect" – yet I not being <u>quite</u> a fool, and of course <u>feeling</u> where the shoe pinches more than mere spectators possibly can do – I saw, – and knew Mr Wheeler <u>thoroughly</u>; – therefore had I not been thought too great a cipher in my own affairs to be worthy of being consulted in the matter; – Mr Ironside -should have written him a <u>very</u> different sort of letter – to the one you thought so splendid! – and so, would have avoided receiving this affront, from that low bred <u>parvenu</u>,[4] – for which, I am truly, and deeply grieved, – not only because – I resent insults too keenly myself, – not to resent them for others also; – but because Mr Ironside had incurred this one through his kindness to me pray dont fail to tell him how hurt, and annoyed I am at it, and if ever I can get out of Mr Samuel Wheelers clutches which alas! save by death I am not likely to do; <u>he shall hear of it</u>. I got a note this morning from a Mr Arthur de Noé Walker 55 Upper Berkely St[5] – which I sent on to Sheffield not having one [*sic*] – if it should – be your Mr Walker? – will you beg of Mr Eyre Lloyd to apologise to him for my <u>apparent</u> rudeness in not replying to it; – but while I am trying to scrawl this to you, – I feel exactly as if fiery serpents were lashing my brain – the agony is so excruciating – so now – good bye and God Bless you – I thank from my heart for all the trouble you have so kindly taken on my behalf, – but take no more it is all too late I must turn my face to the wall and try and die quietly – it is not right to even begin to set ones house in order with ones mind in a ferment so no more questions – for God's for Pity's sake I <u>can</u> no more "The words of Job <u>are</u> Ended".[6] The race will soon be too. Ever affectly yours – and gratefully Mr Ironsides for what he has done R Bulwer Lytton.

Of course it is such conduct as Mr Wheelers that has brought my affairs into the frightful abyss they are – and this is what my nauseating repetitions have been trying to dun into Mr Ironside but till a sample came under his <u>own</u> knowledge, he did not seem to think so.

Mr Ironside is wrong again; Mr Walter Weldon never took my "surplus"! I defy <u>any</u> <u>one</u> to do <u>that</u>! had I only a surplus – anyone and every one should be welcome to it; and I hope would not have to ask for it – no, he like a god among other authors && only took my <u>non</u> plus[7] – with hardly a thank you.

HALS
1. Mr Hartcup, Revd Sandby's solicitor.
2. Another solicitor.
3. Mr J. E. Jenkinson. See RBL, 14 August 1857.
4. Upstart (French).
5. Arthur de Noé Walker (*c.* 1821–1900) was a physician, who had been a captain in the Madras army. He was a friend of Walter Savage Landor. See RBL, 20 June 1858.
6. Job 31:40.
7. No more (French).

To Rebecca Ryves

[August? 1857]

When I sealed my letter I had not seen your copy of the Bradford letter – They are quite welcome to continue the cry – of "Bulwer says nothing" (which of course is very kind of <u>him</u>! considering how <u>much</u> he <u>has</u> to say! almost as kind as Mr Ironsides promise not to breathe to mortal my criminal habit of besotting myself with opium!!!) Aye truly <u>let</u> <u>them</u>, – (now my friends have discovered the <u>real</u> cause of my having no friends! – my quarrelsome disposition and nauseating repetition of my grievances) – continue the howl – of "Bulwer says nothing, – faults on both sides, – better let it alone" – or, if they like to vary it with – <u>oh!</u> <u>entirely her</u> fault – no man <u>could</u> live with such a woman – look at her ungrateful conduct to her Husband! his relations!! and even her own son!!! to say nothing, of all the friends who have been <u>so true</u>! – <u>staunch</u>! <u>and devoted to her</u>! – she! who never did a kind thing by any one – while it is Easy to see by Sir Edwards writings what a faultless and charming person <u>he</u> is!" – yes let them say this; and as much more as they please – the lies – of the originaters or the imbecility of their Echoes, can never equal – my profound indifference to, and contempt for them and their vetos. I am neither "Mêlius pejus, prosit, obsit, nil vident nisi quad blinerit"[1] as Terence[2] has it, or in plain English I am neither better, nor worse for their favor – or their falsehoods as they see, or say, nothing but what they <u>please</u> – that is, what they think will tend to their advantage – Amen Ever affectly yrs

RBL.

P.S: I have read Mrs Wigfield![3] The language might have been more Elegant certainly – but still, it is difficult for women to speak on the subject of their concrete, and world old wrongs – and in their anxiety to find language at all adequately strong – keep to that which is unexceptionable. I tell you what <u>would</u> do a great deal of good – as Mr Ironside did send her my Pamphlet; if any one woman would give Mrs Wigfield, and the women of Leicester a hint to burn Sir Liar in Effigy on the market Place at Leicester because <u>then</u> <u>that</u> fact would travel the wide world over; – such a hint would have a far better Effect coming from a man – and might be sent by any man – with with [*sic*] <u>Hawthornes</u> – panegyric "Bulwer nauseates me he is the very pimple <u>on</u> (not of!) the Ages Humbug, – there is no hope for the public as long as he finds – an admirer – a reader – or a Publisher."[4] – This; might serve at once as an inaugural address! – and Funeral oration at the burning and would do more to thoroughly <u>unmask</u> the wretch <u>publicly</u> – than all the private execration – which only amuses <u>him</u> and plays his game – while it tantalizes and goads me on to distraction. <u>All</u> are agreed as to belling the cat – i.e. as to the necessity of belling his infamy into the Public ear but who is to do it? here is a capital opening and opportunity – but like all others no doubt like a stone flung into a pond – it will sink to rise no more – amen. – I have just seen in the Bath paper that old Mountebank Walter Savage Landors[5] recantation of his Libels on Mrs Yescombe[6] – of course that ineffable Blackguard Mr John Forster advised him to slink out of the lies he could not substantiate – as he always advises his other worthy friend Sir Liar to do, and so justice is bulked, and people can get no redress – the plan being to <u>hush</u> up every thing at the 11th hour and screen the Liars <u>Coûte-qu'il-coûte</u>[7] I told you of old Lander's in my drawing room at bath volunteering the most horrible imprecations on his own head if anything ever induced him to sit in the same room with such "a w<u>oo</u>nderful scoundrel"! as Sir Liar, and 4 days after! Mr John Forster, and my Lady Blessington arranged that he, and Sir Liar should be bandying compliments, and asking each other to take wine at a dinner at my Lady Blessingtons! and when he returned to Bath – and was astonished that I would not let him into my House and Mrs Paynter[8] said "Good Heavens Mr Lander how could you expect it – after volunteering to take such a horrible oath that you would never sit in the same room with Sir EBL?" His cool answer was "God bless my soul did I? I'm sure I forgot all about it" –!! They are a nice set one and all – truly and much chance! I have against such ceaseless – unscrupulous and never blundering infamy. – I see that poor Mrs Belli of Princes Gate[9] is dead and also Delane[10] the Editor of "The Times" – as the last Post office order I sent Mr Weldon was only for £1"10"0 (all I had) I suppose he did not think such a trifle from me worth acknowledging; as he never has done so but as it was another gift, of course a man may do as he likes with his own. – RBL

HALS

1. 'Better or worse, beneficial or otherwise, men see nothing but what they desire', Terence, *Heautontimoroumenos*, 4.1.30.
2. Terence (*c.* 190–158 BC) was a comic playwright in ancient Rome.
3. Mrs Wigfield, who was speaking on women's rights, was the wife of a framework knitter. RBL was actually mentioned in the newspaper report of the speech dated 24 July 1857. See RBL, 3 August 1857.
4. See RBL, 21 July 1857.
5. The *Bath Express and Literary Observer* (1855–75) carried an account of the trial on 27 December 1856, 3 and 10 January 1857. RBL had originally dedicated *Cheveley* to the poet Walter Savage Landor, but he asked for it to be withdrawn when he realized that the novel was an attack on EBL.
6. In June 1857, Landor published two pamphlets: *Walter Savage Landor and the Honourable Mrs. Yescombe* and *Mr Landor Threatened*, claiming that he had been duped by Mary Jane Yescombe (former wife of Baron Massy) into parting with money to help out her protégée, Geraldine Hooper. When Mrs Yescombe sued him for libel, and gained the support of the press, Landor fled to Italy.
7. Cost what it will (French).
8. At Villa Landor on the Fiesolan hills, Landor met Mrs Paynter early in the decade of 1830–40. She was the mother of Rose Paynter, with whom Landor extensively corresponded between 1838 and 1863. She became Lady Graves-Sawle and was one of the most beautiful of women in society.
9. South Kensington, London.
10. John Thadeus Delane (1817–79) was the first editor of *The Times* (1841–77) to pay attention to obituaries. He did not die until nearly twenty years after this letter appears to have been written.

To Rebecca Ryves

[*c.* August 1857]

... I see, on re-reading your letter that often as I have nauseated with my repetitions – none of you understand Sir Liar – and Loadens relative positions yet;

Loaden is to Sir Liar what "Le Saint Eloi"[1] was to the "Bon Roi D'Agobert"![2]
– paid to take the onus of all Sir Liars infamy on himself – (Loaden) – he! owns
to being the person who had me turned from my childs death bed of course! Sir
Liar must not be held accountable for anything of the sort!!! though Loaden was
not within twenty miles of the place – and did not know of my being there; till
they had finished their work! the fiends of Hell – and now if the ruffianly old
monster is frightened with anything the next dodge will – be that Loaden has
made him a confession!! that he Loaden has been decieving him Sir Liar about
me for years poor dear guilless soft easily led man! and that now he is undecieved
– and Loaden has confessed!! what did I write that long letter to you some time
ago reccommending Mr Ironside to go to Loaden but because, that Sir Liar
would do nothing unless he had a plastron[3] to shift the onus; – of his concession,
or the odium of his aggressions upon, – but until they are both curtly told that
not one word they utter will – or can from their known characters be believed on
oath – nothing will be done with them and with regard to my infamous conduct
– (which strange to say never transpired in any place I have been in out of Sir
Liars or Loadens den) what a more than fool I must have been! to have done the
Devils work without wages! and been in the state of utter debt, and destitution I
am in – when all the "other"!!! W's in England are so flourishing Mother Norton
with her 2 pensions[4] – Lady Palmerston[5] Lady Harriet D'Orsay (now Cowper)[6]
– Lady Molesworth[7] Lady Dundonald[8] – Duchess of Inverness[9] – Lady Dufferin[10] Mrs Fox Lane – and inshort the whole strumpetocracy – either provided
for or re-husbanded by some of their paramours – really Sir Liar – ought at least
to provide me a permanent shelter in an asylum for Idiots – for the rest of my life
– as my bad conduct! coupled with my bad circumstances must surely entitle me
to this boon – if indeed I have a right – to anything but suffering calumny – outrage, and persecution in this world. as Lord Justice Knight Bruce is still living – I
think he ought to be asked if he ever wrote or dictated such a letter? because you
know at the time, when I told it to every one – both Sir Liar and Bean denied,
that any such letter had ever been written or such proposition made!! – as for
Talfourd! he would have lied through any thing, and I always considered his falling back dead on the Bench after denouncing a perhaps far less guilty criminal,
as an awful judgement on him and should not be astonished if his friend Sir Liar
met with a similar one. Don't forget to tell me in your next if Mr Walker is dark
or fair? – dark I hope for no fair person is to be trusted.

HALS

Incomplete letter.

1. St Eligius (Eloi) (*c*. 590–660), Bishop of Noyon-Tournai and patron saint of gold-
   smiths.
2. Good King (French), Eloi (see above, n. 1) became chief adviser to Dagobert, King of the
   Franks in 629.
3. Flat part of a shell of a tortoise.

4. See RBL, 1 March 1858.
5. See RBL, 0D019RR21.
6. Charles Cowper, a younger son of the fifth Earl Cowper, was nephew to Lord Melbourne
    and became a stepson to Lord Palmerston. Later he married his mistress, Lady Harriet
    d'Orsay, Count Alfred d'Orsay's widow, and was obliged by the stuffy attitude of his
    neighbours in Norfolk to leave the county. See RBL, 15 December 1852.
7. See RBL, 0D019RR21.
8. Katherine Corbett Barnes (1796–1865) secretly married Thomas Cochrane, tenth Earl
    of Dundonald. The validity of the marriage was in doubt and they married twice more in
    1818 and 1825. Lady Dundonald had an affair with Lord Auckland, who was acting as
    her husband's trustee while he was serving as a naval officer in Greece.
9. Cecilia Underwood, Duchess of Inverness (*née* Lady Cecilia Letitia Gore) (*c.* 1785–
    1873), married the Duke of Sussex in 1831 in a ceremony not valid under the Royal
    Marriages Act. Since it was considered legally void, she could not be called the Duchess
    of Sussex. She was created Duchess of Inverness in her own right by Queen Victoria in
    1840.
10. Helen Selena, Lady Dufferin (*née* Sheridan) (1807–67), author and songwriter, was
    Caroline Norton's sister.

To Rebecca Ryves

Sunday August 9th 1857

My dearest Rebecca I thank you from my heart for your kind letter and am
grieved with more additional grief than I have room for; at all the trouble and
anxiety I cause you – I assure you Mr Ironside cannot over rate your kind good
heart, or even rate it as highly as I do; – only he might have done so without
heaping brutal [ill] upon me – however he is an Englishman – and they never
can manage more than one civility at a time, that without a heavy mortgage of
rudeness to somebody else upon it. – He sent me a copy of his letter to Sir Liar
– yesterday, – but I think a part of it must have been left out, as it seemed so
unconnected, – I was so ill I could scarcely read it, but did try and scrawl a few
important suggestions on it – for a mere catalogue raisonné[1] of his infamies
– would have no effect upon the monster and the mere curt item of 4th J your
Richmond letter he would not have even understood as most probably he has
drank that infamy out of his memory long ago; – so I added – "after making
your teeth meet in her cheek"[2] – Mr Ironside had written some extraordinary
name – for that of my French Council, – and Fanny had been jabbering about
De Beriot Malibrans[3] Husband to show you the state my poor head is in, – I
having this jumble in my ears, altered Mr I's[4] bevu[5] into the equal one of Beriot,[6]
– but the proper name (which as it is one of [ill] celebrity one ought to know) is
Berryer[7] which I have already written over and over again in the reiteration of my
"nauseating commonplaces" which indeed are of little avail since they are never

remembered and notwithstanding this delicate compliment – if dying I must rouse up to repeat them again as I have done in the letter I now send – in answer to that insolent Knave Hartcups – all of which I have said over and over again before – and if my nauseating commonplaces were only digested, and combined – I dont think any one need be at a loss – what to say – or do in the business but as they are not – I may venture to say that – I think it a very important point that both the scoundrel Loaden, and his Infernal Client should – be asked what they think public opinion is – at that infamous wretch Mrs Beaumont alias Miss Laura Deacon the street walker for whom I was turned out of my home on the wide world to struggle with every privation degradation – insult, and temptation that a human being could be exposed to should be now – in the month of August 1857 showing forgeries from her infamous paramour purporting to be letters from me!!! overflowing with affection for her!!!! After – the wretch has done her infamous Keepers dirty work – by dragging my name through the mire of Europe – and branding it with her iniquities – and though my poor murdered Emily refused to sit down to dinner with this [ill] Walker (than whom there was no one that her loathsome Father the Fiend! would rather entrust his daughter to!!) yet his son who is in every way worthy of him is aux petits soins[8] to her! – at least so she boasted to Mrs Braine. – Now here is more of my nauseating reiterated common places yea verily! – for they constitute my whole case, – they are the concrete torture of my whole life, – they are Me! and the very earth worms in my grave will have to be nauseated with them – more especially if when I try to lie still and cold – and to take refuge in the calm of death – they lash me up – with "but I want to know this? – and I want to know that?" all of which, when they have been knawing my brain for months, they ought to know as well as me. – Forgive me for boring you with all this who really may well be haunted with it, – I am grieved to hear that good Mr Walker has torments but truly as you [say] good accounts for [nothing] in this world [and] does appear to be a patent for suffering – and wickedness one for prosperity – and immunity from all ills. – I am grieved too at giving you all so much trouble – from which I feel that my usual nothing will result but the trouble – for recollect that none of Sir Liars infamies in the way of robbing – and swindling me, are perfectly Legal – and all his other abominations which would have gained him an unenviable notoriety in the Old Testament – are not only winked at, and tolerated – but adulated and defended in English society! so what has such a man with a purse sufficiently long to pay for unlimited puffs, and perjuries – to fear from exposure? – Poor dear kind old Dr Price– wants to honour that £100 to repay Augusta – but that I wont hear of – it will be bad enough to have to honour the £10 from him – for the interest and premium. I fear you wont be able to read this scrawl – which I am not able to write – the burning – constant and excruciating pain in my head affects my Eyes, and makes me nearly blind – God Bless you – Ever affectly [and] gratefully yrs Rosina Bulwer Lytton

---

HALS
1. Descriptive catalogue (French).
2. A reference to EBL's violent assault on RBL in July 1834.
3. The soprano Maria Malibran (1808–36) married Charles August de Bériot (1802–70), the composer and violinist.
4. Isaac Ironside.
5. Blunder [*bévue*] (French).
6. See above, n. 3.
7. M. Berryer was a lawyer acting for RBL in the Paris libel of 1840.
8. Has few cares (French).

To Rebecca Ryves

Sunday 6 P.M. 9th August 1857

More last words – I just write while I think of it to say – (that you may be prefaced with the truth) Augusta Evidently wishes to se poser en victim[1] and imply – that old Prosser[2] has given them this congé[3] – on account of my having used her name in my book!!!! now the truth is that Fanny has been loudly expressing her determination to leave this – for the last six months – and if old Prosser has given them their Congé? no doubt it is, that she wishes to take the initiative but of course, (not that God knows – ill, or well; – I am ever idle!) poor I must be the root of all evil! I do hope Mr Ironside will have the goodness to write to Mr Wheeler or Mr Hodgson; – that is to perceive that something must be done – I am unable to do anything – even to reply to all this, and it must be patent – even to the most sanguine – and with the most celtic Economy – that having been plunged into this abyss – of pecuniary difficulty – and deprived of every power of extracting myself from it – by earning my bread – that even anything Mr Wheelers kind!! and considerate offer!! of paying him only £5 this quarter and £42 for the Policies (ie £67 –) and £2 to Mr Hodgson for receiving the money £69 – that would leave me exactly £21"14!! to live! and pay all I owe with! and the munificent sum of £41 – each alternate quarter when Mr Wheeler recieves the £50 – would certainly be quite inadequate to make up the deficit, – such cruel facts must be met by deeds not words, – surely the proper, and dignified mode of proceeding to have represented to that monster that his infamous conspiracies at Llangollen – crowned with this suppression of my last book, – had put the finishing stroke to the 15 years ruin he had been entailing upon me, and that if he did not pay the expenses his villainies had made me incur – and give me sufficient to live upon; – a public exposure should be made of him, – and a public subscription set on foot for me – how does Mr Ironside or any one else think I <u>am</u> to go on <u>for ever</u> without one shilling, – and fresh and fearful expenses eternally entailed upon me? – and it is not – giving the brute an additional triumph – and Every reason to laugh at the Emptiness of my arsenal by firing such ridiculous Pop guns as Parker's[4] and Mrs Boates letters![5] – that will achieve any thing but additional humiliation for me God help me between friends! and foes, I am cruelly tortured – there is no use in Mr Ironside telling me that many persons have lived and are living on Half a crown a week if they have, they were <u>not</u> married to Sir Edward Bulwer Lytton – and had an <u>Ever increasing</u> debt entailed upon them. I know as well as any one can tell me that if I had not married him – and <u>if</u> I had not made over to him all my property and <u>if</u> I had not been bullied into signing that infamous deed of separation – and <u>if</u> I had had any one to kick him all this would not have happened but Even Job![6] had better comfort than this. –

HALS
1. To pose as a victim (French).
2. Miss Prosser. See RBL, 12 February 1857.
3. Leave (French).
4. Godfrey Parker. See RBL, 31 July 1857.
5. Mrs Wellington Boate.
6. The holy man in the Bible, whose suffering are recorded in the Book of Job. See RBL, 29 December 1853.

To Rebecca Ryves

Monday August 10th 1857

My dearest Rebecca will you give the enclosed note from Mrs Jermyn back to Mr Ironside and say everything kind to him from me – for his great goodness in going to London on my account, and alas! I fear in vain – for it is a melancholy fact that my kindest champions with all the most devoted, and indefatigable zeal – and a world of trouble to boot never <u>do</u> seize the salient, and unanswerable points of my miserable and outrageous case – and so give my Enemies – a vantage ground – they never otherwise could have acquired. – I have just read your letters in the S.F.P.[1] (the last of which the Printer has made a hash of) dont think me ungracious – I cant say ungrateful – for <u>that</u> I am not – feeling most deeply the kindness of your always kind intentions, but forgive me if I say I wish – you had never written – those letters – I send you what I would have written; – I never degrade my friends by what is called "defending" them – when I know them to be calumniated – I always make short work of it, and decapitate the calumny with a fact – Deeds, not words, – being – my principle on all occasions; – for <u>words</u> are only the weapons of unkindness – and deadly ones they are! but actions are the sole arsenal of kindness, – therefore I have plenty to be grateful to you and Mr Ironside for, and I shall never cease to be so – even should no result but additional misery ensue from the efforts you are so kindly making on my behalf; – I feel it is little matter what betides now – I cannot suffer much longer. God Bless you both Ever affectly yrs Rosina Bulwer Lytton

---

HALS
1.	The *Sheffield Free Press.*

To Rebecca Ryves

Tuesday August 11th 1857

My dearest Rebecca Though up to day to see my Taunton Blister Easton – I am so ill – I really can scarcely hold up my head – to thank you Mr Ironside Mr Eyre Lloyd and Mr Walker which I do from my heart for all your kindness alas! Cui bono?[1] I dont know what St Lawrence suffered on his gridiron[2] but I dont think it could equal the broilings I have to endure on mine – it is very easy to know the influence at work through that humbug of a Manchester Committee[3] – Sir Liar through that equal blackguard – though not equal monster Milner Gibson[4]– this I told Mr Ironside from the first – in my nauseating commonplaces – but I am a fool, and not the best judge of my own case – and between this really nauseating and cruel twaddle, – and floods of theoretical talk that falls wide of the mark – it is written as the Turks say, that I am to be engulfed on all sides. Mr Walker[5] seems indeed a sensible practical man, – and what I like, right for rights sake, – his not going to Knebworth shows that; will you give the enclosed order for an appeal to Mr Ironside he will do nothing with the ruffian Loaden[6] – or his infamous client – without the most uncompromising and stringent threats, – if he continues on the cold civility tack he better, cut my throat at once. I wish you would send me that Blackguard Jenkins's[7] letter to Mr Ironside as the latter sent you a copy of it – I dont like being kept in the dark about what so vitally concerns me, or only being sent copies of letters after all the mischief is done and the originals sent. I sent that letter of Dr Prices to be shown to Mr Ironside as he spoke so highly of him in it – why on earth should he not see it? – The room is turning round and round with me so that I cannot write – so good bye and God Bless you Ever Gratefully and affectly yrs R B L.

HALS
1.	Literally: 'good to whom' (Latin); for whose benefit?
2.	St Lawrence was martyred by being burnt on a red-hot gridiron.
3.	The Manchester Committee incorporated RBL's petition in its report on the opening of letters at the post office. See the *Sheffield Free Press* for 18 July 1857.

4.   Thomas Milner Gibson was a Liberal politician.
5.   Arthur de Noé Walker. See RBL, 6 August 1857.
6.   William Loaden, EBL's solicitor.
7.   Mr J. E. Jenkinson, Isaac Ironside's friend.

To Rebecca Ryves

Wednesday August 12ᵗʰ 1857

My dearest Rebecca What is the use of a heartful of gratitude to you <u>all</u>, – when even the nerves of ones hand are too much relaxed to trace the verbal expression of it? but God bless you all! – Mr Ironside and that noble hearted clearheaded Mr Walker[1] will soon see, that such a brace of Fiends composed of the very <u>dregs</u> of Hell – as Sir Liar and Loaden would be – quite ready and capable of getting tools to perjure my life away in a Court of Justice – as they have tried to do before, and I, am quite ready again to defy them at that Game, as I <u>do</u> believe there <u>is</u> a God in Heaven, though He does for some inscrutable purpose allow the Devil to reign triumphant on Earth. – One additional favour I have to beg of Mr Walker and of you, which is, that you will <u>never</u> again on <u>any</u> <u>account</u> or under <u>any</u> circumstances Blister my Ears, by mentioning the name of Sir Liars son to me, whom I think <u>ten thousand</u> times <u>worse</u> than his Fiend father, and for whom there is, or can be no excuse in Heaven or Earth, – for he must long before this, have known of <u>what his father is capable</u> if the young viper – is married?[2] all I can say is, God help the wretched woman that ventured on his fathers son and his fathers pupil!!!! It is not his conduct to me, so much as <u>the nature that has made him capable of it</u>; that I loathe, and despise; – were he to come on his bended knees from the worlds end to me – nothing <u>now</u> could ever induce me to see him: – though I forgive him – with that abstract Christian forgiveness – which is drawn in Heaven and cannot be met here, God Bless you ever affectly yrs RBL

HALS
1.   Arthur de Noé Walker. See RBL, 11 August 1857.
2.   In 1856, Robert proposed to Caroline, the Dutch daughter of the wealthy Baron Groenix van Zoelen, who turned him down. He resumed his courtship and, in November 1858, Caroline agreed to marry him, but in June 1859 she declined. Robert eventually married Edith Villiers in 1864.

To Rebecca Ryves

Friday August 14th 1857

My dearest Rebecca I am so ill so sore, so outraged so more than hopeless that I have scarcely strength left to write to you – Again I cry out of the agony of my too cruelly crushed heart – God defend me from my friends! – it is this accursed abstract universal benevolence mongering without a particle of human feeling individually for poor wretched me! that puts me <u>so</u> completely at the mercy of those infamous and unscrupulous Demons! – I have read Mr Ironsides report! and can only say I feel as if I were skinned from head to foot ! – and he could sit <u>coolly</u> and listen to all this! and find no better answer to it than to write <u>me</u>! a beast of an official letter calling on <u>me</u>! to refute these infamies! which he had ample <u>means</u> of doing and should have done – with curt summary and uncompromising indignation on <u>the spot</u>. – I have now sent him my affadavit that every word that Fiend Loaden uttered was a base black – and utter <u>falsehood</u> but of course he was as usual amusing himself by cramming "the fools I get hold of" as they <u>truly</u> call them! with as many lies as he found they had <u>patience</u> <u>politeness</u>! and <u>imbecility</u> to <u>listen to</u>! Even my poor Sisters grave[1] was desecrated by the monster! and there was no body to kick him! The poor soul died of lingering consumption at Paris – and that Fiend – Loaden, never once saw me with my children – so much for the lie about the "Bulwer up!" and Mr Ironside had not even presence of mind enough to say because he had not sufficient feeling to do so in refutation of the infamous lies – about my poor murdered child who <u>never</u> <u>saw</u> me, and did not even <u>know</u> I was in England much less in the house, and the whole of the Planché family could be suborned to disprove that gross lie![2] I see that Fiend Marshall Hall died at Brighton the day before yesterday I hope the old monster thought of her death bed on his! – Then what a glorious opportunity Mr Ironside had of silencing the monster Loaden once and for Ever – when he the reptile presumed to ask whose money I was spending at Bath! but <u>no</u>! not a syllable – he can hit upon nothing better than writing to me officially to contradict them! thereby [ill] of ruffians Loaden and his client but as I now feel that Mr Ironside by his apathy towards me and his gentlemanlike delicate deferential forbearance to them sending the perjured Liar Loaden his report of the conversation!! to [ill] that he might not do those dear creatures the [ill] injury of misrepresenting a word of theirs! while he had not one word to day for me! – As Mr Ironside has I say by this inconceivably ill judged conduct cut my throat I can only wish he had done so with a less blunt saw ... [rest of page illegible]

... whereas had the matter been treated with the summary <u>contempt</u>, and determination which I <u>know</u> is the way – and the <u>only</u> way to deal with these wretches they would very soon have been made to knock under and I saved all these additional outrages! – and <u>then</u> to crown the whole – to set a common report! to take down and of course disseminate these outrages – and infamous lies – truly – Mr Ironside <u>has</u> no feeling – or he would have its shadow – <u>some delicacy</u> – but his mode of "dealing with my case" as he calls it from the first has been to tear of[f] my skin, and lard me with poisoned arrows, – on all occasions! of course he <u>wont</u> write the letter I have sent him to Sir Liar which would be the <u>only</u> sort of one that could do me; the least good verily Mr Easton that Mr Ironside so laughs at – would not, and has <u>not</u> acted in the coarse cruel way Mr Ironside has done – nor yet with such utter want of judgement! – I wrote to day to Mr Walker to <u>day</u> thanking him for all his kindness – apologising for the liberty – I had taken in requesting him and Mr Eyre Lloyd – to have the goodness to <u>take</u> that letter to Knight Bruce[3] – and get his affadavit respecting it, but still <u>imploring them to do so</u> as it is the only thing to be <u>done</u> – as all this accursed talk – and cross post consultations, is wrecking – ruining and torturing me – besides I am <u>not</u> asking – or wanting any ones <u>advice</u> I will back my <u>own</u> knowledge and judgement for knowing how – to deal with those two wretches – against <u>all</u> the cleverest heads in Europe if I could only get people to do what I want – and not what <u>they</u> think! and for God's sake do not as you are omnipotent with him – allow Mr Ironside to finish me! by sending that most offensive and cruelly ill judged letter beginning "Madam" to Sir Liar and degrading me by saying that they accused me of killing my child and I must refute it! in a court of justice if I expected my friends (pretty friends!!) to associate with me – Why in the name of common sense and common honesty – did he not tell the Fiend Loaden on <u>the spot</u> "Don't Sir presume to insult me by such language! – when you must be perfectly <u>aware</u> of the damning facts – we have to bring out about your client on <u>that</u> head alone" – But no – it was all mismanaged with the same inconceivable assery and apathy that made him <u>publish</u> Jenkinsons[4] first letter about me thus <u>injuring</u>, and offending <u>all</u> parties, from the general Philanthropy plan – of not individually caring a jot about any of them verily so cruelly crushed – and outraged a spirit as mine required a little more human and – and personal feeling a little more delicate handling than Mr ironside has given it – God help me! God have mercy on me! of course the next blow, and blunder will be – that you have left Town and that Messrs Walker and Lloyd cannot get the letter to take to Knight Bruce – Oh if only Mr Ironside would only wait till I am dead and buried for all these futile consultations! I should be very much obliged to him – for a person who had sufficient presence of mind to say "Boo" to a goose when it hissed <u>intimating</u> to the charming Mr Loaden and his amiable Client that he, and all my soi-disant[5] friends (??!) quite believed them till I refuted them in a court of justice! – never of course troubling his head – how – or where, – that is <u>whose money</u>!!! I am to spend – to take those proceedings and fish up the witnesses of 18 years! then this said brute of an official letter – begins "Madam" – as much as plainly to say to Sir Liar: – "you see <u>I</u> have no interest what ever in this woman; – I am merely an <u>agent</u> asked by her to arrange her affairs; – and consequently I have stirred up the puddle afresh – and set you again at on[e] another, – so now fight it out between you, and I'll look on and see the fun"

Commonplace – and nauseating as much as he pleases – But why in the teeth of my every prediction being <u>fulfilled</u> <u>to the letter</u> – should Mr Ironside think me such a fool? (except indeed for differing from him) did I not say that Genl Thomson would do no more and that the Glasgow papers would not print his correspondence with Boyd? did I not tell him from the first the influence at work in the Manchester Committee? did I not tell you – when you thought Mr Ironsides letter to Mr Wheeler so "splendid" how <u>injudicious</u> it was, – and what the result would be? – knowing Mr Wheelers character rather better than either you or Mr Ironside could possibly do: – and did I also not tell you from the vague manner he wrote to Hartley[6] offering to pay his charges! that the rogue – would make a demand for his dead letter fraudulent bill; and even while I was writing this ! was not his letter travelling to Sheffield to do so? Why then am I such a fool?

Now I am sorry to nauseate you by repeating for the 500th time – that Mr Loadens invariable Cheval de Bataille[7] – on which to meet those infamous letters of Sir Liars (and all his infamies) is a shrug – and "Oh forgeries of hers"! now anyone going to this wretch (knowing what his is and has been for years) in a mild! temperate – impartial spirit, as they would to arbitrate between you and I in a misunderstanding convinced that however angry or mistaken we might be we should both state the truth from which they could draw an equally true inference and thereby come to a just judgement had better stay away – for unless a person is thoroughly prepared to tell him in the <u>fewest</u> and <u>plainest</u> words possible that both he; and his client are now too well known to be believed on Oath – they can but injure me let his Fiend client accuse me of murder if he pleases but it <u>shall</u> be openly in a Court of Justice

PS: as I have told Mr Ironside in his <u>abstract</u> and <u>per se way</u> of viewing the matter he will argue that <u>telling</u> Sir Liar – he meant to make his conduct public comprised <u>Every</u> <u>thing</u>! but to <u>that</u> man it does <u>not</u> C'est le tou qui fait la musique[8] – and even among the <u>ordinary</u> race of human beings – it makes <u>all</u> the difference in <u>what</u> language – the same announcement is conveyed – that is whether one man says to another "Sir your conduct is not that of a gentleman – and I shall take care to publish this fact" or whether he says "you are an infernal Blackguard and I'll post you as such every where" and I <u>know</u> the latter is the <u>only</u> way to produce <u>any</u> effect, upon that brace and not in his or Loadens Den. I made the former quail and turn pale in the court at Paris and hang his hidious head – and could I only see his fool Fiend Client I think I could look the monster straight into that Hell he has passed his infamous life in Earning

Then the beautiful and insulting cant after sending me such a tissue of dastardly outrages of telling me to keep myself cool!!

verily if my pretended <u>friends</u>! were a little <u>less</u> cool I might be more so – and it would be infinitely better ...

... at him would do me more service – that is less deadly – and irreparable injury – God Bless you don't think me unkind or ungrateful but when one is being broken on the wheel one cannot gauge or even moderate ones groans

　　R B L

---

1. Henrietta Wheeler was buried at Père-Lachaise Cemetry, east of Paris. See RBL, 28 May 1853.
2. Emily Bulwer died in a small lodging house in Pelham Terrace, Brompton, from typhus fever in April 1848. When her mother saw her, she was too ill to recognize her. Kate Planché was a witness to the tragic events.
3. James Lewis Knight Bruce (1791–1866) was a conservative judge.
4. Mr J. E. Jenkinson was the chairman of the Bradford Committee. He published a letter in the *Sheffield Free Press* for 18 July 1857, supporting EBL's attempts to suppress RBL's books on the grounds that her husband was protecting her from exposing herself as a bad writer.
5. So-called (French).
6. A solicitor. See RBL, 6 August 1857.
7. War horse (French).
8. It takes all the instruments to make the musical effect (French).

To Rebecca Ryves

Saturday August 15th 1857

Alas! My dearest Rebecca More delay! more blundering, more torture – why did you not give the <u>original</u> letter as I begged – and prayed of you to Mr Eyre Lloyd? – Surely surely! it would have been as safe with <u>him</u> – (such a letter as that he <u>would</u> have taken care of) as safe as trusted through the Post from Dover! and any thing but the <u>original</u> will be of no more use than all the other blunders! – that are elaborately performed with an immense waste of inverse trouble, to torture me I am grieved to see the controversial twaddle of word splitting you are getting into – just like Mr Ironside – when <u>action</u> is vitally necessary – what on earth does it, or can it matter whether I can <u>swear</u>! whether Sir Liar knew Knight Bruce or not at that time? what on earth am I sending or <u>wanting</u> to send which alas! is a very different thing – that letter to Knight Bruce and have his <u>affidavit</u> on it one way or the other but <u>to</u> ascertain <u>effectually</u> and incontrovertibly whether he <u>did</u> know him or not, or had anything to do with that infamous letter or not? which would do me rather more good than all the talking matches in the world even if Mr Ironside with his usual <u>judgement</u>!? <u>delicacy</u> good <u>feeling</u>

and <u>discretion</u>! had them afterwards copied and proclaimed by the Town Crier – as a specimen of his judgement – and that equal absentee his feeling – just look at that insulting – and <u>imbecile</u> letter he presumed to write to me to be shown to Sir Liar! for it is a gross insult for any one even pretending to espouse my cause – to even <u>admit</u> much less to <u>assume</u> – that any thing – such unscrupulous monsters and notorious Liars as Loaden and Sir Liar could say of me now could with any one injure my character – and make it necessary for <u>me</u> to clear myself from such contradictory and too ridiculous lies – before my acquaintance could continue to associate with me!!! though for 20 years these lies known <u>to be such</u> have never done me the least injury instead – of <u>as</u> my pretended friend taking the diametrically opposite and true phase of the question <u>urging</u> me to <u>expose</u> <u>them</u> – and not insult me – by supposing it was due to <u>me</u> to be cleared from any aspersions such wretches could be spatter me with – all of which Mr Ironside had the means of refuting – but never thought fit to raise his voice to do so now this letter I consider as degrading to himself – as it is insulting to me – for it stamps the writer a heartless fool; – he is very fond of telling other people – that they are in a "highly immoral state!" but that <u>he</u> is there can be no doubt for any man living in the flash of lightning hurry that he does and undertaking so much more than any one, or any 20 could do – must necessarily butcher every business he undertakes from not having time even to <u>feel</u> much less to think. I wish I <u>did</u> know Mr Walker – for he at least Independent of his sense – intelligence and <u>knowledge of the worl</u>d would at least have the tact, and bearing of the <u>gentle-</u> <u>man</u> towards one <u>so</u> crushed – and outraged at every point as I am – and not as Mr Ironside has done – after flinging me into the illimitable vague of one of his <u>baseless</u> <u>planless</u> chimeras! hammer away at my poor shattered nerves and har-assed spirit – as if I were a Kitchen range – of which the clumsy scrawl – could <u>not</u> be <u>driven in too tight</u>! Oh! what a pity! what a mistake! that Mr Walker did <u>not</u> go with him to Loadens – as I could with a safe conscience take my oath that Loadens report to Sir Liar was "Pooh! <u>that</u> man! we can do what we like with <u>him</u> why I clearly saw, – that if I had said <u>she</u> was the person who had really intrigued with, and poisoned Liangeler <u>he</u> would not have had a word to say in her defence – only – "well – you must prove it"; – for his game <u>evidently</u> was a <u>neutral</u> one to keep himself aloof – from her interests, – and merely act as an <u>impartial</u> and <u>uninterested</u> <u>employed</u> agent; – "and this you know my dear Sir Edward is the way we have <u>always</u> got her more and more, into toils – she does as you say get hold of such precious apathetic fools! – who have no pride even as to their own diplomacy!" God have mercy on me – and take me – for I <u>can</u> bear no more. Good bye God Bless you I hope you will enjoy yourself at Dover Ever affectly yrs RBL

———————

HUNT

To Rebecca Ryves

Monday August 17th 1857

My dearest Rebecca I am <u>so</u> outraged and so <u>disgusted</u> – at the inconceivable folly of which poor I am made the Victim and Mr Ironsides – rubbish of <u>your</u> being responsible! for this life and death case to me which he undertook with such assurance – and now treats – as if it were a mere political squabble to be talked to tatters week after week between the cross Posts of Sheffield and Brad-ford[1] – I have written once for all to tell him – that though he may have done enough to drive me mad! I am not quite a drivelling idiot – and neither want your nor any one elses judgement – in this affair. I <u>know</u> no ones judgement can possibly compete with my own if I could but get minded and listened to – instead – of outraged and set at naught; – nothing I <u>feel</u> can ever <u>undo</u> the fatal! effects that will be produced by that vulgar – ungentlemanlike and under the circumstances utterly <u>idiotic</u> letter (the Madam one) – instead of saying that at this time of day my Character would need no defence – therefore <u>I</u> had every thing to gain by the Ecclesiastical court[2] the Fiend every thing to lose – for even if he by dint of perjury made my life out to be as infamous as his own <u>he</u> could get no redress – and having condoned their <u>pretended</u> evidence! against me for 20 years – <u>that</u> alone would put him out of court – and yet the <u>fools</u> my pretended advocates! are letting slip all the strong points of the case and thereby not only outraging and <u>degrading</u> me – but what is <u>worse</u>, letting <u>them</u> see what folly! I as usual have to play into [their] hands. – I have written Mr Ironside word what even <u>now</u> he <u>ought to do</u> – if he dont; my destruction be on his head:- for I have tried to impress upon him that not having a <u>sixpence</u> in the world to commence law proceedings – the <u>great</u> thing would be to so manage it – (which with <u>com-mon</u> sense might be done – having <u>all</u> the trumps in his own hand) so as to bring the ruffians to their knees, – <u>before</u> that; – oh! the cursed folly of delaying <u>one moment</u> to go to Knight Bruce; – before he was tampered with! – it was the only thing that perfect strangers like Mr Walker and Mr Eyre Lloyd <u>could</u> have served me in, and <u>now</u> the letter is not to go to them till to day! And Knight Bruce perhaps out of Town at the end of the season before tomorrow! God help me – God keep my reason Thank heaven Loaden has <u>now</u> stuck one of his poisoned arrows into Mr Ironside – so <u>now</u> that his own withers are wrung, he can write as he <u>ought</u> to him; but even here mark the imbecile oversight he upbraids Loaden with his infamy in fishing up filthy evidence – and doing dirty work for his client – to which – their natural and ready answer would be – that every husband sus-pecting his wife had a <u>right</u> to do these things, instead of working the wretches upon the <u>really</u> strong point of the case he never even touches! I mean the damn-ing fact of their so hermetically sealing up this pretended Evidence for 20 years!! and never daring to bring it forward! <u>if</u> Mr Ironside will even <u>yet</u> <u>do</u> what I have

pointed out I may even now be saved, but if more time is to be lost in <u>consulting</u>
– and flummerising you – and Mr Walker – and Mr Lloyd – who with all their
great kindness – <u>cannot</u> be expected to know how to act in such an exceptional
case and with 2 such – unexampled Fiends – then am I indeed lost. I have tried
also to bring Mr Ironside <u>if possible</u> – out of the clouds of ultra theory, down to
the <u>hard</u> <u>cruel realities</u> – that like so many vultures – are preying on my vitals
– by reminding him that October will be here immediately when Mr Wheeler,
and all the rest of the world will be down upon me again immediately, – so that
instead of 12 Tons more talk! Sir Liar ought instantly to be informed that I am
<u>now</u> living at <u>his</u> expense – I also told him he ought the first thing have written
to Mr Hyde – Of <u>course</u> as I have also told Mr Ironside in my "nauseating repetitions" that that Life of Lady Blessington[3] <u>proves</u> the Llangollen conspiracy as
when I wanted it again that Blackguard Monk[4] the librarian <u>one</u> of the Jacques
and Davies[5] gang, said he had sold it to Mr Jacques of the ginshop for 5 guineas!
– this low blackguard Jacques having been formerly connected with the press
and minor Theatres (and who from <u>every</u> crime had narrowly escaped the gallows) distinguished himself as Sir Liars emissary at Llangollen – by getting all
the abuse of me from Mr Ironsides friend "The Liverpool Albion"[6] New Quarterly[7] && – copied into local papers headed with large Capitals "Lady Bulwer
Lytton!" He it was also, that took the spy Barnes alias Leighton to the Chester
races[8] – and helped him to concoct that infamous anonymous letter – beginning he had the Queen's permission to sleep with me! and signed the King of the
Gypsies! – Any man that was not a perfect fool – or what amounts to precisely
the same thing, – that had not so many irons in the fire that he had not time to
know his right hand from his left like Mr Ironside with <u>such</u> weapons in his hand
– would smash those wretches in 24 hours – therefore if he goes on – <u>reversing</u>
the positions – and giving them the vantage ground as he has hitherto done
– God have mercy on me! – I also informed him – what he either ignores or in
his usual chimerical way of disposing of every thing does not trouble his head
about that no one can have the <u>entrée</u>[9] to the Ecclesiastical court without a Proctor[10] and each fee to a Proctor is 130 guineas! – But my cup of miseries is never
full enough – and that little Reptile Easton, who not only took my verbal thanks
but accepted my elaborate written gratitude! it appears never gave the Deeds at
all! and as they are for £600! The poor Boys's[11] have had to scrape the £100 to pay
them rather than let them remain in his hands while I have had to borrow the
money from Dr Price to pay the interest and premium! so much for my obligations! to him – which indeed are very similar to those I am generally laid under
producing nothing but humiliation and additional ruin to me! – and to mend
the matter I see between them all nothing will be done with that swindler Clarke
for Mr Easton flings me to Mr Ironside to sue him and Mr Ironside back to Mr
Easton – with a why – don't I <u>make</u> Mr Hyde do it! Mr Hyde to whom I have

never paid a sixpence – and who told me a year ago – he <u>wont</u>, and <u>cant</u> work – and whom I suppose had he gone to Loadens with Mr Ironside the excitement would have killed him. – God – help me – Job – had <u>his</u> comforters[12] – and I have <u>mine</u>; – but the sending me that beastly report! was too much! – Mr Hyde never desecrated my poor dear Sisters and murdered childs grave! but when people have no time to think – how can they feel or act as common humanity would dictate. – I am sorry you are so uncomfortable at Dover, but am myself in such a state of superhuman misery – that I cannot even <u>imagine</u> a state of comfort – God Bless you and help me. Ever, affectly yrs RBL.

HALS
1. A Yorkshire town, north-west England.
2. The ecclesiastical court had jurisdiction over rights of marriage, actions for divorce, restitution of conjugal rights, etc.
3. RBL had annotated by hand *The Literary Life & Letters of the Countess of Blessington*, 3 vols (1855), held at Llangollen library which at that time was situated above the post office in Bridge Street.
4. Charles Monk was a bookseller on Bridge Street, Llangollen, who also ran a circulating library.
5. George Davies was the Llangollen postmaster, who ran the post office, next door to The Eagles tavern in Bridge Street. It was not run by a Mr Jones, though this may have been the name of one of the staff. RBL may be referring to Edward Jones, who ran the Red Lion tavern, which was also on Bridge Street, Llangollen. RBL believed that Mr Jones and Mr Davies were intercepting her mail on behalf of EBL.
6. A Whig weekly newspaper, published in Liverpool (1825–59).
7. The *New Quarterly Review and Digest of Current Literature, British, American, French and German* (1842–62) set out to take note of everything of importance in the book world, but the pace soon slackened off. In 1857, there was a marked increase in the political content.
8. The racetrack was at the Roodee in Chester, an historic city near the border of north Wales.
9. Entry or priviliged access (French).
10. RBL hired the services of two ecclesiastical proctors. See RBL, 0D39II.
11. Fanny and Augusta Boys.
12. See Job 16:2 and RBL, 29 December 1853.

To Rebecca Ryves

Tuesday August 18th 1857

My dearest Rebecca

I am too ill to be bored with word splitting I <u>never</u> meant to write to Mr Walker or <u>any</u> <u>one else</u> that I <u>would</u> swear Knight Bruce did not know Sir Liar then, but if I <u>had</u> written to him "I could swear Sir L did not even know Knight Bruce" Mr Walker nor no one else would have been so obtuse as not to have understood so <u>very common</u> a façon <u>de parler</u>[1] – I have heard nothing of or from Mr Walker what a fatal mistake letting Mr Ironside go alone to Loadens – <u>any</u> one would have done for a witness – . What another fatal mistake Mr Walkers acting separately from Mr Ironside – and <u>pretending</u> ! to know nothing of Mr I's movements! (so likely!) when all the world know "union is strength" Mr Ironside <u>now</u> actually tells me he sent that Park Lane letter to me to see – before it was sent he did indeed asking me to make any suggestions or alterations – I made 3 – not one of which were adopted ! why then insult my common sense by telling me I was consulted? I must say I think it more than unfeeling actually unprincipled – in Mr Ironside after getting me into this quagmire throwing all the onus upon you! for if he had not had your "giant intellect" to fall back upon – would he – or could he have answered it to his conscience to wash his hands with such apathy of me and my fate, and not care what the deuce supervened as long as <u>he</u> had no responsibility and was out of the scrape, as that infamous vulgar – and disgusting letter he wrote to me! to be shown to my Enemies to whom it will be <u>such</u> a triumph! clearly evinced

I hope to God you have not further degraded me by so <u>very</u> silly! and injudicious a proceeding – as writing to Green and Partridge!![2] to undertake my case – which would be precisely as if at the commencement of the Crimean War – England had humbly sued the Czar – to lend her some Troops from the Don![3] but if you <u>have</u> done so – of course I shall be again told that I was consulted! because informed of it when I had no means of preventing it. I do not wish to be, and am sorry to appear ungracious – but you must suppose tortured as I am at every pore – beset with <u>ruin</u> on every side – it is <u>too</u> great an aggravation of my misery – to have my fate bandied like a shuttle cock backwards and forwards between cross posts – without any earthly interest or fixed purpose concerning it – and I laid under heavy obligations for being additionally wrecked and outraged – God have mercy upon me

affectly yrs R B L

HUNT
1.   A manner of speaking (French).
2.   Solicitors.
3.   Don Pacifico was a Portuguese moneylender whose house in Athens was pillaged. After being refused compensation from the Greek government, he sought aid from Palmerston on grounds that he had British citizenship since he had been born in Gibraltar. Palmerston sent ships to blockade the Greek coast without consulting France or Russia, who were the joint guarantors of Greek independence.

To Rebecca Ryves

Thursday August 21ˢᵗ 1857

Indeed my dearest Rebecca I am <u>not</u> ungrateful for all (more especially <u>your</u>) kind motives but knowing the <u>incarnate</u> and <u>exceptional</u> not to say unprecedented Fiend that wretch is – you cannot wonder at my doubting <u>every ones</u> judgement in the matter – when it is <u>more</u> than a matter of life and death to me. Were it otherwise – I should of course let things quietly take their course only feeling and expressing gratitude for their kind efforts and intentions to serve me. But when one <u>is</u> – drowning – ungrateful as it may appear on first law of nature principles – one doesn't study how to dig ones nails into the arm stretched out to save one if one feels or fancies it is letting one sink – therefore was it that I felt and still feel so indignant at that coarse vulgar and <u>injudicious</u> letter of Mr Ironsides – degrading to me <u>only</u> in so much as it would give such wretches a glorious handle against me – from seeing how <u>completely</u> and fully he took up a totally <u>wrong</u> position. – Of one thing I am <u>very</u> <u>certain</u> so well do I know those <u>utter</u> <u>Blackguards</u> – who would be quite capable by forgery and perjury of swearing – mine, or any body elses life away – that however Mr Walkers gentlemanlike – Jesuitical – astute mode of proceeding – may <u>nominally</u> gain the victory if one <u>is</u> gained – ??? the <u>real</u> defeat to them will have been in the black blunt unvarnished <u>truths</u> and supreme contempt contained in Mr Ironsides last letter – to Loaden for <u>that</u> is the only sort of leaven wherewith to knead such natures. I also feel convinced that if they <u>do</u> succeed in extorting any pecuniary redress from that monster for me – he will <u>effectually</u> contrive to poison me in less than six months, as I am sure that he would rather part with his infamous life than his money – therefore I never can believe that they will succeed in extorting a farthing from him. <u>I</u> still feel that it was <u>wrong</u> not to go <u>instantly</u> to Knight Bruce – but shall only be too happy to <u>own</u> myself wrong – should events convince me, that I was. Truly may they say that it is the <u>last</u> straw that breaks the Camels back! for that last £100 of the poor Boys's gnaws – grinds – saws and screws – me more than all the <u>rest</u>, and has thrown me into a most deplorable state – a pity the amiable Mr Loaden does not know it; or he could say he had proofs of my having miscarried and Mr Ironside might diplomatically tell <u>them</u> it was doubly necessary for <u>me</u> to vindicate character in the Ecclesiastical court!!. – however I drink your health now in <u>Tumblers</u> of claret, it is excellent, and I really think it saves my life – for which I hope you wont expect me to be grateful to you. I told that Boulogne woman whose letter I sent you yesterday – that the reason Miss Landons Brother[1] – or any of the other wretches did not bring actions for Libel against me – was for the same reason that Mrs Beaumont![2] will not bring action – against the Boulogne people for all they are now saying of <u>her</u> – and I then proved to her that I had not calumniated L.E.L Mr Ironside will send you a very kind letter I got this morning from a Mr Wrightson[3] making me a curious proposal (not of marriage!) had he made it last year – I should have listened to it, now, I could, not if I would. I am so tired with writing this, that I must say good bye and God Bless you. Ever gratefully and affectly yrs RBL. –

HALS
1.   Whittington Henry Landon (1804–83) was LEL's only brother.
2.   Laura Deacon, EBL's mistress.
3.   Mr Wrightson made friendly overtures to RBL. She later suspected him of being in league with EBL.

To Mrs Jermyn[1]

Clarkes Castle Hotel Taunton
Thursday August 21st 1857

They say sunshine cannot cheer a grave, not true, for your letters dear kind Mrs Jermyn come, and cheer like so many sunbeams – all my poor dead withered life – God bless you! and all kind Samaritan Spirits like you. – I am still fearfully ill, and weak, – and if you <u>knew</u> or could imagine what I have gone – and am going through – your only wonder would be that I am such a <u>consommé</u>[2] of <u>Cats</u> – as to have still any life left in me. –

Good Mr Ironside– and others who are working for me – seem – now quite elated, and this morning send me a hope (which however I am afraid to indulge in) by telling me to go to sleep and not trouble myself about any thing – till they wake me up; – it appears by their barefaced – contradictory lies and their asinine folly in inculpating persons of note in their infamy – the <u>great</u> Man! and "Most sublime of rascals his Attorney" have got themselves so tightly into one of their <u>own</u> <u>springes</u> that they would give their black souls, to save their ugly necks; <u>nous</u> <u>verrons</u>;[3] but the moment I have any good news, you, dear kind Mrs Jermyn shall be one of the very <u>first</u> to hear of it. I am perfectly inundated with letters about that infamous wretch Mrs Beaumont – alias Miss Laura Deacon[4] – the creature I and my poor children were turned out of our home for – she has taken up her abode at Boulogne with the present <u>lie</u> of her infamous Paramour – being the guardian of her and his Bastards! and actually dares to show a letter from the Fiend, in which my poor murdered Emily's grave is desecrated by this blasphemous forgery "you know my dear Mrs Beaumont my daughter Emily's high esteem (!) and deep affection for you"!!! the wretch I hear has her rooms hung with Portraits of her infamous Paramour and a picture of Knebworth which she points to saying "As soon as that horrid wife of his is dead I shall be Mistress of that magnificent place" – You may guess how all these letters, and details from perfect strangers harrow me up – but since my Book and "Appeal"[5] they say they are <u>determined</u> to hunt her out of Boulogne, being as you may suppose furious – at having been entrapped into visiting, and recieving in society – a common Prostitute, of the very <u>worst</u> kind; but they really deserve it, for she <u>talks</u> very big – of all the Royalties!! and fine people she knows, as no gentlewoman would brag; – but <u>Humbug</u>! is to English people what Manna was to the Israelites in the wilderness a sort of miraculous food that sustains them under everything[6] – with this difference that it is not exactly <u>Angels</u>! food, but quite the <u>reverse</u>. Ten thousand thanks – for the offer of the Chocolate, but I dare not touch any thing, at all rich – but as I plainly see that great large kind heart of yours, is bent upon sending me half Liverpool! I'll tell you what you shall send me, if you can get them? and what I will gratefully accept – is half a dozen (mind not <u>one more</u>) large ripe Pears – but be <u>sure</u> and tell your servant <u>not</u> to pay the Carriage – as if he does – the odds – are I shall never get them; but if this be a troublesome or an <u>impossible</u> commission (as it would be <u>here</u>, where there is no fruit of any sort to be had) <u>pray</u> do not give it a second thought – But Believe dear kind Mrs Jermyn that nothing can increase or diminish the grateful affection of your sincere Friend

     Rosina Bulwer Lytton

     alas!

HARV
1. See RBL, 3 July 1857.
2. Thin soup (French).
3. We will see (French).
4. EBL's mistress. See RBL, 16 June 1854.
5. *Very Successful!* and 'Lady Bulwer Lytton's Appeal to the Justice and Charity of the English Public'.
6. The Lord provided the Israelites with this miraculous food for forty years. See Exodus 16:35.

To Rebecca Ryves

Saturday August 22nd 1857

My dearest Rebecca of course whether they succeed or not I shall be always grateful – most grateful – to Mr Walker – and Mr Eyre Lloyd – beginning with <u>you</u> the <u>cause</u> – and to Mr Ironside also – though I could wish the latter had not shaken me up quite so roughly – for to be good and disagreeable <u>is</u> as Elizabeth Smith[1] says high Treason against virtue, and this High Treason Mr Ironside is always committing. I need not say – that <u>if</u> Mr Walker succeeds you need never want a home – and you need not thank me for I shall owe you <u>more</u> than <u>that;</u> – and hope should such a thing ever come to pass – not to cancel the boon to you – à l'anglaise[2] by making it as uncomfortable to you as possible. My only fear is, that by going on <u>general</u> principles – Mr Walker is mistaking his ground – and is <u>deluded</u> by Sir Liar's <u>continuing</u> the <u>correspondence</u>! which I see clearly is simply <u>pour battre la chamade</u>[3] & <u>spin out the time</u> till the 11th hour, – when he will throw him over, and go back on every word he <u>promised</u> <u>if</u> he <u>does</u> promise anything I had a letter from Mrs Greene of Boulogne this morning – who had applied to the Galignanis![4] the chief tools of the Brothers Bulwer – to translate Very Successful who of course would not!! – I told Mrs Greene – I did not in the least pity the English who had made that vulgar bragging patent Prostitute, the <u>soi-disant</u>[5] Mrs Beaumonts – acquaintance as <u>Humbug</u> was to the English what manna had been to the Israelites in the wilderness[6] – a miraculous susten-ance! – that enables them to bear anything. – It is <u>good</u>!! Sir Liar having given out at Boulogne – that he meant to answer my Pamphlet!! but even there they looked upon this, as a <u>canard</u>[7] – but ask Mr Ironside to send you her letter, and Galignanis – which I sent him today – between the fever suspense despair! and heat – which is Earthquakey – I am fearfully ill. Good bye, God Bless you Ever affectly & gratefully Yrs R Bulwer Lytton

The greatest obstacle of all, to my getting anything is, that that Fiend would rather lose his right hand, than give me the means of being <u>freed</u>! from the tor-tures he has taken <u>such pains</u> and spent <u>so much money</u> to entail upon me and the <u>gentlemanlike</u>! will never achieve anything with him though the vulgar fear of uncompromising exposure might

---

HALS
The end of the letter is missing.
1.   See RBL, 24 December 1836.
2.   In the English way (French).
3.   A form of surrender (French).
4.   A French publisher.
5.   So-called (French).
6.   Exodus 16:35.
7.   A lie (French).

To Rebecca Ryves

Monday 24th of August 1857

My dearest Rebecca I am suffering martyrdom from what I believe is called " a surfeit" – IE – a terribly red – angry rash – not in my face – but all over my neck and shoulders, and worse still <u>under</u> my arms – which alternately burns, and itches like a blister! all brought on by my own folly in drinking a glass of cold water, when I was very warm – of the torture these blisters are under my arms I can give you no idea – moreover – every thing fatigues and knocks me up – or rather down – for the least exertion prostrates me – and last Evening that Mr Wrightson[1] who is so urgent that I should give lectures on the Queens – of England – came over from Bristol[2] to see me – he is not only an <u>ugly</u> man of the most florid style of ugliness but a mixture of <u>all</u> the ugliest men I ever knew, – Sir Liar! Lord Montfort! and Sir Henry Leeke![3] – got up most elaborately, – and regardless of expense! – and his only beauty – a pair of snow white, and beautifully shaped hands – were greatly disfigured by enormous rings, – one of which had a strong family likeness – to the jewel of the Philippine Isles[4] – that Camilla gave Gil Blas[5] – or a Dessert spoonful of red currant jelly. – I am so used to be underrated – more especially by my friends and advisers – that when any one – says – that they admire my books – my first impression is, that they are laughing at me – but this man spouted out so many passages from them – and analysed them with such verve – pointing out – the original delineations where (he said I had achieved little gems) in comparison with Sir Liars – stilted bungled plagiarisms – in the same arenas – that I – was compelled to end by believing that he really was – misguided enough to be sincere in his very extraordinary, and unusual Enthusiasm – which – from its novelty had such a strange effect upon me – that I think it had more to do with throwing out this surfeit upon me, than even the cold water. – He seemed to have a proper horror of that Blackguard Forster – and that fellow Dilk[6] of the Athenaeum[7] – he had just been to Bath by old Loadens invitation to see him but Savage Walter[8] was ill in bed, – This Mr Wrightson brought me as a present some Engravings from Bristol – I am sure Fanny and Augusta – must have been surprised at the Estimation this man appeared to hold me in as ones friends (?) who for the most part have the lowest possible estimate of one in every way – are always astounded to find there are people with whom one is a Prophet. He said he had been Private Secretary to Lord Cloncurry[9] – oh! then said I, I must have met you at Lyons[10] – "No", said he – "I always remained at Maritimo" – He was so urgent, about the lecturing Plan – that I was at once obliged to negative it, by saying that no-one could undertake those sort of things without a shilling in their purse – whereupon – "Oh all that he had in the world was at my disposal! as he was sure – that in one week – I should clear enough not to owe a shilling in the world" (??!!!) but this, as you may suppose I peremptorily declined – as fate appears to be rapidly (in my case) abusing the indisputable privilege she has – of tampering with the destiny of mortals, by laying me under heavy obligations to perfect strangers – who, on the strength of it, of course think they have a perfect right to use me as coarsely – and as roughly as they please; – and I God forgive me would rather not be served, than skinned and scalped at the same time. – That poor dear kind Mrs Jermyn who was always wanting to send me semolina, or chocolate – or something, – to appease her I at length said well you may send me 6 pears – and to my shame, and dismay – the result was this morning – a box, containing – a large Queen Pine – an immense shaddock & 2 dozen of large Pears – how I wish you were here to eat them. – She also sent me in her letter a most beautiful Irish point collar, I said I had often heard the Irish speak of Potatoes & <u>point</u> and if <u>this</u> was a specimen of their point, they might keep all the Potatoes and give me the <u>point</u>! I have read those Free presses you sent me – it appears formerly to have been much more of a paper – that "Country Concert" by "Veritas"[11] is very good – but to my taste I never read a more <u>bald</u>, hop – and go – one – style than those letters signed "Caritas"[12] and the matter certainly does not redeem the manner. – I send you Mr Ironsides dispatch of this mg returning – me a letter of Dr Prices – it is as concise – and not more explicit than usual – I'll not close this till the 5 o'clock Post comes in. No letter from you – or any one else. – I think if the ...

HALS
The end of the letter is missing.
1. See RBL, 21 August 1857.
2. A city in south-west England.
3. Sir Henry John Leeke (1794–1870), naval officer.
4. A ruby ring given to Camilla by her uncle, who had been governor of the Spanish settlements in the Philippine Isles. See below, n. 5.
5. The hero of the picaresque novel by Alain-Rene Lesage, *The Adventures of Gil Blas of Santillane* (1715–37). See RBL, 23 November 1833.
6. Charles Wentworth Dilke (1789–1864) was a newspaper editor and writer.
7. Dilke became editor of the *Athenaeum* in 1830 until 1846. See above, n. 6.
8. Walter Savage Landor (1775–1864), poet and author.
9. Valentine Brown Lawless, second Baron Cloncurry (1773–1853), was a radical Irish politician and landowner.
10. Cloncurry lived in Lyons, under Lyons Hill, Ardclough, County Kildare, Ireland.
11. Truth (Latin).
12. Love (Latin). Harriet Urquhart's pseudonym for the political articles she published in the *Morning Advertiser* and the *Sheffield Free Press*.

To Rebecca Ryves

Wednesday August 26th 1857

In bed – awfully ill
My dearest Rebecca

I am truly sorry to hear of all your <u>contretems</u>, and <u>mécomptes</u>[1] for the last 3 days – the more so, that it is so typical, of my own miserable Hell upon Earth state of existence

I sent you (Post office Dover which I hope you will write for) a packet describing that Mr Wrightsons visit and sending you a letter from that good kind Mrs Jermyn. – You know as much about my affairs as I do – I can tell you nothing

– except that I am too – too wretched and too much tortured to live – and it <u>is</u> cruel to keep any poor wretch in such suspense, when more than their existence is at stake – Mr Ironside inclosed in a black cover – this morning – one of Mr Walkers short mysterious notes – which I never understand and of course am not meant to do so till plunged into some fresh mess – the note I returned, as it was sent without a word to Mr Ironside – all it contained as well as I remember was

"Dear Sir

some of our lady friends seem to think Sir E will over reach me by subtlety I dont think that likely I offer him a pleasant alternative which I dont think he will accept – proceedings then can be taken"

Remember I quote this <u>satisfactory</u> Epistle from memory – it was dated Monday – now all I can make out of this is, <u>that as usual</u> an an [*sic*] immensity of time has been lost in obstinate, and chimerical shadow hunting that my ruin is now <u>sealed</u> that it was a fatal, and irreparable mistake, <u>not</u> going to Knight Bruce at once who of <u>course</u> will <u>now</u> be tampered with, as every man in England <u>can</u> be; – that as I said from the <u>first</u> the <u>gentlemanlike</u>! would never achieve anything with such a Blackguard upon whom <u>fear</u> is the only thing to act – and seeing as <u>usual</u> the deferential and creep mouse tone pursued with him; what <u>would</u> have caused fear, vigorously carried out in the first instance now resorted to as a pis aller[2] (knowing as he <u>now</u> <u>does</u> that I have not a farthing to carry on law proceedings) will be laughed at, and hailed as it will be, as an additional triumph to that monster. – Mr Walker of course knows nothing about me – and little more of my case – Mr Ironside was so nauseated with it, that it was in at one ear and out at the other so that he had not a word to say in reply to Mr Loaden and could hit upon no less cruel and insulting plan of sinking me – than writing me that vulgar brutal degrading and idiotic letter – over which Loaden and his Fiend Client must have roared – and chuckled and which they of course keep as a sinking stone against the next whirlpool <u>my Friends</u>! in their heartless conceit plunge me into – for while Mr Walker – and Mr Ironside – are enjoying the <u>excitement</u> of the <u>game</u> – of which I am the stake – for such it is to them – and inflating themselves with an exaggerated idea of their own indomitable <u>cleverness</u> it is of course of little <u>import</u> what superhuman tortures I am writhing under ...

_____

HUNT
Incomplete letter.
1.　Hitches [*contretemps*] and miscalculations (French).
2.　Last resort (French).

To Rebecca Ryves

Thursday September 3d 1857

"Tell me what you wish!!! and I will write to Ironside"!!! only <u>now</u> to be let to die in peace and not kicked to death by grass hoppers the <u>one</u> thing – that I have begged and <u>pray'd</u> far more than I would beg and pray for my miserable life <u>wont</u> be done; – and in order to add insult to injury as is usual with me – not the least notice ever taken of it! in your rigmarole of to day I should think your prig friend Mr Walker would suit Sir Liar admirably, and I hope all this noodling will pave the way, to an advantageous <u>liaison</u> between them; – of <u>course</u> Sir Liar has found out all about <u>him</u>, – for <u>he</u> happy brute can do his <u>own</u> work, – and not be wrecked upon the outrages of charity blundering like his victim – what <u>I</u> wish!! indeed – with your "great mind" on the one side, and the giant apathy – self sufficiency and colossal deference to the great man on the other why should I <u>presume</u>, as you all plainly show me to have a wish? – As after Mr Walkers "careful watching of the Divorce Bill" – it turned out that he knows nothing about it! as I <u>do</u>, I beg to inform him there is not a single clause in it which can benefit any woman breathing, unless she was happy enough to have a father or brother who could <u>feel</u>, and would <u>act</u> for her. In continuation of the usual diplomatic hugger mugger (the only attempt at diplomacy in the matter, and consequently a caricature of it) one is not even given the satisfaction of knowing <u>where</u> the great man is? and verily if he is only at Knebworth; for anyone <u>else</u> but me! – he would be quite as accessible as if in London – but what am I dreaming about! When astuteness and caution! does not reach to the possibility of an <u>important</u> <u>vitally</u> <u>important</u> letter being forwarded to <u>Mister</u> Knight Bruce! by which address it would certainly never reach him amen.

HALS
Incomplete letter.

To Rebecca Ryves

Monday September 7th 1857

your letter of Saturday just come

No – my dearest Rebecca – Mr Walkers creep mouse deferential mode of proceeding <u>never will</u> do any thing with that Fiend and I am far too deeply wrecked, and outraged – to feel grateful to people who only intermeddle in my affairs to injure me more through their cursed self sufficiency apathy, and obstinacy. <u>Of course</u> I cannot expose Sir Liar more than I have done; – nor does he care <u>One</u> <u>fig</u> about <u>my</u> exposing him! – but he would quake to his craven soul if <u>others</u> did so; effectually – and <u>really</u> that is if there was <u>one</u> true – and courageous man in in [*sic*] England, – but they are one, and <u>all</u> sneaks and cowards – and when it comes to the point; – make the most prudent discovery that after all! they have <u>no right</u> to interfere in a gentlemans private vices! – even Mr Ironsides theoretical valour cooled, and his courage like Bob acres,[1] oosed out of his fingers the moment he had to come to close quarters with the great man! the superiority of whose rank in life immediately awed him! though – being his <u>victim</u> there was <u>no</u> respect or deference for me, or no insult, and outrage too coarse, and too free, and easy to fling at me! –

Sir liar of <u>course</u> don't care one lie – for having his infamies recapitulated to him – <u>sub rosâ</u>![2] – or told what tortures he has inflicted upon me of which he is perfectly <u>aware</u>; <u>that</u>, having been the successful aim of his life: – but c'est <u>le tou qui fait la musique</u>,[3] and other men telling him, – <u>not</u> in <u>mild</u> gentlemanlike Jesuitical murmurs! – but in stringent uncompromising terms, the effect, it had upon <u>them</u>, and that <u>they</u> were determined to expose it; is <u>a very</u> <u>different thing</u> – and would soon bring him to his senses. But my miserable fate is consistent from the smallest , to the greatest things, if I only send a person for a quire of paper; – that I am in urgent want of; – they'll come back with a dawdling – "I <u>told</u> them to send it; they said they <u>would</u>; – and what can <u>I</u> do more?" – my way is always a shorter, surer, and more consciencious way;- to bring <u>with</u> me the thing I am sent for; or not come away till I have seen that it <u>is</u> done; – I never depend upon I <u>tolds</u> and I <u>thoughts</u>, – I did not when your room had to be furnished in a day at Thurloe Cottage, – I sat up all night helped to do it; and saw that it was done; – and I believe you found it comfortable when you went into it; though I was so <u>immoral</u> as your friend Mr Ironside would say; as to go in debt for every stick of furniture in it, not having a penny on earth then, any more than now – and dearly I paid for my immorality for that cheat Smith who furnished it, was the fellow who set all the people on, at me. – There is no use in saying it is <u>my fault</u>! that Knight Bruce was not instantly applied to!! – for when I wrote to Mr Walker to urge and <u>implore</u> it; thinking I had <u>some right to see my own interest</u> as no one <u>else</u> did; – his creep mouse and I think rather cool and certainly cruel answer was – "when – the time came"! or he saw fit, – or some prig of a sentence like those (for I have not the note at hand) he would apply to <u>Mr</u>! Knight Bruce of <u>course</u>, when I thought K: Bruce, was in England, and I begged and prayed, he might <u>be gone</u> <u>to</u> – I insisted on the necessity of the <u>Original letter</u> being <u>taken</u> to him and of <u>course</u> equally no one in their senses, – would – or at least <u>ought</u> to send the <u>original</u> letter through the Post! – as you wanted to do from Dover much less, abroad! – but once for all – I tell you – I could take my <u>Bible Oath</u> with a safe conscience, that Knight Bruce never <u>saw</u> or <u>heard of that letter</u>; – and <u>there in</u>, was no great strong hold! that all these twaddling talkers! could not see! and

<u>now</u>, unless the <u>exact</u> letter I wrote is written to him, applying to him on the subject, will do <u>more harm</u> than good – for one of Mr Ironsides, short, unintelligible, and offensive curt chops, – which he, and you are welcome to think as "masterly"! as you please (when <u>more</u> than my existence is not at stake, – will only affront, and irritate Knight Bruce, – and additionally injure me; – but it is easy to see how Mr Ironside (doubtless at the instigation of Mr Walkers mild – gentlemanlike stagnant pool – system, for like you Mr I, – marvellously affects new people, and thinks the last speaker an Oracle!) is drawing in his horns, for last week I sent him a paragraph from an Edinburgh paper that had been sent me, which said that Miss Madeleine Smiths[4] Education had been perfected by going from her catechism to the study of Bulwer's Lucretia[5] <u>asking</u> him to reprint this in The S.F.P.[6] – which he never did. – I sent him a paper signed "Ajax"[7] yesterday – I dare say he'll not publish that either as it certainly is not written, in the bold, chop Guillotine style, he so much admires. – How differently <u>dear</u> Sir Liar does his work! we have now found out, that that infamous blackguard Clarke (about whom of course nothing will be done) had his orders to leave my book open on his Counter – at the name of Prosser,[8] and tell every one that it was Miss Prosser of Mount House! that I had shown up – and the Boys in the street were set to call out this after her, the plot being of course to get the poor Boys's[9] as they kindly got me that £100 deprived of the means of Earning their bread – which he has as usual succeeded in; – but it is partly their own fault, as <u>I</u> wanted six months ago to have written to Miss Prosser expressly denying this calumny but <u>they</u> thought it better to let it blow over (I knowing it was <u>not</u> better as common sense, and common feeling told me that if the woman thought herself aggrieved; I owed her an explanation and apology) – and the event, has proved I was right; as I wrote to her on Friday, to that effect, and she replied saying – my note had completely satisfied her, and set the matter at rest. – Yet so sapient are my friends! (?) who effectually do Sir Liars dirty work better even than his paid tools – that I have no doubt that Mr Ironside 10 years hence – hearing from such high authority as the Liverpool Albion – Penny a liner – or the sapient Mr Jenkinson – of the Asinine Manchester Committee that the <u>reason</u> Sir Liar had tried to suppress very successful was – that it would make Enemies for me in Taunton! by my having ridiculed the Tauntonians! he would have the wisdom to repeat this to you as a fact! adding "no doubt <u>that was</u> the case"!!! – why, the very circumstance of that villain Loaden so soon Eating his own words! and saying Mr Ironside had "dishonestly falsified them" would have put any <u>one else</u> on the <u>qui vive</u>, given them the clue to the whole web of lies, – and shown them the <u>urgent</u> necessity of <u>instantly</u> making known to Knight Bruce <u>what</u> <u>he had</u> <u>been accused of</u> – but there is no sense like the sense of feeling – and as Mr Ironside <u>only</u> acts in deference to your "giant intellect" – and went to Loaden solely because your

attractions had prevailed with him I feel that I owe him nothing but the additional misery of yrs affectly

    R Bulwer Lytton

HUNT
1. Bob Acres is a character in Richard Brinsley Sheridan's *The Rivals* whose name is a synonym for a coward.
2. In secret (Latin).
3. It takes all the instruments to make the musical effect (French).
4. The woman on trial in Glasgow for poisoning her lover. See RBL, 10 July 1857.
5. EBL's novel. See RBL, 23 January 1856.
6. *Sheffield Free Press*.
7. The Greek hero of Homer's *Iliad*, noted for his strength and courage.
8. See RBL, 12 February 1857.
9. Fanny and Augusta Boys.

To Rebecca Ryves

Wednesday September 9th 1857

My dearest Rebecca I wrote you a long (and to <u>me</u>) important letter on Monday, which you ought to have had on Tuesday Morning if it is lost; I will recapitulate the contents – simply because I am quite tired of being treated, and written to as if I were the greatest fool under the sun, – otherwise for all the good I get, by begging as if it were for my very life to get anything done I might as well quietly submit to this sort of Irish Post Bedlam broke loose sort of work. In Haste yrs affectly R Bulwer Lytton

---

HALS

To Rebecca Ryves

Thursday September 17th 1857

I was not able yesterday (and am not much more able to day) to say all I wanted, but I do, think it is quite on a par – with the rest of the idiotic folly going to Mr Hyde! <u>now</u>, who has so evidently <u>backed</u> out of my case, since he has known, what an <u>utter</u>, and <u>hopeless</u> beggar I am; – and who as a Lawyer will roar! to hear of what Mr Ironsides 4 months back flourish of Trumpets, has ended in ie in going back to him to know how I can be in <u>formâ pauperis</u>![1] after having again – and more degradingly than ever been wrecked by that disgusting and idiotic letter of Mr Ironsides – and Mr Walkers inane creep mouse obstinacy – in giving dear Sir Liar, all the gentle and gentlemanlike warning possible; <u>time</u>, and prevention being <u>everything</u> <u>to such</u> villains the <u>modus operandi</u>[2] having been while every advantage and emollient anodyne, that could be applied to <u>him</u> unsparingly; – Mr Ironside was to <u>pound me</u>, with one of the bars of the Kitchen ranges he used to work at, – and as the fashion is among my friends! to proclaim all my affairs, in the coarsest and most incautious manner by the first Reporter, or Town Crier, that can be caught; – of <u>course</u>, that ineffable Blackguard Mr Stocquiler,[3] – can <u>now</u> report to Sir Liar, – the <u>ne plus ultra</u>[4] Fools nest I have tumbled into – I would rather have to deal with all the villains unhanged, – provided I was <u>let</u> to deal with them as <u>common sense</u> dictated, than such inconceivable asses. I cannot like you, imitate the "judgement and clear Eye"!! jargon but I will borrow one of Mr Ironsides cant phrases and say that it <u>was</u> most "<u>grossly immoral</u>" of him to write to a poor ...

HUNT
Incomplete letter.
1. In poverty (Latin).
2. Way of working (Latin).
3. Joachim Heyward Siddons Stocqueler. See RBL, 10 July 1857 and RBL to Rebecca Ryves, 30 October 1857.
4. The ultimate (French).

To Rebecca Ryves

Friday September 18th 1857

My dearest Rebecca I am sorry if I said anything to annoy you, but really, I am <u>so</u> goaded hunted and tortured that the feeling I have is, that if I had ever possessed even <u>one</u> – true friend I could not be in the <u>awful</u> position I am, and – there are moments when I <u>hate</u> the whole world; I am <u>not</u> such a hard, selfish, ungrateful beast, as to <u>only</u> value peoples services, as they <u>succeed</u> God forbid! since it is "<u>not</u> in mortals to command success,"[1] – and if people "do their spiriting – gently – "[2] – any just, or generous mind – is equally grateful for their <u>intention</u> however wide it may fall of the mark; but what I <u>do</u> resent in all this, is, the utter way I have been set at naught and every supplication of mine disregarded and every feeling outraged, – all of which is <u>double</u> folly – for had they but complied with my wishes – then if failure had been the result; no one would have been to blame <u>but</u> me; – and even now! that that letter is <u>still to be</u>! extorted from that obstinate Prig Mr Walker no doubt the <u>only</u> thing that <u>could</u> make it available ie the letter I wrote being written with it to Knight Bruce will <u>not</u> be done; – but it will be flung to him, in some curt, priggish way, – that will <u>personally</u> offend him; and totally mystify him, as to what is required of him. – Had that Mr Walker been a French man![3] – I know what he would have done, and done effectually before now; – what that is; I certainly shall not tell you at present; if I am alive six months hence, perhaps I may; but he is an Englishman! and therefore has almost as much feeling as a Stone, as much judgement as a Steam Engine, and as much energy as a Tortoise. – I cannot also help feeling poignantly just now, when I am so denuded of all earthly hope, and help, that I feel grateful if a fly's wing fans me, and writhe if it touches me; – how completely Mr Ironside – after having shaken me nearly to death, has contrived with his "Judgement!?! – and his clear Eye!" to alienate every one from me, who Even professed good will, and zeal, Walter Weldon – who really had, and could serve me in a way very <u>important</u> to me, – was completely put off it, by having it incessantly pointed out to him what fools he, and I were? how <u>I injured</u> him by giving him, the means of getting bread! – and how he injured me, by doing the only service anyone can do me defending me against the infamies of a paid press gang like Mr Ironsides penny a liner friend Mr Neill! – and Mrs Jernyn who was so demonstrably kind to me (and after that first point Callas sent me a really magnificent <u>garmiteur</u> of point,[4] which Day said he would give me Twelve guineas for) in an evil hour wrote to Mr Ironside to know if any thing was doing about my affairs? – upon which, he said to me "I have <u>written her!</u> fully on the subject" I can well imagine what his writing her <u>fully</u> would be! perhaps sending her a copy of that charming letter he <u>dared</u> to write to me! however the result is; – that I have never heard from her since: – however kind perfect strangers may be; it shows such, <u>good</u> judgement!! and such a clear eye to tell – all the calumnies of a set of unscrupulous Fiends, – against their victim, when – there is neither time, nor opportunity, to explain the real state of the case; – but from first, to last, his zeal, in propagating <u>everything</u> that could <u>degrade, injure</u> and <u>insult me</u> – has been unbounded! as in the case of that blackguard Jenkinsons letter,[5] – could Sir Liar – or Loaden have done more than <u>publish</u> such a letter in a news paper!? – and then, as usual! – the <u>pretended apology</u> – is a <u>private</u> <u>hugger</u> <u>mugger</u> in an ill written muddle of a letter, from one of his oracles a Mr Crawshay,[6] the <u>insult</u> having been made (not even by the fellow who offered it but by <u>my pretended friend</u>!! Mr Ironside, as public as possible; – and then this ass of a man (Mr Ironside) who has left no coarse outrage and insult unheaped upon me; – (as I will some day or other convince you of) writes to me, saying that he fears from Mr Crawshays "clear eye!! and purse, and <u>sensative</u> mind"! – he may feel insulted – at my calling Jenkinson a low Blackguard – as implying that he, Mr Crawshay associated with Blackguards!!!! but he had no such tender scruples – as to what <u>I</u> might feel, when he <u>published</u> that Blackguard Jenkinsons insulting letter; – or when he handed over to my unscrupulous enemies that outrageously insulting, and <u>ultra</u> idiotic letter he presumed to write me after his interview with the infamous wretch Loaden! – now when with his <u>actions</u>, I couple his former unbounded protestations of service; – and championship and his reiterated blasphemous "By G—ds you <u>shall</u> be got out of it" you cannot be surprised at the bitter, indignation, and contempt I feel for him. What an ass his friend Mr Urquhart seems to have made of himself at the Manchester meeting last Sunday Miss Dyke goes to Town today, and I would send you – some sticks of sealing wax by her; but that I take it for granted you would not like her to know where you are. – Nothing has been heard of poor George Willoughby, but the confirmation – of his death, I am glad the Governor General in Council[7] had the grace to pass a Eulogyium upon his heroic services;[8] for he or his; are not likely to reap any reward in <u>this</u>, beast of a country; – for Englishman collectively or individually, are <u>the</u> greatest and most inanely apathetic brutes under the sun. Poor Edward Willoughby[9] has also had his leg shattered which he fears will oblige him to leave the service Oh! that £100 of the poor Boys! I would cut of[f] my right arm if I could only get <u>that</u>! – But not having <u>one</u> <u>hope</u> on Earth; I now commit myself implicitly to God – I can <u>do</u> no more my physical life is ebbing – in all directions, so I do trust he will have mercy on me and release me soon from this too cruelly unequal life-long torture He has seen fit, unarmed and single handed to appoint me to struggle against, and then Mr Ironside and Mr Walker can go down upon all fours and worship Nena Sahib,[10] as abjectly as they please – yours affectly R Bulwer Lytton .

HALS

1. Joseph Addison, *Cato*, I.ii.
2. 'Do my spriting gently', Shakespeare, *The Tempest*, I.ii.298. A reference to the spirit Ariel.
3. This remark may also have been prompted because Arthur de Noé Walker has a French-sounding name. See RBL, 6 August 1857.
4. 'Trimming, etc., added to dress' (*OED*).
5. J. E. Jenkinson. See RBL, 14 August 1857.
6. George Crawshay. See RBL, 22 September 1857.
7. The Governor-General of India was the head of the British administration in India.
8. There was a memorial plaque placed by the government of India at the former entrance gate of the magazine in Delhi, which George Willoughby helped blow up. His family erected a memorial for him at Bath Abbey.
9. There is a Lieutenant Edward C. P. Willoughby, who was killed in action at Rooya on 15 April 1858.
10. Nena Sahib (known also as Nana Sahib), whose real name was Dhundu Pant (b. *c.* 1821), was a Hindu nobleman. He betrayed the trust placed in him by General Sir Hugh Wheeler (1789–1857), RBL's uncle, that led to the massacre at Cawnpore in 1857 and the General's death.

To Rebecca Ryves

September 19th 1857

My dearest Rebecca What ever peoples, <u>intentions</u> may be, they can do me no possible good in the fearful abyss; in which I am; – where I feel as if I were being torn limb, from limb by wild beasts, and that the laceration might be sufficient! having all the raw places stung by Hornets. What ever Mr Ironsides intentions are, or rather <u>were</u>, he has shown himself a considerable Ass, in my affairs, and a considerable brute, towards me; and he is so totally devoid of all delicacy, tact, and judgement (for it is always the weakest point in any man, where he invariably thinks himself the wisest!) that I confess I do dread his <u>gaûcheries</u>[1] in writing to any one, and I only know that I have lost the proffered good will, of all with whom he has had any communication. My dread of Mr Hyde being applied to, is that, if God himself felt when on earth that those who were not <u>for</u> were <u>against</u> him; what must I feel? – and Mr Hyde who for the last 4 years has backed out of my wreck, as much as he could; – and seeing the bubbles and <u>chimeras</u> Mr Ironsides flourish of Trumpet proffers of service, are based upon lawyer like, he would be much more likely to throw cold water upon them and put a supererogatory spoke in my wheel to say nothing of his now having that venal – treacherous blackguard Stocquiler at his Elbow; which makes me feel, as if I were only being pushed into a fresh Hornets nest.- Irreparable and incalculable injury, has Mr Walker done me (as I foresaw he would) by the terrible delay in having Knight Bruce written to and this worse than dead loss of time – in these futile creep mouse appeals to Sir Nena Sahib,[2] – which only gave <u>him</u> ample warning <u>time</u> – and means to concoct fresh villainy, and in all probability tamper with Knight Bruce. – I might <u>mean</u> – to try and recover Massy's Estate, from the Encumbered Estate's Court – and give myself an immense amount of perfectly useless trouble and lay you under heavy obligations – in my ostentatious attempts to do so; – but if, in spite of your superior knowledge of the <u>Carte du Pays</u>[3] – the details of the matter, and the exceptional peculiarities of the persons to be dealt with I <u>would</u> run counter to all your urgent entreaties – and you saw that instead of recovering your estate my Pig headed obstinacy was jeopardising the mouldy crust you had for your subsistence you could <u>not</u> feel very grateful! to me – now my position is this, – I am suspended by a single thread over a Precipice – at the bottom of which, is a foaming torrent therefore the matter is urgent, but the way this urgency is met by my sapient friends! (?) reminds me, of a gentlemans illustration of Edmund Keans[4] – exaggeratedly lengthening pauses in his Shakespearian characters – "On a certain day Mr Browne, was riding through a certain part of the country when suddenly he turned round and said to his groom

"John; do you like Eggs?"

"Very much sir." Nothing more was said then, but on <u>that day twelvemonth</u>. – Mr Browne again riding through that part of the country; again turned round, and propounded the following query – of relation to the matter –

"Poached; or boiled John?" John's reply on this occasion is not recorded; but of course another – Twelvemonth elapsed before either plan was resorted to, to gratify John's gastronomic taste, I have passed my life in serving others, not when

I had the means of doing so, but chiefly when I really had not, but never have I found much real service, in my hour of need. – I should have more faith in your kind suggestion, about Mrs Tyler, among the Indians, and Members of the Stock Exchange than any thing if she really would exert herself but though she could tell me tales of £1, 500 being raised in two days for some Governess, I am very different – however cruel, complex and treacherously, brought about they may be; they never excite anything more than a little verbal compassion from any one. – Amen! As for "Chevely"[5] they may put it in the fire if they like, and indeed I think it would be the best thing such conscienceless noodles could do – any other mortal would in the natural routine of things, – be told who was to re-publish it; and be put in communication with the Publisher; – touching the projected mutilation of the Book; – leaving out all the Epigraphs or headings – of Chapters, I should not in the least mind; – but leaving out the French, <u>unless</u>, it was replaced by <u>correct</u> English translation, – would be very like – cutting off ones legs, because there was not room to stretch them in an English Railway Carriage; – <u>this</u> for a book of <u>mine</u> as Mr Neill! and his friend Mr Jenkinson I would tell Mr Ironside is no earthly matter; and were they also, – to tell him – "that what annoyed "Bulwer"! in me, was my nose, and Ears, and that if I would cut them off, – I should <u>look</u>, and he would act a great deal better." Mr Ironside, like all Empty echoes, who have no opinion, would implicitly believe this, and <u>solemnly</u> advise it – but as I am not quite a fool – it is too ridiculous talking to me about the French! look at Mrs Gores[6] books! Thackeray's![7] Sir Liars – ! and above all the much be-puffed Miss Brontes[8] books! which latter – are perfectly <u>suffocated</u> with French Ah! had I lived any where but in this most odious – heartless and brainless of all countries, instead of being put <u>down</u> with an <u>Echo</u>, I should have been <u>taken up</u> – by some one who had a <u>voice</u>; and a judgement of their own; and the brains God has given me, with only common <u>fair play</u> would not only have given me bread, but luxuries; – however, the brayings of those asses have made me feel what I <u>can</u> do; and I have no hesitation in saying, that if anyone <u>else</u> not even of the Clique, but who was not <u>me</u>; wrote the book I am now writing there would not be steam engines enough to puff it; – including – the sapient Mr Isaac Ironside – and hard work is it! on the rack both in body, and mind; and obliged to hold a handkerchief to my mouth, least the blood should gush out, and blot the words as fast as I write them; – but that £100! of those poor girls – who work as hard as I do, for a miserable existence – it haunts me night and day! and I cannot die till <u>it</u>, at <u>least</u> is paid my only hope, and chance of getting this book published is through that Mr Wrightson– and yet, with all his hyperbolical admiration and prof<u>essions</u>! he may fail me like the rest, in any thing I <u>want</u>, or that could really serve me. Yesterday I had the most flummerising letter from him, and after a lament upon the stagnation of my miserable and wasted existence here; – and calling me a lost Pleiad![9] – he proposes an excursion to

Manchester before the Exhibition[10] closes, telling me "his purse, and person!!" were both, at my service at which I replied that were I not now unmistakeably an old woman I should feel greatly offended at his proposition; as in the whole course of my life! I had never accepted of any mans "purse or person!!" though being yoked! to one of the meanest brutes of men this mean age, – the <u>former</u> was certainly a great Temptation! I wonder if I lived till 90 (which God forbid!) whether English men would still be brutes enough to insult me? As that poor Sir Hugh Massy Wheeler was <u>born</u> at Bally Wire[11] in 1789 and was the son of Mr <u>Frank</u> Wheeler[12] by Margaret sister[13] of the first Lord Massy[14] – he must have been a younger brother of my Fathers and consequently my uncle! – I envy his brave daughter,[15] the good use she made of her revolver! the <u>Wheeler</u> and the <u>Colt</u>,[16] – did good havoc among the sepoys[17] – could I but <u>choose</u> my men, <u>I</u> should like to try my hand at a revolver too. I really would put on Mourning for that brave old soldier, had I the means, but as I have not, I must only philosophise, as the Irish man did, when reproached for not going into mourning for his Grandmother, "sure divel, a <u>wan</u> of <u>me</u> relations never put on a rag o'mourning for <u>me</u> yet, and why <u>wud</u> I, be after blackening <u>me</u> self for <u>dem</u>?"- I did read your brother Willy's very interesting but harrowing letter from Agra;[18] – horrible as it all is; I keep wishing myself there for then I should soon be put out of my misery, which combines, every <u>antipodes</u> of trial, and torture, acuteness and <u>giant</u> <u>strength</u> in its agonies. Stagnation! and utter helplessness in its <u>quality</u>; – But I ought to apologise to you (new style!) for so long "nauseating you with my commonplaces." Ever affectly yrs Rosina Bulwer Lytton

Had not Mr Ironside with his judgement! and his clear Eye! better instantly write to Loaden to tell him of Mr Wrightsons offer of his "<u>purse</u>! and <u>person</u>!" for <u>that</u> would be a strong point for Sir <u>Liar</u> when the Law proceedings commence!

HALS
1. Awkwardnesses (French).
2. See RBL, 18 September 1857.
3. Lie of the land (French).
4. Edmund Kean was the famous actor. See RBL to Rebecca Ryves, 30 October 1835.
5. A new edition of RBL's novel *Cheveley* was published in 1858 by Charles Skeet.
6. The novels of Catherine Gore. See RBL, 6 July 1853.
7. William Makepeace Thackeray (1811–63) was a leading novelist, whose panoramic social satire, *Vanity Fair*, began serialization in 1847.
8. The novels of Charlotte Brontë.
9. In the Pleiades star cluster, only six of the stars shine brightly, the seventh is hard to see with the naked eye. In Greek mythology, these are personified as the seven daughters of the Titan, Atlas.
10. The Art Treasures Exhibition of 1857 was the first international exhibition of its kind.

11. Hugh Massy Wheeler was born on 30 June 1789 at RBL's family home, Ballywire in the parish of Clonbeg, County Tipperary, Ireland. He had been Commander of the British forces at the time of the Indian Mutiny of 1857. See above, n. 2.

12. This was RBL's grandfather, Captain Francis Hugh Massy Wheeler of the East India Company, who was promoted to major, as reported in the *Bombay Times* of 19 December 1838.

13. Margaret was the second daughter of Hugh, first Lord Massy. See below, n. 14.

14. Hugh Massy, first Baron Massy (1700–88), was the son of Colonel Hugh Massy and the elder brother of General Eyre Massey, first Baron Clarina. He was a member of the Irish House of Commons for County Limerick. In 1776, he became Baron Massy of Duntrileague in County Limerick.

15. Hugh Wheeler married Frances Matilda (d. 1857), the Anglo-Indian widow of Thomas Samuel Oliver, at Agra on 6 March 1842. They had a son, Godfrey, decapitated during the Siege of Cawnpore by a roundshot, and two daughters; Margaret Frances was also killed but his eighteen-year-old daughter, Ulrica, was rescued by an Indian cavalryman who later married her.

16. Artemus Wheeler had patented designs for a flintlock revolver in 1818, while Samuel Colt patented a type of revolver in England in 1835 and, the following year, a revolving gun in America.

17. Indian soldiers, who were employed by the British army.

18. Rebecca Ryves's brother Lieutenant William Ryves, 12th Native Infantry, arrived in Agra from Gwalior in India.

To Rebecca Ryves

Tuesday September 22d 1857

Really my dearest Rebecca The more I think over the frightful abyss, into which I have been plunged, by the heartless fools, who have presumed to thrust themselves into my affairs, without either sense, <u>interest</u>, or means, to conduct them; – the more indignant and disgusted, I am for it <u>is</u> a <u>monstrous</u>! piece of impertinence, to intermeddle in a persons fate, where you have neither the means, nor even the <u>zeal</u> (which often invents means) to serve them, and where they set the chief person concerned in those affairs completely at naught, and aside, and instead of <u>consulting</u> merely outrage their feelings at every point As you require to have <u>every</u> thing pointed out to you, and put into you; and you can feel, or perceive nothing but what is; – I will once for all, <u>show</u> you, <u>clearly</u>, as <u>noon</u> day, – <u>how</u> <u>utterly</u>, and <u>irremediably</u> – Mr Ironsides brutality idiocy, and vulgarity have ruined me when he saw that blackguard Loaden, the sort of letter, any thing <u>human</u>, half a brain in their head, would have written to me for <u>them to see</u>; – would have been simply this –

"My dear Lady Lytton I am too disgusted with my interview with Mr Loaden to even insult you by repeating – his palpable, and contradictory lies – he and his client, must only take the consequence; – of the nice springe they have got themselves into – for I now see your only protection against the unparalleled infamy you have so long and so defencelessly been the victim of; – will be to fully expose it, in a court of Justice; – which as we have now got all the links of the Evidence complete, we will lose no time in doing." – Such a letter as this, would have effectually terrified both the wretches and completely, and powerfully, mystified them as to – the weapons I might have against them, and the resources I might be [ill] with to use them. Whereas the vulgar, insulting – idiotical never to be forgiven letter that unfeeling brute presumed to write me, to send to them!! showed them at once, the bare black, horrible truth! that they had nothing to fear, – for that I had not a farthing, or a friend, in the world, – and was again, by the most flagrant species of fool a superhumanly vain, and utterly heartless one, thrown completely under [their] Chariot wheels; – to drive over, and once more mangle as they pleased; – but fool as I know Mr Ironside to be, from his exaggerated, and over weaning opinion of himself, his preposterous vanity! – and his being so totally absorbed in himself, his rag of a paper, – his ass of a committee, Mr Urquhart and Russia! I do not think that it was entirely folly, that dictated – that inhuman and ruinous letter; – but a paltry contemptible, infernal spite; – because I did not choose to submit to being treated like a woman of the Town by him, – and think it – great honour to boot! – and even now, they are doing nothing they ought to do; – for that ass of a circular, particularly worded, and mismanaged as they will be sure to mismanage it will not get two pence half penny – it will only give Loaden, and the Park Lane Fiend another triumph, and a good roar, by assuring them (as that seems the noodle tactics of my meddlers in all things) that the poor pauper, has not a single weapon, no not even a straw to fight them with, and has at the 11ᵗʰ hour! to go a begging to the stones again for chimerical means to even attempt it; so that they may forthwith rub up their villainy – and furbish up their perjuries and conspiracies as soon as possible; – for their victim is utterly friendless farthingless; and defenceless all the writs in the world served on Sir Liar – would not frighten him now – with that brutal idiotic letter of that self sufficient ass Ironsides in my possession guarantee him, as strongly as it was possible to do, – that I was more helpless friendless, and penniless, and consequently more at his mercy than ever; – this coupled with the time, and chart as it were; if my defenceless position given him by Mr Walkers – priggish, creepmouse, overtures; has made him, and Loaden feel as sure, and safe, as if they were embedded in the Rock of Gibraltar;[1] – added [ill] cruel fools – never having written to Knight Bruce! which depend upon it those astute clever villains who never bungle, have ascertained long, long ago. Now, the first thing that would strike any one of common sense and therefore of course will neither strike – Mr Prig Walker, or Solomon Scaramouch[2] Ironside is that Mrs Bruces[3] deposition ought to be immediately taken (if she is still living at Church St Fulham)[4] as to the state of things at my poor murdered childs death bed –

prior and independent, of her being subpoenaed in Court if I ever get there? Ibid[5] Byrnes (living at her brothers Mr Paul Byrnes Hairdresser ... Hemel Hempstead[6] Hertford to his personal cruelty – neglect of – and brutality while I lived with him, and his notorious adulteries then and ever – and I must say, – in common honesty as you so glibly (I am sure meaning all that was kind) entered into all this ruinous bungling, and hugger mugger against me; – you should without transmitting my just execrations to the man if you fear to offend him; – point out to him late as it is; verbatim ad literatim,[7] – the exact state of the case, as I have set it forth in this letter; and if possible excite in him some glimmering of human sense, and human feelings to try as much as may be (which alas! is about as a drop compared to the sea!) to atone for the cruel supererogation of tortures insults, and difficulties he has wrought for me – not being a system monger (thank God!) nor a self constituted Lord God almighty; – I have always thought – that one could not be too guarded, when we spoke to, or acted for, those crushed, and writhing under a great affliction much less a fight of afflictions as sorrow, and dejection! pre-disposes the heart made morbid by long suffering to interpret bitterly and unkindly every act, and every expression that does not breathe the greatest gentleness, – and most exuberant kindness, but the Kitchen range maker thought differently and hammered me accordingly what first gave me an insight into the mans want of sense, and want of feeling – was his letters to Weldon pointing out my folly! in dwelling!! on my misfortunes! – when every day he was stirring up the cess pool – to rake out materials for the present bungle! – and when I was in such a quick set hedge of ruin – that I must have been as unfeeling as himself – if I did not think of the ruin I had brought on others as well as myself – Then by flying at me for reading such rubbish, as Douglas Jerrolds Paper[8] – which I never do read; and had only bought for the nonce, on account of my name being coupled with Ld Lyndhursts. Next his good sense! and good feeling! in publishing Mr Jenkinsons blackguardedly and gratuitous insult to me, whereas, the tardy apology was strictly private, and hugger mugger, – and his only fear, least Mr Crawshay[9] – or Postchay or whatever the mans name is, should have his feelings hurt! – but all this, I could forgive – but the insult he offered me here, and that infamous letter, so carefully forwarded to Loaden , – I never can forgive, and you may concieve the sincerity of my detestation; when I tell you – by comparison with Mr Ironside – Sir Liar appears to me friendly and humane; – for with all the good will, in [the] world – he never had it in his power to insult, and degrade me, – as this low, arrogant, self sufficient, unfeeling brute has done and his ridiculous, and insulting letter about the opium!! will remain a monument of his arrogant absurdity – long after he has passed away. – Judging by her crabbed – ill written printed things – what an odious prig of a woman that Mrs Urquhart must be! – those "Caritas" affairs,[10] always give me the idea of [ill] Parmigianinos[11] Early pictures painted with bad paint, on rough wood, into which he had not the sufficient space to cram all the common, ungainly things, he dragged into them for it is exactly as if she wrote with an iron pen, dipped in starch on, an unplained deal board. – Now for Heaven's sake – dont to adulate Mr Ironside, and that set; go imitating her bad grammar, and vulgar English, of "the similar ones"!! similar ones, – is the correct phrase, and expresses every thing; – the participle, is quite out of place, – and vulgarises – the sentence down to a par with "the like"! and "such like"! – I am almost mad – for want of sleep – and think I shall soon have to take either to laudanum, or Prussic acid in good Earnest – for this hell of body – and mind night and day – day – and night! helpless, hopeless! and alone, neither, Angel – nor Devil could bear. – Why do they not send some Irish Regiment to Arrah[12] – to quell the insurrection there; and they'd soon say "Arrah! be aisy" I got some of Dr Lococks [Pul]monic Lozenges, said to stop spitting of blood and cure coughs, – but as yet, they have done neither me, nor my Tib, any good – though I give the poor little Doatskin 2 a day, dissolved in water – No letter from you to day – so I suppose they have made some fresh mess, which you are afraid to tell me, and so, it will go on God forgive them. – No [ill] like from Mrs Jermyn nor wont be – now, ever again affectly yrs R B L

HALS

1. A limestone promontory located in Gibraltar which, since 1713, has been under British sovereignty.
2. In the Bible, King Solomon is seen as a personification of wisdom. Scaramuccia is an unscrupulous and unreliable servant, who was a stock character of the Italian theatrical form of Commedia dell'arte.
3. Charlotte Bruce had nursed Emily Bulwer Lytton on her deathbed.
4. Mrs Bruce lived at 1 Church St, Fulham, London.
5. Same (Latin)
6. A town in Hertfordshire where Rosetta Byrnes, RBL's former lady's maid, lived.
7. As spoken (Latin).
8. Douglas Jerrold edited *Lloyd's Weekly Newspaper* from 1852 until his death in 1857. The newspaper's circulation climbed to 582,000. See RBL, 16 June 1854.
9. The first issue of the *Free Press* in Sheffield was financed by George Crawshay (1821–96), an ironmaster and politician.
10. The letters, which Harriet Urquhart published in the *Sheffield Free Press* under the pen-name of 'Caritas'. See RBL, 24 August 1857.
11. Girolamo Francesco Maria Mazzola (Parmigianino) (1503–40) was a prominent Italian Mannerist active in Florence, Rome, Bologna and his native city of Parma. By the time he was eighteen years old, he was working on a number of religious paintings: *Saint Francis* for the church of the Frati de'Zoccoli, and the *Mystical Marriage of Saint Catherine* for San Pietro in Viadana, Italy.
12. Arrah city, located in north-east India, was the scene of fighting during the Indian Mutiny of 1857 when the British were attacked by Kunwar Singh. Other centres included Delhi, Kanpur, Lucknow, Bareilly and Jhansi.

To Rebecca Ryves

Saturday September 25th 1857

My dear Rebecca It is very little matter to me what "you think"! or the fools who are your oracles; and whose vulgarities you so studiously ape with "my sister in Law writes me! to go out with her – " I know, and feel, that I am irreparably injured; – and how could it be otherwise? – with the cross purpose hugger mugger that goes on among you all, – from which I m carefully excluded, – till some fresh mischief is accomplished – when I am appraised of it by Homeopathic globules; – when it can only serve to additionally torture me. I repeat, – that I know what Mr Walker had he been a Frenchman would have done at once and effectually; but he would never have let me know it; – at least till long after; because if made a party to it; – I should have of course indignantly refused it; – but a French man, would have felt and known this, – and done the thing, well delicately and effectually for all parties; – but such ideas, never enter an Englishmans head, because they must first pass through the heart, and they have no hearts for them to pass through. The very fact – the damning fact! of Sir G telling him how it would injure his career if he took up my cause!! would be a powerful! an all powerfully crushing weapon against him, – in the hands of any high minded courageous – singled purposed man; – but find such a thing in this loathsome land of cant, Humbug, arrogance, Public life! Bosh! – as for "Cheveley", as I have never been consulted about it but in the usual offensive round about, hugger mugger way through you, your "giant mind" can decide with the Sheffield savage, about mutilating it, or putting it in the fire, or any other way you may like to flummerise each other on your conglomerated bother – and further injure, and insult me R B L

of course Oh! giant mind! that can always see the Dome of St Pauls,[1] as soon as it is built! The appeal let Sir Sodomite know that I had not a Farthing – but it might also have mystified him into thinking that it had got me a great many Farthings but for Mr Ironsides ruffianly – and Blackguardly letter

---

HALS

1.   St Paul's Cathedral in London, which Christopher Wren started building after the Fire of London in 1666, took over thirty-five years to complete. The dome is the second largest next to St Peter's Basilica in Rome. Both domes were based on that of the Pantheon, built by the ancient Romans.

To Rebecca Ryves

Saturday after my first letter September 25th 1857

I had another letter from Boulogne the other day, – announcing that Mother Beaumont had been drummed out of Boulogne – which she left, vowing vengeance against the inhabitants and saying that "in three months, she should return there a very great Lady!" when the people – who had then turned their backs upon her; would be going down upon their knees to visit her!" – No <u>doubt</u> of it they were English! – I repeat it, had your pompous prig friend Mr Walker, been a French man the <u>natural</u> course he would have taken to serve me, – would have prevented this humiliating and, worse than useless! <u>re</u>-appeal – to the same stones that were deaf to my former one; – and certainly would <u>not</u> have "injured his future career!!" But what a comfort it <u>ought</u> to be to me to think, that Mr Ironside sends <u>you</u> Mrs Jermyns – or Mrs Any – body elses letters, about me, as of <u>course</u>, – both my affairs, and my feelings, even the empty breath of a kind word – that might in this solitary confinement mitigate them <u>must</u> concern <u>you</u> so much more, than they can possibly do me! – Truly "you may bray a fool in a mortar and his folly <u>not</u> depart from him."[1] R B L

No, certainly – a parcel of creep mouse deferential ultra fools! will never terrify Loaden and his <u>clever</u> Client! – moreover as they say "Hell is paved with good intentions!" <u>they</u> may have reason to be grateful to them; but <u>I</u>, have none.

HALS
1.   'Though thou shouldest bray a fool in a mortar among wheat with a pestle, yet will not his foolishness depart from him', Proverbs 27:22.

To William Hartcup

True copy To W. Hartcup Esqr Ditchingham Lodge Bungay Suffolk
October 1st 1857

Sir, Having been extremely ill; Mr Ironside of Sheffield (much to my regret) has only <u>now</u> forwarded me your mendacious, and impertinent statement of the 19th of August. It is easy to make blasphemy of the Bible by leaving out the context, and equally easy, through chronological anachronisms, to make a truth <u>per se</u> a falsehood <u>de facto</u>.[1] If I only <u>now</u>, – to quote your own most insolent words "pretended to be indignant" at the outrageous proposition you <u>presumed</u> to make me from Mr Beavan – why should you have written to me, at the time in reply to my bitterly, and justly indignant letter "really such reproaches you should address to Sir Edward and not to your solicitor"? whereupon, not <u>then</u> being as well aware, as I am now, that when thrown out of ones sphere, in this most vulgar minded of all countries – one should come down to the level of those one is thrown amongst; and divest oneself of all the nice feelings of a gentleman, or a gentlewoman, but <u>not</u> having done so, I did write you in answer to your irate letter the one you have copied disclaiming all intention, of saying anything personally offensive to <u>you</u>; and I did also ask to have your Bill of costs; not chusing to be under an obligation, to any one connected with poor henpecked Mr Sandby who at the instigation of his worthless and ungrateful wife, had behaved so shamefully to me; – for <u>very</u> differently did I treat her, in my house. But when I saw your bill! considering what you had done; and the way in which you had done it; I was astounded and told Mr Hartley, I considered it most extortionate! – Alas! Mr Hartley was serving (?) me gratuitously; and when that is the case with English people they think, there is no liberty, they cannot take with you; no no [*sic*] coarseness, or no impertinence, they may not be guilty of; and above all, that they may move you about like a Chessman without the <u>slightest</u> reference to your wishes, feelings, or superior knowledge of your own position, its intricacies, or its exceptional points; and so, cruelly saddle you with the curse of responsibility; without the justice of free will. – Mr Hartley, pooh, pooh'd your bill to me said he would settle it, and what passed between you on the subject (till I have now read your garbled extracts from his letters, which <u>I</u> never authorised him to write) I knew not; all I <u>do</u> know is, that he sent me a reciept of yours for £20 telling me, he had compounded with you, for that sum, and that an Eminent London solicitor said, – he, would not even have paid that; I also – know, that for months after the murder of my poor dear child, I was <u>incapable</u> of communicating with Mr Hartley or <u>anyone</u>; – but I perfectly recollect, when I was apprised of your cool demand for £600! on the part of Mr Sandby I indignantly asked what I now repeat – how dare Mr Sandby; – in the teeth of Mr Erringtons,[2] – noble, and high minded letter to me – declining the interest of the £400 <u>he</u> had in so chivalric, and unprecedented a manner (for an English man!) lent me, declining to recieve even the principal till it was perfectly convenient to me; when he added like a true gentleman "then of course I should not offend you by refusing it" I say, I indignantly asked, – how dare Mr Sandby or you, presume – to interfere with Mr Erringtons noble conduct? My ceaseless prayer, has been to be able to repay <u>this</u> money out of <u>gratitude</u>; – though were it paid, with interest, and compound interest; I never could repay Mr Errington what I owe him; – and shall feel proud in proclaiming to Every one that I <u>do</u> owe him as long as I have life; – I was also from <u>far different</u> motives, equally anxious to be out of the Sandby debt of the £200, and <u>should</u> have been so long ago – as god knows I have worked hard enough for it! but for Sir Liar Coward Bulwer Lyttons ceaseless and ever increasing conspiracies; – but the interest he <u>has</u> recieved every year punctually though a few months later – than the stipulated time. If you wrote to Mr Hyde on the subject of your Bill I wonder in your grateful statement you did

not insert his answers? – Recently a Pettifogging country solicitor I had occasion
to Employ – in a most deliberate falsehood – not only made out that I was under
a heavy obligation to <u>him</u>; but cruelly calumniated the person, who had really
rendered me this service: under this <u>false</u> impression not content with thanking
him verbally, – I wrote him a most elaborate and heartfelt letter of thanks – for
his noble conduct!!! when I discovered the <u>truth</u>, in unlimited disgust. I wrote
him a very different sort of letter, ten years hence, like a contemporary fellow as
he is – it will be very Easy for <u>him</u> to concoct a <u>garble</u> by suppressin[g] – my last
and producing the first letter of Rosina Bulwer Lytton

HALS
1. Intrinsic ... factual (Latin).
2. RBL owed him money.

To Rebecca Ryves

October One 1857

My dearest Rebecca Hethot is convinced against his will, of the same opinion
still and there is no use in pointing to the blind; or screaming to the deaf – you
dont see that I have been injured in any way; by all this cruel muddle, delay and
<u>false moves</u> – but <u>I</u> <u>know</u> – and <u>feel</u> that I am what I <u>know</u> Mr Walker <u>would</u>
have done if he had been a French man <u>had nothing to do with threats, nor even
with Sir L</u> and as I said before, six months hence if I'm alive which God forbid!
I'll tell you. – my real wreck from first, to last, has been my penniless position
and the millstone of debt it has entailed upon me, had Mr Hyde been a <u>paid</u>
solicitor – <u>he</u> <u>would</u> never have let slip the strong and damning evidence that
has past through <u>his</u> hands alone – but my own firm conviction is, <u>that</u> since
his <u>re</u>-connection he is playing double or quits with me iE – running with the
Hare, and hunting with the Hounds. I also firmly believe that with unlimited
money and consequent perjury at his command – and <u>knowing</u> that <u>I</u> have not
one Farthing on Earth, to insure even real witnesses and an honest defence and
that my pretended advocates have not even zeal – let alone brains, to atone for
the want of financial means, – that Sir Liar will only be <u>too glad to get</u> me into
what under the circumstances will be the fresh, and finishing snare, of a Court of
Humbug and that this new and final springe is what both Knaves and fools are
playing up to for him. – As for the new Humbug Divorce Bill from all <u>I</u> can make
out of it – it may benefit common women with Police magistrates and the only
thing in it having a shadow that would be likely to benefit me is article XCIII
– though by that time I might be dead and burried which I should much prefer
you cannot of course see, how that unfeeling ass Mr Ironsides throwing me back
into the hands of that cheating, and insolent blackguard Clarke can injure and

<u>degrade</u> me but <u>I</u> do. The great charm of my miserable – ultra miserable position is the way I am insulted and set at naught by <u>every</u> fool I have to deal with: being perfectly <u>ashamed</u> of the shillings and pence I have had to borrow from Anne I wrote twice – to Mr Hodgson explicitly forbidding him to recieve my next ensuing parish allowance from that infamous Loaden, or his still more infamous Client, but that as he had recieved and appropriated the greater portion of the last, contrary to my wishes that I now authorized him to pay Mr Sandby the one £10 remaining in his hands and send me the other £10 <u>neither</u> of which letters has he taken the slightest notice!!

After plunging me into – and leaving me in this frightful abyss – only poking – and stirring me up from time to time, with a poisoned spear whenever I was particularly exhausted, and lacerated, I suppose your amiable and sapient friend Mr Ironside would – even now <u>now</u> have the idiotic effrontery to repeat, that if <u>he</u> had had the management of my affairs I never should have been in debt!! or in difficulties!!! As you press me for my opinion of that Circular which otherwise as a useless waste of ink I meant to have kept to myself – I think the only result it is likely to produce is to additionally degrade, and injure me without extracting one penny whereas a well organized subscription beginning at a penny in all the great Towns of the leading commercial Districts could hardly have failed. Look at the nice mess Mr Hartley's cringing – degrading falsehoods to Mr Hartcup have got me into! this is what comes of people managing my affairs in <u>their</u> way – and throwing my feelings, and judgement overboard "Ten years hence of course Mr Clarke of Paternoster Row can say – that to prove <u>he</u> had never dealt unfairly by <u>me</u> – <u>my friends</u>(?) had almost gone on their knees to him to re-issue Chevely stipulating that <u>he</u> was not to be brought into contact with <u>me</u>!! after <u>my</u> violent letters to him!! Oh God preserve my reason at having <u>all</u> my outrageous <u>reversal</u> and <u>I</u> made to bow down to my Enemies, and insulters, and put additionally in their power R.B.L.

HALS

To Edward Bulwer Lytton

Sir E Bulwer Lytton M P! For The woman Beaumont Alias Laura Deacon Strumpet and Spy To That Loathsome and Ridiculous Old Ruffian Sir Liar Coward Bulwer Lytton Knebworth Park Stevenage Herts [on envelope]

Taunton
[October 3 1857]

If you don't like these sort of truths addressed to you on the superscription of a letter? <u>Don't presume</u> to send any more of your low tools and infamous spies to add outrages to all the injuries you have heaped upon me, for as <u>sure</u> as you do; you shall hear from me in this way as I have no brother to kick you

---

HALS

To Rebecca Ryves

October 4th 1857

My dearest Rebecca

I can indeed feel for your shock! about poor Willy – but thank God it was only a false alarm with regard to the subject of my last letters – there is no use in saying any more upon the subject – of course you and every one else are like the King and <u>can</u> do no wrong! it is only I from my insane habit of blurting out the truth and speaking my mind on all occasions – who am <u>always</u> wrong

Going to sue Mr Fred Clarke in November it cannot be done before as Term dont meet. young Hodgson has been from home he told me in two lines yesterday – I send you his letter of to day – as I <u>can</u> own myself in the wrong – I apologised to him for the words "unwarrantable liberty" which I had written under the erroneous impression that Mr Ironside had in an explicit and business like way appraised him of the intended proceedings against Sir Liar and given him due notice <u>not</u> to recieve my pittance, and therefore I had concluded that my refusing to give a receipt for it, was sufficient notice from <u>me</u>. – I said all I could – about his not judging of Mr Ironside by the ordinary rules of civilised society, as me – whom he had so generously, and disinterestedly gone out of his way to serve – he never the less flayed and scalped – in a way that a Cherokee[1] chief – might despair of emulating. – Thank God this cheque of young Hodgsons will enable me to pay the servants, & the washer woman and to get 2 Flannel petticoats – which I am now shivering for want of – I told young Hodgson I am very certainly having all Mr Hertslets correspondence <u>somewhere</u> – but with this horrid spitting of blood – which the slightest exertion brings on – I cannot go and kill myself to look for them. Your not being able to see how mortifying and degrading it is to me to be put again in the power of a shuffling lying fellow like that Clarke of Paternoster Row – is only an other proof that while the most unscrupulous astute and indefatigable villainy is ever at work against me – Blundering oblivion apathy and obstinacy, is all the forces I can muster – Of <u>course</u> Mr Easton was not wrong either! his ridiculous quibble to the Boys – was that what he meant was that <u>he</u> would not take [h]is £1"6"0 fee!!!!!!!! and when they said – and I in one breath what on earth could <u>that</u> have had to do with jeoparding your Fathers £100!? – and could you suppose Lady Lytton would have written you such an elaborate letter of gratitude for £1"6"0!!! or even have laid herself under an obligation to you by not paying it? the little reptile had not a word to say – and the next day had the noodleism to go to Augusta and say he hoped so angry as I was with him, that I should not be offended if he sent me some game! I said it was superfluous – as I made so much of him – nevertheless he sent me a leash of half fledged Tom Tits like himself which he called Partridges. However here is the truth that I should indeed be sorry to do any thing to wound or annoy his Fathers son for whose memory I had the greatest regard, and respect. I also by this mornings Post recieved 3 post office orders – amounting in all to £1"6"0 for the 3 copies of the Sheffield Free Press – which I have sold since May – this being their years subscription the way it amounts to £1"6"0 is that I have made them pay 2d for each paper to include the stamp – next year – they will forward their subscriptions again – when they fall due in May – I will get the 3 orders converted into one tomorrow – and forwarded to you to send to Mr Ironside but if you omit to explain to him about the 2d he will not understand how they come to £1"6"0 – I have had two very kind letters from Mrs Jermyn She it was who sent me the Divorce case – I send you a letter from Augusta – on account of Lalla's account of the quietness of India – which I cannot understand. I sent for poor Mrs Clarke the moment I found out I had no earthly hope of even moving in the quagmire I am in before January! Nothing could be kinder than she was – saying – "Oh never mind me – I am sure to see the way you suffer – and the way you work – morning noon and night – nothing out of Hell could add to your sufferings – at least I'm sure I wont" Oh! shall I even have the power of being able to repay her – for her forbearing kindness – and to prove to her that I dont forget it. – She brought me up the inclosed elegant scrawl – which she said she did not answer or take any notice of – being Certain it was some spying blackguardism – and indeed it smacks strongly of the Pyke caligraphy, and eloquence du billet![2] I am afraid you will not be able to read this scrawl but writing is a terrible exertion to me, as I am obliged to write with my head leaning back as bending forward so hurts my chest – and brings on that blood

    Yrs affectly R B L

HUNT

1.   Native American of the Charokee tribe, whose ancestral lands were North Georgia and the Carolinas. Scalping was a practice that had taken place in the pre-historic period but had continued to a limited extent into more recent times. Cherokee members of the Thomas Legion had been accused of scalping Union soldiers during the Civil War.

2.   Of the love letter [*billet-doux*] (French).

To Rebecca Ryves

Tuesday October 6ᵗʰ 1857

My dearest Rebecca For Heaven's sake <u>dont</u> be so provokingly <u>obtuse</u> <u>car</u> <u>rien</u> <u>n'enrage</u> <u>come cette espére de donce enté le vent avec la quelle vous me tuer à</u> <u>petit fau</u>[1] Once for all and for the 20ᵗʰ time of repeating its <u>not</u> on the score of the <u>money</u>! that I care about that Blackguard Clarke of Paternoster Row having a book of mine[2] – but the gross insult it was to <u>me</u>, to place me – and that swing to [ill]!!!!! again in the fellows power – and if I made 20, 000 by it would not reconcile me to so gross an insult. "Mr Walker thinks that letter was submitted to Knight Bruce,[3] to know if he might <u>legally</u> so threaten his wife?"!!!! Mr Walker is a genius! – and an <u>acute</u> one too! not to see that no gentleman – much less any man wishing to rise in the legal profession – <u>would</u> allow himself in <u>any</u> way <u>to be made a party to even</u> a coal heaver sending such a letter to <u>any</u> woman; – even a woman of the town; – and if you <u>will</u> allow me to <u>know</u> the Fiend I am tied to, <u>rather</u> better, than all your united Imbecilities put together can possibly do; – I could with a safe conscience take my Bible oath, that <u>not</u> only Knight Bruce, but <u>even the Blackguard Loaden</u> – or any <u>human</u> eye but Sir Liars, ever <u>saw</u> that letter before it was sent to me; – <u>I know Sir Liar better</u> he is <u>too cunning</u>, and would have cut off the infamous hand that wrote it before <u>he</u> would have <u>let mortal see it</u>, and only like all over cunning brutes, – over-shot his mark, and reckoned without his host in sending it to me, thinking <u>I</u> would either fall down in a fit, on reading it, or put it in the fire – but fear is for the lying, the cowardly and the infamous and <u>I</u> foiled, and astounded! him by showing it to <u>every one</u> – and as I said before, could, with a safe conscience swear – that <u>I</u> was the first that ever show'd it to <u>any one</u> Then "Knight Bruce <u>may</u> be a friend of his"!! exactly so; and it was for <u>that</u> <u>very reason</u> that he ought to have been <u>gone</u> to the <u>very moment</u> Mr Ironside left Loadens; – now dont write me back, an idiotic and irritating rigmarole of six pages – to say he <u>was</u> then even at that time in Switzerland (which he was <u>not</u>) but granting even that <u>he was</u>; <u>that</u> made it the <u>more incumbent</u> that the <u>instantaneous</u> <u>visit</u>, should have been <u>followed by an</u> <u>instantaneous</u> <u>letter</u> explaining the circumstances; and <u>courteously</u> but <u>imperatively</u> demanding his immediate <u>reply</u> – as it <u>makes all the difference</u> if he <u>is</u> an an [*sic*] <u>acquaintance</u> of Sir Liars (for he has no friends) to have given the latter 2 clear months to tamper with him oh! my God it <u>does</u> make one hate people who <u>so</u> torture one, on the brink of so terrific a precipice! and insult one with their idiotic – blundering pig-headed obstinacy besides! How I <u>do</u>, – pity that Mr Urquhart! – for having such an <u>unthinking injudicious echo</u>, – as Mr Ironside; which only serves to weaken his strength, and throw a ridicule on his sense, for Mr Urquhart though evidently from his arrogance, a disagreeable, and repulsive person; – <u>is</u> <u>unquestionably</u> – a man of <u>great</u> depth, and breadth of mind, – a stalwart grasp of intellect, and a whole- mine of solid – and original ideas, how it <u>must</u> irritate him to have the <u>manner</u> (which is their only objectionable part) <u>imitated</u>, without the matter ever being caught; – inshort his – gold – done into base coin! – I sent you Mr Hydes Humbug yesterday – and return his note to you Walter Weldons rigmarole I have neither time, nor patience to read this morning I see he is <u>very</u> <u>grateful</u> (via words) for Mr Ironsides trumpery loan (which after all was not his, as I was "so immoral" as to send him the £1"10"0) but he is not the least grateful for having skinned me of £5 notes all the summer – and as the last farthing I had was £1"11"6 I had got for a stray copy of my book he from that day to this, did not think it worth his while to acknowledge even the reciept of it – neither has he ever returned me "The Nemesis"[4] – Thank you very much for the prescription, but as I only <u>wish</u> to die seeing too plainly I have nothing to live for, – and shall have nothing to live on; – I shall let nature take its course, and only hope <u>she</u> will not dawdle over her work. yrs affectly

    R B L

HALS
1. Nothing is so enraging like this hope of killing me by degrees [slightly inaccurate] (French).
2. The second edition of *Very Successful!* was published by C. H. Clarke in 1859.
3. James Lewis Knight Bruce was a judge. See RBL, 14 August 1857.
4. Nemesis is the Greek goddess of retribution and indignation against those who commit crimes with apparent impunity. Appropriately, it is the title of RBL's unpublished autobiography, which Louisa Devey drew on for her biography.

To Rebecca Ryves

Friday Night October 9th 1857 9o'clock

The <u>only</u> thing that would, or <u>could</u>, have the least chance of doing me any good, in that Circular, would be setting forth, and <u>wringing</u> the <u>exact</u> <u>truth</u>; ie that it has been Sir Liars successful conspiracies for years (beginning with Bentley and "Cheveley" as there is Judge Haliburtons letter to me to prove) not only with <u>Publishers</u> to Burke, and prevent the <u>sale</u> of my books; but with the <u>Venal Critical Press</u> white was black in regard to them and thus <u>prevent</u> my earning the bread he would not give me; – which conspiracies have further entailed upon me for 18 years, such fearful! expenses as to have mortgaged the beggarly pittance he <u>does</u> give me; down to about £15 a quarter! which <u>no</u> one in the false position of a <u>nominal</u> gentle woman hampered with a beggarly title! and also the <u>nominal</u> wife! of a rich man, <u>could</u> exist upon. But these <u>true</u>, and <u>legitimate</u> pleas; of course a low-born, cowardly man like Mr Ironside, the friends of two such craven Blackguards as a Mr Neill and a Mr Jenkinson will fear; to set forth; or!! if he does it will be, in such a <u>vague</u>, <u>casual</u>, <u>apathetic</u> way; as to have worse than no effect; – ie an <u>injurious</u> one, – instead of making <u>this</u> the <u>whole</u>, and <u>all powerful</u> pivot upon which the appeal turned. But for God's sake no nonsense about my living <u>now</u> on the charity! and kindness of friends! unless they want to drag me <u>more</u> through the mire, which would be too cruel a work of supererogation Even for Mr Ironside RBL

HALS

To Rebecca Ryves

Tuesday October 13th 1857

Oh ! yes – I see clearly through the whole thing – having had a taste of Mr Bryces[1] quality before – who is Disraelis Myrmidon and the plan is to get those parts about that vulgar old strumpet Mrs Disraeli[2] left out, but I assure you it will take far cleverer diplomatists than such clumsy Bunglers as Mr Ironside and his vulgar brute of a friend Mr Neill – to hoodwink me – all the low blackguard printers and reporters in the kingdom may return thanks to Mr Ironside for his zealous endeavours to drag me under their chariot wheels – <u>only</u> there is this little drawback that he can neither fool, nor make a tool of the chief person concerned for <u>not one</u> word will I curtail of Cheveley – they may put it in the pie, make greased Carteridges of it – light their pipes or do anything else they please with it. – I do not care one straw – but they shall not hugger mugger and dispose of <u>my</u> free will. – Thank goodness I have now made arrangements – to prevent my books for the future being Burked, and have friends who are <u>not</u> afraid that Sir Liar Coward Bulwer Lytton will <u>know</u> that they are my friends – I want no such sub rosâ[3] sneaks, and only wish I had died the day Mr Ironside entered this house, while I think of it I <u>must</u> beg that you will in time, that is <u>directly</u> to prevent that hot-headed, cold hearted system monger sending me that degrading ass of a circular open like a <u>newspaper</u> which is what he would be quite <u>capable of doing</u>, as I do not want it to be read down in that Bar below – to entail more insults, and arrogances on me, as I have already more that I can bear. I wanted you to have sent that insolent letter of Braggs[4] to your friend Mr Ironside so of course you did not – I have sent the bracelet – in the little jar and wooden box you were kind enough to send me the <u>Foie gras</u>[5] in – I did <u>not</u> prepay it thinking you would get it more safely – but I inclose a Shillings worth of stamps. – I am now so ill – that I keep hoping Every day will be my last as for the 2d"p! "looming in the future!!" to be got from Disraeli's Publishers Bryce turned Clarke, or Clarke turned Bryce! <u>that</u> is not exactly a thing to live for R B L.

If they charge <u>more</u> than 1s for the parcel pray let me know. Beg of Mr Ironside not to give himself any trouble about getting my "trash" republished the day will come when it will be published fast enough, despite his blackguards Neill, Jenkinson and co.

HALS

Incomplete letter.
1. David Bryce, 44 Paternoster Row, London, is Benjamin Disraeli's publisher.
2. Mary Anne, the wife of Benjamin Disraeli.
3. Secret (Latin).
4. William Bragg (1802–81), librarian, printer, publisher and bookseller at the Parade in Taunton, was distantly related to the Lyttons. See RBL, 0D063RR21.
5. Goose liver pâté (French).

To Rebecca Ryves

Tuesday October 13ᵗʰ 1857

I hope that you will clearly understand that I dont <u>want</u> to have my books rebuked as they would be <u>sure to be</u> – by the sort of wretches, who are now hugger muggering and <u>lying</u> for so many months over One! still less, do I want to be laid under obligations!! to a pack of wretches whom I cordially despise: – for being additionally injured in my vocation. For as I told you long ago – which of course went in, at one ear and out at the other, – as there was nothing to flatter your giant intellect, and Mr Ironsides giant muddle in the matter, that the only way that a re-issue of my books, could be of any service to me, and not injure <u>them</u> and degrade me additionally, – would have been to have the <u>whole</u> series properly re-issued as <u>other</u> <u>peoples are</u> and extensively advertized with a <u>new</u> analytic Preface – quoting the impartial reviews (from "The Times") and other journals at the period of their publication and also – the infamous – swear white is black reviews (– many no doubt written by that Blackguard Mr Neill himself) to <u>expose</u> the infamous system of crushing that had gone on with regard to them <u>this</u> was a service that Mr Weldon could well and Easily have rendered me, but which thanks to Mr Ironsides usual arrogant Pig headed brutality <u>he</u> effectually prevented and you may assure him from me, that a solitary mutilation of Cheveley – hugger muggered, and re-issued still born from – the press, under the Back-door auspices of Mr Neill!! for fear of offending that great man Sir Sodomite Bulwer Lytton can <u>only</u> additionally outrage, and injure me, at all events, I'll see them all hanged – before they'll get me to be willingly a party to my own additional humiliation Rosina Bulwer Lytton.

I have no doubt I have still interest enough with Sir Liar to get him to take Mr Neill as a Footman – which would be a rise in life to him after being a penny a liner, and I shall be happy to Exert this influence in his behalf <u>under the rose</u> – in return for the kind <u>secret</u> service he has done me with Bryce! and Clarke. The brutes! how I do despise them.

HALS

This incomplete letter may be part of the one above.

To Rebecca Ryves

Wednesday October 14th 1857

My dearest Rebecca I am sorry to hear of your domiciliary discomforts – for I can feel for any one who has an uncomfortable <u>no</u> Home – an uncomfortable <u>Home</u>, being bad enough. Tib says – that by your description the Maltese Cur, must be a Maltese <u>Cross</u>.[1] – I pity the poor Indian Ayah[2] – in a London Lodging!!! I have just hereby burst a blood vessel, with indignation, at having recieved a letter all civility! from that incestuous ruffian Loaden! saying to prevent all mistakes, <u>he</u> thinks it better to inform me that <u>he</u> "holds Sir E. Lyttons Cheque for my quarters allowance of £97"1"8 – which he will pay over either to me, or my order – as I please!" This shows the fright the cowardly brutes are in; two such ruffians as he, & his Client, in France would have been kicked back to their native Hell long ago; but My Lord Mansfields infamous Maxim that "truth is a libel"!]3 has made of every English – man, a sneak, and a coward. Any <u>man</u> deserving the name of one, would soon settle two such contemptible ruffians as Loaden and his still more infamous Client. I sent this precious Epistle dated from Romsey[4] in Hampshire, on to Sheffield – if Mr Ironside <u>dont</u> answer it as it <u>ought</u> to be answered, <u>I</u> shall, and <u>direct</u> it too. You must indeed miss – Massy's two great virtues <u>cleanliness and neatness</u> – for my idea of Hell, is dirt, and disorder. – I inclose the note to Blackburne if you will have the goodness to post it. How very "immoral" of you to owe him £3"0"0 I thought I was the only person so improvident, and so wicked as to get into debt! especially with nothing, and compound interest on it to live on yrs affectly R.B.L.

HALS

1. A cross-bred Maltese breed of dog.
2. An Indian nurse or lady's maid.
3. William Murray, first Earl of Mansfield (1705–93) was a jurist and leading politician. While he was Lord Chief Justice, he invented the dictum: 'The greater the truth the greater the libel', presumably to protect himself and his colleagues from exposure by the press.
4. The town of Romsey lies near Southampton in Hampshire.

To Rebecca Ryves

Thursday October 15th 1857

My dearest Rebecca I am sorry to write harshly to you; but I confess your letters, do irritate me; because however Mr Ironside, or people who know nothing about me and care ditto, may probe, rip me up, and skin me on all occasions I do think it is very obtuse of you, not to see and feel even without my telling you (instead of always joining them, in their hugger mugger operations) that it does make me writhe additionally to be continually dragged under the Chariot Wheels, of a pack of low wretches who have either swindled, insulted, or otherwise injured me; and that without even the puerile, and grovelling excuse of deriving the slightest pecuniary or other advantage from it! – you nor Mr Ironside I suppose could not understand why that ruffian Loaden's presuming to write to me yesterday – threw me into a fit; – and would doubtless argue with your usual inverse logic, which always argues from the wrong point that a mere sheet of paper with so many written characters scrawled over it could not, and ought not possibly to produce such an effect! which is as about as wise, and as humane! as to argue with a poor wretch in a delirium upon the non existence of the Phantoms that are terrifying them! – and I am in a constant delirium of chronic and complex misery, which makes me fear every wind that blows; – knowing that my danger is certain and always on the increase, and that I have not only no defence equal to the attack; that first fundamental of all warfare; social or military; – but that my soi-disant[1] allies(?) with the best intentions in the world; from ignorance, and self sufficient obstinacy, are eternally playing into the hands of my Enemies – However, as you have now the advantage of being in the house with a Senior Wrangler (Miss S:) I hope your logic will improve. I wanted you to send that insolent letter of Braggs – to Sheffield that you might say to Mr Ironside that, that was a slight speciman of the insults and degradations which my present agreeable situation subjected me to; – which as I certainly will not write to a man , who after placing me in it, has insulted me in every coarse way he could; and talked of my "nauseating letters" I thought you might; but here again, is a part and parcel of that obtuseness of which I complain. I did not want you to do anything with that list of appeals, I only sent it to show you the amount that had been sold irrespective of Sheffield and 3 have been sold since I sent it to you.

Sunday Morning

Now I feel my dearest Rebecca that I have been ungracious to you, and Massy about the wine – but I meant to be so for though fully appreciating the great, and constant kindness of your motives – it does distress and annoy me beyond measure, when he, and you do such things – knowing how ill you can afford it, why will you not take example by my millionaire friends (?) and never do, or

think of doing any thing for me? but as you want, you shall never get anything
but abuse from me for such doings and as that vile old woman Queen Elizabeth
in what is called her golden speech,[2] to wit the last she ever made her "Faithful
Commons" took care to tell them that all the glories of her reign were her own,
and and [*sic*] that whatever had gone wrong or been amiss in it was "all their
<u>culps</u>" – (an old English word for faults – from which culpability is derived) so
my bearishness on these occasions is all your <u>Culps</u>? – I saw the Execution[3] had
taken place as I recieved Capt and Mrs Dents cards yesterday – God grant that
they may be happy – my best love and wishes to all in Leinster Terrace.[4] I have
not the Shrewsbury Paper – but send you a Plymouth one – which though not
quite so well put contains nearly the same thing. – I wonder when Walter Weldon's – long threatened <u>resumé</u> review of all my poor Burked Books (the <u>only</u>
thing that could do them or me any good) is to appear – I suppose the year after I
am buried – to put a little more money in the Publishers pockets – well it <u>is</u> hard
to see the utter <u>trash</u> that is puffed into a name and a fame, and be compelled to
starve on better things – while even ones best friends all in wishing to serve one
dont know how – and of course only – estimate ones capacity by the – failures
ones infamous and indefatigable but clever and astute enemies have achieved for
one – Amen. Here is that horrid Post – Oh! My God! – what <u>am</u> I to do -? under
this ever increasing and insupportable weight of misery? – truly the Psalms of
this morning were prophetic – "Turn thou unto me, and have mercy on me, for
I am desolate, and in misery."
"The sorrows of my heart – are enlarged: O bring thou me, out of my troubles"
"Consider mine enemies how many they are: and they bear a tyrannous hate
against me"[5] –
What <u>am</u> I to do? I cannot take council of my only companions the Spiders,
and the Flies – who are always enacting my own history before my eyes – of the
wiley aggressor and the powerless victim – I do not even understand about this
accursed money of Mr Wheelers – I thought the Policy <u>was</u> paid up every quarter, and that I was only in arrears to him the interest – would you kindly write
one line to Hodgson saying I am too ill to reply to his letter but that it <u>shall</u> be
attended to – and then send it to Mr Ironside, and beg of him at <u>once</u> to set Mr
Wheeler at Sir Liar – for the sooner people know I am utterly ruined the better
– I <u>cannot</u> and will not go on swindling people any longer – and what <u>am</u> I to
do – ? and this being for ever without a farthing to meet even my petty trumpery current expenses; – is sinking me <u>deeper</u> and <u>deeper</u> and <u>hopelessly</u> – in the
mire! and <u>words</u> <u>wont</u> meet this fearful avalanche of <u>hard</u> <u>remorseless</u> <u>realities</u>
– I am in the position of a person up to their waiste in a quagmire, and sinking
a foot a minute, and being told that a bill has been passed by both houses, for
draining it, and that the work actually has commenced at the other extremety
of the Swamp, – is little consolation! when it is immediate main force to pull

me out that is wanted. – The poor woman and good Samaritan Miss Dickenson – does not press on me like the millionaire, it is true – but for that very reason – my debt to her weighs on me all the heavier – then look <u>because</u> I am helpless and penniless how I am treated – and tortured – on every side – not a word can I hear from that ass Mr Easton of what he is doing with that vile swindler Clarke? Or whether he is doing <u>anything</u>! and <u>writing</u> to him to <u>ascertain nothing</u> (as is the invariable result of my communications with him) is only [ill] his infamous bills – and that of <u>course</u> is the meaning of all these infamous delays, – so that to add <u>to all the rest</u>! I am in a fever about poor Augustas £100 – and read the exhilarating letter! I have – had from her this morning – no, – <u>it is too much</u>, and lasts too long – for any one poor weak wretch to bear. Marius only <u>sat</u> amid the ruins of Carthage,[6] – but I feel crushed <u>under</u> the ruin of a plurality of world – my own outer, and iner one you <u>would</u> – pity me if you knew the physical agony alone that I am suffering – I was getting calmer from sheer <u>exhaustion</u> – but since that letter came of Mr Hodgsons – fire seems to be crackling in my brain and my feet and limbs have grown so suddenly, and deadly cold that I cannot feel them – Oh! it <u>will</u> – it must soon End – for I can bear no more – Forgive the trouble I am entailing upon you of answering young Hodgsons letter, – but I <u>cannot</u> answer it, – I have struggled like twenty Gladiators for the last 8 months single handed and alone, – I am now fairly over powered – and can do or hear no more – God Bless you Ever gratefully and affectly yrs Rosina Bulwer Lytton.

I send you Judge Haliburtons letter – about Sir Liars – <u>threats</u> to Bentley if he published for me – which I think Mr Ironside <u>ought</u> to have – I also send you <u>16</u> more letters I have found from people who wrote for the appeal, you can give them to Mr Walker.

HALS
1. So-called (French).
2. Delivered on 30 November 1601, to 141 members of the House of Commons.
3. RBL's name for a wedding.
4. There is a Leinster Terrace in Westminster, London.
5. Psalms 25:15–18.
6. The Roman general Gaius Marius (155–86 BC), having been exiled from Rome, sought refuge from Sextilius, a Roman governor in Africa. He was warned that he would be treated as an enemy of Rome if he landed on African soil, to which Marius replied, 'Go tell him that you have seen Caius Marius sitting in exile among the ruins of Carthage', a scene depicted by John Vanderlyn in *Caius Marius Amid the Ruins of Carthage* (1807).

To Rebecca Ryves

Sunday October 19th 1857

My dearest Rebecca I am so ill to day from the cold I caught star gazing (which I
will tell you about presently) and from being up 2 nights with my poor Innocent
suffering Tibby (who though a long time about it like me <u>is</u> dying and it is fearful to see a poor animal suffer so and not be able to relieve it) that I can scarcely
hold up my head to write to you. I pity you sincerely for your domiciliary nui-
sances – but in London lodgings it is far easier to have a Bug-gy! than a Brougham
– What remark was there to make on that Fiend Loadens letter but that it was like
every thing he, or his infamous client ever said or wrote <u>a lie</u> – for there are such
Mr Hydes letters to prove <u>how</u> punctually – that swindling pittance has been paid
even within the last 2 years – to say nothing of the Geneva conspiracy when it
was not paid at all,[1] and from the <u>first</u> quarter instead of being paid in advance as
is <u>always</u> customary on such occasions, I was kept 4 months penniless waiting for
it and so it has gone though Mr Ironside would never have let me get into debt!!!
Well then the plain and true reasons, why I will not acknowledge the Alms that
may be produced from that circular – which I am convinced will not exceed 13!
more postage stamps each if that ??? – is that I really could not afford 2 or 300
postage stamps – to say nothing of paper and envelopes – as you may see from
Briggs bill – which is chiefly for postage stamps paper etc etc what acknowledging
these doles in the first place cost me! and now as I have no means of going in debt
for them – <u>nothing shall make me do so</u>. The torture I feel at being a complete
swindler! – with only two months before me, till the storm bursts – and the Days
and Clarkes, and those who are kindest to me will find I have nothing but Moon
shine to pay them with is quite sufficient – and I can bear no more – I see my dear
Rebecca – there is <u>no</u> use in my saying anything – for when I am in the East, you
are in the West, so we can only talk Antipodes at each other – all the barristers in
England, headed by the solicitor, and attorney Generals – could not plead my case,
without evidence, any more than a cook could dress a dinner without provisions
and <u>I</u> am talking of an attorney having – been employed 4 months ago – to collect
this evidence <u>ready</u> for Council and you are talking of at the 11th hour fishing up
some stray Barrister – <u>if</u> this 2p can be collected from this chimerical circular when
supposing it <u>were</u> to realise £2, 000 – there is no brief even <u>prefaced</u> for council so
then another 6 months would have to be lost – and you cannot suppose creditors
however humane, and forbearing will wait for ever?

In fact it would be just as were to say – you <u>must</u> give a public dinner to 300,
or 400 – and when told but I have no money – to reply "Oh you only collect the
guests, and when they are all assembled – we'll see about sending out and getting
the provisions"!!! But as I said before God alone <u>can</u> extricate me from so fearful!
an abyss so fiery a furnace – and to Him I leave it; and in Him I trust – but if feel-

ing cut up piecemeal <u>could</u> pay what I owe – and release me from this crushing, and degrading load, I would cheerfully submit to it; – for hell itself cannot exceed in torments – what I endure every hour of the day, and night, in mind, body, and estate. but enough of me and my hopeless miseries: – Poor Dyke yesterday sent me a beautiful bouquet of Hot house flowers and a very characteristic note, which I send you. On Friday night, though ill from the thought of it, and miserable to leave my poor Tib, and the night raw, and cloudy – I sallied forth with poor Dyke for I would not allow Day – to send the carriage for me – I was recieved by <u>la famille</u> Day[2] – really as if I had been the Queen, in their very pretty country house, and without any Tauntonian free, and easy vulgarity – the whole family being better mannered, and infinitely better bred, than half the <u>soi-disant</u>[3] <u>ladies</u> and <u>gentlemen</u>! one meets, Mrs Day <u>mère</u>[4] a good looking fair woman – <u>very</u> like Mrs Kitchener, in <u>expression</u> but not her beauty: – Day himself I found highly <u>liter-ary</u>! scientific, philosophical, archaeological, and even metaphysical! – but "Mr Frank"[5] the second brother – so dreadfully like Disraeli! that I am <u>sure</u> the mother must have been frightened by him 20 years ago when he stood for Taunton,[6] and escaped from it as an old woman. With my usual luck Professor Adam (you know he it was who discovered the new Planet)[7] was Telegraphed back to London a quarter of a hour before I arrived, – but the Telescope was there, and a magnificent one it is – Jupiters three belts were very plain – and looked – like bands of <u>vapeur</u> colored ribbon with white edges his satellites did their best to shine, but like all satellites, looked poor contemptible things beside him – the double stars, are very beautiful – hanging like deep purple sapphires suspended as it were from the sky. – As for Saturn, I would not have accepted his ring, had he offered it to me; and the Pleiades,[8] appeared to me a sort of celestial Erysipelas,[9] a perfect rash of stars. – when we returned to the house, we found a handsome spread, and microscopes stethographs and all sorts of things to amuse but of all the beautiful, marvels of creation! – commend me to the <u>eye</u> of a fly, seen through a microscope it is like a large piece of red brown arras <u>thickly</u> studded, with bright new silver pin heads – and were I ever again to possess such a thing as a dining room, I would take the hint, and have it for the walls, and chairs. But after all de thing that interested me most, was, a poor innocent honesty of a sheep dog – Mr Rover, who after having sniffed all round my dress, to inquire after my poor doatskin put his poor innocent rough head in my lap; – Mrs Day said – that about a year ago – he followed her husband – home one night, and poked him cold nose into his hand – seeming quite to consider him as his own: – I said, and so he was for of course Rover knew, dat every dog, has hims <u>Day</u>; – as a little wit goes a long way in a country Town, dis was greatly applauded, and even Rover wagged hims tail at it. – I was particularly struck by one piece of <u>absence</u> of vulgarity in Mrs Day – looking at all their Pho-tographs, I very vulgarly said, I thought "Gentlemen"! made better Photographs than "lady's" – of course had I been at Devonshire or Stafford House I should have talked of men and women; but I did not know whether people of the class of the Days, in England, might not be offended at being designated by those primative appellations, but Mrs Day immediately said, "Yes, I I [*sic*] think men, do, make better photographs than women" – There was no vulgar fuss – or parvenu pride about their luxurious house – and no cringing servility in their manner – but a well-bred respect, that one seldom meets from any class in this essentially vulgar minded country. – I should be ashamed to repeat to you Mr Days – hyperbolical expressions, and professions of esteem, respect, admiration and sympathy for me – however I need a strong dose of this kind occasionally to counteract, the coarse abuse, and calumnies, generally hurled at me; the only danger in all this is, that I shall begin to fancy the mantle of that great Conqueror of creditors! the Vicomte de Letorière![10] has descended upon me; – to be adulated by persons to whom you have lent money – is as common as black berries – but to be so by those to whom you have owed it for a scandalously long time! – is something like the Rocks Egg[11] – in the Arabian Nights, a thing never heard of out of a Fairy Tale – and really had he been the Dey of Algiers![12] he could not have recieved me more munificently: – ah! what will these poor people, and all the others think of me in January when they find I am no nearer to paying them than ever! God have mercy on me. – As I said before I do wish Day would marry poor Miss Dyke; – it would make her so very happy; – and would be so easy for him to do. – will you ask Mr Ironside to send me 2 appeals, I want them for Miss Dyke, and inclose you 2 stamps for them. and to morrow when I can get another dozen; I will send them to you for the 16 letters you had to forward for me to Mr Ironside. I wish Mr Ironside would have the goodness to write to that Weldon to return my nemesis saying that I did not write myself – as he had never acknowledged the reciept of my last letter. – You will think that my pen is made on the model of Myneheer Von Woodenblocks wooden leg, and that once set going it cant stop; – but I thought you'd like to hear all about the vortex of dissipation! in which I have been plunged – and though I have been in bed ever since, with the most excruciating spasms in my chest, and the spitting of blood worse than ever, I tried to write it to you. – Hoping you may find your new lodgings more comfortable and have no [ill] Believe me Ever affectly [R] B Lytton

That Mr Ironside may not be again unprovided with an answer if Loaden wants to know whose money I am spending now? he had better say Massy's; – and what makes the case more clear! that I have even the effrontery to take his hand! as that Ticket is made out in the name of Mrs Ryves!! so if I would retain my acquaintance! xxxxxx!

HALS

1. RBL's allowance due from EBL was not paid while she was in Switzerland because he was being sued by a Swiss hotelier for her hotel bill. RBL believed that this had been

contrived by EBL as a way of preventing her from leaving Switzerland at a time of civil unrest.
2. The Day family (French).
3. So-called (French).
4. Mother (French).
5. Brother to Mrs Day, the Taunton draper.
6. Benjamin Disraeli lost the Taunton by-election in April 1835.
7. John Couch Adams (1819–92) became Regius Professor of Mathematics at St Andrews University in October 1857. He had predicted the existence of a new planet, which turned out to be Saturn.
8. A constellation, also known as the Seven Sisters. See RBL, 19 September 1857.
9. Erysipelas (Greek for 'red skin') is an acute streptococcus bacterial skin infection, resulting in inflammation.
10. A character in Giuseppe Verdi's opera *La Traviata*, first performed in 1853.
11. In Sinbad's voyage, the eponymous hero discovers a huge white dome, which turns out to be the egg of the giant roc. The island he is on turns out to be its nest.
12. Hussein ben Hassan, the last dey of Algiers. See RBL, 23 November 1833.

To Rebecca Ryves

Tuesday October 20th 1857

My dearest Rebecca I hope your present quarters will be more comfortable and less instinct with <u>animal</u> life! as beds of roses are more agreeable than beds of the other things. – For three nights have I been up with my poor suffering Innocence; and it was too terrible to see him panting, and gasping for breath, and the dear beautiful eyes – saying as plain as they could – "oh! mud – mud surely you might think of <u>something</u> to Ease me?" and last night as a <u>pis aller</u>[1] I thought of mesmerising him – which I did for 3 hours till I thought my arms would have dropped off but at length he fell, into a profound quiet sleep – he has slept without <u>moving</u> for 15 hours – Anne crying and wringing her hands over him saying she was <u>sure</u> he was dead though I had my hand on his heart and felt its innocent beatings. This morning at 12 de darling paws – were stretched out de bootiful eyes opened bright and well, de tail wagged, – de breathing free, de muds hand licked – and de dog, who had neither slept nor eaten before for a week Eat with ravenous hunger half a Partridge what was so terrible was that on account of these asthmatic gaspings – he could not lie down, but was obliged to sit with hims poor darling head thrown up to catch the air – Him is now thank God stretched out at the foot of my bed full length, quite at hims ease. – Mr Hyde would not have told me years ago about an attorney – collecting Evidence – for what <u>then</u> kept Mr Hyde back – was the fear of plunging me into the <u>horrible</u> position I am now in; – knowing I had no resources to live on <u>ad intrium</u>;[2] – and now Mr Hyde is old, – and too ill to be bothered with a pauper Client: – <u>all</u> the documents (excepting Thomas's letters, – which Mr Hyde hang back as he may; can be subpoenad to give Evidence on. –) Mr Ironside and Mr Walker have – but a cartload of such Evidence is of no more use, than so much air, – <u>without</u> the <u>collected Evidence</u> of an attorney – that I have tried in vain to impress upon you Mr Hyde never even told you -what I now tell you; – and what if <u>asked</u> he could not deny; – iE that <u>even</u> under the <u>old system</u>, – as far as <u>legal proceedings</u> <u>against Sir Liar went</u>, which you are all making such an impotent pother and <u>talk</u> about now, – I <u>could</u> then, <u>as now</u>, have sued him <u>In Forma Pauperis</u>[3] without a shilling – but then, as <u>now</u>, – a Barrister must have a <u>Brief</u>, – and no brief could be properly and <u>effectually</u> drawn up, without the collected Evidence aforesaid. – Mr Ironside insulted me grossly, – and brutally, and never even expressed the slightest contrition, or made me the shadow of an apology for so doing; – nothing therefore could induce me to write to him again for I have quite enough to suffer – and contend against daily and hourly – without bringing this gratuitous and impotant torture upon myself – he sides cui bono?[4] while I was in direct communication with him, he treated me like a complete fool, I was not to have a feeling, or an opinion, of my own, upon matters that were vitally, and exclusively mine, – all was to be referred to your superior wisdom (and of course greater matrimonial! and legal experience!) now had this been only with reference to the choice of a dress – or a bonnet, however superior your taste might be <u>per se</u>,[5] – as the dress and the bonnet were for <u>me</u>, and <u>to be worn by me</u>, – such conduct would have been offensive and ridiculous in the extreme, – but as it was! with <u>more</u> than my existence depending upon the issue, of the mess he has plunged me into, it was <u>brutal</u>, and to use one of his own cant phrases, "grossly immoral". – Besides Even if he <u>had</u> more feeling, and common sense, – it is <u>not</u> my business – or my tortures he is troubling his head about; – word splitting with, and for, Mrs Urquhart is his <u>One</u> idea, his <u>one</u> feeling and his <u>unique</u> aim, end and occupation – amen! and God forgive him for the thoughtless – heartless and unwarrantable manner in which he intermeddled and thrust him self into my affairs – only to achieve the inhuman miracle! of adding to my torments, and deepening my despair! He can see Mr Dickens meddling infamy in the Jerrold case[6] plain enough though Dickens (from vanity I am very sure – still he <u>exerted</u> <u>himself</u>) did work and collect for them £2000 – but of course he cannot see his own much greater enormity towards me. And now since none of your wonderful wisdoms see <u>that</u> either! I'll tell you what this new "Matrimonial Causes Bill"[7] will do for me; – and <u>all</u> (with the sort of people I have to ultra muddle my affairs for me) that will do for me – by it married slaves are allowed to Trade – recieve and Transfer property from themselves as if they were <u>Fenner Sole</u> – the natural sequence of which is that they are also <u>responsible</u> <u>for their own debts</u>, which they were not before – So my <u>only</u> prospect, or rather my only <u>certainty</u> is that of ending my days in a debtors Prison – and were it not for the bitter, bitter pang – of swindling those, who believed in and would have trusted in me to any amount – the sooner – that communication took place the better pleased I should be, for this <u>too cruel</u> because – too brutally unequal struggle – would be Ended – for what I have gone and am going through – would convert an angel itself into a Demon yours affectly R B Lytton

HALS
1.　Last resort (French).
2.　In the meantime (Latin).
3.　As a pauper (Latin).
4.　Literally: 'good to whom' (Latin); for whose benefit?
5.　Intrinsically (Latin).
6.　Dickens's rather high-handed fundraising for the family of Douglas Jerrold after his sudden death in June 1857 raised a total of £2,000, according to his announcement in *The Times* (1 September 1857). See RBL, 16 June 1854.
7.　The Matrimonial Causes Bill was intended to made divorce easier for a limited section of the population. The subsequent Act contained clauses protecting the earnings of a deserted wife; allowing married women to inherit and bequeath property like single women and to make contracts and to sue and be sued. Not all of these provisions would have suited RBL since, under the new legislation, EBL would no longer be liable for her debts. See RBL, 3 April 1857.

To Alfred Edward Chalon

Thursday October 22d 1857

Dear Mr Chalon
　　I shall be delighted to have my hand back
　　　　Yours Thankfully
　　　　R Bulwer Lytton

HUNT

To Rebecca Ryves?

[October? 1857]

P.S:
　　Recollect you tell me in your letter <u>to day</u>, – but <u>only to day</u> – what Mr Ironsides intentions to serve me were but from your <u>other</u> letters, the impression left <u>on my mind</u>; was, that after the 2 outrageous insults I had recieved from him, and all his brutal letters, – <u>nothing</u> now was to be <u>attempted</u>, but there the matter was to end, and I left to struggle through this fearful maelstrom of misery – with only my creditors curses to accompany my dying groans. Now it

neant to do, that I have <u>all along written and</u>

eley" has of selling! when it has never been
ss this was the stipulation upon which it was
great man!
st son! and the Boots here his brother, yester-
stle. – All can manage to die but me, I cannot

t the Taunton Giles Castle Hotel. See RBL, 13 June

To Rebecca Ryves

Sunday – October 25th 1857

My dearest Rebecca I wrote to you yesterday in great haste, "and said <u>in my haste</u>"
as the Psalmist did before me "all men are liars";[1] but I really <u>was</u>, much annoyed
at the vulgar conglomerated, and brusque tone of that letter to Knight Bruce;
– and it is not only vulgar, but <u>extremely</u> <u>rude</u> and <u>offensive</u> to end a letter to an
utter stranger and one in a superior social position to the writer with

"I have the Honor to Be your obedient servant" Instead of as courtesy exacts – I
have the Honor to be <u>Sir</u> your obedient servt -

I do long and <u>entreat</u> – you will have the kindness <u>to copy</u> the <u>formula</u> of what I
said about asking Judge Halliburtons permission to make use of that information
about Bentley because <u>merely</u> <u>casually</u> writing to Mr Ironside 3 weeks hence, and
saying I thought Judge H's permission ought to be asked; – he will as usual either
make a point, of setting my wishes – judgement and knowledge of the world at
defiance, or will write him such another brusque offensive missive, as the one to
Knight Bruce to whom instead of saying as I had put it "as I feel the honor of a
person of your high character and position is compromised" he says "you have
now an opportunity of vindicating your honor!!!" for which I have no doubt
– K.B. will feel inclined to kick him – I have just recieved the inclosed from that
dear delicate minded fine porcelain Mrs Jermyn with another £5 stuffed into the
letter without a word but which I shall certainly return, [telling] her she must
not <u>encroach [on] my goodness</u>!! in this way – poor dear soul, even <u>she</u> forgets
that Beggars cannot be chusers! and marvels my Dr should be so far off – My Dr
like every thing else is on Charity! would <u>it</u> were farther and <u>he</u> nearer poor man;
for this cold rainy day, has set me coughing and bleeding terribly again, and poor
innocence panting fifty times a day I wish we were both in our last home. – The

wrapper to "Chevely" is quite in the vulgar Dickens style; and as far as I remember the book in no way illustrates any part of it unless it be Lord De Clifford[2] horsewhipping Campobello, when he catches him with the French governess[3] at Naples. The girl, and old man, at the back, I suppose are meant for Mary Lee,[4] and her Father. Was my sandalwood fan ever converted into a large green one? if so? and you will send it down – and let me know what it comes to? I will send up the money yours affectly R B L

HALS
1. Psalm 116:11.
2. A man with a whip is depicted as violently grabbing hold of another man, knocking him out of his chair. RBL suggests that it is most likely to be George Grimstone, Lord de Clifford, the villainous husband in the novel.
3. In *Cheveley*, Lord de Clifford had been flirting overtly with the French governess.
4. Mary Lee is a seamstress, who is seduced by Lord de Clifford. He pretends to be a gentleman farmer and tricks her into a mock marriage. Driven insane when she discovers the truth, she is supported by her elderly father throughout her ordeal.

To Rebecca Ryves

[29? October 1857]

That loathsome wretch Beaumont having arrived here yesterday – by the one o'clock Train – Calling herself Mrs Seller! née Hauteville de Hauteville![1] – and spelling the née wrong with an accent over each é – she had the impertinence to send up this card saying she wanted to see me – as she was most intimate with some friends of mine abroad!! Mrs Clarke was out at the time – she arrived from London – pretending she came to give lectures here (which we have found was all a lie) without a shred of luggage – even a night cap – though she slept here last night! and was very urgent to know the numbers of my room and to be just near me!! Anne very properly forgot my number and could not put her near me, as the rooms were full, still she urged it saying – she was afraid to sleep in a room near a gentleman!! Anne rather impertinently told her, that she thought she might very safely even sleep in the same room with one! and that no harm would happen [to] her – This morning Mrs Clarke has turned her out – but first the following coloquy took Place

"Beaumont
    I've moved in such a very different sphere to what I do now – in fact in the very highest circles abroad where I was acquainted with some of Lady Lyttons most intimate friends – I'm sure she'd see me if she was well enough"

Mrs Clarke – "I'm sure she'd do no such thing, for I am very certain you never knew any <u>friends</u> of Lady Lyttons however you may be <u>employed</u> by her <u>Enemies</u>"

"Ah! poor thing – <u>I</u> can feel for her, for <u>I</u> have also a wretch of a husband from whom I am separated and if they would only let one alone, – <u>one</u> would let them <u>alone</u>; but they hunt, and persecute one so: – and what can a poor woman do without <u>money</u>? if I had only <u>money</u> – I'd <u>sue</u> my wretch in the ecclesiastic Court, but you know its <u>impossible</u> without?"

Mrs Clarke – "Ah! well, luckily Lady Lytton has found <u>both</u> money and friends – as her wretch will find – before he is many weeks older." –

Beaumont – "Indeed! do you know where Sir Edward is now?"

"Mrs Clarke – "No I dont; nor do I want to know; but every one knows where such a villain <u>will</u> be."

"Beaumont – Dear me, – you seem very warm in Lady Lyttons cause"

Mrs Clarke – "Not more than any honest person who <u>knows</u> her, and what she has gone through, and is going through and how uprightly she acts by every one, – ought to be. And now I'll thank <u>you</u> to leave my house – and if ever you are sent down here <u>again</u>, to go some where else"

And out walked Beaumont and her basket – now Mrs Clarkes – is the sort of head a person ought to have upon their shoulders and as for the <u>lie</u>! about my having money! to fight Sir Liar – I am very certain – that even if the Recording Angel was inclined to note it against her the avenging Angel would blast it out with one sweep of his wing. – Had she sighed and shaken her head, and said "Oh! poor thing that is very <u>true</u>; a woman <u>can</u> do nothing to to [*sic*] right herself without money, and that, that villain knows – ." She might have <u>meant</u> just as kindly by me – but would have injured <u>me</u> irreparably and that vile wretch Beaumont would not have returned without her errand as she has <u>now</u> done. But when I think of the <u>ceaseless</u> <u>active</u>, and unscrupulous villainy of that Fiend, I am indeed in despair! for what chance – has my <u>stagnant</u> poverty against it? – of course the monsters object in getting these wretches to <u>see</u> me, is that they may report – how near my grave I am – and as to the great anxiety to know <u>which</u> <u>side</u>, and where my rooms are? – I <u>fully</u> expect to be shot some night through the window which is a little job – that any ticket of leave fellow for a trifling annuity and a free passage to America would do – and as to the "is it likely twaddle?" is it likely that after a horrible murder – a <u>woman</u>! would be sent with the mutilated bones in a Carpet bag! and the head in a brown paper parcel! to throw over such a public thoroughfare as Waterloo bridge! yet <u>likely</u> or <u>not</u>; the fact remains, that it <u>was done</u> and though every thing was as clear as <u>noon</u> day – against that wretch Spollen[2] for the murder, and robbery of Mr Little[3] and his wife <u>confessed</u> <u>it</u> – is it <u>likely</u> he would be acquitted? yet he <u>is</u> – and poor mangled Mr Little moulders in his unavenged grave. How Provoking! The advertizement of "The Square of Beechwood"[4] is neither in to day's "Times" nor "Punch" and I cant get yesterday's or last weeks, but no doubt it will be in <u>tomorrows</u> and I'll cut it out and send it. I see Skeets sneaking out with another novel "Maulevere's Divorce – A Tale Of Woman Wrongs"![5] I do indeed pity you, having to move again on Saturday! – Poor Massy I am very sorry to hear he is again ill – do beg of him to try Dr Lococks Pulmonic Lozenges – they have really done me, and poor Doat-skin good. But I cannot tell you how that wretch Beaumont coming here has – worked me up, and put me in a fever. <u>Pray</u> don't forget to tell Mr Eyre Lloyd – <u>how</u> grateful I feel for his kindness, Ever affectly yrs

    RBL

HALS
1. EBL's mistress, Laura Deacon. See RBL to Rebecca Ryves, 30 October 1857.
2. James Spollen was acquitted for the murder of Mr Little at his trial on 7–11 August 1857.
3. Mr George Samuel Little was murdered at the Broadside Terminus of the Midland Great Western Railway, Ireland.
4. *The Squire of Beechwood: A True Tale of Scrutator* [pseud.] by Knightley William Hor-lock. See RBL, [*c.* 27 April 1857].
5. Emma Robinson, *Mauleverer's Divorce: A Story of Woman's Wrongs*. See RBL, 16 October 1854. Devey wrongly attributes this to RBL. See Devey, *Life of Rosina*, p. 432.

To Edward Bulwer Lytton

To Sir Liar Coward Bulwer Lytton

October 30th 1857

As the moth flits round the candle to its distruction, so you far more con-temptible reptile will to the last; pursue your course of fabulous, yet impotent blackguardism. As there can be no doubt from the description of the thin hay-coloured hair, the aquiline nose, the jaded meretricious look, the coulisse theatrical manner, the vulgar braggadocio,[1] about the fine people she knows!??? – the fine outside and the shabby under clothes, that the soi-disant[2] Mrs Seller! (and I don't think you <u>can</u> sell her any more;) is <u>One</u>, and the same with your old strumpet Mrs Beaumont![3] (?) lately drummed out of Boulogne. I <u>warn</u> <u>you</u> that if you <u>persist</u> in this to the <u>last</u> hunting, and outraging me, with your infamous cast off mistresses, it will be the <u>worse for you</u>, when the Mountebank Mask, is torn from your hidious face in the Ecclesiastical Court[4] next January. Can you not be content with having achieved the miracle, of writing what are generally considered, as two incompatible antipodes! Execration and ridicule? For you are never mentioned by any class – but as "that ridiculous and execrable brute

Sir E Lytton." Or are you determined <u>never</u> to stop till ridicule, is swallowed up in public odium? You little dream, of the pretty quagmire! the bare-faced and asinine lies of that incestuous Ruffian your accomplice and jackal Loaden has prepared for you. With every feeling of execration contempt and defiance I remain for the present your legal victim

    Rosina Bulwer Lytton alas!

HALS
1. 'An empty, idle boaster; a swaggerer' (*OED*).
2. So called (French).
3. One of the names of Laura Deacon, EBL's mistress.
4. This court dealt with matrimonial disputes, including adultery.

To Edward Bulwer Lytton

Friday October 30th 1857

Was it not enough you monster! to turn me out of my home for this vile creature? – hunt me through the world and starve me out of it with your infamous conspiracies that have beggared me, but you must crown the whole by sending <u>this</u> wretch to insult me by asking to see me!!! But thank God the days of your infamous reign are numbered.

    Rosina Bulwer Lytton

True copy of the Laura Deacon Beaumont flam – After telling Mrs Clark she wanted to hire the Assembly Rooms to give <u>lectures in</u>! but luckily for us poor honest fools liars, like yourself, and your tools, have <u>short memories</u>. Then no doubt she thought it a master stroke of cunning! – pretending she had not money to pay for the insertion, of this sham advertisement while even Bragg[1] who is a great goose saw that it was a flimsy pretext of getting out of the Town – (which was getting too hot for her) under color of being what she <u>originally</u> was, before she took to street walking; a teacher of music. Truly your myrmidons are <u>such</u> <u>bunglers</u>! That they must be as besotted with brandy and Profligacy as yourself. Turn over.

"<u>Singing and elocution</u>"

(To say nothing of spying; & pr<u>ostitution</u>!)

Madame Seller (?) (née de Hauteville!?? (and who with her employer <u>ought</u> to be kicked <u>de</u> <u>Haut en bas</u>) Pupil of Signor Bordogni principal maestro of the Scala at Milan and of the Conservatoire of Paris – and Royal Academy of London – and of the celebrated composer Alexander Lee,[2] has some hours disengaged during the week which she would be glad to fill, by giving lessons in singing and elocution at Taunton – (she had <u>better</u> that's all) and its neighbourhood. Applications as to terms to be addressed to Madame Seller – to be left at Whereats Library,[3] Weston Super Mare

Madame S is sister in law (so the real Mrs Seller may be) to the Rev W H Seller late of Trul— whom Sir E B Lytton's Trull Miss Laura Deacon – is perfectly aware left this neighbourhood some time ago or she would not have ventured to use his name. October 30th 1857.

HALS
1.　William Bragg is a Taunton printer. See RBL, 13 October 1857.
2.　George Alexander Lee (1802–51) was an English composer and conductor, who wrote much stage music, including many popular songs.
3.　This library was owned and run by Joseph Whereat (1812–65). See RBL, [6? November 1857].

To Rebecca Ryves

Friday 3 O'clock October 30th 1857

As I find, the wretch to carry on the sham – has ordered £5 worth of things from Days to be sent here for her, and that she would return for them (?) and as there is no use in all this casual creep mouse and waiting till the year – 300057 – till – villains come forward and make voluntary confessions of their own infamy! and till "something turns up"! I have sent Mrs Clarke off to Weston[1] – to make inquiries about the wretch calling herself Mrs Seller![2] and as to any twaddle – about my dreadful language! I am past all that – for that Fiend has not just ,unsexed, but unsphered me – and as his Blackguardism – exceeds that of the lowest, and most vicious – Swells mobs man – the only language to address him in, is that of Billingsgate! I shall not close this till the Train returns from Weston – but for poor Mrs Jermyns kindness – I could not even – have done this much! – if any thing – could add to my misery – it would be a letter, I have this moment got from Mrs Jermyn – of [ill] as I was always averse from Mr Hydes being gone to on every account – but more especially – on account as I told you from the first of that Blackguard Stocqueler being in his Employment who would betray – all the miserable and hopeless helpless of my position confided to Mr Hyde! – to Sir Liar! – of course – the Pigheaded obstinacy would persevere, in spite of me, in betraying me to a a [sic] person, whom I had good reason no longer to trust! and now as "you do not like his letter"! it has like all the rest only to be hugger muggered into a profound – secret from me! as for that ridiculous and degrading circular Mrs Jermyn views it in the same light, that any person of common sense would – God have mercy upon me but it is cruel to wantonly butcher any poor wretches Fate – as mine has been

9 at night – Mrs Clarke just returned – the wretch has taken lodgings at <u>Weston</u> <u>for</u> <u>the next 2 months</u>!!! has not got a single <u>pupil</u>, Every one asking <u>who</u> she is, as there are <u>these</u> strange rumours about her. But she'll not come <u>here</u> <u>again</u> R B L

---

1. RBL's landlady Charlotte Clarke has gone to Weston-super-Mare, a seaside town in Somerset, where Mrs Sellers is residing.
2. RBL alleges that EBL's mistress is calling herself Mrs Maria Sellers (*née* Hautenville) of 14 Woburn Place, Russell Square, London, and is posing as a music teacher.

To Rebecca Ryves

Saturday Night October 31st 1857

I have written to find out the <u>present</u> address of the late Rev W H Seller[1] – late of Trull[2] – and shall instantly write to him – a <u>full</u> <u>description</u> of his sister in law – née Hauteuville de Hauteuville!! and though I <u>know</u> what his answer will be as well as if it was before me – <u>that</u> Even is not enough – if I knew a man worth a grain of salt – which I dont – when I've got his address they would go for him, bring him to Taunton, and I they and a Magistrate and a Police man (which could be got at Weston) would go over to Weston and take the wretch in her lair – that is the way <u>other</u> peoples business is <u>done</u> – for <u>talk</u> never yet did anything but fester wounds, and put an Enemy on their guard, and of <u>course</u> – hearing Mr Ironsides "Judgement"! that is his want of it, slapdashed off – under the waifer of an Envelope from Sheffield or 20 months hence – that Mr Walker – had actually arrived at the conclusion! that <u>perhaps</u>??? she really might <u>not</u> be the person she represented herself to be – and <u>even</u> might be the woman Beaumont! but it would not be well to move in the matter till the day of Judgement arrived – when she <u>must</u> confess it before an assembled world! is very little service or comfort to me! but what ever you do – dont commit the asinine and to me insulting blunder of consulting Mr Hyde!! to know "what he <u>thinks</u> on the subject" – as I <u>think</u> and know, him to be a Traitor that he plainly proved to me in the Lyndhurst affair – and I am almost mad by being dropped for ever by bungling fools – into the open jaws of my devouring Enemies Again! I must <u>entreat</u> you <u>not</u> to compromise me any more with Mr <u>Hyde</u>! – between Mr Ironsides high hand arrogant assumption of omnipotence! in the first instance, his then coolly shuffling me off upon you! and all the obstinate blunders, and delays – I have been thoroughly wrecked – so have nothing for it, but to lay down with my ruin in the old year and rise up with my disgrace in the new – so God have mercy on my soul. Mr Hyde informed you 3 weeks ago that raising money for law was illegal! and now you repeat this to me as a great piece of news! – and nonentity as I may be among you all – pray understand after so <u>many</u> "<u>nauseating</u> repetitions" on my part that it is not whether Mr Walker will see Mr Hyde! to bungle the matter and perform the work of supererogation of swamping me a little more – but whether <u>I</u> – even nonentity <u>I</u>! will allow him to do so and as my wishes have never been consulted or my consent asked about <u>any</u> thing, I now volunteer to say <u>I WONT.</u>

HALS
1.   The supposed relative of the so-called Mrs Sellers, who RBL claims is Laura Deacon, mistress of EBL. See RBL, 30 October 1857.
2.   A parish in Taunton, Somerset, 3 km south-west of Taunton. It is also the name for a strumpet.

To Rebecca Ryves

Saturday October 31st 1857

In bed, and in torture from head to foot.

I must <u>beg</u> and <u>entreat</u> that I may not be <u>more</u> wrecked, by having all my Naked wounds exposed to a Knave, and a Traitor which <u>every</u> thing proves Mr Hyde to be; – were he a paid solicitor he would tell you a very different storey – and he must have <u>even</u> a more exalted idea of the fabulous idiotcy it is the curse, and the aggravation of my unexampledly miserable fate to be wrecked amongst – To <u>presume</u> to talk such nonsense as "The Infant State!! of this Bill" is not an act of Parliament <u>once</u> <u>passed</u>; an accomplished and <u>matured</u> fact, that <u>cannot</u> be altered or added to – and therefore, as matured the <u>first</u> <u>hour</u> <u>it comes into operation</u>; as it will be at the end of 500 years; – its <u>only</u> <u>wisdom</u>? perhaps being that it is so far like Minerva[1] that it starts in to life – at full maturity and armed <u>cap à jue</u>[2] – it's not a tree, or a child; to talk of its infant state!!! if he had called it a swindle and a juggle, like every thing else English – <u>that</u> would have been a different thing. – Mr Hyde has <u>evidently</u> been brought over <u>by the party</u> (<u>his</u> party) to choke the fools I have to deal with with [*sic*] Chaff – and he <u>may betray</u> a defenceless wretch like me, who am at every ones mercy – but he cannot <u>decieve</u> me. As for that degrading and asinine circular, it did not require Mr Hyde or any other Lawyer (honest if there is such a thing?) or roguish to point out its futile absurdity – Of <u>course</u> Mrs Clarke was a <u>fool</u> to let the woman Beaumont go; but when have <u>I</u> to deal with any thing <u>but</u> fools, it is not that that Fiend <u>is</u> so clever! <u>far</u> from it, he is too great a villain to be consistently and segaciously clever, and I could foil his flimsy – snares any day – could I only get <u>others</u> to act as <u>I</u> know they ought – but which Either their <u>cowardice</u> or their folly prevent their doing – However as I have no human being to <u>protect</u> me against any villainy – but only with their cursed and maddening <u>talk</u> – to plunge me into fresh troubles, each succeeding one more horrible, and hopeless than the last! – I <u>did</u>

the only thing <u>to be done</u> my object being not to <u>talk</u> for a month of Sundays in a percentage of impotent conjectures? – as to <u>who</u> the wretch was? and how? when? and where she came from? but to <u>rid</u> the neighbour hood of the pollution and misery of the maddening outrage of her proximity – as I am <u>perfectly</u> <u>certain</u> <u>who</u> <u>she is</u>, to frighten her dastardly and infamous Employer – as I <u>have</u> <u>done</u> by the <u>public</u> <u>exposure</u> of the superscription of that letter. the people at Weston told Mrs Clarke that every one there thought her a very odd, and a very improper person as she had arrived there so mysteriously – and there was such a round about hugger mugger in all her ways. – So for God's sake spare me your respective Twaddles – that I should <u>not</u> have written to Sir Sodomite in that way without I had had the Parish register to certify! that she <u>was</u> Miss Laura Deacon. I am just as <u>morally</u> certain of it as I was of Miss <u>Gettings</u> mission – when in spite of the cowardly creep mouse remonstrances of the people there to <u>want</u> to be <u>sure</u>?!!!!!! I turned her out – of the Hotel – giving her – her redress – by telling or rather <u>entreating</u> her to bring an action against me; if I had accused her falsely? <u>has she</u> Ever done so from <u>that day</u> to this? or have <u>one</u> of the infamous gang? – from Sir Sodomite down wards ever <u>stirred</u> to refute all the vast outrageous <u>libels</u> (since by our iniquitous Laws "the greater the truth, the greater the libel") <u>no</u> ten thousand Devils no – and Mr Hydes telling you Mr Ironside might be proceeded against for that circular – <u>proves</u> him to be a double Traitor – for he knows did any one ever Publish Sir Sodomites exploits at Nice, in "The Times"! <u>could</u> the Times be got to publish them – he the loathsome rotten ruffianly coward would never <u>dare</u> to stir as for the soi disant³ Mrs Sellers printed card, – you have got it and it would be very easy for any <u>man</u> in London to make enquiries at 14 Woburn Place Russell Square⁴ – a "Mr James Hopkins" lives there now; but <u>a</u> Mrs Seller <u>may</u> (or may not) have lived there formerly – and it is very easy for street walker adverturesses like the wretch Beaumont either to steal a real persons visiting card; or get one with a mythlogical name and address – printed as that one with its (<u>née</u>! Hautenville de Hautenville) <u>evidently</u> <u>was</u>. To such a pompous puffed up Char[l]atan as Sir Liar – my calling him <u>Ridiculous</u>! on the superscription of 2 letters sent through the public Post! – will go farther to dig his Felons grave, than even – a steady course of Antimony – and as every one has such a cringing dread! and deference for the great <u>mans position</u>! <u>I</u> must be permitted to evince <u>my</u> respect for it in <u>my own way</u>. Mr Walker is extremely <u>obliging</u>! – but pray assure him – that <u>great</u> as he – and other <u>men</u> (or <u>gentlemen</u>! for there are no <u>men</u>! now a days) might consider the <u>honor</u>!! <u>I</u> could starve 20 times over, – or beg about the streets before I would accept even <u>one</u> drop of water were I in Dives Post mortem position from so craven – so wicked – so unnatural, so unchristian, – and so <u>utterly contemptible</u> a wretch, – as Sir Edward Bulwer Lytton's <u>worthy</u> <u>son</u> nor were he to walk on his bended knees – from China to Taunton would any earthly power ever induce me to see him, for it is not so much his conduct to his mother, as the <u>nature</u> that would dictate – or <u>even</u> – <u>be</u> <u>coerced</u> <u>into it</u>; that is so utterly abhorrent to me. Indeed I am not fond of being patronised even by Kings upon their Thrones, much less by Dunghill birds on their Dunghills – and therefore, am not <u>even grateful</u> for the <u>sub rosâ</u>[5] patronage!! of a set of low Penny a liners who have passed their dirty lives in abusing me and who at Mr Ironsides intercession would kindly, all in heaping on me a few additional insults, make a parade of re-burking one of my books – <u>provided</u> the great man! did not know it!!!! In reply to the inclosed rigmarole from Mr Weldon, would you be kind enough to write him 2 lines saying I am too ill to write to him which I really <u>am</u> – and return him his 2 circulars – you see how quickly he has dropped the long ago – promise – of an Elaborate review of all my Books – for the Dublin Quarterly[6] of 1858! January and now gives me a <u>réchaufée</u>[7] of moonshine – on the stale dogs trick of Publishing the <u>facts</u> of my case – faugh! how sick – sick at heart I am. They say the water torture in the Inquisition, is maddening! I am sure it never can be <u>so</u> maddening as the <u>Talk Torture</u> I have been subjected to! – I quite agree with him as to the distinguishing and unwarrantable impertinence of Mr Ironsides letters! were God almighty only half so arrogant – and dictatorial He never could be loved, and as to being worshipped <u>that</u>, would be out of the question. I am very glad you have got good accts from India, and hoping poor Massy will be better; and you more comfortably <u>settled</u>. Believe me affectly yrs R B L.

HALS
1. The goddess of wisdom, who sprang fully formed from the head of Zeus.
2. Armed to the teeth (French).
3. So-called (French).
4. Bloomsbury, London.
5. Secret (Latin).
6. This is probably the *Dublin University Magazine*, which was published monthly and then quarterly. See RBL, 1 January 1837.
7. Rewarmed (French).

To Rebecca Ryves

Sunday November 1st! 1857

"Blessed be the Lord my strength; who teaches my hands to war, – and my fingers to fight"[1] since I have no other to fight for me. – of <u>course</u> the first thing I did was to try and get Mr Sellers address, in order to write to him – and of course as usual, there is a delay in my doing so – but I have this morning sent my letter to Augusta – detailing the wretch Beaumonts arrival to Miss Comer that she may see <u>why</u> I want Mr Sellers address <u>immediately</u> – It is very little matter – what all England thinks of me the brutes! and you can Echo that; and every other twaddle till you are black in the face – or get an original idea, But do not for God's sake muddle, and mistake, what I say, wish – and do – I did wish and want long before I ever wrote that appeal, to have had a well organised penny subscription, got up for me in every town in England – I never and you know I never thought of this circular in any other light but as futile and degrading. But to show you the mistake of garbled extracts – and opinions upon letters – one does not see I thought from your saying you "did not like Mr Hydes letter at all" that he had now proved himself the blackest Traitor that ever was – since I have read his letter, I dont exactly think that, but I do think him very false, and very shuffling and that he has been tampered with – and anyone of common sense would ask him – "pray Mr Hyde – how came your views upon Lady Lyttons wrongs and rights – that she could enforce – all of a sudden to be so very much modified? and what sort of a figure do you think your own very differently expressed letters within the last 2 years in Mr Ironsides possession would cut in a court of Justice, compared with the lukewarm – if – and but – one you have just written to me? But the real thing – to do, as any one of common sense, and human feeling would know – would be, to go to knight Bruce; who must be in England this month for the November Term. – It ought to be Mr Ironside, – and luckily his appearance is far from being as vulgar, – and revolting as his letters; – but any one knowing the facts would do; – if he has any pretention to being a gentleman – (of which the race in England is, nearly if not quite extinct) he would understand the case himself. Were I in London; – or within reach of it; – I would of course go to him myself – But for God's – for mercy's for pity's sake – dont let the next bungle be to consult Mr Hyde!!! who (has so evidently sold me) upon the expediency of going to Knight Bruce? as he might even have the effrontery to suggest as a cogent reason for not doing so, – ! that perhaps Knight Bruce might be out when they called! and with the sapient, and energetic friends(?) I have they would no doubt consider this as an all sufficient reason to deter them, from making the attempt! as all persons – intermeddling in my affairs – seems to be thoroughly imbued with, and to act upon, Talleyrand's[2] advice, to the Charge d'affaires[3] "Sur tout, mon ami! point de zele!"[4] – Oh! yes – its very much beneath me! to publicly use the only sort of coarse language – that will effectually frighten and deter that lowest of all low blackguards Sir Liar Coward Bulwer Lytton but it is not beneath him to outrage me at every point? – oh dear no and Mr Walker, and the rest of the conventional Creep Mouseocracy – may treat the great man! with as much deference as they please, and even lick the dust off his feet if – they like; – but I will not have the dregs of my miserable and wrecked existence maddened – by the spying of this vile strumpet – for whom I was turned out of my house – and to whom Sir Liar Bulwer Lyttons charming son! – whom Mr Walker admires so much!! is <u>aux petits soins</u>,[5] while he leaves his mother to starve – and to be outraged by every wretch that chuses to do it. Oh! for Gods sake spare me the echo, – of this cursed twaddle about my coarse language, – let <u>them</u>, let <u>you</u>, – be outraged as <u>I</u> am and see what you would do? – the fear is that Mr Seller is in Italy – or that vile wretch would never have presumed to take his name. Suppose a poor wretch were suffering martyrdom with a cancer, which for certain causes all the faculty had pronounced incureable; and a man came and with great authority tore off all the bandages in the rudest manner, thereby, skinning you, and considerably adding to the original wound; – you telling him the while, – <u>all</u> the reasons that <u>others</u> had <u>given</u> for not being able to cure you; – and his only reply was. "Pooh! pooh! I am not surprised at such a set of <u>fools</u> as <u>you</u> have laid about you doing you more harm than good – but you only be quiet; – and leave it <u>to me</u>!" you then begin to hope, against hope – but the very first time the wound – comes – to be dressed; – he is evidently frightened at the least serious of the symptoms <u>all of which</u> – he had been pre-warned of: – and says, "we must ask Dr Quackhum what <u>he</u> thinks had best be done?" and when it is objected, that Dr Quackhum had <u>formerly</u> done all he <u>could</u>, – and having been left, – was not likely to exert himself upon being re-called in; – still he <u>was</u> appealed to; – and the wound growing worse while it was being <u>talked</u> over – and someone suggested that white lilies growing in the Botanical garden at Kew[6] would give immediate relief – "not <u>now</u>, – we'll try <u>that</u> by, and bye, if <u>necessary</u>; but <u>I</u> think the Creep mouse appeal, – to the stone that caused the cancer, had better be continued a little longer?" The <u>stone</u> as might have been foreseen from the first continuing as deaf <u>as</u> a stone! – Then Kew is applied to; but the Head gardener is abroad; – and they must <u>wait</u> a few months longer! and the arrogant gentleman that so rudely tore off the bandages – sapiently suggests, that they should be looked for in, and fished out of the dust hole! and <u>re-applied</u> – as <u>perhaps</u> there might be still sufficient virtue remaining in the ointments to do some good!!!! Now – I am the cancer patient, and this, is precisely the way in which Mr Ironside has treated me. – But setting all treachery aside it, was repugnant to my common sense, and revolting to my pride, to have Mr Hyde – a man who had never for 16 years recieved a shilling of my money and who after the most hot, and apparently disinterested zeal – all of a sudden, cooled down and did every thing he could to back out of the case and to throw cold water upon it, – but still despite <u>all</u> this I am to be additionally injured, and humiliated – by having him <u>nolens</u>, <u>volens</u>[7] <u>dragged into it</u>! – where as, – any first rate Chancery Barrister for a £5 Consultation Fee (which I would have sold all I had to raise) – would have given a <u>clear</u>, <u>impartial</u> and <u>astute</u> opinion of the case – had it been properly placed before him – you must remember in mitigation of my violence! and my coarse language – all the kind, good, trusting people – that I am swindling!!! that it is not simply <u>my</u> fate that is at stake! that I am stabbed in the back and outraged at every point, helpless on a sick bed – and writhing in bodily pain R B L

HALS
1. Psalm 144:1.
2. Charles Maurice de Talleyrand-Périgord, Prince de Benevente (1754–1838), was regarded as the Prince of Diplomats.
3. In charge of business (French).
4. 'Above all, my friend! point of zeal!' (French).
5. Has few cares (French).
6. The Royal Botanic Gardens are located at Kew in Richmond, Surrey.
7. Whether willing or unwilling (Latin).

To Rebecca Ryves

2 November [1857]
Monday November 2nd My Birth day! could I afford mourning
God knows with what <u>sincere</u> <u>sorrow</u> I would put it on.

My dearest Rebecca – Pray <u>again</u> assure Mr Eyre Lloyd how <u>grateful</u> I am to <u>him</u> (and I dare say <u>you</u> also) for his very kind thought of writing a Review of "very successful" – but <u>indeed, indeed</u> – I would <u>far rather</u> it did <u>not</u> appear in the S.F.P much less be laid under an obligation – to Mr Ironside, for the room it will take up – even had it appeared 11 months ago – when the Book came out it would have done me <u>no</u> good in that paper, and I think even the Advertizing the Book constantly in that Paper – and in <u>no</u> other has done it and me harm – because really instead of "The Free Press" it ought to be called the Urquhart Bully – talk of "nauseating repetitions"! I'm sure there cannot be a finer sample extant of them, and I really am sick at heart – of being placed under humiliating obligations – for what <u>only</u> injures, and degrades me; – could any one by the most abject means get me £50, 000 from Meyer de Rothschild[1] I might then consent (though I doubt it?) to quietly pocket 50, 000 insults with it; for I should at least have an equivalent for them, <u>Pray</u> <u>pray</u> above <u>all</u> <u>don't</u> compromise me any further with that traitor Mr <u>Hyde</u>, for you surely <u>cannot</u> be so stolidly obtuse as not to percieve, that if Mr Hyde had been <u>true to me</u> – putting all <u>Law</u> out of the question what ever it may; or may <u>not be</u> – when Mr Ironside told him of that ruffian Loadens <u>presuming</u> to say Knight Bruce had written that infamous letter after for 16 years, telling Mr <u>Hyde</u> it was a forgery of mine!!!!! Mr Hyde would have been the first to <u>volunteer</u> to say – "oh <u>I'll</u> soon settle <u>that</u> I'll go to Knight Bruce myself, and tell him what they have been saying <u>till now</u> – and instead of asking what <u>evidence</u> I had against Sir Liar – he at all events would have <u>volunteere</u>d to publicly state – what he knew – and what <u>he</u> had written – <u>even</u> within the <u>last two years</u>. – He would also as I <u>begged</u>, and entreated him to do, <u>as</u> my solicitor have written a letter to "The Times" – on the purloining of the Lyndhurst letter! not <u>one</u> of those things did he do – which years ago – before Sir Liar had ratted, and when he called – himself a Whig – Mr <u>Hyde</u> would have been <u>too</u> glad to have done – for he never <u>then</u> had such <u>strong</u> and such <u>glorious</u>! opportunities yet, <u>how</u> he fought and battled and <u>exposed</u> them for a fraud; – <u>I</u> can <u>see</u> <u>it</u> <u>all</u> and must <u>insist</u> upon not being <u>further</u> wrecked with this heartless Traitor because <u>you</u>, and Mr Ironside don't <u>see</u> it in that light Mr Ironside is not troubling his head about the matter – and it is not your Eyes that you use, but your <u>Ears</u>, that you are <u>always</u> lead by – "he <u>says</u>, and they say" and you never have the nouse to compare this – with what he or they said before; and see how it agrees with it. Having <u>piously</u> cursed the day I was born! – I cannot but end my prayer – with "Save, oh! save me from my friends!" as but for Traitors and fools! – to do their work; I think I could soon master such ultra Blackguard Enemies, as mine! – I send you a letter I have just got from Augusta I <u>told</u> her at the time I had nothing on earth to do, with the advertizement of the squire of Beechwood[2] being put into The S.F.P[3] that it was Entirely Mr Ironsides own volunteer – and I'll write, and tell her so again – to day – she has sent me some lines – a just tribute to poor George Willoughby and "The Delhi Nine"[4] I have sent them to the Times, and hope they will insert them. I am so ill from having braved the night air on Friday to go to the Post office that God knows – when I shall be able to leave my bed. – <u>Never</u> if God has mercy on me – I can only account for Mr Hydes extraordinary <u>insult</u> about my not getting <u>less</u> than £400!! to his meaning if I got a Divorce? – Hoping you may be comfortably settled at last? Believe me Ever affect'ly yrs

　　　R Bulwer Lytton

HALS

1. James Mayer de Rothschild (1792–1868) was a banker and a member of the prominent Rothschild family.
2. *The Squire of Beechwood: A True Tale* (1857) by 'Scrutator' (Knightley William Horlock). See RBL, [29? October 1857].
3. The *Free Press*.
4. The other men included William Shaw, John Buckley, John Scully, William Crow, Sergeant Benjamin Edward and Peter Stewart. On 11 May 1857, they defended the magazine of Delhi for more than four hours against the rebels. Five of them perished when they fired the magazine, destroying many of the enemy. See RBL, 1 July 1857.

To Rebecca Ryves

9 Tuesday Night November 3d 1857

Miss Comer has just been here to say the wretch Beaumont had left Weston in a great hurry (whether she returns or not is another affair) has <u>not</u> paid Mrs Clarke, or any one <u>here</u> – was living [at] a <u>school</u>[1] at Weston [ill] Major Sympson[2] ("who had been a very gay man"! as <u>all</u> the Brutes are) had <u>met</u> the soi-disant[3] Mrs Seller in the street and said – he had known her formerly (no doubt) and knew her to be a [most] extensively improper person" and that if she presumed to call at the Hotel – wanting his wifes patronage which she might have acute effrontery enough to do – she was on <u>no</u> account to be let in – Mrs Seller has [but] <u>one</u> son the ... [ill] Miss Comer is to write [to] Mrs Seller <u>Mère</u>[4] tonight telling her of her charming daughter in law that she has so long ignored!

    yrs affectly
    RBL

HUNT
1.   5 South Terrace, Weston-super-Mare.
2.   Joseph Dyer Sympson. See RBL, 17 December 1857.
3.   So-called (French).
4.   Mother (French).

To Rebecca Ryves

[6? November 1857]

... Rogers's Hotel[1] which by the bye is a perfect Palace, like a first rate London Club; – but by the way I called at Whereats Library[2] – and there writing the same little memorandum on the back of one of my own cards, touching the identity of Mrs Seller! arrived at the Hotel I ordered some dinner for Mrs Clarke, and asked to see Mrs Rogers – a very handsome nice woman whose own daughters I understand have a first rate governess, and are thoroughly well brought up. When I opened the session by saying I had been to Miss Rogers's and on what account [Mrs] Rogers said "Oh! from what I have seen of Miss Rogers's school and the way scampish officers stop and flirt, with her young ladies I would not send a cat that I cared for to her." She then told me ...

... that vulgar brute Miss Rogers had the impertinence 2 days after to inclose me! 4s 6d worth of stamps – to pay Mrs Clarke Miss Laura Deacons Bill – the night she slept here! requesting a reciept. Poor Miss Comer was in such a rage! and sent them back to her, asking her how she dare so presume to insult me; so poor Mrs Clarke has not yet been paid. we have found out that there was a Mr Seller who many years ago made an imprudent marriage with a foreigner; who went so completely to the bad, that he refused to allow her anything; now as qui se ressemble [s'ass]emble,[3] no doubt Beaumont knows this creature and has borrowed her name and story to come down here for her present dirty work. I think it was very good, Mr Kinglake[4] offering her a place in a Penetentiary! I am sorry to have bored you with so long ...

... that this wretch Seller, had arrived post at the Hotel, without a stick of luggage and begging the Chambermaid not to put her to sleep next a man! for oh! she could not sleep! if she was within a mile of one! – which when Mr Rogers heard – he said "Oh depend upon it that ugly old baggage is no good" That Mr Sympson[5] is a thorough bad profligate man and managed in the six weeks he was there to debauch 2 of Mrs Rogers' Housemaids. – But [a] day after the arrival of the soi-disant[6] Seller the latter; hearing Mrs Sympson playing on the Piano – knocked at the door tripped into the room – and with great [ill] said – "Oh! I see you are fond of music – I'll sing and play for you" In short, as the common Irish song began putting her comehither upon Mrs Sympson – who was quite frightened at her. – Two or 3 days after this – Mr Sympsom over took a waiter carrying up one of her Mrs Seller cards to his wife,[7] and taking it out of his hand he said – "Pooh! pooh! Mrs Seller indeed! come no more of this nonsense; tell her <u>I know who she is</u>" and forbid her being shown up to his wife but of <u>course</u> like a true English sneak and profligate when I got, Mr Kinglake to write to him, asking her real name – or under what name he had known her, and her anticedents – he of course knew nothing against her character! – if I only [ill] man in London worth 2d and as much brains in his head as a chicken, he would call at 7 Golden Square[8] – and soon worm the truth out of the fellow, without of course putting him on his guard by writing <u>my</u> name ...

HUNT

Incomplete letter.

1. In 1851, Rogers's Hotel was known as the Reeves' Hotel and in 1861 it became known as the Royal Hotel. The hotel was run by Thomas Rogers and his wife Elizabeth at Weston-super-Mare. RBL is told that Mrs Sellers had stayed one night there.
2. Joseph Whereat was a bookseller, publisher and owner of a public library with a public reading room, which is on the corner of Regent Street and the Esplanade in Weston-super-Mare.
3. Those who resemble assemble (French). The equivalent of the proverb: 'Birds of a feather flock together'.
4. Alexander William Kinglake (1809–91) was elected the MP for Bridgewater in 1852. See RBL, 15 December 1857.
5. Joseph Dyer Sympson, a solicitor. See RBL, 17 December 1857.
6. So-called (French).
7. Amelia Louis Sympson.
8. Mr Sympson's London home. See above, n. 5.

To Rebecca Ryves

November 8th 1857

Will you beg of your coarse vulgar brute of a friend Mr Ironside not to send any more of his papers to me; – people do <u>not</u> care to read such over strigged?? trash, – and I can ill afford the 2[d] a week they cost me, to forward them obtuse as you are, and requiring Everything to be pointed out to – and dunned into you – you cannot surely be <u>such</u> a fool as not to see the way in which this vulgar arrogant brute of a man has with his insulting patronage (<u>his</u> patronage!) gone out of his way and out of the <u>regular</u> <u>routine</u> – even of advertizing to injure, and insult me he can advertise the squire of Beechwood[1] <u>Properly</u> as all Books <u>are</u> advertized, giving quotations – from the opinions of the Press respecting it <u>even</u> adding one – from his own slap dash Review now though <u>he</u> never noticed my Book for which I am <u>truly</u> <u>thankful</u> there were plenty of laudatory and <u>advantageous</u>, – quotations from <u>other</u> Reviews, that might and ought in the <u>regular</u> <u>routine</u> have been appended to the advertizements – this he has carefully avoided doing and <u>this</u> alone – and <u>only</u> being advertised in his rag of a paper, would be <u>quite</u> enough to effectually damn any book. – I must therefore <u>insist</u> that he does not continue to advertise it in his Paper – and if ever ruin overtakes him and his family – may <u>he</u> find such a friend as himself!! – and the poor creatures, something <u>rather</u> better RBL

If he sends any more of his Papers after this I shall return them so you had better prevent his doing so.

I wish to goodness he and Mr Urquhart Sir Liar and all the other beastly Humbugs would go to India, or to a hotter place together.

HALS
1.   *The Squire of Beechwood: A True Tale* by Scrutator (Knightley William Horlock).

To Rebecca Ryves

Tuesday November 10th 1857

As Lord Justice Knight Bruce <u>sat</u> yesterday in Lincolns Inn – of course it will take the noodleocracy 99 – more years to ascertain in some round about wheel of fortune way through some men who may, or may not be met in the street whether he is in England! and 99 – more, – to jibbet their inanity on cross Posts – to come to a conclusion – upon this <u>conjecture</u>! and of course it is quite out of the question (and never was such a thing heard of!) as being able to ascertain whether a man had recieved a letter imperatively requiring an answer when he was Blackguard enough <u>not</u> to answer it; though the letter may have been (and most probably was) so Blackguardedly both as to wording and appearance that he thought it beneath him <u>to</u> answer it. The more I think over Mr Ironsides brutal, – and <u>too</u> <u>idiotic conduct to be natural imbacility</u> – the more I am concerned; that through the Blackguards by whom he is surrounded, Neill Jenkinson and Co! with an impetus from that inflated Frog Mr Urquhart, the more I am convinced I say, he has been – bought over to do Sir Liars dirty work – for a pompous self sufficient ass is the easiest thing possible to convert into a tool <u>without their being the least aware of the fact:</u> – and the Brute never could have gone out of his way to offer me the wanton outrages and gratuitous insults, he has and to give the <u>coup de grace</u>[1] to slurring a book – he <u>affected</u> to advertize! if this were <u>not</u> the case. All this is of course <u>unpardonable in me</u>! but <u>facts</u> are <u>stubborn things</u> – and I am <u>not</u> a fool; – though condemned to be handcuffed and muzzled with them in all directions ...

HALS
Incomplete letter.
1.   Killing blow (French).

To Rebecca Ryves

Wednesday November 11th 1857

I am sorry if I said anything to annoy you and beg your pardon but really I am stuck so full of poisoned arrows that I cannot help in my agony occasionally tearing out one, and flinging it back – upon those who aimed it: – and just look at the fearful! the sickening – the <u>hopeless</u>! abyss I am in? – and and [*sic*] the cruel – wanton – and irritating manner I have been mocked, and tortured with <u>talk</u>! for 8 months – and not a thing <u>done</u> – however important – as in the Instance of Knight Bruce and every feeling I have set at defiance – and every wound ripped up and laid bare – and now a dose of Sheffield vitriol poured into them Even you must feel that <u>no</u> one had they the moral imperviousness of an armadillo – <u>could</u> bear – an eternal Flourish of Trumpets – of threatened obligations never conferred! – look at the Cheveley Humbug alone, – for which I have been as much annoyed, and humiliated, – as if it had been to secure me a £1, 000 for the Copyright of Each of my books, – and all <u>Bosh</u> like the rest. As I before said, – I am very grateful to Mr Eyre Lloyd for his kind thought and intention, – but it <u>is</u> too degrading and humiliating to be threatened with a review – 11 months after date! in a penny Provincial Paper! and laid under a mighty obligation! to its coarse and pompous Editor for it never to appear – and who has been assiduously doing all he could to swamp an already wrecked book, by his <u>invidious</u> and <u>unprecedented</u> mode of advertizing it. – If any one – will hit upon any plan to pay my debts and prevent my being branded at the gallies of my own remorse, as an ungrateful, and unprincipled swindler! they may then kick and spit upon me for ten years together, and I will neither resent it nor complain; – but I cannot bear all these wanton insults, – and <u>theoretical obligations</u>! without a single equivalent and in proportion to the kindness and forbearance I have recieved from <u>all</u> my creditors, will of course be the terrible! reactions of their just indignation – when six weeks hence – they find not a <u>thing</u> has been <u>done</u> towards paying them, or extricating me from this cruel whirlpool yrs affectly

 R B L

May I ask if it is not an impertinent question? as I cannot help feeling anxious on the subject what notice Sir Liar took of Mr Ironsides returning <u>him</u> the Fiend Loadens letter to me? or whether he took any?

———————

HUNT

To Rebecca Ryves

Saturday November 14th 1857

You ask me my dear Rebecca How<u>I</u> should like being called any mans Patent Blundering Machine? Whether I liked it or not I should have the candor to own I deserved the appellation had I been a Miss of your age, totally void of all knowledge of the world, and of human nature, which I could have had no possible means of acquiring – and arrogantly set – by a man of Mr Ironsides calibre! over a person – of double my age – and fifty times – my knowledge – and experience, as an autocrat, an oracle! and umpire! to whose fiat (without giving them any option in the matter) – they were implicitly to defer, and to succumb; – and that I had in achieving <u>nothing</u>, done every thing not only contrary, but in <u>defiance</u>, – of their wishes – feelings, – and experience. When <u>I</u>, hurt peoples feelings, it is that I am <u>lashed</u> stung, and goaded, into the retaliation of doing it, and therefore I <u>mean to do so</u>; at the time, however sorry I may be for doing so after; <u>you never mean</u> to hurt peoples feelings, – and yet from total want of <u>tact</u>, and want of <u>thought</u>, are <u>incessantly doing</u> – so; for the undigested garbage of a Circulating Library – can neither give <u>savoir vivre</u>, nor <u>savoir faire</u>;[1] – and like most imitative persons lacking the stamina of originality, – you have no <u>observation</u>, – that best of all teachers, <u>after</u> experience – and therefore, – if you lived with a person 99 years, you would go on (<u>unwittingly</u> which makes it the more provoking) treading upon a persons gouty feelings – and – and scraping the wrong way of their Cut nerves – and then be all astonishment! at their writhings and wincings; – and like all intensely idle people, you never have <u>time</u> to do anything as it <u>ought</u> to be done; – if it were even to make a pen and ink sketch. (though always paper spoiling in this way –) and <u>words</u> – alone – however <u>kind</u>

never have, and never <u>will</u> constitute – either kindness or good feeling. Believe me, no natures (unless the <u>very</u> <u>blackest</u>, like Sir Liar Coward Bulwer Lyttons;) <u>are</u> ungrateful, for <u>benefits</u> <u>conferred</u>; – but what <u>every</u> one winces under, – and what the authors of these wincings <u>call</u> ingratitude! are benefits long – <u>coarsely</u>, and humiliatingly <u>threatened</u>, – and <u>never</u> conferred! Now had I last April when first all this bungling torture commenced, – said – that it was of vital importance that I should attend, the Birthday Drawing room – but, that alas! I could not do so; – not having the means of getting a dress; – I'm sure Mr Ironside, would have said, in his usual hand over head – capacious faith in his own omnipotence "Then by G—d you shall go to the Drawing room, and you <u>shall</u> have a dress", and then would have followed 50 letters – never telling me what the dress was to be, or who was to make it; – and if I ventured to beg the train might not be crimson – as it was summer his wise answer would have been – "Are <u>you</u>, the best judge of what becomes you? – Rebecca is commander in Chief, <u>she</u> must decide: – what <u>she</u> says must be our guide" – Well, – in this irritating and tant soit peu ridicule!² much ado about nothing – muddling, – not only the Birthday, – but the whole season is past away; – but by <u>next</u> mng, arrives a vulgar scarlet and yellow 3s 6d cotton gown! by way of a court dress! so badly made that I cannot get into it and I farther discover that the person <u>you</u> recommended to make it – was Mrs Littlejohn, the woman who – had spoiled seven dresses for me- and who I had dismissed – for extreme insolence! and when I complain of this, and of the barbarous cotton never even having been tried on! I am told it was by the greatest <u>favor</u> Mrs Littlejohn was <u>induced</u> to make the (ie spoil) the dress for me and she expressly stipulated that <u>she</u> <u>was not to be brought into contact with me to try it on</u>!!!!!!! and <u>that</u> was the reason it did not fit and then, for all the trouble!! you and Mr Ironside have had to achieve this bungle! and this humiliating insult! I am ungrateful! yea verily I am <u>more</u>, ie indignant and disgusted <u>beyond measure</u>. Now – <u>you</u> do not understand what I mean by your total want of <u>tact</u>; – which few persons – without great knowledge of the world ever <u>do</u> possess, – unless, nature has given their perceptions a very fine Edge indeed. – Now I will give you an instance of it, – and I do it with a <u>sincere</u> wish to <u>benefit</u> and <u>not to annoy</u> <u>you</u>; because I know you have a fine, and noble heart, – and <u>excellent</u> abilities if they were but properly cultivated, disciplined and above all – darned together, with a little needle work, and other womanly knowledges – The instance of your <u>terrible</u> want of <u>tact</u>, that <u>first</u> jarred upon me – was 5 years – ago; – the first, Evening – you ever saw – Augusta; – because you had heard <u>me</u>, who had known her all her life, call her Jenkins; – the moment she came into the room, you, who had never seen her! immediately accosted her as Jenkins!! – this of course annoyed her; and made me, feel, as if I should sink into the earth! and yet, – <u>you</u> only thought you were making yourself facetious; and agreeable! Now again, – in your letter to day, – <u>sans vous en douter</u>!³ you say; you will send! <u>me</u>! the review Mr Lloyd was good enough to write of one of my books! to see if I like it! before it is printed! now never in this world, was such a thing done except in cases like Sir Liar who writes <u>his own puffs</u> but to any one else, sending them a Review of their books to read in M:S: is about as <u>delicate</u>, a proceeding as – to make them a <u>present</u> of a dress, – or a Bracelet and send them the bill with it!!! I must therefore beg to decline – reading this critique in M.S. which I am very grateful to Mr Lloyd for having written. – and equally grateful that it is <u>not</u> to appear in Mr Ironsides Paper – where

"Praise too short doth blot"[4] Oh! how true is it! that "The well intentioned, but <u>injudicious</u> actions, of what are called, <u>well meaning</u> people, – are apt to remind us of an ill regulated clock – whose hands always point to the right hour, – but whose stroke, is <u>invariably wrong</u>. It is – this terrible want of tact and moral obtuseness – and the hurry skurry – of the <u>only</u> event of your day – getting ready to go out! – that prevented your percieving, how <u>annoyed</u> any <u>gentlewoman</u> in my <u>unique</u>, – and <u>exaggeratedly</u> miserable! position, – would be, at reading Lady Glamis's[5] coarse note, with her dole of £5; which – if it got me out of <u>one</u> of my difficulties, however my feelings might wince, my <u>necessities</u> at least would be grateful; but when it does not; – <u>both of course</u> are outraged; though to do the woman justice – she of course never intended <u>me</u> to see such a note! – It is for this reason – from this same obtuseness – and <u>want</u> of <u>thought</u> that when you are with me, I have continually to say dont say this; – and dont say that; – before so, and so; – for I never saw any one so devoid of <u>discretion</u> (yet with plenty of <u>secretiveness</u>) and its active principle <u>tact</u>: – and the worst of it is, I never <u>can</u> get you to understand the <u>moot</u> point; it is <u>always</u> upon its <u>inverse</u>; that <u>you</u> argue. – Charles Matthews[6] tells, a story of – a man at a public dinner – (dirty Pig) using a silver tooth pick – and laying it down beside him – a still dirtier pig who sat next him; took it up and used it! Matthews naturally supposing – that this was done in a fit of absence; – thought it would be charity to tell him – that the tooth pick belonged to, and had just been used by his "next neighbour". – "Well Sir! said the indignant borrower "I'm not going to <u>steal</u> it; I mean to <u>return</u> it!!!" <u>Et voila où nous en sommes,</u>[7] <u>always</u> arguing about totally <u>opposite premises</u> – This gentleman only thought of defending – his <u>unimpeached</u> honesty, – while Matthews, was only disgusted at his <u>cochourie</u>.[8] – I should be much obliged to you to get, for me the Anonymous £5 – Mr Ironside "holds", as you will see by the inclosed; that Dyer is dunning for the Chair (the £2"16-) I so "immorally" got, for Mr Ironsides comfort, – that fatal day he came here; and Mrs Jermyn's £5 – (which is already diminished by £2"10 – for fares, – and journeys – of Mrs Clarke to Weston,) I must keep, – for the Laundress, and the sharks of the Hotel at Xmas. The only thing, – I was anxious to hear, – about; and because it naturally keeps – me – in a low fever, (– which however thank God, is rapidly bringing me to the only place where I shall have peace) you of course say nothing about; – I mean Knight Bruce! that other great, and <u>chief</u> cause of my base ingratitude! – to my kind friends, who have shown such <u>zeal</u> in forwarding my interests, and where they could not do <u>that</u>, in sparing – my feelings! and mitigating – the cruel tenterhooks, of suspense, upon which they have hung me amen! – I am sorry to bore you so often about it but if my sandal wood fan is done (which at the end of so many months I should think it ought to be) I should be glad to have it. you may keep Mrs Epps's[9] book as she sent me 2 – when <u>such</u> [a] namby Pamby gets puffed! <u>I</u> may well feel aggrieved – yrs affectly Rosina Bulwer Lytton

---

HALS
1. Knowledge of living, nor knowledge of doing (French).
2. Irritating and that is to say a little ridiculous (French).
3. Without you no doubt! (French).
4. Shakespeare, *Love's Labours Lost*, IV.iii.237.
5. This may be Charlotte Bowes-Lyon, Lady Glamis (1797–1881).
6. An actor who was a popular theatre entertainer in London.
7. And here where we are together (French).
8. Rubbish [*cochonnerie*] (French).
9. Mrs Ellen Elliott Epps (1809–1876) wrote *Practical Observations on Health and Long Life* (London, 1855) and had some success as a novelist. She was the wife of Dr John Epps (see RBL, 27 June 1857) and after his death in 1869 published the *Diary of the Late J. Epps*.

To Rebecca Ryves

Clarkes Castle Hotel
Thursday November 25th 1857

To The Taunton Post Master
Lady Bulwer Lytton Has this morning recieved a letter from London, informing her that her letters sent from Taunton generally arrive torn completely open, and re-sealed! at the Taunton Post Office! The first time this occurs <u>again</u> Lady Bulwer Lytton will make a stringent complaint to the Post Master General, and even should it be proved that this infamy originates in London, and that Sir Edward Bulwer Lytton is at his dirty work again; both he, and his tools and myrmidons at Taunton may depend upon being well and <u>publicly exposed</u>.

Of course! Because you have been told 199 times that even the <u>Taunton</u> attornies say there would be no earthly use in sueing – or trying Clarke <u>here</u>! – and that it to have any avail must be done in London – you with your usual kind! <u>considerate</u> <u>feeling</u>! got rid of the matter by recommending Mr Trenchard!!!![1] Just as Mr Ironside in <u>his</u> slap dash – devil may care way to get rid of the matter – recommended my accepting a compromise! after all this infamy of injustice of

£29!!! which would <u>go so far</u>! towards paying the poor Boys's £100. – Of <u>course</u> Sir Sodomite <u>seeing</u>, and <u>knowing</u>, the inhuman fools – (and <u>worse</u>) that I have to deal with; is <u>quite</u> willing to stand the exposure of law proceedings! knowing that there is <u>not</u> a man; a Christian, or a gentleman amongst them <u>to expose him</u>, – or he would soon knock under, and also knowing, of course from this ceaseless, and active villainy – of spying and tampering with all my letters, that <u>nothing</u> has been done, <u>or is going to be done</u>, as now on the 25th of November 1857 the noodleocracy are still <u>talking</u>!! of attempting some sort of subscription in the year Four thousand and one! – and the only thing <u>you</u>! think Mr Ironside was wrong in; &&& – whereas any one of common sense, or <u>human</u> feeling – could see the fearful iniquity of any man's not better informing himself of the <u>details</u> of so cruel and complicated a case, before he arrogantly – and <u>oracularly</u> announced his <u>power</u>!! and determination of righting it. God forgive you! one and all, – not for <u>failing</u>; – but for the brutal arrogant obtuse, apathetic and self sufficient way in which you have failed – and done every thing you possibly could to add to my tortures.

HALS

This letter is a copy.

1.   A solicitor.

To Rebecca Ryves

Tuesday November 26th 1857

Will you have the goodness to answer this inane unfeeling letter of Mrs Wheelers which came on Sunday but which I have not been able to open till now and tell her that if she, or her husband will take a knife and cut my throat, I shall be <u>really</u> <u>grateful</u> <u>to them</u>; – but that even then they will only get blood (and not much of that now, and not money out of me – and that untill this Tragical farce! is concluded one way or another – I can say or do nothing – Poor Mrs Tyler kindly got the millionaire to give up the £100 a year of the <u>principal</u> when I was at Llangollen 4 years ago – and <u>that</u> in the Liberality! his wife alludes to – the <u>interest</u>, and double insurance on the Fiends <u>life</u>, and <u>mine</u> – has been paid up regularly till this <u>last</u> <u>October quarter</u> which I refused to take of course. Knight Bruce could not be gone to as he ought to have <u>been from the first</u>, and so the matter will be left by the inhuman brute who has kicked me into this abyss and left me there God forgive him! – <u>He</u> advised a <u>compromise</u> with Mr Clarke! he did indeed with his usual arrogance and off hand never troubling his head about either my interests, my feelings – or even my <u>business</u> – and it was indignantly refused – it was <u>indeed</u> – as <u>my</u> motive for suing the ruffian Clarke – was not to get the money he had swindled me out of by wholesale nor even <u>merely</u> to publicly Expose <u>him</u>, – so much as to expose Sir Liar, and the Whittakers[1] whose idiotic and unprincipled tool he was – and how would accepting the slap dash compromise of £27 (a drop in the sea as to the <u>money</u> part of the fraud even for Mr Clarke who <u>does not</u> keep a circulating Library had been hiring out my book at 2d a vol to read! and never even accounted for the 39 copies he said he had sold and said he had never been paid for!!!!) how I say would this idiotic, and degrading compromise of accepting £27 even could it have been got out of him which it could not – how could <u>this</u> have affected my object of public exposure and through it some <u>little</u> <u>redress</u>? – but <u>that</u> of course was of little consequence my feelings interest – and salvation having been thrown overboard – from the first in this Vanity Fair Butchery Mr Ironside has amused himself carrying on at my expense <u>I do not believe</u> that Knight Bruce ever <u>saw</u> or <u>heard</u> of that infamous letter till Mr Ironside sent it to him – and I <u>do</u> believe that his sole reason for not answering it is that as usual M[r] Ironsides letter was so vulgar – curt offensive, and unintelligible; that he thought it was from some maniac and so took no notice of it – Stone wallish as you are in your <u>perceptions</u> it is odd it does not strike you – that were there a grain of <u>sincerity</u> – or even of human justice I will not say <u>feeling</u> as English people have none that in a matter of such <u>vital</u> importance to me your <u>honest</u>! friend Mr Hyde – or your talking Prig Mr Walker would have <u>gone</u> to Knight Bruce aye – and gone till they <u>did</u> find it out; – because they cannot be <u>quite</u> such fools or believe me to be quite such a fool – as to sit down under the conviction that this <u>cannot</u> be ascertained <u>because</u> a man does not answer what may have been to him an incomprehensible and even perhaps an illegible communication I wrote to that little reptile Mr Easton on Saturday a letter – that anything human would have answered immediately – but then to be sure there is nothing human about English men on sending to his office this morning he was out with the Harriers! but would send an answer this Evening! if he does I'll inclose it. It is Easy to order me to write to Augusta – as Easy to order me to rebuild Taunton but though I have not the means of living (which my dear friends seem to think an unnecessary superfluity) I must be allowed sufficient leisure to die – for the poor old hack has dropped at last nothing can I keep on my stomach not even water, or breath, which makes me retch – till I faint That horrid journey to Weston finished me but it was worth it to ascertain what I did. Of course the talking! and sensible part of the world will think me a great fool, and the Canters very wicked! but I <u>cannot</u> get over my loss it was <u>all</u> I had in the world the <u>one</u> spot of soft green moss on the miserable hard cold stone of my barren and ragged existence which thank God – must now soon be ended – I do hope poor good Mrs Clarke wont be coolly left the additional expense of burying me. Oh! if it were not for her! the poor Boys's and poor kind forbearing <u>pennyless</u> ! Miss Dickenson – I dont think I <u>could</u> keep from cutting my throat – the fear of wronging them <u>more</u>! keeps me from this irremedable sin – but my God! My God the suffering is <u>too</u> much. – I hope you will soon hear from poor Massy R B L.

HALS
1.   RBL's London publishers.

To Rebecca Ryves

November 27th 1857

I can stand this cruel fooling no longer and so have written to K Bruce[1] myself – if he does not answer <u>now</u>; and perhaps he wont? for all Englishmen that I have ever known without a single exception are such <u>utter</u> Brutes liars, cowards sneaks knaves, and unredeemed Blackguards – I think he ought then be apprised that his disgraceful conduct would be made public – But after that vile old profligate Lord Lyndhursts infamy to me, I can be surprised at <u>nothing</u> – and my valiant! soi-disant[2] champions?? instead of <u>steadily</u> exposing such iniquity which would end it; get cowed, and frightened by it and sneak off – leaving me to be torn to pieces at the leisure, and pleasure of the Blood hounds ever in pursuit of me. Truly says Charles Reade[3] in one – of his incomparable books "If you want to be crossed, thwarted, and vexed, set your heart not on a thing you can do <u>your-self</u>, but on something somebody else is to do; if you want to be tormented to death, let the wish of your heart depend upon <u>two</u> people, a man and a woman! neither of them yourself. – Now do try this remedy you will find it an excellent one"![4] <u>Probatem Est</u>![5] – It was a brilliant idea! that (like most that I am mocked with to meet a Legion of gigantic demoniacal difficulties, <u>one</u> of which would make a strong man blow his brains out) but it <u>was</u> a bright idea that! of writing to Augusta – who has been already bothered to death and swindled out of a hundred pounds by that little reptile Eastons lies and shuffles – to write to him! or to look out for another rogue for me! <u>she</u> who with many others is in a fools Paradise, (and only keeps quiet on that account! God help me!) that Mr Ironside! – undertook to settle my affairs! and <u>is</u> settling them!! when in reality he has done <u>nothing</u> but outrage, insult and <u>injure me additionally</u>, in every way he could. – I am well aware, that there are cases where <u>nothing</u> can be done, but even in such cases – kind words do a great deal, instead of making it a point of goading, and irritating one to madness with an insulting and stolid obstinacy – that could Revolutionize a stone from its gravitation, – like writing me 6! letters – about an 11 months after date! review in a provincial Penny Paper! and when I tried to explain to you the unheard of <u>coarseness</u> of sending a person a Review to read in M.S. and therefore explicitly said – <u>I must beg to be excused from doing so</u> – <u>forthwith</u>! with your usual, offensive and disgusting obstinacy and obtuseness you make a point of sending it to me!! – and that at a moment of such intense misery – and total bereavement that unless I had been as totally devoid of feeling as Mr Ironside himself – I could not have looked at a consecutive series of puffs in all the leading Reviews of Europe. Take my advice once for all, and remember when I am gone; – never unless you want to make yourself insupportably odious irritate people with the machinery of your services, even after they have been successful, for if they have succeeded to do so, cancels them – and if they have not; – this sort of se faisait valoir;[6] – being the most humiliating of all insults – is more deserving of kicks, than thanks. Now if a person were fool enough to want – or wish for an invitation to a State Ball – you would do a great deal that could not by any possibility succeed! to get them one, torturing them with letters every day for six months telling them of your fruitless efforts! and as a climax! saying you had even employed the Laundress! and the Footmen!! at the Palace to try and get a card filled up in their name!!!! – now – I, should never breathe a word to them of my intention to beg for an invitation, till I had got it, and even had I stooped to get it via the kitchen for them, I should take especial care, not to let them know this! otherwise, I should have the commonsense to feel that what might appear to them a triumph and a compliment which ignoring the means by which it was achieved apprised of those humiliating means would be converted to a gross, and unpardonable insult. – I only know had you been here fretting your heart out with your whole fate upon less than a crust! and crumbling avalanches – in all directions – every moment ready to fall, and crush you, – and had set your whole soul – upon what any ones common sense – would have told them was of such vital importance in so critical brutal, and complex a fate. – I would have said nothing to any one – but gone to Mrs Kitchener – and got her to drive me Either to Roehampton,[7] or Lincolns Inn[8] – till I saw Knight Bruce; – with her as a witness, her Beauty would have done much, and by the mans countenance upon being asked the question – whether he had had any hand in that infamous letter – more of the truth, would have been gleaned, than from a thousand letters. But then to do these sort of things, or indeed to do any thing, – requires – the strength of feeling which always gives the feeling of strength – but weak, washy – unstable people who only – Echo, or follow in the footsteps of others of course – never think of much less – venture upon any decided, – effectual measure – besides – as every day's experience shows us actions of any kind, whether civil, military – moral – or immoral – gain the performer very little pro – or con –"But talk! talks the thing

That makes the subject – 'Cause it lauds the King!"

But really – had you the wisdom of Solomon – Solon[9] and Socrates rolled into one, and a golden heart with golden arteries – the Treadmill – sort of Locomotion in which you live would be enough to muddle them – and I should think the £5 a month! you mentioned must be more than expended in cab hire removing luggage. Have the goodness <u>not</u> to lose the copy of my letter to Knight Bruce, which I inclose – for if he does not answer within a reasonable time, his disgraceful conduct <u>ought</u> to be made Public therefore of course it <u>wont</u>. I hope you have heard from Massy? yrs affectly R B L.

HALS

1. James Lewis Knight Bruce was a judge.
2. So-called (French).
3. Charles Reade (1814–84) was a novelist and playwright, who became friendly with RBL. His best known novel is *The Cloister and the Hearth* (1861). His novel *Hard Cash* (1870) about the so-called trade in lunacy resonated with RBL's exposé of wrongful incarceration in an asylum in her *A Blighted Life*.
4. RBL has 'remedy' instead of 'recipe' and some differences of punctuation. Charles Reade, *The Course of True Love Never Did Run Smooth* (London: Richard Bentley, 1857), p.173.
5. It is proved [*probatum est*] (Latin).
6. A valuable service (French).
7. South-west London.
8. Lincolns Inn is one of four ancient Inns of Court where members qualify for the rank of barrister.
9. Solon (*c.* 638–558 BC) was a famous Athenian statesman, lawmaker and lyric poet.

To George Douglas Campbell, Duke of Argyll[1]

Clarkes Castle Hotel Taunton
December 3d 1857

(True Copy)

Lady Bulwer Lytton Presents her compliments to the Duke of Argyll and in his capacity of Post Master General begs to inclose him a speciman of the manner (when not entirely intercepted) in which her letters are treated! as every <u>packet on business</u> which she sends to London is invariably torn open <u>there</u> and resealed at the Post office. In making this complaint – she is perfectly aware, that she has not the <u>s[l]ightest</u> chance of <u>investigation</u> into the matter and still less of redress; – as gentlemens (?) Blackguardism, in "moral! England"? <u>must</u> of course <u>coûte qu'il coûte</u>;[2] be <u>protected</u> ie screened, and hushed up; more especially; in the case of so convenient and unscrupulous a doer of dirty work – for <u>any</u> and every government – as the bran new Baronet Sir Edward Bulwer Lytton. Besides, what chance of redress in <u>any way</u>, could a <u>really</u> outraged woman have; where the dregs of English Profligacy are the men appointed to to [*sic*] make – break – and administer the ecclesiastical Laws? – a Lord Lyndhurst![3] to wit, who could not be made Ld Chancellor! till his own <u>crim con</u> damages with my Lady Sykes were paid by the present Ld Ashburton[4] (for the job of getting his own Peerage;)

– which creditable ex Ld Chancellor; keeps the unities of his edifying career! by jobbing a Divorce Bill through Parliament, – for an infamous woman like Mrs Norton! – Then, was there not a Judge Talford![5] – and is there not – as a further brilliant speciman of Legal Morality! a Sir Alexander Cockburn![6] – <u>cum mul-tumalui</u>.[7] Such being the case; Lady Bulwer Lytton is perfectly aware, that she has no chance of redress in any way. – Still, whenever her letters <u>are</u> torn open, she must beg leave to go through the official farce – of troubling the Post Master General on the subject.

HALS
The end of this letter, which is a copy appears to be missing.
1. George John Douglas Campbell, eighth and first Duke of Argyll (1823–1900), was a writer and prominent politician, who served as Postmaster-General (1855–8).
2. Cost what it costs (French).
3. Lord Lyndhurst, who was Lord Chancellor (1827–30, 1834–5 and 1841–6), had an affair with Henrietta, Lady Sykes (d. 1846), whose other lovers had included Benjamin Disraeli and the painter Daniel Maclise.
4. Alexander Baring, first Baron Ashburton (1774–1848), was a financier and MP for Taunton (1806–26).
5. Sir Thomas Noon Talfourd was a judge and MP, who introduced the Custody of Infants Bill to Parliament. See RBL, 18 March 1838. The Bill was passed by the House of Commons but rejected by the House of Lords in 1838. The following year, Talfourd sent a copy of Caroline Norton's *A Plain Letter to the Lord Chancellor on the Law of Custody of Infants* (1839) to every MP. This time the Bill was successful and the ensuing Act gave mothers of good character the right of custody to children under the age of seven, subject to the agreement of the Lord Chancellor.
6. Sir Alexander James Edmund Cockburn, twelfth Baronet (1802–80), was Lord Chief Justice of England. In 1856, he became Chief Justice of the Common Pleas. He also prosecuted the poisoner William Palmer. See RBL, 23 January 1856. RBL quotes Denison, the reporter from *The Times*, who said that Cockburn was 'the most unprincipled man in England' (Bulwer Lytton, *A Blighted Life*, p. 6). RBL accuses him of having borrowed money from EBL for intriguing with a tradesman's wife with whom he had an illegitimate child. See ibid., p. 69.
7. With much evil (Latin).

To Rebecca Ryves

Decr 13th 1857

For God's sake! if you want an <u>additional</u> specimen! of that most brutally, <u>culpably</u> <u>unthinking</u> and reckless mans mode of <u>serving me</u>! <u>Look</u> at the notice of Chevely in to day's S F P[1] "The incidents are supposed to be those of the authors own life!" <u>Ergo</u>[2] Mowbray[3] was my lover!, and I was Lady De Clifford![4] but no <u>matter</u> – as long as <u>his</u> fling at Lord Palmerstons tool is served; – how poor <u>I</u> am butchered! – then it is the <u>best</u>!! of my novels which <u>he</u> knows nothing about (what a dolt I must be then, he had far better have said in <u>print</u> as he had the <u>good taste</u> to tell me, – that he had heard in London (of course from his Neil[1], and Jenkinson Clique) that it was "horridly vulgar trash" a man saying <u>these</u> sort of things <u>wantonly</u> and gratuitously to <u>another</u>, and that other a woman! is knocked down when a truth is wrung – aye – <u>racked</u> out of another to <u>him</u>! Luckily no one sees the S.F.P. – or this brute of a notice! would be an effectual spoke in the wheel of my next book <u>though</u> that I hope is in better hands. The great run of Cheveley arose from its personality – its having been written in 2 months, and its being my first book. RBL

HALS
1. The *Sheffield Free Press*.
2. Therefore (Latin).
3. The hero Augustus Mowbray was the fictional suitor of the married Lady de Clifford in RBL's novel *Cheveley*.
4. The heroine Julia Neville is the long-suffering wife of the cruel Lord de Clifford.

To Rebecca Ryves

December 15th 1857

Will you have the goodness after reading the inclosed letter to that inhuman brute, and cowardly <u>liar</u> Mr Ironside, to <u>post it</u>? – or if <u>you</u> do not like to do this? return it to me <u>instantly</u> as I am determined he shall have it. – My first impulse was to forward it to Mr Walker or Mr E Lloyd – but recollecting that this man had <u>begun</u> by doing me a kindness in reprinting my appeal, I <u>still</u> do not wish to expose him, to <u>others</u> unless he <u>goads</u> me to it; but you must be aware, that if left in the cruelly brutal position, in which he has placed me; – I <u>must</u> in <u>self-defense</u> appeal to others to extricate me? and show <u>his</u>, and <u>my letters</u> <u>to them</u>, in order that they may do so. – I confess I am cruelly disgusted at finding this man (like all men under the circumstances, a mean liar thinking a poor, wretched woman has no witness to prove his infamy not so Mr Ironside!) and <u>you</u> know him as <u>I</u> do too well, not to know that he is too fond of blowing the coals in the most treacherous manner and <u>repeating</u> even in print, what one says of another to burn my letter from what I said of <u>you</u>!! which most persons make a point of honor of <u>not</u> doing; – you may take your oath I never said a word to Mr Ironside of you that I have not said to you, and should not <u>now</u> have done so to <u>him</u>, had I not been goaded by his putting you in authority over me! <u>doing nothing</u> and like a sneak and a liar, shifting the onus of his disgraceful do nothing upon you whom I was to bow down to! I ask your <u>truth</u>, and common sense, and every <u>body elses</u> – if any man in this world, ever wrote such a disgusting! and insulting letter, as <u>his</u> about me to Mr Sandby after having <u>volunteered</u> – to arrange her affairs, and made her take them out of the hands of others, in the most summary and peremptory manner and were witness to the insulting; and disgusting letter this fellow wrote me ordering me to leave off opium!!!! I want Mr Hodgsons letters back from him – Despite this mean cowardly brute there <u>is</u> still a God in Heaven and to him I still trust. RBL

To Rebecca Ryves

Tuesday December 15th 1857

My dearest Rebecca I thank you with all my heart, or rather with all the fragments of it, for your kind, noble and affect letter, which has made me shed the first tears not blood, and gall, which I have shed for many months, as I am <u>not</u> Mr Ironside or any other brute of a man thank God! – I never am nor never will be, guilty of the meanness and tenfold injury of denying any wrong I say or do – I frankly tell you, torn up as I am by the roots, with every nerve laid bare and quivering for every breath – much less every <u>blast</u> to fester into torture – I <u>did</u> wince under what I thought your patronising manner of (bearing with me) because that pompous brutal Empty ass Mr Ironside had sent you in authority over me – and I would rather you had simply done as I should in our relative positions have said – "Well yes, of course I bear with her and do what I can to help her, for she helped me in my hour of need which never was half so dark, complex and terrible as hers is now." – But all this is pasted over and never will I again say to, or think, an unkind thing of you, – for as muriatic acid tests gold – my <u>misery</u> atic acid has tested you – and if I do not tell you a la slap dash that you have a "giant intellect" I tell you, you have what is much better, a deep – kind generous heart – and a broad, honest mind. – As for me – I am besotted with misery – and <u>despair</u> (not opium! even that spurious relief being denied me) – you saw the Earth quake of Lisbon[1] at the Cosmorama[2] – you said the sea turned inside out and all its world old dead, and dregs flung up despairingly to heaven. – And in so seeing you may have some idea of the throes of the Moral Earthquake under which I poor wretch hunted, single handed, pillaged, and alone! am writhing – "I looked for some to have pity on me; but there was no man, <u>neither found I any to comfort me</u>."[3] If such a state of things, was hard for the King of Israel[4] to endure; – what must it be to the penniless woman scape goat of England!! where I know, and <u>feel</u> that, Mr Ironside, (as I told him in my first letter – setting aside his two gross and unpardonable insults to me) has behaved <u>so inhumanly</u> to me, was writing to me in his usual curt, authoritative manner for a <u>schedule</u> of my debts, and then putting me in a fools Paradise that he had some sure mode of arranging them by writing me back word he could only allow my £150 – a year had he said £50 I would have [ill] only to have been taken out of this Pandimonium of debt and difficulty! – now asking even a pauper in a workhouse, much less a gentle woman for a schedule of their debts in that authoritative manner was <u>most</u> coarse, and unwarrantable <u>unless</u> he had the <u>power</u> and determination to settle them instead of which he has left poor me to battle with and bear the brunt, of every difficulty his false hopes and flourish of trumpets have increased – upon me for all the persons to whom in my gratitude I boasted of his interference – have implicitly pinned their faith upon <u>his</u> fighting my battle, and seeing me righted in January! and on that account, and that only have had mercy on me till then! How unlike! as I also told him, in the letter he got rid of by burning! the poor dear kind man whose son he wanted me to fly at like a tigress – because <u>he</u> had first insulted him with one of his overbearing and insolent letters. As poor dear old Mr Hodgson when he got me that £1000 like a gentleman, and a Christian – further in the apportioning of it saved me every trouble <u>he</u> could with my creditors and when often goaded to madness – I have been annoyed at his creep mouse timidity in some things and have written to him in a manner perfectly unwarrantable, considering our relative positions, <u>his</u> gratuitous and constant services, and the many obligations I was under to him – <u>his</u> was always the soft word that turneth away wroth, the additional kindness that disarms suspicion – Thank God the last letter I wrote to him – 2 days before <u>his</u> death – was filled with my real feelings for him which can never end but with <u>mine</u>. – But for the Sheffield Executioner there is a coarse old English proverb, he would do well to remember before he ever sits down to write a letter, or sends his rag of a Paper to Press, – which is that "Arrogance is a weed that always grows on a dung hill. – of <u>course</u> as I told that arrogant self sufficient man from the <u>first</u> – My poverty <u>is</u> and has been all along the great the insuperable barrier to my getting redress in this infamous Country where gilded infamy is always triumphant – and it was <u>that</u> as I wrote you word – that wretch Beaumont – was sent down to impress upon the people here – that on account of my poverty Sir Liar was safe from me and I could do nothing! – Tomorrow I will send you my correspondence with Arthur Kinglake (Eothen's author)[5] about this infamous wretch – or rather his letters he has done all he could to hunt her out of Weston – she actually went through the farce of getting a low Bath attorney about a fortnight ago – to write me a letter threatening an action for defamation!! and told Mr Kinglake I must besides send her £50!! I told Mr Kinglake to tell her that Sir Liar could well afford to pay his own mistresses and tools – and that the sooner she brought her action the better pleased I should be The blasphemous wretch (<u>so</u> like her vile Hypocrite of an Employer) was smuggled into Weston by the low Church set, and talked of her being "regenerated"! and " a new creature"! I wrote back word – no – the <u>old</u> creature and no mistake only with a <u>new name</u> She let out to Mr Kinglake that she <u>had</u> been at <u>Boulogne</u> this summer – she bragged about being able to show the <u>arms</u> of her family! I said she had much better show the <u>legs</u> and take herself off as soon as possible. But my last <u>worry</u> is (for I have never Enough!) that Mr Lovibond[6] is detained in London for a fortnight! then come the Xmas holidays and so I am dashed by wave after wave from one rock to another – from incessant crying, and want of sleep – I literally can eat nothing that is keep nothing on my stomach poor Dr Price sends me an expensive prescription to bathe my head and back every two hours in hot eau de cologne take three grains of Calomel twice a week and leave off cold water and drink nothing but claret or weak brandy and water:- this is about as <u>practical</u> as all the other advice I get! – God Bless you, forgive all I, or rather my agony has said, or done, and believe me yrs ever Gratefully and affectly R B Lytton

[newspaper cutting]

It may be well asked what connection is there between Bucolics and Bravery, when this week we find several of our legislators ruralising and giving utterance at great agricultural meetings to the most martial and inspiring sentiments.

    At St Albans,[7] Sir EDWARD BULWER LYTTON, referring to the affairs of India, and the Spartan fortitude and Spartan endurance of our troops, spoke enthusiastically of what might be accomplished by the military genius of the youth of England, advocated the formation of Volunteer Corps. This, he suggested, would supply the Army with cavalry, which the Militia did not, and would be a means by which they could at all times keep up the strength of the standing army – The speaker evinced his sincerity by offering, if the young man wanted an example from men of position and rank, to volunteer himself and fight for outraged and injured women. Who takes SIR EDWARD at his offer? * Impulse has ere now produced heroes; and though the learned baronet can never, in his own person, realise the aspirations of one of his poetic creations, and become "a general at two-and-twenty", a K.C.B.[8] at fifty- three would be no small honour if bravely won. SIR EDWARD, in course of his speech, gave utterance to some patent truths. He said that this revolution, which appeared to them sudden, could not have occurred without giving to the Government some signs of its approaching outbreak; if an explosion were to take place it could not be done without breaking the ground, placing the powder, laying the train, and other signs by which the catastrophe might be foreseen; and yet they asked this country to believe that no foresight could have foreseen and no energy prevented it. He believed the public were more to blame than the Government for its inattention to Indian affairs.

[addition in Rosinas hand:]

*oh the too loathsome brute! and the more loathsome brutes who cringe! and creep mouse to such a wretch!

It is a shame my letters should be opened at the <u>Post office</u> as there is no end to the sympathy of all the Post office people for me, <u>they</u> have bought more of my books and appeals than anyone.

HALS
1. The Great Lisbon Earthquake of 1855 was one of the most destructive in history, destroying much of Portugal's capital city.
2. The Cosmorama was located at 207 and 209 Regent Street in London, exhibiting views of remarkable scenes in different parts of the world.
3. 'But there was no man, neither found He any to comfort Him', Psalms 69:20.
4. King David.
5. Alexander W. Kinglake was a historian, who wrote about Asia in *Eothen* (1844). See RBL, 6 November 1857.
6. Probably George Lovibund, the solicitor. See RBL, 30 January 1858.
7. A town in Hertfordshire, about 15 km from EBL's family seat at Knebworth.
8. Knight Commander of Bath is one of two divisions of the Most Honourable Order of the Bath (1725), an honour for conspicuous services to the Crown.

To Rebecca Ryves

December 16th 1857

[newspaper clipping]

A BOX AT THE OPERA. – In the Court of Queen's Bench, a case involving the liability of a husband for the debts of his wife, living separate from him, was tried in the Court of Common Pleas on Wednesday. Mr Mitchell, the publisher in Bond Street, sued Mr Morris a member of the Stock Exchange, for 259l. 19s., the balance of a debt incurred by Mrs Morris, for boxes at the Opera and several theatres supplied to her, and for other things. A portion of the debt was not contested, as Mr Morris <u>admitted his liability</u>. But he took exception to an item of 300 guineas for a box at the Opera, and put in evidence to show that he had duly warned Mr Mitchell that he was to give no credit to Mrs Morris, and that the hiring of the box took place without his authority, and after the separation. Mr Mitchell offered to take back the box, but Mrs Morris would not surrender. It was left to the Jury whether Mrs Morris had any authority to take the box; and they found for the defendant.

I wish to heaven, I had done this sort of thing – but of course if <u>I</u> had got only a penny roll, <u>my</u> case is warranted <u>beforehand</u> to differ from every body elses, as verily! with a vengeance! it <u>does</u>

I forgot to put this in my big packet – I had such a horrible! dream this morning I wish you could consult any "wise man"? or "cunning women" to interpret it? – as we all know there are no Josephs![1] nowadays I dreamt I was young, again and in St James's church[2] being married over again to Sir Liar![3] and there stood my poor darling old uncle[4] looking pale, and sad, as he was that fatal morning he gave me away – I thought Sir Liar made a snatch at this great diamond Star of the Bath[5] and my uncle said "no, not that; but took his diamond order of the Crescent from round his neck and said – that one if you like" – The marriage then began – the church was very cold – and very dark I saw no bridesmaids nor any one but my Uncle, Sir Liar Mr Bentinck[6] and myself:- and when it came to putting the ring on my finger – Mr Bentinck had to tell him (as was the case at the real execution) to do so; – as it touched my finger – every bit of flesh I thought fell from <u>his</u> bones and he knelt there a horrible skeleton! the next minute, the bones all fell to pieces, with a terrific crash! but were nowhere to be seen strewed about: – I thought my poor dear Uncle, then took off his large Star of the Bath, fastened it on my left breast – kissed me, – and said God bless you my poor child – you've suffered enough! but now, – you may go any where I woke, crying bitterly, and still feeling his kiss upon my cheek, and his God Bless you! in my ear. – Was it not a strange dream? at least it has haunted me all day and made me feel if possible still more wretched. Yours Ever affectly R B L

HALS
1.   In the Bible, Joseph interprets the dreams of the Pharoah (Genesis 41:12–57).
2.   St James Church, Piccadilly, London.
3.   RBL was married to EBL on 29 August 1827.
4.   Lieutenant-General John Doyle.
5.   He was made a Knight of the Grand Cross in the Most Honourable Order of the Bath with the postnominal GCB on 2 January 1815.
6.   RBL and EBL were married by the Hon. and Revd William Bentinck.

To Rebecca Ryves

Thursday December 17th 1857

My dearest Rebecca I am so ill to day – I can scarcely lift my head off the pillow to write it is easy to say keep up! but verily – I dont see how, or what, I have to keep up with! and each succeeding miserable day that brings me nearer to utter disgrace and being deprived of a roof over my head; – the more I feel the loss of the only thing on earth that cared for me. God help me! and let me soon rejoin it. – Now you must <u>give me your solemn word of honour that you really sent my letter to Mr Ironside</u> – and if not send <u>it back to me</u> for it is <u>important</u> to me that he should know the things there in contained, and I am tired oh! tired unto death at being wrecked and re-wrecked – tortured and re-tortured by persons who have neither the time, the feeling nor the capacity to judge for one – a thing which by the bye even if people had the power to serve and <u>did</u> effectually serve one, is always a most offensive, and generally injurious thing except in the case of confirmed lunatics or idiots and you have just had a flagrant example of the fruits of all this – in the matter of Mr Sandbys money and Mr Ironsides vulgar brutal and unwarrantable letter to me. – That very intemperate chimerical non judging man has no doubt heard that cutting a nerve is good for <u>tic doulerureux</u>[1] – and my species of <u>tick</u> being the most <u>doulureux</u>[2] of any – he has slap dash – cut open all my nerves, and left them to fester in the frost after. There was one <u>strong tangible</u>, <u>legitimate</u> plan made of exposing Sir Liars infamous conspiracies against me, the last of which has brought me into this appalling ruin! – namely by bringing Mr Clarke before the public foot lights – and in exposing <u>his</u> share in the plot, exposing <u>all</u>; – but no! – did he, did you did any of you see it, though begged and intreated; – all he did was to help the Fiend with his blackguard Neills and Jenkinsons – to crush, and prevent my Earning my bread a little more, & take up this <u>most</u> important <u>link</u> of the conspiracy at the <u>wrong</u> and <u>feeble</u> end, of the mere L.S.D! and fling the whole struggle of it on poor bed-ridden me; and I have no doubt when Mr Lovibond is at length caught – he will say it is too late! and the time has gone bye! God forgive him again I say – and all who so wantonly tamper with the fate of any poor wretch as mine has been tampered with! – How <u>can</u> you be so silly as to say you wish that brute of a woman <u>would</u> bring an action against me! – of course if she were Mrs Seller, she would have done so long ago – but Being Mrs Beaumont alias Miss Laura Deacon and spy of Bulwer Lytton of course she neither can nor will, the game as usual being to – stab me in the back – spring a mine under my feet – drag every penny out of my pocket and then run away and laugh at me. And the Fiend has had a glorious proof in the affair of Clarke and Whittaker alone! that <u>he</u> has nothing to fear from the ultra fools who have undertaken to weaken, and fling away my unprec-edentedly strong and flagrant case. I did <u>not</u> direct to Knight Bruce what I wrote on the Envelope of the copy I sent to you, and pray be careful <u>not</u> to break the seal, of my original letter to him, which I now inclose in his cover as if <u>broken</u> it would be no Evidence in a Court of Justice and will you always have the good-ness to put the day of the <u>month</u>, and date of the <u>year</u>, to your letters, as there is nothing so horribly muddleing, troublesome and inefficient as sticking merely "Monday" or "Tuesday" on letters – of <u>any</u> sort, but more especially on business. And when you send large packets if you only put <u>one</u> seal in the centre, instead of 3 – that is one, at each corner they are nearly <u>sure</u> to get torn open. I wish you would also tell me what excuse you made to Mr Wheeler for this Land of Egypt darkness[3] – I am kept in about all my affairs till the crash comes! adds, cruelly, and unnecessarily to the extreme horrors of my hopeless position in a way that I am sure you would be sorry for, if you gave yourself time to think about it. yours affectly R B Lytton

It is long before any man amongst them pretending to serve me would go to that Mr Sympson 7 Golden Sqr[4] and worm out of him the identity of this wretch or in fact <u>do</u> anything but <u>Talk</u>!!!

HALS
1. Facial neuralgia (French).
2. Painful (French).
3. Darkness was the ninth of the ten Plagues of Egypt sent by God in order to persuade the Pharaoh to allow the Israelite slaves to leave (Exodus 7–12).
4. Joseph Dyer Sympson, a solicitor of 7 Golden Square, London.

To Mrs Henrietta Wellington Boate

Clarkes Castle Hotel Taunton
December 22nd 1857

(True copy)

Madam I much regret, that you should have experienced any annoyance from having my name among the subscribers to your Poems, and must beg, that you will <u>instantly</u> withdraw it; as not only from having all my life had a great objection to figuring in a printed subscription I am annoyed, at doing so now; but I am doubly annoyed ay finding my name, in the same page, as that, of such an ineffable Blackguard as the present Duke of Wellington; whose <u>worthy</u> friend! – Sir Liar Coward Bulwer Lyttons infamous conspiracies have brought me to such a state of complete destitution, that it is rather incongruous, and highly injurious to me just now, to have my name figuring in a subscription! though I was quite willing – to help you, as far as I was able, (and indeed rather further) in my usual way of helping people; as long as the matter remained, unrevealed, between them, and me. I thank you for the copy of your Poems sent this morning – but do not require the other two copies, which will do for some other subscriber, from the list of which, I must beg you will instantly have the goodness to withdraw – the name of Madam your obedient servant Rosina Bulwer Lytton

To Mrs Wellington Boate.

8 Great College St Westminster London   Dec 21st 1857

My Dear Lady Lytton By a compromise I have succeeded in getting a few copies of my little volume from my cruel publisher and I hasten to forward you <u>one</u> all I am able to send at present. I trust your health is quite restored. I would have written to ask about you but was prohibited doing so by your friend in Charles

St[1] who answered my last letter to you Would you kindly acknowledge the safe receipt of the vol herewith sent I send an envelope for that purpose that I may know it in the postmans hand I shall tell you more again at present I am too over-powered with business, fatigue and weakness. <u>I have had some sad annoyance</u> by <u>having you as a sub</u>scriber to my book, I however who know your kindness shall be ever proud of your name, and I defy the mean heartless creatures who have attempted to injure me. Sincerely wishing you restoration of health and a happy Christmas I am yours Ever Sincerely and Truly <u>Henrietta Boate</u>

P.S. – As soon as I can I shall send your other two copies In haste.

HALS
This letter is a copy.
1.　EBL lived at 8 Charles Street, Berkeley Square, London.

To Rebecca Ryves

Taunton
Wednesday December 30th! 1857!

Thank God my dearest Rebecca I have heard from you at last! for when one is in such an abomination of desolation as I am, compassed round about on every side, with snares and springes, – and not a loop hole to look out at, but what has despair at the end of it! the aggravation of a dead silence – which makes one fancy all sorts of additional horrors! is really cruelly insupportable – and hearing nothing from you I had been fearing you had had some dreadful news from India, or from Massy – and not knowing <u>where</u> to direct I could not write, though I have been almost frantic! since Sunday when I got that letter from Mr Hodg-son – knowing and feeling only too acutely <u>what it portends</u> for God's sake! for mercy's sake! dont treat this, with your usual oblivious apathy; – I am not asking what you think of it? – because I know you never see or think anything <u>till</u> the avalanche falls and crushes one – I am only <u>imploring</u> that it may not be treated, as a matter of no import like my paying Mr Sandby– of course in your estimation it is of no import that I should be further lacerated by getting such disgusting and unwarrantable letters from that most brutal and idiotic man, but to <u>me</u> it is what the water torture is to a poor wretch on the rack a culminating point of agony! at which human endurance fails. – I cannot help smiling bitterly I own – at the obtuse apathy of your cool observation! of Mr Ironsides having been too sanguine! as if he had merely undertaken to get me some mignionette seed, and failed, never seeing the <u>intense</u> infamy of a man rushing hand over head into such a case without a <u>single</u> resource to cope with unlimited money power and unscrupulous infamy – <u>and when warned of it all</u>; pooh poohing it, with an

arrogant self sufficiency truly monstrous! any man with a <u>grain</u> of <u>common sense</u>
human feeling, or <u>good faith</u>, would as the very <u>first step</u> in <u>such a case</u> have consulted, a Proctor of Eminence submitting to him the enormities, and intricate
infamies of the case – and setting <u>him</u> to find out how they might be met, and <u>he</u>
would (if not a <u>Conservative</u>! which should have <u>also</u> been ascertained before he
was consulted) have <u>soon</u> brought Sir Sodomites <u>notorious</u> and therefore <u>more</u>
<u>tangible</u> than most mens infamy <u>successfully</u> to bear upon it. – But no! – this
vain Empty talking fool, frittered away the mortal fate fraught hours; in puffing
himself, flummerising you; and insulting, and crucifying me upon all the blundering hugger mugger of these cross Posts no verily! it is <u>not</u> that Sir Liar is so
clever! but that he <u>knows</u> that the mass of English are such truckling servile lick
the dusts to wealth and power, and that those who run themselves into my affairs
are not only deficient in <u>capacity</u>; and <u>patient research</u> but also take the first
scarecrow he, and Loaden set up. – for an armed legion! that it would be madness to contend against! and <u>their</u> weakness it is and <u>nothing</u> else; which makes
<u>his</u> strength; – for a position so <u>rotten</u> with wickedness and corruption as his,
– would <u>crumble to pieces</u>, at the first <u>properly</u>, and vigorously directed thrust;
– but the brutal and vulgar imbecility like Mr Ironsides – that goes out of its way
to injure, and degrade me, of course furnishes a foundation of fictitious adamant
to his <u>rotten</u> tottering super structure. How soon <u>my</u> mode of <u>acting</u> not <u>talking</u>,
drove that wretch Beaumont out of Weston. – and the matter could be clenched
by any man going to that Mr Sympson of 7 Golden Square and <u>cleverly</u> getting
the truth out of him; – but as I have no one to <u>do</u> this, or to <u>see</u>, or <u>feel</u> the
importance of it. – I must only submit, as I cannot do <u>this</u> myself. I am indignant
and disgusted, but <u>not</u> surprised at Mr Lovibonds conduct; and <u>there</u> it was, <u>last</u>
year that Mr Hyde so decidedly showed the Cloven foot, and how little I had to
expect from faith in him! when he refused to issue the writ against Clarke for as
Mr Easton at the time remarked "<u>as</u> Mr Hyde so clearly points out the way for
<u>me</u> to act in the case; why does he not do it <u>himself</u>?" and that's what <u>all</u> these
pettifoggers say; – <u>as</u> he has transacted for himself for 16 years and knows, it
all, <u>why</u> should <u>he</u> not do it; or why should <u>they</u> risk offending Sir Liar and his
Cliques powerful infamy; for what cannot bring them <u>pecuniary</u> gain; – and it
was <u>because</u> I so writhed under this treachery and desertion of Mr Hydes; and
saw through the beastly <u>party</u> motive of it so clearly; – that the <u>Praetons</u>,[1] and
Dictators! at whose mercy I am, so obstinately insisted upon flinging me <u>back</u>
upon Mr Hyde any thing! no matter, as long as the trouble was shuffled off of
themselves! and Mr Ironside who as a <u>man</u> might have explained to a London
solicitor (and therefore get him to do it) that we only wanted the writ issued, to
springe Sir Liars <u>refusal</u> – insults my misery with one of his usual asinine system
mongelifications – merely writing on the cover of my note to Mr Easton "and
this is the man we address dear Sir Hypocrisy"! which is all the <u>help</u> I get, but of

course I ought to be very <u>grateful</u>!! for having been beguiled betrayed insulted, and tortured, in a manner that I think even Nena Sahib[2] would have shrunk from torturing one of <u>his</u> victims .

What a brilliant discovery! you have made my dear Rebecca that you have heard persons remark that the <u>construction</u>!! of the French phrases were wrong in my books! "<u>prodigious</u>!!" what <u>the deuce</u>! <u>else</u> do you think I am complaining of? the <u>spelling</u> could not well be so, otherwise. But conceit, and self sufficiency are <u>always</u> the meddling marring attendants upon English peoples ignorance – and these Compositors having as much French as an indifferent Dictionary can help them to – of course decide, that they know the language better than a person whose childhood, and most of their after life were passed in France. – Thus, in the very first page of Chevely instead of as I wrote it "C'est un triste metier, que çe lui de femme"[3] they look in the dictionary and because <u>femme</u> is femenine the[y] forth with change it to c'est un triste metier que <u>celle</u>!! de femme. you, I recollect, favored me with a long argument about the variability! of French orthography, – I tried to make you understand that there was nothing in <u>this</u> world on the contrary <u>so</u> <u>immutable</u>? (unless it might be Sir Liars villainy) and that what you took for difference of orthography – was only the different terminations of the masculines, and feminines, singulars and plurals. – Il plait – he pleases <u>Ils</u> <u>plaisent</u> – they please Elle est <u>jolie</u> – she is pretty Il est <u>jolie</u> – he is pretty and so on. – But "It's a pity when charming women talk of things they don't understand." – Wishing you many happy – and happier new years (though I wont abuse even this one!! having for the last 10, found Each succeeding one, infinitely worse! than its predecessor) Believe Me affec[t]ly yrs Rosina Bulwer Lytton.

Let me have "The Birds capital letter back?

HALS
1.   These may be the Praetorian guards, used by Roman emperors.
2.   The Indian mutineer. See RBL, 19 September 1857.
3.   It is a sad way, that of a woman (French).